The Three Jewels II

THE COMPLETE WORKS OF SANGHARAKSHITA
include all his previously published work, as well as talks, seminars, and writings published here for the first time. The collection represents the definitive edition of his life's work as Buddhist writer and teacher. For further details, including the contents of each volume, please turn to the 'Guide' on pp.715–19.

COMPLETE WORKS 3 FOUNDATION

Sangharakshita
The Three Jewels II

EDITED BY VIDYADEVI

Windhorse Publications
169 Mill Road
Cambridge
CB1 3AN
UK

info@windhorsepublications.com
www.windhorsepublications.com

Cover design by Dhammarati
Cover images © Clear Vision Trust Picture Archive (flap);
The Buddha Amitabha in the Western Paradise, Tibet, 18th century,
courtesy of the Trustees of the Victoria and Albert Museum (front)
Typesetting and layout by Ruth Rudd
Printed by Bell & Bain Ltd, Glasgow

**British Library Cataloguing
in Publication Data:**
A catalogue record for this book is
available from the British Library.

ISBN 978-1-909314-79-5 (paperback)
ISBN 978-1-909314-83-2 (hardback)

CONTENTS

Part III: The Network of Personal Relationships

Conclusions:
Can the Spiritual Community Save the World?

FOREWORD

1968 marked a turning point in the life and work of Sangharakshita
and the Buddhist movement he founded. On Sunday 7 April, the first
twelve members of the Western Buddhist Order were ordained. A week
later, during the Easter retreat, Sangharakshita gave a series of three
talks, 'Introducing the Three Jewels of Buddhism'. 'Who is the Buddha?'
was given on one evening, then the next morning came 'The Meaning
of the Dharma', and on the evening of the same day, 'The Sangha, or
Buddhist community'. In the space of twenty-four hours the men and
women attending the retreat were thus given an intensive introduction
to the essence of Buddhism. The urgency is palpable. The new Order
members attending the retreat, and the others present who might feel
inspired to commit themselves to Buddhist practice, to 'Go for Refuge
to the Three Jewels' in the traditional phrase, needed to understand, and
quickly, what that really meant. There was no time to be lost. At the end
of the third talk, after quoting the *Dhammapada* on the 'fire of spiritual
practice', Sangharakshita exhorted,

> Many of us feel very strongly indeed that unless and until in this
> country there is a real, genuine, united spiritual community of
> Buddhists, not just a distant ideal of Enlightenment, not even
> just a teaching, much less still just societies, organizations in the
> ordinary sense, but unless and until there is a spiritual community
> of people who are committed and dedicated and actually

following the path in varying degrees, unless – in other words – there is an Order, a Western Buddhist Order, there is no real future for the Buddhist movement in the West. This is why, as many of you know, we have just very recently established this Western Buddhist Order as the latest formulation along traditional lines of the *sangha*, the spiritual community.

Enticingly, before beginning to speak on the theme 'Who is the Buddha?' Sangharakshita mentioned a talk given the previous day, 'Living Buddhism'. No recording of it exists, as far as we know, but that theme is the subtext of the series of three that followed it, which fortunately *were* recorded. It is these three talks, from the very beginning of the Buddhist movement whose fiftieth anniversary this publication marks, that are the nucleus of the volume now in your hands.

Around this nucleus have been gathered other talks given on many other occasions over the following twenty years or so, and covering many topics dear to Sangharakshita's heart, to form the three books collected here (first published in the 1990s). The content and organization of the books (which was of the original editors' choosing, not that of the author) is a little idiosyncratic, one must admit. There can't be many accounts of the sangha that include chapters on Nietzsche, evolution, the artist as true individual, and parenting. In *Who is the Buddha?*, which was first published in 1993 to coincide with the release of a new film, Bertolucci's *Little Buddha*, is to be found the seminal talk 'Karma and Rebirth' (which might otherwise have found a natural home in *What is the Dharma?*), included in the hope that that juicy topic might appeal to potential purchasers intrigued by the exploration of the theme in *Little Buddha*. History does not relate whether that attempt at a cunning marketing ploy had any effect, but it is certainly true that these three volumes have found their way to many readers in many countries in the years since they were first published. I was very touched to hear, when recently visiting a small meditation group in the far north of Maine, close to the Canadian border, that *What is the Dharma?* is a firm favourite there, and some or all of the three books have been translated into languages including Dutch, Portuguese, Russian, Swedish, Turkish, Polish, Spanish, French, German, and Hindi.

If you would be interested to read the transcripts of the various lectures from which these books have been woven together, they are currently available at freebuddhistaudio.com and also in printed form in Urgyen Sangharakshita, *The Collected Lectures* vols. 1 and 2, from lulu. com. A list at the back of this book shows which lectures have provided the material for each chapter. The text prepared for this volume is very substantially the same as originally edited to produce the three books it contains; a few changes and corrections have been made here and there, but the main difference is the revision of the original endnotes, and in a couple of places the text has been amended slightly to reflect new light shed by researching a note. We have also included many new endnotes. When giving these talks Sangharakshita was drawing on an intimate acquaintance with the Buddhist tradition, decades of close reading, and constant reflection on the Buddha and his teachings – a great river of doctrines, scriptures, stories, and anecdotes. We have sought to trace as many quotations and references as possible, to help the reader follow the river back to its source in Buddhist tradition and follow up particular interests. We have been fortunate to be able to consult Sangharakshita himself several times in the course of research.

The plethora of endnotes certainly doesn't signify any attempt to make this volume into an academic work. It could be thought of as a companion to volume 2 of the *Complete Works*, which includes *The Three Jewels*, first published in 1967 and based on a series of encyclopaedia entries Sangharakshita was commissioned to write. This expertly lays out the doctrinal background and implications of what the subtitle calls 'the central ideals of Buddhism', and one would guess it may have been the Dharma book most read by Sangharakshita's audience in April 1968. The talks he gave on that retreat, and in the following years, showed another aspect of his skill as a Buddhist teacher – his gift for storytelling. All the stories from the Buddhist tradition and references to concepts and culture with which his listeners were more familiar were chosen carefully to help the members of the growing sangha make personal connections with the teachings, and support them in their efforts to put them into practice.

A characteristic of the Buddha's teaching method from the very beginning was the identification of wrong views; the starting point is often not the communication of new knowledge, but the dismantling of whatever the listener thought he or she already knew. Who was – is – the Buddha, really? And what, really, is the Dharma? What distinguishes the true follower of the Buddha's teaching? These are not new questions; they cropped up in the Buddha's own time and the *suttas* record the Buddha's responses to them, many of which are to be found in this volume. We are also shown the Buddha's encouraging approach in a whole sequence of chapters (in *What is the Sangha?*) which begin with the Buddha's advice to a young man called Sigāla whom he finds by the river preparing to 'worship the six directions'. It is not in that way, the Buddha advises, that the directions should be worshipped – and he proceeds to outline a more metaphorical, less literalistic, and thus more spiritually productive way of honouring an ancient convention.

Following this tradition, Sangharakshita likewise often takes the approach of surprising the listener or reader with a challenge to conventional wisdom or expectation. When he began teaching in the West, he discovered that people had already acquired all kinds of views about what Buddhism was, and he set about challenging those views. So in this volume we learn, perhaps to our surprise, that Buddhism can be thought of as heroic, and that the Buddha's first instinct after his Enlightenment was to feel grateful to the Dharma. The author begins an exploration of Nirvāṇa with a teasing account of what a lecture on that subject would conventionally include, and then deconstructs that approach in favour of something potentially much more useful. Elsewhere, he explains how a talk on 'a Buddhist view of current world problems' could meet with universal approval and still get no one even an inch closer to solving the problems identified; again, another approach is needed. Likewise, we learn that to find out what a guru is, we need to start by considering what a guru is not.

Thus we are shown, now from this angle, now from that, sometimes how to 'start where we are', sometimes to see things afresh, to think again – and encouraged not to remain satisfied with where we are, but to see how to change and develop, and feel inspired to do so. A great range of cherished topics are approached with love and the desire to have them clearly understood; and, again, to overturn common misunderstandings. For example, a once little known formulation, the five *niyamas*, is used to show the multivalent nature of conditionality and guard against any tendency to see karma in a fixed, mechanical way. Another teaching, the twelve positive *nidānas* (the spiral path), encourages a positive approach to the spiritual life that cuts completely across the idea that was prevalent in the West at one time that Buddhism took a grimly pessimistic and negative view of things. These and many other themes have been further developed and reflected on by Sangharakshita and other members of the Triratna sangha over the years, but that takes nothing away from the powerfully transformative energy, passion, and original expression of these early works.

If Sangharakshita were to address those attending an introductory retreat today, he might choose to focus on different topics, in response to whatever he judged his listeners' needs to be (it would be interesting to consider what such topics might be), or he might cover just the same ground. In a sense we're listening in on words addressed to a particular audience at a particular time and place. This has been characteristic of the Buddhist tradition from the very beginning. The Buddha described the Dharma as being 'of the nature of a personal invitation' (*ehipassiko*), and a crucial aspect of Buddhist practice is to learn to understand what we personally need to learn from the words we hear or read, the emphasis being on what we need to learn, not what we want to hear. Although the Buddha advised us to evaluate teachings in accordance with our own reason (and with the testimony of the wise – an important extra criterion), given that the aim of Dharma practice is to examine our views and let go of those that stop us from seeing how things really are, we need to stay alert to teachings that present us with an entirely new way of seeing things – teachings that prompt us to feel as the scriptures tell us people felt in the earliest days of Buddhism, and as people have continued to feel ever since when the light suddenly dawned. As Sangharakshita describes it in *Who is the Buddha?*:

> Some went away as ignorant as they came, others went away with some food for thought, but for many, their lives would never be the same again. They would marvel aloud: 'It is as if someone were to set up what had been knocked down, or to point out the way to one who had got lost, or to bring an oil lamp into a dark place. ... I go for Refuge to the Buddha, the Dharma, and the Sangha.'

That's the traditional description of Going for Refuge to the Three Jewels, and that's what it still feels like: the feeling of something set right, a path found in a wilderness, light in the darkness. Even one such moment, sparked by something in the pages that lie ahead, would be enough to show the way – and perhaps there will be many.

This volume is being launched as part of a celebration of the fiftieth anniversary of the founding of the Friends of the Western Buddhist Order – now the Triratna Buddhist Community. At the time I am writing this there are more than two thousand Order members. Of those first twelve, some of whom 'made themselves useful' (as Sangharakshita put it) at the Easter retreat just after their ordination, the only one still in the Order has just had his forty-eighth Order birthday. His name is Ananda and, like Sangharakshita, he is a poet. Indeed, in the few days between two very public events, the ordinations and the retreat in April 1968, the two poets spent a few days together in solitude, writing, 'watching the incense burn in this quiet room', as Sangharakshita wrote. Later, Ananda published a poem called 'Easter Retreat' in which 'an avalanche falls/ in a remote and unknown valley'. Something momentous clearly occurred on that first retreat of the fledgling sangha, quietly and at first unperceived, but powerfully, though emerging from such simple conditions. From those days to these, from those first intimations of a shift, so much has happened. In celebration of that are these gathered words. Another characteristic of the Dharma is that it is timeless (*akāliko*). These words are not just a historical record of something that happened once upon a time, or a textbook to be dutifully learned; they are living sparks, to ignite the fire of spiritual practice, and keep it lit.

Vidyadevi
Herefordshire
August 2016

Who is the Buddha?

I

THE EVOLUTION OF A BUDDHA

'Who is the Buddha?' This question has always been crucial to the Buddhist quest. Through it, Buddhists determine their ideal, their goal in life, and their whole spiritual path. It is as an essentially practical question in this sense that it appears as the title of this book. We shall be examining, through the following chapters, some of the significant events in the Buddha's life, as it occurred 2,500 years ago. However, the question 'Who is the Buddha?' is not answered by a simple biography – at least not in a very helpful sense. Besides, matters of historical fact are not fundamental issues to Buddhists. Scholars continue to dispute over whether certain details in the various traditional records may or may not be regarded as true statements of what actually happened. But for those who follow in the Buddha's footsteps the facts of his life, such as they are, are secondary to their significance as a guide to the spiritual path. Many biographies of the Buddha, both popular and scholarly, have appeared before now, and some of these are both informative and inspiring. But our approach here is different. Our aim is the specific one of reflecting on the Buddhist conception of who the Buddha is.

We will therefore take each of the major elements in the Buddha's career as the starting point for a consideration of the ideal and goal of Buddhism as he exemplifies it, and as we also can strive after it. To begin with, however, it will be useful to get an idea of the spiritual context within which the man, Siddhārtha Gautama, became the Buddha. That is, the Buddha cannot be recognized for what he is except from within the context of Buddhism itself. From the Buddhist point of view the Buddha did not arise from nowhere. It is true that Buddhism as we know it starts with the Buddha. But he did not invent or create the Dharma, the truth around which Buddhism developed. He discovered it – or rather he rediscovered it. The Buddha takes his place at the centre – or at the culmination – of a vast pattern or system of spiritual hierarchies. To know who he is we also have to know, in a manner of speaking, where he is. If we cannot get some measure of the scale of the Buddha's achievement against our own human experience, the question 'Who is the Buddha?' cannot realistically be addressed at all. Therefore, not only do we need to take in as comprehensive a view as we can of the Buddhist 'scheme of things', but we should also try to see Buddhism itself in the most far-reaching perspective. 'Who is the Buddha?' is another way of saying 'Where does Buddhism propose to lead us?' To answer it we need to have some idea of where we are now – and even of how we came to be here. Before we look at where the human quest ends, we should also, perhaps, look back at where it began.

In the beginning, life was a mystery. That, at least, was how it seemed to primitive humanity. Without formulating it as such, people felt, as though in the blood, that life was strange, incomprehensible. Then later on, though still during humankind's unrecorded past, people began consciously, explicitly, to think about life. Our ancestors apprehended that they were – without knowing how or why – in the midst of what seemed to be a strange and even hostile world, surrounded by all sorts of things that they could not understand or control. In the morning they saw the sun rise, and in the evening they saw it set. But why the sun rose and why it set, and what happened to it when darkness fell, they just did not know. Sometimes there were great storms – the world grew dark, rain fell, thunder seemed to crack open the earth and the sky would be lit up by an intermittent and terrible glare. But what caused these disturbances no one could tell. The days might be long and warm, or they might be short and freezing, but why they should be so was, again, a mystery. Eventually, they discovered that they could strike two stones together to make fire – and here was another mystery.

Sometimes people felt acutely miserable, and their bodies were racked with terrible pains. Why? They didn't know. And sometimes something even stranger happened. Someone would be found lying on the ground, quite still. Usually it would be an old person, but not always; sometimes it would be a child. When you called them they did not answer. You saw that their eyes were fixed and staring, but they did not recognize you. When you drew near, when you placed your fingers near their nostrils, you discovered that they no longer breathed. When you touched them you found that their flesh was cold and hard. If you left them where they were, sooner or later you noticed a dreadful smell coming from them. And this was the greatest mystery of all.

Almost as soon as these mysteries arose, it seems, they would have been named and given a place in a larger pattern of meaning whereby people could make some sense of their lives. And this world-view – the particular view of the world held in any one society or social group – would satisfy people for perhaps a very long time indeed. But eventually some inconsistencies would appear, some aspects of the world or of themselves would be discovered that could not be explained within that system. Some people would then simply choose to muddle along with the old system, making a few adjustments here and there, while others would dismantle the whole apparatus and start again from a completely different governing principle.

What has changed today is that people have now, in most places in the world, a very considerable range of world-views – of beliefs, myths, and philosophies – to choose from and learn from. This can only be a good thing. As Kipling shrewdly demanded of an earlier, nationalistic age, 'What should they know of England who only England know?'[1] You can hardly be said to know your own culture if you have nothing to compare it with, and the same goes for anything else one wants to know: knowledge is essentially comparison. You cannot really understand even your own religion except in relation to other religions. Of course, one hasn't always had the information one needed to make these comparisons. Fifty years ago you hardly ever heard another religion apart from Christianity even mentioned – you were not given to understand such religions existed at all. But today all this has changed. Kipling's aperçu now seems almost a truism, and one finds one can learn a great deal about one's own faith from studying other systems of belief. Things we would have taken for granted in the past we can now see for what they are by comparison with different things of the same nature. And one appreciates and understands them all the better for it.

Side by side with this development, however, and linked with it, we have seen a break-up of the old unified culture in which there was a commonly accepted overall view of things. We live in an era of the specialist, of the person who knows more and more about less and less. Although we have developed areas of densely cultivated knowledge, they don't link up into any kind of network of ideas. The central split is of course between science and the humanities, but the fissures extend and proliferate within these 'two cultures' to produce a seriously fragmented system of knowledge.[2] This very modern problem of isolated specialization presents us with the acute difficulty of having to try to make sense of our knowledge piecemeal. It's as though we have just four or five pieces of a jigsaw puzzle and we can't make out what the whole picture is supposed to be.

There is, therefore, for anyone who is at all reflective, a pressing need – as much as there was for our primitive ancestors – to find the other bits of the jigsaw. There are, of course, many people willing to supply the missing pieces. The Roman Catholic Church, for example, is an ancient and venerable institution, and in the course of 2,000 years it has worked out all the answers. You only have to buy a copy of the latest catechism to find all the questions and all the answers neatly set out. Should any fresh questions arise, these will be swiftly answered by an encyclical from the Vatican. Many people find that this system deals with the mystery of life very satisfactorily. The same goes for Islam, which also lays down a conclusive and thoroughgoing context of meaning for human life. Marxism too, in its various forms, provided – at least until recently – a comparatively all-embracing world-view that explained everything in terms of economic evolution leading to a political and social utopia.

Those whom the more established systems of thought fail to satisfy can turn to any number of 'cults' or fringe religious groups, even psychological and political movements, for something that will validate their aspirations and make them feel positive and progressive. And it is possible to go from one to another, to change your direction, as often as you like. I knew an Englishwoman in India who claimed to have changed her religion seventeen times. She had started off as a Roman Catholic and had worked her way through the Vedanta and the Swedenborgian Church and the Ramakrishna Mission and many others. By the time I knew her, when she was middle-aged, she was a Seventh Day Adventist, and even then thinking of moving on to something else, because this religion prohibited the consumption of tea. I remember visiting her once (this was in Kalimpong), and while we were having a nice cup of tea together there was a knock on the door and she turned pale. 'My God,' she whispered, 'That's the minister', and quickly hid the teapot. I believe she went on to Australia, but whether or not she found something that suited her better I don't know. One may laugh or one may cry at the sort of predicament she was in – but she was at least searching for the truth in her own way.[3]

The fact is that, whether one is making a point of searching for the truth or not, it is simply not possible to avoid the practice of philosophy altogether. Everybody has a philosophy of some kind. It is just that some people are good at philosophizing and others are not. You can meet all sorts of people who have developed, without any academic training of any kind, an articulated philosophy of their own that is consistent and integrated. But whereas these individuals may have worked out a clear conceptualized version of their attitude towards life as a whole, others may have only a very rudimentary or embryonic idea of what they take to be the central reality and purpose of life. Like it or not, we all begin as our remote ancestors did in a state of confusion and bewilderment, but it is up to us where we go from there.

It is as if you woke up one day to find yourself in a strange bed in some kind of inn. You don't know how you got there and you don't know where you are – except that it's somehow a temporary place to stay, with people coming and people going. All you know is that it's not your own place and you don't recognize the road it's on. You've just woken up and you're bewildered and confused and wondering what's going on. This is surely more or less how we feel about finding ourselves in the world at all. Here we are with a body, two eyes, two ears, a mouth, a nose, thoughts ... dropped off in the middle of England or wherever, dumped down in the tail-end of the twentieth century. What brought us here, we just don't know. We just wake up and here we are.

When you wake up in this imaginary inn all you want to know is where you go from here. You need someone to give you a map showing the surrounding country, so that you can see the route you have come by so far and the direction you need to take to reach your destination. And this, as one might expect by now, is where Buddhism comes in. It is when the human condition is looked at in these quite elementary, even existential, terms that the teaching of the Buddha seems to come into its own.

Encountering Buddhism, what we discover, essentially, is a very comprehensive system of thought. (The word 'thought' is not ideal, but it must do for the time being.) This is not to say that the different forms of Buddhism that have arisen over more than 2,000 years all necessarily hang together neatly. But as well as being used as a blanket term covering the whole range of different approaches to the teaching, 'Buddhism' needs also to be appreciated in essential terms as representing a consistent and complete philosophical scheme.

Encountering Buddhism concretely, however, coming into contact with actual Buddhist groups, meeting flesh-and-blood Buddhist individuals, we find only too often the same sort of piecemeal approach that characterizes modern knowledge as a whole. There are a lot of schools in Buddhism (and they are 'schools' rather than 'sects') – Theravāda, Zen, Pure Land, Tiantai, Gelug, Kagyu, Nyingma, and so on. But it is rare to find followers of one school of Buddhism knowing anything much about the teachings of any other school. I have had a good deal of contact with Theravāda Buddhists, for example (admittedly, in most cases, a very long time ago), and my experience was that – whether they came from Sri Lanka, Burma, or Thailand – they knew absolutely nothing about Zen. In the vast majority of cases they had not even heard of it. Conversely, one can meet Zen monks – even Zen masters – who haven't a clue about what the Theravāda might be. As the world becomes a smaller place this is gradually changing, but one has to be careful when picking up a book on Buddhism, or listening to someone talk about Buddhism, that one isn't just getting the version of Buddhism put forward by one particular school.

Within Buddhism there is also a tendency to present a partial and unbalanced account of the teaching. A particular set of doctrines may be set out very clearly, but they are not related to other doctrines that perhaps look at the same issue from a different angle. For instance, there is the teaching of *duḥkha*, that human existence is inherently unsatisfactory, that it can never be quite as we would like; that, indeed, even if we got everything we wanted, life would still be unsatisfactory. It is a fundamental doctrine, without which the whole of Buddhism rather loses its point. However, if it is not always firmly located within the context of the four noble truths which go on to summarize the way to transcend it, the teaching of *duḥkha* will seem just a rather sour fact of life.

Take another doctrine, that of the *tathāgata-garbha* – literally the 'womb of Enlightenment' – according to which all sentient existence carries within it the 'seed' of Buddhahood, of supreme and perfect Enlightenment. If this doctrine of universal potential Buddhahood is not related to the Noble Eightfold Path, which lays out the necessary steps to be taken in order to realize Enlightenment, we can come away with the notion that we actually have Buddhahood in the palm of our hand, as it were, and that all we have to do is wake up to the fact. Such teachings, if not put in their proper context and related to an overall framework, can be quite misleading.

This goes for meditation too. We can no doubt very usefully take up meditation as a purely psychological exercise, but as soon as we begin to see it as more than just a profane training, as soon as we begin to acknowledge that it is some sort of sacred or spiritual practice, we need to acquire some understanding of the general framework or context within which its practical spiritual purpose is defined. In the East it doesn't matter so much, because there the whole culture, the whole society, provides that framework, and if one has close personal contact with a good teacher then one doesn't need to know very much about the doctrine intellectually. But that situation does not obtain in the West, and if we are to take up Buddhist meditation we must have some knowledge of the general principles of Buddhism.

Buddhism is a vast subject, and putting it in a context which is familiar to the modern Western mind is not to be taken too literally – it is not like finding a big box into which we can fit a smaller box. It is a matter rather of laying out the Buddhist system of thought as a whole in terms that should be sufficiently familiar to all of us as a way of looking at the world as not to require much explanation. And the idea that functions most comprehensively in this way is the principle of evolution, derived from the biological sciences. The fact that the Christian faith in particular has become reconciled to this principle only with the greatest difficulty makes it also a useful tool in highlighting some of the more distinctive features of the Buddhist vision. Nothing like the kind of *tour de force* we meet with in the works of the Catholic thinker Teilhard de Chardin is required to bring Buddhism and modern evolutionary ideas together.[4]

We now know that the theory of evolution was anticipated by a number of thinkers, by Kant, Hegel, and others – and even, according to some, by Aristotle himself.[5] But Darwin was the first to trace the operation of evolution in detail within the field of biology. To attempt to refute the principle of evolution in that field today would be like saying the earth is flat. It is the given basis for all the biological sciences. If anything, the idea has invaded all sorts of other disciplines, from politics to astronomy, so that one could fairly say that just as the Elizabethan age was dominated by the concepts of order and hierarchy, so the modern world is dominated by the concept of evolution.

In taking up an idea that is generally understood in scientific or at least academic applications and applying it in a spiritual context, we have, of course, to draw some precise boundaries. Scientific knowledge depends on the evidence of the senses – but, just because Buddhism has never tried to resist the evidence of the senses, that does not make it a 'scientific religion'. It is certainly true that Buddhism's appeal in the West owes much to the spirit of empirical, open-minded inquiry which the Buddha laid down as axiomatic to the spiritual quest – and this lack of dogmatism does align Buddhism in some important respects with the Greek scientific spirit rather than with the dominant religious traditions in the modern West. Equally axiomatic to the Buddhist notion of the spiritual quest, however, is the recognition of a transcendental Reality – which is not, of course, a provable scientific hypothesis. As a practising Buddhist one starts, in accordance with the Buddha's advice, from the evidence of one's own experience, and this will tend to support more and more the idea of a spiritual order of evolution. It is on the basis of this evidence that biological evolution carries conviction – not the other way round. If we see human beings as in any way constituting some kind of key to the universe, then on the basis of our own experience of progression we may fairly conclude that progression is in some way inherent in the universe.

In this respect, at least, Buddhism inclines more towards a traditional, pre-scientific viewpoint. If we look at a traditional civilization, we find that everything, every activity, every piece of knowledge, is linked with ideas of a metaphysical order. Ordinary things, ordinary events, accepted ideas, are not just of practical use. They have a symbolic value, they point beyond themselves, they have meaning. Amidst our own fragmented, 'specialist', economically defined culture we may find it difficult to appreciate this attitude, but it is the basis for the Tantra, and it was the world-view of our own society until comparatively recently.

According to this view everything is interconnected and nothing can ever really be ordinary – in the sense of being without a deeper meaning – at all. Rather than look for scientific proof of spiritual realities, we may say, paraphrasing G. K. Chesterton, that it is because we no longer believe in the gods that we no longer believe in ourselves.[6] Our project as Buddhists must be to replace a mechanistic universe with one that has meaning, that carries throughout its fabric intimations of spiritual values.

Buddhism therefore looks at the rational knowledge derived from the senses in the light of a knowledge that is derived not from the senses and reason alone, but from a fusion of reason with emotion in a higher faculty of archetypal knowledge which we may call 'vision', 'insight', or 'imagination'. It is not a question of justifying Buddhism in scientific terms, but rather of understanding sense-derived knowledge by means of knowledge that is not sense-based. In other words, the knowledge that is derived from the senses fits into a much larger pattern of knowledge that is not derived from the senses. From a Buddhist point of view, there is a hierarchy of levels of being and consciousness, a hierarchy of degrees of spiritual attainment, which seems to be reflected in, or as it were anticipated by, the whole process of biological evolution. It seems to make sense, therefore, to regard both biological evolution and the hierarchies of spiritual development as being – from the Buddhist point of view – in their separate spheres, exemplifications of a single law or principle.

It is clear that according to the principle of evolution life is not just existence. It is a process – a process of becoming – and humankind is not something apart from the rest of nature, as the theistic religions usually teach. Humankind itself also comes under the operation of this great process of becoming. It too is evolving and developing, not just towards new forms of existence and organization, but towards new and higher levels of being.

There are two different ways of looking at any evolving phenomenon: in terms of its past or in terms of its future; in terms of what it was or in terms of what it may come to be. The first of these ways of looking at phenomena – in terms of their origins – is traditionally called the genetic approach; the second – in terms of their destination or purpose – is the teleological method. So if we take an example of humankind at its best – someone who is intelligent, self-aware, morally responsible, sensitive to others and to the world around them – we should be able to look at them from each of these two perspectives. From a genetic perspective, we can look back at the complex evolutionary process described by Darwin, including that critical point at which self-consciousness – or more precisely, reflexive consciousness, which is roughly identifiable with specifically human consciousness – emerges from simple animal sense-consciousness. This whole process we can characterize, from the Buddhist point of view, as the 'lower evolution'. But there is also the teleological perspective: we can also look at what an aware human being may develop into, what they are in process of developing into, and this development we may distinguish as the 'higher evolution'. We have got so far in evolutionary terms propelled by the unconscious urge to grow and develop which fuels the origin of species, but to enter into the higher evolution takes conscious effort, or what we call spiritual practice. The lower evolution is the province of the biological sciences, leaving the higher evolution to be mapped out by the religions of the world, especially, of course, by Buddhism.

This sort of model of Buddhism is crucial to an understanding of who the Buddha is and what our own relationship to him might be. By means of it we can locate our own situation, which is probably a little short of our central figure of the fully integrated human being, and thus somewhere in the upper reaches of the lower evolution. We can also see the evolutionary process stretching ahead of us as far as Buddhahood – and beyond, inasmuch as Buddhahood is not a terminal point, but is by its very 'nature' limitless. And somewhere in the midst of this continuum we can envisage another critical point, where Insight into the nature of Reality – Insight with a capital I – replaces our faint, confused, and intermittent apprehensions of something that transcends our common perception of things. In this way, we know where we stand, we know the direction we must take, and we have something to aim for.

Before focusing on those stages in the evolutionary process that concern us as individual human beings we can restate what has been said so far in traditional Buddhist terminology. According to Buddhism the nature of existence consists in change or 'becoming'. It is not simply some 'thing' that is subject to change – existence itself is change. The specific manner of that change was expressed by the Buddha in a formula known in Sanskrit as *pratītya-samutpāda* and translated as 'conditioned co-production' or 'dependent origination'. This formula or law goes as follows: 'This being, that becomes; from the arising of this, that arises. This not being, that does not become; from the ceasing of this, that ceases.'[7] So if existence is change, change is conditionality. Existence is seen as an infinitely complex and shifting pattern of physical and mental phenomena, all coming into being in dependence on certain conditions, and disappearing when those conditions disappear.

Pratītya-samutpāda is not traditionally invoked as a cosmological principle, but there is no reason why it should not be. In the *Dīgha Nikāya* of the Pāli canon there is a very long discourse delivered by the Buddha, the *Aggañña Sutta*, which deals with the evolution of the universe and the origin of humankind.[8] But for our present purposes we may say simply that in dependence upon the lower evolution arises the higher evolution.

What this does not mean is that the higher evolution is entirely the product of the lower evolution. *Pratītya-samutpāda* expresses the middle way between seeing the lower evolution as essentially the same process as the higher evolution and seeing them as completely different processes. The basic Buddhist approach is in this sense scientific – it describes what happens without necessarily committing itself to an interpretation of those facts.

Within this universal framework of conditionality, however, there are two types of conditionality. On the one hand there is a 'cyclic' mode of conditionality, a process of reaction between opposite factors: death arising in dependence on birth, good in dependence on evil, happiness in dependence on suffering – and vice versa. It is a characteristic of human experience that is all too familiar – as Keats puts it: 'Ay, in the very temple of Delight / Veil'd Melancholy has her sovran shrine'.[9] This is *saṃsāra* or the round of existence, as depicted in the Tibetan version of the wheel of life.

On the other hand there is a cumulative development of positive factors progressively augmenting each other, and this 'spiral' mode of conditionality provides the basis for the spiritual life. Thus in dependence on the arising of faith, joy arises, and so on in an ascending series of mental states all the way up to Enlightenment itself. The essential characteristic of a positive mental state is that it does not produce a negative reaction but instead produces a further positive factor. An act of true generosity, for example, is not succeeded by a niggling resentment when your gift does not seem to be appreciated. You simply derive joy from giving. It hardly needs saying that the cyclical principle governs the lower evolution, while the spiral mode of conditionality comprises the higher evolution.[10]

The Buddha's working out, in his first discourse after his Enlightenment, of the principle of *pratītya-samutpāda* as the four noble truths[11] can be correlated with the evolution model equally simply. The first and second noble truths, which are that pain is inherent in sentient existence and that this pain arises in dependence – ultimately – upon craving, are concerned with the lower evolution. The third and fourth noble truths, which are, respectively, that this pain ceases with the ceasing of craving, and that the way to bring about an end to craving is by undertaking the Noble Eightfold Path, take us into the higher evolution.

By taking an evolutionary perspective we can discern some absolutely fundamental practical principles of the spiritual life. Within the lower evolution forms of life develop as a group – evolution works as a collective process – whereas the higher evolution is necessarily individual, which means that one individual can outstrip the rest. It is for this reason that self-awareness, mindfulness, is the starting point – the growing point – of the higher evolution. It is as though self-awareness generates a degree of energy sufficient to carry you through the whole process of the higher evolution in a single lifetime. Buddhist practice is concerned solely and exclusively with the development of the individual, that is, with the higher evolution. Once this is clear we can bring the whole range of Buddhist teachings into focus.

The Buddha lays down a path of practice leading to Enlightenment, but then he says very emphatically, 'You must walk the path yourselves. I've walked it for myself, but I can't walk it for you. No one can save another. No one can purify another. It's up to you to do it for yourselves.'[12] In this sense Buddhism is a do-it-yourself religion. The corollary of this is that anyone who makes the effort can obtain the same results. There aren't some chosen few who can do it and others who can't. If no one is going to do it for you, this also means that if you make the effort, you will make progress. You don't even have to call yourself a Buddhist. If you accept the principles and follow the path, you will infallibly get the right results.

This is one reason why Buddhism is, by its very nature, a tolerant religion. Buddhists are not tolerant out of sheer indifference or apathy, but because everybody has to find out the Truth for themselves. This is the nature of the Buddhist path. You have to allow others the same freedom that you claim for yourself – freedom to grow, to develop spiritually, in their own way. Therefore there is no conception of religious war or religious persecution in Buddhism. For example, the king of Thailand, who is the Buddhist king of a largely but not wholly Buddhist country, has as one of his titles 'Protector of all Religions'.

So there is no compulsion. The Buddha's teaching, the Dharma, is called, in Pāli – the ancient language in which much of it was first written down – *ehipassiko dhamma*, that is, 'the teaching (*dhamma*) of come (*ehi*) and see (*passiko*)'.[13] It is the teaching that says come and see for yourself. Don't accept it on trust. Believe it because you can understand, experience and verify it for yourself. Don't believe just because the Buddha tells you to. The Buddha himself is recorded as saying: 'Monks, don't accept what I say just out of respect for me. Just as gold is tested in the fire, so test my words in the fire of spiritual experience.'[14]

When the Buddha's aunt and foster-mother, Mahāprajāpatī Gautami, asked the Buddha directly to give her a teaching she could practise, the Buddha replied that she could work out for herself whether any of the spiritual practices on offer were in accordance with his teaching: 'Whatever teachings you can be sure conduce to tranquillity and not to greed and hatred; to freedom and not to enslavement; to decrease of worldly ties and not to increase of them; to contentment and not to covetousness; to solitude and not to social distractions; to energy and not to sluggishness; to delight in good and not to delight in evil; of these teachings you can be sure that they constitute my Dharma.'[15]

One of the most prevalent ways in which some Buddhists take a one-sided view of the Dharma is in thinking of it in an exclusively negative manner, as just a matter of rooting out the whole of the lower evolution and leaving it at that. But it is quite clear that the Buddha's own conception of it was one of positive growth, of a conscious effort to evolve and progress as an individual. As well as leaving the lower evolution behind, we need also to take some positive steps in the direction of the higher evolution. As well as giving up meanness we want to cultivate generosity. As well as avoiding being harsh and callous we want to develop kindness. And there is a set of four meditation practices that are specifically concerned with developing the whole range of positive emotion. These are the four *brahma vihāras*, 'the abodes of the gods'.[16] The first consists in the development of *maitrī* or love towards all living beings – a desire for the well-being of others, a wish that they may grow and develop. The second *brahma vihāra* is *karuṇā* or compassion for those who are stuck, whose growth is stunted. Thirdly there is *muditā* or 'sympathetic joy' in the happiness of others – which is like when you go out into the garden in early summer and see the flowers all springing up and blooming. And the fourth is *upekṣā*, equanimity or peace, an experience not of sitting back and putting your feet up, but of a vibrant spiritual equilibrium.

The four *brahma vihāras* do not come naturally; they are not endowments of the lower evolution. They have to be consciously developed, for, as we have seen, spiritual development is the development of consciousness. Whereas the lower evolution is an unconscious development on the material level, the higher evolution is a conscious development on the mental level. At the same time the whole of evolution, lower and higher, is a continuous process. Of the two general scientific theories of evolution, that it is a mechanistic, random process, and the opposite view, that it could not have taken place without some kind of purpose or direction, the Buddhist approach is more akin to the second view. It is very broadly 'vitalist' in that it recognizes a will to Enlightenment somehow present in all forms of life and manifesting in any gesture of consideration or act of intelligent good will. With the beginning of the evolutionary process you get the impression of a sort of fumbling, with a lot of false starts – it seems a bit hit-or-miss. But then as you follow it further, whatever it is that stands behind the evolutionary process seems to become surer of itself, as it were, and to define itself more clearly as time goes by. And with the emergence of the aware individual human being undertaking the spiritual path it becomes fully conscious of itself, thereby speeding up the whole process.

The Buddhist has to tread very lightly in this area to avoid misunderstanding. Evolution is just a metaphor or model for Buddhism, a temporal model. In speaking of some 'thing', some reality *behind* the evolutionary process, we are simply using a different model, a spatial model. If we speak in terms of developing from one stage to another, that is to look at reality in temporal terms. But if we speak of what is there all the time, the absolute reality which is always here and now, that is to speak in spatial terms. So this is the function of the 'will to Enlightenment' or *bodhicitta*, in this context – to transcend these spatio-temporal models. It is not the life-force of the universe, or any kind of causative first principle, but rather a liberation principle, a will to transcend the universe or *saṃsāra*.

We may say, in fact, that self-transcendence is what the whole of evolution, from the amoeba upwards, is about. We can say further that this evolutionary principle of self-transcendence is expressed in its highest and most fully self-conscious form in the figure of the bodhisattva, the one who, according to Mahāyāna Buddhism, dedicates himself or herself to the cause of helping all sentient existence to Enlightenment. The will to Enlightenment of a bodhisattva is a fully committed volition to perpetual self-transcendence. And from the bodhisattva to the Buddha there is only, as it were, a step.

It is from this perspective, seeing spiritual development in terms of perpetual self-transcendence, that we can best appreciate the often half-understood Buddhist concept of *anātman*, or 'no-self'. This is sometimes interpreted as meaning that we don't really exist, that there's a sort of hole where one imagines one's self to be. In fact, the point of this teaching is that we have no substantial unchanging self, no soul. Indeed, putting it more dynamically and experientially, we can say that for radical change, radical development, to take place – for a fully conscious self-transcendence to be possible – there *can* be no unchanging self.

We may look at Buddhism from a purely academic perspective as just an activity or philosophical position of a number of individuals calling themselves Buddhists. On the other hand, we can take the vast and awe-inspiring perspective of the Buddha's teaching itself. From this latter perspective, we are all frail, impermanent beings, born into the world and passing out of it with apparently little to show for our trouble – but at the same time we embody the universal possibility of Enlightenment. Just as the scientific concept of evolution involves a progression towards new biological organisms through periods of time that are practically unimaginable, so, according to Buddhism, our own lives take their place in a context of literally unimaginable temporal duration, in which, however, they are of literally cosmic importance. For among all the life-forms in the universe, from the amoeba to the highest realms of the gods, it is only the kind of sentient life to which human beings conform that can be, in the words of Lama Govinda, 'the vehicle for the rediscovery of the transcendental and inconceivable nature of mind or consciousness'[17] – that can become, in short, a Buddha.

2

THE WAY TO ENLIGHTENMENT

All human beings are capable of evolving into Buddhas, but one man alone opened the way for the rest of humanity to follow. To be strictly accurate, we should say '*re*-opened', because traditionally speaking there had been other Buddhas, many other pioneers on the path of the higher evolution, before him. But when we speak of *the* Buddha we refer to Siddhārtha Gautama, who discovered the path on the full-moon day of the lunar month of April/May, in the year 542 BCE. The way he himself put it was this: 'Suppose a man wandering in a forest wilderness found an ancient path, an ancient trail, travelled by men of old, and he followed it up, and by doing so he discovered an ancient city, an ancient royal capital, where men of old had lived, with parks and groves and lakes, walled round and beautiful to see. So I too found the ancient path, the ancient trail, travelled by the Fully Enlightened Ones of old.'[18]

Hence the very special place in the Buddhist calendar of Vaiśākha Pūrṇimā, the full-moon day of the Indian month Vaiśākha. Vaiśākha in Pāli is Vesākha, and this translates into Sinhalese as Wesak, which gives its name to the most important of Buddhist festivals. At Wesak Buddhists celebrate what they regard as being the greatest event on record, the occasion when, for the first time in recorded history, an unenlightened being, a man, became an Enlightened being, an Enlightened man. They commemorate the day when Siddhārtha Gautama finally freed himself from all human conditionings, all human limitations, to become as it were one with Reality, to become even, we may say, a living embodiment of the Truth, a Buddha.

It might seem surprising, therefore, that there should be a certain amount of confusion as to what is really being celebrated at Wesak. However, whenever I used to be invited to take part in a Wesak celebration in India, whether as a speaker or in some other capacity, what I used to be asked to do was to honour (or grace) with my presence – such is the Indian style of courtesy in such matters – 'the Thrice Sacred Day (or Festival)'. So why 'thrice sacred'? Surely once is enough? Either something is sacred or it isn't – so you might think. But of course there is a reason for this designation. According to some sources the Vaiśākha Pūrṇimā is the anniversary of not one but three events: the Buddha's birth, his attainment of Enlightenment, and also his final passing away or *parinirvāṇa*. They are all supposed to have taken place on the same day – in different years of course, but by quite a coincidence on the same full-moon day. It must be said, however, that this tradition of a thrice-sacred Vaiśākha Pūrṇimā rests on a very late tradition originating in Sri Lanka and thence spreading to other Theravāda countries. The rest of the Buddhist world, the Mahāyāna Buddhist countries, celebrate the Buddha's birth and his *parinirvāṇa* on other days of the year, and this does seem to have been the earlier – and also the more reasonable – arrangement.

As well as having different ideas about whether or not Wesak marks anything besides the Buddha's Enlightenment, Buddhists in different parts of the world have different national traditions in the way they go about marking it. In Sri Lanka and Burma you will find people lighting candles and offering them in homage to the Buddha's memory. In Tibet it will be butter lamps, and it will be a particular number of butter lamps – 108 or 1,008 of them. In many Buddhist countries you will hear people chanting verses in praise of the Buddha, sometimes for hours on end, even all day and all night. In other places there will be lectures and discussions, and some people of course will simply be meditating. On a more social level you will find monks being fed – in some Buddhist countries this is a very popular pastime on any festive occasion. You gather together as many monks as possible, line them up in rows on the floor and give them food. Monks are traditionally supposed to have very healthy appetites and in some Buddhist quarters the amount of merit you get from feeding a monk is said to be directly linked to the amount of your food the monk eats. In these circumstances, therefore, hospitality is not stinted, and certainly not refused. Buddhists in the West follow the lead given by these older traditions, of course, but many of them are in the process of developing their own cultural tradition of celebrating Wesak.

At whatever level and in whatever fashion Buddhists celebrate Wesak they are unified by its one central theme and purpose, which is to rejoice at the emergence of a Buddha in the world. In this they are following a tradition which goes back a very long way indeed, and we have only to look among the earliest examples of Indian Buddhist stone carvings to find evidence of this. A particularly striking composition places the Buddha, in symbolic form, on a throne, surrounded by monks, nuns, and lay-people all with their hands joined together above their heads and all making offerings of garlands, fruits, scarves – all sorts of offerings being made in all sorts of ways. What is really notable about this scene is the expression of absolute joy that all these figures wear. The impression one gets is that an event of overwhelming, cosmic importance must have taken place to be celebrated in this exultant and spectacular manner. It would hardly be an exaggeration to say that the artist has made these worshippers look positively crazy with joy.[19]

Such is the only emotional response – as this artist proposes, at least – that can do justice to the Buddha's realization of the ultimate possibility of human development. Yet the deep roots of the joy expressed by his followers at Wesak lie not just in the fact that he attained Enlightenment for himself, as it were. They lie in the fact that he opened the way, he blazed the trail, for others to follow after him. The question of how the Buddha became Enlightened is therefore not just theoretical. Of course, you can approach it theoretically if you wish, as you can approach any question theoretically, but essentially it is a question of the greatest practical importance. The Buddha did not inherit Enlightenment; he was not born to be Enlightened. He attained Enlightenment only after many years of struggle – and even after making mistakes. Through his own efforts in his own life he showed how we too by our own efforts can gain Enlightenment.

This provides an entirely new approach to the Dharma, the Way to Enlightenment. You can, as already suggested, think of it in terms of evolution, of progressive stages to be followed like a sort of road, with milestones along it marking the distance you've travelled. There are the three great stages of the path – ethics, meditation, and wisdom – as well as many other ways of subdividing and classifying the Way to Enlightenment. But you can also approach it from a more unusual angle – that is, in terms of the events of the Buddha's life.

To contemplate the biographical details of the Buddha's early life is to be concerned not just with the spiritual path followed by a man who lived 2,500 years ago. It is to contemplate a path which one can follow here and now, a path that one is committed to following if one is a Buddhist, if one has Buddhahood as one's ultimate goal. In other words, when as Buddhists we celebrate the Buddha's Enlightenment, we are not just rejoicing in a thing of the past. We are reminding ourselves that it is high time we started to think of our own Enlightenment, if indeed we have not already done so – and if we have, to think of it more persistently, more seriously, and more deeply.

I will therefore run through the salient events of the Buddha's early life, to get a general idea of the way to Enlightenment, and then take up for more detailed examination certain crucial episodes or features of his biography that have a definite bearing on our own process of development towards Enlightenment. Like the story of the Buddha's life as a whole, these notable elements are in substance historical, inasmuch as we know they actually did happen. However, the versions that have come down to us contain a certain amount of legendary material, and it is this legendary material that helps to bring out the universal significance, the inner spiritual dimension, of the external events. The mythical aspect makes it clear, among other things, that these events are concerned not with one man's spiritual career, but with the career of every man and woman who aspires to grow and develop as an individual.

It is very often said that Siddhārtha Gautama, who became the Buddha, was born in India, and a hundred years ago this would have been true. But owing to changing political boundaries we would have to say today that his birth took place in the southern part of what is now Nepal. He was born into a tribe called the Śākyans, who had inhabited that particular area in the foothills of the Himalayas for many centuries. Nor is it quite true – as it is, again, often said – that his father, Śuddhodana Gautama, was the king of the tribe. He did certainly hold the title of rajah at the time of Siddhārtha's birth, but today he would probably be called a president. Like other small tribes in north-eastern India at that time, the Śākyans had a semi-republican form of government, with a leader elected from the clan assembly for a fixed period of twelve years. Towards the end of the Buddha's lifetime the little republics of India were swallowed up by the developing Magadha empire, but at the time of his birth they were, for the most part, in a flourishing condition.

Siddhārtha's mother, Māyādevī, was the daughter of the chief of a neighbouring tribe, the Koliyas. It was then the custom, as it still is in many parts of India, for the first child to be born in the house of the mother's parents. When she felt her time approaching, therefore, Māyādevī set off from Kapilavastu, the Śākyan capital, to make for her father's city, carried, as far as we know, in a palanquin. She was still only halfway there when, seized with the pangs of labour, she dismounted, and in a grove of sāl trees at a little place called Lumbinī gave birth to the future Buddha. She died shortly afterwards – seven days later, according to tradition.[20]

Siddhārtha was reared by his maternal aunt, Mahāprajāpatī Gautami, whom his father had also married. We know little more about his childhood, but a single authentic incident stands out, one that took place when he was five, six, or perhaps seven years old, on the occasion of the annual ploughing ceremony. In primarily agricultural civilizations all over the world, the sowing of the first seed in the spring was a matter of magical and mythical significance, and the first ploughing was always undertaken by the king or chief. It was one of the duties of the old emperors of China, and until quite recently the emperor of Japan used to inaugurate the ploughing every year. It was thus one of the jobs that fell to Siddhārtha's father to carry out. Later accounts tell us that it was done with a golden plough drawn by beautiful white oxen (storytellers love to embroider their material). But leaving that aside, what we can say with confidence is that Siddhārtha's father performed this ceremony and that Siddhārtha was brought along to watch.

The little boy was put on one side on a bank in the shade of a *jambu* or rose-apple tree, and it was there that he had what we would describe nowadays as a spontaneous mystical experience. According to the Buddha himself, as he reminisced to his disciples a great many years later, what he experienced beneath the rose-apple tree was a sort of superconscious state known as *dhyāna*. So deep was his absorption that he never saw the ploughing at all, and he had still not emerged from the experience when they came to take him home.

It is at this point that an interesting legendary anecdote finds its way into the episode. The legend has it that although it was noon when the ploughing started, and evening by the time the ceremony was over, the shadow of the rose-apple tree had not moved during that time. On a literal level this would be what we call a miracle, but it is perhaps more meaningful if we take it symbolically. The obvious implication is that the sun stood still; and the implication on the symbolic level is that for the young Siddhārtha time itself had stopped.[21]

Later on, as we shall see, the memory of this experience was to have a crucial bearing on the direction of Siddhārtha's spiritual career. But meanwhile, mystical experience or no mystical experience, he was a Kṣatriya, a warrior, and he would have been brought up like one. That was his caste – the caste of the whole tribe – so he was literally born a warrior, as others were born Brahmins (priests), Vaiśyas (traders and farmers), or Śūdras (labourers) – just as they are today, although these four castes are now subdivided into some 2,000 subcastes.[22]

The future Buddha spent his formative years not in the close study of philosophy or in religious practices, but acquiring the arts of archery and spear-throwing, swordplay, and the skilful handling of a war-chariot. With his patrician background he would have received the best martial training available. He would also have been initiated into the various traditions, customs, beliefs, and superstitions of the tribe, and he would have learned a little history and genealogy too. Of course, whatever he learned would have been by word of mouth from the elders of the tribe. It is not clear whether the Buddha ever learned to read or write. We must imagine him as a man who was cultured, educated, and well-bred without ever having attended anything like a school (it is, in any case, questionable whether education has really anything to do with going to school). He led on the whole a quite comfortable, well-to-do life, had no particular responsibilities, and was doted on by his father.

Siddhārtha's upbringing was not, however, quite so simple and straightforward as all that. Shortly after his birth, his father took him to see a *rishi*, the sage Asita, to have his horoscope cast. This was common practice, as it still is in India today. There is hardly anybody, even among the Westernized so-called élite, who does not have this done for their children – especially for their sons. You want to know what is going to happen to your child, what sort of a career he or she will have, so you go to an astrologer. It is not known exactly how Siddhārtha's horoscope was cast, but we know that he was placed in the arms of Asita, and that the *rishi* made his calculations. He predicted that the child would have a remarkable future: Siddhārtha would either become a great Kṣatriya, a great warrior and ruler, or else he would give it all up and become a great spiritual master.[23]

Śuddhodana was deeply disturbed at this prognostication, of course. He liked the idea of his son becoming an illustrious conqueror – he liked it very much – but he was appalled at the idea that the lad might take it into his head to retire from the world altogether and devote his talents to the spiritual quest. The older Siddhārtha grew, the more Śuddhodana turned the matter over in his mind. He thought, 'I want him to grow up like me. I want him to be brave and strong and extend the territory of the tribe, and – if the *rishi* is right – to become a great ruler and maybe conquer all of India. He must not be allowed to waste his time over all this religious nonsense. Therefore he must be prevented from thinking too deeply about anything; he must not be introduced to the more unpalatable facts of life – at least not too early. His heart must be set firmly on worldly things.'

So Śuddhodana was determined that the young prince should want for nothing, that all he should learn about life should be how to enjoy it to the most refined pitch of sensual pleasure. The Buddha later related in one of his autobiographical discourses how his father had provided him with three beautiful mansions, one for each season, so that he should never feel discomfort from the heat or the cold or the rains. And he recounted also how these mansions were filled with alluring dancing girls and bewitching singing girls, and how his days and nights were spent in drinking, dancing, and singing, one pleasure succeeding another, with hardly a moment for sadness.[24]

At sixteen he was married off to a cousin, Yaśodharā. It was an arranged marriage, of course, just as in India today a marriage is usually negotiated by the families of the bride and bridegroom rather than by the young people themselves. He settled down happily enough and in this way for many years his life went on. All the same, though, he seems to have had an underlying sense of dissatisfaction with the life he was leading. When the news was brought to him that his wife had given birth to a son his reaction was not the usual one of a proud father. Asked what the boy should be called, he said, 'A fetter has been born to me. Call him Rāhula,'[25] for this is what the name Rāhula means – 'fetter'.

(A fetter is a chain or manacle used to tie down a prisoner.) It was as if he sensed what his father had been trying to do all his life. Somehow he knew that Śuddhodana was trying to bind him down: with pleasure, with property, with power, with family, with wife and child. Realizing what was happening, he neglected his martial exercises and lost interest in the amusements and distractions laid on for him. Domestic life held no joy for him.

Increasingly he took himself off for long periods in order to think, and at some point he evidently had some sort of spiritual crisis – though this is not of course how the early scriptures put it. This psychological and spiritual turning point is known among Buddhists everywhere in the form of a dramatic narrative called the four sights. Whether this is a legend, whether it is an external projection of an experience arising out of intense inner questioning, or whether it actually happened in something like the way the story has come down to us, it is impossible for us to say for sure. What is certain is that the story of the four sights crystallizes in a very powerful form some of the fundamental teachings of Buddhism, as well as throwing light on the Buddha's own early spiritual development.

The story goes that one bright morning Siddhārtha called his charioteer to harness the horses for an outing. 'Let's see what is going on in the world, see what people are up to,' he said. The charioteer shook his head. 'I'm afraid we can't do that. I'll get into trouble. You know the king has said you are not to go out among the people.' But the young prince insisted: 'Don't worry. I'll take full responsibility. If the king has anything to say about it, let him say it to me. But let's go.' So the horses were whipped up and away they went. They drove out into the village and Siddhārtha saw life going on much as he might have expected – until his attention was arrested by the sight of a very old man.

The traditional accounts give a graphic description of this old man's appearance – feeble, withered, and bent over, his bones sticking out, tottering along on a stick. He had a long white beard and the rheum was trickling from his eyes. If this seems to be laying it on a bit thick, it would not seem so in India. There, old people, even today – because of the climate and the hard life – can sometimes look very old indeed. We have to remember that according to the legend his father had deliberately secluded him from anything unpleasant about life, and this included old age. So when Siddhārtha saw this very old man, he pointed at him and said, 'Who ... what ... is that?'

The charioteer thought, 'Well, he'll have to find out sooner or later,' and he said, 'It's an old man.' 'But why is he like that? Why is he so bent? Why do all his bones stick out? Why is that fluid trickling out from his eyes?' The charioteer was not used to fielding this sort of question, except perhaps from children. He said simply, 'Well, he's just an old man.' Obviously Siddhārtha was not satisfied by this: 'But how has he got like that?' 'It just happens,' the charioteer explained gently. 'You don't have to do anything to get old – you just get old. It's natural, I'm afraid – everybody gets old.' The young prince felt his flesh creep. 'What, everybody?' he asked, and the charioteer said, 'Well, yes, of course. Everybody.' 'What about me? Will I become like that?' The charioteer nodded: 'The king, your father, the queen, your mother, your wife, myself, and you too – all of us – are subject to old age.'

We are told that Siddhārtha received this intelligence like an elephant struck by a thunderbolt[26], and he broke into a cold sweat with the shock. 'What is the use of being young?' he lamented. 'What is the use of this vitality and strength, if it all ends in such emaciation and frailty?' He was sick at heart. 'That's enough for today. Let's go home,' he said, and as they rattled back to the palace he brooded over the knowledge he had been given.

This, then, is the legend of the first sight. Siddhārtha may or may not have literally clapped eyes on an old man for the first time in this way, but there is no mistaking the real significance of it. He might have seen many old men before, but somehow missed really seeing them. That day, perhaps, he saw an old man *as though* for the first time. This is how life is, of course. We may see a thing every day of our lives, just as we see the sun rising and the sun setting, but we don't really see it because we are not aware and we don't think. We see but we don't see. For example, one might work in an old people's home for years without taking in the fact of old age to any great depth. Then when we develop some awareness, some clarity, we can find that things appear to us in such a fresh light that it is as if we never saw them before. So Siddhārtha realized, truly realized for the first time in his life, that there was such a thing as old age, and that youth would be brief, even for him.

Shaken as he was by this realization, Siddhārtha went out again a few days later – so the legend has it – and again he saw something he had never seen before. What he saw was a sick man, lying by the roadside with an attack of fever or something of that sort, tossing this way and that. Again Siddhārtha asked the charioteer to explain what was going on: 'What has happened to this man? What is wrong with him? Why is he shaking and shivering? Why are his eyes rolling so wildly? Why does his face look so ghastly?' Of course the charioteer had to tell him, 'Well, he's ill.' And Siddhārtha, who had apparently enjoyed blooming health up to that time, wanted to know whether he too would be likely to suffer in this way: 'Does this happen to other people? Will it happen to me?' So again the charioteer drove the point home: 'All men, all women, are liable to sickness. It might come at any time. At any moment strength and health may go from us and then we must suffer sickness.' So again Siddhārtha had something to think about as he returned to the palace.

After a few days, they went once more in the chariot, and this time he saw four men coming towards them carrying something on a sort of stretcher, the poles of which were balanced on their shoulders. Lying on the stretcher there was a man wrapped in a yellow sheet. His face was exposed, but there was something odd about it. He didn't move a muscle. The face was quite expressionless, stiff-looking, and the eyes were closed.

Of course, you can still see this sight any day of the week in India. An Indian funeral is rather different from what most of us are used to in the West. Here, when you die you are smuggled away in a box, and that's that. You are just quietly disposed of; you're put into the incinerator or into a hole in the ground and covered over. But in India it isn't like that. In India you are laid out in the best room of the house and all your friends and relations come round to have a good look and say, 'Well, he looks quite happy, quite peaceful. Goodbye then, old fellow.' They shed a tear and throw a few flowers onto the corpse, and then it is hoisted on the shoulders of four strong men and borne through the streets with the face still uncovered. As the corpse is jolting along, crowds of people following behind in the heat, the people passing by look and say, 'Oh, there's old so-and-so – didn't know he had died.'

This sort of procession is what Siddhārtha saw, and he said to the charioteer, 'That's very strange. Why are they carrying that man like that? What's he done?' The charioteer replied in his usual laconic style, 'Well, this is a dead body.' We have to remember, of course, that death was one of those matters Siddhārtha was supposed to have been kept in the dark about, so he was mystified by this explanation. 'Dead? What do you mean?' And the charioteer again had to expatiate a little: 'Well, you can see, he's stiff, lifeless, doesn't breathe, doesn't see, doesn't hear, he doesn't feel. He's dead. They are taking him to the burning ground. They are going to burn the body. It's what happens at death.' Siddhārtha gasped with horror: 'Does this too happen to everybody? Will everybody come to this death, as you call it? Will I too come to death?' The charioteer drew a long sigh. 'Yes. Your father, your mother, your wife, your child – they must all die one day. I must die. You must die. Everybody who is born must die. There have been millions of men and women born since the world began and every single one of them has died. No doubt there will be millions more born in the future, but every single one of them will die. No one can escape the cold hand of death. Death is king of all.' More sad, more thoughtful, more anguished than ever, Siddhārtha ordered the charioteer to turn round and head back to the palace.

Over these three outings with his charioteer he had come up against what nowadays might be called existential situations: facts of existence from which you cannot escape. You don't want to grow old but you can't help it. You don't want to fall sick, but it happens. You don't want to die, but die you will, like it or not. So you start asking yourself questions: 'How do I come to be in this condition? I want to go on living for ever, young and strong and healthy, but it isn't going to be that way. How is it that I have been given this urge to live when I am given not the remotest chance of escaping death? It's a riddle. But why am I presented with this riddle at all? Why this mystery? Is it God who is responsible? Is it fate? Or is this just the way it is? Is there an explanation? Or is there no explanation?'

Siddhārtha was wrestling with the fundamental questions of life and death in this way when he took in the last of the four sights. Driving out again in his chariot he saw a man dressed not in the usual white garb, but in a yellow robe, and shaven-headed. This man was walking calmly along the village street with a begging-bowl, going from door to door. There was something in his mindful gait that Siddhārtha found quietly compelling, and he asked the charioteer, 'What manner of man is this that looks so at peace with himself and the world?' The charioteer replied, 'This is one who has gone forth.' 'Gone forth?' said Siddhārtha. 'Gone forth from what?' 'From the world,' the charioteer explained.

'Gone forth from his home, from his family. He has simply left it all behind to devote himself to the search for Truth. He's trying to find an answer to the riddle of existence. To do this he has given up all worldly ties, all domestic responsibilities, all social and political obligations. In this way he has gone forth.'[27]

You may find such people in India even today, still wearing the saffron robe. They are called sadhus, which simply means 'good people', and supporting them with alms is considered very meritorious. People give them food, invite them into their homes, and look after them. Very much the same system is still in operation after 2,500 years. And it was the sight of just such a figure that awoke in the young Siddhārtha the inspiration to go forth himself. The ultimately unacceptable limitations of human life had impressed themselves upon his consciousness too forcibly for him to be able to ignore them, to put them aside and just 'get on with his life'. You can choose not to see them, but they are there all the time, and he knew this. But now he knew also that there was a way of penetrating through to the meaning of it all. After spending a long time thinking things over, he decided that there was nothing for it but to become a sadhu himself. He felt that these questions had to be answered and that he could not rest until an answer was found.

So one full-moon night when everything was quiet, Siddhārtha bade a last farewell to his sleeping wife and child.[28] He was not happy to leave them, but there could be no alternative. He had told no one about his decision except his faithful charioteer, who saddled the horse for him to ride out of the palace as a prince for the last time. We are told that the charioteer, whose name was Channa, seized hold of the horse's tail and trotted behind,[29] and that they travelled as far as a river marking the border of the Śākyan territory. There, Siddhārtha cut off his beard and his long, flowing black hair. Just then – it was the crack of dawn – a beggar came along, and Siddhārtha offered to swap clothes with him. It did not take the beggar long to agree to this proposal, eccentric as it seemed, and he went on his way blinking with delight at the richly embroidered robes he now wore, the gold and silver buttons and buckles on them gleaming in the first rays of the sun.[30] Siddhārtha made his farewells to his faithful charioteer and his faithful horse, and watched them go. Then he plunged on into the jungle, alone.

First he went in search of teachers who he hoped might have penetrated to the ultimate mystery of existence. In those days in India, as much as in India today, there were many who illumined the ways to the attainment of Truth. He went from one teacher to another; he practised according to their instructions and mastered what they had to teach. But he was not satisfied. Good and profound as their teachings were, he knew that there was something beyond all they knew, something beyond all they had realized. He had no name for it. He did not know what it was. But he had to find it – he had to know it. He had to carry on his search.

He was grateful for all that he had learned, but he moved on. He began a programme of terrible austerities. This was a common practice in India, as it is still today, for it was thought that the thinner the veil of the flesh, as it were, the more transparent it was to the light of the spirit. For years Siddhārtha mortified the flesh, and no one in India exceeded him in self-torture. It was said that 'the fame of his great austerities had spread like the sound of a great bell hung in the canopy of the skies',[31] and he began to gather followers of his own. Eventually, however, something happened to make him wonder if perhaps he was heading in the wrong direction. He fainted and collapsed into a river, from which, not having the strength to save himself, he was fortunate to be rescued.[32] When he recovered he said to himself, 'This is ridiculous. I'm getting no nearer to the Truth, for all this asceticism. I've been wasting my time. It's all been a big mistake.'

So Siddhārtha Gautama the great ascetic started taking regular meals again. His five disciples were not at all impressed. The fact was that they were not so much disciples as admirers, hangers-on. They relied on him to make the effort, and just stayed around in the hope that his achievements would somehow rub off on them. They thought that when he achieved his goal by virtue of his austerities they would be the first to benefit. So it was obviously a great disappointment to them when he made the decision to give his body the nourishment it needed. 'He's backsliding,' they said to one another, 'He's gone back to the luxurious ways of the world. Clearly he's not the man we thought he was.' And they trooped off in disgust. Once again, Siddhārtha was on his own.

It was six years after he had left the palace when he came to the place that would mark the end of his quest. At a spot in the present-day state of Bihar called Uruvelā, now known as Bodh Gaya, he found a copse of beautiful trees beside a river. It seemed an ideal location in which to sit and meditate. Then as he sat there in the shade, with a cool breeze blowing, he remembered something that suddenly seemed to show the way forward. He recollected his experience of thirty years before, sitting beneath another tree, while his father initiated the season's ploughing. He gently felt his way back to that integrated state of concentration – not trying to force it, but just letting it come, and letting go of whatever hindered its arising. As he did so a cowherd's wife from a neighbouring village brought him some milk-rice, which he took, and he was nourished and strengthened by it. A grass-cutter also came up to provide him with a heap of *kuśa* grass to sit upon, and he made himself comfortable on it. Then he settled down and gave himself to his meditative experience.[33] He plunged deeper and deeper into it, through level after level of superconscious states.

How long he sat there we do not know. It may have been days; it may have been weeks; it may even have been months. All we do know is that on the night of Vaiśākha Pūrṇimā he saw the solution to the problem upon which his mind had been bent ever since the four sights had awakened him to it. He not only saw this solution, but understood it, plunged into it, became one with it, and realized it. Full illumination arose within him and he became Enlightened.

Some of the early texts try to give us some idea of the content of that experience,[34] but this is by no means an easy thing to attempt. Enlightenment is inherently ineffable. It cannot be understood by the rational mind. However, to begin with, we can say that it is a state of pure, clear, radiant awareness. And it is sometimes specified that in this state of awareness one no longer makes any emotional distinction between oneself and others. That sense we have of an inner world set against the world outside ourselves is entirely transcended. There is just one continuous, pure, and homogeneous awareness extending freely in all directions. It is, moreover, an awareness of things *as they really are.* This means an awareness of things not as objects, but as transcending the duality of subject and object. Hence this pure, clear awareness is also spoken of as an awareness of Reality. It is a state of knowledge – knowledge not in the ordinary sense of someone accumulating notions of things, but rather a seeing of 'things' directly and truly, unmediated by any separate subject doing the seeing. It is a spiritual vision – even a transcendental vision – which is free from all delusion, all misconception, all wrong, crooked thinking, all vagueness, all obscurity, all mental conditioning, and all prejudice.

However, this is not the end of it. Enlightenment can be described as full illumination, as transcendental awareness, as Wisdom. But it is also an overflowing of profound love and compassion for all that lives. It is described, too, as supreme bliss, or complete emancipation – the bliss of release from the subjective ills and limitations of conditioned existence. It is thus also characterized by inexhaustible energy continually bubbling forth, total spontaneity, uninterrupted creativity. At the same time none of these aspects of Enlightenment function separately. Therefore the actual experience cannot be described at all. Only by reflection on the Dharma – reflecting on the Buddha's teaching as well as on his example – by deep communication with friends, and above all by meditation, can we get some real intimation of what the Enlightenment of a Buddha consists in.

The traditional accounts say that the Buddha's Enlightenment arose or blossomed gradually as the full-moon night of Wesak wore on. According to one account,[35] in the first watch of the night the Buddha looked back into the past, into 'the dark backward and abysm of time'.[36] He looked back over the whole course of human history, over millions of years of evolution. We are told that he was able to survey all his previous lives and see what he had done and what had arisen in consequence of his actions. He saw the conditions he had laid down and the results that had followed from them. And he saw that it was all done with, all ended. He had transcended the whole process of conditioned existence.

Then in the second watch of the night he looked, as it were, all around him, all around the universe, and he saw beings of every kind – human beings, animals, even beings in higher worlds. He saw how each one came into being, became what it was, in accordance with what it had done – in other words, how beings were reborn according to their karma. He saw this happening at every level of mundane existence, from the deepest abyss of the hell realms to the highest sphere of the gods.[37]

Finally, in the third watch of the night, he directed his mind to the destruction of the *āsravas* – literally 'biases'. The *āsravas* are the natural biases of the mind, the deep-rooted tendency of the mind towards conditioned existence rather than towards that which is Unconditioned, towards unreality rather than towards Reality. There are three *āsravas*: the bias or inclination of the mind towards sensuous experience; the bias towards existence as a separate, ego-centred personality; and the bias towards spiritual ignorance, that is, ignorance of Reality. So he turned his mind in the purity of its concentration to the elimination of the *āsravas*, and in the morning, when the sun rose, he knew that for him the *āsravas* had been destroyed completely.[38] Enlightenment had been attained. Siddhārtha Gautama had become the Buddha.

3
THE HIDDEN TEACHINGS OF
THE BUDDHA'S EARLY LIFE

When Siddhārtha Gautama became the Buddha at the age of thirty-five, a great many things had taken place in his life, and each and every incident recorded in the early accounts of it is in some way deeply significant for us. It is not easy to select from the riches of such a unique and momentous biography; the previous chapter is no more than a summary of his progress to Enlightenment. Even from this bare outline, however, we can draw some specific principles of the Buddhist path through focusing on a few incidents. Here we will concentrate on just six: the four sights, the going forth from home into homelessness, the exchange of princely robes for a beggar's rags, the performance of austerities, being abandoned by companions, and the acceptance of help. Each one of these events is in substance historical, but at the same time has become the nucleus of a whole rich complex of myth and legend. Each one therefore assumes a universal significance; each one, that is to say, has a direct bearing on the condition of every evolving, or potentially evolving, human being.

First, then, let us consider the four sights: Siddhārtha's seeing for the first time – or as if for the first time – an old man, a sick man, a corpse, and a holy wanderer. Up to this point his father had apparently managed to seclude him from the world by occupying him with his martial exercises by day and entertaining him with singing girls and dancing girls in one of his three mansions by night. In a sense Siddhārtha had been secluded from real life, secluded even from reality. In Buddhist mythical literature the father sometimes represents ignorance, while the mother may represent craving (one being the more intellectual poison, and the other the more emotional source of suffering). So Siddhārtha had been confined by ignorance, the universal father of those beings who live without awareness. Lacking the wider perspective, he had lived in a world of his own. He had been hardly aware that there was a world outside at all – not so as to make any difference to the way he had occupied himself, anyway. The existential reality of his situation had not yet broken in upon his little world.

The same theme is given a different treatment in the parable of the burning house from the *Saddharma Puṇḍarīka*, or *White Lotus Sūtra*. In a huge crumbling mansion, a lot of children are engrossed in their various childish games when a fire breaks out. But while the fire blazes merrily and gradually takes hold of the ancient fabric of the building, the children pay no attention to the acrid smell in the air, or the smoke curling up from under the door, or the crackle and roar of the flames and the creak and crash of falling timbers. They are simply not aware of the danger. They just go on amusing themselves with their toys. We are not concerned with the rest of the story here – suffice to say that the children are eventually saved.[39]

The point of the opening of this parable hardly needs labouring. The burning house is this world, blazing with old age, disease, and death, while the children, of course, represent ourselves. The cosmos, conditioned existence itself, is on fire with existential suffering, yet we remain immersed in our trivial pursuits, our distractions and amusements. Most of us are occupied, much of the time, with matters that are simply unworthy of the attention of a moderately aware human being. Though we may catch glimpses of our real situation, of a real purpose to our existence, it is only too easy to slip back into the old ruts carved by social pressures and long habit.

Even when we are passionately absorbed in trivial things, however, even as we waste our time over distractions and diversions, sooner or later something happens. One day, something catastrophic happens, and our little world is shattered or so badly cracked that we can never again be really comfortable living in it. It's as though we had, until then, never been born, like a chick in its egg; but suddenly our little world is broken open, and we find ourselves looking out into another, wider world. Reality has finally started to break in. We begin to see things as they really are. We feel as though we have grown up, and are no longer entranced by the toys and tales of childhood. Or it is as though we have woken from a dream. When we are immersed in our dreams, whatever happens seems as real, as vivid, as our waking experience. But when we wake up, the dream world rapidly fades. After a few minutes, or perhaps after a few hours, it is nothing, usually not even a memory. In the same way, when reality irrupts into our sleepy, cosy existence, we look back at our old life, all the old pursuits for which we have lost the appetite we once had, and we think, 'How could I have lived in that way? Was that really me? Was I really so foolish, so deluded?'

As a result of this sort of experience our behaviour changes, just as an adult behaves differently from a child. People may notice that we've changed. They may even wonder if there's something wrong with us. 'Is anything the matter?' they may ask, not unkindly – though privately they may think we're not quite in our right mind, because we're no longer taking any interest in the sort of things that we used to like, no longer doing the things that other people like to do.

The event which shatters one's private world is very often unpleasant – it may be a bereavement, or the loss of a job, or being dropped by a lover, or discovering the infidelity of a spouse. On the other hand the breakthrough can come about in a more agreeable fashion – you get a sudden insight through art, perhaps, or music or poetry. Then again, it can occur through an experience that is neither pleasant nor unpleasant, nor even sudden: you just become discontented and dissatisfied. But whatever serves as the trip-wire, the experience which follows tends to be painful, disturbing, and all-consuming, because the old patterns are disrupted, the old moulds are broken. This is the sort of experience that Siddhārtha had, as illustrated by the four sights.

The second of the six incidents is the 'going forth from the home life into homelessness'. What this means in essence is that you separate yourself from what we may call 'the group'. It is not easily done, because the group, the collectivity, is the world most people inhabit most of the time. It is the world in which relationships are based on misunderstanding, on mutual exploitation and projection, in which people do not see each other as they really are, in which there is no genuine communication. But when the shell of your conditioning is broken and you catch a glimpse of a richer world beyond this narrow one, you can no longer function as a member of the group that defines who you are. You have to separate yourself from it. In the case of the Buddha he literally left home. He left parents, wife, and child, he left the tribe, he left the tribal territory, even – and he left at night so no one could see him going. When you forsake the group, you are, metaphorically speaking, stealing away in the night, because the people in the group do not really see the person who is leaving it. They do not really know what you are doing. You are incomprehensible to them.

So what does it signify for those who follow in the Buddha's footsteps, for those who call themselves Buddhists? It is probably fairly obvious. It means that you start to dissociate yourself from the group, to shake off your identification with humanity as a mere collectivity. How you go about doing this depends, of course, on the nature of the group or groups to which you belong.

The group that springs to mind at once is the family – the blood group – and you leave the family when you leave home. At least, you begin to leave it when you leave home, and maybe everybody should literally leave home as soon as they are able to do so. Once you've left home in the straightforward sense of moving away, you start to get your family into perspective because you are no longer immersed in it. You begin to get a better view of your parents – just as, conversely, they get a better view of you. When you are at home with your parents you tend to think of them just as your parents, but of course they are much more than that – just as you are much more than someone's child. Seeing them simply as your mother and father you don't really see them, you don't really know them at all. But after you've moved away and stood on your own two feet for a time you are more likely to be able to see your relations for who they are, for whatever individuality they may possess. Not only that, you can also insist on being treated as an individual yourself, and not just as a daughter or son (or sister or nephew or whatever). It's a curious phenomenon, but when people visit their parents they very often, without being able to help it, slip back into relatively infantile attitudes – as a reaction, perhaps, to their parents slipping into corresponding parental attitudes. They accept the role of son or daughter again, they identify with that role, and thus cease to be themselves. So going forth from the family means being watchful for our own tendencies – and those of our relations – to slip into well-worn grooves whenever we come back into contact with family life.

The family is by no means the only group you take leave of when you go forth, however. There is also the social group. Going forth, you drop all the conventional, run-of-the-mill social activities, because you see that parties, clubbing, or whatever social functions you used to like are generally quite worthless, trivial, and dull. This perception of social activities should not be confused with the antisocial pose sometimes adopted by people who are simply socially awkward. The question is whether you hanker after the merry social whirl at all. If you do, it means that your individuality is not yet well enough defined to enable you to step away from the social group. However, even if you stay away from the more institutionalized forms of the social group, there is still a great deal of merely social chit-chat and gossip in most ordinary social circles. When Siddhārtha went forth into the homeless life he was also going forth from this sort of thing – although when he became the Buddha, he found that his own sangha was not entirely free of unmindful nattering. He even went so far as to say to his disciples on one occasion, 'When you meet together, either keep quiet altogether, or talk to some spiritual purpose, about the Dharma, about things that are helpful to your individual development.'[40]

Then there is the economic group. You're connected with this mainly through your job, if you have one. To develop as an individual, therefore, you have to avoid identifying yourself with the work you do. Unfortunately, this identification is established in common parlance: instead of saying they do this or that kind of work, people say 'I am a bricklayer,' or 'I am a stockbroker.' Not only this, but people sometimes identify very strongly with the firm they work for, or with a trade union. There are, of course, some jobs which are vocational, and which it may be entirely appropriate to regard as a genuine expression of creativity or compassion. That's a different matter. You may also be able to work with other Buddhists on a project or within a business which has some kind of altruistic dimension to it. In this case, too, a full personal commitment to one's work will form part of one's spiritual practice. But if you do a straightforward job as a money-generating enterprise, that is not something with which to identify yourself.

Going forth from the economic group involves, in fact – and this is an idea that goes against the flow of a major current in our conditioning – doing as little work as possible. When you are really serious about being a Buddhist you have to make time for spiritual practice. This means, if possible, getting a part-time job. Then – and this is the difficult part – you have to resist the temptation to spend all your spare time reading the newspaper, watching television, chatting idly, window-shopping, and so on. Going forth from the economic group is about making proper and creative use of whatever spare time you can make for yourself and dissociating yourself from whatever you do to earn a living.

What I mean by 'the group' should now be becoming clear. Another quite fundamental one is the cultural group. You emancipate yourself from the cultural group into which you have been born in two different ways: by study and by travel. By studying the products of other cultures, familiarizing yourself with the literature, the music, or even the social customs of another culture, you broaden your outlook and your sympathies, ceasing to identify with a particular culture. Travelling on your own, or simply observing the different ways of ethnic groups within your own society, also naturally tends to loosen up your attitudes. Particularly if you can go and live in a completely different society, you soon realize how many of your habits and ways of thinking are just a product of your environment. There is no inherent validity in them at all. It is no more a basic law of the universe, say, to eat with a knife and fork than it is to eat with one's fingers.

The group is not of course necessarily large. What is often nowadays the most insidious type of group is the group of two – what the French call *égoïsme à deux*. The basis for what is apparently seen to be the ideal form of sexual relationship nowadays is mutual emotional dependence, mutual exploitation. And unless the sexual relationship is put in its proper place in one's scheme of things, unless it is seen as a not immensely important relationship, it can only hinder one's development as an individual. Unfortunately, as sexual relationships tend to be by their very nature volatile, this condition is seldom fulfilled. So this is yet another implication of going forth – leaving the group of two.

The group operates in many different ways, but these examples should suffice to give a rough idea of how we as individuals can move away from it, and an idea, therefore, of what Siddhārtha's going forth means to us in practice.

Following on from the going forth, we come to the third of our six incidents: the exchange of clothes with the beggar. Leaving home for Siddhārtha meant leaving his position in society. In those days one's position in society was signalled, to a far greater extent than it is today, by one's dress. In giving up his princely robes, Siddhārtha gave up his social identity, his identity as a Kṣatriya, as a member of the Śākya tribe. He gave it up because it was not his real identity, and he knew it, though what his real identity was he did not yet know. Ideally, perhaps, he should have gone without clothes at all, but it was later on, in his ascetic period, that he went naked. For now, he wore the clothes of a beggar, because on the social scale a beggar is nobody – he doesn't count, he doesn't exist. If you haven't got anything – no property, no money, no influence – you're nothing, nobody. Siddhārtha gave up his social identity by changing clothes with someone who had no social identity.

To use a term from Jungian psychology, Siddhārtha surrendered his persona. Persona literally means 'mask', and the term is used to refer to the psychological mask one wears when dealing with other people. Some people have many masks which they use on different occasions – and putting them on becomes an instinctive, barely conscious way of guarding themselves in any interaction they may have with another person. They wear masks because they are afraid of being seen as they are. They think that people will disapprove of them if they drop the mask, that they will be rejected. Ideally, you should be able to fling aside your persona, at least with your friends, but in any case you have at least to try to be aware of your mask and thus be aware also that you are not your mask. One way in which people reinforce their masks is, of course, by wearing a particular style of dress or uniform. Useful as a uniform may be in assuming a necessary social role, one cannot identify oneself with that role without damaging oneself as an individual. So when Siddhārtha cast off his princely clothes he was casting off his persona, his mask.

As for his performance of austerities, the fourth event we have isolated from the Buddha's early biography, it may be difficult to imagine what possible significance this spiritual cul-de-sac – which he explored so exhaustively – might have for us. The closest most people in the West come to practising austerities is probably trying to give up smoking. Self-torture is not a spiritual error we are in any danger of falling into. However, we need to look at what was underlying Siddhārtha's practice of austerities. What was he really trying to do in pushing himself to the very limits of his endurance? In a way it's obvious. He was trying to gain Enlightenment by force of will, by sheer force of ego-directed effort. His conscious mind took the decision to realize Enlightenment, and then tried to force this decision on to the rest of his psyche. Of course, the rest of his psyche refused to cooperate in this enterprise, noble as it was, so all that effort turned out to be useless.

The point of this is not that we should stop making so much effort. That isn't it at all. The key to what he was doing when he was practising austerities lies in what happened when Siddhārtha sat down under the bodhi tree and started to meditate. What happened then was that he recollected his early mystical experience – and the significance of this experience was that it was spontaneous. It was a product of his psyche as a whole. The effort we put into our development needs to be directed towards the growth of the whole psyche, not just a part of it. We need to unify our energies, and this means enlisting the cooperation of our unconscious energies – by means of myth and symbol, and by the exercise of imagination and devotion. The rational approach will not do on its own. This is what Siddhārtha realized when he saw that his ascetic efforts were getting him nowhere.

The fifth incident is the abandonment of Siddhārtha by his companions. They were also looking for the way to Enlightenment, but they depended on Siddhārtha to do their work for them, to lead the way. At the same time they had fixed ideas of how he ought to go about leading them forward; so their notion of how to make the best use of their association with him was quite mixed up. Instead of accepting his guidance and following his example as best they could, they sat on the sidelines hoping to benefit from his discoveries while clinging firmly to their own views.

It has to be said that Siddhārtha's experience has a bearing on our own situation as Buddhists that we need to take into account. Sometimes you find yourself following the same path as other people so you naturally go along together for a while. But then what if you begin to have doubts about the path you are all following? What if you want to change direction, or retrace your steps? And what if your companions disagree with your perception and think you are giving up? The hard fact is that if others are not willing to go with you, you have to go on alone. The position may even be that you are agreed on which way the path goes but your companions are simply not willing to follow it very far, or make the effort to keep going. Then, too, you have to go on alone. This is often the position when a spiritual tradition becomes fossilized and the majority of the 'followers' of that tradition are satisfied with a more or less nominal observance of its principles and practices. If you decide to take those principles and practices more seriously, you are going to find yourself in a minority – perhaps in a minority of one.

The fact is that anyone who decides to become a Buddhist, to commit themselves to the principles of Buddhism – or, in the traditional idiom, to go for Refuge to the Three Jewels, to the Buddha, the Dharma, and the Sangha – is not joining a group. The sangha, the Buddhist community, is not there to make decisions or do your thinking for you. It is a community of individuals who take full responsibility for their own actions. Only if one is ready to be on one's own is one going to be ready to be a member of the sangha.

Our final incident, Siddhārtha's acceptance of help – milk-rice from the cowherd's wife and *kuśa* grass from the grass-cutter – might seem a rather minor detail in the build-up towards his Enlightenment. However, it reflects a crucial change of attitude on Siddhārtha's part. We cannot afford to think lightly of any help we receive, even the smallest gesture. Some people speak very slightingly of whatever is provided to aid spiritual practice. They say, perhaps, that shrines are not necessary, because you should be able to meditate anywhere; or that Buddhist scriptures are not necessary, because you should be able to discover the Truth for yourself. Well, maybe we should – but the fact is that in practice we can't. In any case, the way to Enlightenment is difficult enough already. There is no need to make it more difficult still. If Siddhārtha could accept help, we might as well do the same if we truly want to reach our goal as he did.

These, then, are the six incidents in the Buddha's progress that have a particular relevance to our own development. They are, so to speak, the hidden teachings of the Buddha's early life. Beginning with the four sights, we have to get at least a glimpse of our existential predicament, of things as they really are, of the world outside our daily concerns. In going forth from home into the homeless life, we cease to identify with the group in any of its various forms. Siddhārtha's surrender of his princely clothes represents the surrender of his persona, and we too need to look for the reality behind our masks, to disclose not just our psychological identity but our spiritual individuality. Then we have to realize, as Siddhārtha did when he renounced the way of austerity, that the conscious mind cannot impose itself on the rest of the psyche by sheer effort of will, that the hidden forces of the unconscious must be harnessed, not overborne. His companions deserting him illustrates the fact that we have to be prepared to go it alone if necessary. On the other hand, as Siddhārtha's acceptance of help clearly shows, even if we are self-reliant, we should accept with gratitude every little bit of help we can get.

The image of an Indian prince from ancient times wandering off into the forest may seem remote, even alien, to us. However, beneath the exotic surface details of his early life there lie some fundamental patterns which we can identify in our own experience. Beneath the apparently prosaic and contingent circumstances of our own lives there are hidden teachings too, and this must surely give us confidence in our own spiritual potential. If we can recognize in Siddhārtha's story our own deepest strivings for ultimate liberation from the confines of conditioned existence, and the first steps we are already, perhaps, beginning to take in order to fulfil them, then we can also see that what Siddhārtha finally realized is what we too can realize, eventually, for ourselves.

4

THE HEROIC IDEAL IN BUDDHISM

Although very few people in the West have so far had the opportunity to study or practise Buddhism to any great depth, most of us will have formed some sort of impression of it. We will have formed, too, some sort of impression of the Buddha. We meet or hear of people who have become Buddhists, we read articles about Buddhism in the newspapers, we hear people talking about Buddhism on the radio or the television. There's even the occasional film in which an actor plays the part of the Buddha. Some of the impressions of Buddhism we get may be quite positive, even quite accurate, but inevitably there will be others which are very misleading and, once established, misconceptions are notoriously difficult to eradicate.

Some of the most persistent misconceptions derive from the earliest Western interpreters of Buddhism, who naturally saw it from the stand-point of their own religious tradition, a Victorian version of Christianity. It was natural enough for this first wave of Western literature on Buddhism to explain it to largely Christian readers by making use of Christian concepts, but the misconceptions they generated have unfortunately lasted a long time.

One of these misconceptions was the idea that Buddhism was not a religion in the full sense of the word. According to this view it could be regarded as an impressive system of philosophy, like that of Plato, or Kant, or Hegel; or an admirable scheme of ethics; or even a system – a remarkable system – of mysticism; but as no more, really, than that. Roman Catholic scholars in particular (for some reason or other Roman

Catholics have always tended to make a bit of a speciality of Buddhism) damned it with faint praise in this way and somehow suggested that there was a whole dimension missing in Buddhism which was supplied in full within Christianity.

Another equally tenacious misconception was that Buddhism was a specifically oriental religion, inextricably tied up with various oriental cultures. This is evidently quite a difficult idea to see through; even today people find it hard to distinguish the essence of Buddhism from its cultural expression – exotic, colourful, and attractive as these expressions often are. But if the practice of the Buddhist path is to be established in the West, we will have to find ways of integrating the Dharma with our own, more humdrum, grey, and familiar culture.

The particular misconception to which this chapter is addressed originated in the Victorian perception of the Buddha himself. They naturally tended to see him as a sort of oriental Jesus, and the popular Victorian conception of Jesus was a rather weak version of the real thing. It has been said that for the Victorians Christ was a ghostly figure in a white sheet gliding around Galilee and gently rebuking people for not believing in the Nicene Creed. So a Victorian Buddha was likewise installed in the popular imagination as a ghostly figure in a yellow sheet gliding around India and gently rebuking people for not being kind to animals.

In this way, Buddhism began to be perceived as a rather passive, negative, or gutless teaching and tradition. This impression, unfortunately, can only be reinforced, perhaps unconsciously, by any acquaintance one may have with later Buddhist art, in which decadent phase the Buddha is depicted as a sweet, dreamy, effeminate figure. As for the mass-produced representations of the Buddha that are turned out today, their attempts at the smile of Enlightenment leave the Buddha with a kind of coquettish simper. Such images are sure to influence the way we see the Buddha in our own minds.

Another factor we have to take into account is that Buddhism is a religion of Indian provenance. While Indian culture is respected for its 'spirituality' it has also sometimes been looked upon as backward, slow, unprogressive, and unenterprising, and therefore epithets of this sort seem naturally to attach themselves to Buddhism.

We also have to recognize that a good deal of contemporary Buddhist teaching in the East, particularly from Sri Lanka, Burma, and Thailand, has tended to be rather negative. You are told not to do this and to refrain from that and abstain from the other, but you are not nearly so often told what you can do to cultivate positive qualities and develop in a positive sense. The oldest Buddhist scriptures recognize that you can't have one side of a coin without the other, and carry a forthright positive emphasis as well as an uncompromising negative one,[41] but the teaching has been too often presented in the West in terms of avoidance rather than engagement, escape rather than commitment.

In order to redress this imbalance we need to take a fresh look at what Buddhism is about, and in the process perhaps we will have to rethink our whole attitude to the spiritual life. The aim of Buddhist teaching is the attainment of Enlightenment, or Buddhahood, a state of moral and spiritual perfection, and this ideal calls for the exercise, on the moral and spiritual plane, of heroic qualities. When we speak of the heroic ideal in Buddhism, we are not speaking of anything distinct from – much less still opposed to – the spiritual ideal. We are speaking of the spiritual ideal itself – an ideal that is not just about meekly refraining from this, that or the other, but requires heroism in the highest degree.

Of course, we may not find that at all inspiring. The whole concept of the 'heroic ideal' is unfashionable these days, and having ideals may suggest 'alienation' and 'lack of acceptance', to use the fashionable terminology. As for the hero or heroine, the idea of nobility, of a kind of real superiority, may be objectionable to modern taste, which much prefers the celebrity culture that seems to represent fame without any need to make an effort to achieve anything.

In the nineteenth century this took quite a different form. Of course the Victorians also had a taste for celebrity, but it tended to take the form of a kind of hero-worship that seems unthinkable today. Almost anyone who had risen to some eminence in public life might be revered, even worshipped, as a hero. It was for this reason, perhaps, that the person representing their highest spiritual ideals, Jesus, should have been so ethereal a figure – to distinguish him from the more mundane objects of public adoration. Thomas Carlyle's lectures *Heroes and Hero-Worship*, first published in 1841, established as axiomatic the view that 'history is the biography of great men'. Thackeray was able to label his novel *Vanity Fair* as unique among the mass of fiction being run off the presses at the time (1848) by subtitling it *A Novel Without a Hero*.

On the mantelpiece in any home in the country you would find china figurines of highly esteemed public figures. Alfred Lord Tennyson, Florence Nightingale, Gordon of Khartoum, Gladstone, and Disraeli were admired as pop stars are today, and no sooner were they dead than out came at least three, and sometimes six or seven, thick – one might say monumental – volumes of memoirs and letters. Victorian biographies were exercises in hagiography: they were intended to exhibit the great man in all his glory, striking the pose or attitude in which everybody wanted to remember him. This is why the great Victorians appear, even in retrospect, so very much larger than life.

The First World War was sold to the man in the street as an opportunity to be heroic himself, and it was probably the association of the heroic pose with incompetent generals and mass slaughter that destroyed the heroic ideal. Biographies became exercises in showing how petty and ordinary so-called great men really were. The classic example of this new type of biography was Lytton Strachey's *Eminent Victorians* (1918), in which no fewer than four great Victorians suffered the indignity of being packed together in one slim volume.

Today, heroes and heroines may still be found in the more commercial works of fiction, but rarely elsewhere, and certainly not in politics. When you recall that people used to write to Gladstone or Disraeli asking for a lock of the great man's hair to wear in a locket, you have to admit that times have changed. It would be difficult to find anyone involved in determining the important public issues of our day who would be regarded in quite this adulatory light. No doubt this is as it should be. Victorian hero-worship was certainly a bad case of projection, and their ideals can sometimes look like hypocrisy. 'No man is a hero to his own valet,' we observe sagely.[42] However, if we replace ideals with cynicism, we deny the possibility of change. And if we take a valet's eye view of the hero, if the whole idea of the hero seems to us a little ridiculous and absurd, if we refuse to look up to someone of exceptional qualities, we deny reality as surely as the Victorians did. It means we cannot take seriously someone of extraordinary ability who has ideals, that is to say someone who is serious and cares deeply about something important.

I have introduced the concept of the hero at some length because although it is an unfashionable word in English, it accurately translates one of the titles by which Siddhārtha Gautama was known after his Enlightenment. We know him as 'the Buddha', or sometimes 'the

Compassionate One', but the Pāli and Sanskrit texts also apply to the Buddha the epithets Mahāvīra, which means 'Great Hero', and Jina, which means 'Conqueror'. In fact, the title Jina is almost as common in the earliest Buddhist texts as the one we are so familiar with, 'the Buddha'. He is the Conqueror because he has conquered the whole of conditioned existence within himself. He has conquered the world by conquering himself. According to the *Dhammapada*, 'Though one should conquer in battle thousands upon thousands of men, yet he who conquers himself is (truly) the greatest in battle.'[43] Later, medieval Buddhism produced the idea of the Trailokya Vijaya, 'the conquest of the three worlds' – conquest, that is, of the world of sensuous desire, the world of archetypal form, and the world of no form.[44] So the Jina's victory is over these three inner worlds.

By virtue of this conquest the Buddha becomes, of course, a king. Having subdued all the realms of conditioned existence within his own mind, he is called the *dharmarāja*, 'King of the Law', or 'King of Truth'. It is as a king that the Buddha is often portrayed in Buddhist art; we know this because he is shown bearing the insignia of royalty. These insignia are actually quite curious, at least to Westerners. In Britain the corresponding insignia are, of course, the orb and sceptre, the symbols of the reigning monarch's authority. But in India, and wherever the Buddhist cultural tradition has penetrated, they comprise instead the parasol and fly-whisk.

In India in the Buddha's day an ordinary person never used a parasol or umbrella. You certainly didn't use one for keeping off the weather – you would probably have used a leaf. A real umbrella could only be used by the king or some other noble and eminent person. According to Lama Govinda this goes back to when the elder of the tribe or village used to sit under a tree in the evening with his back against the trunk, dispensing advice and settling disputes.[45] The umbrella became, if we accept this interpretation, a sort of artificial tree held above you as you went about, as a symbol of your social position. Following this line of thought, we can link this symbolic umbrella ultimately with the cosmic tree which, in mystical terms, overshadows the whole world, the whole of existence.

The fly-whisk is a more straightforward symbol. It is made from the tail of the yak, a plume of very soft white hair, about two feet long, and very beautiful. The tail is mounted in a silver handle, and royal personages are gently fanned with it to keep off the flies. It is still used in Hindu ritual worship. There's a stage during the *āratī*, the evening worship, when the fly-whisk is waved in front of the image of the deity – Rama or Krishna or whoever it may be – because he is being treated, for the time being, as a king as well as a god.

Therefore, just as Jesus is often represented seated with the orb and sceptre in his hands to signify his divine kingship, so in Buddhist art the Buddha is depicted with an umbrella held over him – sometimes by divine beings – and with gods flanking him, equipped with fly-whisks. These symbols show that he is king of the Dharma – king, if you like, of the spiritual universe. The Buddha being king, his chief disciple, Śāriputra, was known as his Dharmasenāpati, which means 'commander-in-chief'.[46]

If that sounds surprisingly military, we could reflect that this royal symbolism and military terminology are perhaps not unconnected with the Buddha's original social background. As a Kṣatriya, he belonged, according to the Hindu reckoning, to the second of the four castes, the Brahmins or priestly caste coming first in terms of status. But the Kṣatriyas didn't see it like that. While the other castes accepted this ordering of the hierarchy, the Kṣatriyas regarded themselves as the top caste. This is also the way the castes are arranged whenever they are mentioned in the Pāli canon, with the Kṣatriyas first. So in the early Buddhist texts the warrior is given pre-eminence, from a purely social point of view, over the priest.

We know that when Siddhārtha was growing up, Brahmanism had not penetrated into Śākyan territory, so we can be fairly sure that he was educated purely and simply as a warrior – and a warrior, in a sense, he remained. There is a legend that when he became betrothed to Yaśodharā some of her kinsmen objected that he wasn't good enough at fighting, and of course he had to prove his worth by defeating them all in contest.[47] Clearly, as a nobleman it was not enough to be a warrior – he was required to be an exceptional warrior, a hero.

It is quite significant that this should have been the background of the person who would become the prime exemplar of the spiritual life. It is clear that the heroic qualities he had been trained to exhibit on the battlefield were drawn upon at every step of his spiritual quest. We know that he left home when he was about twenty-nine. He left everything he had been taught to believe in as the good life, everything he had been taught to believe was worthwhile, everything he had been taught to believe was his duty. It must have been a great wrench to leave his family and his tribe, to go out alone into the darkness, into the forest, going he knew not where, knowing only that he went in search of the Truth. But this is what he did.

Then for such a man to support himself as a mendicant called for no less a degree of fortitude. The traditional procedure of the almsround was simple enough, as it still is today. You take a big, black begging-bowl, and moving from door to door you stand for a few minutes at each house, and people come out and put a few scraps of food in your bowl. When you feel you've collected enough for your meal, you go off to a quiet spot outside the village and sit down to eat it. Not a demanding way of providing for oneself, you might think, but there is a rather poignant touch in the Buddha's own account of his first almsround which shows what it can be like when you aren't used to it. What he apparently told his disciples, according, that is, to the scriptures – but the story has the ring of truth to it – is that the first time he sat down outside a village with his bowl, he took one look at the heap of disparate scraps of food in it and vomited. Having been used to the choicest quality of absolutely fresh food prepared by the best cooks, he found himself gazing down at the coarse leftovers of peasants and his stomach turned. But he did not allow his own delicacy to stand in the way of his quest. If the price of his freedom was to subsist on this sort of diet he had to overcome his disgust. And that is what he did.[48]

His clothing was rough and ready too, of course. Going around the modern Buddhist world you can easily get the impression that the Buddha went around in brand new, beautifully laundered, clean and neat yellow robes, but this seems highly unlikely. He almost certainly wore rough yellow garments, stained and ragged. It's a sad fact nowadays that in some Buddhist countries a monk who goes around in a rather old robe is considered a bit of a disgrace. I myself remember coming down to a monastery in Calcutta from Kalimpong one time and – I have to say – I did not think to dress up for the occasion, but some of my monk friends were quite scandalized because I happened to be wearing a very old robe. To them it was terrible: 'What will people think?' they said. We have to imagine that the Buddha himself would have had a completely different attitude. For him, what he wore would have represented a complete break from his previous way of life, in which his secure social position was clearly reflected in the way he dressed.

Having gone forth, Siddhārtha quickly mastered the teachings that were made available to him;[49] he did not rest on his laurels, but took his way alone again. In his old age he used to reminisce about this critical period in his life. He described how he would be in the depths of the jungle at night, when everything was dark and silent, with no one for miles around, and he would hear a twig break or a leaf fall, and a terrible panic, fear, and dread would come over him. Those who have practised meditation know that this can happen sometimes – fear just wells up. It isn't that there's anything objective to be afraid of, and there seems to be very little you can do about it. And this is what Siddhārtha used to experience. He would be seized with a nameless terror. So how did he subdue this fear and dread? What did he do to break its hold? What he realized was that he had to do literally nothing. He said, 'If the fear came while I was walking up and down, I continued walking up and down. If it came while I was sitting, I continued sitting. If while I was standing it came, then I continued standing. And if I was lying down when it came, I continued lying down. The fear would pass away as it had arisen.'[50] In other words, he didn't try to escape it. He let it come, he let it stay, and he let it go away. He did not allow his mind – his essential mind – to be disturbed by it.

Though Siddhārtha took on every difficulty and adversity that lay in his way, these had presented, so far, relatively minor hardships. It is a measure of his heroic character that he then chose to take upon himself the most arduous spiritual path he could find. Not only this, but having taken up the practice of austerities he followed that path more rigorously than any man alive at the time. He was experimenting, searching for the Truth by trial and error, and when he tried something he followed that method to the limits of his human capacity. So he went about naked, even in the bitter winters of the Himalayan foothills, with snow lying thick on the ground. He stopped using a bowl, and just took what little food he ate in his hands. He had heard it said that if you cut down your food to a few grains of rice or barley, and a little water, this would bring you to the brink of Enlightenment, so he did this. There is a terrible description in the scriptures of the emaciated state this regime brought him to, and it is the subject of a famous Gandhāran stone carving which portrays Siddhārtha at this stage in his career as a seated figure consisting of no more than skin and bone and tendons.[51]

It may be difficult for us to admire this sort of endeavour – it probably seems simply perverse. But you have to remember that he was doing it with a very clear purpose in mind, and that the consensus at that time favoured the practice of austerities as highly efficacious if you had the heart for it. Even today in India some people are very much impressed by austerities, and it was the same in the Buddha's time. By going to such extremes, Siddhārtha attracted followers who greatly admired his fortitude. So to give up other people's expectations of him, to put up with their scorn when, as it seemed to them, he gave up his heroic resolve, to go back once again to being a nobody, required great psychological and spiritual courage. It is so much easier to do anything, however difficult, when you've got other people around, idolizing and applauding you, saying, 'Look how heroic he is!' But when no one likes what you are doing and your admirers flounce off in disgust,[52] that is a very testing time, and there are very, very few people who can handle it. Jesus, one might say, had something of this experience in the garden of Gethsemane.

Finally, having realized for himself what the true path was – that it led through the stages of meditation – Siddhārtha fixed his resolve on the goal with an unshakeable resolution. At this point a beautiful and dramatic verse is put into his mouth by some compilers of the scriptures: 'Let blood dry up, let flesh wither away, but I shall not stir from this spot till Enlightenment be attained.'[53] He did not say, 'Well, I'll try this for a few days, and if it doesn't work, I'll just have to try something else, I suppose.' His commitment, once he had seen the way clear before him, was total and uncompromising. Nothing less would do for the purpose he had set himself, which was to overturn conditioned existence itself. The Buddha's Enlightenment is therefore very often described in simple heroic terms as a victory – a victory over Māra, the Buddhist embodiment of evil. The name 'Māra' literally means 'Death', and he personifies all the forces of evil existing within our own mind, our negative emotions, our psychological conditionings and so on, everything that binds us to repeated suffering – in short, our craving, our hatred, and our ignorance. On account of his victory over Māra, another of the Buddha's titles is Mārajit, the conqueror of Māra.

Given that the Buddha's attainment of Enlightenment was so conspicuously the expression – the ultimate expression – of the heroic ideal, it is no surprise to find that his teaching puts such a stress on self-reliance. The Pāli scriptures record him saying: 'All that a teacher could do have I done for you. Here are the roots of trees. Sit down, meditate – the rest is up to you.'[54] He was always asking the monks how they were getting on, never letting them slacken off, always inspiring them to greater efforts, and most of them responded by showing great determination. Others got a bit tired of it all, and resisted keeping up the pace – but they soon left to find an easier teacher.[55]

The Buddha knew from personal experience that following the spiritual path was no easy matter. On more than one occasion he spoke of the spiritual life in terms of a battle. 'We are Kṣatriyas, warriors,' he told his disciples. He did not mean that they were of the Kṣatriya caste, because his disciples were from every caste, from Brahmins to Untouchables (caṇḍālas), and no distinction of caste was respected in the sangha. He said, 'We are warriors because we are fighters. And what do we fight for? We fight for śīla, the ethical life; we fight for samādhi, higher consciousness; we fight for prajñā, Wisdom; and we fight for vimukti, complete spiritual emancipation.'[56] In passages like this the Buddha comes across as the embodiment of fearlessness and self-confidence. There is no false humility or bravado about him. His utterance is spoken of as his siṃhanāda, his Lion's Roar.[57] We all know people who bleat like sheep, even people who 'baa' like little woolly lambs, and we know people who bark or yap like dogs. But the Buddha's preaching is likened to the roaring of a lion because, according to Indian mythology, when the lion roars every other beast in the jungle falls silent. When the Buddha expounds the Truth, no one can stand against it.

You don't have to cast your net very wide to find the heroic ideal being extolled or put into practice in the Buddhist scriptures. However, for a more direct and immediate impression of the fundamentally heroic nature of the Buddhist ideal, you have only to look at some of the more powerful images in Buddhist art. I am not thinking here of the Gandhāran tradition of sculpture, which is not purely Indian and is sometimes a bit cloying, but of the Mathura tradition, named after a place not very far from where Delhi is today, and the earliest purely Indian art, in which is emphasized vigour rather than gentleness, confidence rather than tenderness, strength rather than sweetness. Characteristic of this artistic movement is a standing portrayal of the Buddha as a powerfully-built man in the prime of life, firmly erect, like a great tower or a massive tree, and making with his hands the *abhaya mudrā* – the gesture of fearlessness.[58]

Buddhist art does not, of course, focus solely on the Buddha himself, nor is the heroic ideal embodied solely in the person of the Buddha. From the Mahāyāna development of Buddhism emerged, as its most important contribution to the Buddhist vision, the figure of the bodhisattva. As an archetype, the bodhisattva became a symbolic manifestation of a particular aspect of Enlightenment; and one of the most important and revered of these archetypal bodhisattvas is Mañjuśrī, who represents Wisdom. Just as in the *Dhammapada* the Buddha describes the Dharma-farer as destroying the hosts of Māra with the sword of Wisdom,[59] so Mañjuśrī is depicted – in the form known as Arapacana Mañjuśrī – as brandishing aloft in his right hand a flaming sword, the sword of knowledge, or Wisdom. Later still in the historical development of Buddhism, the central figure of Tantric Buddhism is the figure of the wrathful Vajrapaṇī, who represents, in his graphically fearsome aspect, the heroic, fearless energy of the Enlightened mind. In his right hand he brandishes a *vajra*, an indestructible weapon of irresistible power.

The bodhisattva ideal, the determination to guide all sentient beings to Nirvāṇa, is the epitome of the heroic ideal as exemplified in the Buddha's own life. In the Mahāyāna literature the bodhisattva is likened to the new moon:[60] as the new moon is to the full moon so the bodhisattva is to the Buddha. As the new moon waxes to full moon so the bodhisattva grows towards Buddhahood, and he or she does this by the practice of the six *pāramitās*, the six transcendental virtues of generosity, ethics, patience, energy, meditative concentration, and Wisdom.[61] These virtues are all to be practised, according to the Mahāyāna texts, on a truly heroic scale.[62] It's not just a matter of an occasional burst of generosity, a momentary awareness of the ethical dimension in one's choice of action, a reasonable degree of patience, a fitful stirring of spiritual energy, a modicum of meditative absorption once or twice a week, and the odd moment of reflection and contemplation on the Dharma.

Take generosity, for instance. The bodhisattva gives not just material things, but even life and limb if necessary. It is against this sort of background that we can understand the self-immolation of Vietnamese monks who wanted to draw attention to the terrible spiritual plight of their country. And the bodhisattva practises all the virtues or perfections, not just during one lifetime, but (according to the heroic vision of Mahāyāna Buddhism) over an enormous number of lives spanning three *kalpas*, or aeons.

The bodhisattva as hero is delineated particularly clearly in a passage from the *Aṣṭasāhasrikā*, the 'Perfection of Wisdom in 8,000 Lines'. As usual in the *Prajñāpāramitā sūtras*, the Buddha is addressing his disciple Subhūti:

> Suppose, Subhūti, that there were a most excellent hero, very
> vigorous, of high social position, handsome, attractive and most
> fair to behold, in possession of all the finest virtues, of those
> virtues which spring from the very height of sovereignty, morality,
> learning, renunciation and so on. He is judicious, able to express
> himself, to formulate his views clearly, to substantiate his claims;
> one who always knows the suitable time, place and situation for
> everything. In archery he has gone as far as one can go. He is
> successful in warding off all manner of attack, most skilled in all
> arts, and foremost, through his fine achievements, in all crafts.
> He has a good memory, is intelligent, clever, steady and prudent,
> versed in all the treatises, has many friends, is wealthy, strong of
> body, with large limbs, with all his faculties complete, generous
> to all, dear and pleasant to many. Any work he might undertake
> he manages to complete. He speaks methodically, shares his great
> riches with the many, honours what should be honoured, reveres
> what should be revered, worships what should be worshipped.
> Would such a person, Subhūti, feel ever increasing joy and zest?
>
> *Subhūti:* He would, O Lord.
>
> *The Lord:* Now suppose, further, that this person, so greatly
> accomplished, should have taken his family with him on a
> journey, his mother and father, his sons and daughters. By some
> circumstances they find themselves in a great, wild forest. The
> foolish ones among them would feel fright, terror and hair-raising
> fear. He, however, would fearlessly say to his family: 'Do not be
> afraid! I shall soon take you safely and securely out of this terrible
> and frightening forest. I shall soon set you free!' If then more and
> more hostile and inimical forces should rise up against him in
> that forest, would this heroic man decide to abandon his family,
> and take himself alone out of that terrible and frightening forest

– he who is not one to draw back, who is endowed with all the forces of firmness and vigour, who is wise, exceedingly tender and compassionate, courageous and a master of many resources?

Subhūti: No, O Lord. For that person, who does not abandon his family, has at his disposal powerful resources, both within and without. On his side forces will arise in that wild forest which are quite a match for the hostile and inimical forces, and they will stand up for him and protect him. Those enemies and adversaries of his, who look for a weak spot, will not gain any hold over him. He is competent to deal with the situation, and is able, unhurt and uninjured, soon to take out of that forest both his family and himself. And securely and safely they will reach a village, city or market-town.

The Lord: Just so, Subhūti, is it with a bodhisattva who is full of pity and concerned with the welfare of all beings, who dwells in friendliness, compassion, sympathetic joy and impartiality.[63]

This, then, is an account, from the *Prajñāpāramitā* tradition, of the bodhisattva as hero, leading all sentient beings out of the deep forests of *saṃsāra* to the city of Enlightenment. If we turned to other traditions – Zen, or Tantric Buddhism – we could produce many other examples of the heroic ideal in Buddhism. But perhaps enough has been said to dismiss the notion of Buddhism as a disengaged, bloodless, or effete teaching and tradition. We may say, on the contrary, that it asserts the heroic ideal to a degree that ought to render it quite unfashionable. And as Buddhists we should be prepared to question fashionable ideas and attitudes. To a Buddhist it must seem a pity that the heroic ideal has been discredited or degraded in our century, because people really need something to live for, and, if necessary, to die for. So fundamental, indeed, is it to Buddhism, that we may say that the heroic ideal is coterminous with the spiritual life itself. Heroism is intrinsic to the quest for Enlightenment, and it is therefore at the very core of the essential nature of the Buddha.

5
FROM HERO-WORSHIP TO THE
WORSHIPPING BUDDHA

If the Buddha is, by his very nature, a hero, and if the Buddhist ideal is a heroic ideal, where does this leave us? How does the heroic ideal relate to us, or how do we relate to it? Is there an essential difference between one who is a hero and one who is not? It might help to answer this if we bring in another term here, if we say that the hero is also the genius – the cultural hero. So where does the difference between the genius and the ordinary person lie? The way we use the term 'genius' tends to suggest that the difference is one of kind, that the genius is almost of a different species to an ordinary person, but in fact the difference is simply one of degree. It is as though what is undeveloped or hardly developed in ourselves is highly or fully developed in someone we call a genius.

Take music, for instance. Clearly, anyone who is not deaf has, in some degree, the capacity to appreciate it. Dr Johnson used to confess, or rather – more characteristically – used to pride himself, on the fact, that he was unable to recognize the tune to *God Save the King*. It is questionable, however, whether the musical faculty can really be *totally* missing from a person's make-up. In the case of a great musician that faculty is simply – by virtue of an innate or developed capacity, sheer application, parental encouragement, natural talent, and force of character – converted into what we call genius. The same goes for literature. A great poet or novelist uses words just as we do when we write a letter, but they take their use of language to the highest possible pitch of expressiveness. And it is said that the most wretchedly painted signboard of a village inn shows that a Rembrandt once lived in the world.

This principle may be applied to almost any subject. Some people are good philosophers and others are poor philosophers, but no one can be said to be without a philosophy at all. A great philosopher simply philosophizes with greater rigour and imagination than the rest of us. If the difference between the genius and the ordinary person were a matter not simply of degree, but, in some sense, of kind, we should be unable to appreciate the productions of genius. We can appreciate music, or poetry, or philosophy, only because there is music and poetry and philosophy already in us. We have an affinity – however undeveloped – for these things. In a poem, Goethe compares the affinity of the eye with the sun to the affinity of the human soul with God. Just as the eye could not behold the sun unless the eye had in it something that was like the sun, he says, so the human soul could not perceive the divinity unless in the human soul there was something of the divine.[64] So we cannot appreciate Mozart unless there is something of Mozart in us. We cannot appreciate Shakespeare unless there is something of Shakespeare in us. And, as we shall see, we cannot appreciate the Buddha unless there is something of the Buddha in us.

Such appreciation does not come easily, of course. We may be stretched and challenged to our limits by the output of a creative artist. Indeed, it may be beyond us altogether to appreciate their work. Even in the case of Mozart, who is not commonly regarded as a revolutionary, some of his contemporaries thought they detected in his later works mistakes of harmony, whereas in fact he had simply moved beyond the conventions of the time. He had outstripped the general level of sensibility. To begin with, the creative genius is on his or her own, but then gradually more and more individuals catch up with their vision, until eventually there is a general raising of cultural sensibility. Almost anyone becomes able, with a little effort, to appreciate the work of great individuals of the past.

A corresponding process takes place in the opposite direction. The general level of cultural achievement provides the raw materials with which the exceptional individual expresses his or her genius. It is no coincidence that Mozart grew up in an intensely musical society, or that Michelangelo appeared at the height of the Italian Renaissance, or that Shakespeare honed his skills amidst a galaxy of dramatic poets, or that

Plato cogitated within a city humming with philosophical inquiry. The same must go for the originators of spiritual and religious traditions. They are the product, in some degree, of favourable cultural milieux, and it is no surprise to find that the Buddha appeared at a time of intense spiritual inquiry. Cultural development, however, takes place largely through the efforts of individuals working on their own or in contact with a few friends. Groups, schools, and institutions tend to stifle creativity.

In terms of cultural evolution, then, the genius or the hero is the forerunner, a few steps ahead of the rest of humanity, but leading the way for others to follow. This brings us back to our evolutionary model of human development: on the one hand we have the Buddhist model of spiritual development, and on the other we have the scientific model of evolution. As we have seen, the two models may, from a Buddhist viewpoint at least, be put together, so that the Buddhist vision can be seen as in some sense developing on from the scientific vision to produce one continuous process of development. So we start with the 'lower evolution', governed by a 'cyclic', reactive, or unconscious conditionality, and we develop by a 'spiral' principle, constituting creative, conscious action, on to the 'higher evolution'.

If we accept this overall scheme, we can then break it up into stages. First there is the subhuman stage of biological evolution. Then the specifically 'human' stage starts with the point at which self-consciousness emerges. Following on from this, the higher evolution opens with the 'superhuman' stage, characterized by the heroic individual or the genius. Finally, there is the stage starting from the point at which Insight into the nature of Reality is sustained at a sufficiently deep level to direct the individual's consciousness irreversibly towards Enlightenment. This point is traditionally called 'Stream Entry', and it marks the beginning of what we may call the 'trans-human' stage.

We can, therefore, see what our general position is. People are at a wide range of levels of development between the human stage and the superhuman. As Buddhists our agenda is to progress from wherever we are towards and through stage three, the stage of heroism and genius. It may come as a surprise, but our path lies not in the direction of a slow attenuation of the self, or an abandonment of the self, but in the development of a strong and heroic individuality. After all, if there is one thing that distinguishes the hero and the genius from comparatively ordinary people it is their individuality. They are not units in a mass. They stand alone.

We like to think that we are individuals, but most of the time we are not. You may even try very hard to be different – you may try to look different, behave differently, or even outrageously, but none of this will make you an individual (though it may, in some cases, be a start). We have to recognize that individuality is rare, because real awareness is rare. To become truly individual we need to make a conscious effort to become more deeply aware: of ourselves, of others, of the environment around us, and of Reality itself.

Statistically, numerically, we may be individuals, but very, very few of us are individuals in a psychological and spiritual sense. Most people are simply not sufficiently aware to be classed as real individuals. So when Buddhists talk about going beyond the 'self' and realizing the truth of 'non-self', they are talking about something that is quite out of the question for most of us. Most of us have not even developed a self yet, never mind realizing the non-self. If one has not developed a self that is distinguishable from a group mentality, if one's self is little more than an amorphous mass of conditionings, if one has not yet learned to be truly oneself, then nothing is really there to transcend. It is for this reason that the Buddhist path goes by way of the kind of ardent dedication and vision – the individuality – we find demonstrated by the great artist, the genius, and the hero.

If we know who or what we mean by a hero or genius, we can get a clearer idea of what a Stream Entrant is, and even what it means to speak of a Buddha. We may say that the genius, the cutting edge of a culture – the cultural hero – represents, to a greater or lesser degree, what the average person can become, from the point of view of cultural development. The Stream Entrant then represents what this kind of true individual can become spiritually. And the Buddha represents the goal towards which the Stream Entrant is irrevocably bound. They together constitute one continuous process of development within the higher evolution.

We can thus begin to see an analogy – and perhaps not just an analogy but a real correspondence – between the cultural hero and the Buddha. The Buddha is the first historical example of what all men, all women, potentially are. The Buddha is different from other beings not in kind, but in degree of development, in the degree to which he manifests his inner potentiality. In the scriptures this crucial point is made by way of a typically homely image: 'Suppose', the Buddha says, 'a hen has laid a number of eggs, and suppose the hen sits on these eggs patiently, until they start hatching. What happens then?' Clearly, the chicks don't all hop out simultaneously. What happens is that one egg hatches first. So when this first chick emerges and stands clear of the eggshell, what does it do? It starts tapping with its little beak on the other shells, helping the other chicks out into the world.[65]

The meaning of this simile is not difficult to fathom. The egg is the state of unawareness, the womb of spiritual darkness and ignorance within which we sleep. The Buddha is the first chick to break out of his shell, and having done so he then rouses the others, tapping vigorously on their shells. Maybe he hears a muffled tapping coming back at him, and he taps more vigorously, to be answered again by a more eager tapping from within until the shell cracks and a fellow chick hops out.

Yet another of the Buddha's titles, therefore, is Lokajyeṣṭha. The common translation, 'World-honoured One', does not give the full flavour of this term, because *jyeṣṭha* really means 'first-born son'. So, *loka* meaning 'world', *lokajyeṣṭha* means the first-born of the world, the elder brother of humanity, and it refers to the first human being to be spiritually reborn. This means that the only difference, spiritually speaking, between the Buddha and his Enlightened disciples (the question is explicitly raised and answered in the scriptures) is that he attained Enlightenment first, by himself, whereas they attained it subsequently with his help.[66]

In the scale of the higher evolution, the Buddha appears at the apogee – not a finite point, but, as it were, an infinite extension – of the trans-human stage. He is neither human, strictly speaking, nor even superhuman, but simply fully Enlightened. However, the higher evolution does not exclude the lower evolution; the Buddha is still human, still a man – only, at the same time, something more than that, something more, even, than a superman.

But why bring the idea of the 'superman' into a discussion of the Buddha? Are we trying to interpret Buddhism along Nietzschean lines? In fact, there is no need to bring in Nietzsche here. The 'superman' or *Mahāpuruṣa* was evidently a quite important idea in India during the Buddha's lifetime, and an entire *sutta*, the *Lakkhaṇa Sutta*, is devoted to a full description of this ideal figure.[67] The characteristics

– *lakkhaṇa* in Pāli – of the *Mahāpuruṣa* (Pāli *Mahāpurisa*) amount to thirty-two major marks or signs, and eighty-four minor ones, and they quite clearly embody the highest aesthetic, cultural, and religious ideals of the time. It would seem that the Buddha was regarded by his contemporaries as conforming to this ideal, and this is quite significant because it shows that the Buddha did not bypass human perfection, even physical perfection, but incorporated it into the higher perfection of Enlightenment.

We like to distinguish human beings from animals, but in fact humanity does not exclude the animal. Our nature incorporates the animal in subordination to the truly human in us. We develop all our truly human characteristics and functions, qualities, and attitudes not so much by rejecting the animal as by integrating the animal into the human. And just as human beings, even at the highest pitch of their development, include the animal in their make-up, so Buddhahood includes and integrates the human in subordination to the Enlightened personality.

The point to grasp from all this is that cultural attainment and spiritual development are analogous, that they represent the lower and the higher levels of an overall spiritual process, the higher evolution. They are both the work of *individuals*, in advance of, and helping, the rest of humanity. To get anywhere ourselves, then, we must acknowledge that there are men and women who are more developed than we at present are. Hero-worship, or the hero-worshipping attitude, is by no means a bad thing, provided it is directed towards those who really are more highly developed than the rest of us, rather than towards the media-generated icons of contemporary popular culture. The tendency to cynicism, a determination to uncover the feet of clay, must be seen for what it is – a vice. Unwillingness to believe in anything like high ideals, or to respect those who devote their lives to the serious pursuit of those ideals, or to recognize greatness in an individual, is soul-corroding and spiritually corrupt.

By contrast, Buddhists try to cultivate a spirit of admiration, of respect, of reverence and devotion. This reverence is not only for certain individuals as they are, on account of the level of spiritual development they have already attained, but also for everybody else, on account of what they are capable of becoming. A comparison is drawn in the scriptures with the convention in a monarchical system of respecting the heir to the throne even as a baby.[68] Though this child may be playing with his rattle now, you know that one day he is going to be king, and thus you treat him with the reverence due to a king. Buddhism encourages such an attitude towards all sentient beings. They may be anything now – they may be thieves or prostitutes, financiers or politicians, but one day they are going to be Buddhas. However degraded their present condition, however limited their outlook, however enmeshed they are in their own evil deeds, you need to respect them on account of what they are in potentiality, which one day will surely be realized.

No case is so desperate that you can ever say that they will never get out of the hell they have created for themselves. The classical villain of the Buddhist scriptures, for example, is Devadatta, the Buddha's cousin. In some ways he was one of the brightest of the Buddha's disciples – he had all sorts of psychic powers – but he was ambitious and jealous. One day he went to the Buddha and said, 'Lord, you are getting old. Don't exert yourself any more. Take it easy, retire. I shall look after everything for you. I shall lead the sangha.'[69] When the Buddha made it plain what he thought of this idea, Devadatta tried to initiate a split in the sangha, which is regarded in Buddhism as a truly heinous crime.[70] When this failed he even made attempts upon the Buddha's life. He had a mad elephant let loose upon the Buddha on one occasion, and another time he sent a boulder rolling down a hill towards him. All these attempts failed, of course, and some time later Devadatta died of disappointment – and we're told that after his death he went to an unpleasant place.[71] But the Mahāyāna scriptures tell us what Devadatta's name will be when he becomes a Buddha, and exactly when this will be.[72] Whether or not you accept the precision of these forecasts, the principle is clear. Even someone like Devadatta has the seed of Buddhahood in him, and when he has purified himself he too will become Enlightened and liberate other sentient beings. No one is ever completely and hopelessly lost. If Devadatta can bounce back, anyone can.

Buddhists revere their spiritual teachers in particular, because their teachers represent what they can become, what they want to become, what indeed they will become when they have made the necessary effort. If we have no reverence for our ideals as embodied in the form of human beings, whether still alive or long dead, whether we meet them through personal contact or through the pages of a book, it will hardly be possible for us to attain that ideal for ourselves. Devotional practice, the whole question of worship in Buddhism, has to be understood as proceeding from this basis.

This means that we have to dissociate the word 'worship' from notions of churchgoing or praising a universal creator figure. It is easy for people who associate religion exclusively with the worship of God to jump to the conclusion that if Buddhists worship they must be worshipping a god. The confusion arises out of the limited sense in which the word 'worship' is used in the West. In India, by contrast, one word serves to denote the respect you pay to anyone, whether to the Buddha, your parents, your elder brothers and sisters, your teachers – spiritual and secular – or any senior and honourable person.

When Buddhists bow down and make offerings of flowers, candles, and incense to the image of a Buddha or a bodhisattva, they are honouring the Buddha as an Enlightened being, not worshipping him as a god. This does not mean that worship plays a minor or even dispensable role in Buddhism, although those who present Buddhism as merely a rational philosophy would like to think so. The expression of gratitude, of rejoicing, of respect – in short, worship – is fundamental to Buddhism. Just how fundamental becomes startlingly apparent when we take up again the account of the Buddha's life and find out what it was that occupied the Buddha's thoughts as he sat by the River Nerañjarā after his Enlightenment.

He remained in the same area for some seven weeks after attaining Enlightenment, sitting beneath the trees – a few days beneath one tree, then a few days beneath another. In this way the weeks passed by, and during this time he hardly bothered to eat. There is just one reference to food in the scriptural account – apparently, two wandering merchants offered him some honey and rice cakes[73] – but we can assume that he was above all bodily considerations.

It wasn't just that he had gained Enlightenment. That was a tremendous thing in itself, but it wasn't just that. He had something else to do, something which was if anything even more difficult. For seven weeks he was intent upon the task of absorbing the Enlightenment experience, allowing it to transform and transmute every atom of his being. After all, what had happened to him was literally the most tremendous thing that can possibly happen to a human being. The transformation from an unenlightened to an Enlightened being is so overwhelming that, in a sense, when one becomes Enlightened, one ceases to be, in the ordinary sense, a human being at all. An Enlightened human being, a Buddha, has entered an entirely new and different category of existence.

The Buddha was the first person in the course of human history to undergo this transformation. No wonder that he was staggered by his own achievement. And it seems that he found himself faced with one or two dilemmas – or, at least, certain teachings have been presented in the form of dilemmas that exercised the newly awakened mind of the Buddha. One of them is quite well known and forms the basis for the next chapter. The other, which we are going to look at now, has been almost completely overlooked by commentators on the life of the Buddha. So far as I know, no one has remarked on the extraordinary and clear implications of the passage. Both episodes are found in the *Saṃyutta Nikāya*, 'The Book of the Kindred Sayings' – that is, sayings of the Buddha on the same subject – but the first is found elsewhere in the Pāli canon as well. The more obscure – and quite surprising – dilemma comes straight after the more famous one in the text, but it actually happened before it, having apparently occurred five weeks after the Enlightenment.

The Buddha's reflections at this point went as follows: 'It is ill to live paying no one the honour and obedience due to a superior. What recluse or Brahmin is there under whom I could live, paying him honour and respect?'[74] Now this is surely remarkable. The Buddha has just attained supreme Enlightenment – and here we find him wondering to whom he can pay honour and respect. In our own time, it is unusual for anyone to pay honour and respect to anyone else. Instead, we demand equality; we want to make sure that no one is regarded as superior to anyone else. Some of us may try to be polite and courteous, but the idea that respect benefits the person who offers it rather than the person to whom it is offered runs right against the grain of current social values. Not only that, the Buddha's attitude also seems to upset traditional Buddhist ideas about the Buddha, and even about Enlightenment itself.

But let us continue with the episode. Perhaps things will become a little clearer. The Buddha continues to reflect, and his reflections are concerned with four things: the training in ethics, the training in meditation, the training in insight or wisdom, and the training in contemplation of knowledge of emancipation. What he sees is that there is no one in the universe – no one among the gods, even Brahmā

Sahāmpati, lord of a thousand worlds, and no human being, no holy or wise man anywhere – who is more accomplished in these things than he is himself. He sees that in terms of spiritual insight and understanding he himself is the highest living being in the universe. This is how the Buddha sees himself, and if we don't see the Buddha in this way, then we don't really see the Buddha at all.

Having realized for the first time who he really is, the Buddha sees that there is no one 'under whom he can live, paying him honour and respect'. That, surely, is clear enough. One lives 'under' someone in order to learn from them. As the Buddha is more highly developed than any other living being, he has nothing to learn, spiritually speaking, from anyone. But the crucial point here is that he doesn't give up. He still requires a focus for his devotion. So he reflects further: 'This Dharma, then, wherein I am supremely Enlightened – what if I were to live under it, paying it honour and respect?' And at this very moment, Brahmā Sahāmpati appears before him and approves of the Buddha's decision, telling him that all the Buddhas of the past lived under the Dharma, honouring and respecting it, and that all the Buddhas of the future will do likewise.

This is really an astonishing episode. It shows that even a Buddha 'needs' (not that the Enlightened mind can literally be in need of anything) to honour and respect something. Even a Buddha needs to offer worship. So worship is not just a spiritual practice to be taken up as a means to an end, and then discarded once Enlightenment is attained. Worship is an integral part of the Enlightenment experience itself. The Enlightened mind is a worshipping mind no less than it is a realized mind or a compassionate mind. We are all familiar with the image of the meditating Buddha, and there are images of the teaching Buddha, and even the standing or the walking Buddha. But we must add to these the much less familiar image of the worshipping Buddha.

The text tells us that the object of the Buddha's devotion is the Dharma – but the Dharma the Buddha worships is not the Dharma as we usually think of it, in the sense of the Buddha's teaching. For one thing, when this particular episode happened the Buddha had not, as yet, taught anybody anything. The Dharma referred to here is the Dharma as *principle*, the Dharma as the Law, the Truth, or Reality. The Dharma we know about is the Dharma as a conceptual formulation – expressed in accordance with people's needs – of the Dharma as Reality itself. What the Buddha worships is the object or content of his own experience of Enlightenment.

When we think about it, however, a further difficulty confronts us here. If you worship something, what you worship is necessarily higher than you are. If the Buddha worships the Dharma, then the Dharma is higher than the Buddha. But in what sense can this be the case? Has not the Buddha penetrated the Dharma, mastered it, so to speak? What is left for him to worship in the Dharma? To solve this puzzle we shall have to take a closer look at the most fundamental formulation of the Dharma, *pratītya-samutpāda*: 'conditioned co-production' or 'dependent origination'. As we saw in the first chapter, this principle consists in the fact that one thing is conditioned by something else, that whatever happens takes place by way of a cause. And conditioned co-production is of two kinds, one being a circular process symbolized by the wheel of life, and the other generating a spiral of spiritual development. The first of these the Buddha has clearly left behind him: he is free of the wheel of life. What we are concerned with at this point is *pratītya-samutpāda* in its spiral form, the form of the successive stages of the spiritual path.

The best-known formulation of this sequence of positive mental states or experiences, known as the chain of positive *nidānas*, runs as follows:

In dependence on suffering arises faith. In dependence on faith arises joy. In dependence on joy arises rapture. In dependence on rapture arises calm. In dependence on calm arises bliss. In dependence on bliss arises concentration. In dependence on concentration arises knowledge and vision of things as they really are. In dependence on knowledge and vision of things as they really are arises dispassion. In dependence on dispassion arises withdrawal, or disentanglement. In dependence on withdrawal, or disentanglement, arises freedom. In dependence on freedom arises knowledge of the destruction of the *āsravas*, or all unskilful, negative states.[75]

This sequence is the second of the two processes by which the principle of *pratītya-samutpāda* works out, and it represents the rationale of the spiritual life. In turn, it also divides into two sections: one mundane, the other transcendental. The first section consists of the first seven *nidānas*, or links, up to 'the arising of knowledge and vision of things as they really are'. All these *nidānas* except the seventh are – though positive, though skilful – still mundane. They are mundane because after having attained them you can still fall back to the wheel. From 'the arising of knowledge and vision of things as they really are' onwards, however, through the five links that comprise the second section of the 'spiral', you cannot fall back – you can only go forward. And you cannot fall back from them because they are transcendental attainments.

This makes the seventh *nidāna* the crucial one. The arising of 'knowledge and vision of things as they really are' marks the transition from the mundane to the transcendental. It constitutes the arising of transcendental Insight, or Stream Entry – that is, it is the point at which you enter the stream that leads unerringly to the ocean of Nirvāna. It is also, for obvious reasons, known as 'the Point of No Return'.

The *nidāna* chain gives us a clue to solve the mystery of how it is the Buddha worships the Dharma as higher than himself. The culmination of the *nidāna* chain is the arising of knowledge of the destruction of the *āsravas*. This is what happens when one attains Enlightenment. At this point one becomes a Buddha. But is it literally the culmination? Is the twelfth *nidāna* literally the last one? We can get a clue to the answer to this question from a scriptural account of conditionality put forward by the brilliantly gifted nun, Dhammadinnā, whose exposition, we should add, the Buddha assented to in full. It is sometimes thought that Dhammadinnā expounded the teaching of the twelve positive *nidānas*, but this is not indicated in the scriptures. Rather, as we learn from the *Cūḷavedalla Sutta* of the *Majjhima Nikāya*, she gave examples of two different kinds of conditioned relationship, indicating movement in oscillation and progressive order. Questioned by her former husband Visākha about the 'counterparts' of various mental states, she answered him until he asked, 'What is the counterpart of Nibbāna?' At this point she said, 'Friend Visākha, you have pushed this line of questioning too far; you were not able to grasp the limit to questions.'[76] Along the same lines, we could perhaps say that the progressive spiral of conditioned co-production stops at this point simply because it has to stop somewhere. Perhaps there is no reason why the spiral process should not continue indefinitely. In that case, attaining Enlightenment does not mean achieving a fixed, determinate state, however high. It means becoming involved in an irreversible and unmeasured transcendental process.

So, even though the Buddha was the highest living being in the universe, even though he had progressed further along the spiral path than anyone else, he saw that there were still reaches of that path, there were still developments of that progression, which he had yet to explore. This is why it was possible for the Buddha 'to live under the Dharma, paying it honour and respect'. The Dharma here is the law, or reality, of *pratītya-samutpāda*. And for the worshipping Buddha, the Dharma is especially this law or reality as represented in unnamed and as yet unrealized *nidānas* – *nidānas* which from our point of view are literally inconceivable. The fact that one of the first things the Buddha thinks of when he has gained Enlightenment is to look for something to worship, and that even he is able to find something to worship, should be enough in itself to convince us of the central importance of worship within Buddhism.

In this episode from the *Saṃyutta Nikāya*, the word for 'honour and respect' is *gārava*, which means, according to the dictionary, 'reverence, respect, honour, esteem, veneration, worship'. The term clearly suggests the kind of positive attitude which we naturally adopt towards something or someone we see or experience as being higher than ourselves. Obviously there are the Buddhas and Bodhisattvas – but is there anything else that can be an object of honour and respect for us?

As it happens, the Buddhist tradition provides a list of six *gāravas*, six objects that are worthy of reverence, respect, and worship.[77] They are: *satthā, dharma, saṅgha, sikkhā, appamāda*, and *paṭisanthāra*. The first three of these can be more or less taken as read: they are known collectively as the Three Jewels. The central act of becoming a Buddhist, and of affirming one's commitment to Buddhism, is traditionally termed 'Going for Refuge to the Three Jewels', usually abbreviated to just 'Going for Refuge'. You go for Refuge to the Buddha as the ideal of Enlightenment, to the Dharma as the fundamental spiritual principle discovered by him, together with its formulation in a body of teachings, and to the Āryasaṅgha as the spiritual community of those who really follow those teachings.

In the context of the *gāravas*, however, the first of the Three Jewels is termed Satthā, which is yet another title accorded the Buddha, the full honorific usually being *satthā devamanussānaṃ*, 'teacher of gods and men'. Why the term Satthā appears here instead of 'Buddha' is probably because we experience the Buddha through the scriptures mainly as a teacher – as the supreme teacher, the teacher of gods and men. Also to be considered is the fact that in ancient India, as in almost all ages apart from our own, anyone who earned the title of 'teacher' automatically commanded great honour and reverence. It is still the case in India today – you call even your primary school teacher your 'guru' – and it is, of course, a term of great respect. In the Buddhist tradition, parents are often called 'the first gurus' – or to use another term with an equivalent meaning, 'the first *ācāryas*' – because they are the first people from whom you learn anything. And again, this represents a posture of respect. You respect your parents not only because they brought you into the world, but also because they were the first people from whom you learned anything.

The remaining three *gāravas*, after Satthā, Dharma, and sangha, are less familiar. The fourth, *sikkhā*, is study, training, or discipline. Study is a *gārava* inasmuch as we cannot study Buddhism effectively unless we see it as something higher than we are, as having the power to help us to grow and develop, just as the rain and sunshine help plants and trees to grow. In Buddhism there are traditionally three objects of study or training: the higher ethics, the higher states of consciousness, and the higher wisdom. These are the pre-eminent sources from which we learn, grow, and develop. But there are all sorts of other things that benefit our human development – friendship and the fine arts, for example – and these too can be aspects of Buddhist study and training, and thus worthy of honour and respect. The basic principle implied by the idea of study as a *gārava* is that if we are unable to honour and respect something, it isn't really worth studying, because it won't help us.

The fifth *gārava* is *appamāda*, or 'non-heedlessness' – that is, mindfulness or awareness. So why is mindfulness to be venerated? Why is it one of the six *gāravas*? The answer is quite simple. We have to respect those qualities that we are trying to develop. If we think rather lightly of them, if we don't really take them seriously, we won't get anywhere with them. In other words we need to bring an attitude of reverence to our own spiritual practice, whether we are taking up mindfulness or any other discipline. *Appamāda* or non-heedlessness is named as the fifth *gārava* in an essentially representative sense, in the sense of being the key to all other Buddhist practice.

With the last of the *gāravas* we are introduced to a rather interesting word with a wide range of associated meanings: *paṭisanthāra*. It comes from a root meaning 'to spread', and its literal meaning is 'spreading before'. This probably leaves us none the wiser so far as identifying it as an object of respect is concerned. However, there is an old-fashioned English idiom that takes us a little closer to the nature of this *gārava*:

'laying out a good spread', meaning providing a good meal. A spread is a sort of feast, and *paṭisanthāra* has much the same kind of meaning. According to the dictionary it means 'spreading before' in the sense of 'friendly welcome, kind reception, honour, goodwill, favour, friendship'. This 'spreading before' can be material, or it can be spiritual. If you take it as meaning a 'kind reception' you can see that, as well as gastronomic feasting, it could suggest a feast, say, of music, and even 'the feast of reason and the flow of soul'.[78] At the highest level, it is a 'spreading' of spiritual abundance before people. Thus *paṭisanthāra* covers a rich, important aspect of human life, including spiritual life, and we will not be able to draw nourishment from it if we take it for granted. As well as honouring mindfulness, the heart of Buddhist practice, we also need to honour the whole expansive richness of the Buddhist life.

The significant place of reverence and worship in the spiritual life is made explicit in the teaching of the six *gāravas*. But as we have seen, it is clear from the evidence of the Buddha's own life, too, that worship is a spiritual requirement of every Buddhist, however highly developed. In fact, the greater the place we can give to worship in our own lives, the more certain we can be of one day attaining to whatever the Buddha himself attained, and of worshipping as the Buddha himself worshipped.

6

THE WORD OF THE BUDDHA

So the Buddha attained Enlightenment. He reached the end of his heroic quest. His aspiration was fulfilled. Then what? Enlightenment may have been in a sense the end of something, but it was also the start of something. It was the start of what we know as 'Buddhism', the emergence of the Dharma into the world. But in order for the Dharma, the Truth, to spread, the Buddha had to find a way of communicating his experience to other people. And, according to the traditional account of what transpired after his Enlightenment, the Buddha's decision to teach was not inevitable.

What he had realized seemed so tremendous, so overwhelming, that he began to wonder whether he could ever make it known to anybody else. Reality, in all its heights and all its depths, was so sublime, so unfathomable. It could never be reached through mere reasoning or dialectic. It was deep, delicate, and subtle. Only the truly wise would ever be able to understand it, because it went right against the grain of the world. And who had that kind of wisdom? Ordinary men and women were so absorbed in the pleasures of the senses that they couldn't take anything else seriously. What would be the point of trying to communicate his discovery to them? Even if he managed to speak to them on their own level, there would be nothing in their experience remotely like his own. How could he possibly get through to them?

The more he thought about it, the more inclined he was to hold his peace and leave the world to its own devices. But then, as he sat there under one of the trees at Bodh Gaya, enjoying the bliss of the Enlightenment experience, something happened to change his mind. In fact, according to the legends, it was some*one* who changed his mind. It was as if he saw a great light, heard a great voice; there appeared before him the great god Brahmā Sahāmpati. And the god spoke to him (we should note, by the way, that even he, lord of a thousand worlds, defers to the Buddha) saying, 'Let my Lord the Exalted One teach the Truth. For there are in the world at least a few people whose eyes are covered with but little of the dust of the passions. They will surely understand the Dharma, if you will only teach it to them.'[79]

That is what the scriptures say happened. Of course, as with so many events from the Buddha's life, you can take the incident either literally or symbolically. Either it happened more or less as described, or else the sublime figure of Brahmā Sahāmpati simply represents the level in the Buddha's mind at which this thought arose, a level that for all its sublimity was lower than that of Buddhahood itself. The voice, wherever it came from, was saying, 'Well, you've reached your goal. You're Enlightened. You're at peace. You have perfect knowledge and perfect bliss. But what about those who are still struggling? What are you going to do for *them*?' As the Buddha heard this voice, as he saw, as it were, this radiant figure in supplication before him, a great surge of compassion took place in his heart.

More prosaically, we may say that as the Buddha applied himself to the task of assimilating the Enlightenment experience at all levels of his being, one very important aspect of that process was the development of what we call *karuṇā*, or compassion. The compassion of a Buddha is directed towards all those beings who are not Enlightened, who are suffering from their own ignorance, psychological conditioning, bewilderment, and confusion. So as he assimilated the Enlightenment experience in the deepest emotional aspect of his being, his ordinary human emotion was transformed into a transcendental quality of mind, into *karuṇā*.

Then, with the supernormal power of his 'divine eye' the Buddha looked out over the world, and he perceived that the beings of the world were at widely differing stages of development. As he saw it, the world was, in this respect, like a muddy lake full of lotus plants. Some folk were deeply immersed in the world, like lotus buds buried deep in the mud. Others were not so completely engrossed in worldly things, and were beginning to emerge, like lotuses, from the muddy waters of the world. And there were a few who stood clear above those waters, ready to burst into bloom in the sunlight of the Truth.

Convinced at last that there were people in the world who would be receptive to the Truth, the Buddha addressed Brahmā Sahāmpati in verse. The English translation doesn't really capture the rhythm and beauty of the original Pāli, but it is still very striking: 'Wide open are the gates leading to the deathless state. Let those that have ears to hear release their faith.'[80] So saying, he decided to go out into the world, and teach the truth he had discovered.

But having decided to teach, the next question was: whom should he teach? He cast his mind back to the earliest days of his going forth, and he thought of his first two teachers. They had not been able to show him the Truth themselves, but they had helped him as far as they could, and they were assuredly high-minded, noble individuals. If anyone could grasp what he had to teach, they could. But then the Buddha perceived that it was too late, that they were both dead. So then his thoughts turned to the five disciples who had followed him in the days when he was practising austerities. Although they had eventually left him in disgust, they had been very helpful to him for a time. Why not share his discovery with them first?

It is notable that the Buddha is motivated in his initial attempts to teach not only by the fact that these particular individuals are ripe for the Dharma, but also by his gratitude towards them. It is interesting, in fact, that gratitude is clearly one of the keynotes of the Buddha's post-Enlightenment experience. Apparently, when he arose from the foot of the tree where he had become Enlightened, he walked some distance away from the tree, turned and looked at it for some hours together, and then bowed to it. By this he was saying, in effect, 'This tree sheltered me, it shaded me while I gained Enlightenment. I pay respect and express gratitude to it.'[81]

It was in such a spirit of gratitude that the Buddha determined to find his five former followers. Perceiving in his mind that they were living at a place called Sarnath, seven or eight miles out of Benares, the Buddha set out, leaving Bodh Gaya at the end of the seventh week after his Enlightenment.

Sarnath was about a hundred miles away – it must have taken a good week to get there – and he found the five ascetics living in the deer park, a sort of game sanctuary, also known as 'the resort of the seers'. They saw him coming, and recognized him while he was still some way off. They hadn't forgotten *him*. 'Here comes that fellow Gautama,' murmured one. 'You remember – we really thought he was special, until asceticism got too tough for him and he went back to the easy life. Look, you can see how well-fed he is, even from here.' Another said, 'Well, let him come if he wants to. He needn't think we're going to pay him any particular respect, though. We can't pay homage to the poor fellow as we used to when he was Gautama the great ascetic.' So the Buddha came nearer and nearer. And as he approached, the ascetics found themselves unable to keep to their resolution to ignore him. It was as though some strange force compelled them to rise to their feet, greet him, take his bowl and spare robe, and offer him a seat. Even though they disapproved of him – even though he had, as they thought, betrayed their ideal – there was still something about him. It was something strange, something they'd never seen before, to which they could not help responding.

After the preliminary greetings were over, the Buddha came straight to the point: 'Listen. The Deathless has been attained. Let me teach you the way to reach this goal for yourselves.' But the five ascetics wouldn't believe him. They said, 'Even when you were practising all those austerities, even when you were mortifying the flesh with extremes of self-torture, you couldn't gain Enlightenment. How can you possibly have done it now, when everyone knows you've fallen by the wayside?' But the Buddha persisted. He reasoned with them, he argued with them, and in the end he managed to persuade them at least to listen to what he had to say. It was exactly two months from the date of his Enlightenment, and so it is this day, the full-moon day of June/ July, which is celebrated as Dharmacakra-Pravartana Day, that is, the anniversary of the Buddha's first turning of the wheel of the Dharma. (We usually just call it Dharma Day.) The rains had just begun, and throughout the months of the rainy season they talked, they debated, and they meditated. By the time the rain stopped, all five disciples had also gained Enlightenment.[82]

Although the Buddha taught the five ascetics for all those months, it so happens that we simply don't know what it was that he taught. The oldest accounts simply say that he discoursed with them, and leave it at that. At a later date it was suggested that the Buddha taught the five ascetics the Four Noble Truths and the Noble Eightfold Path, but while he may well have done so we don't know for sure.[83] Some people don't like anything unknown, so they prefer to fill in the blanks, and this is what seems to have happened here. What really took place remains a complete mystery, and perhaps it is best left that way.

Somehow or other, the Buddha had succeeded in communicating the ineffable, or rather, he had succeeded in leading his five disciples to their own direct experience of the ineffable truth of the Dharma. But this was only the start. For the next forty-five years he must have taught hundreds or even thousands of people, from all walks of life, up and down the length and breadth of north-eastern India, right up to the time of his death, or as we say, his *parinirvāṇa*, at the age of eighty. From the scriptures emerges a succession of countless unique occasions and encounters, each of which draws out a fresh insight into the Dharma:

- An important Brahmin comes to see the Buddha to ask him how best to conduct a great sacrifice of many hundreds of animals. Courteously and systematically, the Buddha convinces him that the most perfect sacrifice is a bloodless one, consisting in the practice of ethics, meditation, and wisdom.[84]
- A well-to-do farmer is busy organizing the sowing of his fields when he sees the Buddha standing there with his begging-bowl, and says to him, 'Why don't you try working for a living?' The Buddha gives a brilliant discourse, describing the spiritual life in terms of work. The farmer offers to reward him with a bowl of delicious food, but the Buddha refuses it; he is not to be hired or paid for his teaching.[85]
- A number of monks overhear a wanderer speaking abusively of the Buddha and finding fault with the Dharma. The Buddha warns them not to get angry or upset on this account, nor to be pleased when people praise him and his teaching; but simply to acknowledge what is correct and explain what is incorrect in the views of others.[86]
- One of the Buddha's lay-followers suggests that the local people would take to the Dharma much more readily if the monks could be persuaded to perform superhuman feats and miracles. The Buddha explains that the only miracle that is of any real use is the miracle of instruction in the Dharma which brings an end to suffering.[87]
- Two novice monks from Brahmin backgrounds admit to the Buddha that Brahmins have been reviling and abusing them for renouncing

their caste in order to join the sangha. The Buddha reassures them: there is no real distinction to be drawn between members of different castes, either physical, moral, or spiritual; but anyone whose faith is unshakeable becomes a true son and heir of the Buddha and the Dharma.[88]

- A king is inspired by the beauty of a moonlit night to go with his retinue to seek peace of mind from the Buddha.[89]
- A monk comes with the news that a raucous and intemperate dispute has broken out among the Order.[90]
- A great crowd has gathered to listen to a discourse, and the Buddha sees that there is only one among them, a leper, who is really going to hear what he has to say.[91]
- An old woman, distraught with grief at the death of her granddaughter, comes to the Buddha for comfort.[92]

In this way people kept coming and the Buddha responded to them according to their individual spiritual needs. Some went away as ignorant as they came, others went away with some food for thought, but for many, their lives would never be the same again. They would marvel aloud: 'It is as if someone were to set up what had been knocked down, or to point out the way to one who had got lost, or to bring an oil lamp into a dark place. ... I go for Refuge to the Dharma and the Sangha.' And then they would ask to be accepted as a lay-follower or ordained as a monk or nun.

The Buddha's last disciple was someone who came to see him when he was literally on his deathbed. Ānanda, the Buddha's disciple and attendant, was all for sending this person (his name was Subhadda) away. The Buddha was dying. This was hardly the time to ask him for yet another teaching. But the Buddha overheard their talk and said to Ānanda, 'Let him in. Whatever he wants to ask is for the sake of knowledge, not to cause trouble. What I tell him he will quickly understand.' So in he came, the last person to be personally instructed by the Buddha.[93]

After the Buddha had passed away, his disciples carried on the teaching, passing it on to their own pupils, who then, in time, passed it on to theirs. They passed it on, of course, by word of mouth. People didn't start writing books about Buddhism, or even taking notes. In fact, the teachings were not written down in any form for hundreds of years.

If you wanted to learn about Buddhism, you had to find someone at whose feet you could sit and learn about it. People only started to write down the Buddha's teaching about 500 years after his death, perhaps because by that time people's memories weren't as good as they had been in earlier days, and there was a danger that the Dharma would be lost.

The teaching that the Buddha taught personally to his disciples, and which was transmitted orally for so many years before eventually being written down in the form of scriptures, is known as *Buddhavacana*. 'Buddha' is a title meaning 'One who knows', while *vacana* means 'word' or 'utterance' or 'speech'. So Buddhavacana is the word, the utterance, the speech, of one who really does know. It is no ordinary speech. It is quite unlike the speech of anybody who is not a Buddha. This is because Buddhavacana is the expression in terms of human speech of an Enlightened state of consciousness.

There is much more to this than one can imagine. We tend to assume, perhaps unconsciously, that the Buddha speaks in much the same way that an ordinary person does, because, after all, he uses much the same language as everybody around him. But behind the common mode of communication there is something in the Buddha's speech that is not there behind our own speech. Informing the Buddha's words, standing behind them, as it were, there is the Enlightened consciousness, the Buddha-mind, and 'for those who have ears to hear', the words of the Buddha express that Buddha-mind. However, those words cannot be said to express the Buddha-mind directly. In fact, although words are the most obvious medium of communication, they provide only one of the ways – perhaps the least direct way – in which the Buddha expresses Enlightenment. Between the Enlightened state of consciousness and its expression in terms of ordinary human speech there are several intermediate levels of communication, and these levels are also implicit in our use of the term Buddhavacana. They represent the deeper – or at least some of the deeper – implications of the term.

First of all there is the level – if we can call it that, because it is a level beyond all levels – of the Enlightened mind, the Buddha-mind itself. We use this expression 'Buddha-mind', but actually it is very difficult for us to get any idea of what the Buddha-mind is like, because in it there is no subject and no object. All that we can say about it – and even this is misleading – is that it is pure, undifferentiated awareness, absolutely void, absolutely luminous. It is one continuous 'mass' of spiritual luminosity. If this manner of speaking leaves us none the wiser, we can take a different approach. We can say that this level of experience is completely, deeply, ultimately, absolutely, satisfying, that it comprises peace and bliss beyond all human understanding. Another way of putting it would be to say that the Buddha-mind is above and beyond space and time. Or, to put it yet another way, we could say that at that level of experience everything is known because in it there is nothing to be known.

So is that clear? Well, no. We can hardly express in words what is by definition utterly beyond them. The consciousness of a Buddha is inconceivable to us in our ordinary state of consciousness, dominated as it is by the subject–object distinction. Perhaps the nearest we can get to it is through metaphor, by describing the Buddha-mind as a vast and shoreless ocean in which millions of universes are just one tiny wave – or even just a fleck of foam – in the midst of that boundless ocean.

So now we have to try to conceive of there arising, within this inconceivable Enlightened mind, the desire to communicate. Again, this is not strictly conceivable, because we have to speak in terms of time ('arising') and space ('within'), even though the Enlightened mind transcends space and time. Nor is it truly feasible to use the word 'desire' of a mind that is totally at peace. However, as we have already recounted, the desire to communicate in some sense did arise within the Enlightened mind of the Buddha. And what the Enlightened mind desires to communicate is, of course, itself. It can hardly communicate anything else. In fact, we may say that the Enlightened mind is an Enlightenment-communicating mind. And this desire on the part of the Enlightened consciousness to communicate with the non-Enlightened consciousness, on whatever level the non-Enlightened consciousness is found, is what we call compassion.

This communication at the highest level is very, very subtle. There is nothing obvious about it at all. It's like a sort of tremor, a sort of vibration, that passes between the Enlightened mind and the mind that is just a little short of Enlightenment. Speaking quite metaphorically, this tremor or vibration is *like* an extremely subtle sound. It is not sound in the ordinary sense, not sound of the kind you can hear with your physical ears, or even sound you can hear inside your head. It is a kind of primordial sound, something on the spiritual plane which corresponds to what we know as sound. This tremor, this vibration, this soundless sound, is the Buddhavacana in the highest sense of the term. This is the sound emitted, as it were, by the Buddha-mind – even by Reality itself. And because the Buddha-mind is not limited by time or confined by space, there is no moment or place where it does not give out this vibration.

Some Indian traditions identify this primordial, cosmic sound with the mantra *om*. This is not a syllable pronounced by any human tongue. It is a subtle, inner, spiritual sound which can sometimes be heard in higher states of consciousness such as those attained in meditation. If you are attuned to it, you can hear it coming from all things, all phenomena of the universe, because the Buddha-mind is as it were behind them all, even within them all, and shines through them, sounds through them.

When you hear this sound, you hear in its most subtle form the word of the Buddha. Hearing it, you hear that everything is in this sound, and you understand everything. No words are necessary. No thoughts are necessary. There isn't any need for images. There's just this one primordial, undifferentiated vibration sounding forth from the Buddha-mind, the Buddha-consciousness, from Reality. You hear all, understand all, realize all, just from this sound *om* coming from everything, everywhere, all the time. This is Buddhavacana in the highest sense, on the highest level.

As we can imagine, this level of communication is almost unimaginably lofty, so the Enlightened mind has to come down, so to speak, step by step, to relatively lower levels of communication. And the next step down is the level of archetypal images: images of the sun and the moon and the stars, images of light and darkness, images of the heavens and the earth, images of birds and beasts and flowers, images of rain and wind and thunder and lightning; images of Buddhas and Bodhisattvas, images of gods and goddesses, images benign and wrathful, images of all sorts of monstrous shapes; perhaps above all, images brilliantly coloured, shining, luminous.

These images are not created by the individual human mind, nor even, perhaps, by the 'collective unconscious'. Indeed, they are perhaps not created at all, but coeval, co-eternal, with the Enlightened consciousness itself – at least, so far as this particular level of communication is concerned. They arise out of the depths of infinite space, and like the primordial sound, they reveal everything, tell everything. They image forth the Buddha-mind throughout the universe in terms of form and colour. Here in the world of images, no thoughts are necessary, no ideas, no words are necessary. Communication is not so subtle as it is at the level of mantric sound, but it is still far subtler and far more comprehensive than anything we ordinarily experience.

Coming down one step further, the Enlightened mind also expresses itself on the level of conceptual thought. Conceptual thought is common to both the Enlightened and the unenlightened mind, in that it is created by the unenlightened mind, but it can be used, taken over, even transformed, by the Enlightened mind in accordance with its own higher purpose. This is what essentially distinguishes what is sometimes called Buddhist philosophy or Buddhist thought from what we normally think of as philosophical thought. 'Buddhist thought' does not consist of the speculations of ordinary, unenlightened Buddhists. Doctrines like conditioned co-production are not intellectual theories. In the true sense, Buddhist thought is a series of attempts on the part of the Enlightened mind – whether that of Gautama the Buddha or that of other Enlightened beings – to communicate with unenlightened minds through the medium of concepts.

It may come as a surprise to find that below the conceptual level comes that of words, the lowest level at which the Enlightened mind communicates. Some people would say that it is not really possible to separate words and thoughts. Certainly the connection between the two is very close, closer than that between thoughts and images. Nevertheless, thoughts and words are not quite the same thing. We do sometimes have thoughts which we do not, or cannot, put into words.

We can now see the enormous gulf that separates the Enlightened mind from its expression in terms of ordinary human speech. We can see through how many levels the Buddha had to descend, as it were, before he could communicate himself to the five ascetics. No wonder it took him eight weeks to make the transition. We can think of this as 'coming down' in a way, but it is not that he left the previous levels behind. It is more like an extension of his range of communication. So Buddhavacana, the word of the Buddha, consists of all these levels of communication – primordial mantric sound, archetypal images, concepts, and words – and on all these levels the Dharma, the Buddha's teaching, is transmitted. The Dharma as the Buddha's teaching is not just a matter of words and concepts.

The Tantric tradition of India and Tibet explicitly acknowledges this point, that Buddhavacana is more than just words. It emphasizes it in a rather different way, but with much the same meaning. What it does is identify three modes of transmission of the Dharma. First of all there is what the Tantra calls the mind transmission of the Jinas, or 'Conquerors'. Here the transmission takes place from mind to mind, from heart to heart, from consciousness to consciousness. There are no words. There is no thought. The communication flashes directly, intuitively, telepathically, from one mind to another. The Buddha looks at you, as it were, and you know it. That's the end of the matter. Neither of you says anything, neither of you thinks anything. The transmission takes place on a purely mental or even spiritual level.

The second mode of transmission is the transmission of the *vidyādharas*. The *vidyādharas* are the great Tantric initiates, the Tantric masters. They are not fully Enlightened, like the Jinas, but by ordinary human standards they are spiritually developed to an inconceivably high level. On this level the transmission is through actions and gestures. In the Chan (or Zen) tradition of China a famous story is told of the Buddha's silent sermon. He simply holds up a golden flower. He says nothing, he just holds up a flower, and somebody understands. The gesture is lost on the rest of the audience, who are all ears, waiting for the Buddha to say something profound. But for one of them, Kaśyapa, this simple gesture is enough.[94] There are some Tantric initiations, even today, in which the master just points. He doesn't say anything, or explain anything. He just points, and that's that. If the disciple is receptive enough, he gets what has been literally pointed out. There are no words, there is no discussion, but if you're really alert, you get the point, there and then.

Thirdly and lastly, right at the bottom of the list, there is the transmission through words by the *ācāryas*. The *ācāryas* are ordinary teachers of Buddhism, people who are not fully Enlightened, but have some measure of insight, and faithfully hand on the teaching through the medium of ordinary human thought and speech.

All these are valid transmissions. You can get the spirit of the Dharma, the heart of the Dharma, through telepathy, through signs and gestures, and through words, but, of course, the lower the level of transmission, the greater the possibility of misunderstanding. If the communication flashes directly from mind to mind there is no question of misunderstanding, because there is no question even of understanding – and if there's no understanding, how can there be misunderstanding? With a gesture there is a little scope for confusion, because you may not quite see what is being pointed at; you may see something a bit different. On the level of words, however, the chances of misunderstanding are very great indeed.

The first safeguard against misunderstanding the Dharma as expressed in words is to ensure that both the letter and the spirit of the teachings are faithfully recorded. For many years this was the responsibility of the monks who memorized the teachings and passed them down through the generations by word of mouth. Even when people did start to write things down, it was a very gradual process – so gradual, in fact, that apparently some things were never written down at all, and are still being transmitted by word of mouth right down to the present day.

As soon as an oral teaching is committed to writing, it becomes a 'sacred scripture', and these sacred scriptures, the literary records of what were originally oral teachings, are known as the word of the Buddha, Buddhavacana. In fact, the term 'word of the Buddha' is often used almost exclusively in the sense of the scriptures, and its deeper implications rather forgotten. But although they are only one aspect of Buddhavacana, it is important to have an awareness of the canon of Buddhist literature – which has, over the centuries, grown very large indeed. We will consider the scriptures in their main categories, roughly in the order in which they appeared as literary documents – which is over a period of nearly a thousand years. Broadly speaking, the more exoteric teachings seem to have been written down first, while the more esoteric ones were recorded later on, or perhaps even not at all.

The first category of teachings to be written down is certainly the most exoteric. This is the monastic code, the Vinaya, which consists essentially of rules of conduct for monks and nuns. The rules of the Vinaya are of two kinds. There are rules for those monks and nuns leading a wandering life and living off alms: these rules are known as the *bhikṣu prātimokṣa* and the *bhikṣuṇī prātimokṣa*. And there are rules known as the *skandhakas* or 'chapters' for monks and nuns living in permanently residential communities. The chapters cover all sorts of subjects. There's a chapter on ordination, a chapter on the fortnightly gatherings of the wanderers, and a chapter on how to observe the rainy season retreat. There are rules about medicine, food, and material for robes; there are sleeping regulations and rules for sick monks. There are rules about dwellings and furnishings – they seem to have acquired furnishings rather quickly – and there's even a chapter on the use of leather for shoes. Other rules cover the order of precedence among monks, how to settle disputes and schisms, and the duties of monks under suspension. All these disparate topics, and lots more, are covered.

The Vinaya does not just consist of a list of rules. It also includes explanations of the rules, plus historical, biographical, and anthropological material. Altogether it comprises a bulky corpus of teachings and information. In fact, the Vinaya literature is probably our richest source of information about the general condition of north-eastern India in the Buddha's time. You also find, dotted here and there, quite a few discourses. As far as modern scholars can discern, some of the material in the Vinaya – and this includes some of the rules – cannot be counted as literally the actual word of the Buddha, but was added later by disciples. This later incorporation of extra material is not unique to the Vinaya, incidentally, but applies to practically all branches of the scriptures.[95]

The second category of scriptures consists of the dialogues and discourses of the Buddha. There are about 200 of these, some long and some short, and most of them are arranged in two great collections: the *Digha Nikāya*, the 'Long Discourses' and the *Majjhima Nikāya*, the 'Middle-Length Discourses'. In the Pāli recension, there are 34 long discourses and 152 middle-length ones. Between them, they cover all aspects of moral and spiritual life. Some are of anthropological interest, some of mythological interest, and some even of autobiographical interest, because in them the Buddha recounts the experiences of his own earlier life. It's a rich and rather miscellaneous collection.[96]

Thirdly, there are the 'anthologies' – anthologies of sayings of the Buddha, of which the most famous is the *Dhammapada*. This Buddhist classic is quite short, but there are two particularly large anthologies, containing between them thousands of sayings, all systematically arranged. One of them, the *Samyutta Nikāya*, is arranged according to subject matter, bringing under one heading all the Buddha's sayings on a particular topic. There's a collection of sayings on the gods, one on Māra the Evil One, one on Vangīsa, who was one of the Buddha's most gifted disciples and a fine poet, and one on Maudgalyāyana, another of the Buddha's disciples, famous for his psychic powers. There are sayings on nuns, sayings on Brahmins, sayings on the heavenly musicians, plus others on Stream Entry, on views, on the defilements, and on the Four Foundations of Mindfulness.[97]

Another anthology, the *Aṅguttara Nikāya*, arranges sayings numerically. For instance, in the section on 'the fours' you get the four things leading to liberation from conditioned existence, the four kinds of purity of a gift, the four kinds of thoroughbred (thoroughbred horses, apparently), the four *dhyānas* (states of higher consciousness), the four *brahma vihāras* (love, compassion, joy, and equanimity), and so on. Similarly, you get 'the ones', 'the twos', and so on up to 'the elevens'. The arrangement would clearly have been a useful mnemonic device in the days of oral transmission.[98]

The fourth category is that of the *Jātakas*, or 'Birth Stories', and the *Avadānas*, or 'Glorious Deeds'. These are perhaps the most widely popular of all Buddhist scriptures; they are especially loved by the lay people in all traditional Buddhist countries, from Sri Lanka to Tibet. This is not surprising, since they consist entirely of stories, many of which are enthralling enough to stand up well just as stories. The *Jātakas* are all about the Buddha, while the *Avadānas* recount fables relating to his closest disciples, but they are stories with a difference, in that they concern the *previous* lives of these various individuals. They effectively illustrate the workings of the law of karma, the law of moral and psychological recompense over a whole series of lifetimes, showing how one's moral and spiritual gains are conserved, as it were, from one life to the next.

The *Jātakas* are much more numerous than the *Avadānas*, and the biggest collection of *Jātakas*, 550 of them – some the length of short novels – is in Pāli. Most of the stories follow a standard pattern of four parts. An introduction describes the particular occasion on which the Buddha is supposed to have narrated this particular *Jātaka* story to his disciples. Then there's the *Jātaka* story proper. Thirdly, there are some verses which generally follow on from the prose story. Lastly, the Buddha identifies the characters in the story; he says, for instance, 'Well, Ānanda, you were so-and-so in the story, and I was so-and-so – and Devadatta was so-and-so.' Sometimes the stories aren't very complimentary even to the Buddha himself. He is certainly no saint in some of his past lives, and in one story he is even a robber, which shows there's hope for everybody.[99]

Many *Jātaka* stories are old Indian folk tales, taken over by the Buddhists and adapted to their own particular purposes. T. W. Rhys Davids has gone so far as to describe the Pāli *Jātaka* book as 'the most complete, the most authentic, and the most ancient collection of folklore in the world'.[100] What is beyond doubt is that the *Jātakas* and the *Avadānas* have exerted an enormous moral and spiritual influence in the Buddhist East. Right down to recent times dramatic versions of them were staged on special occasions in the courtyards of the big monasteries of Tibet – probably the most effective way of moving and inspiring Tibetan herdsmen, traders, and mule-drivers with the word of the Buddha.

Our fifth category is something very different. In the Abhidharma there are no stories at all, and even figures of speech are utterly banished. The purpose of this literature is the definition of technical terms (which is much more important, when you think about it, than it sounds) and the analysis and classification of mental states. It attempts also to give a complete systematic account, mainly in psychological terms, of the whole path to Nirvāṇa. So the task the compilers of the Abhidharma set themselves was to gather together the teachings found in the dialogues, discourses, and anthologies, and to analyse them. All personal references were edited out. History, biography, mythology, poetry, and rhetoric were eliminated. The results still make a good shelf-full, though.[101] The word Abhidharma is usually explained as the 'higher' or 'further' teaching of the Buddha. Some schools take the view, however, that while there are some traces of the Abhidharma method in the dialogues and anthologies, the Abhidharma itself should be treated, not as the literal word of the Buddha, but as the product of later scholastic activity.

According to the schools of early Buddhism (the so-called Hīnayāna tradition, the 'Lesser Way'), this is as far as the word of the Buddha can be said to go. At this point we leave behind the Pāli canon and move on to scriptures that are accepted as canonical only by the Mahāyāna tradition. However, the Mahāyāna *sūtras*, the sixth category, form one of the largest and richest divisions of the Buddhist scriptures. They deal, of course, primarily with specifically Mahāyāna teachings – *śūnyatā* (the voidness), the bodhisattva ideal, the One Mind, the Trikāya (the three bodies of a Buddha) and so on. But they are also called '*sūtras*' and are thus records of discourses given by the Buddha. Out of several hundred Mahāyāna *sūtras*, some are very long indeed, consisting of several volumes, while others run to only a page or two. Some of them are written in a quiet, philosophical style, while others are full of myth and symbolism, marvels and magic.

A brief résumé can hardly do justice to the Mahāyāna *sūtras* – all we can do is mention a few of the most famous ones. First, there's *The Perfection of Wisdom in 8,000 Lines*. This is one of the oldest texts from the Perfection of Wisdom tradition, dealing mainly with *Prajñāpāramitā*, 'the wisdom that goes beyond'. It deals also with the person who strives to develop this Perfect Wisdom, the bodhisattva, and with the focus of Perfect Wisdom – *śūnyatā*, the Void, unfathomable Reality. Making relentless use of paradox, the text stresses again and again the subtle, elusive, trans-conceptual nature of this wisdom.[102]

Next, a totally different Mahāyāna *sūtra*. From a literary point of view the *Saddharma Puṇḍarīka*, the 'White Lotus of the Real Truth', is one of the most marvellous, impressive, and magnificent of them all. It conveys a profound spiritual meaning, but it conveys it for the most part in entirely non-conceptual terms. It contains no abstract teaching, no philosophy, no conceptual statements. Instead, it is full of parables, myths, and symbols, and through these it expresses two great teachings: that in essence the Buddha is eternal, above and beyond space and time; and that there is just one great way to Enlightenment for all beings – the Mahāyāna. According to the *White Lotus Sūtra* all living beings, whether they know it or not, are following this path, and will in the end gain Enlightenment. It thus emphasizes the spiritual optimism of the Buddhist vision at the highest possible level.[103]

The *Laṅkāvatāra Sūtra* is said to have been expounded by the Buddha in the course of a visit to the mythical island of Laṅka (not to be confused with the modern Sri Lanka). It teaches, among other things, that the whole of conditioned existence is ultimately nothing but one mind, one absolute and ultimate consciousness to which everything can be reduced, and of which everything, in one way or another, is the manifestation. The emphasis in this text is on the need actually to realize this. It is not enough just to talk about it, or to think about it, or even to meditate upon it. One needs to realize for oneself, within oneself, that everything is just mind. What the *Laṅkāvatāra Sūtra* also stresses is that in order to do this one needs to undergo a radical transformation. One's whole mental apparatus, one's whole psychological system, must be put into reverse, turned upside-down, transformed. This transformation the

Laṅkāvatāra Sūtra calls the *parāvṛtti*, the 'turning about in the deepest seat of consciousness', a turning about from the split, fractured mind to the One Mind.[104] This is the ultimate message of the *Laṅkāvatāra Sūtra*.

The vision of the universe we get in the *Gaṇḍavyūha Sūtra* is different again. It gives an account of a young pilgrim called Sudhana, a seeker after truth. In the course of his pilgrimage, all over India and beyond, he visits more than fifty teachers, and they are of many kinds. They include bodhisattvas, monks, nuns, and householders; there's a physician, a sailor, a perfume seller, two kings, several children, a number of deities, and also a hermit; and Sudhana learns something from each and every one of them. Eventually, at the end of his long journey, he comes to the Vairocana Tower in southern India. There he meets the bodhisattva Maitreya and receives his final 'initiation'. Within the tower he has a vision of the Absolute Truth. Mysteriously able to see the whole cosmos and everything in it, he perceives that everything in the cosmos reflects everything else, that everything in the universe interpenetrates with everything else like mutually intersecting beams of light. He sees that things are not separate, demarcated, solid, but fluid and flowing; every thing flows into every other thing, all the time, everywhere.[105]

The *sūtra* upon which Edwin Arnold based his famous poem, *The Light of Asia*, is the *Lalitavistara*, which means 'the extended account of the sports'. This might seem like an odd title for a biography of the Buddha, even a highly imaginative and poetic biography, as this one is, but it emphasizes an important aspect of the Buddha's nature, because the word 'sports' is meant to indicate the playful spontaneity of the Buddha's actions. After his Enlightenment there was no question of being conditioned, or determined by anything, or being subject to karma. It was all free, creative, playful manifestation of his Enlightened essence. And this is what the title *Lalitavistara* is getting at.[106]

This is no more than a glimpse of a few of the very many *sūtras* of the Mahāyāna – even a catalogue of their titles would run to many pages. And it is even more difficult to offer an adequate account of the seventh and last branch of the Buddhist scriptures, the Tantras. They are not systematic treatises or discourses. They are written – though this word makes them sound more like literary compositions than they really are – in a cryptic, even deliberately misleading way. You're not meant to be able to read a Tantra and understand it – as will be obvious if you manage to get hold of a Tantric text. You're not supposed to read, let alone practise the content of, the Tantra at all without initiation by a guru. The guru takes from the Tantras what he thinks you need, organizes it to suit your personal practice, and initiates you accordingly. That is all one can usefully say about this particular branch of Buddhist literature.

These seven categories of the Buddhist scriptures – the monastic code, the dialogues and discourses, the anthologies, the birth stories and heroic deeds, the Abhidharma, the Mahāyāna *sūtras*, and the Tantras – constitute between them the Buddhavacana, the word of the Buddha, in its most external and exoteric sense. Altogether, these literary records of oral teachings amount to a small library. At present they exist in three main collections: the Pāli Tipiṭaka, the Chinese Sanzang, and the Tibetan Kangyur. The Pāli Tipiṭaka is the scriptural basis of the Buddhism of south-east Asia – mainly Sri Lanka, Thailand, and Burma – and it is of course in the Pāli language, which is based on an old Indian dialect. It contains versions of the first five categories of scriptures – practically all of it by now translated into English – but nothing else. The Chinese Sanzang is even more voluminous than the Pāli Tipiṭaka, and it contains versions of all the categories of scriptures except the Tantras (although one or two Tantras are included in early *sūtra* form). It consists of translations into Chinese, mainly from Sanskrit. And the Kangyur, which consists of translations into Tibetan from Sanskrit, is in a sense the most complete collection of Buddhist scriptures, because it contains all seven categories. However, very little of either of these collections has been translated into English.

It is very easy to get lost among all these Buddhist scriptures, even among the English translations, comparatively few as they are. It is very easy to get confused about what to read and what not to read. It is even easy to forget what the word of the Buddha is in a deeper sense. Among all the words we can lose the Word itself. Reading and studying so many scriptures, it is so easy to forget the spirit of the Buddhavacana. Under these circumstances we need a teacher to help interpret all these texts, to show us a clear path for us as individuals to follow. On our own we will see a multiplicity of teachings before us, some of which are appropriate to where we are now and some of which are not. We need someone with greater experience than we have, who can help us through difficult patches and suggest where we might change the emphasis of our practice or change direction altogether. Otherwise we can lose heart, or even lose ourselves up blind alleys. No one, not even the Buddha, has ever been incapable of making mistakes, and these can sometimes be big mistakes.

Above all, we need our spiritual friends, that is, friends who relate to us on the basis of a shared spiritual commitment to a common spiritual ideal. In our communication with those who relate to us on the basis of what is best and highest in us, we can turn the theory of the Dharma into practice. It is only in relation to other people that we can really gauge the effectiveness of our own spiritual practice, and it is those who know us at our best as well as at our worst who can provide the most helpful and precise advice. So important and delightful is communication that the Buddha's attendant Ānanda was once moved to suggest that 'spiritual friendship is half the spiritual life'. The Buddha replied, 'Say not so, Ānanda. Spiritual friendship is the *whole* of the spiritual life.'[107] Indeed, Enlightenment itself, inasmuch as it communicates itself, exemplifies spiritual friendship at the highest level, most notably in the Buddha's relationship with Ānanda. Despite their inequality in spiritual attainment, they looked after each other with mutual kindness for the last twenty years of the Buddha's life.

The Buddhavacana can only come alive in the context of the sangha. Otherwise it remains a dead letter. This is why the integrity and harmony of the Order of monks was the Buddha's first concern. If his followers lived in concord, with open and clear communication with one another, and with friendliness and care for each other's welfare, the spirit of the Buddhavacana would be preserved.

However, there is more to the sangha than meets the eye. We can also connect with the spirit of the Buddhavacana by leaving behind, for a moment, the world we are familiar with, and approaching a different realm, that of archetypal images. There we will find that the Buddhavacana appears embodied in the figure of the bodhisattva Mañjughoṣa, the Bodhisattva of Wisdom. His name means 'he of gentle speech', and he is also known as Vāgīśvara, which means 'Lord of Speech' (the root of this name, *vag*, is also, by the way, the root of *vacana*). Vāgīśvara, sovereign of speech, appears in the midst of the dark blue, midnight sky in the form of a beautiful youth, sixteen years of age, and a rich yellow in colour. Seated cross-legged on a lotus, he is clad in silks and jewels, and has long, black, flowing hair. In one hand he wields a sword streaming fire, and in the other he holds a book which he presses to his heart, a book which contains the Perfection of Wisdom scriptures. He is surrounded by an aura of golden light, which is in turn surrounded by rainbows. This is Mañjughoṣa, Vāgīśvara, Lord of Speech, and he is the embodiment, the archetype, of the word of the Buddha.

We can go even further, even higher, than that. The word of the Buddha is embodied not only in the figure of a bodhisattva, but in the figure of the Buddha himself, the Buddha of the *White Lotus Sūtra*. In that *sūtra* we are told that the Buddha is seated eternally on the spiritual Vulture's Peak, the very summit of mundane existence. There he eternally proclaims the Dharma – not in words as written down in the text of the *sūtra*, nor even in images as described in the text of the *sūtra*. He proclaims it in terms of pure mantric sound, as the primordial vibration, so to speak, of Reality itself. Whether we are meditating or reading the scriptures, whenever we are silent and still, we can pick up that vibration, coming, as it were, from the Buddha-mind, on the furthest pinnacle of existence. As we pick it up we can ourselves begin to vibrate very subtly in harmony with it. We too can hear in that way, to that extent, in the very depths, in the very heights, of our being. In the deepest, highest, truest, most comprehensive sense, we can hear the word of the Buddha.

7

KARMA AND REBIRTH

Old age, sickness, and death were the spurs to Siddhārtha Gautama's quest, and what he realized when he became the Buddha somehow put an end to these things. It was not just that he came to terms with death, or looked forward to death. He *realized* something – not intellectually but by way of direct perception – that transformed him into a new species of being to whom birth and death simply did not apply. As we saw in the previous chapter, the Buddha doubted at first the possibility of communicating this alchemical insight – what he called 'the truth of *pratītya-samutpāda*' – to anyone else. But communicate it he did, deep and subtle as it was. And though his seminal formulation of *pratītya-samutpāda* engendered, over the years, a vast and rich array of teachings, it remains the basis, the very foundation, of all of them. In philosophical terms, at least, it is the realization of this truth of universal conditionality which constitutes the essence of the Buddha's Enlightenment. Hence we describe it as the fundamental principle of Buddhism.

It originally took the form in his mind of a laconic, even bleak statement: 'This is conditioned by that. All that happens is by way of a cause.' However, the most renowned version of this principle derives, perhaps significantly, from an occasion when it was being *communicated* – and with dramatic success. In this instance it was communicated not by the Buddha himself, but by one of his disciples, and it was imparted to a seeker after the truth who was to become the Buddha's chief disciple.

It was a few months after the Buddha's Enlightenment. A young Brahmin from Bihar called Śāriputra had gone forth from home, just as the Buddha had, along with his childhood friend Maudgalyāyana. He was now on his own because the two of them had agreed that they would go off in different directions, and that whichever of them found an Enlightened teacher first would tell the other, thus doubling their chances, so to speak.

In the course of his travels, Śāriputra happened to meet one of the Buddha's first five disciples, called Aśvajit, who had by this time become Enlightened himself and gone forth to teach the Dharma. Very much impressed by the appearance of this wandering monk, who radiated tranquillity and happiness, Śāriputra approached him, greeted him, and asked, 'Who is your teacher?' This might seem to us a rather direct way of addressing a total stranger. In Britain we generally open a conversation with a remark like 'Nice weather we're having,' or 'Looks like it's beginning to clear up a bit now.' But in India they tend to come straight to the point. So Śāriputra asked the question that people in India still sometimes ask each other, and Aśvajit answered, 'My teacher is Śākyamuni, the Sage, the Wise One of the Śākya tribe, the Buddha.' Śāriputra then put to Aśvajit the second standard question – standard, but in this case momentous: 'What does he teach?' Aśvajit said, 'Frankly, I'm a beginner. I really don't know much about the Dharma. But I can tell you in brief what it's about.' And what he then said has since become famous throughout the Buddhist world in the form of a short Pāli verse of just two lines. He said:

Of all those things that proceed from a cause, the Tathāgata[108] has explained the cause, and also its cessation. This is the teaching of the great śramaṇa.'[109]

It seems that this stanza made a shattering, and at the same time liberating, impression on the mind of Śāriputra. He had an instantaneous glimpse of the truth that it embodied, Transcendental insight arose in him, and he became a Stream Entrant on the spot. Obviously, the ground had been so well prepared that this most compressed exposition of the Dharma was enough to tell him his quest was at an end. He could go to his friend, Maudgalyāyana, and tell him with confidence that he had found the Enlightened teacher they were looking for.[110]

This verse of Aśvajit's is recorded, honoured, and worshipped all over the Eastern Buddhist world. In Tibet, China, Japan, Thailand, and Sri Lanka, it is found carved on stone monuments and clay tablets, printed on strips of paper to be stuffed inside images, and inscribed on plates of silver or gold. It is, we may say, the credo of Buddhism. If it seems rather dry and abstract, academic, uninspiring even, it certainly did not seem so to Śāriputra. And when you really think about the principle of *pratītya-samutpāda* – in whatever form it is expressed – when you meditate on it, when you really follow through its implications, you begin to understand the extraordinary impact it has had on the world. Whatever comes into existence, on whatever level, does so in dependence on conditions, and in the absence of those conditions it ceases to exist. This is all it says. But if anything is Buddhism, this is Buddhism.

What it is saying is that, from the viewpoint of the Enlightened mind, the outstanding feature of all phenomena, whether physical or psychical, is that they are conditioned. The unceasing flux of things, both material events and states of mind, is a process of interdependent stages, each of which comes about through the presence of conditions and, in its turn, conditions the stages succeeding it. Rainfall, sunshine, and the nourishing earth are the conditions from which arises the oak tree, whose fallen leaves rot and form the rich humus from which the bluebell grows. A jealous attachment will have consequences that may lead to murder. Nothing phenomenal is spontaneously produced without preceding conditions, or itself fails to have consequences. And it is the process of becoming aware of this law of conditionality that gradually liberates us from all conditions, leading to the freely functioning, spontaneous creativity of Enlightenment.

If we are reasonably clear about what it was that constituted the Buddha's realization, we can move on to look at how it actually dealt with the questions that Siddhārtha originally set out to answer. What about old age, sickness, and death? Where do the immutable facts of our physical decay fit into the whole process of conditionality? Does this 'unceasing flux of things' continue beyond death – or is death the end? These questions, of course, are not abstract or theoretical for us. The mystery of death which so troubled primitive humanity is still a mystery. Even these days, when we apparently know so much, you only need to give a talk called 'The Tibetan Book of the Dead' or 'What happens after death' or 'Where you go when you die' to draw record crowds, and there is always a healthy market for books about death and dying. We may think things have changed immeasurably since primitive times, but they haven't changed much when it comes to our understanding of death. Indeed, if anything, the 'problem' of death has become more pressing.

We are not, however, talking about one single problem of death common to everyone. The way we feel about death, and the way we personally come to terms with death, or fail to do so, is not exactly the same as the way other people feel about it, and people's feelings and ideas about death have changed over time, over the centuries, as well. Putting the problem of death into some kind of historical perspective, we may say that it all really began when mankind first started growing crops, in the age of the great river valley civilizations. This was perhaps ten or fifteen thousand years ago. At that time the world began to take on an aspect that was less hostile and mysterious, but people were still in the dark about the greatest of all mysteries – death. The mystery, in fact, grew deeper and darker, and it seemed to weigh on people's minds more oppressively than ever before. And there was a reason for this. People no longer lived a nomadic life; they lived in villages and towns, even in great cities. Civilization had begun. Life had become more secure and comfortable, and people enjoyed it more. And having begun to enjoy it, they wanted to go on enjoying it. They didn't want to leave their wives or husbands, their children, their houses and their neatly cultivated fields, their singing and their dancing, their games of chance and their religious rites – but one day they would have to leave it all, and they knew it. The thought of death threw a shadow over the sunlight of their lives. What was life for, if it had to end so soon? You had just a few short years of youth, pleasure, and prosperity, and after that, just a blank, a void, with nothing apparently surviving – perhaps some ghostly wraith twittering in the darkness, but nothing more.

What could you do about it? It seemed that you could do nothing at all. Most people just tried to forget about it and enjoy life as much as possible while they could. 'Eat, drink, and be merry, for tomorrow we die,' expressed the substance of their philosophy. A few who were made of sterner stuff immersed themselves in action. They performed heroic deeds – went about slaying monsters, fighting battles, conquering kingdoms. They tried to make a name for themselves so that even though they might perish – probably sooner rather than later – their names would live on after them, so they hoped, for ever. But even these heroes, in their more reflective moments, saw that this was all a bit pointless.

Human life, it seemed, was not just a mystery, but a tragedy. This mood is reflected in the traditions and tales of ancient cultures, which were eventually written down to become the earliest examples of literature. We find it in the Babylonian epic of Gilgamesh, from around 3000 BCE, and in Homer's account of the fall of Troy, the *Iliad*, composed over 2,000 years later. It is there in the Anglo-Saxon epic poem *Beowulf*, dating from the eighth century, and it is even more powerfully and bitterly expressed in the Bible, in the Book of Ecclesiastes, the 'Book of the Preacher'. The vanity of human ambition in the face of death, the great leveller, is a favourite theme in ancient literature, and has inspired the same sort of thing in more recent times:

The boast of heraldry, the pomp of pow'r,
And all that beauty, all that wealth e'er gave,
Awaits alike th'inevitable hour:
The paths of glory lead but to the grave.[111]

But this was not the whole story. It was only half the story – the western half. Further east, people had started to take a different attitude, and had, in fact, arrived at some sort of solution to the mystery of death, which of course also meant some sort of solution to the mystery of life. What they perceived was that death was not the end. Human beings did not just vanish. After a time, they came back in a new body, in accordance with the nature of the deeds they had performed in their previous life. This perception made its first appearance in India at about the time of Homer (c.800 BCE), and from India thereafter spread widely. The first clear reference to it is found in the Hindu *Brihadaranyaka Upanishad*, in which the idea is represented as a highly esoteric teaching, to be communicated only to the chosen few. But as the idea spread, it became known, in a more organized, systematized form, as the teaching of karma and rebirth.

When people in the West go flocking along to a lecture on karma and rebirth, or the *Tibetan Book of the Dead*, what they really want to know is: 'What is going to happen to me when I die? Is death the end, the absolute full stop, or not?' The fact is, if we could be assured that death was not the end, there would be no problem at all. If people knew with absolute certainty that they weren't going to just disappear when they died, they would be a lot less inclined to go and hear a lecture on karma and rebirth. For us, death is the problem. But in the East, especially the Hindu and Buddhist East, it is rather different. People are not so bothered about death there. For them, death is natural and inevitable – and so is rebirth. You die and you are reborn, you die again and you are reborn again – that's just the way it is. It's not a matter for speculation at all. In the East it is not death that is the problem. The problem is how to escape from the whole process of birth and death. How can you reach a state in which you will no longer be subject to birth and death? The problem is dying and being born time and time again, through endless ages. So the question is carried a stage further: what for the West is a solution of the problem is for the East a problem in itself, requiring a further solution. And this is where the Buddha's discovery of the universal principle of conditionality comes in.

When, in the course of the Enlightenment experience, the Buddha surveyed the whole vast range of conditioned existence, he saw that everything, from the lowest to the highest, was subject to the universal law of conditionality.[112] And he also saw that this universal law operates – as we have already seen from the point of view of our evolutionary model – in two distinct modes: a cyclical mode and a spiral mode. In the cyclical mode, there is action and reaction between opposites. We experience pleasure and pain, vice and virtue, birth and death – and usually what happens is that we swing back and forth between them. Life is followed by death, which is in turn followed by new life. Pain is followed by pleasure which is again followed by pain. At all levels of life – physical, biological, psychological, sociological, historical – this same cyclical process can be found to be operating. Empires rise only to fall; growth must be succeeded by decay; health, wealth, fame, and status have old age, sickness, death, loss, and oblivion as their inevitable outcome.

In the spiral mode of conditionality, on the other hand, there is the possibility of real and permanent growth. Each factor in this process, rather than reversing the effect of the previous one, increases its effect. For example, instead of an oscillation between pleasure and pain, you go from pleasure to happiness, then from happiness to joy, from joy to rapture, from rapture to bliss, and so on indefinitely. And this spiral mode can be applied to life and death just as much as to anything else. The Buddha saw that as well as being subject to the endless round of birth and death, it was possible for human beings to enter the spiral path of spiritual development, which was 'the way to the door of the Deathless', the way beyond the opposites of life and death.

When applied to the process of life and death, the principle of conditionality gave rise to one of the most famous and important – and most frequently misunderstood – of Buddhist teachings: karma and rebirth. The first thing to understand about karma is that it is simply an application of the principle of conditionality. Nothing mysterious, nothing odd, nothing strange, nothing occult. Karma, in the most general terms, represents the law of conditionality at work on a certain plane of existence. This has to be emphasized because one major source of confusion seems to be the idea that karma *is* the Buddhist teaching of cause and effect, and that it is universal – which is not the case. The universal principle is conditionality, and karma is only one of the ways in which conditionality operates. This point may be clarified by referring to a Buddhist teaching which dates from considerably later than the Buddha's own lifetime. It comes, in fact, from the analytical and systematizing philosophical tradition of the Abhidharma, and it is the teaching of what is called the five *niyamas*. These five *niyamas* are a very useful formulation because, as is the way with the Abhidharma, they draw together strands which are otherwise rather loose and disconnected as we find them in the original *suttas*.[113]

The word *niyama* is a term common to Pāli and Sanskrit meaning a natural law, a cosmic order. According to this teaching there are five of them, showing the law of cause and effect at work on five different levels. The first three are straightforward enough, as they can be related to Western sciences. Firstly, there's *utu-niyama*. *Utu* means non-living matter. Nowadays people are beginning to doubt whether there is any such thing as non-living matter, but let's call it that for the time being. In other words, this is the physical, inorganic order of existence. *Utu-niyama* is therefore the law of cause and effect as operative on the level of inorganic matter. It very roughly embraces the laws of physics and chemistry and associated disciplines.

The second *niyama* is *bīja-niyama*. *Bīja* means 'seed', so *bīja-niyama* deals with the world of living matter, the physical organic order whose laws constitute the science of biology.

Then there is *citta-niyama*. *Citta* is 'mind', so *citta-niyama* is conditionality as operative in the world of mind. The existence of this third *niyama*, therefore, implies that mental activity and development are not haphazard, but governed by laws. It is important that we understand what this means. We are used to the idea of laws operating on the level of physics, chemistry, and biology, but we are not so used to the idea that similar laws might govern mental events. We are more inclined, in the West, to the view that mental events just happen, without any particular causation. To some extent and in some quarters, the influence of Freud has begun to shift this assumption, but the idea that mental phenomena arise in dependence on conditions is not one that has yet penetrated deeply into popular thinking. It is there in Buddhism, however, in this teaching of *citta-niyama*, the law of cause and effect as operative in the world of mind – and we may say that it is a concept which corresponds to the modern science of psychology.

Fourthly: *kamma-niyama*. *Kamma* (Pāli) is of course more popularly known in its Sanskrit form, *karma*, and it means 'action', but in the sense of deliberately willed action. So it is traditionally, and paradoxically, said sometimes that karma is equivalent to *cetanā* (volitional consciousness), that is that action equals volition: 'for as soon as volition arises, one does the action, whether by body, speech, or mind.'[114] *Kamma-niyama* therefore pertains to the world of ethical responsibility; it is the principle of conditionality operative on the moral plane.

It is perhaps difficult for those of us with a background of Western thought on morality to understand how this works. In ordinary social life, if you commit a crime, you are arrested and brought before the judge or magistrate, tried and convicted, sentenced, and sent to jail or fined. Committing the crime and being punished are quite separate events, and there is someone or something – society, the police, the judge, the law – who punishes you. Our tendency is to apply this legal model when it comes to morality as a whole. We think of sin and the *punishment* of sin, virtue and the *reward* of virtue. And traditionally we have tended to think in terms of a judge too: somebody who sees what you do, and punishes or rewards you accordingly – the judge being, of course, God. People imagine God as holding a sort of tremendous courtroom trial, with everybody hauled up in front of him, and the angels and demons standing around like police witnesses. It is still official Christian doctrine that when you die you face your judge, and this is a terrible thought for the orthodox Christian – that you are going to be put in the dock before the Transcendental Judge and then bundled off wherever he sends you. The dramatic possibilities inherent in the doctrine have made for some terrific literature, music, drama, and art – Michelangelo's tremendous painting of the Last Judgement in the Sistine Chapel is just one notable example. But it also makes for rather poor philosophy, and a mode of thinking from which we are still suffering a ghastly hangover.

The Buddhist point of view is totally different, and it may seem distinctly odd to us, with our approach to ethics – almost whether we like it or not – tending to be underpinned by Christian theology. In Buddhism there is a law but no lawgiver, and no one who administers the law. I have heard Christian missionaries arguing with Buddhists and insisting that if you believe in a law, there must be a lawgiver – but this is quite specious. After all, there is a law of gravity, but there isn't a god of gravity pushing and pulling things. The law of gravity is just a generalized description of what happens when objects fall. In the same way we don't have a god of heredity, or a god of sexual selection. These things just happen; they work themselves.

It is much the same on the moral plane, according to Buddhism. The law administers itself, so to speak. Good karma naturally results in happiness, and bad karma naturally results in misery. There is no need for anybody else to come along, look at what you've done, and then fit the punishment or the reward to the deed. It happens of its own accord. 'Good' and 'bad' are built into the structure of the universe. This might sound dreadfully anthropomorphic – and I am putting it rather crudely here – but what it really means is that from the Buddhist point of view the universe is an ethical universe. Putting it more precisely, the universe functions according to conditionality, and this operates at the karmic level in a way which we could describe as ethical, in that it conserves ethical values. This is *kamma-niyama*.

The fifth and last *niyama* is *dhamma-niyama*. Dhamma (*dharma* in Sanskrit) is a word with a number of different possible applications, but here it means simply spiritual or transcendental as opposed to mundane. So the principle of conditionality operates on this level too. Exactly how it works, however, has not always been made very clear, and some of the more popular traditional explanations of this *niyama* are a bit childish and superficial. For example, many legends report that when the Buddha gained Enlightenment, and also when he died – and indeed on other momentous occasions – the earth shook and trembled in six different ways; and this, according to some commentators, was due to the operation of *dhamma-niyama*.

In fact we do not have to look very far in order to locate a more sensible and helpful interpretation. The obvious key, it seems to me, is in the distinction between the two types or modes of conditionality. The first four *niyamas*, including *kamma-niyama*, are all types of conditionality in the cyclical sense, in the sense of action and reaction between pairs of opposites. But *dhamma-niyama* corresponds to the spiral type of conditionality. As such it constitutes the sum total of the spiritual laws which govern progress through the stages of the Buddhist path.

Thus karma is not the law of conditionality in general, but only that law as operating on the ethical level, the plane of moral responsibility. This means we cannot assume that what befalls us necessarily does so as a result of our past actions, because karma is only one of the five levels of conditionality. What happens to us may be a result of physical, biological, psychological, ethical, *or* spiritual factors. In all likelihood, it will involve a complex *combination* of factors, bringing several of the *niyamas* into play.

But how does karma actually work? If there is no judge handing out sentences, what does happen? The Abhidharma, that most precise school of Buddhist philosophy, gives us a very clear picture of karma, classifying it from seven different points of view.[115] These are: ethical status; 'door' (what that means will be explained when we get to it); appropriateness of resultant experiences; time of taking effect; relative priority of taking effect; function; and the plane on which the karma matures. Let's look at these seven ways of classifying karma one by one.

Firstly, how is karma classified 'according to ethical status'? The main point to be grasped here is that the ethical status of a willed action is determined by the state of consciousness in which it is performed – this is absolutely axiomatic for Buddhism. This state of consciousness can be what Buddhists call 'skilful' or it can be what is called 'unskilful' – and this terminology is significant because it emphasizes that the practice of Buddhist ethics is a matter of intelligence as well as benevolence. Our unskilful mental states are those dominated by craving (neurotic desire), by aversion (hatred, resentment), and by ignorance. We are not punished for them – they simply make us miserable, inasmuch as unskilful states of mind involve a contraction of our being and consciousness which we experience as misery. Skilful mental states, by contrast, are characterized by contentment, love, understanding, and clarity of mind. And again, there are no prizes handed out to reward us for these. Skilful actions – whether of body, speech, or mind – result by themselves in a sense of expanded being and consciousness which we experience as happiness. In a sense, skilful action *is* happiness.

So Buddhist ethics are psychologically based. Action is skilful or unskilful not because it conforms with an external set of rules, but because it accords with a certain state of being. There are 'rules' – well, they are usually termed 'precepts'; they are rules only in the sense of being rough and ready guides to indicate the way you might normally behave if you were in a certain state of being. The 'rules' are not ends in themselves; they are not imposed by the religious 'group'; they are simply there to be of use towards a specific end, which is Enlightenment. The Buddha, moreover, distinguished between 'natural morality' (Pāli *pakati-sīla*) and 'conventional morality' (*paṇṇatti-sīla*).[116] Natural morality is universal, and based on the facts of human psychology, while conventional morality varies from place to place, and is based on custom and opinion. And it is only natural morality which comes under the operation of the law of karma.

Some schools of Buddhism are very much concerned to safeguard this psychological and spiritual basis of Buddhist ethics. In order to counter the danger of ethical formalism – the belief that you are good just because you are following the rule-book – Zen and the Tantric schools insist on drawing out a surprising, even shocking, implication of the Buddhist approach to morality. They go so far as to maintain that in principle the Enlightened man or woman is quite capable of committing apparently unethical actions. It is the state of consciousness that counts, they say, not the action itself, because it is the state of consciousness that determines the ethical value, and therefore the karmic effect, of the action – not the other way around. The way these Tantric and Zen schools look at it, such is our propensity to grasp at the easy answers provided by ethical formalism that we have to be positively scandalized into seeing that Buddhist ethics operate on a different basis from conventional morality. So they come up with some bizarre stories, of which one of the most extreme examples is the following from Tibet.

Once upon a time, so the tale begins, there was an ancient and holy hermit who lived all by himself in a mountain cave – and as this was

Tibet we should probably imagine it as being just above the snow-line, thus bitterly cold. So he lived just like Milarepa, the famed poet and ascetic, except that he did not live just on nettles, which was Milarepa's staple diet. Though he was very strict and austere, he didn't live on nettles because just a few miles away there lived an old woman who used to supply him with meals every day, so that he could get on with his meditation without having to bother about food. Every day she used to approach the mouth of the cave, with great faith and devotion, and set the food down in front of the old hermit. He would eat it silently and give her a blessing. Then she would silently take away the empty dish and go back home, while he returned to his meditation.

This old lady had a daughter who was also devoted to the old ascetic, and sometimes she sent the girl to give the hermit his meal instead of going herself. One day the daughter went up as she often did and placed the food in front of the hermit. But this time, to her great surprise, instead of eating it quietly as usual, the hermit leapt up and tried to rape her. Considerably surprised, and even more considerably annoyed, she resisted his assault stoutly. As she was a hefty country wench, and the old hermit was feeble and weak, she had no trouble in beating him off and running home unscathed. 'Mother!' she cried, as soon as she had her breath back. 'What do you think? That old man we've been thinking all this while is so holy – what do you think he tried to do?' And she told her mother all about it. Her mother was certainly outraged, but for a quite unexpected reason. 'You foolish girl!' she scolded, 'You wicked girl! Have you no faith? A holy man like that does not try to rape someone for fun. There must have been some important meaning to it – don't you understand? Go back at once, apologize, and say, "Here I am. Please do as you wish."'

So the girl went back and found the hermit sitting in front of his cave. She bowed in front of him and said, 'I am very sorry I was so foolish a little while ago. Here I am; I am at your service.' But the hermit said, 'You're too late!' She said, 'What do you mean? Too late for what?' And he said again, 'Too late! What a pity! Too late!' The girl was very puzzled, and asked again, 'Too late for what?' So the old hermit said, 'Well, since after all you were involved – or very nearly involved – I will tell you what was going on. You know just around the hill there's a big, wealthy monastery? Well, the abbot there was a very wicked man. He wasn't a good monk at all. He didn't care about the Dharma, he never studied anything, and he was very greedy for money and food and possessions.

'Now the fact is, the abbot died just a few hours ago, and as I was meditating, I saw his spirit hovering in the air. It was in a terrible condition, so sad and miserable, and I could see that it was gravitating towards a lower birth, a really unpleasant future life. There were no other people around, but at that moment you turned up. Out of compassion I wanted to give that unhappy spirit one more chance. I thought, "If I move fast perhaps I can help him at least to be reborn as a human being." But unfortunately you ran away – and do you know what happened? In that field over there, just after you left, two donkeys copulated – and so, yes, you are too late! The abbot will be reborn as a donkey.'[117]

The Tibetans tell this story whenever they get the chance. It's one of their favourites – and it does illustrate the point. It is, indeed, the sheer unlikelihood of a compassionate act of rape that makes the point. Whatever the ethical rule, however straightforward it may seem, though it may cover many, many instances, it can never be regarded as absolute. The state of consciousness in which an action is performed is what determines its ethical value.

Of course, this teaching – though it is crucial – can easily be misunderstood. It is only too easy to make it mean 'If it feels good, do it,' – but this is a complete distortion of the Buddhist ethic. After all, quite a lot of people feel good even when they are doing something which is unskilful in every sense. It's not a question of following your instincts or feelings willy-nilly, but of trying to achieve the most positive mental state possible and acting from that. The ethical 'rules' or precepts are always there to provide a guide to the kind of action that will support positive mental states, even when your mental states are less than positive. But the aim of Buddhist ethics is to succeed in acting from a positive, skilful mental state – one of contentment, love, compassion, peace, tranquillity, joy, wisdom, awareness, and clarity of understanding. So much for the classification of karma according to ethical status.

Next, the classification of karma according to 'door'. This picturesque expression refers to the door through which, as it were, the karma is performed. Traditionally, Buddhism divides the human being into three aspects – body, speech, and mind – and these are the doors. For it is not only physical actions and actions in the form of speech that have karmic consequences. Mental actions, that is, thoughts and feelings, do too. But any action, of whatever kind, will only have a karmic effect if it is intentional. If you didn't mean to do something, or if what you say is misinterpreted, that action does not produce effects under the law of karma. Here Buddhism differs from Jainism. Jainism holds that if, for example, you take life by accident – even if you have taken all possible precautions against doing so – that action still has karmic consequences which will cause you to suffer in the future. In other words, the Jain system of ethics is based on rules – very complicated rules – whereas the Buddhist system is based on psychology.

Thirdly, karma can be classified 'according to the appropriateness of resultant experiences'. Putting it crudely – and indeed unbuddhistically – this is saying that karma works by making the punishment fit the crime. For example, if you adopt an attitude of reverence for life, if you guard and protect living beings, you will be reborn in a state of happiness in which you will enjoy long life. If, on the contrary, you deliberately take life, you will be reborn in a state of suffering, and your life will be short. In the same way, if you practise generosity, you will be reborn in comfortable circumstances, but if you are mean, you will be reborn poor and destitute. If you show respect and honour for others, you will be reborn in a high social position, but if you look down on others and treat them with contempt, you will be reborn at the bottom of the social scale.

Sometimes this principle is applied in a way that may seem to us in the West a bit ludicrous. For instance, one of the texts says that if you gossip unkindly about other people, you will be reborn suffering from halitosis. There's also the story of the *Arhant* who was born a dwarf. Apparently the Buddha had a disciple who was a dwarf. He was Enlightened, his Dharma knowledge was immense, he was a wonderful preacher – but he was a dwarf, and a hunchback too. The story goes that one day the Buddha's disciples began to discuss the case of this dwarf. He must have done many good things in previous lives to have been reborn as a disciple of the Buddha, but what could he possibly have done to be born a dwarf? To satisfy their curiosity, the Buddha is supposed to have told the following story.

Thousands and thousands of years ago, in a certain remote world period, there was a Buddha, in fact a *pratyekabuddha* – that is, a 'private' Buddha, one who gains Enlightenment but does not teach. When this

Buddha died, the whole community decided to erect a magnificent monument to commemorate his life. As they discussed the project, some people said the monument should be twenty feet high, while others thought it should be at least forty feet high. And as this discussion was going on, the person who was to be reborn as a dwarf came along and said, 'What on earth does it matter? Surely a small monument will do.' It was as a result of that very bad karma that he was reborn as a dwarf.[118]

I remember this story being told very solemnly in a Burmese Buddhist magazine. At the time some Buddhists – I was one of them – were suggesting that instead of spending all their money on gilding monuments, the Burmese might usefully devote some of it to printing books on Buddhism. They trotted out this apocryphal story to show the terrible karmic consequences we were apparently creating for ourselves by suggesting such a thing, and it just shows the rather silly way in which this principle has sometimes been applied. Despite such slightly tendentious applications, however, the principle is quite clear. We could put it another way: whatever we do to other people, we are in the long run also doing to ourselves. This is not just Buddhist theology; it's good sound psychology. We could even put it the other way round and say that whatever we do to ourselves, we are in the long run doing to other people.

The fourth way of classifying karma is 'according to time of taking effect'. In this sense, there are three kinds of karma: those that take effect in the present life – that is, the results accrue during the life in which the action was committed; those that take effect in a subsequent life; and those that do not take effect at all. This third category may come as a surprise. In some popular expositions, the idea is put forward that karma is an iron law from which nothing escapes. It is suggested that even if you did a very small action – good or bad – millions of years ago in some remote existence, it will catch up with you in the end. The idea that you never escape, that you will ultimately have to pay for everything you have done, clearly appeals strongly to some people.

It is not, however, the Buddhist teaching. According to Buddhism, some karmas, whether skilful or unskilful, are just cancelled out in the course of time. They may be counterbalanced by opposite karmas, or simply lose their force. Lacking an opportunity for expression, they may just fade away. So there is no 'iron law' of karma; some karmas do not produce any effect at all.

The fifth way of ordering karma – 'according to relative priority of taking effect' – brings us to the question of rebirth. Rebirth is the result of karma, but karma is of many different kinds. When you have died and are about to be reborn, there are all sorts of karmas in the background crowding in, so to speak, waiting to produce their effect. So in what order of priority do they influence the nature of your rebirth?

According to this mode of classification, karmas basically line up in four groups of relative priority. Firstly, under the heading of 'weighty' karma are gathered those karmas which embody conscious volitions, whether skilful or unskilful, which are so strong that they modify and affect your whole character. The example usually given of an unskilful weighty karma is that of the deliberate taking of life – murder – especially if the victim is spiritually advanced. An important skilful weighty karma, on the other hand, is meditation, but we have to be clear what this means in this context. The word meditation is often used, even among Buddhists, to mean *trying* to meditate, rather than actually experiencing higher states of consciousness. As a skilful weighty karma, meditation is not just a dreamy, passive sort of wool-gathering. It is an action that modifies your whole being, your whole character, your whole consciousness, both here and now, and in the future. When you have been meditating you shouldn't end up in a sweet, gentle, slightly abstracted state of mind. If you do, you may have been having a pleasant little reverie, but it will not have been meditation. Meditation is something much more dynamic, more challenging, even more shattering; afterwards, you should feel full of power and energy and life. Weighty karma, whether skilful or unskilful, exerts a tremendous influence.[119]

Second in the scale of influence over one's rebirth is 'death-proximate' karma. This means a sort of mental image which appears at the time of death, usually one that connects in some way with your activities and interests in life. The example commonly given in this regard is that of the butcher, who, we are told, is very likely to see visions of slaughter at the time of his or her death. He or she may well see an animal being butchered, or hear its cries, and see blood and meat cleavers: obviously, his or her mental state will not then be a very happy one. A painter, by contrast, might see beautiful colours and shapes, while a musician might hear music. Whatever you experience, however, does not necessarily have to be connected with your previous life. The image you see at this time may be connected with the place of your future rebirth. If you see a beautiful lotus flower, white or pink or golden, this is said to indicate rebirth on a higher plane of consciousness, a 'heaven realm'. If, on the other hand, you see flames, this of course indicates rebirth in another place.

The third category of karma which has an effect at this time is 'habitual' karma, that is, any action which one has repeated a number of times during one's life. A very great part of one's life is probably made up of habitual karmas, things we do over and over again, often without realizing the effect they are having on us. The action itself may not amount to very much – it may not take up much time – but if we do it every day, perhaps several times a day, it has its effect, like drops of water wearing away a stone. All the time we are creating karma, either forging a sort of chain that binds us, or planting seeds of future growth. And it need not necessarily be repeated physical action. Even an action which we do only once, but on which we continually reflect, mentally re-enacting it again and again, counts as habitual karma. There is no need to offer examples of this; I am sure they will spring to mind.

The fourth and last class of karma, distinguished 'according to relative priority of taking effect', is called 'residual' karma, which constitutes any willed action not included under the other three headings. The Abhidharma is nothing if not tidy.

So when we are between death and rebirth, between one life and another, hovering on the brink, these karmas come into effect and determine the nature of our rebirth in this order. According to the Abhidharma, the weighty karmas take effect first. If you have to your debit or credit a weighty karma, it is this that will decide initially the kind of rebirth you will have. One can now begin to appreciate the importance of meditation from the karmic point of view. If you have meditated a lot during your life, if you have dwelt in a higher state of consciousness consistently, or even from time to time, or even once – if you have really penetrated to some higher level of being during your lifetime, even for just a few minutes – it is that factor which will initially determine the nature of your future rebirth. Other factors will take effect afterwards.

If, however, you have committed no weighty karma, either skilful or unskilful, in your previous life, your rebirth is determined by the death-proximate karma. In the absence of death-proximate karma, it is determined by habitual karma, and in the absence even of habitual karma – this would be very unusual – it is determined by residual karma. At least, some Abhidharma authorities give this order of priority, while others say that habitual karma takes precedence over death-proximate karma – but despite this difference of opinion, the general picture is clear.

Karmas can overlap these categories, of course: a particular karma could function in all these ways. For instance, if you have meditated during your lifetime, that's a weighty karma. If at the time of your death you think of that meditation experience, it becomes a death-proximate karma. And if during your lifetime you have meditated many, many times, it will also be a habitual karma. If meditation is your weighty karma, your death-proximate karma, and also your habitual karma, then obviously meditation is going to be very much the determining factor when it comes to your next rebirth. You are likely, according to Buddhism, to be reborn in a higher state of consciousness, even in a higher world, than before: you will be virtually a born yogi, living in a world fit for yogis to live in.

The sixth classification of karma, after 'according to relative priority of taking effect', is 'according to function'. This refers to a fourfold disposition of karmas: 'reproductive', 'supportive', 'counteractive', and 'destructive'. Reproductive karmas are those which are directly responsible for the production of a new life after death, so this category refers to the way we create tendencies which will result in our being reborn, the way we indulge our craving, aversion, and ignorance. Supportive karma refers to the way we set up and reinforce those tendencies. Counteractive karma refers to the process by which the effects of our actions can be offset, countered, or cancelled by other actions. Thus weighty positive karma like meditative concentration would be counteractive karma inasmuch as it cancelled out weighty negative karma like gross breaches of the ethical precepts. Finally, destructive karma is any experience of Insight into Reality sustained deeply enough to destroy negative karma at the root.

There is a traditional simile which illustrates this classification. Reproductive karma is compared to a seed planted in a field – the new life is, as it were, 'planted' in the mother's womb. Supportive karma is like the rain and manure that nourish the seed and help it to grow into a plant. Counteractive karma is like a hailstorm that falls upon the growing crops and damages them. And destructive karma is like fire that burns up the whole field so that the crop perishes.[120] So from the point of view of function, karmas are of these four kinds.

The seventh and last classification of karma is 'according to the plane on which the karma matures'. This is very important, and again it is closely connected with the whole question of rebirth. In the Buddhist world picture, the universe is conceived in terms of space-time and also in terms of what we might call depth, or the spiritual dimension. Space-time represents the objective, material aspect of conditioned existence, whereas the spiritual dimension represents its mental, subjective aspect. The first of these aspects we usually refer to as the world or sphere or plane in which we exist, while the second we refer to as our state of mind or experience of that existence. In the microcosm of the individual human being these two poles or dimensions are represented by body and mind, body being the human entity in terms of space and time, and mind being the same human entity in terms of depth or spiritual dimension.

All this is illustrated by the *Tibetan Book of the Dead*, which, among other things, tries to answer the question 'What happens when we die?' It describes how the senses gradually fail. You no longer hear, or see, or smell, or taste, or feel. Eventually consciousness detaches itself from the body. The body loses its heat. Then even the subtle psychic link that exists between the body and its non-material aspects snaps. At that point you are really and truly dead. And then – according to the Buddhist teaching exemplified in great detail by the *Tibetan Book of the Dead* – in that first instant after you are completely dead, you find yourself face to face with Reality itself. It is as though throughout your life the body, the senses, the lower mind, sheltered you from Reality all the time, shutting it out, or at least filtering it, so that you only experienced a very little of it at a time. But after death, when the body is no longer there, when the lower mind is no longer there, or is at least suspended, Reality dawns, and flashes upon you for one dreadful instant. I say 'dreadful' because most people cannot bear it – they shrink back in terror. 'Human kind', as T. S. Eliot puts it, 'cannot bear very much reality.'[121]

When the human consciousness finds itself face to face with Reality, this can be a terrifying experience from which the mind flees, retreating to lower and ever lower levels until at last it finds itself on a level where it feels at home. On that level it grasps a body, and in that body it is then, as we say, 'reborn'. Of course, we should not be misled by words. We speak of the consciousness coming and going – we even speak of it passing from one body to another – but there is no real coming and going of consciousness. It does not occupy space in a literal sense; it cannot 'enter' a body. Mind and body are like the two ends of a stick: you grasp one and the other automatically follows.

So these are the seven classifications of karma, and together with the five *niyamas* they give a comprehensive picture of the nature of karma. Karma is one's own deliberately willed action and the results that follow from that, as well as the law by virtue of which the one follows upon the other. It is not fate; it is not destiny. Neither is it the law of cause and effect in general. As the teaching of the five *niyamas* makes clear, karma is just one kind of conditionality – albeit a very important one – along with four others. It is therefore wrong to say that whatever happens is the result of karma. Some people imagine that if, when something happens to them, they say, 'Ah well, that must be my karma,' they are being very pious, very Buddhist – but this is not in fact the Buddhist teaching. Buddhism teaches that whatever happens happens as a result of conditions, but that not all those conditions are karma. Karma is only one among the five kinds of conditionality at work in the universe. Events may be the result of karma, or they may not. How we find out is another question altogether.

A difficulty that crops up sometimes is the relationship between rebirth and the *anātman* teaching, the teaching that there is no self, or no soul. One might think, 'If there is no soul that passes from one life, one body, to another, how does rebirth take place?' It might seem that you've got to sacrifice either the *anātman* doctrine or the teaching of rebirth – you can't have both. But this is an artificial difficulty. *Anātman* does not, as we saw in the opening chapter, mean no soul in the sense of no psychic life at all. It means no *unchanging* soul, no *unchanging* self. When it comes to rebirth, there is a substratum of mental activity that 'flows' from life to life – now linked with this body, now with that. It is the linking of a fresh body with this 'stream' of mental activity that constitutes what we call rebirth. So there is no contradiction; you can have *anātman* and rebirth side by side.

By this stage in a discussion of karma one can sometimes find oneself thinking, 'That's all very well. It hangs together beautifully. It all sounds very plausible. But is it true? How can we know? What is the proof?' The average Western mind wants hard evidence, and this is slowly but assiduously being gathered. Teams of researchers are systematically investigating the cases of people who claim to be able to remember their previous lives. Records are gathered and published of ordinary people – not saints or sages or meditators – who claim, for no apparent reason, to remember a previous life. They usually go into all the details, too – their name, where they lived, what they did, what illness they died of, and so on. And it seems that these details are found to tally with what is still known about the lives – ordinary humdrum lives for the most part – that they claim to recall. The scientists tend to be particularly interested in the many cases of curious recollections of this kind on the part of children. The possibility of coincidence or fraud or imagination has been ruled out completely in many cases, and researchers seem inclined to admit that a hypothesis of rebirth, or reincarnation, would provide the simplest explanation for the facts. As more and more evidence of this sort comes to light, I have no doubt that it will eventually convince all open-minded people of the truth of the teaching of karma and rebirth.[122]

Some people point to further evidence for karma and rebirth in the existence of child prodigies. When you get a child like the young Mozart who could play, sing, and compose at a very tender age, it is hard to believe that this degree of knowledge and proficiency could possibly have been acquired entirely in the present life; it must, so it is argued, have been carried over from a previous life. But this brings up the whole question of heredity: there is no general agreement as to what can and cannot be inherited in the genes. The issue is complicated besides by all sorts of other factors, both personal and cultural, so that particular line of argument is hardly as convincing as the evidence of recollection.

The idea of karma and rebirth certainly resolves many more questions and problems than it creates, but this is not to say that there are no loose ends in the teaching. In my opinion, the traditional doctrine needs a thorough reformulation, taking account of various matters that have not so far, apparently, been considered in the East. For instance, there is the whole question of the relation between karma and rebirth and time, and between karma and rebirth and the individual consciousness. Karma and rebirth operate within time – so what is time? Karma and rebirth pertain to the individual consciousness – so what is that? There is also the knotty question of population explosion. Where have all the people come from? Has there been a sort of fission of souls, or have they come from other realms, or other worlds? Some Eastern Buddhists would say loftily, 'Of course they have come from other realms and worlds. Everybody knows that.' But is this the only possible solution? These and similar questions will have to be given full consideration in a new formulation of the traditional Buddhist teaching of karma and rebirth; and this reformulation will perhaps be one of the works of Western Buddhism.[123]

In the end, we have to admit that there will be for some time, perhaps, a certain amount of resistance in the West to the idea of karma and rebirth. As we have seen, it cuts across a lot of our Western assumptions about some of our deepest concerns. So an important question for a lot of people is this: do you have to believe in karma and rebirth to be a Buddhist? The simple answer is 'Yes.' But an answer that might be more illuminating is 'No – but on one condition. You need not believe in karma and rebirth provided that you are willing to go all out for full Enlightenment in this life.' This is certainly true, and might satisfy some people. But it also shows at once how difficult it might be to practise Buddhism seriously without installing karma and rebirth as part of one's mental furniture, so to speak.

The teaching of karma and rebirth does provide an answer – perhaps *the* answer – to certain questions. It helps to solve the mystery of death, which is also the mystery of life – and very few people can follow the path to Enlightenment without bothering, at least sometimes, about such questions. A few may be happy to get on with their meditation and not worry about philosophy, but most people require some answers. They really want to know, and it is only within the framework of this sort of knowledge that they can practise at all. They need to have some general philosophical framework, however rudimentary or sketchy, within which to follow the path. The teaching of karma and rebirth does give, at least in part, such a framework.

If we do not accept karma and rebirth as a solution, we are going to have to find another one, and that, I think, will not be easy. I personally believe that the teaching of karma and rebirth is the most satisfactory answer to many of the questions raised by the fact of death and the nature of human life and existence. It is not only true; it gives meaning and purpose to life. It makes it clear that human beings are pilgrims through a succession of lives, and that by changing our consciousness – something which is, according to Buddhism, very much within our power – we can determine our own destiny, not only in this life, but in future lives as well. This means that no real effort is ever wasted. The good is conserved from life to life. There is no question of reward, and there is no question of punishment. By performing a consciously willed action we modify our own consciousness, both here and now, and for the future – and that is surely reward or punishment enough. I would say personally that the teaching of karma and rebirth is an integral part of Buddhism, and that for most people it would be difficult to be a Buddhist without accepting it, at least in principle.

Traditionally, the truth of the teaching of karma and rebirth is said to become clear in the light of higher states of consciousness, and especially in that highest of all states of consciousness – so high that it is not really to be called a state of consciousness as such – the Enlightenment of a Buddha. In the East it is held that there are some truths – call them 'spiritual truths' if you like – that cannot be perceived by the ordinary rational mind.

This, of course, is a point of view that we in the West usually find completely unacceptable. We tend to take it for granted that anything that can be understood or seen can be understood or seen by our ordinary conscious 'everyday' mind. This mind, we assume, is capable of understanding anything that can be understood at all. But Eastern tradition, especially Indian tradition, says that there are some truths – some laws or principles, if you like – that cannot be understood by the ordinary human mind. If you want to understand them you have to raise your level of consciousness, in the same way that if you want to see a long way you have to climb a mountain. Buddhists take the view that if you climb the mountainside of your own consciousness you will see, spread out before you, as it were, spiritual truths which in your ordinary state of consciousness you could not have perceived.

According to Indian tradition, the teaching of karma and rebirth is one of these truths. Our ordinary, rational consciousness cannot apprehend it. We may be able to understand it when it is explained to us, but we cannot really see the truth of it directly. Karma and rebirth in all their details, all their workings, all their ramifications, are perceived only by a Buddha. This means that the hard facts, as it were, are not really available to us.

However, in the course of the thousands of years of the development of Buddhism, all the Buddhist sages and yogis have testified to the truth of karma and rebirth. There has never been a school of Buddhism or a prominent Buddhist teacher who has questioned it – which is interesting. If the teaching of karma and rebirth had been just a doctrine, a philosophical idea, a speculation, surely someone in the Buddhist world at some time would have denied it, or at least doubted it? Buddhists have complete freedom of thought – there is no ecclesiastical power to coerce them into orthodoxy – so Buddhist history is full of the questioning of doctrine. Why, then, has the teaching of karma and rebirth never, apparently, been questioned? I suggest that this is because karma and rebirth is not a matter of speculation and philosophy, but one of experience and perception. As the great yogis and meditators increased in spiritual understanding and insight, they would have seen more and more clearly the truth of this teaching. They may not have perceived it as fully as the Buddha did, but they saw enough of it to be convinced of its truth. So in the East the evidence of the superconscious perception of the Buddha and other Enlightened teachers is considered conclusive proof of the truth of karma and rebirth. For practising Buddhists, at least, this should provide sufficient basis for their faith until they can perceive the truth of karma and rebirth directly for themselves.

Karma and rebirth are complex subjects, but some understanding of the teaching is essential to an understanding of who the Buddha is. The Buddha's primary Insight into the nature of Reality, the realization of which made him who he was, arose out of his direct perception of the workings of karma and rebirth. On the night of his Enlightenment, as he was seated beneath the bodhi tree, the Buddha saw, in a flash of illumination, the whole series of his previous existences – tens of thousands of previous lives. Not only that: he could see, stretching back into the past, the previous lives of other living beings – and on that night, and whenever he wished subsequently, he could see their future existences too.[124] The Buddha taught the doctrine of karma and rebirth not as a philosophical teaching, something he had worked out logically, but as something he had experienced, something he had seen. This faculty, this ability to see previous lives, one's own and other people's, is technically known as *pūrvanivāsa-smṛti* – literally 'recollection of previous abodes'. It is reckoned as one of the five or six *abhijñās*, the 'superknowledges',[125] and we are told that it can be cultivated on the basis of the practice of meditation by anybody who cares to make the effort.

8

THE 'DEATH' OF THE BUDDHA

The 'death' of the Buddha wasn't an ordinary death, because the Buddha was not an ordinary person. Even during his lifetime, his very closest disciples were sometimes perplexed by the question of the Buddha's nature. Who was the Buddha? What was the Buddha? And what would happen to the Buddha when he died? We don't know why, but apparently in the days of the Buddha quite a lot of the disciples, and quite a lot of members of the public, were very interested in this last question. So many people, indeed, seem to have been fascinated by it that there came to be a standard way of putting it. People used to come to the Buddha and say, 'Lord, after death, does the Tathāgata (that is to say the Buddha) exist, or does he not exist, or both, or neither?' And the Buddha would always give the same reply. He would always say, 'It is inappropriate to say of a Buddha that after death he exists. It is inappropriate to say of a Buddha that after death he does not exist. It is inappropriate to say of a Buddha that after death he both exists (in one sense) and does not exist (in another). And it is inappropriate to say of a Buddha that after death he neither exists nor does not exist. All ways of telling, all ways of describing, are totally inapplicable to the Buddha.'[126]

From this it becomes clear that the Buddha's death is not death in the ordinary sense at all. This is why in the Buddhist tradition it is usually termed the *parinirvāna*. We don't say the Buddha died; we say he attained *parinirvāna*. Nirvāna, of course, means Enlightenment, and *pari* means 'supreme', so *parinirvāna* means 'supreme Enlightenment'.

What then is the difference between *nirvana* and *parinirvana*? Well, none at all, really. When a Buddha attains Nirvāṇa, this is traditionally called the 'Nirvāṇa with remainder', because the Buddha still has a physical body. *Parinirvāṇa*, on the other hand, is known as the 'Nirvāṇa without remainder' because the physical body is then no longer attached. This is the only difference – and this difference only affects other people, notably his unenlightened disciples. The Nirvāṇa is just the same. From the Buddha's point of view, there is no difference at all between the two states. Before death or after death, the experience, whatever it is – and we cannot know or describe it – is exactly the same.

His attainment of *parinirvāṇa* may not have been an event of much consequence to the Buddha personally, but it is important to those of us who are unenlightened. His last days are recorded in the Pāli canon in greater detail than any other part of his life after his Enlightenment.[127] His followers evidently thought that the way he died taught them a great deal about him, about his teaching, and about the nature of Buddhahood.

He felt the sharp pains of his final sickness come upon him in a village near the great city of Vaiśālī. It may have been the sudden change in the weather with the beginning of the rainy season that brought them on. But by an effort of will he recovered sufficiently to undertake a gruelling 'farewell tour'. 'My journey is drawing to its close,' he said to Ānanda. 'Just as a worn-out carriage can only be kept going by being held together with straps, so this body can only be kept going by being strapped up. But my mental and spiritual vigour is undiminished.'[128] His body, like all conditioned things, was subject to decay, but his mind was beyond birth and death.

Taking leave of his disciples in Vaiśālī – a city very close to his heart – he set off on a final round of visits to other places where he would be able to offer some last words of encouragement. Despite the constant physical pain he endured, and despite his knowledge of his impending death, he was as outward-going and concerned with the needs of others as he had ever been. The scriptures also note that he was as aware of his surroundings as he had ever been, expressing an appreciation of the beauty of certain places they passed through, certain groves where they rested. He delivered discourses in towns and villages, continued to accept new disciples, and issued his final instructions to the sangha. Reaching a village called Pāvā, he took what was to be his last meal, provided for him by the local smith, called Cunda. It gave him severe dysentery. With the last of his physical strength he made the journey to a place called Kuśinagara, in north-eastern India. Resting by a river on the way, he told Ānanda to comfort and reassure Cunda the smith that he should not be troubled in his mind at having inadvertently given the Buddha food poisoning. So, far from being blameworthy, to provide a Buddha with his last meal before his *parinirvāṇa* was in fact highly meritorious.[129]

Just as he was born in the open air under a tree and gained Enlightenment in the open air under a tree, so the Buddha attained *parinirvāṇa* in the open air under a tree. There are shrines, places of pilgrimage, at the site of each of these events, and the shrine to the *parinirvāṇa* is at Kuśinagara. The scriptures make it clear that Kuśinagara was honoured in this way by no kind of accident. It was his conscious choice to die in this 'miserable little town of wattle and daub in the back of beyond', as Ānanda rather fretfully called it.[130] The Buddha was no more a victim of circumstance in his death than in any other aspect of his life.

Just outside Kuśinagara was a grove of sāl trees where the local people had built a stone couch for the elder of the village assembly to sit on. On this couch the Buddha lay down. He then sorted out the funeral arrangements. Ānanda and the other monks were not to concern themselves with these at all, he said, but just get on with their spiritual practice. The lay followers, however, were to be enjoined to deal with his remains as they would those of a great king.

All this proved too much for Ānanda to bear, and he went away and wept. The Buddha called him back and said, 'Enough, Ānanda. Do not grieve so. It is in the very nature of all things most near and dear to us that at some time or other we must be parted from them. For a long time, Ānanda, you have shown unstinting and wholehearted loving-kindness to me in your actions, your speech, and your thoughts. Maintain your practice and you will surely attain liberation from the defilements.' The Buddha then extolled Ānanda's virtues before the whole company of monks.[131]

After this the Buddha dealt with one or two points concerning monastic discipline. For example, he instructed that his old charioteer, Channa, who had joined the order but had proved wilfully errant in his practice, should be 'sent to Coventry' (that is, no one should speak to him) until he came to his senses – which he did eventually. In this way the Buddha was able to focus his mind with clarity and compassion on the welfare of specific individuals right up to the end. Indeed, his last address to the monks amounted to an invitation to any individuals among them with doubts or uncertainties about his teaching to bring them up there and then, while he was still there to resolve them. When the company remained silent, he uttered his last exhortation: 'Decay is inherent in all conditioned things. With diligence, strive on.'[132] Then he entered into meditation and passed away.

The force of this final scene, more than any other in the Buddha's life, is most tellingly captured, not so much in the words of the Pāli canon, but in paintings by the great Chinese and Japanese artists of the medieval period. Against a beautiful forest backdrop, the trunks of the sāl trees are seen rising like columns, straight and tall, to a crown of broad green leaves and large white flowers. The Buddha is resting on his right side, with the sāl trees showering white blossoms down upon him. He is surrounded by disciples, his closest followers sitting near his head in their yellow robes, and all sorts of other people – Brahmins, princes, ministers, ascetics, fire worshippers, merchants, peasants, traders – crowding round where they can. Not only people, but all sorts of animals as well – elephants, goats, deer, horses, dogs, even mice and birds – have gathered to look their last on the Buddha. Up in the clouds the gods and goddesses complete this cosmic deathbed scene. What the best paintings of that scene show is that this is no ordinary conclusion to someone's life, but an event of universal significance which the whole of creation has come to witness.

The general mood is, as you would expect, tearful. Even the animals are weeping, and you particularly notice the elephant's big, fat tears rolling down his cheek. In fact, the only ones who aren't weeping are a few of the disciples, those sitting closest to the Buddha, and the cat. The cat remains unmoved out of fabled feline nonchalance, but the closest disciples stay perfectly calm because they are able to see beyond the physical body, and know that really the change from *nirvāṇa* to *parinirvāṇa* is no change at all.

This is the scene that Buddhists bring to mind each year on Parinirvāṇa Day, held on 15 February. It is, of course, a day of grateful celebration for the example and teaching of the Buddha's life. However, the mood is different from that of other festivals, because the real point of commemorating this event is to focus our minds on the fact of death – and not just the Buddha's 'death', but our own. So the mood is sober – not sombre but reflective, meditative. We reflect, indeed, that the fact of death is present not on one day of the year only, but every day of our lives, and that the recollection of this fact should be an intrinsic aspect of our daily spiritual practice. The Buddha's *parinirvāṇa* reminds us to renew our whole meditation practice in the light of the ever-present reality of death. But in particular it can spur us to take up meditation practices which are specifically concerned with death.

There is, of course, such a thing as an unhealthy, morbid fascination with death, and we have to be clear that the recollection of death as a meditation practice bears no relation to anything like an unwholesome or gloomy mental habit. It should, in fact, be undertaken on the basis of a highly positive and clear mind. As the development of mindfulness and positivity are the specific province of other practices, meditation on death cannot properly be presented except in the context of a systematic approach to meditation. In the course of this chapter, therefore, we shall see where the recollection of death fits in with other methods of meditation.

Initially, we will look at the general nature of meditative experience, its function and purpose – that is, the sort of ground meditation covers – before going on to examine the various specific practices by which we enter upon that experience. In short, we will answer the question 'What do we mean by meditation?' The word is in common usage nowadays, but most people would be hard pressed to say what it is really all about.

Very broadly speaking, the word meditation can be used in three main senses, corresponding to three successively higher levels of experience. First of all, there is meditation in the sense of the integration – the bringing together – of all our psychic energies. This is the first step. Human beings, like other living things, are essentially embodiments of energy. We may not always look like it, but this is what we essentially are. The reason we don't always look like embodiments of energy is that our energy is split into many different streams. Some flow in one direction, some in another, some meander happily, others rush and pour and tumble. A lot of the time these different streams of energy, instead of flowing together harmoniously, move in opposite directions. The result is either a whirlpool or stagnation: a lot of energy rushing around going nowhere, or a total energy shut-down. Because we are struggling against ourselves, divided within ourselves, our energies cancel each other out. This is a not uncommon state for people to find themselves in, their energies so scattered and distracted that they cannot do very much or achieve very much.

The first function of meditation, therefore, is to bring all these energies together and get them flowing in the same channel, get them flowing more and more smoothly and sharply, cutting deeper and deeper into this single channel so that it carries those energies more and more surely and steadily towards their goal. Gradually through meditating we integrate all our psychophysical energies, so that there is no longer any conflict or discord, and we experience peace and harmony and a sense of everything coming together.

The next level of experience to which we refer when we speak of meditation is the experience of superconscious states, termed within the Indian tradition *dhyānas*. These are states of progressive superconscious simplification. What this means is that – according to tradition, supported by the experience of anyone who puts in the work – you experience in the first *dhyāna* a number of mental factors, and this number is progressively reduced as you move into the three higher *dhyānas*.

In the first *dhyāna*, you experience not only integration – carried over from meditation in the previous sense – but also bliss and joy, as well as subtle mental activity of various kinds. But as you ascend to the second *dhyāna*, the mental activity gradually fades away. You don't think *of* anything, you don't think *about* anything. All mental functioning in this sense entirely ceases. But although the mind is stilled in this way, at the same time you are perfectly aware, perfectly conscious – more aware and more conscious than ever. The mind becomes like a vast lake in which every ripple has died away. Instead of being tossed into waves, it's perfectly calm, level, shining, and serene. At the same time it is as if the lake is being fed by an underground spring, so that you may experience degrees of intense but subtle psychophysical pleasure and joy welling up as certain energies are released. This is the experience of the second *dhyāna*.

Just as the mental activity faded away to give rise to the second *dhyāna*, so, on the higher level of the third *dhyāna*, even the experience of joy, which is comparatively coarse, fades away, and what you have left is simply intense bliss and peace. Then eventually there is not even a feeling of bliss. At this fourth level all the elements of your being, all your energies, are unified in a sort of vast ocean of integration, of mental harmony, with an overwhelming knowledge of absolute peace which far surpasses any experience of happiness or even bliss.[133]

In this way the *dhyānas* develop from lower to higher and ever higher levels of experience, and one should be prepared for all sorts of things to happen on the way. What I've described represents a standard pattern, but there are all sorts of additional dimensions, all sorts of byways of experience which people may find themselves entering, according to their different temperaments and backgrounds. Some people have visions of archetypal images: visionary landscapes float before them; jewel-like forms, mandalas, even gods, goddesses, Buddhas, and bodhisattvas emerge, as it were, from the depths of their own minds. Then again, other people, as they progress through the *dhyānas*, can discover various supernormal faculties developing – telepathy, for example. They may find they are aware of what is going on in other people's minds, or at least uncannily sensitive to how other people are feeling. They may hear or see things going on in other places. Some people even have the odd flash of what seems to be a recollection of a previous life.

Whatever unusual side-effects meditation may throw up, the Buddhist tradition is quite clear about how to deal with them. Basically, you don't. You pay no particular attention to them. In general, you treat them as a very subtle form of distraction from the job in hand, which is to try to extend and deepen your experience of meditation by moving from the lower to the higher *dhyānas*.

The third and highest level of meditative experience is that of insight into the true nature of existence. As higher levels of consciousness become more familiar, your experience becomes not only more integrated, blissful, and peaceful, but also more and more objective. You become less and less influenced by your own subjectivity, less and less influenced by the pleasure principle. You begin to rise above the distortions of subjective factors, like an aeroplane emerging from the clouds into the clear blue sky. You begin to see conditioned existence spread out, as it were, below you, its essential patterns becoming more apparent. You begin to see it as it is. Now you're in some degree clear of it, to some extent free of it, you can see it much more objectively. You begin to see things as they really are. You begin to see Reality. In other words, you develop at least the beginnings of Insight, or Wisdom, which leads directly to Enlightenment.

The word meditation clearly covers a great deal of ground, operating as it does on these three very different levels. The first level is concentration, really, rather than meditation; the second is meditation proper; and the third is contemplation, one could say. Being realistic, we have to say that most people are going to be occupied for a very considerable time with the first two: meditation as concentration and meditation as meditation. To start with, you simply need to integrate all your scattered energies. You need to pull yourself together, to become one person, not a number of conflicting selves. You don't want to waste your energies in internal and external discord; you want to be whole and harmonious. Only in that way can you deploy your energies effectively and be really happy.

When you have achieved this concentration of energies, the next step is to raise your consciousness above the usual – what we like to think of as our 'normal' – level. Here, you come to the nitty-gritty of meditation and the spiritual life: the transformation of consciousness. The point has already been made that we are embodiments of energy. It could equally well be said that we are embodiments of consciousness. We are what our state of consciousness is; our state of consciousness is us. So in the course of our spiritual life in general, and our meditation practice in particular, we are concerned with changing our state of consciousness – and it's not easy. Indeed, for those who are not spiritually gifted from the beginning, it is very, very difficult. There are all sorts of hindrances and obstacles. There are plenty of exterior ones, obviously, but there are even more obstacles in our own mind, our own present state of conditioned consciousness. These hindrances or obstacles, which prevent us from rising to a higher state of consciousness, the Buddhist tradition summarizes under the general heading of the five 'poisons' or 'defilements'. Strong words, perhaps, but the fact is that they defile and poison the whole of our existence, and, if we're not careful, even bring about our spiritual death – not in the positive sense in which that term can be used, but the slow death of all spiritual aspiration.

The five poisons are distraction, aversion, craving, ignorance, and conceit, and for each of them there is an antidote in the form of a specific method of meditation.[134] So if one particular poison predominates in us, we need to concentrate on the meditation practice which remedies that poison. If we find that one particular poison is predominant one week and another the next, we can change our method of practice accordingly.

The five 'antidotes' are the five basic methods of meditation – one of which, as we shall see, is the recollection of death.

From the point of view of meditation, however, the first and fundamental practice to undertake, without which any other practice will prove heavy going, is one that counters the poison of distraction. Particularly this is the case under the conditions of modern life: techniques of attention-grabbing seem to be brought to a fresh pitch of sophistication with every year that passes. You may be trying to do something, but your attention is taken away by so many things. Almost anything you see or hear seems capable of starting some train of thought or action which seems all the more inviting when you have set yourself to do something requiring a bit of concentration. Sometimes it seems practically impossible just to settle down and concentrate on one thing at a time. Someone can come to the door and you forget all about what you were supposed to be doing. There's always some fascinating distraction on hand to drag your attention away – if it needs to be dragged. In fact, what seems to be an unwilling submission to some irresistible outside force – 'I was distracted' – is actually a condition of one's own mind.

This inability to concentrate is very much to do with non-integration. Because one's energies are not all pulling in the same direction, it is impossible for one stream of volitional consciousness to decide to concentrate on something without another part of oneself popping up and taking an interest in something else entirely. We become distracted when, after a struggle, the first self succumbs and the second self takes over. As far as the first self is concerned, the mind has wandered and one has become distracted. If anything is left of the first self it is just a nagging sense of unease.

The antidote to all this is simple. It lies in the method of meditation called the mindfulness of breathing. Through the various stages of this practice one's concentration on the natural rhythm of one's own breathing gradually gets deeper and more subtle. One gets more and more absorbed in the flow of the breath until eventually the breath seems to disappear, and one is just concentrated without concentrating on anything. The mind is just like a sphere resting on one non-dimensional point – perfectly at rest and perfectly mobile at the same time. With regular practice of this meditation technique one gains some measure of control over what one is doing. One also finds that the ability to put the whole of one's energies behind doing one thing at a time is the source of a relaxed and happy state of mind.

Having at least lessened the effects of the poison of distraction, we are now ready to apply the antidotes to the others. The next one is aversion, or hatred, and this is overcome by the practice of the *mettā bhāvanā*. *Bhāvanā* simply means 'development', but *mettā* is more difficult to translate, since there is really no word like it in the English language. The usual translation is 'universal loving-kindness'. In the meditation technique designed to help one develop universal loving-kindness, one works to cultivate an attitude of positive emotion towards all living beings – a disposition towards feelings of friendliness, love, compassion, sympathy, and so on.

Like the mindfulness of breathing, the *mettā bhāvanā* proceeds through a number of stages. Starting by establishing a warm, positive regard for yourself, you then explore and connect with the feelings you have towards a good friend. In the context of the affectionate interest you have for your friend, you bring to mind someone for whom ordinarily you have very little feeling. When you have found you are able to experience genuine concern for this individual as well, you go on to extend this sense of care and goodwill to include someone you don't like. Finally, you establish the non-exclusivity of your sympathy and fellow-feeling by finding it in your heart to feel a real sense of kindness, of *mettā*, towards everyone, whoever and wherever they are – and indeed, towards all living beings. This practice is not about thinking vaguely beautiful thoughts. The aim is the cultivation of powerful, focused, precise positive emotion, as an antidote to a specific and powerful poison: aversion or hatred.

The third poison is craving. This is intense, neurotic desire: lust to possess this, that, and the other. It is a primordial, cardinal defilement, very difficult to overcome. Perhaps in recognition of the power it wields over us, not one but three meditation methods are prescribed as antidotes. First, the recollection of impurity. This is a rather drastic method that very few people have recourse to nowadays. It's usually supposed to be practised only by people like monks and hermits rather than lay-folk; and in any case it calls for rather special facilities, to which not many people have access. The practice consists in going to a burning ground – one of the Indian type, with corpses and bones strewn everywhere – and contemplating corpses in different stages of decay. This meditation is still practised by some people in the East, but obviously you need strong nerves and a strong spiritual resolution to be able to do it.

The second method of dealing with craving is the same sort of thing, only milder. This is the recollection of death, which must be undertaken on a firm foundation of mindfulness and emotional positivity. When you take up the practice of the recollection of death, your mind must already be relatively free of discursive thought, integrated, peaceful, harmonious, and happy – conditions you can most effectively establish with the help of the mindfulness of breathing and the *mettā bhāvanā* meditation practices. If you don't do this, the recollection of death meditation can even be harmful.

If, for instance, without being aware of how you were really feeling, or mindful of what you were doing, you began the practice by thinking of people near and dear to you who had died, you might start feeling sad, not in the positive sense of an objective sorrow, real compassion, but simply depressed, which is not the point of it at all. Or if, on the other hand, you happened to think of somebody you disliked who had died, you might find yourself feeling faintly pleased, thinking 'Well, thank goodness he's gone!' – which would also do more harm than good. Then again, you might bring to mind people who had died, or who were undergoing death, and feel a certain indifference – not in the positive sense of equanimity, but in the sense of uncaring insensibility. This too would undermine the practice.

To avoid feelings of depression or *schadenfreude* or simple indifference, one is very strongly advised to start this practice in a mindful and positive frame of mind – if possible, in a higher state of consciousness, a state of serenity and happiness. Then, on that basis, you start reflecting that death is inevitable. This is a truism, of course, but though one may acknowledge its truth at a certain superficial level, it is another matter to absorb it sufficiently deeply to realize its truth as pertaining to one's own, most personal interests. So you begin this practice by allowing the simple truth to percolate down through your mind: 'I'm going to die. Death is inevitable.' It's as simple as that.

Simple to say, but far from simple to realize. Other factors being equal, the younger you are, the more difficult it is. When you are very young, it's virtually impossible. You have the irrational feeling that you're going to go on living for ever and ever. You may see people dying all around you every day, but it may still not occur to you to apply the fact of death to your own self. You can't grasp it. You can't imagine it. It seems so absolutely remote, absurd, and ridiculous, this fact that you're going to die. But it is a fact, and the older you get, the more clearly you see it. And when you see it, you begin to see, too, that until now you had never seen it, you had never understood this simple fact at all.

So at the beginning of this practice this is all you do. In a serene, happy, concentrated frame of mind you just let the thought of death, the thought that you are going to die, sink in. You say to yourself 'I'm going to die,' or, more traditionally, and even more succinctly, 'death … death', like a sort of mantra. Again traditionally, it's said to be helpful actually to see dead bodies, but this tip must, as always, carry a health warning. It's no use looking at corpses if your mind is unconcentrated, agitated, liable to depression, and so on. You've got to have not only steady nerves in the ordinary sense but real inner calm. Otherwise, if you start looking around for corpses, you can, such is the power of meditation, do yourself real damage.

In most Western countries, of course, there's little chance of catching a glimpse of a corpse anyway, never mind being able to sit down and contemplate one. But another, less extreme, option is to keep a skull by you. One of the reasons the Tibetans make and possess skull cups and thighbone trumpets and ornaments made of human bone is to familiarize themselves with the idea of death by handling these bits of people who were once living and breathing and feeling and are now dead. So if you don't want to go the whole hog and contemplate a corpse, you can get hold of a skull, or even just a fragment of bone, as a constant reminder of death. Some people in the Buddhist East have malas, or rosaries, made of human bone – they come in discs rather than round beads. But once again, there should be nothing morbid or ghoulish about this. The indispensable basis for meditating on mortality is a serene state of concentration.

The next step in the practice, if the simple methods so far described don't seem to be producing results in the way of deepening your awareness of death, is to start thinking systematically of the precariousness of human life. You reflect that all the time life is hanging by a thread, that its continuance depends on any one of a number of factors. For one thing, you need air. If you stopped breathing for more than a few minutes, you'd die. You are totally dependent on that pair of bellows inside the chest called the lungs. If they stopped pumping air – finish. If all the air were suddenly sucked out of the room – end of story. In the same way, you are dependent on a certain degree of warmth. If the temperature went up a little, we would all die, quite quickly. If it went down a little, we would be dead in no time. If the Earth was to wander just a little out of its orbit, that would be the end, for all of us. Life is so precarious, so contingent, it's a marvel that anybody is alive at all. Every moment of our lives is a step on a tightrope over an abyss. It's so difficult to be alive, and yet we are alive – we've managed it somehow – so far.

Another challenging angle on the matter, which can bring home to us how close we are to slipping from that tightrope, is the reflection that there is no special set of conditions for death. It's not as though you die at night but you don't die during the day. There's no time of the day or night when you can say to yourself, 'Well, I'm safe for a bit now.' It isn't like that. You can die during the night or during the day. And it isn't that if you are young you can think 'I'm young, so I'm not going to die. I'll only die when I'm old.' No, you can die either when you're young or when you're old. You can die when you're sick or when you're healthy. You can die in your home or outside. You can die in your own country or in a foreign land. There is no set of conditions within which you can be sure that you are not going to die. Death doesn't abide by any conditions. There is nowhere you can go to escape it. There is no time at which you can be sure that, because of such-and-such conditions, you're not going to die at that particular instant. You never know. There's absolutely no barrier between you and death at any time, in any place. So this can be quite a sobering subject for reflection.

You can also reflect upon the fact that everybody has to die. Every single member of the human race, however great, however distinguished, however noble, however famous – they all have to die one day. All the great men and women of the past have gone this way, even the Buddha. And if even the Buddha himself had to die, then you can be sure that you yourself are not going to escape.

Implicit in the practice of the recollection of death is the idea of impermanence. However, you can, if you like, make this broader principle the subject of your meditation. This is the third practice for the overcoming of the poison or defilement of craving. The recollection of the impermanence of all things is the mildest of the three antidotes to craving, but if you are sensitive and imaginative enough it can have a powerful impact. In the end, you always have to gauge which meditation is most suitable for you to practise at any one time on the basis of individual temperament and mood. This one, the recollection of the impermanence of all things, is fairly self-explanatory. Everything changes. Nothing lasts. Evidence of impermanence is around you all day, every day, if you look for it. Again, you just have to bring a calm and positive sense of awareness to the meditation. Gradually, as the fragility of things and their inevitable decay becomes apparent, so does the falsity of the perception underlying the craving to possess become more and more obvious.

The fourth basic method of meditation is the one designed to overcome the poison of ignorance. Ignorance here means not lack of intellectual knowledge, but lack of awareness, the refusal to see things as they really are. The meditation which overcomes this culpable ignorance is the contemplation of a formulation of the truth which we have already come across: the chain of conditioned co-production.

This consists of twelve *nidānas* or links. Between them they represent the whole process of the reactive mind as it operates throughout this life – and not only this life, but the past life, the present life, and the future life. Basically, this chain of conditioned co-production is a framework by means of which one can get some understanding of the process of birth, death, and rebirth.

To enumerate the twelve links briefly, first of all there's ignorance – this is where it all starts. In dependence on ignorance there arise *saṃskāras* or volitions. In dependence on volitions there arises consciousness. In dependence on consciousness there arises the whole psychophysical organism. In dependence on the psychophysical organism there arise the six organs of sense, one mental and five physical. In dependence on those six organs of sense there arises contact with an external world. In dependence on that contact with an external world there arise feelings of various kinds: pleasant, painful, and neutral. In dependence on pleasant feeling there arises thirst or craving for the repetition of that pleasant feeling. In dependence on that thirst or craving, there arises grasping – the attempt to hang on to the pleasant feeling, and the object that created it. In dependence on that grasping and clinging, there arises becoming, which is the whole process of psychological conditioning, the whole process of the reactive mind itself. In dependence on becoming, there arises birth. And in dependence on that, there arises decay and death, and further rebirth.

These are the twelve links in the chain of conditioned co-production.[135] To do the meditation practice, you first have to learn them off by heart – in the original Pāli and Sanskrit if you like, or in English translation – it doesn't really matter. Then, having first established yourself in a state of concentration, you say to yourself, 'In dependence on ignorance arise volitions. In dependence on volitions arises consciousness. In dependence on consciousness arises the psychophysical organism,...' and so on. However, you don't just repeat the words. You don't content yourself with merely understanding the formula in an intellectual sense. You try to see what is really happening – because it's happening to you, it's happening in you. It's your own reactive mind that you are studying with the help of this framework.

What goes on in your mind as you do the meditation might be something like this. As you say to yourself, 'ignorance, ignorance,' you see in your mind's eye, if you like, a sort of great, pitch-black darkness. This is the darkness of ignorance. No light. No awareness. Consciousness has not arisen. And as you ponder on this, you see emerging out of this darkness, arising in dependence upon this darkness and blindness and ignorance, various actions of will, various strivings and volitions. But you see that these volitions are dull and dim and blind because they emerge out of that darkness. In this way, you see very clearly in the meditation all sorts of unaware, blind, thoughtless actions arising out of the fundamental, primordial state of ignorance which is within oneself.

Then you see how, as those volitions stumble on, as they bump into this and that, they get a bit more sensitive, a bit more aware, and just a tiny glimmering of consciousness arises. You see the little seed of individuality, tiny, frail, and flimsy, and how it gradually develops into a psychophysical organism – into a mind and body. You see the psychophysical organism developing different senses – of reason, of sight, of hearing, and so on. Then, as the organism comes into contact with the world through those senses, you see it experiencing all sorts of sensations – some painful, some pleasurable. You see it shrinking away from the painful sensations and trying to hang on to the pleasant sensations, becoming attached to them, and finally enslaved by them –

conditioned by them. This process goes on and on like a wheel rolling. And so the wheel of life takes another turn.

As you continue to meditate, you see how your own mind works in this way. You see how you experience sensations – sights, sounds, smells, tastes, feelings, thoughts – and react to them. You like this, you want more of it. You feel sad or angry when it's over. You don't like that, you want to avoid it – you even hate it. The more you can see your own psychological conditioning at work in this way, seeing it objectively at the same time that you are experiencing it subjectively, the more you become free from it. You become free from your own psychological conditioning to the extent you see it. You become aware to the extent that you see you are unaware. And you can do this with the help of the traditional formula of the twelve links of the chain of conditioned co-production. You can certainly achieve the same sort of results with the help of a more contemporary psychological analysis of the process, if that is more appealing. What is essential, however, is to be able to see that your mind is not spontaneous and creative, but merely reactive, machine-like, and unaware. It is through seeing this that you gradually free yourself of spiritual ignorance.

Until we have completely freed ourselves from ignorance in this way, our death is simply the prelude to our rebirth, which takes place on account of the residue of craving, aversion, and ignorance left in the individual stream of consciousness at the time of death. In other words, if you have died with your passions unexhausted, if there is something that you still want, if there is something for which you still crave, something to which you are still attached – whether it is spouse and family, or riches, or name and fame, or even Buddhism perhaps – then you will have to come back. You will be drawn back by the power of your desire into a new body and a fresh incarnation.

But in the course of spiritual practice, one is gradually able to eliminate these three poisons. Cravings are attenuated, aversion is abated, ignorance is dispelled. In the end there is only a state of peace, a state of love, a state of wisdom. One is no longer bound to the wheel. One no longer has to come back. When one dies, when the consciousness slips out – or flashes out – of the physical body, there is nothing to draw it back. It remains on the higher, archetypal, even transcendental plane of existence. It remains in Nirvāna, the state of undisturbed Buddhahood. In other words, there is no need for any further rebirth.

At this point, according to Mahāyāna Buddhism, two possibilities, two different paths, disclose themselves. Having got this far, one alternative is just to remain there. One can allow oneself to disappear into Nirvāṇa, to disappear from the ken of the world, slipping into Nirvāṇa like 'the dewdrop ... into the shining sea.'[136] Or, on the other hand, one can turn back and decide quite voluntarily to be reborn – not because there is any residue of karma left unaccounted for, but out of compassion, so that one can continue to help other living beings in the world through the spiritual experience which one has gained.

This is the story told, for instance, about the great bodhisattva Avalokiteśvara, whose name means 'the one who looks down' – looks down, that is to say, in compassion. It is said that many, many centuries ago, Avalokiteśvara was a monk, a yogi, who practised meditation in a cave in the Himalayas for many years – in fact, for the greater part of his life. Then at last a moment came when he found himself on the very brink of Enlightenment. He ascended from one stage of superconsciousness to another, going further and further and further away from the world. He passed through all sorts of archetypal, paradisal realms, and saw all sorts of glorious figures. Then all these experiences faded away, and he came to the shore of a great ocean of light. He could see and hear nothing but this ocean of light, and he experienced tremendous joy and happiness that at last he was returning to his source, returning to his origins, and was going to be merged with Reality itself. With a great sigh of relief, he started to let himself go, to slip into that ocean of light.

But at that very moment, we are told, he heard a sound, a faint sound which seemed to be coming from a very long way away. At first he didn't know what it was, but it arrested his attention, and he began to listen. As he listened, the sound became a texture of many sounds, many voices, and they were all crying out, wailing, weeping, lamenting, grieving. The sound seemed to get louder and louder, until at last he turned his eyes away from the great ocean of light and looked down. He looked down right into the depths, right down to this world. And he saw in this world millions of living beings, suffering in various ways due to their spiritual ignorance. Then the thought came to him, 'How can I leave these beings? How can I allow myself to merge into this ocean of light, just saving myself, when in the world below there are so many beings who need my help and guidance?' He turned back. He not only looked down – he *went* down. He chose the path that led back into the world.

The option which Avalokiteśvara eschewed, the path of allowing oneself to be merged into Nirvāṇa, is the path of the *arhant*, the one who desires his or her own individual salvation. And the path he took, the path back down into the world, is the path of the bodhisattva, the one who desires not just his or her own emancipation, but the liberation and Enlightenment of all living beings. The bodhisattva is not satisfied until he can gather all living beings in his arms and take them with him into Buddhahood.

The path of the bodhisattva is traditionally regarded as being higher than that of the *arhant*, but the distinction between the two paths is not as black and white as all that. In a sense the bodhisattva path includes and contains the path of the *arhant* because one must at least have the capacity to gain liberation for oneself and remain in Nirvāṇa for one's renunciation of that to have any meaning. Otherwise, following the bodhisattva ideal can turn into a rationalization of one's attachment to the world.

We could say that the bodhisattva ideal was implicit in the Buddha's own experience of Enlightenment, and that his decision to teach was a natural expression of the Enlightenment experience. And the bodhisattva ideal is, as Marco Pallis observes,[137] the presiding idea of Tibetan Buddhism. For Tibetan Buddhists it is a real, living thing, and one which they take very seriously indeed. They believe strongly that there are living in the world people who have made this great renunciation, this great sacrifice, people who have truly turned their backs on Nirvāṇa and who have returned to the world to help in the higher evolution of humanity towards Enlightenment. For the Tibetans, the bodhisattva ideal is a living reality.

Religious differences cannot be judged on this sort of issue. The view professed by a typical Roman Catholic commentator, for example, goes something like this: 'Well, the bodhisattva ideal is very beautiful, but it's a beautiful dream. There are no bodhisattvas in the world. The ideal of Christianity, the ideal of the crucified Christ, is a historical reality, but the bodhisattva ideal is just a sort of spiritual pipe-dream conjured up by the indolent Buddhist, lying on his couch in the East with nothing better to do than dream beautiful spiritual dreams.'

But it isn't like that for Tibetan Buddhists. They regard bodhisattvas as being very much with us, as being bound up with the spiritual economy of the world. They believe very strongly that there are bodhisattvas living in the world, and that it is possible to identify them. Not only is it possible; it is standard practice. Tibetans take it as read that highly spiritually advanced teachers can direct their rebirth. When a *tulku* or incarnate lama dies, his disciples embark on a search for his new incarnation, the young child he has been reborn as. When the child is discovered (or rather the *tulku* is rediscovered) he is given the traditional education in the Dharma that enables him to take up his bodhisattva activity from where he left off in his previous life. The most famous of these *tulkus* is of course the Dalai Lama, whom the Tibetans regard as a manifestation of Avalokiteśvara himself, and who is both the spiritual leader of Tibet and – *de jure* if not *de facto* – its temporal ruler. Through the centuries he has been reborn again and again to give his guidance to Tibet, the present Dalai Lama being the fourteenth in the lineage.

To be drawn back into rebirth, to continue to circle round in the wheel of life, not through the poisons of craving, hatred, and ignorance, but out of compassion, requires spiritual awareness in the highest degree. And this we can begin to develop – remembering that a journey of a thousand miles begins with a single step – through meditating on the chain of conditioned co-production.

The fifth and last poison is *māna*, 'conceit', sometimes translated as pride, but really more like high-mindedness, or even high-and-mightiness. Pride is having a strong sense of 'I', 'me', 'mine', so in overcoming it you need to attack the whole 'I' feeling, especially as applied to the body. The method of meditation by which you launch this attack is called the contemplation of the six elements – these being earth, water, fire, air, space, and consciousness.[138]

You begin, once again, by generating a calm, happy state of concentration. Then, as you're sitting meditating, you start to think about the element earth, and try to get a feeling for what it is. 'Earth. Earth.' It's everything solid, everything cohesive. You can think of all sorts of things in the objective world that are solid – natural things like trees and rocks, man-made things like houses and books – all this is the element earth. Then you think, 'Not only is there the element of earth in the external world; there is also earth in the internal world, the subjective world, which is me. My bones, my flesh, are derivatives of the element earth. Where have my bones come from? Where has my flesh come from? Where has the earth element in me come from? It's come from the earth element outside me. It's not mine. I've borrowed it. I've taken it from the earth element outside myself for a short time and incorporated it into my own being, my own substance, my own body, but I'm not going to be able to keep it forever. After a few decades, after a few years – maybe sooner, who knows? – I'll have to give it back. Sooner or later the earth element in my body will be resolved into the earth element in the objective world. So how can I say of that earth element that it is mine, how can I say of it that it is me? It isn't mine, it isn't me. I've got to give it back. So all right, I'll let it go. It's not me. I can't claim to possess it. I can't identify with it.'

In the same way you take the element water. 'Water. Water.' The water element is in whatever is fluid, liquid, flowing. In the world outside you find it in rivers, you find it in oceans, streams, rain, dew; and within you there's also a water element: blood, bile, tears, and so on. Where have you got that water from? Obviously from outside – and when you die, it has to go back where it came from. It doesn't belong to you, it isn't you – so let it go, cease to identify with it.

'Fire. Fire.' The fire element in the external world is the sun, the source of all the warmth and light of the solar system. There's warmth in us too, but where does it come from? It comes from the fire element in the external world. So again you reflect: 'One day I will have to give it back. I can't hold on to it for long. When I die, I'll go cold. Heat will disappear, leave the body. The fire element in me which is at the moment doing all sorts of things in my body – digesting my food and so on – is not really mine. It doesn't belong to me. I can't identify with it. So let it go. Let the heat element in me go back to the heat element in the universe.'

'Air. Air.' You think, 'There's air in the external world, obviously – there's this atmosphere which envelops the whole earth – and then in me there's the breath of life, which I'm inhaling and exhaling all the time. But I've only borrowed it for a short while. It's not mine. A time will come when I'll breathe in and breathe out, breathe in, breathe out – and then I won't breathe in again. I'll be dead, and there won't be any more breath left in my body. I'll have given it back for the last time. I can't say of the air element in me that it's me or mine. So let it go. I won't identify with it.'

'Space. Space. The body made up of the first four elements, with which I identify myself, occupies space. When the earth element goes from my body, when the water element goes, when the fire element and the air element go, what will be left? Nothing. Just an empty me-shaped space. So what is to differentiate that me-shaped space from the surrounding space? Nothing at all.' The Indian tradition says that just as if you break a clay pot, the space inside the pot merges with the space outside it, so that there's no difference any more; just so, when the body disintegrates, the space that was occupied by your physical body merges back into the universal space. You don't exist any more, so how can you hang on to this physical body which at the moment occupies space? You can't. So let that space which you are occupying merge into the universal space.

Sixthly and lastly, 'Consciousness. Consciousness.' There's the consciousness associated with your physical body. You might say, 'Even if I'm not earth, even if I'm not water, or fire, or air, or even space, surely I am consciousness?' But no. Even consciousness is borrowed. Even what you call your consciousness is a sort of reflection, a gleam, of a higher, more universal consciousness, which is you in a sense, yes, but in another sense is very definitely not you. It's like the relationship between the waking state and the dream state. When you're awake, you can think in terms of 'having' a dream, but when you're dreaming, where are 'you'? It's as though the dream is having you. Similarly, in the case of the higher dimension of consciousness which we identify with 'me', the consciousness is there, but the 'me' has to go. So even individuality in that 'I' sense goes. It's as though the lower consciousness has to merge itself in the higher consciousness – but being consciousness (or at least conscious) without thereby being destroyed. There is no loss of consciousness, but consciousness is no longer centred on the 'I'. At the same time, paradoxically, in another sense you were never more completely yourself.

So this is the contemplation of the six elements, designed to counteract the poison of pride, and the last of the five basic meditation practices. However, there is another meditation practice based on the six elements, or at least the first five of them, and it brings us back to where we began – the Buddha's *parinirvāṇa*. In this practice you visualize the five elements symbolized by different geometrical figures of different colours. First of all you visualize a great yellow cube. This represents earth. On top of the yellow cube, a great white sphere or globe, representing water. Next, on top of the white sphere, a brilliant red cone or pyramid – fire. Then, balanced on the point of the cone or pyramid, a blue saucer-shape: that's air. Finally, in that saucer-shape is a golden flame, which symbolizes space, or ether. And if you like, the tip of the golden flame can be rainbow-coloured – it can end in a rainbow-like jewel – and that will be consciousness.

These are the geometrical symbols of the five or six elements, and when you arrange them in this order, one on top of another, they add up to something else: the stupa – and the meditation is therefore called the stupa visualization. The stupa is of particular significance in this context, because it was originally a funeral monument of a rather special kind. Sometimes it contained ashes, and sometimes these ashes were those of someone held in very great reverence. In Buddhist history and tradition, the stupa is especially associated with the *parinirvāṇa* of the Buddha. In fact, in early Buddhist art, the stupa is the symbol of the *parinirvāṇa* itself.

This symbolic representation of the Buddha is an interesting and significant feature of archaic stone carvings by Buddhist artists – and the stupa is just one of a rich iconographic series. Sometimes he is represented simply by a pair of footprints, but there are all sorts of other symbols. In the case of a treatment of the Buddha's birth, the place of the infant Buddha is taken by a lotus flower. Where you get Siddhārtha leaving home, going into the jungle in quest of truth, you see the horse charging out of the palace gate, but there's only an umbrella over the horse's back to indicate where the figure would be. In the scene of the Buddha's Enlightenment, you see the bodhi tree, you see the throne, but the throne is empty – or there may just be a trident representing the Three Jewels. In the scene of the Buddha's first discourse, there are the five monks listening, there is the seat of the teacher, there are deer around, but what the five monks are apparently listening to is a wheel, a *dharmacakra* – the wheel of the Dharma. In other contexts the Buddha is represented by the bodhi tree under which he gained Enlightenment – so you would have, say, the figure of Māra, the evil one, raising his club against the Buddha, but with no sign of the Buddha's presence in the scene apart from the bodhi tree. And likewise, in the earliest depictions of the Buddha's *parinirvāṇa*, instead of the figure of the Buddha lying on the stone couch under the sāl trees which you see in the art of the later Chinese and Japanese traditions, there is just a stupa to represent the presence of the Buddha.

There is, of course, a reason for all this. The early Buddhists, it seems, felt very strongly that the Buddha is incommensurable, unrepresentable, transcendental. A Buddha's nature is beyond thought, beyond speech, beyond words. When you come to speak of it, all you can do is remain silent. When you are drawing or carving a scene from the Buddha's life, and you come to the Buddha himself, all you can do is leave an empty space, or just a symbol. You can't represent the Buddha; the Buddha is beyond representation.

Although later artists did feel able to represent the Buddha, symbols like the wheel of the Dharma, the bodhi tree, and perhaps particularly the stupa, have remained potent expressions of Enlightenment. Stupas built in various architectural forms are distinctive parts of the landscape throughout the Buddhist East, and small ones cast in brass or turned in wood are often kept in their homes by Buddhists as a reminder that one day we must all give the elements which we think of as 'me' back to the universe. All of us – even the Buddha – must die.

9
WHO IS THE BUDDHA?

By now we know a good deal about the Buddha. We know that he was born in the Lumbinī garden, we know how he was educated, we know how he left home, how he gained Enlightenment at the age of thirty-five, how he communicated his teaching, how he founded his sangha, and how, finally, he passed away. And there is a good deal more we could find out. The traditional biographies give us all the facts. We could find out the names of the Buddha's half-brothers and cousins, the name of the town where he was brought up, the name of the astrologer who came to see him as a baby. But although his life is fully documented, although we've got the whole story, does his biography really tell us who the Buddha was? Do we know the Buddha from a description of the life of Gautama the Buddha?

What do we mean by 'knowing' the Buddha anyway? In what sense, really, do we know anybody? Suppose you are told all about some-one: where they live, what they do – the sort of things people always want to know about a person – how old they are, and so on. In some sense you have an answer to the question, 'Who is this person?' You know their social identity, their position in society. Gradually you can fill in any number of details – how tall they are, their accent, their background, their taste in food and music, their political affiliations and their religious beliefs. You can then say you know *about* this person. But however much you know *about* someone, you would not claim to *know* them until you'd met them at least once, and perhaps a few times. You'd then know them *personally*. This deeper knowledge would be based on a relationship, on communication: you know someone, properly speaking, when they also know you. Eventually you may claim to know this person very well.

But is it really so? Do you really know them? After all, it sometimes happens that we have to correct our evaluation of someone. Sometimes we are taken completely by surprise. They do something quite unexpected, quite 'out of character', and we say to ourselves, rather surprised and sometimes a little hurt, 'Well, I never would have expected them to do that. They're the last person I'd have thought would do such a thing.' But they did it, and this shows how little we really know other people. We are not truly able to fathom the deepest springs of their action, their fundamental motivation. This happens even with those who are supposedly nearest and dearest to us. It's a wise child that knows its own father, as the saying goes – and it's a wise father or mother who knows his or her own child.

Particularly, perhaps, it is a wise husband who knows his own wife, and a wise wife who knows her own husband. Sometimes I've had the experience of meeting – separately – a husband and wife, each having come to talk to me about the other. And usually what happens is that each gives a picture of the other that I would never have recognized. The impression I've had is that neither really knows the other. It's as though the so-called closeness gets in the way, and what we know is not the other person to whom we are supposed to be so close, but only our own projected mental state, our own quite subjective reaction to that person. In other words, our ego gets in the way.

In order really to know another person we have to go much deeper than the ordinary level of communication – which means, in effect, that ordinary communication is not real communication at all. It's just the same when it comes to knowing the Buddha. We may know all the biographical facts about his life, but are we thereby any nearer really knowing the Buddha? Well, no. The question continues to arise: Who was the Buddha? This question has been asked since the very dawn of Buddhism.

For example, the scriptures tell us about an occasion when someone had the opportunity to ask the Buddha directly, 'Who are you?' The man who asked the question was a Brahmin called Doṇa, who, walking along the road one day, found himself following in someone's footsteps. It was the footprints that attracted his attention, in fact; there was something about them that was extraordinary. Indeed, they were marked with the thousand-spoked wheel which is said to be one of the marks of a Buddha. It is said that the Buddha sat down to meditate by the side of the road, so Doṇa, following his footprints, caught up with him. Seeing this calm, serene, joyful figure seated there, Doṇa couldn't help asking him, 'Who are you?' There was no opening preamble: 'Lovely weather we're having,' or 'Where are you from?' He just blurted out, 'Who are you?' If you were standing at the bus stop waiting for the bus into town and someone came up and said, 'Who are you?' you'd probably think they were being rather impertinent, but in India, it's different, and Doṇa could put this question without fear of giving offence. The point is that Doṇa was not asking who the Buddha was in social terms; he was not asking what sort of a human being the Buddha was. He was, in fact, wondering whether the figure in front of him was really a human being at all.

The ancient Indians believed that the universe was stratified into various levels of existence. There were not just human beings and animals, as we tend to think. There were also gods and ghosts and *yakṣas* and *gandharvas* – all sorts of mythological beings – inhabiting a sort of multi-storey universe. The human plane was just one out of scores of planes of existence. Doṇa's first thought, therefore, impressed as he was by the appearance of the Buddha, was, 'This isn't a human being. He must be from – or on his way to – some other realm. Perhaps he's a sort of spirit.' So he asked the Buddha, 'Who are you? Are you a *deva*?' – a *deva* being a god, a divine being, a sort of archangel. The Buddha simply said, 'No.' So Doṇa tried again. 'Are you a *gandharva*?' This creature is like a kind of celestial musician, a beautiful, singing, angelic figure. The Buddha again said, 'No.' 'Well,' said Doṇa, 'Are you a *yakṣa*?' A *yakṣa* is a sort of sublime spirit, rather a terrifying one, who lives in the jungle. But the Buddha rejected this designation as well. Then Doṇa thought, 'He must be a human being after all. That's strange.' So he asked, 'Are you a human being?' (the kind of question you could only ask in ancient India) and once again the Buddha said, 'No.' 'Well, that *is* odd,' Doṇa thought. 'If he isn't a *deva*, or a *gandharva*, or a *yakṣa*, or a human being, what on earth is he?' 'Who are you?' he asked, now even more wonderingly. 'If you are none of these things, who are you? What are you?'

The Buddha said, 'Those conditions (perhaps a better translation would be 'those psychological conditionings') on account of which I might have been described as a *deva* or a *gandharva* or a *yakṣa* or a human being have been destroyed. Therefore am I a Buddha.' It is, as we have seen, these conditioned mental attitudes, volitions, or karma formations as they are sometimes called, which according to Buddhism (and Indian belief in general) determine our rebirth, as well as our human condition here and now. The Buddha was free from all this, free from all conditioning, so there was nothing to cause him to be reborn as a god or a *gandharva*, or even a human being. Even as he stood before this Brahmin, therefore, he was not any of these things. His body might appear to be that of a man, but his mind, his consciousness, was unconditioned, and therefore he was a Buddha. As a Buddha he was a personification, so to speak – even, if you like, an incarnation – of the Unconditioned mind.[139]

What Doṇa tried to do is what we all try to do when we meet something new. The human mind proceeds slowly, by degrees, from the known to the unknown, and we try to describe the unknown in terms of the known; which is fair enough so long as one is aware of the limitations of this procedure. And we may say that the limitations of this procedure are most pronounced when it comes to trying to know other human beings.

There always seems to be a basic tendency to want to put people in categories and think that we have thereby got them neatly pigeon-holed. When I lived in India I was often stopped in the road by someone just passing, and they would say, 'What is your caste?' – without any sort of preamble. This used to be, and I'm afraid sometimes still is, an important question in India. If someone can't classify you according to caste, they don't know how to treat you. They don't know whether they can take water from your hand or not, whether they can get to know you or not, whether you might marry their daughter or not. In Britain people are much more indirect in their approach, but they try to worm out of you the same sort of information. They want to know what sort of job you've got (and perhaps from that they try to work out your income), they want to know where you were born, where you were educated, where you live now, and by taking these various sociological readings, they gradually narrow down the field, and think they've got you nicely pinned down.

So likewise, when Doṇa saw this majestic, radiant figure, and wanted to know who – or what – it was, he had at his disposal various labels – *gandharva*, *yakṣa*, *deva*, human being – and he tried to stick these labels on what he saw. But the Buddha wouldn't have it. His reply said, in effect, 'None of these labels fit. None of them apply. I'm a Buddha. I transcend all conditionings. I am above and beyond all this.'

Doṇa may have been one of the first people to puzzle over the Buddha's nature, but he was certainly not the last. We have already come across four of the Fourteen Inexpressibles: whether the Buddha would exist after death, or not, or both, or neither. Although the Buddha was constantly being asked about this, he would always say that it was inappropriate to apply any of those four statements to a Buddha. And he would go on to say, 'Even during his lifetime, even when he sits there in a physical body, the Buddha is beyond all your classifications. You can't say anything about him.'[140]

This point is easily made, of course, but very difficult to accept, and it evidently needed to be constantly hammered home. The most suggestive and evocative repudiation of any attempt to grasp the nature of the Buddha is found in the *Dhammapada*: 'That Enlightened One whose sphere is endless, whose victory is irreversible, and after whose victory no (defilements) remain (to be conquered), by what track will you lead him (astray), the Trackless One?'[141] According to this verse, there is absolutely nothing by which a Buddha can be identified or tracked down or classified or categorized. You cannot trace the path of a bird's flight by looking for signs of its passage in the sky – and you cannot track a Buddha either.

If this is clear, however, it has not really been understood. It is somehow the nature of the human mind to keep on trying, and to imagine that, having understood what is being said, it understands what it is that is being spoken of. So if we turn to the *Sutta Nipāta*, we find the Buddha saying:

There is no measuring of man,
Won to the goal, whereby they'd say
His measure's so: that's not for him.
When all conditions are removed,
All ways of telling are removed.[142]

When all psychological conditions are removed in a person, you have no way of accounting for that person. You can't say anything about the Buddha because he doesn't have anything. In a sense, he isn't anything. In fact, we are introduced in this *sutta* to an epithet for an Enlightened being that says just this. *Akiñcana*, usually translated as 'man of nought', is one who has nothing because he is nothing. And of nothing, nothing can be said.[143]

Although many of the Buddha's disciples gained Enlightenment, and themselves went through the world leaving no trace, as it were, they still worshipped the Buddha. They still felt there was something about the man who discovered the Way for himself with no one to guide him that was mysteriously beyond them and unfathomable. Even his chief disciple, Śāriputra, floundered when it came to estimating the Buddha's stature. He was once in the presence of the Buddha when, out of an excess of faith and devotion, he exclaimed, 'Lord, I think you are the greatest of all the Enlightened Ones who have ever existed, or will exist, or exist now.' The Buddha was neither pleased nor displeased by this. He didn't say, 'What a marvellous disciple you are, and how wonderfully well you understand me!' He just asked a question: 'Śāriputra, have you known all the Buddhas of the past?' Śāriputra said, 'No, Lord.' Then he said, 'Have you known all the Buddhas of the future?' 'No, Lord.' 'Do you know all the Buddhas that now are?' 'No, Lord.' Finally, the Buddha asked 'Do you even know me?' And Śāriputra said, 'No, Lord.' Then the Buddha said, 'That being the case, Śāriputra, how is it that your words are so bold and so grand?'[144]

So even the closest of his disciples didn't really know who the Buddha was. To try to make sense of this attitude, they put together, after his death, a list of ten powers and eighteen special qualities which they attributed to the Buddha just to distinguish him from his Enlightened disciples.[145] But in a way this was just an expression of the fact that they simply could not understand who or what he was at all.

This fact that the Enlightened disciples of the Buddha, enjoying personal contact with him, did not understand who he really was does not say much for our own chances in the matter. However, at a certain level, we can build up a collection of hints and clues, and the episode with Doṇa offers an important lead. What it suggests is that we have to step back and bring in a whole new dimension to our search for the Buddha. He is untraceable because he belongs to a different dimension, the transcendental dimension, the dimension of eternity.

So far we have seen him very much in terms of time – his birth, his Enlightenment, his death – his historical existence. We have, in fact, been looking at him according to the evolutionary model we introduced in the first chapter, which model is, of course, one of progress through space and time. This, however, is only one way of looking at things. As well as looking at the Buddha from the standpoint of time, we can also look at him from the standpoint of eternity.

The problem with any biographical account of the Buddha is that in a sense it deals with two quite different people: Siddhārtha and the Buddha – divided by the central event of the Enlightenment. One tends to come away from the biographical facts with the view that his early life simply built up to this point, and that after it he was more or less the same as he was before – apart from being Enlightened, of course. If we had been around at the time we should probably have been none the wiser. If we had known the Buddha a few months before he was Enlightened and a few months after, we should almost certainly not have been able to perceive any difference in him at all. We would have seen the same physical body, probably the same clothes. He spoke the same language and had the same general characteristics. This being so, we tend to regard the Buddha's Enlightenment as a finishing touch to a process which had been going on for a long time, the feather that turned the scale, the final piece of the jigsaw, that little difference that made all the difference. But really it isn't like that at all – not in the least like that.

Enlightenment – the Buddha's or anybody else's – represents 'the intersection of the timeless moment'.[146] We need to modify T. S. Eliot's analogy a little, because strictly speaking only a line can intersect another line, and although we can represent time as a line, the whole point of the timeless – eternity – is that it isn't a line. Perhaps we should think rather in terms of time as a line which at a given point just stops, just disappears into another dimension. It's rather like – to use a hackneyed but (if we don't take it too literally) rather useful simile – the flowing of a river into the ocean, where the river is time and the ocean is eternity. Perhaps, indeed, we can improve on the simile to some extent. Suppose we imagine that the ocean into which our river is flowing is just over the horizon. From where we are, we can see the river flowing to the horizon, but we can't see the ocean into which the river is flowing, so it seems as though the river is flowing into nothingness, into a void. It just stops at the horizon because that is the point at which it enters the new dimension which we cannot see.

The point of intersection is what we call Enlightenment. Time just stops at eternity; time is succeeded, so to speak, by eternity. Siddhārtha disappears, like the river disappearing at the horizon, and the Buddha takes his place. This is, of course, from the standpoint of eternity. Whereas from the standpoint of time Siddhārtha *becomes*, evolves into, the Buddha, from the standpoint of eternity Siddhārtha just ceases to exist, and there is the Buddha, who has been there all the time.

This difference of approach – in terms of time and in terms of eternity – is at the bottom of the whole controversy between the two schools of Zen, the gradual school and the abrupt school. In the early days of Zen (or rather Chan) in China, there were two apparently opposing viewpoints: there were those who believed that Enlightenment was attained in a sudden flash of illumination; and there were those who believed that it was attained gradually, step by step, by patient effort and practice. In the *Platform Sūtra* Huineng tries to clear up the whole controversy. He says it isn't that there are two paths, a gradual one and a sudden one; it is merely that some people gain Enlightenment more quickly than others, presumably because they make a greater effort.[147]

This is true, but we can go deeper. The abrupt attainment of Enlightenment, we may say, has nothing to do with speed within time. It doesn't mean that you begin the usual process of attaining Enlightenment and get through it more quickly. It doesn't mean that whereas you might normally spend fifteen or fifty years on the gradual path, you are somehow able to speed it up and compress it into a year, or even a month, or a week, or a weekend. The abrupt path is outside time altogether. Sudden Enlightenment is simply the point at which this new dimension of eternity outside time is entered. You can never get closer to eternity by speeding up your approach to it within time. Within time you just have to stop. At the same time, of course, you can't stop without first having speeded up. So Enlightenment can be looked at from two points of view, both of which are valid. It can be regarded as the culmination of the evolutionary process, a culmination which is reached through personal effort. But Enlightenment can also be regarded as being a sort of breakthrough into a new dimension beyond time and space.

There is a rather picturesque story which vividly illustrates the paradoxical meeting of these two dimensions. It concerns a famous bandit, called Aṅgulimāla, who lived in a great forest somewhere in northern India. Aṅgulimāla's speciality was to ambush travellers on their way through the forest, murder them, and chop off one of their fingers as a trophy. These fingers he strung into a garland which he wore round his neck; hence his name, Aṅgulimāla, meaning 'garland of fingers'. It was his ambition to have one hundred fingers on his garland (some versions of the story say a thousand), and he had got to ninety-nine when the Buddha happened to pass through that forest. The village folk had tried to dissuade him from entering it, warning him that he was in danger of losing a finger – and his life – to the notorious Aṅgulimāla, but the Buddha had carried on regardless. The sight of him just about made Aṅgulimāla's day. He had been getting so desperate to find the last finger for his garland that he was even considering killing his mother. He was on his way to find his poor old mother when he saw the Buddha coming through the forest and saw his chance to get that last finger.

It was a beautiful afternoon, a gentle breeze stirring the tree-tops and the birds singing, when the Buddha came walking along the little trail that wound through the forest. He walked meditatively, slowly, thinking to himself or, perhaps, not thinking at all. Aṅgulimāla emerged from the forest, and stealthily began to follow the Buddha, creeping up on him from behind. He had his sword drawn ready, so he could make very quick work of his prey when he got close to him. He loped along smoothly and rapidly to cut down the distance between them before he was seen. The last thing he wanted was a long, messy struggle.

After he had followed the Buddha for a while, however, he noticed that something rather odd was happening. Although he seemed to be moving much more quickly than the Buddha, he didn't seem to be getting any closer to him. There was the Buddha way in front, pacing slowly, and there was Aṅgulimāla shadowing him and trying to catch up, but not getting any nearer. Aṅgulimāla quickened his pace until he was running, but he still got no nearer to the Buddha. When Aṅgulimāla realized what was happening, he apparently broke into a cold sweat of terror and astonishment and bewilderment. But he was not a man to give up easily – or to stop and think about things either. He just lengthened his stride till he was sprinting along in the wake of the Buddha. The

Buddha, however, stayed just the same distance ahead, and if anything he seemed to be going even more slowly. It was like a bad dream.

In desperation, Aṅgulimāla called out to the Buddha: 'Stand still!' The Buddha turned round and said, 'I am standing still. It is you who are moving.' So Aṅgulimāla, who had considerable presence of mind despite his fear – for he was a bold fellow – said, 'You are supposed to be a śramaṇa, a holy man. How can you tell such a lie? Here am I running like mad, and I can't catch up with you. What do you mean, you are standing still?' The Buddha said, 'I am standing still because I am standing in Nirvāṇa. I have come to rest. You are moving because you are going round and round in saṃsāra.'[148]

Of course, Aṅgulimāla became the Buddha's disciple, but that, and what happened afterwards, is another story. The point I want to make is that Aṅgulimāla could not catch up with the Buddha because the Buddha was moving – or standing still, it is the same thing here – in another dimension. Aṅgulimāla, representing time, couldn't catch up with the Buddha, representing eternity. However long time goes on, it never comes to a point where it catches up with eternity. Time doesn't find eternity within the temporal process. Aṅgulimāla couldn't have caught up with the Buddha even if the Buddha had come to a complete halt. He could still be running now, after 2,500 years, but he still wouldn't have caught up with the Buddha.

When the Buddha attained Enlightenment, he entered a new dimension of being. There was no continuity, essentially, from the person who was there before. He was not just the old Siddhārtha slightly improved, or even considerably improved, but a new person. This is a very difficult thing for us to grasp, and needs reflecting on, because we naturally think of the Buddha's Enlightenment in terms of our own experience. In the course of our lives we may add to our knowledge, learn different things, do different things, go to different places, meet different people, and life teaches us things – but underneath we remain fundamentally and recognizably the same person. Whatever changes take place don't go very deep. In the poet Wordsworth's phrase, 'The child is father to the man' – that is, what one is now is determined to a remarkable degree by what one was as a child. One remains much the same person as one was then. The conditions for one's fundamental attitude to life were set up a long time ago, and any change that takes place subsequently is comparatively superficial. This even applies to our commitment to a spiritual path. We may take to Buddhism, we may 'go for Refuge' to the Buddha, but the change isn't usually very deep.

But the Buddha's experience of Enlightenment wasn't like that. In reality it wasn't an experience at all, because the person to have the experience wasn't there any more. The 'experience' of Enlightenment is therefore more like death. It is more like the change that takes place between two lives, when you die to one life and are reborn in another. In the Zen tradition Enlightenment is sometimes called 'the great death', because everything of the past dies; everything, in a way, is annihilated, and you are completely reborn. In the case of the Buddha, it is not that he was a smartened up version of Siddhārtha, Siddhārtha tinkered about with a bit, reissued in a new edition. Siddhārtha was finished. At the foot of the bodhi tree Siddhārtha died and the Buddha was born – or we should say, rather, that he 'appeared'. At that moment, when Siddhārtha dies, the Buddha is seen as having been alive all the time – by which we really mean above and beyond time, out of time altogether.

Even to talk in this way is misleading, however, because it is not as if, being outside time, you are really outside anything. Time and space are not things in themselves. We usually think of space as a sort of box within which things move about, and time as a sort of tunnel along which things move – but they are not really like that. Space and time are really forms of our perception. We see things through the spectacles, as it were, of space and time, and we speak of these things that we see as phenomena – which are, of course, what make up the world of relative, conditioned existence, or *saṃsāra*. But what we call phenomena are only realities as seen under the forms of space and time, and when we enter the dimension of eternity, we go beyond space and time, and therefore we go beyond the world, we go beyond *saṃsāra*, and, in the Buddhist idiom, we enter Nirvāṇa.

Enlightenment is often described as awakening to the truth of things, seeing things as they really are, not as they appear to be. The Enlightened person sees things free from any veils or obscurations, sees them without being influenced or affected by any assumptions or psychological conditionings, sees them with perfect objectivity – not only sees them, but becomes one with them, one with the reality of things. So the Buddha, the one who has awoken to the Truth, the one who exists out of time in the dimension of eternity, may be regarded as Reality itself in human form. This is what is meant by saying that the Buddha is an Enlightened human being: the form is human, but in the place, so to speak, of the conditioned human mind, with all its prejudices and preconceptions and limitations, there is Reality itself, there is an experience or awareness which is not separate from Reality.

In the Buddhist tradition this crystallized eventually into a very important distinction which came to be established with regard to the Buddha. On the one hand there was his *rūpakāya* (literally 'form body'), his physical phenomenal appearance; on the other, there was, or rather *is*, his *dharmakāya* (literally 'body of Truth' or 'body of Reality'), his true, his essential, form. The *rūpakāya* is the Buddha as existing in time, but the *dharmakāya* is the Buddha as existing out of time in the dimension of eternity.[149] Where the true nature of the Buddha lies, in his *rūpakāya* or his *dharmakāya*, is declared definitively in a chapter from one of the great Perfection of Wisdom texts, the *Diamond Sūtra*. In it the Buddha says to his disciple, Subhūti:

Those who by my form did see me,
Those who followed me by voice,
Wrong the effort they engaged in.
Me those people will not see.

From the Dharma should one see the Buddhas,
From the Dharma-bodies comes their guidance.
Yet Dharma's true nature cannot be discerned,
And no one can be conscious of it as an object.[150]

The Buddha is found to be equally emphatic on this point in the Pāli tradition. According to the *Dhammapada Commentary* there was a monk called Vakkali who was very devoted to the Buddha, but his devotion had got stuck at a superficial level. He was so fascinated by the appearance and the personality of the Buddha that he used to spend all his time sitting and looking at him, or following him around. He didn't want any teaching. He didn't have any questions to ask. He just wanted to look at the Buddha. So one day the Buddha called him and said, 'Vakkali, this physical body is not me. If you want to see me, you must see the Dharma, you must see the *dharmakāya*, my true form.'[151]

Vakkali's problem is one that most of us have. It's not that we should ignore the physical body, but we should take it as a symbol of the *dharmakāya*, the Buddha as he is in his ultimate essence. That said, it must be admitted that the word Buddha is ambiguous. When, for instance, we say, 'The Buddha spoke the language of Magadha,' we are obviously referring to Gautama the Buddha, the historical figure. On other occasions, however, 'Buddha' means the transcendental Reality, as when we say, 'Look for the Buddha within yourself.' Here we don't mean Gautama the Buddha; we mean the eternal, time-transcending Buddha-nature within ourselves. Broadly speaking, the Theravāda School today uses the word Buddha more in the historical sense, whereas the Mahāyāna, especially Zen, tends to use it more in the spiritual, trans-historical sense.

The shifting usage of this word only adds to the confusion Westerners are liable to feel when it comes to identifying the Buddha. Like Doṇa, we want to know who the Buddha is, we want to slap a label on him. But our Western, dualistic, Christian background provides us with only two labels: God and Man. Some people tend to say that the Buddha was just a man – a very good, holy, decent man, but just a man, no more than that. He's someone rather like Socrates. This is the view typically taken, for instance, by Catholic writers about Buddhism. It's a rather subtle, insidious approach. They praise the Buddha for his wonderful piety, charity, love, compassion, and wisdom, and they agree that he's a very great man. Then, on the last page, they carefully add that of course the Buddha was just a man, and not to be compared with Christ, who was, or is, the son of God. This is one way in which the Buddha gets mistaken. And the other way people fail to see him is by saying, 'The Buddha is a sort of god for the Buddhists. Of course, he was originally a man, but then, hundreds of years after his death, those misguided Buddhists went and made him into a god, because they wanted to have something to worship.'

Both these views are wrong, and the source of these misconceptions probably lies in a general misunderstanding of what religion is about. People for whom the idea of a non-theistic religion is a contradiction in terms will always want to resolve the question of how the Buddha stands in relation to God. Christ is said by his followers to be the son of God, Mohammed is supposed to be the messenger of God, the Jewish prophets claim to be inspired by God, and Krishna and Rama are claimed to be incarnations of God. Indeed, many Hindus think of the Buddha as a god as well. They look upon him as the ninth incarnation, the ninth *avatar*, of the god Vishnu. This is how they see him because the category of *avatar* is familiar to them. But neither the Buddha nor his followers make any such claim, because Buddhism is a non-theistic religion. Like some other religions – Taoism, Jainism, and certain forms of philosophical Hinduism – in Buddhism there is no place for God *at all*. There is no supreme being, no creator of the universe, and there never has been. Buddhists can worship as much as they like, but they will never be worshipping their creator or any conception of a personal God.

The Buddha is neither man nor God, nor even a god. He was a human being in the sense that he started off as every other human being starts off, but he didn't remain an ordinary human being. He became an Enlightened human being, and according to Buddhism that makes a great deal of difference – in fact, all the difference. He was an Unconditioned mind in a conditioned body. According to the Buddhist tradition, a Buddha is the highest being in all the universe, higher even than the so-called gods or devas who are certainly part of the world of traditional Buddhism. (In Western terms we would probably call them angels, archangels, and so on.) Traditionally the Buddha is called the teacher of gods and men, and in Buddhist art the gods are represented in a very humble position, saluting the Buddha and listening to his teaching. Therefore there is no possibility, whether on a philosophical or a popular level, of confusing the Buddha with any kind of god.

For those of us brought up to imagine that if anyone is the highest being in the universe that person is God, it is natural to want to place the Buddha in that position. Even if we don't believe in God, we see a God-shaped empty space. Of course, the Buddha as truly seen simply does not fit into that space. After all, he has not created the universe. We see the Buddha in this way because there's a category missing, we may say, from Western thought. If, therefore, we are to perceive who the Buddha is we have to dispel the ghost of God, the creator of the universe that looms over him, by substituting for God something completely different.

After all this, are we any nearer to answering the question, 'Who is the Buddha?' We've seen that Buddha means Unconditioned mind, Enlightened mind. Knowing the Buddha therefore means knowing the mind in its Unconditioned state. So the answer to the question 'Who is the Buddha?' is really that we ourselves are the Buddha – potentially. We really, truly come to know the Buddha only in the course of our spiritual life, in the course of our meditation, in the course of actualizing our own potential Buddhahood. It is only then that we can really say, from knowledge and experience, who the Buddha is.

We can't do this all at once. It certainly can't be done in a day. First of all we have to establish a living contact with the Buddha. We have to arrive at something intermediate between mere factual *knowledge* about Gautama the Buddha – the details of his career – and on the other hand, the *experience* of Unconditioned mind. This intermediate stage is what we call Going for Refuge to the Buddha. And it means not just reciting '*Buddhaṃ saraṇaṃ gacchāmi*' ('to the Buddha for Refuge I go'), though it doesn't exclude that. It means committing ourselves to the goal of Enlightenment as a living ideal, as our ultimate objective, and striving to realize it. It is only by Going for Refuge to the Buddha, with all that this implies, with all that this means, that we can answer from the heart and the mind and the whole of our spiritual life the question: 'Who is the Buddha?'

What is the Dharma?

Introduction
WHAT IS THE DHARMA?

I once visited Delphi, the place in Greece to which, in ancient times, people flocked to consult the oracle of the god Apollo. As I walked up the hill through the olive trees I came across a spring, bubbling vigorously from rock to rock in a little cascade. At first I didn't pay much attention to it; but the same little cascade reappeared higher up – it was falling down from level to level – and then higher up still. As I eventually discovered, this was none other than the famous Castalian Spring – famous because the drinking of its clear waters was said to make one a poet on the spot. Continuing my ascent, I at last came to the source, the point at which the water welled out from between two enormous rocks in a rather mysterious way, so that you couldn't quite see where it came from.

In the same way we can trace Buddhism back to its own deep and mysterious source. If we trace that great river, with its many tributaries, back to its point of origin, we find that it all springs from the Buddha's spiritual experience: the experience of Enlightenment. The connection may not always be obvious. Sometimes the living waters of Buddhism get lost among the stones and the sand. But if you follow them upstream you come, sooner or later, to this ever-living source and fount, the Buddha's experience of supreme perfect Enlightenment, by virtue of which he became the being we call the Buddha ('the Enlightened', or 'the Awake').

What we call Buddhism, but for which the more traditional, Sanskrit term is the Dharma, is essentially the sum total of the different ways in which the Buddha and his disciples after him tried to communicate some hint, some suggestion, of the experience of Enlightenment to others, so that they too might eventually come to have that experience. If we put to one side the complexities of Buddhism – the schools and the systems, the philosophical theories and the doctrinal analyses – it is really very simple. Buddhism or the Dharma is nothing other than the means to this experience. It is *the way to Enlightenment*.

But what is Enlightenment? What was it that transformed the man called Siddhārtha Gautama into 'the Buddha'? It's difficult to express it in words – the Buddha himself at first despaired of being able to do so, as we shall see – but one way of putting it is to say that the Buddha saw the true nature of existence. He didn't just have an idea; he didn't just work out the true nature of existence in his head, intellectually. He saw 'the way things really are' *directly*, and this direct seeing transformed his whole being, in its depths and in its heights.

THE MEANING OF THE WORD 'DHARMA'

The word *Dharma* is used to refer both to the reality the Buddha experienced and also to his conceptual and verbal expression of that experience, his teaching. These two usages are closely connected; indeed, they refer to two aspects of the same 'thing'. The first – Dharma as truth or law or principle or reality – refers to the objective content of the Buddha's experience of Enlightenment. And the second – Dharma as doctrine or teaching – refers to the Buddha's expression of his experience for the benefit of others. The experience, we could say, corresponds to the wisdom aspect of Enlightenment, and the expression to the compassion aspect – wisdom and compassion being, as D. T. Suzuki says, 'the twin pillars of the whole edifice of Buddhism'.[152] From our point of view we can distinguish between experience and expression, wisdom and compassion, but in reality – from the point of view of a Buddha – they are indistinguishable.

These are not the only meanings of the word 'Dharma' in Buddhism, although they are the principal ones. It is a rich term, with many connotations. In India it is commonly used to refer to one's duty as a member of a particular hereditary class, and thus it is associated with the caste system. It is not used in this way in Buddhism, which repudiates the idea of caste, but there are many other definitions of the term.

To deal first with the two I have already mentioned, we find an example of 'Dharma' used to mean 'law, principle, or truth' in the classic Buddhist text called the *Dhammapada*, where it says, 'Not by hatred is hatred ever pacified here [in the world]. It is pacified by love. This is the eternal law.'[153] The word for 'law' here is Dharma. It's in the very nature of things that hatred does not cease by hatred, but only by love. This is the principle, this is the law, this is the truth. Here, Dharma is a psychological and spiritual law – a spiritual principle, one might say. Then there's Dharma as doctrine or teaching – at least, these English words approximate to what is meant. It's not quite 'doctrine' in the theological, 'I believe in', sense; and it's not quite 'teaching' – it's more like an exposition, a making clear, a presentation. One Sanskrit expression is *dharma deśanā*, which means 'exposition of the Dharma', and another is *dharma kathā*, 'talking about the Dharma'.

And – just to touch upon other definitions – *dharma* (here with a small D) can also mean simply thing (or 'phenomenon', to be more technical and philosophical). Used in this way, the word can refer to any kind of thing, whether physical, mental, spiritual, or transcendental. Again in the *Dhammapada*, there's a well-known verse that says 'All things [whatsoever] are devoid of unchanging selfhood.'[154] What 'devoid of unchanging selfhood' might mean we shall see later. The point here is that the word used for 'things' in the original is *dharma* (the Sanskrit form of the word) or *dhamma* (the same word in Pāli, the ancient Indian language in which many early Buddhist texts have come down to us).

Dharma can also mean 'mental object'. In the West we usually speak of five senses, but the Indian tradition, including the Buddhist tradition, counts six: as well as the five sense organs – eye, ear, nose, tongue, and body (skin) – there's a sixth, mind. Just as the eye has material form as its object, and the ear has sound, so the mind has ideas or mental objects – and the word used for 'idea' in this context is *dharma*.

Lastly, *dharma* can mean a state or condition of existence, as in what are known as the eight *loka dharmas*. *Loka* means 'world', so these *loka dharmas* are the 'eight worldly conditions': gain and loss, fame and infamy, praise and blame, and pleasure and pain, and we're advised, of course, not to allow ourselves to be blown around by them. (They are also sometimes called the 'eight worldly winds'.) The *Maṅgala Sutta* says that the greatest of all blessings is to have a mind that cannot be disturbed by any of these eight *loka dharmas*.[155] It is a great blessing to be – or rather to learn to be – unmoved whether we win or lose, whether we're famous or infamous, whether people blame us or praise us, and whether we experience pleasure or pain. Of course, one can think of many other such pairs – for example, whether we're young or old, resting or working, well or sick. All these states or conditions are *dharmas*.

Thus the term 'Dharma' is very rich in meaning, and one has to be very careful in studying the original texts to sort out the appropriate meaning of the word if one is to make sense of what is being said. In this book we are going to be focusing on the Dharma as principle or truth and the Dharma as teaching or path. One could say, perhaps, that we will be looking at the theory and the practice – except that really the whole of Buddhism is about practice.

THE NATURE OF THE DHARMA

We get a strong sense of the practical nature of the Dharma from the way it is described in one of the traditional Buddhist formulas. The *Tiratana Vandanā*, or 'Salutation to the Three Jewels',[156] is chanted and recited by many thousands of Buddhists throughout the world. As often happens with things that are done regularly, even habitually, its meaning is sometimes forgotten; but this is a shame, because in just a few words it tells us a great deal about the nature of Buddhism. The section on the Dharma, in a few adjectives, gives us a clear idea not so much of the content of the Buddha's teaching as of its character, its nature.

First of all it describes the Dharma as *svākkhāto*. This literally means 'well-taught', or 'well-communicated', and it suggests that the Buddha is in touch with other human beings. He knows their needs, he knows their mental states, he knows how to help them, he knows how to put things to them in a way they can understand. The Buddha was neither an ordinary man nor a god or a son of a god, but an Enlightened human being. Being Enlightened, he had many sublime qualities: supreme purity, great wisdom, and absolute compassion. And it was out of that compassion that he communicated with other human beings, to help them grow and develop. The Dharma is the communication of the Enlightened individual to the non-Enlightened individual, the encouragement of the spiritually free individual to the individual who is not yet spiritually free. Or, more simply, it is one human being talking to another, encouraging another, trying to help another.

An early record of the Buddha's teaching to his disciples is found in the Tipiṭaka or 'Three Baskets' of the Pāli canon, which comprises about forty-five printed volumes and contains accounts of teachings given to people in all sorts of ways.[157] Sometimes we find the Buddha giving a short and simple explanation, in just a few words. Sometimes he doesn't say anything – he just sits in silence – but nevertheless meaning is communicated. On the other hand, sometimes we find him giving a long discourse, spending an hour, two hours, or even a whole night explaining things in detail. Sometimes he gives teachings of an ethical nature, sometimes psychological teachings, sometimes teachings about spiritual life, and sometimes, even, teachings about politics in the sense of the principles of communal existence.

Sometimes we find him explaining matters in abstract general terms, but sometimes he makes use of beautiful illustrations, speaking of the trees and the flowers, the sun and the moon, animals and ordinary human life. Often we find him telling stories, because sometimes people understand things more easily in the form of a story. The Buddha taught in all these different ways, in order that his message should be understood by everybody.

For the same reason he insisted that his teaching should be made available to people in their own language. One day two disciples of his who were of Brahmin birth and 'of fine cultivated language and fine eloquent speech' came to the Buddha and requested permission to put his words into Vedic, the exclusively brahmanical language out of which Sanskrit later developed. But the Buddha refused to allow this. People were to learn the Dharma in their own language or dialect.[158] This principle has been followed throughout Buddhist history. There is no one sacred language. When the Buddha's teaching went to Tibet, the scriptures were all translated into Tibetan. When it went to China, they were translated into Chinese. In fact, wherever Buddhism went it gave a stimulus to the local language and literature. The basic idea is that the Dharma is to be shared with everybody in a way that they can understand. Some religions have a priestly class with a sacred language and in this way knowledge of the scriptures is confined to a small circle of people, but the Buddha insisted that his teaching should be spread as widely as possible, in as many ways as possible. This is what is meant by that teaching being *svākkhāto* – 'well-communicated'.

Next, the Dharma is described as *sandiṭṭhiko*, which can be translated as 'immediately apparent'. In other words, you will see the results of your practice of the Dharma yourself, in this lifetime. Some religions teach that you will taste the fruits of your spiritual practice only after death – your reward will be in heaven – but according to Buddhism we needn't wait that long. Sometimes, indeed, we can see the results in five minutes. Enlightenment, the ultimate goal of Buddhist practice, may be a long way off; but spiritual change, a move in the direction of Enlightenment, can happen almost straight away. Indeed, if one is practising Buddhism and not experiencing any result, one needs to ask oneself whether what one is practising is really Buddhism.

The next description of the Dharma is that it is *akāliko*, which means 'not connected with time'. The Dharma was practised for the first time 2,500 years ago, and it changed, even transformed, people's lives. It has the same effect today; and in 10,000 years' time, if people do the same practices, they will experience the same results. The Dharma is not limited by time. It is also universal, in that you don't have to live in a particular country or culture to practise it. I have noticed in visiting Buddhist centres in different parts of the world that they all have the same kind of atmosphere. The culture may be different, manners and customs may be different, but the Dharma is the same, because the minds and hearts of men and women are the same everywhere.

One might think that this is true of all religions, but in fact some religions are very much tied to a particular place or culture. For example, the Ganges in India is sacred to Hindus, so that if you're a Hindu who happens to live in England, you will have to rely on the international postal service if you have to perform a ritual involving holy Ganges water, and this may be inconvenient, or impossible. But you can practise Buddhism anywhere. Even if you happened to go to the North Pole you could practise Buddhism there. The Dharma is limited neither by time nor by space.

Then, the Dharma is *ehipassiko*. *Ehi* means 'come' and *passiko* derives from a word meaning 'see', so *ehipassiko* means 'come and see'. The implication is that we need not take on the Dharma in blind faith, or believe it because somebody tells us to believe it, or because it is written in some holy book, or because some great guru tells you that you should.

Perhaps the vogue for gurus of the sixties and seventies has worn off a bit now, but there are still a few around, and most of them say the same kind of thing. They say that they are God, or, if they're a bit more modest, they say they have been sent by God. And they say they know everything. 'Ask me any question, and I will know the answer. All you have to do is believe in me, follow my teaching, do whatever I say, and you'll be all right. Don't think for yourself, just come to me, I'll save you.' This is the typical line of the average great guru. And some of them have a lot of followers, because people are very confused and frightened, and they want to be saved.

But there is nothing like this in Buddhism. Even the Buddha didn't speak in this way. He just said, 'I'm a human being, and I've had a certain experience. Listen to what I have to say, by all means, but listen to it critically, test it in your own experience.' He even went as far as to say, 'Just as the goldsmith tests the gold in the fire, so you should test my words.'[159] No other religious teacher, perhaps, has dared to say this.

Next, the Dharma is *opanayiko*, which means 'leading forward' or 'progressive' – not progressive in the modern, scientific sense, but in the cultural and spiritual sense, in that it leads the individual human being to higher and higher levels of human development. This is quite simply what the Buddha's teaching is for: to lead us forward, to lead us up, to make us happier, kinder, wiser, more full of energy and joy, more able to help others.

Finally, the *Tiratana Vandanā* describes the Dharma as *paccataṃ veditabbo viññūhī* – a phrase which can be translated 'to be understood individually, by the wise'. This means that the Buddha's teaching is to be experienced by each person for himself or herself. You can't practise the Dharma at second hand. You have to do it yourself: it's *your* life. You can't ask a priest to do it for you. You can't pay anybody to do it for you. Even a great guru can't do it for you. The Buddha himself can't do it for you. He shows the way, but it is you who must tread that way.

THE BUDDHA WAS NOT A PHILOSOPHER

All in all, the *Tiratana Vandanā* gives the impression of the Dharma as being eminently practical. But, one might think, isn't Buddhism all about theory and abstract thought? What about all those volumes of Buddhist philosophy and doctrine? Well, it's true that some schools of Buddhism have developed, and refined, elaborate philosophical systems, but these systems were developed in the context of spiritual practice by people for whom the Buddha's words were not just of academic interest but of vital spiritual concern. And the Buddha himself – let us be very clear about this – was not a philosopher. In the scriptures he at one point says emphatically, 'I have no views' – that is, no views on 'metaphysical' subjects such as the eternity or non-eternity of the cosmos.[160]

Hence the Buddha has nothing to teach, and that is why he is sometimes said to have remained silent from the night of his Enlightenment to the night of his death.[161] Of course, this is not to be taken literally; as the scriptures make clear, he spent those forty-five years talking to people and teaching the Dharma – but at the same time he had nothing to teach. One could say that, in a way, there's no such thing as Buddhism. There's a language, but there's nothing to communicate – because what you're trying to communicate is beyond communication. The only purpose of attempting to communicate is to help the other person realize that what you're trying to communicate is beyond communication. When they see that, then you really have communicated!

This isn't easy for us to grasp. We like to think that we've got Buddhism *here*, in a book, or a list of important teachings or principles, or a certain tradition of practice. And when we think we've got it, of course we hang on to it. But the Buddha's hands are empty; he isn't holding anything, not even Buddhism. In other words, Buddhism is only a means to an end. In Mahāyāna Buddhism there are what appear to be philosophical systems, what appear to be metaphysics, but they are not quite philosophy in the Western sense – though there are exceptions even in Western philosophy. In his 'Seventh Epistle' Plato solemnly declares that no treatise by him on the higher subjects exists or ever will exist, for 'It is not something that can be put into words like other branches of learning; only after long partnership in a common life devoted to this very thing does truth flash upon the soul, like a flame kindled by a leaping spark, and once it is born there it nourishes itself thereafter.'[162] Students of Plato's dialogues tend to be rather disconcerted by this. They have the idea that Plato ought to be teaching a definite, consistent system that can be given definitive written form; but Plato says plainly that he has no such system. He is only trying to strike a spark, so that the disciple will be able to see things for himself.

It's the same with Buddhism. It's no use thinking that when one has acquired the teaching about karma and rebirth, the teaching about the three characteristics of conditioned existence, the teaching about śūnyatā, and a handful of concentration techniques, then one has 'got' Buddhism – not at all. One has learned the language of Buddhism, but one hasn't started speaking it. And some people never get round to speaking it at all. Of course, one should not confuse this silence of ignorance with the Buddha's silence of wisdom.

THE PARABLE OF THE RAFT

This is all by way of a warning as we embark on a study of these very teachings and practices – a warning that the Buddha himself was very concerned to give. On one occasion he gave it in the form of a parable: the parable of the raft.[163] 'Suppose', he said, 'a man were to come to a great stretch of water, a great river. If he wanted to get to the other shore, the opposite bank, but there was no ferry to take him across, what would he do? He'd chop down a few saplings, lash them together, and make a raft. Then, sitting on the raft and plying a pole, or using his hands to paddle with, he'd get across to the other side. Having arrived there, what would he do with the raft? He'd abandon it. He wouldn't, thinking how useful it had been, out of gratitude load it on to his shoulders and continue his journey with it. He'd just leave it where it was.'

'In the same way,' the Buddha said, 'the Dharma, my teaching, is a means to an end. It's a raft to take you to the other shore of Nirvāṇa. It's not an end in itself; it's the means to Enlightenment.'

This is one of the most striking and important of all the Buddha's teachings: that Buddhism itself, the Dharma itself, is just a raft. Religion is just a raft. It's for getting across the water, not for carrying with one when one has reached the further shore. That's one extreme one may go to. But of course there's another extreme to be avoided – one that is much more common – and that is not actually using the raft to cross the river at all.

Some people board the raft but don't do anything to make it move. In fact, they tend to forget that they ever intended to cross the river. Their main concern is to make the raft a bit more comfortable. They start building walls on it, and maybe a roof; then they install furniture and cooking utensils; and then they bring on board their family and friends.

In short, they turn the raft into a house, and they moor it securely to this shore. And they don't like any talk about releasing the mooring or pulling up the anchor.

There are other people who stand on the bank and take a good look at that raft. 'It's a fine raft,' they say. 'It's magnificent– so big, so solid, so well constructed, so impressive.' And they take out their measuring rod or their tape, and they measure it. They can tell you its exact dimensions, the sort of wood it's made of, and where and when that wood was felled. They may even produce a learned book about rafts which is an immediate best-seller. But for all that, they've never set foot on the raft, let alone thought about crossing the river.

Others, again, stand around on the bank, saying, 'No, the raft isn't very well made. Twelve saplings should have gone into its construction, not ten, and they ought to be lashed together more securely. And I don't like the way the raft floats on the water. I'd build it bigger and better.' So they remain on the bank – speculating, discussing, disputing, but going nowhere. There are yet other people who think the old raft's a bit plain and unattractive, a bit rough and ready. After all, it's just a lot of logs lashed together. So they paint it and decorate it and cover it with flowers and make it look quite pretty. But they don't ever get on board – don't ever start using that pole and ferrying themselves across to the other shore. There are also people who claim they've inherited the raft. It's their ancestral property, it belongs to them, so they don't have actually to make use of it. It's enough that it's theirs.

The shore we are standing on represents our present, ego-bound existence, with its suffering and its disharmony. The other shore represents what we aspire to be, or what we ideally are; it represents our goal – Enlightenment, Nirvāna, or whatever else one cares to call it. Buddhism is simply the raft that carries one over the intervening waters. That's its only function. 'The raft,' the Buddha declared, 'I teach as something to be left behind.'

Later in the history of Buddhism, in the Japanese Buddhist tradition, we find the beautiful image of the finger pointing to the moon. The pointing finger helps you to see the moon, but once you have seen the moon, that becomes the focus of your attention, and you need to make sure you don't mistake the finger for the moon. In the same way, you pass from a religious teaching to a spiritual experience. You don't remain stuck with that teaching or doctrine, that practice or method, making it the focus of your attention. No, you look beyond the finger to see the moon shining in the heavens.

One might say that the Buddha perhaps took greater precautions against the possibility of his followers mistaking the finger for the moon than the founder of any other religion. So far as I know, Christ never warned his disciples not to take his words too literally. Nor did Mohammed ever explain that when he spoke about the delights of heaven it was only as a skilful means. But in Buddhism the point is insisted upon again and again, because human nature is such that, especially in matters of religion, we always tend to cling to the means and treat it as though it was the end itself.

WHAT IS THE DHARMA?

The parable of the raft makes the function of the Dharma clear. But of what should the raft be made? These days there are so many spiritual teachings around that it can be hard to know what is really going to help us. This is not a new problem. Even in the Buddha's day one could become quite confused about what Buddhism really was. There were so many apparently contradictory versions, one disciple saying this, another that. Fortunately, help is at hand in the form of the answer the Buddha gave to a question from his aunt and foster-mother Mahāprajāpatī Gautami. She had followed in the Buddha's footsteps and become a homeless wanderer, and one day she came to him wanting to hear from her nephew's own lips a teaching that she could practise in her solitary life dwelling in the forest. From the nature of the Buddha's answer we can gather that perhaps she had heard many interpretations of the Buddha's teaching and wanted to be certain of what he himself had to say.[164]

And what the Buddha said was, 'Take it like this. Whatever you find in practice, in terms of your own experience, conduces to peace of mind, purity, seclusion, fewness of desires, contentment, insight and wisdom, detachment from the world, and an understanding of the transcendental, take that as my Dharma, take that as my teaching.' In other words, the criterion is not logical or philosophical, but pragmatic and empirical – though the pragmatism is spiritual and the empiricism is a transcendental empiricism.

If we can only remember this, it can save us a lot of trouble. There are many forms of Buddhism in the world. It is a very old religion, having now been going for 2,500 years. In the East it has spread from the snowy tablelands of Tibet to the sweltering jungles of South-east Asia, from the beautiful islands of Japan to the deserts of Central Asia and the tropical plains of India. Everywhere it has travelled, it has changed in accordance with local conditions, so that there are many different forms of Buddhism, many different presentations. In the West we have been deluged in recent decades by presentations that are apparently in conflict. One teacher may assure us that Buddhism's essential message is 'Rely on your own efforts. You are the one who has to do it; no one can do it for you – no God, no Buddha', but then we may hear that there is one school of Buddhism that says 'You can do nothing. Only the Buddha Amitābha can do it for you, in fact has already done it. Rely on him, trust in him.'[165]

If we are bombarded by conflicting interpretations such as these, and not sure what to think, it is very helpful to remember what the Buddha said to his aunt: 'If it works, if it helps you spiritually, it's my teaching.' If you find in your own experience that it helps you become more concentrated, more sensitive, more intelligent, wiser, kinder, more understanding, it is the Dharma, it is the true teaching, it is what the Buddha really taught and really meant.

The great emperor Aśoka, who lived a century or two after the Buddha, inscribed in his Rock Edicts this memorable saying: 'Whatever the Buddha said was well said.'[166] But the Mahāyāna *sūtras*, which were written down a little later than Aśoka's time, reversed this to say, 'Whatever is well said, that is the word of the Buddha.'[167] In other words, whatever helps you, take that as the word of the Buddha, because in principle that's all that the word of the Buddha is: that which helps you across, that which helps you on your journey.

Sometimes people say, 'Well, such and such' – it might be t'ai chi ch'uan, perhaps, or drawing classes, or one of any number of things – 'helps me in my spiritual life. I feel much better for it; it helps me to concentrate – but it isn't anything to do with Buddhism, it isn't part of the Dharma.' But in fact if it helps you spiritually it is essentially, by definition, part of the Dharma.

Of course, we need to keep asking the same question – 'Is this helping me to grow spiritually?' – of Buddhism itself, or of whatever is presented to us as being Buddhism. If we want to be sure whether any form of Buddhism – whether it's Theravāda or Tibetan Buddhism,

Tendai, Shin, or Zen – is authentic, we have to ask ourselves whether it really helps people towards Enlightenment or whether it is a venerable museum piece – ancient, beautiful, admirable, but for the museum, not for real life. It's only the Dharma if it's alive, if it works, if it still helps people to follow the spiritual path.

We must resist the temptation to think that the Dharma is this teaching or that teaching. Provisionally that may be true but not in the long run. You may be familiar with the credal statements of Christianity: 'I believe in God the father almighty, maker of heaven and earth...' and so on, but we find no such statements in Buddhism. There are formulations, there are presentations, but they're all provisional; they're fingers pointing to the moon.

As Buddhism develops in the West, it is unlikely to follow any existing Buddhist pattern, because our needs, our approach, and our background are different from those of any Eastern country. We need to draw upon the essence, the inner spirit, of the Buddha's teaching as preserved in all schools. We need to take the best – not just in an eclectic way, or just intellectually, but drawing upon the teachings deeply, and blending them all into one great stream of spiritual tradition adapted to our needs. This is really the task before us. It won't be easy; it will demand a great deal of effort and spiritual experience on our part. And to do it we will need to bear in mind that the Dharma represents not this doctrine or that teaching, but a great current of spiritual life, in which we can participate, in which we can help others to share, and which bears us on in the direction of Enlightenment.

In this book are gathered not an exhaustive collection, but a basic starter kit, if you like, of Buddhist teachings and practices – enough, certainly, to help one make a start. They are, on the whole, of the very essence of Buddhism, not specific to any one school or culture. And they all have the same intention: to help us towards Enlightenment.

PART I
THE TRUTH

I

THE ESSENTIAL TRUTH

In the Buddha's time, in a village near Nālandā – which later became the site of a great Buddhist university – there lived two young men called Śāriputra and Maudgalyāyana. They had been close friends since childhood; and now they made a pact. They decided to leave home in search of the truth, in search of a great Enlightened teacher – not an unusual thing to do at that time in India. The pact between the two friends was that they would start their search by going in opposite directions. Whoever found an Enlightened teacher first would go and tell the other, and they'd become his disciples together. So Śāriputra went in one direction and Maudgalyāyana went in the other.

Śāriputra was the lucky one. He hadn't gone far, or wandered for many weeks, before he saw someone coming in the distance who seemed – well, he hardly dared hope that this was true – but there was something about this man that seemed special. Could he be Enlightened? As the stranger drew nearer, Śāriputra was still more impressed by his appearance, his bearing – so much so that he didn't hesitate to put to him a question which is *the* question in India, even today. People don't tend to remark on the weather or anything like that. They don't even necessarily enquire about your health. As Śāriputra did on this occasion, they come straight to the point and ask, 'Who is your teacher?'

In the East, especially in India and Tibet, it has been the tradition for thousands of years that everybody has a spiritual teacher from whom he or she has received some kind of religious practice. It is not so much the case these days, perhaps, but people still often have the attitude that if you don't have a spiritual teacher, you hardly exist as a human being. You might just as well be a dog or a cat as be a human being and not have a spiritual teacher. Hence the first thing you want to know about anybody is what lineage of spiritual practice they belong to.

So Śāriputra asked the stranger, 'Who is your teacher?' Now the stranger, as it happened, was one of the Buddha's five original disciples, a man called Aśvajit. After his Enlightenment, the Buddha had decided to seek out five former companions of his and share with them his experience of the truth. He had caught up with them at a place called Sarnath and – after some initial resistance on their part – he had managed to communicate his experience to them. Indeed, in a short while these five men too became Enlightened. Other people came to hear the Buddha teach, and they also became Enlightened. Before long there were sixty Enlightened beings in the world. And the Buddha said to them, 'I am free from all bonds, human and divine. You also are free from all bonds, human and divine. Go now and teach all beings for the benefit and the happiness of the whole world, out of compassion, out of love for all living beings.'[168] So they scattered in all directions, and they traversed the length and breadth of northern India, everywhere trying to communicate the teaching of the Buddha.

So Aśvajit said at once, 'My teacher is Gautama who has gone forth from the clan of the Śākyas, the Enlightened One who is now the Buddha.' Śāriputra was of course overjoyed to hear this, but he still wasn't quite satisfied. His next question – predictably enough – was, 'What does the Buddha teach?' This is obviously the second thing you are going to want to know.

Aśvajit had himself gained Enlightenment, but he was a modest man. He said, 'I am newly converted. I don't know much of the teaching. But what little I do know I shall tell you.' And so saying, he recited a verse which has since become famous all over the Buddhist world. 'The Buddha has explained the origin of those things which proceed from a cause or a condition. Their cessation too he has explained. This is the doctrine of the great śramaṇa.'

That was all he said. But when Śāriputra heard this verse, his whole being rose up in a sort of flash of insight and he knew that this was the truth. Whatever arises does so in dependence on conditions; when those conditions are no longer there, it ceases. Seeing this, Śāriputra at once became what is called in Buddhism a 'Stream Entrant' – that is, he entered the stream leading ultimately to the liberation of Enlightenment. And, of course, he immediately went to find his friend Maudgalyāyana, to tell him that they had found their teacher. The two friends subsequently became the Buddha's two chief disciples.[169]

The verse that Aśvajit recited, and which had such a tremendous effect on the young Śāriputra, is to be found all over the Buddhist world. You find it in India, stamped on the base of images. You find it on clay seals in the ruins of monasteries: thousands and thousands of little clay seals just stamped with this verse. You find it in China, you find it in Tibet. In Tibet, when they consecrate a Buddha image, very often they print hundreds of thousands of tiny copies of this verse and stuff them all inside the image, as part of the consecration.

This verse is really the essence of Buddhism; on the doctrinal level there's nothing more basic. It is common ground to all the Buddhist schools, whether Theravāda or Mahāyāna, Zen or Tibetan. They all have their origin in the great law of conditionality, *pratītya-samutapāda* in Sanskrit, sometimes translated as dependent arising, or conditioned co-production. This is the single source to which all Buddhist teachings can be traced back, the most basic conceptual expression of the Buddha's spiritual experience.

THE DECISION TO TEACH

We find an early reference to this great teaching in the *Ariyapariyesanā Sutta* (the 'Discourse on the Noble Quest') of the *Majjhima Nikāya*. This is a sort of autobiographical discourse, one of several in the Pāli canon, in which the Buddha, as an old man, relates some of the experiences of his younger days, describing how he practised asceticism, how he gained Enlightenment, his thoughts and doubts, the way he began to teach, and so on. Thus the Buddha here relates the story of how after his Enlightenment he wasn't sure whether or not to try to make known the truth he had discovered.

The text represents him as saying to himself, 'This Law [Dharma] that I have attained to is profound and hard to see, hard to discover; it is the most peaceful and superior goal of all, not attainable by mere ratiocination, subtle, for the wise to experience.' And then he goes on to reflect: 'But this generation relies on attachment, relishes attachment, delights in attachment. It is hard for such a generation to see this truth, that is to say, Specific Conditionality, Dependent Arising [*pratītya-samutapāda*].'[169]

When the Buddha said to himself, 'It's going to be difficult for humanity to understand what I have discovered,' the way he described his discovery was in terms of universal conditionality, conditioned co-production. This is the first presentation of the Buddha's insight. It's as if, when the Enlightened mind looks out at all existence, at the whole of the phenomenal universe, the first thing that strikes it, the most obvious thing about the universe, is that it is conditioned. It arises in dependence on conditions, and when those conditions cease it disappears. This is the basic insight, as it were, about the world, from the standpoint of Enlightenment.

The story goes on to explain how it happened that the Buddha did decide to teach after all. Here is the account given in the *sutta* itself.[170] It involves, I should warn you, the sudden appearance of 'Brahmā Sahāmpati', who, in traditional Buddhist mythology, is 'the ruler of a thousand worlds'.

Then Brahmā Sahāmpati, having known with his own mind the reflection in the Blessed One's mind, thought: 'Alas, the world is lost! Alas, the world is to perish, in that the mind of the Tathāgata, the Arahant, the Perfectly Enlightened One, inclines to living at ease, not to teaching the Dhamma.' Then, just as quickly as a strong man might extend his drawn-in arm or draw in his extended arm, Brahmā Sahāmpati disappeared from the brahma world and reappeared before the Blessed One. He arranged his upper robe over one shoulder, knelt down with his right knee on the ground, raised his joined hands in reverential salutation towards the Blessed One, and said to him: 'Venerable sir, let the Blessed One teach the Dhamma; let the Fortunate One teach the Dhamma. There are beings with little dust in their eyes who are falling away because they do not hear the Dhamma. There will be those who will understand the Dhamma.'
This is what Brahmā Sahāmpati said. Having said this, he further said this:
'In the past there appeared among the Magadhans
An impure Dhamma devised by those still stained.
Throw open this door to the Deathless! Let them hear

The Dhamma that the Stainless One discovered.

    'Just as one standing on a mountain peak
Might see below the people all around,
So, O wise one, universal eye,
Ascend the palace made of the Dhamma.
Being yourself free from sorrow, behold the people
Submerged in sorrow, oppressed by birth and decay.

    'Rise up, O hero, victor in battle!
O caravan leader, debt-free one, wander in the world.
Teach the Dhamma, O Blessed One:
There will those who will understand.'

    Then the Blessed One, having understood Brahmā's request, out of compassion for beings surveyed the world with the eye of a Buddha. As he did so, the Blessed One saw beings with little dust in their eyes and with much dust in their eyes, with keen faculties and with dull faculties, with good qualities and with bad qualities, easy to teach and difficult to teach, and a few who dwelt seeing blame and fear in the other world. Just as in a pond of blue or red or white lotuses, some lotuses might be born in the water, grow up in the water, and thrive while submerged in the water, without rising up from the water; some lotuses might be born in the water, grow up in the water, and stand at an even level with the water; some lotuses might be born in the water and grow up in the water but would rise up from the water and stand without being soiled by the water – so too, surveying the world with the eye of a Buddha, the Blessed One saw beings with little dust in their eyes and with much dust in their eyes, with keen faculties and with dull faculties, with good qualities and with bad qualities, easy to teach and hard to teach, and a few who dwelt seeing blame and fear in the other world.

    Having seen this, he answered Brahmā Sahāmpati in verse:

    'Open to them are the doors to the Deathless:
Let those who have ears release faith.
Foreseeing trouble, O Brahmā, I did not speak
The refined, sublime Dhamma among human beings.'

    Then Brahmā Sahāmpati, thinking, 'The Blessed One has given his consent [to my request] regarding the teaching of the Dhamma,' paid homage to the Blessed One and disappeared right there.[171]

That's the episode – and it represents a crucial point in the Buddha's life. To communicate or not to communicate, that was the question. It was a crucial question not only for him, but for the whole world. Without it, what we know as Buddhism would not exist. A lot could be said about this episode, the episode of Brahmā's request, as it's generally called. It contains a lot that one can reflect and meditate upon. There is, to begin with, the question of who Brahmā is, what he represents. And then, why did the Buddha have to be requested to teach? What does that mean?

THE RAIN OF THE DHARMA

In this context I want to draw attention to just one feature of the episode. The simplest way to put it is that the story represents the surging up of compassion in the Buddha's heart, as if to say that the wisdom of Enlightenment is inseparable from compassion. Then, the image of the pool of lotuses shows that, however difficult it may be to communicate the experience of Enlightenment, it can be done. Human beings are capable of growth, of development, of transformation; and each of us is at our own stage of the process.

We find the same kind of simile in the *White Lotus Sūtra*, which is one of the great Mahāyāna *sūtras* – Mahāyāna *sūtras* being canonical texts that purport to record the words of the historical Buddha Śākyamuni. I say 'purport' because according to modern scholarship many of the *sūtras* do not so much record the actual words of the Buddha as try to recast in contemporary format something of the essence, the spirit, of the Buddha's teaching as it had come down through the centuries. The *White Lotus Sūtra* was committed to writing in about the first century CE and it is full of beautiful parables, myths, and symbols which are of absolutely epochal importance for Buddhist spiritual life throughout the Far East. And of its parables perhaps one of the most important is the parable of the rain cloud, also known as the parable of the plants.

The parable describes how, just as a rain cloud pours refreshing rain on all the plants of the earth without discrimination, so the Buddha teaches the Dharma to all living beings. The rain of the Dharma falls on all equally – not more to some and less to others.[172] In other words, the Buddha does not discriminate. We know that the historical Buddha taught his Dharma to all alike: to princes, to peasants, to men, to women, to merchants, to outcasts, to murderers, to robbers.

And those on whom the rain of the Dharma falls, the living beings – in other words ourselves – grow. But we each grow in accordance with our own individual nature. When the rain falls on a palm tree, the palm tree grows into a bigger palm tree. When the rain falls on a rose, the rose grows into a more luxuriant rose. But the rose doesn't become a palm tree, and the palm tree doesn't become a rose. Each grows nourished by the same rain, but it grows in accordance with its own nature. In the same way we all learn and practise the same Dharma, but we develop spiritually each in our own way; though at the same time we all grow towards Enlightenment.

This is illustrated by another passage in the Pāli canon in which the Buddha is talking to and about his disciples, enumerating their distinctive qualities. Sometimes people think that a teacher's disciples must all be alike, just copies of the teacher, and sometimes Buddhist art reinforces this impression. You see a picture of the Buddha with yellow robe, shoulder-bag, bowl, and uṣṇīṣa (that's the bump on his head, the 'bodhic protuberance'), and then you see a whole row of little disciples, and they all look exactly like the Buddha, except for the uṣṇīṣa – same shaven head, same yellow robe, same shoulder-bag, same begging-bowl, same meek expression. But this idea that disciples are more or less clones of their teacher is a big mistake, as we see in this passage in the Pāli canon where the Buddha is praising his disciples.

We might think that the usual thing is for the disciples to praise the teacher; and sometimes they do. But on this occasion the Buddha praised his disciples. He said 'Look, there's Śāriputra. Śāriputra is the greatest of you for wisdom and for ability to expound the Dharma. And Ānanda? – well, he's the greatest for popularity and friendliness.' (It was Ānanda, by the way, who made it possible for women to join the sangha, the spiritual community of the Buddha's followers, so women in the sangha thereafter regarded him almost as a sort of patron saint.[173]) Then the Buddha singled out another disciple as the greatest for austerities; another as the greatest preacher. And, because some disciples naturally had greater qualities than others, in the end the Buddha had to scrape the barrel a bit, and he mentioned one disciple as the disciple who always managed to collect the greatest quantity of alms when he went on his almsround. Even he was the best at something.[174]

In this way the Buddha praised his disciples for their distinctive qualities. And this distinctiveness is borne out throughout the Pāli scriptures. If you read them simply as documents of the lives of human beings, you come across so many of the Buddha's disciples, and they're all so different. Śāriputra and Maudgalyāyana, though great friends, are completely different from each another. Ānanda is amiable and popular, while Kaśyapa's a bit grumpy – or at least that's the impression one gets. Some disciples are shy and retiring, while others are outgoing and active.

It's always the same. If you're a true follower of the Dharma you'll grow in accordance with your own nature. And this is what the parable of the rain cloud and the plants brings out very well. When the rain falls the tree grows and becomes a bigger and better tree. But an oak tree will never grow into an apple tree, however much you water it; and an apple tree will never become an oak.

In the same way, someone of a more devotional temperament will not usually become predominantly intellectual; and someone of an intellectual nature will not usually become predominantly devotional. Although both may develop the opposite quality to some extent, their temperaments will stay pretty much the same right up to the point where they both gain Enlightenment. One will be an Enlightened devotee, and the other will be an Enlightened intellectual – or even an Enlightened academic, though that's rather harder to imagine. One person may be an Enlightened monk; another may be an Enlightened householder – but they will both be Enlightened. It might sound like a paradox, but as people on the spiritual path grow towards Enlightenment, they don't grow more like one another; they grow more different – though at the same time communication between them improves.

The simile of the lotuses and the parable of the plants also remind us that human beings can change. They can change from worse to better, and even from better to best. To take a few examples from the scriptures and Buddhist history, Aṅgulimāla murdered nearly a hundred people, and then managed to become an *arhant* – in other words gained Enlightenment – all within the same lifetime.[175] That should give us a great deal of food for thought. Then in Tibet in the eleventh century there was a certain black magician who had been guilty of the death of about thirty people, but he became the greatest of the Kagyupa saints. That, of course, was Milarepa.[176] And from Indian history we can take the example of Aśoka, who wanted to unite the whole of India under his rule. He slaughtered hundreds of thousands of people; but then he experienced remorse, and started going against the grain, as it were. He changed. In the end he became known as Dharma-Aśoka, 'righteous Aśoka', one of the great benefactors of Buddhism.[177]

This change in these and so many other people was brought about not by the grace of God, but by a change in the direction of the human will, a change originating within the human psyche itself. We are responsible for our own spiritual destiny. We are free to develop or not to develop, just as we wish. Circumstances may hinder us, may even appear to crush us, but no circumstance can ever deprive us of our basic freedom of will. This is what the Buddha saw when in his mind's eye he saw that pond of blue and red and white lotuses; and this is what the parable of the rain cloud and the plants also tells us.

BRIDGING THE GAP

But although the Buddha had this vision, which gave him such confidence in the spiritual potential of human beings, we may not – on the strength of what I've said about it so far, at least – feel convinced that we are going to realize our own potential through the apprehension of the law of conditionality. As we've seen, the reality to which the Buddha attained was 'profound and hard to see'.[178] It was 'the most peaceful and superior goal of all'. Not only that. It was 'not attainable by mere ratiocination'. It was 'subtle' – incredibly subtle. And it was 'for the wise to experience'.

So what are *we* to make of this great truth? For Śāriputra – who must have been very receptive – the mere, bare statement of it was enough to give him insight into the truth, but it is hardly likely to have the same impact on us. Indeed, it may be hard for us to make any sense of it at all. As we have seen, the Buddha himself anticipated this difficulty. Buddhism may essentially be a communication – a communication from the Buddha to those who are not Buddhas, from the Enlightened mind to the unenlightened mind – but such a communication is not easy to make, even for a Buddha, because between the Buddha and the ordinary person there is a tremendous gap.

We can't really conceive how tremendous that gap is. It's all very well for us to say – as some Buddhists do say, rather glibly – that we're potentially Buddha, we're potentially Enlightened. But those are usually just words. We don't realize the vast extent of the gulf that separates us from the Buddha. Sometimes people talk about the Buddha in a very familiar way, almost as though he was their next-door neighbour and they knew him well – knew about his realization and his Enlightenment, and just what it consisted in. But this is really a sort of profanity. We don't really know or understand the Buddha. There's a vast gulf between his ultimate realization and our own unenlightened experience.

It's very difficult even for a Buddha to bridge that gap, to make real contact with the unenlightened mind. Mahāyāna Buddhism has powerful myths of bodhisattvas like Avalokiteśvara and Kṣitigarbha descending into the depths of hell to help the beings there.[179] That hell isn't necessarily another world – it can be this world; and the myth of the descent represents the difficulty that the Bodhisattva or the Buddha has in establishing real contact with our unenlightened, mundane mentality. But – and the Buddha felt this as a burning compulsion – contact has to be made, the truth has to be communicated. A bridge, however frail, however slender, has to be flung across the abyss separating the Enlightened from the unenlightened mind. So how did the Buddha do this?

BUDDHISM IN A NUTSHELL

There are two principal modes of communication: through concepts and through images. In the Pāli scriptures the Buddha tends to make greater use of concepts, though images – parables, myths, similes – are by no means lacking. In the Mahāyāna scriptures, on the other hand, he tends to make much greater use of images, though here again concepts are by no means absent, and a few of the Mahāyāna *sūtras* are communicated almost entirely through them.

The story of the Buddha's decision to teach given in the Pāli scriptures is communicated through a mixture of concepts and images, as we have seen. But when it comes to referring to the reality he had experienced, the Buddha chose to express it in terms of a concept: the concept of conditionality, as we've come to call it in English. This, as we have seen, is the basic concept of Buddhism. To the extent that Buddhism is reducible to a concept, it's reducible to the concept of conditionality, and the whole of Buddhism, both theoretical and practical – philosophy, meditation, the Buddhist life itself – is founded upon it.

Or, at least, Buddhism is founded upon the experience of which it is an expression. Conditionality isn't something that the Buddha thought out; it's an expression, a direct expression, of his Enlightenment experience. And though I've said that Buddhist philosophy is based on it, this is not philosophy in the Western sense. Buddhist 'philosophy', as we call it, is no more than an attempt at the further, more detailed elucidation of the Buddha's vision of reality.

The Buddha felt compelled to communicate his experience of reality somehow. He had to give expression to it in conceptual terms if he was to say anything at all. At the same time, he had to find a way of putting it that would be intelligible to ordinary unenlightened people, and that would provide a basis upon which the ordinary person could eventually gain insight into the true nature of reality. The concept he chose was universal conditionality – of which we can certainly gain at least an intellectual understanding, at least up to a point.

The formula usually given in the scriptures is as follows. It is, in fact, almost exactly what Aśvajit said to Śāriputra. The language the Buddha uses is simple, abstract, almost mathematical. He simply says, 'This being, that becomes; from the arising of this, that arises. This not being, that does not become; from the ceasing of this, that ceases.'[180] This is the formula in its highest degree of generality and abstraction; and it holds good for the whole of existence, whether material or mental or spiritual.

So if anyone ever asked you what Buddhism is in a nutshell – not in one word, because that word would be 'conditionality', but in one phrase – you could just tell them 'A being present, B arises. In the absence of A, B does not arise. That's the essence of Buddhism.' Then you could leave them to work out the implications for themselves. If one thought about it for long enough, one could work out the whole of Buddhism from this simple statement. Of course, they might think that you were being deliberately obscure. Perhaps most Buddhists, if asked to summarize the teaching of the Buddha so succinctly, would say, 'all things are impermanent' or 'actions have consequences'. But it doesn't take much reflection to see that both these statements spring from this same fundamental truth: conditionality.

THE IMPLICATIONS OF CONDITIONALITY

The Buddha, you may be glad to hear, chose to make a few concessions and explain conditionality in rather more detail. Probably the best known formulation of the principle is that of the four noble truths: the truth of suffering or unsatisfactoriness; the truth of the cause of suffering, which is craving; the truth of the cessation of suffering, cessation being the equivalent of Nirvāṇa; and the truth of the way leading to the cessation of suffering, the way leading to Nirvāṇa – which is the Noble Eightfold Path.[181] In other words, in terms of this formulation, craving being present, suffering arises; craving not being present, suffering does not arise.

I should perhaps mention that the 'suffering that does not arise' is mental suffering, not physical suffering. There's a passage in the Pāli canon to which one of my teachers, Bhikkhu Kashyap, with whom I studied Pāli and Abhidhamma, was very fond of referring. In this passage, the Buddha is seated cross-legged teaching his disciples; and after he has been teaching for a long time, his back starts aching. Even a Buddha's back aches. And the Buddha didn't just put up with it, as some people might say we ought to. He said to his disciple Śāriputra, who happened to be present, 'Śāriputra, my back is aching. Please take over the teaching. I'll just lie down.'[182] My teacher, Kashyapji, used to be fond of referring to this incident because, as he emphasized, it illustrated the humanity of the Buddha – not in the sense that the Buddha had human weaknesses in the mental or emotional sense, because he didn't, but he had physical weaknesses. He had an ordinary human body, and that body, as he grew older, caused him pain.

In Buddhism a distinction is made between physical pain and mental pain. When you gain Enlightenment you no longer experience any mental pain, or emotional turbulence, or anything of that sort, but you are still subject to physical pain – which you bear, as the Buddha did, with equanimity. Anyway, that's by the way. The basic point is that craving not being present, suffering – mental suffering, avoidable suffering – does not arise. Incidentally, this is *not* to say that all suffering is the result of craving; this would amount to karmic determinism. There are some sufferings – especially physical sufferings – that are *not* due to one's previous unskilful mental actions, whether in this life or in any previous life.

THE CIRCLE AND THE SPIRAL

Elaborating further on this concept of conditionality, the Buddha said that it has two principal trends: a cyclical trend and a spiral trend. The first, cyclical trend is an oscillation between pairs of opposites. In dependence upon pleasure there arises pain; in dependence upon pain, pleasure. In dependence upon loss there arises gain; in dependence upon gain, loss. In dependence upon winter, summer; in dependence upon summer, winter.

In traditional terms the whole process of cyclical action and reaction is called the round of existence, or the wheel of life – that is to say, the wheel of birth, death, and rebirth, best known in its Tibetan iconographic form.[183] If we look at a picture of the Tibetan wheel of life it gives us a detailed presentation of the whole cyclical mode of conditionality. It depicts all living beings, all sentient existence, as involved in the cyclical process, acting and reacting between pairs of opposites, going up and down, round and round, in accordance with the law of karma and rebirth.

With the second, spiral trend of conditionality, you get not oscillation between opposites but a movement between factors which progressively augment one another. In dependence upon happiness you get joy; in dependence upon joy, rapture; in dependence upon rapture, calm; in dependence upon calm, bliss. This is the progressive spiral series. And we can say that the spiral trend of conditionality constitutes, in principle, the spiritual path.

These are the two basic types or kinds of conditionality at work in the universe, at all levels: the cyclical and the spiral. It is the first which keeps us within the realm of the 'conditioned', circling round and round, as the wheel of life so graphically shows. And it is the second which gives us the possibility of growth and development, so that we can transcend conditionedness and ultimately enter the realm of the Unconditioned which is Enlightenment.[184] In a way, the rest of this book is simply an extended consideration of the workings of these two kinds of conditionality. In the first part, we shall explore the nature of the conditioned, in terms of the twelve links of conditioned co-production depicted by the wheel of life and in terms of what are called the three characteristics or marks of conditioned existence, before moving on to consider the nature of the Unconditioned, Nirvāṇa, and the concept of emptiness, sometimes rather misleadingly referred to as 'the Void'.

In contemplating emptiness we shall come to see that ultimately no distinction can be made between the 'conditioned' and the 'Unconditioned'. But at our present level of spiritual development the distinction is very real, so that we have to think in terms of moving from one to the other, in other words in terms of a spiritual path. This is the main theme of the second part of the book.

After an introduction which sees the path in terms of escaping what I call the 'gravitational pull' of the conditioned and responding to the attraction of the Unconditioned, we shall explore various ways of seeing the spiritual path, starting with a consideration of the twelve links of the spiral path, the most explicit demonstration of the way spiral conditionality works. Then we shall consider a few of the many other ways of viewing the path: the Noble Eightfold Path, the seven factors of Enlightenment, the seven stages of purification, the five spiritual faculties, and then, lastly, three chapters each devoted to one of the stages of the threefold path: ethics, meditation, and wisdom. The intention is to show not only the doctrinal context of Buddhist practice but also how the teachings can be applied to everyday life. And, to remind us that there can be no wisdom without compassion, we will finish with a chapter on the bodhisattva ideal, that most sublime expression of the altruistic dimension of Buddhism.

As we consider all these many and varied ways of answering the question 'What is the Dharma?' we should always bear in mind that all these concepts, all these teachings, all these practices, come back to one basic truth, one basic insight: conditionality.

2

THE DYNAMICS OF BEING

'Being' is not a very Buddhistic word. It is rather too static. The word we should be using is 'becoming'. In fact, the subject of this chapter is the underlying dynamics of our 'becoming' that make nonsense of the term 'being' which we commonly apply to this process. In more traditional terms we will be concerned with the 'links' of 'conditioned co-production' which chain us to a continuous cycle of rebirths, and with how the Buddha's analysis of this process offers us an ever-present opportunity to bring this apparently endless cycle to an end.

The topic of karma and rebirth is perhaps not as fashionable in Buddhist circles as it used to be, and in view of the central importance of this teaching to all schools of Buddhism it is probably worth examining how this has happened. If we find that one aspect of the Dharma appeals to us strongly it is usually because there is some imbalance in ourselves, a certain need to which that aspect of the teaching corresponds. If there are aspects of the Dharma that we tend to ignore, that we leave on the side of our plate, so to speak, it may be that those aspects correspond to aspects of ourselves and of our experience that we are not yet prepared to look at. While it is certainly appropriate to follow our own personal inclinations to some extent, we need also to be aware that a bias is there and that an adjustment will need to be made at some point. We can take a balanced view of the Dharma only if we ourselves become psychologically and spiritually balanced.

In little more than a hundred years, the Dharma has come to appeal to people in the West in a wide variety of ways, but the different elements, aspects, and schools within the whole, sometimes bewilderingly complex, body of Buddhist teachings have not always found the same degree of favour. Different teachings, different schools, have come to the fore at different times according to the different cultural conditions in force at any one time.

If we look at how Buddhism came to the West, we find first a period of purely scholarly interest, connected with the growth of 'orientalism'. This fascination with all things oriental arose in the wake of the vast colonial interests exercised by various European states – particularly by Britain. The study of Buddhism was often initiated by civil servants who were simply concerned with gaining a deeper understanding of the local administration. For instance, T. W. Rhys Davids, the great Pāli scholar, developed his interest in Buddhism when, as a judge in Ceylon (now Sri Lanka) in the 1870s, he had to delve into the Vinaya to clear up some rather complex questions of Buddhist law.

Then, at the close of the nineteenth century, a few Westerners began actually to call themselves Buddhists and to take up Buddhism as a way of life. Finally, Buddhism may be said to have definitely arrived in the West when, at about the beginning of the twentieth century, Western *bhikkhus* and *bhikṣus* started to appear, when you got not only Western lay people but also Western monks.

Those aspects of Buddhism that appealed most strongly to the first Western Buddhists are nowadays often of less interest to most people. Judging by the Buddhist literature being produced at the end of the nineteenth century,[185] those Westerners of the English-speaking world who were attracted to Buddhism were mainly interested in three things: firstly, the personality of the Buddha – as a teacher, as a historical figure, as a wise and compassionate human being; secondly, the ethics of Buddhism; and, thirdly, the Buddhist teaching of karma and rebirth. Judging from my own experience, I would say that these are not the things that tend to bring people to Buddhism today.

There are both negative and positive reasons for this change. To begin with, one cannot isolate the history of Buddhism in the West from Western religious history in general. That Westerners should take up Buddhism at all may have seemed eccentric or even bizarre in the eyes of many at that time, but such an exotic development was really a natural part of the Western religious zeitgeist at that time.

During the second half of the nineteenth century this zeitgeist was deeply informed by scientific discoveries, particularly by Darwin's *On the Origin of Species*, by the 'higher criticism' in biblical studies, and by the study of comparative religion. As a result, Christianity in its traditional dogmatic forms became less and less intellectually acceptable to a great many sincere and reflective and even spiritually sensitive people. At the same time, such people retained a strong emotional connection with Christianity. They could emancipate themselves intellectually from the dogmatic, doctrinal side of Christianity, but their heartstrings remained tied to the beliefs, practices, customs, and traditions of their childhood and youth.

For these people, Christianity had originally meant three things. This is especially true of the evangelicals who were prominent in English religious, and even social and political, life in those days. Christianity meant in the first place devotion to the person of Christ as the saviour, as the incarnate son of God. It meant an ethical code by which they could shape their actions: the Ten Commandments of the Old Testament, and the Sermon on the Mount of the New Testament. And finally, Christianity gave them the hope of life after death.

It is hard to appreciate nowadays how strong and pervasive this belief in life after death was in the nineteenth century. But I remember when I was a boy of fourteen I was sent down to the west country to stay with some elderly people in a rambling old house, decorated and furnished in the style of the 1860s and 1870s. And what I came away with above all was a memory of the pictures hanging in the bedroom where I was put. They were huge, framed images of a single religious theme that exercised our Victorian forebears perhaps more than any other. One showed angels welcoming the departing soul into heaven; another was of a bevy of angels having what appeared to be a little gossip; and yet another depicted the heavens opening and a faithful soul aspiring upwards. They were all meant to inspire a hope of the life to come. Probably the best known literary illustration of this sort of thing is Dickens' pathetic description of the death of poor Little Nell in *The Old Curiosity Shop* – how the snow was falling, and as she passed away the voices of the angels could be heard calling her to her everlasting rest. It is all laid on with a trowel, which is how the Victorians liked their sentimentality.

Even after many people felt obliged to abandon Christianity as an intellectual proposition, they still hankered after something equivalent to those three elements in Christianity that had meant so much to them, and some people found them in Buddhism. In the person of the Buddha they found a 'non-theological' Christ: a historical figure with all the virtues traditionally associated with Christ – even, perhaps, a few more – but without the encumbrance, not to say embarrassment, of Trinitarian theology. In the Buddhist precepts they found a code of ethics without any supernatural sanction; with, if anything, a purely humanistic sanction. They found the Sermon on the Mount without the Mount – that is, without the dogmatic, doctrinal background. Finally, they found in the teaching of karma and rebirth what appeared to them to be a more rational basis for their hope in a future life.

It is this final point that would come as something of a surprise to most traditional Buddhists. In the East the idea of having to come back again for another lifetime after the flames of your funeral pyre have died down is accepted implicitly. No one ever argues about it or discusses it; it's just taken for granted that you will keep coming back to the world for lifetime after lifetime. But rebirth is also viewed as a terrible thing. Having to endure all the limitations of a human body, all its pains and sufferings, over and over again, is regarded as a miserable sort of process. The blessed release of Nirvāṇa represents, for most ethnic Buddhists, essentially freedom from rebirth.

In the West, by contrast, a century ago, it was the prospect that after death there would be no life, just annihilation, that was the most terrible thing. The teaching of karma and rebirth even taken in isolation represented some sort of salvation: the possibility of escape from this terrible, post-Christian, nihilistic predicament.

That Buddhism should thus have been effectively treated as a sort of Christianity-substitute is only to be expected at that intermediate stage in the development of Western Buddhism. It is hardly possible to jump all at once into something totally new and strange. You have to go down into it step by step, gradually assimilating it, accommodating it, harmonizing it with what you're used to. You have to go to the unknown from the known.

Today, however, the position is rather different. Most people who come into contact with Buddhism are not so heavily conditioned by Christianity that we are looking – whether consciously or unconsciously – for a Christianity-substitute. We are post-Christian. We are not so much reacting *against* Christianity as simply registering that it just doesn't mean much to us.

We no longer, for example, think of religion in terms of devotion to a person. This was an integral part of religious ideology in the nineteenth century and it is an integral part of the faith of many orthodox Christians even today. But as Western Buddhists we are not likely to think of religion in those terms at all. We are not searching for someone to worship; we are not looking for a relationship with a person.

In a Buddhist this is not just a spirit of rebellion. There is a positive and clear principle involved. To those who were devoted too exclusively to his person, the Buddha used to say, 'He who sees the Dharma, sees me.'[186] It is only when we understand the Dharma, the principles and practices taught by the Buddha, that we can truly see and understand the living embodiment of those principles and practices, the Buddha himself. A further simple reason for the shift of interest from the person of the Buddha to his teaching is that far more of the Buddha's teachings have been translated into European languages than those that were available to people even fifty years ago.

If we are no longer looking for a Christ substitute, neither are we looking for an ethical code. We may need some guidance in the way we lead our day-to-day life, but not a list of dos and don'ts. We get so many conflicting moral messages from various quarters that most of us made the decision long ago to assess for ourselves what is right and wrong. We tend not to pay much attention to systems or codes of ethical behaviour. Most of us work out our positions on moral issues and how to act on them by making up our own minds.

In the case of Buddhists, a more positive reason for the less central importance accorded to ethics is the greater attention paid to meditation. If one had been reading books and articles about Buddhism a hundred years ago one would have found plenty of discussion of ethics, and very little reference to meditation. Nowadays one would find the opposite. It's not that ethics are necessarily neglected, but it is understood that ethical behaviour is important not only for its own sake but because of its effect on the mind, effective meditation being possible only on the basis of a good conscience.

So too with the question of life after death. This is simply not the preoccupation for people that it used to be. In the nineteenth century it was a burning issue, but nowadays many people seem to be able to contemplate with some degree of equanimity the possibility that after death they might not continue to exist. Their interest is centred on their present existence, here and now.

More positively, we may say that the present generation of Buddhists are less interested in karma and rebirth because they are more concerned, at least theoretically, with realization here and now. As a result of this existential emphasis Zen Buddhism gradually replaced the Theravāda in popular esteem from about the 1950s. And while Zen has now perhaps taken second place to Tibetan Buddhism, Western Buddhists seem to remain resolutely uninterested in karma and rebirth and not bothered about the prospect of life after life after life.

However, the process of karma and rebirth as described in Buddhist tradition, and depicted in the Tibetan wheel of life, is worth studying whether or not the question of future lives is an important one for us, because it can be seen not only according to the timescale of lifetimes but on a much smaller scale, reflecting the way life unfolds from day to day, even minute to minute, and suggesting how we can choose the direction our life will take. We will take a brief look at the workings of karma in our chapter on ethics (Chapter 10, and see also Chapter 7 of *Who is the Buddha?*), but here we will focus on the process of rebirth, taking as our guideline the twelve links of becoming, illustrated by the outermost circle of the wheel of life.

THE TWELVE LINKS OF BECOMING

The process of rebirth in Buddhism is analysed and understood according to the principle of 'conditioned co-production', (or in Sanskrit, *pratītya-samutapāda*). As the English translations suggest, this principle explains the origin or production of the various factors of our experience, how they arise in dependence on preceding factors. Thus it represents the application of the general Buddhist philo-sophical principle of universal conditionality to the process of rebirth. It is analysed down into a number of *nidānas* or 'links' in a series, each of which arises in dependence on, or is conditioned by, the preceding one.

A few texts enumerate five *nidānas*, and a few others identify ten, but the standard number is twelve.[187] Such inconsistencies may make the whole way the *nidāna* chain is enumerated seem rather contingent, but this is as it should be. Lists of this sort are not to be taken too literally. It is a mistake to think of a particular subject as being literally divided into a specific number of parts. There is not a literal Buddhist path, for example, consisting of literally eight distinct parts. These are divisions just for practical convenience. Discrepancies between different texts as to how many *nidānas* to count should remind us that conditioned co-production does not divide itself up into a number of actual 'links'. The *nidānas* express the *spirit* of conditionality rather than pinning it down in a set, particular framework. There are innumerable factors operating on the individual at any one moment. The *nidānas* represent simply a selection of crucial ones – and, as conditions do, some of them appear more than once. Of the twelve, the first and second traditionally refer to the previous life, the eleventh and twelfth to the following life, and all the rest to the present life.

1. Ignorance (*avidyā*) is not literally the first *nidāna*, because there is no actual beginning to the chain, but it is in some ways the most important. It is not ignorance in the intellectual sense so much as a lack of spiritual awareness; even, if you like, a lack of spiritual consciousness, a deprivation of spiritual being. Metaphorically speaking, *avidyā* represents a lack of illumination, a state of mental and spiritual darkness. Ignorance in this sense is the direct antithesis of *bodhi* or Enlightenment. Just as Enlightenment or Nirvāṇa is the goal of individual human development – the mountain peak ahead of us – so ignorance, lack of spiritual awareness, represents all that lies behind us in that process, the deep valleys swathed in darkness out of which we are gradually emerging.

More specifically, *avidyā* is made up of various wrong views – wrong ways of looking at things: for example, seeing the conditioned as Unconditioned, or thinking that anything mundane, anything phenomenal, can last for ever. Such a view is not an intellectual conviction, but an unconscious assumption. In clinging on to things that are subject to decay, and therefore becoming unhappy when we finally have to surrender them, we behave as though we believed that they ought to last for ever.

Another specific instance of *avidyā* is belief in a personal God or supreme being. The idea that belief in God is a case of lack of spiritual awareness might raise a few eyebrows; but on this question Buddhism offers the same analysis as does psychoanalysis. According to both, the God figure, the idea of a supreme being, a creator, is a sort of projected father-figure, a glorified representation of the father of our childhood, on whom we depend for help when we get into difficulties. Such belief is seen as a manifestation of spiritually immature dependency and unawareness.

Ignorance can also manifest by way of various beliefs, whether rationalized or not, based upon the assumption that purely external acts such as ceremonies, rituals, and sacraments can have spiritual efficacy or value quite apart from the state of mind with which they are performed. An obvious pitfall to avoid, one might think. However, even today there are, for example, many orthodox Hindus, even educated and Westernized Hindus, who genuinely believe that the waters of the Ganges have a definitely purifying effect, and that if you take a dip in those waters, your sins really will be washed away. And of course it can never be like that at all, as Ramakrishna, the great Hindu mystic who lived at the end of the nineteenth century, used to explain. He didn't like to offend the feelings of the orthodox, but at the same time he didn't like to commit himself to the orthodox belief. He would say, 'Yes, it's quite true that when you take a dip in the sacred Ganges you are purified of all your sins: when you go down into the water, your sins take the form of crows and they perch on the trees nearby; though when you come out of the water the crows disappear and your sins come back to you again.'[188]

It is really quite difficult to dislodge this wrong view, particularly when it is entrenched in a venerable tradition. In the West the sixteenth-century Reformation inaugurated by Martin Luther was basically about this question. It was about whether the whole sacramental side of religion (and in particular, the purchase of indulgences, which relieved the purchaser of the burden of their sins) had value and efficacy in themselves, as purely mechanical, external observances. Luther asserted that it was impossible. Yet it is still one of the teachings of the Catholic Church that the sinfulness of the priest in no way impairs the efficacy of the sacrament he administers.

All this is *avidyā*. Above all it includes ignorance of the law of universal conditionality itself, the law which is exemplified by the principle of conditioned co-production.

2. Karma formations (*saṃskāras*) arise in dependence on ignorance, or *avidyā*. *Saṃskāra* literally means 'preparation' or 'setting up',

and when it appears in the context of the five *skandhas* (i.e. the five aggregates or categories into which the self – or what one thinks of as the self – may be analysed)[189] the term is translated as 'volitions' or 'willed action'. But in the context of the twelve *nidānas* it is generally rendered as 'karma formations'. This means the aggregate of those mental conditions that under the law of karma are responsible for the production, or preparation, or setting up, of the first moment of consciousness in the so-called 'new life'.

Essentially, the *saṃskāras* are acts of will connected with particular states of mind. These states of mind – which may be expressed either in physical action, or in speech, or just in mental activity – are either skilful or unskilful. Unskilful mental states are those dominated by greed or craving, by hatred or ill will, and by mental confusion or bewilderment. Skilful mental states are those dominated instead by contentment, generosity, kindness, and clarity of mind.

Unskilful volitions result in what is popularly called a 'bad rebirth', while skilful volitions result in a 'good rebirth'. However, Buddhism takes the radical view that both these kinds of volition, skilful as well as unskilful, are ultimately rooted in ignorance. According to Buddhism, desire for a good rebirth, or even working towards a good rebirth, is just as much a product of ignorance in the spiritual sense as moving more or less unconsciously towards a bad one. This is because rebirth, even a good rebirth, isn't the goal of Buddhism. The goal is the complete emancipation of the mind – or consciousness or whatever one likes to call it – from conditioned existence itself, from the whole round of birth and death and rebirth.

The traditional image given for the relationship between *avidyā* and the *saṃskāras* (whether skilful or unskilful) is a rather pointed one. *Avidyā* or ignorance is said to be like the state of drunkenness, while the *saṃskāras*, the karma formations, are like the actions that you perform while drunk.

This image suggests that most people in their ordinary everyday actions, even in their so-called conventionally religious actions, are no better – from a spiritual point of view – than drunkards behaving in the foolish ways that drunkards do. This is really the state of most of us. Sometimes it is said that, from a spiritual point of view, we are asleep, but it is just as true to say that we are drunk. We're 'drunk' because we are continuously under the influence of ignorance, so that everything we do, everything we say, everything we think, is the product in one way or another of that lack of spiritual awareness.

A drunkard imagines that whatever he is doing and saying is very clever and witty and wise, when in fact it is simply sottish. We are the same. Whatever we may do or say or think, however we may indulge in all sorts of charitable activities, all sorts of conventional religious practices, it is all done out of lack of spiritual awareness – which is quite a sobering thought, really. And yet in dependence on this 'drunken' activity arises 'consciousness'. So what does this mean?

3. Consciousness (*vijñāna*) arises in dependence on the *saṃskāras* or karma formations. What is meant here is not consciousness in general, but consciousness in a specific sense, called technically the 'relinking consciousness'. After the death of the human organism it relinks the psyche to the psychophysical process in the form of a new life, a rebirth. According to tradition, three factors are necessary for conception of a human being to take place: first, there has to be sexual intercourse; second, the prospective mother should be ready to conceive; and, third, there must be what is popularly described as a 'being' ready to be reborn.

'Being' here means the last moment of consciousness belonging to the previous existence. In other words, it is the relinking consciousness. According to the Theravāda school, there is no interval between death and rebirth, but other schools – the Sarvastivāda, and following them the Tibetans – teach that there is an intermediate state, a *bardo*, in between. (This intermediate state forms much of the subject matter of the *Tibetan Book of the Dead*, or *Bardo Thödol*.)[190]

Which of these views is correct is open to debate. The more important issue is whether or not anyone may be said to be reborn at all. This question exercises many people. In view of the doctrine of *anātman* or no-self, who or what exactly is reborn?

Buddhism offers no facile solution to this conundrum. All one can do is point out two extreme and thus false positions to be avoided. One extreme view is to maintain that the person who is reborn, who reappears in a new existence, is in some essential way the same as they were before in their previous existence. So, if someone is reborn, it's the same Tom or Dick or Harry or Gertrude or Mary as before, but they have a new body. This sort of belief is expressed, for instance, in the Hindu *Bhagavad Gītā*, where Krishna says that rebirth is just like putting on a new set of clothes when you get up in the morning.[191] You cast aside the old worn-out body and take on a new one, but you yourself remain essentially unchanged.

The other extreme view says that you must be an essentially different person in your next life. The influence or the conditioning exerted by the body on the psyche as a whole is so profound – that is, your physical experience is so fundamental to your identity – that you cannot speak in terms of being the same person when you have a different body.

These would appear to be the only alternatives on offer: either the person reborn is the same as the one who died or they are different. However, we can begin to discern the real nature of these two views on rebirth by stepping back to another controversy with which they are connected historically. This is an ancient Indian dispute about the nature of causation, and the two opposing schools survive to this day.

The Satkāryavāda school of thought maintains that cause and effect are identical. It says that when a so-called effect is produced, all that has really happened is that the cause has changed its form. They say that if, for instance, you have a lump of gold which you make into ornaments, then the gold becomes the cause of which the ornaments represent the effect. And in that case both cause and effect consist of the same thing. It is the same gold, whether you call it cause or whether you call it effect. The process is uninterrupted, and there is no specific point at which a cause turns into something different called an effect. Thus cause and effect are one and the same. By contrast, those who follow the Asatkāryavādin line of reasoning say that, on the contrary, cause is one thing, and effect is quite another thing, and they use the example of milk turning into curds to prove their point.[192]

Both these views, if they are pursued logically, in fact make causation impossible. Whether cause and effect are identical, or whether they are quite different, either way there can be no relation between them. Buddhists therefore avoid this whole argument, which they see as proceeding from wrong premises.

Buddhism establishes itself on *pratītya-samutapāda*, or conditionality. According to this principle, any phenomenon whatsoever, whether mental or material, arises in dependence on, or is conditioned by, a complex of other phenomena. But this relationship between the conditioning agents and the object of conditioning cannot be described either in terms of identity or in terms of difference. Neither category fits.

Applying this principle to the question of rebirth, all one can really say on the subject is that in dependence on the karma formations of the last life, consciousness arises. To ask if someone is the same as or different from the person whose karma formations provided the conditioning necessary for their existence is beside the point. The question does not make sense in Buddhist terms. The one who is reborn is neither the same as, nor entirely different from, the one who died. As so often with Buddhism, the really strict, orthodox Buddhist position consists of a paradox: there is rebirth, but there is no one who is reborn. That's the Buddhist position in precise terms.[193]

What no Buddhist should be said to believe in is 'reincarnation' – i.e. getting into a body again and again. This notion assumes that you have a soul, a sort of unchanging essence of yourself that pops into one body after another. Such an idea does not conform with Buddhist principles at all. Technically the correct word is not even 'rebirth', but *punarbhava*: 'again-becoming' or 'rebecoming'.

4. The psychophysical organism (*nāma-rūpa*) – literally 'name and form', but roughly translatable as 'mind and body' – arises in dependence on the relinking consciousness. *Nāma-rūpa* comprises the five *skandhas*: the physical body, feeling, perception, volition, and consciousness. This is a comprehensive link in the chain, representing a basic breakdown of the individual's full experience of himself or herself into these five categories. It is clear from this link that the chain as a whole is not a simple sequence of causation, but a complex chain of conditionality. Certain factors therefore appear more than once in the chain as the crucial element in a whole complex of conditions.

5. The six bases (*ṣaḍāyatana*) arise in dependence on this initially embryonic psychophysical organism. They are simply the five physical sense organs together with the mind, which is treated as a sort of sixth sense organ. Just as our five senses each have their range of objects, so does the mind have its memories, ideas, and projections. The six bases are so-called because they constitute the bases for our experience of the external world, the external universe.

6. Contact (*sparśa*) arises in dependence on the six bases of the psychophysical organism. Contact or impression represents the mutual impact of sense organ with its appropriate object. The eye comes into contact with visual form, the ear with sounds, and so on – and, of course, the mind comes into contact with mental objects or ideas.

7. Feeling (*vedanā*) arises in dependence on sense contact, and we have already met it as one of the five categories comprising the fourth *nidāna*. Feeling or sensation can be pleasant or painful, or it can be neutral, that is, neither pleasant nor painful; and it is an ever-present element of our experience at whatever level, right up to Enlightenment. However, whereas pleasure may be experienced at any plane of existence, pain is possible only in connection with the gross, sensory level.

8. Craving (*tṛṣṇā*) – literally 'thirst' – arises in dependence on feeling. There are three kinds of craving: *kāma-tṛṣṇā*, thirst or craving for sensuous experience; *bhava-tṛṣṇā*, craving for continued existence, especially continued existence after death, in heaven; and *vibhava-tṛṣṇā*, craving for non-existence, for annihilation, the desire for oblivion. This particular link is the crucial one of the whole series – why, we shall see shortly – and it appears as the second of the four noble truths: the origin of rebirth and suffering.

9. Attachment or grasping (*upādāna*) arises in dependence on thirst or craving. One might well imagine that this *nidāna* needs no introduction, that we are all familiar enough with attachment: attachment to pleasures of all kinds, to possessions, to people, and so on. However, what we usually think of as attachment represents only one of four kinds of attachment enumerated by the Buddhist tradition.

The second kind is a particularly significant and characteristically Buddhist idea of what constitutes attachment. It is attachment to *dṛṣṭi*: literally 'views' but meaning also 'opinions', 'speculations', and 'beliefs', including all sorts of philosophical and religious opinions. This is not to say that you shouldn't entertain beliefs or convictions or philosophical or religious opinions – even very strongly – but attachment or grasping or clinging to them is seen as unhealthy.

How is one to tell the difference between a strong, healthy conviction as to the truth of one's views, and an unhealthy attachment to them? In fact it is quite easy. When we are engaged in argument with someone, and they challenge an idea that for us is axiomatic, if we become in the least bit upset or angry, that is a sure sign of attachment to *dṛṣṭi*. If our equanimity is at all disturbed when our belief is challenged, then whether our view is right or wrong is no longer of much consequence. That clinging is a fetter, binding us to the wheel of birth and death. Let us by all means rectify and refine our understanding of the Dharma, and try to put it into practice, but not in such a way that when anyone questions or challenges us, we feel threatened and react in a hostile, unsympathetic manner.

Thirdly, there is attachment to ethics (*śīla*) and religious observance (*vrata*). Again, it is not that one shouldn't practise ethics, meditation, and so on. The mistake is to cling on to one's practice as an end in itself, or to imagine that doing these practices makes one 'different' from other people.

And then, fourthly, there is attachment to a belief in a permanent, unchanging self existing apart from the various and constantly changing elements of one's experience of oneself.[194]

10. Becoming (*bhava*) arises in dependence upon attachment. *Bhava* is life or existence as conditioned by our attachment, on any plane, on any level, from the lowest hell realms to the highest celestial abodes. The term *bhava* can be taken to mean conception, but it also refers to the whole process represented by the *nidāna* chain in both its passive aspect, consisting of the fruits of action, and its active aspect, consisting of the volitions that result in rebirth.

According to some Buddhist schools, including those of Tibet, this link represents the *bardo*, the intermediate state between death and rebirth. Others would say that it represents the intrauterine period of human life – that is, the period between conception and birth.

11. Birth (*jāti*) arises in dependence on becoming (in its 'active' volitional aspect). Some would say that this is literally birth in the sense of becoming physically independent of the mother, but it can also be seen as the simultaneous coming together of the five *skandhas* as a psychophysical organism in the womb.

12. Decay and death (*jarā-maraṇa*) arise in dependence upon birth – together with, the traditional texts say, 'sorrow, lamentation, pain, grief, and despair'. Once you've been born, nothing on this earth can prevent you from decaying, eventually, and dying. We are born out of our attachment to conditioned things, and we must also go the way of conditioned things.

BREAKING THE CHAIN

The wheel of life, and this sequence of twelve links, can be taken symbolically to mirror to us the process of actions and their consequences which drives our behaviour from day to day. The very act of reaching for a biscuit can be analysed in terms of these twelve *nidānas*. But we can also take this sequence as a literal reflection, a pictorial teaching, of the process of birth, death, and rebirth. The twelve *nidānas* cover a sequence of three lives. The first two links, ignorance and the karma formations, belong to the past life, in the sense that it's because of spiritual ignorance and the actions based on that ignorance that we're born again in this life. Consciousness, name and form, the six bases, contact, sensation or feeling, thirst or craving, grasping or clinging, and becoming all belong to the present life. Birth and subsequent decay and death obviously belong to the future life.

These same twelve links can also be subdivided into two groups, known as the 'action process' and the 'result process'. The word for 'action' here is karma, using the word in its simplest sense. The links belonging to the action process represent what we do – they are *volitional* actions, whether of body, speech, or mind – whereas the links belonging to the result process are passive, representing what we experience as a result of what we have done.

Ignorance and the karma formations constitute the action process of the past life; it is as a result of them that we have come into existence in the present life. Consciousness, name and form, the six bases, contact, and sensation or feeling together make up the result process of the present life. They are the given characteristics of existence, the results of our past actions; there's nothing we can do about them now. Thirst or craving, grasping or clinging, and becoming constitute the action process of the present life, because they are all volitional, and therefore productive of future karmic consequences.

Thus we have, over the three lifetimes – past, present, and future – an alternating sequence of action process, result process, action process, result process. Within this cycle there are three points of transition: the point where the action process of the past life is succeeded by the result process of the present life; the point where the result process of the present life is succeeded by the action process of the present life; and the point where the action process of the present life is succeeded by the result process of the future life.

All these three points are extremely important. The first and the third represent the points of transition from one life to the next. The second point, however, is a point of transition which is in a crucial sense even more important: a point of transition – in the midst of our present life – at which we can potentially move from the cyclical type of conditionality to a completely different, spiral type. This is the point at which the wheel of life can cease to revolve altogether, the point at which we can break the chain. But how does this happen?

We have seen that the last link of the result process of the present life is sensation or feeling – pleasant, painful, or neutral. (It is perhaps worth noting at this point that by 'feeling' here is meant no more than the bare sensation. It doesn't mean 'boredom' or 'love' or 'anger', or anything like that; these we could refer to as 'emotions' rather than 'feelings', to make the distinction clear.) There's nothing wrong with feeling, nothing wrong with sensation. In fact, as we have seen, it is part of the 'result process'; we have no choice about whether or not we experience it. Where we do have a choice is in how we respond to that pleasant, unpleasant, or neutral sensation. Of course, we don't usually experience it as a choice. It is usually automatic that in dependence upon feeling arises craving. That's the problem.

Of the three kinds of craving, craving for continued existence and craving for annihilation are impulses – opposite tendencies, really – of which we need to become aware. Generally speaking, each of us tends either to the extreme of eternalism or to the extreme of nihilism – extremes that distort our whole world-view. These tendencies go very deep, but they are clearly in evidence in our everyday life – for example, in that we tend to take either an over-optimistic view of things, or an over-pessimistic one. It is of the utmost importance that we become aware of our own tendency in this respect, and aware that it will be colouring our view of life.

But it is the third kind of craving – thirst or craving for sensuous experience – which gives us the clue as to how we can break the endless circle at this point. Perhaps to speak of 'craving' is slightly misleading, because the connotations of the word suggest that it is simply desire for pleasant experience that is meant, whereas 'craving' here includes three distinct strands. When we experience a pleasant feeling, our usual tendency is automatically to want to hang on to it. When, on the other hand, we experience an unpleasant feeling, our reaction is to push it away, to avoid it. And if we experience a feeling that is neither pleasant nor unpleasant, we are liable just to feel confused. In other words, we are infected by the three root poisons, greed, hatred, and ignorance, symbolized at the hub of the wheel of life by the cock, the snake, and the pig. These are the forces that keep the whole wheel spinning round. When we respond to pleasant feelings with thirst or craving, to unpleasant feelings with aversion, or to neutral feelings with indifference, we set up volitions, we create fresh karma – and round we go again.

This is why this particular link is so crucial. We have to learn to experience feelings and sensations without allowing them to give rise to craving, aversion, or indifference. Here mindfulness – awareness, recollection – is of fundamental importance. It is important that we are able to be mindful or aware of what we are experiencing in the way of sensation or feeling, rather than reacting unconsciously to that sensation and thus setting up unskilful volitions.

Creating this hiatus can be very uncomfortable, because once we become aware at this point, we realize that craving is essentially impossible to satisfy. Although our instinct is to grasp pleasure and push away pain, our longings will not be appeased, nor our pain stilled, in this way. Out of this realization of the essential unsatisfactoriness of mundane things (*duḥkha* is the Buddhist term for it), can arise faith in the possibility of something higher; faith, we may say, is the positive counterpart of craving.

This movement from the awareness of unsatisfactoriness to faith is the first step on the spiral path; and this is the starting point of Chapter 7, in which we will examine another sequence of twelve links, a sequence that forms not the endless round of the wheel of life, but the spiral path – which begins with this moment of awareness between feeling and craving, and which leads us away from the wheel of life through more and more positive states of consciousness all the way up to Enlightenment itself.

These twelve 'positive links', as one could call them, have often been forgotten. They are mentioned in only two or three places in the Pāli canon,[195] and as far as I know they are not mentioned in the Mahāyāna scriptures at all. We hear a lot about the first set of twelve links but we hardly ever hear about this second, positive set. This is unfortunate because it contributes to the impression some people have that Buddhist spiritual practice is primarily negative, consisting simply in getting rid of craving, clinging, and so on. It is very important not to forget the twelve positive links. They represent the spiral type of conditionality, and without them our picture of reality – reality as represented by the principle of conditionality – is incomplete. Moreover, without them the spiritual path has no rationale.

There is also a great deal of value in contemplating the twelve links that make up the cyclical trend of conditionality. Indeed, every serious student of Buddhism needs to be well acquainted with them. We should be able to recite them from memory, almost like repeating a mantra. The Buddhist tradition teaches specific methods of reflecting and meditating systematically on the twelve links (see page 346) and we need to make the effort to do this. One could go so far as to say that otherwise there's not much hope of our really understanding what Buddhism is all about.

3
THE TEXTURE OF REALITY

Reality is a very big word, but it is not really a Buddhist word. We have *śūnyatā* or emptiness, we have *tathatā* or suchness, and we have *dharmakāya*, the 'truth-body', but there is no true semantic equivalent in traditional Buddhist terminology of the word 'reality'.

Reality is not only a big word; it is also an abstract word (which often means a vague word) and on the whole Buddhists have never been fond of abstract terminology. Tibetan Buddhism, for example, takes a very concrete, and even – if one wanted to be paradoxical – materialistic approach to the spiritual life. And Zen Buddhism goes even further: any indulgence in abstractions or vague generalities is met with a piercing shriek or thirty blows or some other such reminder to stay closer to one's own experience.

When I use this word 'reality' in speaking about Buddhism, I am therefore using it in a makeshift and provisional way. It isn't to be taken too literally. Certainly, the connotations that attach to it in general Western philosophical and religious usage cannot be said to apply in a Buddhist context.

It is for these reasons that – while the word 'reality' may be almost unavoidable for an English-speaking Buddhist – I am introducing the idea of its *texture*. This word is almost palpably concrete. Texture is felt, it is handled, it is experienced directly, by touch. Because we have so many nerve endings in the tips of our fingers, we are able to make very subtle distinctions among an enormous range of different textures. We can distinguish between cotton, silk, and wool, or between granite, slate, and marble. And it is possible to discern far more subtle gradations of texture. Chinese experts on jade used to be able to distinguish between hundreds of kinds and qualities of jade – white, black, red, or green jade, mutton-fat jade or dragon-blood jade, or whatever it was – with their eyes closed, simply by feeling the texture of the jade under water.

Reality too, in Buddhism, is something to be felt, touched, even handled – because Buddhism is above all else practical. So, continuing to use the word in a provisional sense, we may say that reality in Buddhism is broadly speaking of two kinds: there is conditioned reality and Unconditioned reality – or more simply, there is the conditioned and the Unconditioned.

THE TWO REALITIES

'The Unconditioned' is the usual translation of the Sanskrit *asaṃskṛta*. *Sam* means 'together', *kṛta* is 'made' or 'put', and *a-* is a negative prefix, so *asaṃskṛta* literally means ' not put together' or 'uncompounded'. 'The conditioned' is therefore *saṃskṛta*, which is a word of particular interest in Sanskrit as it is the name of the language itself – 'Sanskrit' being an Anglicized version of it. According to the Brahmin pundits it is so called because it is the language that has been properly put together, beautifully put together, perfected, in contrast to the rough, crude, and unpolished 'Prakrit' – including Pāli – spoken by the common people (i.e. especially by the non-Brahmins). In modern Indian languages like Hindi, Bengali, and Marathi, *saṃskṛti* means 'culture'. In this way the idea has developed that *saṃskṛta*, the conditioned, is also the artificial, whereas *asaṃskṛta*, the Unconditioned, is the natural, the simple, that which has not been artificially put together.

This connotation to the term 'Unconditioned' receives explicit recognition in Tantric Buddhism. The Tantrics have an interesting word sahaja for reality: *sahaja*. *Saha* means 'together', and *ja* means 'born' (as in *jāti*, 'birth'); so the literal meaning of *sahaja* is 'born with' or 'co-nascent'. Reality is thus said to be that with which one is born, that which is innate, that which does not have to be acquired.

The distinction between the conditioned and the Unconditioned, between the artificial and the natural, is fundamental to Buddhist thought, even though, as we shall see, there is some disagreement among various Buddhist schools as to whether it is an *absolute* distinction or not. And the distinction would appear to go back a long way, even to predate the Buddha's own Enlightenment.

The *Majjhima Nikāya*, the medium-length discourses of the Pāli canon, includes a discourse that is of rather special interest on account of its autobiographical content. This is the *Ariyapariyesanā Sutta*, in which the Buddha describes how he left home, how he became a wandering monk, how he strove for Enlightenment, and, as we have seen, how he deliberated about whether or not to try to teach the Dharma.

What surprises some readers of this *sutta* is that there is no mention in it of the famous 'four sights', of how Siddhārtha Gautama, the future Buddha, sallied forth one fine morning in his chariot with his charioteer, and saw a sick man, and then – on successive occasions – an old man, a corpse, and finally a wandering ascetic; and thus came alive to the existence of sickness, old age, and death, and the possibility of becoming a truth-seeking wanderer.

Instead, this particular account gives a comparatively naturalistic, even humanistic, description of how Siddhārtha came to the decision to give up the household life. It is, so far as this account is concerned, a purely internal process, not connected with anything in particular that he saw or heard. Here he is represented – in his own words – as simply reflecting.

The Buddha relates how one day he was sitting at home in the palace, reflecting alone. We should imagine him perhaps under a tree in the compound; it is probably the early evening, when a cool, calm quiet descends over the Indian scene. He is there simply reflecting, 'What am I doing with my life? I am mortal, subject to old age, sickness, and death. And yet, what do I do? Being myself subject to birth, I pursue that which is also subject to birth. Being myself subject to old age I pursue that which likewise will grow old. Being myself subject to sickness and decay, I pursue that which is subject to the same decay. And being myself subject to death, I pursue that which also must die.'[196]

Then – as the Buddha goes on to relate to his interlocutor in this *sutta*, who is a Jain ascetic – there arose in his mind a different, almost a contrary train of reflection. It occurred to him, 'Suppose now I were to do otherwise? Suppose now, being myself subject to birth, I were to go in search of that which is not subject to birth, which has no origin, which is timeless? Suppose, being myself subject to old age, I were to go in search of that which is immutable? Suppose, being myself subject to sickness, to decay, I were to go in search of that in whose perfection there is no diminution? Or suppose, finally, being myself subject to death, I were to go in search of the deathless, the everlasting, the eternal?'

As a result of these reflections, shortly afterwards he left home. There is no great drama in this *sutta*, no stealing out of the palace by moonlight on muffled hooves.[197] It simply says that although his father and his foster-mother wept and wailed, he put on the yellow robe, shaved his head, cut off his beard, and went forth from home into the homeless life.

This is the story, in brief, of the Buddha's conversion – conversion in the literal sense of a 'turning round', though in Siddhārtha's case it was not an external turning round, from one religion to another, but an internal one, from the conditioned to the Unconditioned. Siddhārtha realized that he was a conditioned being, and that he was spending all his time and energy in pursuit of conditioned things – that is, in the *anariyapariyesanā* or 'ignoble quest'. He realized, in other words, that he was binding himself to the endless round of existence, the wheel of life on which we all turn, passing from one life to the next indefinitely.

So he decided simply to turn round completely and go in search of the Unconditioned instead, to take up the *ariyapariyesanā*, the 'noble quest'. In time, he would realize this quest as the spiral path leading from the endless round to the goal of Enlightenment or Nirvāṇa. But at this point he identified the course before him with this simple but strong, pre-Buddhistic expression, found in the oldest Upanishads: *esana*, urge, desire, will, search, aspiration, quest, pursuit. He could continue with the 'ignoble quest', or he could undertake the 'noble quest' instead.

The Buddha's conversion was not easy, we can be sure of that, because here and there, in other places in the scriptures, we get indications that a terrible struggle went on in his mind before he made his final decision.[198] But stripped of all the legends and myths that have accumulated around it over the centuries, it was as simple – almost classically simple – as this. And it is in this most simple description of the first great insight of the Buddha-to-be that the essence of the spiritual life is to be found. Here we put our finger on the spring that works the whole mechanism.

This spring is the conditioned in pursuit of the Unconditioned, the mortal seeking the immortal: seeking, that is, not immortality of the self, but a self-transcending immortality. What Siddhārtha was looking for was basically the answer to a question, one that we find asked (in the *Majjhima Nikāya*) by a young monk, Govinda, who spends a rainy season retreat – that is, a retreat of about three months – meditating on *mettā* or universal loving-kindness, and as a result has a vision of the 'eternal youth' Brahmā Sanankumāra. The question Govinda asks Sanankumāra in this *sutta* is, 'How may the mortal obtain the immortal Brahmā world?'[199]

This is the essential religious question. How may the conditioned become the Unconditioned; how may the mortal become immortal? How may I conquer death? Now it all sounds very fine put like that, but if one is going to take seriously the question of how to leave the conditioned and go in search of the Unconditioned, one will want the answer to a further question. What exactly does one mean by the conditioned? How do we identify the conditioned?

According to Buddhist tradition, that which is conditioned invariably bears three characteristics, or *lakṣaṇas*, by which it may be recognized as such. These three characteristics are sometimes called the 'three signs of being', but more properly this should be the 'three signs of becoming', as the nature of the conditioned is nothing as static as a 'state of being'.

The three *lakṣaṇas*, the three inseparable characteristics of all conditioned existence, are: *duḥkha*, the unsatisfactory, or painful; *anitya*, the impermanent; and *anātman*, the emptiness of self, of essential being.[200] All conditioned 'things' or 'beings' whatsoever in this universe possess all these three characteristics. They are all unsatisfactory, all impermanent, all devoid of self. Of these three *lakṣaṇas* the first is in some ways the most difficult for most people to come to terms with emotionally, so we shall look at it in rather more depth and detail than at the other two.

SUFFERING

The Sanskrit word here is *duḥkha*, and the usual translation is 'suffering', but a better one – if a bit cumbersome – is 'unsatisfactoriness'. Best of all, perhaps, is to attend to its etymology: though the traditional account of the origin of the word *duḥkha* is no longer universally accepted, it still leaves us with a true and precise image.

Duḥ- as a prefix means anything that is not good – bad, ill, wrong, or out of place; and *kha*, the main part of the word, is supposed to be connected with the Sanskrit *cakra*, meaning 'wheel'. So *duḥkha* is said to have meant originally the ill-fitting wheel of a chariot, thus suggesting a bumpy, jarring ride, a journey on which one could never be comfortable, never at one's ease.

So much for a general picture of *duḥkha*. As we look closer, though, we see that unease or suffering comes in many different forms – and the Buddha usually speaks of seven.[201] First, he says, *birth* is suffering: human life starts with suffering. In the more poetical words of Oscar Wilde, 'At the birth of a child or a star there is pain.'[202] In whatever way it is expressed, this is a great spiritual truth; it is significant that our life begins with suffering.

Birth is certainly physically painful for the mother, and consequently it is often emotionally painful for the father, while for the infant it is, we are told, a traumatic experience. It is very unpleasant to be suddenly thrust forth from the warm, protective world of the womb out into a cold, strange world, to which one is very likely to be welcomed with a slap on the bottom.

Secondly, the Buddha says, *old age* is suffering. One of the discomforts of old age is physical weakness: you cannot get about in the relaxed, agile way you used to. Then there is loss of memory: you can't remember names, or where you put things; you are not as agile and flexible intellectually as you were. Where this degeneration becomes senility it is a tragic thing to observe, most especially in once eminent individuals. Perhaps most painful of all, when you are very old you are dependent upon others: you cannot do much for yourself, and you may even need constant looking after by a nurse or by your relations. Despite all modern comforts and amenities – and often as a result of modern advances in medicine – many of us will experience this suffering, especially if we survive to an extreme old age.

Thirdly, *sickness* is suffering. Whether it is a toothache or an incurable disease like cancer, no sickness is pleasant. It is not just the physical pain that is suffering: there is also the helplessness, the fear, and the frustration of it. Medical science may sometimes palliate the suffering of sickness, but there is no sign at all that we will ever banish it entirely. It seems that no sooner do we get rid of one disease than another comes along. As soon as one virus is defeated, a new, stronger strain of virus arises. And as soon as we feel physically quite healthy, we start to develop all sorts of mental ailments, more and more complex neuroses and mysterious syndromes, all of which involve suffering.

Almost any sense of imperfection in our lives can develop into an illness of some sort: stress turns into heart attacks, fatigue turns into syndromes, habit turns into addictions. So it seems that sickness may change its appearance, but it doesn't go away.

Fourthly, *death* is suffering. We suffer when those dear to us die; we suffer as we watch the life ebbing from a physical body that we have long associated with the life of a loved one. We suffer in the knowledge that our loved ones will die, and we suffer in the knowledge of our own dissolution. Much of our suffering with regard to death, of course, is simply fear. Most of us would put up with a great deal of suffering before we would choose to die, such is our terror of the inevitable conclusion to our own existence:

> The weariest and most loathéd worldly life,
> That age, ache, penury, and imprisonment
> Can lay on nature, is a paradise
> To what we fear of death.[203]

People do not always feel ready to die. They are sorry to leave the scene of their labours and pleasures and achievements. Even if they do want to go, even if they are quite happy to pass on to a new life, or into they know not what, there is still the pain involved in the physical process of dissolution, and with this goes, sometimes, a great deal of mental suffering. Sometimes on their deathbeds, people are stricken with remorse: they remember wrongs they have done, harm and pain they have inflicted on certain individuals; and they may have, in consequence, fears and apprehensions for the future. All this makes death a horrifying experience for many people, and one which, before it comes, they do their best not to think about.

Fifthly, *contact with what one dislikes* is suffering. We all know this. It may be that even in our own family there are people with whom we just don't get on. This is very tragic, especially when it is our own parents or children whom we dislike. Because the tie – even the attachment – of blood is there, we have to put up with a certain amount of contact, and this can be painful.

The work we do can also be a source of suffering, if we do it just because we need to earn a living and it is the only work we can get. Again, we may feel that we have to put up with what we dislike, and perhaps work with people we find uncongenial, for periods of time anyway, even though we would rather do something else.

There are, as well, all sorts of environmental conditions which are unpleasant: pollution, noise, weather. It is obviously not possible for everyone to go off and live in a Greek villa. So there seems to be no way of escape – certainly no way of escaping entirely. You just have to live with people, places, things, and conditions that you don't altogether like.

Sixthly, *separation from what one likes* is suffering. This can be a very harrowing form of suffering indeed. There are people we would like to be with, to meet more often – relations, friends – but circumstances make it simply impossible. This happens often in time of war, when families are broken up – men conscripted and taken to far-off battlefields, children sent away to places of safety, and people simply disappearing as refugees.

I myself can remember how, when I was in India during the war as a signals operator, many of my friends used to get letters from home regularly every week or so; and then a day might come when the letters would stop. They wouldn't know what had happened, but they would know that there were bombs falling in England, so after a while they would start suspecting the worst. Eventually, perhaps, they would get the news, either from another relation or officially, that their wife and children, or their parents, or their brothers and sisters, had been killed in an aerial bombardment. This is the most terrible suffering – permanent separation from those we love. Some people never get over such suffering, and brood over their loss for the rest of their lives.

Seventhly, *not to get what one wants* is suffering. There is little need to elaborate upon this. When you have set your heart on something (or someone) and you fail to achieve your goal, when the prize does not fall to you, then you feel disappointed and frustrated, even bitter. We have all known short-lived experiences of this kind, when we fail to get a job we particularly wanted, or fail to be selected for something, or find that someone else has got to something (or someone) before us.

Some people experience a lifetime of disappointment, frustration, and bitterness if they feel that life has short-changed them in some way – and of course the stronger the desire, the more the suffering. But even in small ways, it is something with which we are acquainted almost every day, if not every hour – for example, when we find that all the cake has gone.

So these are the seven different aspects of *duḥkha* identified by the Buddha. The Buddha once declared, 'One thing only do I teach – suffering and the cessation of suffering'[204] – and emancipation from the bondage of suffering is indeed the keynote of his teaching. In the Pāli scriptures he compares himself to a physician who attempts to relieve his patient of a tormenting disease – the disease of conditioned existence with which we are all afflicted.[205] Of course, we are not always willing patients, as the Buddha clearly found. But on the many occasions when he spoke about suffering, and tried to get people to see it in perspective, he would apparently sum up his discourse by saying that existence as a whole is painful, that the totality of conditioned sentient experience, comprising form, feeling, perceptions, volitions, and consciousness, is unsatisfactory.[206]

Now most people would say that this is going a bit far, that it is a pessimistic, if not morbid, view of life. They would say that human existence can by no means be said to be unsatisfactory and painful all the way through. They will admit to birth being painful, they will agree that sickness, old age, and yes, death, are indeed painful. But at the same time they are reluctant to accept the conclusion that follows from all this, which is that conditioned existence itself is suffering. It is as though they admit all the individual digits in the sum, but they won't accept the total to which those digits add up. They say that yes, there is a certain amount of suffering in the world, but on the whole it's not such a bad place. Why be so negative? There's plenty to smile about. While there's life, there's hope.

And there is, of course. We have pleasant experiences as well as painful ones. But the Buddhist view is that even the pleasant experiences are at bottom painful. They are really only suffering concealed, glossed over, deferred – a whistling in the dark. And the extent to which we can see this, see the suffering behind the gilding of pleasure, 'the skull beneath the skin', depends on our spiritual maturity.

Edward Conze has identified four different aspects of concealed suffering.[207] Firstly, something that is pleasant for oneself may involve suffering for other beings. We don't tend to consider this, of course. If we are all right, if we're having a good time, we don't worry too much or too often about others. The most common example of this is the frank enjoyment with which people eat the flesh of slaughtered animals, without consciously thinking about the suffering of the animals.

But the unconscious mind is not so easily fooled. You can shut out some unpleasant fact from the conscious mind, but unconsciously you notice everything and you forget nothing. You may never be consciously aware of that unpleasant fact, but it will exert an influence on your mental state that is all the more powerful for being unseen. In this way we develop an 'irrational' feeling of guilt, because in the depths of ourselves we know that our own pleasure has been bought at the expense of the suffering of other living beings. This kind of guilt is the source of a great deal of uneasiness and anxiety.

Conze gives the example of wealthy people, who are nearly always afraid of becoming poor. This is, he says, because unconsciously they feel that they don't deserve to have their money. Unconsciously they feel that it *ought* to be taken away from them, and consciously they worry that perhaps it *will* be taken away from them. By contrast, you notice that poor people who may not know where next week's food is coming from are rarely racked with anxiety over it. They are generally much more relaxed and cheerful than the rich.

Wealthy people may suffer from unconscious guilt feelings because they know, however much they may deny it consciously, that the acquisition of their wealth has brought suffering to other people, directly or indirectly. Consequently, they feel a constant need to justify themselves. They say, 'I earn my money, I contribute to the well-being of the community, I offer a service that people want, I provide employment. ...' Or else they say, 'If I'm rich and other people are poor, it's because I work harder, I take risks – at least I don't ask to be spoon-fed. ...'

If the feeling of guilt gets too much then drastic measures are required to relieve it, and the most drastic measure of all is to give away some of that wealth – to the church, or to a hospital or whatever. Hospitals are a favourite option because you can compensate for the suffering you have caused in acquiring the wealth by giving some of it to alleviate suffering. It is called 'conscience money'. If one has anything to do with religious organizations, one soon learns to recognize this sort of donation. Sometimes it is just put through the letter box in an envelope inscribed 'from an anonymous donor'. Then you know that someone's conscience is really biting.

Conze's second kind of concealed suffering is a pleasant experience that has a flavour of anxiety to it because you are afraid of losing it. Political power is like this: it is a very sweet thing to exercise power over other people, but you always have to watch your back, not knowing if you can trust even your best friend, or the very guardsmen at your door. All the time you are afraid of losing that power, especially if you have seized it by force and others are waiting for their chance to get their hands on it. In such a position you do not sleep easily.

The traditional Buddhist illustration of this kind of experience is that of a hawk flying off with a piece of meat in its talons. What happens, of course, is that dozens of other hawks fly after it to try and seize that piece of meat for themselves, and they do this by tearing and stabbing not at the meat itself but at the possessor of the meat, pecking at its body, its wings, its head, its eyes.[208] The highly competitive world of finance and business and entertainment is like this. Any pleasure that involves any element of power or status is contaminated by an element of anxiety, by the sense that others would like to be able to replace you at the top of your own particular dunghill.

The third concealed suffering indicated by Dr Conze is something that is pleasant but which binds us to something else that brings about suffering. The example he gives is the human body. Through this we experience all sorts of pleasurable sensations that make us very attached to it; but we experience all sorts of unpleasant sensations through it as well. So our attachment to that which provides us with pleasant sensations binds us also to that which provides us with unpleasant sensations. We can't have the one without the other.

Lastly, Conze suggests that concealed suffering is to be found in the fact that pleasures derived from the experience of conditioned things cannot satisfy the deepest longings of the heart. In each one of us there is something that is *Unconditioned*, something that is *not* of this world, something transcendental, the Buddha-nature – call it what you like. Whatever you call it, you can recognize it by the fact that it cannot be satisfied by anything conditioned. It can be satisfied only by the Unconditioned.[209]

Whatever conditioned things you may enjoy there is always a lack, a void, which only the Unconditioned can fill. Ultimately, it is for this reason that – to come back to the Buddha's conclusion – all conditioned things, whether actually or potentially, are unsatisfactory, painful. It is in the light of the Unconditioned that suffering, *duḥkha*, is clearly seen as characteristic of all forms of conditioned existence, and of sentient conditioned existence especially.

The second fundamental characteristic of conditioned existence, *anitya*, is quite easily translated. *Nitya* is 'permanent', 'eternal', so with the addition of the negative prefix you get 'impermanent', 'non-eternal'. It is also quite easily understood – intellectually at least. It can hardly be denied that all conditioned things, all compounded things, are constantly changing. They are by definition made up of parts – that is, compounded. And that which is compounded, made up of parts, can also be uncompounded, can be reduced to its parts again – which is what happens, of course, all the time.

It should really be easier to understand this truth nowadays than it was in the Buddha's day. We now have the authority of science to assure us that there's no such thing as matter in the sense of actual lumps of hard solid matter scattered throughout space. We know that what we think of as matter is in reality only various forms of energy.

But the same great truth applies to the mind. There is nothing unchanging in our internal experience of ourselves, nothing permanent or immortal. There is only a constant succession of mental states, feelings, perceptions, volitions, acts of consciousness. In fact, the mind changes even more quickly than the physical body. We cannot usually see the physical body changing, but if we are observant we can see our mental states changing from moment to moment.

This is the reason for the Buddha's (at first sight) rather strange assertion that it is a bigger mistake to identify yourself (as a stable entity) with the mind than with the body.[210] But this is the Buddhist position. Belief in the reality of the 'self' is a bigger spiritual mistake than belief in the reality of the body. This is because the body at least possesses a certain relative stability, but there is no stability to the mind at all. It is constantly, perceptibly changing.

Broadly speaking, the *lakṣaṇa* of *anitya* points to the fact that the whole universe from top to bottom, in all its grandeur, in all its immensity, is just one vast network of processes of different types, taking place at different levels – and all interrelated. Nothing ever stands still, not even for an instant, not even for a fraction of a second.

We do not see this, though. When we look up we see the everlasting hills, and in the night sky we descry the same stars as were mapped by our ancestors at the dawn of history. Houses stand from generation to generation, and the old oak furniture within them seems to become more solid with the passing of the years. Even our own bodies seem much the same from one year to the next. It is only when the increments of change add up to something notable, when a great house is burnt down, when we realize that the star we are looking at is already extinct, or when we ourselves take to our deathbed, that we realize the truth of impermanence or non-eternity, that all conditioned things – from the minutest particles to the most massive stars – begin, continue, and then cease.

EMPTINESS OF SELF

The third *lakṣaṇa, anātman*, encapsulates the truth that all conditioned things are devoid of a permanent, unchanging self. So what does this mean exactly? When the Buddha denied the reality of the idea of the *ātman*, what was he actually denying? What was the belief or doctrine of *ātman* held by the Buddha's contemporaries, the Hindus of his day?

In the Upanishads alone there are many different conceptions of *ātman* mentioned.[211] In some it is said that the *ātman*, the self – or the soul, if you like – is the physical body. Elsewhere the view is propounded that the *ātman* is just as big as the thumb, is material, and abides in the heart. But the most common view in the Buddha's day, the one with which he appears to have been most concerned, asserted that the *ātman* was individual – in the sense that I am I and you are you – incorporeal or immaterial, conscious, unchanging, blissful, and sovereign – in the sense of exercising complete control over its own destiny.

The Buddha maintained that there was no such entity – and he did so by appealing to experience. He said that if you look within, at yourself, at your own mental life, you can account for everything you observe under just five headings: form, feeling, perception, volitions, and acts of consciousness. These are the *skandhas* (Sanskrit) or *khandas* (Pāli). Nothing discovered in these categories can be observed to be permanent. There is nothing sovereign or ultimately blissful amongst them. Everything in them arises in dependence on conditions, and is unsatisfactory in one way or another. These five categories or aggregates are *anātman*. They don't constitute any such self as the Hindus of the Buddha's day asserted. Such a self exists neither in them nor outside of them nor associated with them in any other way.

Seeing conditioned existence, seeing life, in this way, as invariably subject to suffering, to impermanence, to emptiness of self, is called *vipaśyanā* (Sanskrit) or *vipassanā* (Pāli), which translates into English as 'insight'.

Insight is not just intellectual understanding. It can be developed only on the basis of a controlled, purified, elevated, concentrated, integrated mind – in other words, through meditative practice. Insight is a direct intuitive perception that takes place in the depths of meditation when the ordinary mental processes have fallen into abeyance. A preliminary intellectual understanding of these three characteristics is certainly helpful but, ultimately, insight is something that transcends the intellectual workings of the mind.

So in meditation, through insight, you see that without exception everything you experience through the five senses and through the mind – everything you can feel and touch and smell and taste and see and think about – is conditioned: subject to suffering, impermanent, and empty of self. When you see things in this way, you experience what is called revulsion or disgust, and you turn away from the conditioned. It is important to note that this is a spiritual experience, not just a psychological reaction; you turn away not because you are personally repelled by things as such, but because you see that the conditioned is not, on its own terms, worth having. When that turning away from the conditioned to the Unconditioned takes place decisively, it is said that you enter the 'stream' leading to Nirvāṇa.

At this point we have to guard against a misunderstanding. Some schools of Buddhism think of the conditioned and the Unconditioned as though they were two quite different entities, two ultimate principles in a kind of philosophical dualism. But it isn't like that. It isn't that on the one hand you have the conditioned and on the other you have the Unconditioned, with a vast gap between them. They are more like two poles. Some Buddhist schools even say that the Unconditioned is the conditioned itself when the conditioned is seen in its ultimate depths, or in a new, higher dimension, as it were.[212] The Unconditioned is reached by knowing the conditioned deeply enough, by going right to the bottom of the conditioned and coming out the other side (so to speak). In other words, the conditioned and the Unconditioned are, in a way, two sides of the same coin.

This perspective, which is a very important one to take in, is brought into focus by a teaching – common to all schools – called the three *vimokṣas*, or 'liberations'.[213] They are also sometimes called the three *samādhis*, or the three 'doors': the three doors through which we can approach Enlightenment.

The first of these liberations is *apraṇihita*, the 'unaiming' or 'unbiased'. It is a mental state without any inclination in any direction, without likes or dislikes, perfectly still, perfectly poised. Thus it is an 'approach' to the Unconditioned, but it's an approach which is by way of not going in any particular direction. You only want to go in a particular direction when you have a concept of that direction and a desire to go in it. If there's no particular direction in which you want to go, then you just, as it were, stay at rest. This state can be compared to a perfectly round sphere on a perfectly flat plane. Because the plane is absolutely level, the perfect sphere doesn't roll in any particular direction. The *vimokṣa* of directionlessness is rather like this. It's a state of absolute equanimity in which one has no egoistic motive for doing – or not doing, even – anything. So this is an avenue of approach to reality, to Enlightenment.

The second liberation, the second door to the Unconditioned, is *animitta*, the 'signless'. *Nimitta* literally means a sign, but it can also mean a word or a concept; so the *animitta* is the approach to the Unconditioned by bypassing all words and all thoughts. This is a very distinctive experience. When you have it, you realize that all words, all concepts, are totally inadequate. Not that they're not very adequate, but that actually they don't mean anything at all. This is another door through which one approaches the absolute, the Unconditioned. The *animitta* is a state in which one prescinds all concepts of reality. In other words, one doesn't think about reality. I don't mean that one 'doesn't think about it' in the ordinary way in which one doesn't think about reality. After all, we could say that most of us, most of the time, don't give much thought to reality. But on the attainment of this *vimokṣa* one has, as it were, reached the level of reality but one doesn't think about reality. One realizes that no words, no concepts, can possibly apply; indeed, one doesn't even have the concept of non-applicability. This is the *vimokṣa* or *samādhi* of signlessness or imagelessness.

And the third liberation is *śūnyatā*, the voidness or emptiness. In this state you see that everything is, as it were, completely transparent. Nothing has any own-being, nothing has any self-identity. In the language of the Perfection of Wisdom, the Prajñāpāramitā, things are what they are because they are *not* what they are – one can only express it paradoxically. This is the *vimokṣa* of emptiness.

The three liberations represent different aspects of the Unconditioned; that is, they show the Unconditioned from different points of view, which are also different ways of realizing it. You can penetrate into the Unconditioned through the unbiased, through the signless, and through voidness. However, as we have already said, you attain the Unconditioned by knowing the conditioned in its depths. Thus we can also say that you penetrate to the three liberations through paying attention to the three *lakṣaṇas*. That is, each of the three liberations can be reached through understanding deeply enough its corresponding *lakṣaṇa*. In this way the three *lakṣaṇas* themselves can be seen as doors to liberation.

If you look deeply enough at the essentially unsatisfactory nature of conditioned existence, then you will realize the Unconditioned as being without bias. This is because when you see the suffering inherent in conditioned things, you lose interest in the goals and aims and purposes of conditioned existence. You are quite still and poised, without inclination towards this or that, without any desire or direction for yourself. Hence when you go into the conditioned through the aspect of suffering you go into the Unconditioned through the aspect of the unbiased.

Alternatively, when you concentrate on the conditioned as being impermanent, transitory, without fixed identity, then going to the bottom of that – and coming out the other side, so to speak – you realize the Unconditioned as the signless. Your realization is of the emptiness of all concepts, you transcend all thought; you realize, if you like, 'the eternal' – though not the eternal that continues through time, but the eternal that transcends time.

And thirdly, if you concentrate on the conditioned as devoid of self, devoid of individuality, devoid of I, devoid of you, devoid of me, devoid of mine, then you approach, you realize, the Unconditioned as *śūnyatā*, as the voidness. What 'the voidness' is, we shall be going on to consider.

As for the present chapter, however, our aim has been to throw some light on the subject of the three *lakṣaṇas*, the three characteristics of conditioned existence. They are of central importance not just in Buddhist philosophy but in the Buddhist spiritual life. According to the Buddha, we don't really see conditioned existence until we learn to see it in these terms. If we see anything else, that's just an illusion, just a projection. And once we start seeing the conditioned as essentially unsatisfactory, impermanent, and empty of self, then little by little we begin to get a glimpse of the *Un*conditioned, a glimpse that is our essential guide on the Buddhist path.

4
NIRVĀṆA

The first question Buddhists get asked when they meet non-Buddhists is, as likely as not, 'What is Nirvāṇa?' Certainly, when I was a Buddhist monk travelling about India, I used to find on trains that no sooner had I taken my seat than someone would come up to me (for in India people are by no means bashful when it comes to getting into conversation) and say, 'You seem to be a Buddhist monk. Please tell me – what is Nirvāṇa?'

Indeed, it is a very appropriate question to ask. The question is, after all, addressing the whole point of being a Buddhist. You may see Buddhists engaged in all sorts of different activities, but they all have the same overall purpose in view. You may see shaven-headed Japanese monks in their long black robes sitting in disciplined rows, meditating hour after hour in the silence and tranquillity of a Zen monastery. You may see ordinary Tibetans going in the early morning up the steps of the temples, carrying their flowers and their candles and their bundles of incense sticks, kneeling down and making their offerings, chanting verses of praise to the Buddha, the Dharma, and the Sangha, and then going about their daily business. You may see Sri Lankan monks poring over palm-leaf manuscripts, the pages brown with age. You may see layfolk in the Theravādin countries of Southeast Asia giving alms to the monks when they come round with their black begging-bowls. You may see Western Buddhists working together in Right Livelihood businesses.

When you see unfolded this whole vast panorama of Buddhist activities, the question that arises is: Why? What is the reason for it all? What is the moving spirit, the great impulse behind all this activity? What are all these people trying to do? What are they trying to achieve through their meditation, their worshipping, their study, their alms-giving, their work, and so on?

If you asked this of any of these people, you would probably receive the traditional answer: 'We're doing this for the sake of the attainment of Nirvāṇa, liberation, Enlightenment.' But what then is this Nirvāṇa? How is it to be understood or explained? How is it to be fitted in to one's own particular range of mental furniture? One naturally gropes after analogies. If one has a Christian background one will try to envisage Nirvāṇa as a sort of eternal life in heaven after death. If one takes it outside the usual religious framework altogether, one may even think of it as a state of complete annihilation or extinction.

But in fact there is no excuse for these kinds of badly mistaken views. It is not difficult to give a clear account of Nirvāṇa, because the ancient canonical texts are quite clear as to what it is and what it isn't. If one has the job of presenting the topic of Nirvāṇa, one will probably need to begin by discussing the etymology of the word Nirvāṇa – whether it means a 'blowing out' or a 'cooling down'. And one will no doubt go on to explain that, according to the Pāli texts at least, Nirvāṇa consists in the extinction of all craving, all hatred, and all ignorance of the true nature of things.[214]

At some point it is customary to say that Nirvāṇa is a state of incomparable bliss, to which the bliss of this world cannot be compared.[215] And if one wants to get a bit technical one may want to describe the two kinds of Nirvāṇa: the *kleśa nirvāṇa*, consisting in the extinction of all passions and defilements; and the *skandha nirvāṇa*, consisting in the extinction of all the various processes of psychophysical existence, an event that takes place upon the death – as we call it – of someone who has already gained *kleśa nirvāṇa* during their lifetime.[216]

One may then go on to the different interpretations of Nirvāṇa in the various different schools of Buddhism – the Theravāda, the Madhyamaka, the Yogacāra, the Tantra, Zen, and so on. Finally, it is always necessary to emphasize that Nirvāṇa is neither eternal life in the Christian sense, nor annihilation or extinction in the materialist sense – that here, as elsewhere, one has to follow the middle path between two extreme views.

So this is how Nirvāna is traditionally delineated. Above all, perhaps, Nirvāna is conventionally defined as the *goal* of Buddhism. And it is in respect of this particular way of positioning the concept that my approach in this chapter will appear to some people – mistakenly, in my view – to be perhaps rather unorthodox.

THE PSYCHOLOGY OF GOAL-SETTING

There are all kinds of groups of people in the world – religious groups, political groups, cultural groups, charitable groups, and so on – and each of these groups has its goal, be it power, or wealth, or some other satisfaction, and whether it is for their own good or the good of others. And it would seem that Buddhists likewise have their own particular goal that they call Nirvāna. So let us look at what is meant by this idea of a goal to be attained or realized, and then establish to what extent it is applicable to Nirvāna.

It should be clear at once where this procedure is going to lead us. The fact is that whenever terms are used rather loosely, without any lucid consideration of what they mean, you get the beginnings of serious misunderstandings. This is particularly the case when we transfer terms and expressions derived from mundane experience, like 'goal', to spiritual or transcendental experience, like 'Nirvāna'. If they don't quite fit, we need to be aware of this, and if they don't fit at all, we need to think through the whole question afresh.

With this in mind, let us examine the idea of a 'goal' a bit more closely. A goal is an objective, something you strive for. You could, if you like, draw a distinction between striving to *be* and striving to *have*, but actually, the two come to the same thing: 'having' is a sort of vicarious 'being'. A goal is in the end something that you want to *be*. Suppose, for instance, your goal is wealth: you can say that your goal is to *possess* wealth, or that your goal is to *be* wealthy, but obviously the possessing, the having, is reducible to the being, the existing.

There is one really crucial (if obvious) precondition for setting a goal: it must represent something you are not. You don't want to have or to be what you already have or are. You can only want to be what you are not – which suggests, obviously, that you are dissatisfied with what you are. If you're not dissatisfied with what you are, you will never strive to be what you aren't.

Suppose, just by way of example, your goal happens to be money and material possessions. You will have made these things your goal because you are dissatisfied with being poor. Or if, say, you make knowledge your goal, if you want to add to your understanding, investigate fundamental principles, and so on, you want to do this because you are dissatisfied with your present state of being ignorant.

We don't always see it in quite these stark terms, but this is the basic pattern or procedure involved in setting ourselves goals, and it is a quite appropriate way of proceeding on its own level. But we get into a tangle when we extend it into the spiritual life – and by this I don't mean some elevated sphere of experience far removed from everyday concerns. By the spiritual life I mean something very close to home.

Any complex of problems we may have can be boiled down to the most basic problem of all, which is unhappiness in one form or another. A case of bad temper, for example, is a problem because it makes us miserable, and one could equally well say the opposite, that being miserable makes us bad-tempered. Even though we don't usually think of the problem we have as one of unhappiness, that is what it really is.

So we try to get away from unhappiness and attain happiness. The way we go about this is to try to ricochet, as it were, from that experience of feeling miserable or discontented into an opposite state or experience of feeling happy; and this usually involves grasping at some object or experience that we believe will give us the happiness we seek.

When we feel unhappy, what we do is set up this goal of happiness, which we strive to achieve. And as we all know, we fail. All our lives through, in one way or another, we are in search of happiness. No one is in search of misery. Everyone is in search of happiness. There's no one who could possibly say they're so happy that they couldn't imagine themselves being a little happier. Most people, if they're honest with themselves, have to admit that their life consists of a fluctuating state of unease and dissatisfaction, punctuated by moments of happiness and joy which make them temporarily forget their discomfort and discontent. And this possibility of being happy becomes everybody's goal – a goal which can never be realized because happiness is by its nature fleeting. We all continue to set up this phantom goal, however, because the alternative – which is simply to be aware – is too challenging for us.

The setting up of goals – which means trying to get away from one's present experience – is really a substitute for awareness, for self-knowledge. Even if we do develop a measure of self-knowledge, we don't tend to maintain it because to do so would be just too threatening. We always end up setting up goals rather than continuing to be aware.

To take a simple example, suppose I have something of a problem with my temper: I get irritated, even angry, rather easily – even a small thing can spark me off – and this bad temper of mine makes life difficult, and perhaps miserable for myself and others. And suppose that I wake up one day and decide that enough is enough, that it's time it came to a stop. So I set up a goal for myself – the goal of being good-tempered. I think, 'I'm undeniably bad-tempered: my goal, however, is to be sweet-tempered and amiable, always returning the soft answer, always ready to turn the other cheek.'

What actually happens, though? One almost invariably fails. The intention – even the degree of self-knowledge – is admirable. But after a while one's resolve falters. In the face of the same old provocations, one is back again in the same old rut – and probably blaming the same old people and the same old external circumstances for it. So why is this? Anybody who has ever begun to recognize that their problems are, at least to a degree, of their own making will also recognize that this is what happens. But why does it happen?

The reason is that we are continuing to tackle the symptoms rather than the disease. If we try to get away from our unhappiness simply by trying to be good-humoured, we are still unaware of the fundamental cause of our being bad-tempered. And if this isn't resolved, if we don't know why we are bad-tempered, if we don't know what is prompting the angry answer or the violent reaction, then we can't possibly hope to become good-tempered.

Whatever our problem, we automatically – almost instinctively – set up a goal of being happy in order to get away from our unhappiness. Even if a little awareness, a little insight, does arise, it is not sustained. We revert automatically to setting up a goal of one kind or another rather than continuing to be aware and trying to understand very deeply why that problem arises. Setting up goals is an automatic reflex to short-circuit the development of awareness and self-knowledge – in short, to get away from ourselves.

How then do we change this? To start with, we need a change of attitude. Rather than trying to escape from ourselves, we need to begin to acknowledge the reality of what we are. We need to understand – and not just intellectually – why we are what we are. If you are suffering, don't just reach out for a chocolate. Recognize the fact that you are suffering and look at it more and more deeply. If you're happy, recognize it, take it in more and more deeply. Instead of running from happiness into guilt, or into some sort of excitable intoxication, try to understand what the true nature of that happiness is, where it really comes from. Again, this isn't just intellectual; it's something that has to go very deep down indeed.

For some people this sort of insight will come in the course of meditation. Meditation isn't just fixing the mind on an object, or revolving a certain idea in the mind. Meditation really involves – among other things – getting down to the bedrock of the mind, illuminating the mind from the bottom upwards, as it were. It is about exposing to oneself one's motives, the deep-seated causes of one's mental states, one's experiences, one's joy and one's suffering, and so on. In this way real growth in awareness will come about.

But where is all this leading? What has all this to do with Nirvāṇa? It may seem that we have strayed rather from our subject, but in fact we have been doing some necessary preparing of the ground. With some things, if one tackles them too directly, one can easily miss the mark. What we can now do is open up some kind of perspective on the way Nirvāṇa is traditionally described – or rather on the effect on us of these traditional descriptions.

Suppose, for example, I have been going through rather a difficult, upsetting period, and am feeling rather miserable. Then one day I pick up a book in which it is stated that Nirvāṇa is the supreme happiness, the supreme bliss. What will be my reaction? The likelihood is that I will think, 'Good – that's just what I want – bliss, happiness.' I will make Nirvāṇa my goal. And what this means is that effectively I will be making lack of awareness my goal. I will be latching on to Nirvāṇa – labelled as the supreme bliss – because it happens to fit in with my subjective needs and feelings at this particular time. Such a reaction has of course nothing to do with being a Buddhist, but it is the way that a lot of us approach Buddhism, and indeed use Buddhism, in a quite unaware, almost automatic way. Unconsciously we try to use Nirvāṇa to settle problems that can only really be resolved through awareness.

We do not succeed in banishing unhappiness by pretending to ourselves that we are happy, by shoving our misery out of sight. The first step is to acknowledge the reality of our condition: if there is an underlying unhappiness to our lives, we must face up to the fact. It is certainly good to be cheerful and positive, but not at the expense of fooling ourselves. One has only to look at the faces of the people you see in any city to see the 'marks of weakness, marks of woe'[217] that William Blake saw in London two hundred years ago, and yet few people will admit to their misery even in their own minds.

No progress can be made till we come to terms with our actual experience, till we get to know our unhappiness in all its comings and goings, till we learn to live with it, and study it. What is it, at bottom, that makes us unhappy? What is its source? We will get nowhere by looking for a way out of our misery, by aiming for the goal of happiness, or even Nirvāṇa. It is a mistake to postulate the goal of Nirvāṇa too quickly or too unconsciously. All we can do is try to see more and more clearly and distinctly what it is in ourselves that is making us unhappy. This is the only way that Nirvāṇa will be attained.

In this sense Nirvāṇa cannot be seen as an escape from unhappiness at all. It is by trying too hard to escape from unhappiness that we fail to do so. The real key is awareness, self-knowledge. A paradoxical way of putting it would be to say that the goal of Buddhism consists in being completely and totally aware at all levels of your need to reach a goal. We can also say, going a little further, that Nirvāṇa consists in the full and complete awareness of why you want to reach Nirvāṇa at all. If you understand completely why you want to reach Nirvāṇa, then you've reached Nirvāṇa. We can go further even than this. We can even say that the unaware person is in need of Nirvāṇa, but is unable to get a true idea of it. An aware person, on the other hand, is quite clear about this goal, but doesn't need it. That's really the position.

So there we have the basic drawback to conventional accounts of Nirvāṇa as being this or that. We simply accept or reject this or that aspect of Nirvāṇa in accordance with our own largely unconscious needs. If the underlying – and therefore unconscious – drive of our existence is towards pleasure, then we will find ourselves responding to the idea of Nirvāṇa as the supreme bliss. If on the other hand we are emotionally driven by a fundamental need to know, to understand, to see what is really going on, then almost automatically we will make our goal a state of complete illumination. And again, if we feel oppressed or constrained by life, if our childhood was one of control and confinement, or if we have a sense that our options in life are restricted by our particular circumstances – by poverty, by being tied down to a job or a family, or looking after elderly relatives – then we will be drawn to the idea of Nirvāṇa as freedom, as emancipation.

In this way there takes place a half-conscious setting up of goals based on our own psychological or social conditioning, instead of a growing understanding of *why* we feel dissatisfied, *why* we feel somehow 'in the dark', or *why* we feel tied down. Nirvāṇa becomes simply a projection of our own mundane needs.

Hence when we consider the subject of Nirvāṇa, the goal of Buddhism, the question we should be asking is not 'What is Nirvāṇa?' but 'Why am I interested in Nirvāṇa? Why am I reading this book rather than another, or rather than, say, watching television?' Is it curiosity, is it duty, is it vanity, is it just to see how Sangharakshita is going to tackle this thorny topic? Or is it something deeper?

Even these questions will not settle the matter. If it is curiosity, why are we curious about Nirvāṇa? If it is duty, towards what or whom do we feel dutiful? If it is vanity, why do we want to preen ourselves in this particular way? What is underneath our interest? If there is something deeper in our motivation, what is it?

This line of questioning might appear unconventional or unorthodox, and in pursuing it we may not learn much about Buddhism or Nirvāṇa in the purely objective, historical sense. But we will learn a great deal about what the ideas of Buddhism represent. If we follow this particular line, constantly trying to penetrate to the depths of our own mind, we may even get a little nearer to the goal of Nirvāṇa itself.

Sometimes we have to reverse our whole attitude. In the case of this great subject of Nirvāṇa, the abstract, ontological approach is of little use on its own. We have to start examining our own relationship to Nirvāṇa in the way we conceive of it. This is much more likely to bring us nearer to a deeper awareness, and thus to Nirvāṇa, than any amount of purely metaphysical or psychological disquisition. It may also prepare us for something even more profound and important than Nirvāṇa itself – the mystery of the Void.

5

THE MYSTERY OF THE VOID

Primitive Christianity was a religion not of dogma but of 'mysteries' – and indeed the Eastern Orthodox churches still speak of the mysteries of Christianity. Easter, for example, is a celebration of such a mystery, commemorating, according to Christian tradition and belief, the crucifixion and the resurrection of Christ.

The majority of orthodox, practising Christians take both these events in the same literal sense. They believe that Christ was resurrected in the same physical, historical way in which he was crucified, and that he subsequently ascended into heaven, together with his flesh, blood, and bones, and all that appertains thereto. Most practising Christians believe that the whole of his psychophysical organism went up into heaven quite literally and physically, and sat down, presumably on a physical seat, at the right hand of the Father.

Buddhists do not of course believe this. The crucifixion may actually have occurred, but the resurrection and the ascension, from a Buddhist perspective, are most certainly myths. This is not to say that these myths are not true; but whatever truth they possess is spiritual rather than scientific or historical. From a Buddhist point of view the festival of Easter represents a spiritual rebirth after a spiritual death, the triumphant emergence of a new mode of being, even a new mode of awareness, from the old. We may even say that it represents – in Zen Buddhist terms – dying the great death before one can attain the great Enlightenment.[218]

The festival of Easter is, in its origins, a pagan festival. It takes place in the spring, when the trees are bursting into new leaf, when we begin to hear the birds singing again after they have been silent during the long winter months. According to the Venerable Bede, in his *Ecclesiastical History of the English People*, the word 'Easter' is from an old Anglo-Saxon word Eostre, which he says was the name of a pre-Christian, British goddess – presumably a fertility goddess. And of course there is no biblical warrant for the giving of Easter eggs. The unbroken egg is a universal symbol of new, renascent life. It is a symbol of resurrection in the widest sense, found in practically all religious traditions.

For example, in Etruscan tomb paintings dating back to 1000 BCE the dead are often depicted on the walls of their own tombs reclining on classical couches and holding in their outstretched hands an egg, a symbol of their belief that death was not the end, but would be followed by a new life. The same symbol is found in Buddhist literary sources. The bodhisattva, the one who is fully dedicated to the attainment of Enlightenment for the sake of all beings, is spoken of by the Buddha in Mahāyāna scriptures as one who is in the process of emerging from the eggshell of ignorance.[219]

So the mystery of Easter has meaning for us all if we are sensitive to the many overtones of the festival, even though the crudely literal interpretation of its myths is still officially sanctioned, and makes it impossible for Buddhists to celebrate it as Christians do. The festival of Easter is a mystery because its myths represent not a doctrine or a philosophy or a dogma but an experience, something essentially incommunicable. In its universality, it is the greatest of Christian mysteries.

Buddhism also has its mysteries; and perhaps the greatest of them, the one that represents most uncompromisingly an essentially incommunicable experience, is the mystery of the Void, or – in Sanskrit – *śūnyatā*. 'Voidness', or 'emptiness' – or even, in Guenther's translation, 'nothingness'[220] – is an exact translation of *śūnyatā*. One could even translate it as 'zero': in modern Indian languages zero in the mathematical sense is *śūnya*. But all these more or less literal, philologically correct translations can be most misleading, as we shall see.

Śūnyatā is a deep mystery not because it's an abstruse theory or a difficult doctrine or a particularly involved piece of Buddhist philosophy. It's a mystery because it is not a theory or a doctrine or a philosophy at all. One might even say that it is not just a mystery, but 'a riddle wrapped in a mystery inside an enigma' (to borrow Churchill's famous characterization of Soviet policy). *Śūnyatā* or 'voidness' or 'emptiness' is just the word that we use to label an experience – a spiritual, even a transcendental, experience – which we have no way of describing. It is a mystery because it is incommunicable. To speak of *śūnyatā* as though it were a doctrine, a theory, a philosophy, and nothing more than that, is a catastrophic mistake, because it precludes all possibility of greater understanding.

There is undeniably a doctrine of *śūnyatā*, even a theory or philosophy of *śūnyatā*, but we need to remember that these conceptual formulations, like all the others of the Buddhist tradition, are simply for the purposes of communication between the Enlightened (those who have the experience of *śūnyatā*) and the unenlightened (those who do not have any such experience). They represent, in the first place – historically speaking – the Buddha's communication of his experience to his immediate disciples. And, as well as describing the truth of the Buddha's experience, they all, from within their own different contexts, point the way by which we may ourselves experience that truth. All these so-called doctrines, all these formulations, are just components of the 'raft' whose sole purpose is to take us across the waters of birth and death, across the flood of conditioned existence, to the shore of Nirvāṇa. They have no significance apart from that function. They are means to an end, not ends in themselves.

This is something that must always be borne in mind when studying Buddhism, especially in an information-consuming culture like ours. Whatever we may learn about Buddhism, and particularly about the 'philosophy' of *śūnyatā*, it is always essentially a mystery, something to be experienced in the equal mystery of one's own personal spiritual life.

However, it must be said that for something that is so quintessentially a matter of experience, *śūnyatā* has been the subject of an extraordinary wealth and depth of Buddhist literary treatment. In fact, those scriptures devoted to the investigation of *śūnyatā*, known as the Perfection of Wisdom *sūtras*, together represent probably the most important single body of Mahāyāna canonical literature.

There are thirty-odd Perfection of Wisdom *sūtras* in all, some running to several volumes, while others are very short. The most famous of these are the *Vajracchedikā* or *Diamond Sūtra*, and the

Hṛdaya or *Heart Sūtra*, both of which are quite short and are recited daily in the Zen monasteries of Japan, and frequently in Tibetan monasteries as well.[221]

But all these *sūtras*, whether they are famous or obscure, deal basically with just one topic: *śūnyatā*, the Void, emptiness. Furthermore, they all deal with it in basically the same way: not logically, not metaphysically, but as a direct spiritual experience. Most of these texts are presented – as other *sūtras* are – in the form of discourses given by the Buddha, who speaks out of the depths of his own transcendental experience.

They are called Perfection of Wisdom *sūtras* because it is by means of the spiritual faculty of the Perfection of Wisdom, or *prajñā*, that the truth of *śūnyatā* is perceived (or rather intuited). Or, to put it a little more correctly (that is, less dualistically) *prajñā*, the Perfection of Wisdom, represents the subjective pole, and *śūnyatā* the objective pole, of what is essentially the same non-dual experience.

However, it would be a mistake to imagine that, because we are talking about 'an experience', we are dealing with something simple or single. What we call *śūnyatā* consists of a whole vast spectrum of experiences. Any Tibetan monk should be able to rattle off the names of no less than thirty-two kinds of *śūnyatā*, and will be expected to study them as well.

And not only the monks, as I learnt from a friend of mine in Kalimpong (a town in the foothills of the Himalayas where I lived during the 1950s). This gentleman had been at one time governor of the region of Gyantse in Tibet, and he was married to the eldest daughter of the Maharaja of Sikkim, Princess Pema Tsedeun. I remember her on a certain occasion saying (very good-humouredly), 'When we're in Lhasa my husband is never at home. He's always in the monasteries discussing Buddhism with the lamas. I hardly ever see him.' Intrigued, I said to him, 'Well, what is it that you like to discuss with the lamas?' He thought for a moment, and then said, 'Well, usually, after we've worked through this and that, what we really like to get down to – and sometimes we go on all night – is a discussion on the thirty-two kinds of voidness.' (So one knows where to look first for a husband who is out all night in Lhasa.)

However, to begin with it is probably reasonable enough to confine oneself to just four of these thirty-two kinds of *śūnyatā*. These four, which are the principal and most important kinds, are not literally four different kinds of *śūnyatā* as you might have four different kinds of cabbage or daffodil. They really represent four successive stages in our experience of the mystery of the Void, four pin-pointings in a continuous ever-deepening experience of reality.[222]

THE VOIDNESS OF THE CONDITIONED

This is the first of the four *śūnyatās*: *saṃskṛta-śūnyatā*, literally 'emptiness of the conditioned'. To understand this we must appreciate the basic Buddhist distinction between conditioned reality (that which is dependent upon causes and conditions) and Unconditioned reality (that which is not so dependent). Conditioned reality is existence as we know it on this earth, and it is to be recognized by its three fundamental characteristics: it is unsatisfactory, impermanent, and devoid of unchanging individuality or self.

Unconditioned reality (i.e. Nirvāṇa), by contrast, has the opposite characteristics – though these are not all quite the opposite characteristics that one might expect. The first one is straightforward enough: Unconditioned reality is supremely blissful. The second is that Unconditioned reality is eternal – though this characteristic should be understood not in the sense of being everlasting within time, but in the sense of transcending time altogether. As for the third, if the conditioned is devoid of self, then the Unconditioned should, of course, be characterized by self. But here there is a difference among the Buddhist schools – albeit largely a difference of terminology.

The Theravādins, for instance, say that not only is the conditioned devoid of self; the Unconditioned, Nirvāṇa, is also devoid of self. This voidness of self is obviously not quite the same thing in both cases, but the distinction is not always made clear. Some of the Mahāyāna schools indeed speak of the Unconditioned in terms of selfhood, – as *mahā-atma*, the 'great self',[223] or in the Zen tradition, as the 'true' or 'real' self.

Theravādins usually object strongly to this procedure – and with some justification. There is a very great and real danger of hypostasizing the self, that is, making it a concrete reality, when ultimately one wants to get rid of any sense of a separate self whatsoever. Even though it may in a sense be quite legitimate to speak of a higher or greater self – at least in a poetic way – there always remains the danger that instead of aiming at getting rid of the sense of self, one will simply be substituting one self for another, replacing a comparatively gross ego with a more subtle, refined self.

At the same time it is important to bear in mind that all positive statements about Nirvāṇa are really analogies, not to be taken literally. We may speak of Nirvāṇa as the 'supreme bliss', *nibbāṇaṃ paramaṃ sukham*,[224] but it is certainly not bliss as we understand it. Not even if we multiply the kind of bliss we have experienced a hundred or a thousand times will we get even the shadow of an idea of what the bliss of Nirvāṇa is really like. We're using the term 'bliss' analogously.

It should be possible to use the word 'self' in the same way, and this is what the Mahāyānists do. They don't do it very often, and when they do, they do so very circumspectly. They also have some canonical authority for using the word. The Buddha is to be found in several Mahāyāna *sūtras* speaking of Nirvāṇa as the 'great self' – in, for instance, the *Mahāparinirvāṇa Sūtra* (not to be confused with the *Mahāparinibbāna Sutta* of the Pāli canon).[225] It was thought at one time that the term *mahā-atma* appeared in the Pāli canon, in a verse from the *Aṅguttara Nikāya*, the collection of 'gradual sayings', but this was a misreading; the original translator of this text into English misread the Pāli term *mahatta* ('greatness') as *mahā-atta*, 'great self'.[226]

The Tantras go even further than the Mahāyāna: not only the 'great self' but even the 'great passion' and the 'great anger' appear as synonyms for Enlightenment. This has to be understood in a rather esoteric sense – such terms are employed within a certain traditional framework or context, where they may be positively effective rather than dangerous. In the West, where there is not yet a secure tradition in place, there may well be some danger of misunderstanding these usages.

So much for the vexed question of *anātman* or non-self as a characteristic of conditioned existence, and as a different sort of characteristic of Nirvāṇa. But we can now begin to see what the emptiness of the conditioned amounts to. Life as we know it, conditioned reality, is empty of the Unconditioned and its attributes. Bliss, permanence, and true selfhood are not to be found in this world, and if we want these things we have to look beyond this world to a higher dimension of reality. The 'voidness of the conditioned' is in the fact that it is void of the Unconditioned.

If the conditioned is empty of the Unconditioned, what is the Unconditioned empty of? Well, it's obvious really: the Unconditioned is empty of the conditioned. In the Unconditioned, in Nirvāna, there is no suffering, no impermanence, no false selfhood – it is without these characteristics. This is the second of the four śūnyatās: asaṃskṛta-śūnyatā, 'voidness of the Unconditioned' – which consists in the fact that it is void of the conditioned.

The Unconditioned is also 'the transcendental'. This is not an ideal expression, but it translates more or less adequately the Sanskrit and Pāli word lokuttara. Loka means 'world' and uttara 'higher' or 'beyond', so the transcendental is simply that which is above, or beyond, the world. It is not above or beyond in any spatial sense; only in the sense that it is not conditioned. It's beyond all suffering, beyond transience, beyond the sense of self (at least, beyond a false sense of self). It's above and beyond anything we can think of, anything we can imagine or begin to conceive. Contemplating it, the mind stalls and fails. It is almost as if there is only a great blank before us.

This is the Unconditioned, the transcendental reality, the goal of the spiritual life, of the ariyapariyesanā, the 'noble quest' of the conditioned for the Unconditioned. And surely one can't go beyond, or higher, or above, or further than that. Well, as far as some schools of Buddhism are concerned, one can't. The schools of what is called the classical Hīnayāna – the Sarvastivāda – operate with the idea of two mutually exclusive realities, the conditioned and the Unconditioned, a differentiation that provides almost all of us with a quite adequate basis for our spiritual lives. But the Mahāyāna, in the Perfection of Wisdom literature, goes even further than this.

THE GREAT VOID

This is the third śūnyatā: mahā-śūnyatā. It is the emptiness of the very distinction between conditioned and Unconditioned, between the world and the transcendental, saṃsāra and nirvāna. With this stage we experience and realize that the distinction upon which our whole spiritual life has so far been based is in the ultimate analysis only mind-created. It's only a conceptual distinction, not a real one. All things, the conditioned and the

Unconditioned, are equally *śūnyatā*. They are all the same voidness, all the same emptiness, all the same *great śūnyatā*. This *mahā-śūnyatā* embraces within itself all opposites, all distinctions whatsoever.

According to the Perfection of Wisdom teachings, all things and all beings whatsoever, whether great or small, high or low, pure or impure, Enlightened or unenlightened, are the same unique, ineffable, absolute reality, within which there are no distinctions whatsoever. Distinctions are not wiped out or obliterated, but they are provisional, not final or ultimate. Thus this teaching takes a very lofty viewpoint – not actually our own viewpoint at all. But it shows us what our viewpoint might ultimately be.

THE VOIDNESS OF VOIDNESS

Śūnyatā-śūnyatā, the emptiness of emptiness, is the final, and in some ways most important, level of voidness. It reminds us that emptiness is in the last analysis itself only an operative concept. It's not just the conditioned that is empty, it's not just the Unconditioned that is empty; even absolute Emptiness, even the Great Void, is itself empty. It is not a final doctrine or dogma to cling on to at the last. It too must be abandoned.

According to the great dialectician of the Madhyamaka school, Nāgārjuna, the whole teaching – or rather experience – of *śūnyatā* is intended as a medicine for the cure of all possible attachments, whether to the conditioned or to the Unconditioned. It's meant to cure every form of attachment to self, from the most gross to the most subtle, whether it is to the little ego or to the great self. He says that if we then become attached to *śūnyatā* itself we have infected the very medicine that should cure us. If the medicine itself becomes poison, our case is hopeless.

So we have to tread very carefully. Nāgārjuna goes as far as to say, 'Better be attached to a self as high as Mount Sumeru, than be attached to the idea of *śūnyatā*.'[227] If you're attached to the idea of a self, you can always be cured with the medicine of *śūnyatā*, but if you're attached to *śūnyatā* itself, there is no medicine to cure that. And when we begin to consider *śūnyatā* as a dogma, doctrine, or concept, or even as an experience, we begin to settle down with it, to be attached to it. So we must step warily indeed.

Emptiness is beyond even emptiness. Emptiness cannot even be expressed in terms of emptiness. This is the voidness of voidness, *śūnyatā-śūnyatā*. In the end the most appropriate mode of expressing oneself in respect of the fourth kind of *śūnyatā* is to give up long and elaborate explanations and commentaries and sub-commentaries, and to say nothing at all. One may be as eloquent and insightful as one likes, but *śūnyatā* will always remain ultimately a mystery, even the greatest of all mysteries, so far as the Buddha's teaching is concerned. It cannot be explained or even described.

The idea of writing a neat little chapter on the subject, or giving a smooth, well-rounded lecture on it, is really quite ridiculous. At best one can offer broken hints, little suggestions, and just point in its general direction as one would point a finger at the moon. And if we make sure that we do not mistake the finger for the moon, if we do not take these hints and suggestions too literally, then some of them may help to nudge us towards the actual experience of *śūnyatā*, which is coterminous with the experience of supreme Enlightenment itself.

In this way we develop the experience of *śūnyatā* to the point at which words can serve no further useful purpose at all. We begin with our experience of the emptiness of the world. This is the deep realization of the fact that the world as we know it contains nothing, quite literally nothing – *repeat, nothing* – of ultimate interest or real value.

Because this world is empty, one directs one's attention to the transcendental, the Unconditioned. One becomes absorbed in it (as it were) and one finds to one's delight that it is empty of everything mundane. What one found in the world one doesn't find here. In the world there was suffering; here one finds bliss. In the world there was impermanence; here one finds eternity. In the world there was no true individual self; here, by losing oneself, one finds one's true individuality.

Eventually one gets to be so absorbed in the Unconditioned that one forgets all about the conditioned. And then one becomes so absorbed in the Unconditioned itself that one forgets all about the Unconditioned. And having forgotten about the conditioned and the Unconditioned, one loses all sense of distinction between the conditioned and the Unconditioned, the mundane and the transcendental. And after that (though in this realization of the nature of reality there is of course no such distinction as 'before' and 'after') one arrives at a state (though it is no 'state' at all) which may be expressed and communicated only by silence. In that silence one experiences the mystery of the Void.

PART II
THE PATH

6

THE GRAVITATIONAL PULL AND
THE POINT OF NO RETURN

The last of the Indian patriarchs, as reckoned by the Zen school, was Bodhidharma, the founding father of Chan or Zen in China in the fifth or sixth century CE. When he travelled from India to China his reputation seems to have preceded him. In those days great Indian scholars and sages would travel every now and then from India, where Buddhism began, to China, where it was just beginning to take root, and people were very interested to meet them and learn something about Buddhism. It seems that the Emperor of China of Bodhidharma's time was quite an ardent Buddhist, though in rather a conventional sense – that is to say he built and endowed monasteries, allowed monks to be ordained (because in those days imperial permission was necessary if one wanted to enter the Order), and generally busied himself with the outward forms of Buddhism.

So when the Emperor came to hear that Bodhidharma, the great Indian sage, had just arrived in China, he was very eager to meet him and talk with him. An invitation was issued without delay, and before long Bodhidharma found himself being ushered into the palace and into the Emperor's presence. The Emperor apparently wasted no time in getting to the point. He evidently had a rather academic sort of mind, and he was well trained in Buddhist philosophy. So he said to Bodhidharma, 'Tell me in just a few words the fundamental principle of Buddhism, upon which everything else is based, from which everything else follows.' And then he sat back and waited to hear what the great sage would come up with.

Bodhidharma said very calmly, very quietly, 'It's quite simple.' He didn't say, 'This being, that becomes', although, as we have seen, that is one answer to the question. Instead he recited a Pāli *gāthā* or verse from the *Dhammapada*:

Sabbapāpassa akaraṇaṃ
kusalassa upasampadā
sacittapariyodapanaṃ
etaṃ buddhānaṃ sāsanaṃ.

which means 'Abstention from all evil, the doing of good, purification of the heart – this is the teaching of the Buddhas.'[228]

When the Emperor heard this he could not conceal his disappointment. 'Is that all?' he demanded. And Bodhidharma matter-of-factly replied, 'Yes, your majesty, that is all.' But the Emperor just couldn't believe it. He said, 'Are you sure? Simply ceasing to do evil, learning to do good, purifying your heart – is there no more to Buddhism than that?' And Bodhidharma said, 'There's really no more to it than that.' So the Emperor, who had apparently expected some abstruse disquisition on Buddhist philosophy, said, 'But even a three-year-old child could understand that.' Bodhidharma replied, 'True. Even a child of three could understand it. But even an old man of eighty cannot put it into practice.'

And that is the degree of difference between the theory and the practice of Buddhism. The theory is one thing, the practice is another. Quite a lot of students of Buddhism, especially in Western countries, are, it has to be said, rather like the Emperor. When confronted with something apparently simple to put into practice, they often say, or at least they think to themselves, 'Is that all?' They want a long, learned, elaborate lecture, something they can really get their teeth into intellectually, discuss with their friends, and so on.

Of course, the Buddhist tradition has come up with many more detailed descriptions of the path of Buddhist practice than the terse statement with which Bodhidharma confronted the Emperor. In this part of the book we will be considering the Dharma as path or teaching: the twelve links of the spiral path; the Noble Eightfold Path; the seven factors of Enlightenment; the seven stages of purification; the simplest expression of the path, the threefold path; and the six perfections of the bodhisattva. Although the emphasis is different in each case, these are all different ways of describing the same thing: the path to Enlightenment. But whichever one tries to practise, sooner or later – and usually sooner – one bumps into the problem that Bodhidharma was so quick to point out. The theory is fine – but why can't we put it into practice? What is it that obstructs our efforts? Why is it so very difficult to do something that sounds so simple? It is perhaps worth having a look at this before we embark on the path itself.

There are various ways in which one might approach the question. One could say, for example, as I have elsewhere, that the central problem of the spiritual life is to find emotional equivalents for one's intellectual understanding.[229] But one can also think in terms of the relationship between the conditioned and the Unconditioned.

The best-known Buddhist symbol of conditioned existence is the Tibetan wheel of life. We could say that this is a picture of the nature of life, even a mirror in which we can see ourselves. We have already taken a look at the outermost circle of the wheel, which depicts the twelve links of conditioned co-production. Working inwards, the next circle is divided into six segments, which represent the six planes of conditioned existence. In the traditional, almost mythological, terminology these are the planes of the gods; of the *asuras* or titans; of human beings; of animals; of hungry ghosts; and of beings in states of suffering. Then within this circle is another, divided into two halves, one dark, the other light. In the light half are depicted people with happy expressions who seem to be moving upwards towards the realm of the gods, while in the dark half are people tumbling miserably towards the hell realm. And at the hub of the wheel, keeping the whole thing turning round and round, are three animal figures – a cock, a snake, and a pig – which represent the three root poisons: craving, aversion, and ignorance.

This is what Buddhism calls *saṃsāra*, the sphere of conditioned existence. The Unconditioned is also sometimes thought of as a sphere, called the *dharmadhātu*. Here *dharma* means 'ultimate truth' or 'ultimate reality', while *dhātu* means something like 'sphere of operation'. The mandala of the Five Buddhas of the Mahāyāna tradition is, one could say, a depiction of the *dharmadhātu*.[230] A number of Buddhist traditions also speak of what is called the *buddha-kṣetra*. *Kṣetra* means 'field', so *buddha-kṣetra* means 'Buddha-field', and it refers to the area within which there operates the spiritual influence, the spiritual power if you like, of a particular Buddha. This influence is often referred to, especially in the Tibetan tradition, as his *adhiṣṭhāna* – an untranslatable word, but it can be roughly put into English as 'grace'. The Pure Land of the Japanese tradition is also a symbol of the *dharmadhātu*, being that area within which the infinite light and eternal life of the Buddha Amitābha is the dominant influence.

Thus we have two spheres, each of them governed by its own forces: *saṃsāra*, driven by the forces of greed, hatred, and delusion, and the *dharmadhātu*, where the influence, the *adhiṣṭhāna*, of the Buddha is the prevailing force. We can extend this analogy by saying that, just as the earth, the sun, and other heavenly bodies have their own gravitational field, their own area within which they will attract to themselves any smaller body, so the sphere of conditioned existence and the sphere of the Unconditioned each exerts its own gravitational pull. The spiritual path, one could say, is the journey from one sphere to the other, a journey, perhaps, from the earth to the sun. This is one answer to the Emperor's question. The spiritual path is hard to follow because, while we are drawn towards Enlightenment, towards the sun, we are held back by the force of gravity that binds us to the earth. There is bound to be conflict.

We could see our movement towards Enlightenment as having three stages: the stage at which we are still very much within the gravitational field of *saṃsāra*, of conditioned existence; a middle stage, when we are subject to the strong pulls of both spheres; and a final stage, when we are free of the pull of *saṃsāra* and subject only to the increasingly strong influence of the *dharmadhātu*, of Enlightenment. These three stages, one might say, correspond to the three stages of the threefold path, the simplest exposition of the Dharma as path: morality or ethics, meditation, and wisdom.[231] We will be looking at each of these three stages in some detail in later chapters; here I will just give a brief introduction.

MORALITY

First, 'morality' – though before I go any further I should say that there is no such word as morality in Buddhism. Buddhists in the East don't talk about morals; they talk about skilful action. Skilful actions are actions expressive of skilful mental states – that is, mental states that are free from the grosser forms of craving, aversion, and ignorance, and which therefore do no harm either to oneself or others; which may even, on occasion, benefit others. Morality in this sense is of fundamental importance in Buddhism.

At the same time its value is regarded as being strictly limited. Skilful action certainly prepares the way for the experience of the stage of meditation. But – and Buddhism insists on this again and again – skilful action by itself, even skilful mental states by themselves, cannot lead one directly to the experience of the Unconditioned. In the Buddhist view, morality is rather like the launch pad of a rocket. You can't launch the rocket without the launch pad, but once the rocket is launched, once it goes streaking off into the stratosphere, the launch pad is left behind on earth; it doesn't go to the stars. So morality is not identical with the spiritual life. It is only part of it, only a means to an end, the immediate end being meditation, and the ultimate end being wisdom, or even the realization of the Unconditioned.

It should also be mentioned that Buddhism distinguishes sharply between two kinds of morality: 'natural morality' and 'conventional morality'.[232] Natural morality consists of actions expressive of skilful mental states, while conventional morality is simply a matter of local custom or opinion, and has no real moral significance. The first stage of the spiritual path is concerned, of course, not with conventional morality but with natural morality. Morality in this sense, one could say, corresponds to the light half of the second circle of the wheel of life, which leads upwards to the periphery of the gravitational field of the conditioned. But that light segment is still inside that gravitational field. Skilful action alone is not enough to move one beyond the wheel of life.

Unfortunately, this kind of teaching has led to some major misunderstandings. People sometimes think that the Buddha taught a path exclusively of self-interest; and if one is thinking along these lines, then it may seem that skilful action is being advocated simply as a means to one's own ends, that one is expected to behave kindly and generously towards others only as a way of increasing one's own spiritual chances. It was the Mahāyāna phase of Buddhism which made it unequivocally clear once and for all, if there was any room for doubt, that there can be no such thing as self-development without care and concern for the well-being and growth of others. Even the pursuit of Enlightenment is not a matter of individual salvation: one seeks it not just for one's own benefit but for the welfare of all beings. It is this which the Mahāyāna teaching known as the bodhisattva ideal is specifically concerned with pointing out (and we will be going into it in Chapter 13).

MEDITATION

The second stage of the threefold path is usually called 'meditation'. The word meditation is used, even misused, in all sorts of ways, but properly speaking it has three meanings that correspond to three successively higher levels of spiritual experience. To begin with, there is meditation in the sense of concentration of mind, the withdrawal of one's attention from the external world. You no longer see anything – well, your eyes are closed. But you no longer hear anything either, or taste anything, or smell anything. You don't even feel the meditation cushion on which you are seated, or the clothes you are wearing. Your attention is withdrawn from the senses, and therefore also from the corresponding sense objects, and you become centred within. All your psychophysical energies too are no longer scattered and dispersed but drawn together, centred on one point, vibrating, even, on one point.

Next there comes what we could perhaps call 'meditation proper'. Attention has been withdrawn from the senses, from the external world. The energies have been concentrated within, unified, integrated. Then, at this second stage, the energies start to rise, and there is a gradual raising of the whole level of consciousness, the whole level of being. One is carried up, away from one's ordinary physical body, away out of the ordinary, physical, material universe that one knows. One ascends in one's inner experience up to successively higher states or stages of 'superconsciousness'.

As one becomes more and more concentrated, more and more peaceful, more and more blissful, the world becomes more and more distant. Even mental activity fades away, until only stillness and silence is left, within which one begins to see with the inner vision and hear with the inner hearing. These stages of superconsciousness are known in Buddhism as the four *dhyāna* states. This is 'meditation proper': not just unification of one's psychophysical energies but the raising of them to ever higher levels of consciousness and being, so that one is living in a different world, and is indeed a different person, at least to some extent.

Finally, there comes meditation in the highest sense of all: contemplation – turning this unified, elevated state of being in the direction of the Unconditioned, of reality itself. One sees it, or at least has a glimpse of it, and one begins to move towards it, flow towards it, gravitate towards it. One's unified, elevated consciousness begins to come into contact with the very depths and the very heights of existence and being and consciousness.

Meditation as the second stage of the threefold path consists of what I've called 'concentration' and 'meditation proper'; it doesn't include contemplation, which, though it is usually practised within the context of meditation, really belongs to the third stage of the path, the stage of wisdom. Meditation is the intermediate stage of the spiritual path, in which there operate both gravitational forces: the force of the conditioned and the force of the Unconditioned. This, one could say, accounts for two things:

One thing it accounts for is the ease with which we sometimes fall from the heights of meditation right down into the depths of worldliness. Most people who practise meditation have had this experience at some time or other. We enjoy what seems to be a beautiful meditation. We may begin to think that we're really getting somewhere. We may even think we've made it at last, spiritually speaking. After all that effort, we're amongst all these beautiful experiences, floating around us like so many pink and blue clouds. We think, 'This is wonderful, this is going to stay with me all my life, for ever and ever. Here I am, floating on these clouds, timelessly. I'm never going to have any more problems, any more worries. At last I've got there.'

But what happens? Within a matter of minutes – not hours, not days, not weeks, but minutes – we are overwhelmed by what can only be described as highly unskilful mental states. Not only that: we find ourselves even acting in accordance with those highly unskilful mental states, within minutes of floating up there blissfully on those beautiful clouds. In this way we oscillate between the heights and the depths. One minute we're thinking, 'I'd like to devote my whole life to meditation,' and the next minute we are right down in the depths.

When this happens it is only natural to start wondering whether meditation is really worthwhile. One could be forgiven for thinking, 'I make all this effort, spread my wings, and soar up there for a while … then my wings seem to give way somehow, and crash! I find myself back on the earth, maybe with a few damaged feathers. Is it worth it? If only I could get up there and stay there! To get up there only to sink down again is so disappointing.' We begin to wonder whether such a thing as spiritual progress is possible at all. Are we just fooling ourselves? Are we doomed to ricochet in this way between the heights and the depths for ever?

Not necessarily. All this trouble is due to the gravitational pull of the conditioned, from which we can become free in the third stage of the path. But until then, we are liable to fall at any time, from any height, regardless of the length of time we spend meditating. We might have stayed up there for a couple of hours, or even a whole week. It doesn't make any difference – we come tumbling down just as easily.

In India there are lots of stories about this sort of thing, usually stories about Indian rishis. We are told that thousands of years ago Rishi So-and-so went off to the Himalayas, and he spent thousands of years meditating – meditating in caves, meditating in deep forests, meditating in hermitages, meditating on snowy peaks, oblivious to everything. There are all sorts of wonderful stories about how one rishi's beard grew miles and miles long and went flowing over the whole countryside, and how another rishi was so indifferent to what was going on around him that he just went on meditating even when a colony of ants came and built a great anthill over him.

But of course, eventually any rishi has to end his meditation – or at least he decides to end it – and then what happens? It's the same story every time. As soon as the rishi comes out of his meditation, as he comes down from the mountain or emerges from the forest, he encounters a nymph, a heavenly maiden, and within a matter of minutes, despite those thousands of years of meditation, he succumbs to her temptations and he's back where he started.

What do these stories mean? They all mean the same thing. They mean that meditation is not enough, so far as the spiritual life is concerned. It can only take you so far. But though it's not enough, at the same time it's indispensable. It is the basis for the development of wisdom, just as skilful action is the basis for the development of meditation. If morality is the launch pad of the rocket, meditation, we may say, is the first-stage rocket, from which the second-stage rocket is fired when the first-stage rocket has reached a certain height. This second-stage rocket, of course, is wisdom.

Meditation is indispensable because it is only from meditation that one can reach wisdom. One must reach a certain level of meditation experience and sustain oneself at that level, if one can, for a certain length of time at least, and then try to develop wisdom. Once wisdom has been developed, there is no longer any danger, you're no longer at the mercy of the gravitational pull of the conditioned.

This, then, is one thing accounted for by the fact that at the stage of meditation both gravitational forces operate. The other thing accounted for by this fact is that if we've been meditating fairly successfully for some time, we sometimes feel as though we are about to slide down into fathomless depths, or be carried away by a great stream flowing strongly and powerfully within us and beyond us. At such times usually what we're experiencing, however obscurely, and without necessarily knowing it, is the gravitational pull of the Unconditioned. But what usually happens? When we start feeling this pull, when we start feeling ourselves going, slipping, sliding, being carried away, we usually resist. We usually pull back. This is because we feel afraid. Oh yes, we say we want Enlightenment, we want Nirvāṇa, but when it really comes to the point, we don't want to be carried away. We don't want to lose ourselves.

This calls to mind a story about an old woman in Japan. She was a devout Buddhist, and she used to go along to the temple of Amitābha, the Buddha of Infinite Light, who presides over the Pure Land into which – according to Japanese Buddhism – you are reborn after death, if you recite his mantra. She would go along to this temple and worship there every morning, bowing down many times and crying, 'O Lord, O Amitābha, O Buddha of Infinite Light and Eternal Life, please take me away from this wretched, sorrowful, wicked world. Let me die tonight and be reborn into your Pure Land. That's where I want to go, so that I can be in your presence night and day, and hear your teaching and gain Nirvāṇa.' In this way, tearfully and with great sincerity, she used to pray every morning and sometimes in the evening too.

A certain monk in that temple overheard her praying and weeping, and he thought, 'All right, we shall see.' The Buddha image in the temple, like many images in Japan, was an enormous one, about thirty feet high. So when the old woman next came, the monk hid behind the image. As she sobbed, 'Lord, please take me now, let me be reborn in the Pure Land. Take me,' the monk called out from behind the image in a great booming voice, 'I shall take you *now*.' At this the old woman leapt up with a shriek of terror and rushed out of the temple. And as she rushed out she called over her shoulder to the image, 'Won't the Buddha let me have my little joke?'

We say that we want to gain Enlightenment, and we say, with complete sincerity, that this is why we meditate. But as soon as we start feeling that pull, feeling that we're going to be carried away, that we're going to lose ourselves, we draw back. Just like the old woman, we are afraid. We don't want to lose ourselves. But this is in fact just what we must learn to do, whether in meditation or in any other aspect of the spiritual life. We have to learn just to let go. This is the most difficult thing in the world: just to let go. We have to give up – not in the ordinary, everyday sense of the expression, but in a more spiritual sense. To use more religious terminology, we have to surrender to the Unconditioned.

WISDOM

The third great stage of the threefold path is wisdom. This isn't, of course, any kind of mental activity; by wisdom here is meant direct sustained awareness of reality or the Unconditioned. As wisdom is the subject of later chapters, we will put it aside for now.

THE POINT OF NO RETURN

These, then, are the three great stages of our journey from *saṃsāra*, the sphere of the conditioned, to the *dharmadhātu*, the Unconditioned. To begin with, we are going to be battling against the gravitational pull of the conditioned, and the pull of the Unconditioned is going to seem very faint – although it must be there, otherwise there would be no question of our moving towards Enlightenment at all. But there comes a crucial point at which the pull of the Unconditioned, of Enlightenment, becomes the stronger force. This we could call the Point of No Return. Beyond this point our spiritual progress will be assured; there will be no danger of relapse. Clearly this is a very important goal to strive for – remembering all the time that 'striving' for such a 'goal' is this process of continually letting go.

It is said that the ultimate goal of Buddhism is Enlightenment, Buddhahood, Nirvāṇa, whatever one likes to call it, but really these are only words. They are quite unable to convey to us an adequate idea of the nature of the attainment towards which we are supposed to be directing our efforts; it is too far beyond us. But we can set our sights on a more immediate, more comprehensible, more accessible aim: to reach the Point of No Return, the point where the pull of the Unconditioned is stronger than the pull of the conditioned. Once we've reached this point, Enlightenment is in any case assured, and will be attained, according to tradition, within not more than seven more lives.[233]

But although the Point of No Return is within our reach, we will still need to make a great effort to reach it. We should not underestimate the power of the gravitational pull of the conditioned. It operates at many different levels and applies to all aspects of human life. It is owing to the gravitational pull of the conditioned that an artist may conform, or be tempted to conform, even to betray his or her inner vision. It is owing to the gravitational pull of the conditioned that religions lose any sense of their true mission and become merely a matter of custom and tradition. And it is owing to the gravitational pull of the conditioned that we sink down from the heights of meditation, often as soon as we've managed to gain them, or even stop meditating altogether.

It is very important that we see for ourselves the workings of this great force, both in human history and in our own lives. Once we see it, once we realize how powerful, ubiquitous, and extensive it is, we wake up to the fact that we cannot afford to stop making an effort. If we do, we don't just remain where we were – at least not for long. Once we stop exerting ourselves, the gravitational pull of the conditioned inexorably takes over, and before we know what has happened we are back where we started from, maybe months or even years before. We can perhaps afford to have a rest only when we have reached the Point of No Return. Until then, there must be no resting on our spiritual laurels, however brilliant. Hence the Buddha's last words to his disciples: *appamādena sampādetha* – 'With awareness – with mindfulness – *strive*.'[234] He was saying, in effect, that if we can only manage to keep up these two things – awareness and effort – then progress is assured.

The traditional term for the attainment of the Point of No Return found in the Buddhist scriptures is Stream Entry.[235] The 'stream' is the irresistible force of the Unconditioned once you've got near enough to it. So once again we have the image of a river. Once again we are as though standing on a riverbank which represents conditioned existence. In this image the Unconditioned is represented not by the other shore (as in the parable of the raft) but by the ocean towards which the river is flowing.

We could say that the distance from the point where we are standing to the edge of the river corresponds to the first stage of the path, the stage of morality. Then the distance from the edge of the river to midstream corresponds to the second stage of the path, the stage of meditation. Once we've reached midstream and begin to feel the mighty force of the current flowing towards the ocean, we just have to abandon ourselves to it; this is the point of Stream Entry, the Point of No Return. And the distance from there to the ocean itself is the third stage of the path, the stage of wisdom.

The image is reminiscent of one of the parables of Ramakrishna, the great modern Indian saint and teacher. He told this parable to illustrate the relationship between 'grace' and 'works', but it has some bearing on this whole question of Stream Entry as well. He said that it is like rowing a boat right out into the centre of the river, to midstream. The process of getting into the boat and rowing, and with great difficulty making progress to the centre of the stream, represents 'works', karma in the sense of activity. But once you're in midstream, you can hoist your sail; and once you've hoisted your sail it will catch the breeze. Then you can rest, you can put up your oars, for no further effort is needed. All you have to do is steer, as the breeze carries you along.[236] And the breeze represents 'grace' – in other words, the gravitational pull of the Unconditioned.

So, if we are to take Stream Entry as our 'goal', how is it to be attained? This is what the Dharma as teaching or path is meant to explain in detail. We are not simply enjoined: 'be ye perfect', as Jesus advised his followers;[237] neither is Bodhidharma's advice to the emperor the last word on the subject. Throughout his teaching life the Buddha found many different ways of mapping out the journey to Enlightenment, and subsequent Buddhist tradition has added new ways of seeing the same path – not just seeing it, but working out in detail the practical steps one needs to take.

Of all these different ways of describing the path, some make it particularly clear how the Point of No Return, the point of Stream Entry, is to be recognized. For example, just as we can say that in terms of the threefold path it is the point at which meditation shades into wisdom, so, in terms of the twelve links of the spiral path, the Point of No Return is reached at the eighth stage, 'knowledge and vision of things as they really are'. Other ways of seeing the spiritual life – the five spiritual faculties, for example – are conceived more in terms of achieving a balance of qualities. But one thing all these descriptions of the path have in common is that they are all about the cultivation of positive spiritual qualities. A rather different way of looking at how one approaches Stream Entry is in terms of the breaking of fetters.

BREAKING THE FETTERS

The Buddhist tradition enumerates ten fetters that bind us to conditioned existence, each one representing a different aspect of the gravitational pull of the conditioned. If we can only burst them asunder, then we become free, totally free, on the spot. But these fetters are strong and binding, and they usually have to be broken little by little, each one gradually filed through over years of spiritual practice. The ten fetters are (1) self-view or self-belief; (2) doubt or indecision; (3) dependence on moral rules and religious observances as ends in themselves; (4) sensuous desire, in the sense of desire for experience in and through the five physical senses; (5) ill will or hatred or aversion; (6) desire for existence in the plane of (archetypal) form; (7) desire for existence in the formless plane; (8) conceit, in the sense of the idea of oneself as superior to, inferior to, or equal to other people, i.e. making invidious comparisons between oneself and others; (9) restlessness and instability; (10) ignorance – that is, spiritual ignorance in the sense of lack of awareness of ultimate reality.[238]

On breaking the first three of these fetters one becomes a Stream Entrant, so that from now onwards one will be subject more to the gravitational pull of the Unconditioned than to the gravitational pull of the conditioned. The fourth and fifth fetters – sensuous desire and ill will – are said to be particularly strong. On weakening – not breaking, but just weakening – these two, one becomes what is called a 'once-returner'. (All these terms come from the Theravāda tradition.) A 'once-returner' has gone well past the Point of No Return, and is even more strongly drawn by the Unconditioned, feeling the pull of the conditioned comparatively little. As a once-returner you have before you only one more birth as a human being, according to tradition, and you will then gain Enlightenment.

On actually breaking the fourth and fifth fetters, one becomes a 'non-returner'. According to tradition, a non-returner is reborn in one of the 'pure abodes', near the outermost reaches of the gravitational field of the conditioned. The gravitational pull of the Unconditioned is now overwhelmingly predominant; and the non-returner gains Enlightenment directly from the pure abodes without the necessity of another human birth.

These first five fetters are known as the five lower fetters, and they bind one to the plane of sensuous desire, as it is called – in other words, to the innermost circle of the gravitational field of the conditioned, where the gravitational pull is strongest. As for the sixth and seventh fetters, they refer to the 'plane of (archetypal) form' and the 'formless plane'; that is, the middle and the outer circles respectively of the gravitational field of the conditioned. Once the five higher fetters are broken, one is completely free. One experiences only the gravitational pull of the Unconditioned – one is in fact, oneself, the Unconditioned – and there are no more rebirths. Such a person is known, in the traditional terminology, as an *arahant* – a 'worthy one' or 'holy one'.

This, at least, is the traditional way of putting it in Theravāda Buddhism. As we have seen, in the full realization of *śūnyatā* one sees that there is ultimately no distinction between *saṃsāra* and *nirvāṇa*; so to speak of making the journey from the one to the other is only a manner of speaking – and one that may not suit us if we are wary of anything that seems to suggest an abandonment of the world to its fate. Mahāyāna Buddhists would speak of what is basically the same process in terms of the arising of the will to Enlightenment, and the taking of the bodhisattva vow, emphasizing that to move towards Enlightenment is not just for one's own sake, but involves – indeed, is inseparable from – great altruism.

But while they perhaps don't give us the full picture, it can be very useful to think in terms of breaking the fetters. The more advanced ones may be beyond us, but we can usefully focus our attention on the first three, the breaking of which is synonymous with Stream Entry. (And it is said that once one of these three fetters is broken, the other two will also break.)

First, then, the fetter of fixed self-view. This is our habitual acceptance of our present experience of selfhood as being fixed, unchanging, and ultimate. It really amounts to a refusal to accept the possibility of change or progress. We are so familiar with ourselves, so used to ourselves, so used to thinking of ourselves in a certain way. We think, 'This is Me. I'll always be like this – I may change a bit but I'll still be recognizably me, very much so.' We just can't believe that this Self, this Me, this 'I' as I am experiencing it here and now, can ever be, as it were, consumed as though by fire, so that out of the ashes of that old self a new self can arise. We refuse to accept that this can happen even once – let alone many times. Fixed self-view is therefore the negation of the spiritual path. We could say, in fact, that it's a sort of rationalization of the gravitational pull of the conditioned.

The second fetter is doubt or indecision. This is not doubt in the intellectual sense; it is not the suspension of belief or judgement. Doubt here means unwillingness to commit oneself, to take the plunge. It means holding back when there's no reason for holding back, even when one sees good reasons for not holding back. And here the gravitational pull of the conditioned is at work with a vengeance. There are lots of people who are interested in the spiritual life, in a way, but they won't commit themselves, they won't throw themselves in. The tendency is just to stretch out one's toe and dip it into the water, then draw it back. Or, if one does venture in, one fastens oneself securely to a good strong post on the shore so that one doesn't get really carried away, so that, perhaps, one can have the best of both worlds. We find it hard just to throw ourselves in. Very often this is simply because we are afraid. We may agree with everything we hear about the spiritual path, but we won't really try to put it into practice, because we are strongly bound by this second fetter, the fetter of doubt and indecision.

The third fetter is 'dependence on moral rules and religious observances as ends in themselves'. There's a lot that could be said about this, but the main point is that it's the dependence that constitutes the fetter. The Sanskrit here is *śīlavrata-parāmarśa*, which is sometimes rendered by the early translators as 'dependence on rites and ceremonies'. Really, however, this has nothing to do with rites and ceremonies. *Śīla* means 'ethical precepts', as in the *pañca śīla*, the five precepts; *vrata* is 'religious observance'; and *parāmarśa* is 'clinging' or 'attachment', so the third fetter is clinging or attachment to ethical rules and religious observances. Not that these practices are wrong in any way; the problem comes if we come to depend on them too much.

Conventional religiosity, then, is a hindrance to Enlightenment. This is a hard truth for many people to swallow. Indeed, a very great deal, if not the greater part, of ordinary, conventional religious life and activity is simply an expression of this fetter. Religious people tend to become trapped in religion itself. They treat it not as a means to an end – Enlightenment or any other end – but as an end in itself. There's no need to multiply examples; we can find them all around us, even, despite all the Buddha's warnings, within Buddhism itself.

So, let us do pujas, meditate, and study texts, but let us always remember that they are only of value to the extent that they lead us in the direction of Enlightenment. We have to ask ourselves constantly, 'Is what I am doing really helping me in the direction of Enlightenment, or am I going mechanically on week after week, month after month like a hamster in a wheel? Have I just got into a sort of religious conditioning? Am I just settling down comfortably in some sort of religious doctrine or practice or group? Or am I using those facilities in such a way that I do get a little nearer to Enlightenment?'

It's not enough to declare that one is a Buddhist. It's not enough even to keep up one's daily meditation. The point is, are we getting nearer to Enlightenment? Are we making progress? Are the things we are doing a means to an end, or have they become an end in themselves? We need to be on the lookout in this way throughout our spiritual life, always asking ourselves whether we are continuing to do something not because it's useful to us spiritually, but simply because we have always done it that way.

It is necessary to bear these fetters in mind, because until we have broken them we are always going to be subject to their restraint. We are going to need to keep reminding ourselves that we can change, really change. We will need to look out for those times when we feel like giving up on the spiritual path because we are afraid, because we don't know where it's going to take us. And we will need to notice when we are just going through the motions of spiritual practice, clinging on to a particular habit we've got into.

Breaking these three fetters, and attaining Stream Entry, is possible for anyone within their present lifetime. And once this point has been reached, one can only rise higher and ever higher on the path. As one does so, one will feel the gravitational pull of the Unconditioned more and more powerfully. One will, in fact, glimpse the Unconditioned, through all the veils, all the hindrances, all the obscurations of the conditioned, and gradually see it more and more fully, more and more clearly, more and more brightly. As one reaches these heights, the world itself, formerly a veil, formerly a hindrance, formerly an obscuration, will itself be more and more transfigured, more and more resplendent, more and more glorious.

This is the vision before us. But for now we will go right back to the beginning – at least in our imagination – to where it all starts: the first step of the spiral path to Enlightenment.

7

THE SPIRAL PATH

The nature of spiritual development is perhaps most clearly seen in terms of the spiral mode of conditionality, in which it is represented as a certain sequence of experiences, one experience arising in dependence upon another. Just as out of the bud grows the flower, and out of the flower the fruit, so out of one spiritual experience there grows another, out of that yet another, and out of that another still, each one higher, more refined, more beautiful, a little nearer to Nirvāna. Each stage is a spiritual experience in the process of transition to another, more advanced experience. The stages aren't fixed or static; you don't proceed up the spiral path like going up the steps of a staircase, even a spiral staircase. We speak of 'the Buddhist path' or 'the spiritual path', but we mustn't be misled by the metaphor. It isn't that the spiritual path is fixed and we go up it; or that *we* move but the path remains stationary. The path itself grows, just as a plant grows, one stage passing over into the next so that there's a constant upward movement.

This is the way spiral conditionality works; spiritual growth, like everything else, unfolds in accordance with this great law. As we have already seen, the law of conditionality functions in two ways, one 'cyclical' and the other 'progressive'. The cyclical mode is the process of action and reaction between opposite factors – say between happiness and unhappiness, or depression and elation, or birth and death; while the progressive, spiral mode is the process of ever-increasing intensity, so that, for example, you get a progression from pleasure to happiness, from happiness to rapture, from rapture to bliss, and so on.

The concern of Buddhist practice is to break the endless cycle of action and reaction illustrated on the wheel of life as the chain of conditioned co-production. But how? In Tibetan Buddhism there is said to be something of a hiatus between one life and the next – called the *bardo*, the 'intermediate state' – and this *bardo* between lives is said to present a great spiritual opportunity. But we don't have to wait for death in order to find an opportunity for spiritual growth. The chain of conditioned co-production can be broken in the midst of life – indeed, at any moment.

A chain is only as strong as its weakest link. So where is the *nidāna* chain weakest? Where can it be broken most easily? Paradoxically, in this case the weakest link is the strongest. The crucial point is where, in dependence upon *vedanā*, feeling, arises *tṛṣṇā*, craving. It is this link that keeps the whole process going. We don't usually experience feeling in a purely mirror-like way. Craving, aversion, or mental confusion seem automatically to arise in connection with that feeling. But it is in fact possible to break the chain at this point. If we can experience feeling without allowing craving to arise, then the wheel of life is broken; it doesn't revolve any more. Or, to put it another way, one is not reborn.

There are two ways of breaking the chain at this weakest and strongest point – a sudden method and a gradual method. Many of the stories in the Pāli canon bear witness to the fact that there *is* a sudden method – we see people who, like Śāriputra, hear just a few words and undergo an immediate and irreversible transformation.[239] But to be able to break the chain suddenly is very unusual; the gradual method works better for most people. It is 'gradual' not because it is slow, necessarily, but because it consists of a number of successive stages, the order of which is based on a definite principle. If the cyclical type of conditionality is a circle, then the progressive type is a spiral. All versions of the Buddhist path – the Noble Eightfold Path, the sevenfold path of purification, the six *pāramitās*, and so on – are spiral paths, because they are all based upon this progressive type of conditionality. But where does this spiral path begin? It begins at the crucial point of our experience of *vedanā*, the feelings that befall us in the course of our lives.

Some of the feelings we experience are pleasant, some are painful, and some are just neutral. And our reactions to them are usually pretty automatic. We want to grasp the pleasant experiences and hold on to them for as long as possible, and when our experience is painful, of course we try to escape from the pain. We can't cling on to a pleasant experience for ever, it's invariably interrupted, and that interruption usually causes us pain too. So we oscillate between pleasure and pain, pain and pleasure, and in this way the wheel of life continues to revolve.

But we can take a more objective view. If we look at our whole life, all that we've ever thought or known, and then, further, think of all human life, of the way the world is, if we think about it all deeply enough, we see that the whole of it, basically, fundamentally, is unsatisfactory. Yes, there are pleasant experiences. Yes, there are things we enjoy. But there is nothing which is deeply and permanently satisfactory.

This is the sense in which Buddhism says that life is suffering – a statement that has been much misunderstood. In this context 'suffering' means not just individual painful experiences, like having toothache, or cutting your finger, or being bitterly disappointed by someone. As we have already seen, the Sanskrit word being translated as 'suffering' is *duḥkha*, the 'ill-fitting chariot wheel': the sort of discomfort that arises when things don't fit or work together properly, the jarring quality that we experience in the course of our everyday life in this world.

We all know that things are never one hundred per cent right. There's always something that goes wrong, even if it's only a small thing. Even on the most beautiful day, only too often a cloud has to float across the face of the sun. Something goes wrong. Maybe you've been looking forward to this day: you're going to meet someone you like, you imagine things are going to be so lovely. But then some absurd incident happens and it all goes wrong, and you feel utterly jangled. This is how we go through life. Nothing quite lives up to our expectations – or at least not for long. This is what is meant by *duḥkha*, unsatisfactoriness or suffering.

Once one has become sufficiently aware of this, eventually one starts becoming dissatisfied. One may have tried all sorts of things: one may have sought worldly success, or pleasure, or comfort and luxury, or learning. But in the end they are all unsatisfactory. It's a popular belief that material prosperity brings happiness, but only a little contact with people who have it makes it clear that this isn't really true. It's not that you're actually experiencing pain all the time, necessarily, but you're not really happy. You feel a sort of vague discomfort; you can't settle down, you don't feel that you belong. It is a common experience that, in the words of the Bible, 'here we have no abiding city'.[240] It is as though right in the middle of one's heart there is a terrible empty space.

This was certainly the Buddha's experience. If anybody ever had everything, it was the Buddha. Even if we leave aside the legendary additions to his life story, it is clear that he was born into a wealthy, highly respected family, and that everything was laid on for him from his earliest days. He had beautiful mansions to live in, a wife, a child, social position, and even political power, the possibility one day of ascending the throne, succeeding his father. But despite all this he was not happy. He realized that he had everything, but none of it could last. He, and everyone in his family, everyone who was dear to him, would one day sicken, grow old, and die. And so he left it all – his home, his wife, his parents, his child – and went out into the world to seek the answer to the problem of human suffering.[241]

Philosophy shows us how important it is to investigate the causes of things. If we wish to remove some social injustice we must first of all find out its cause. If there is some disturbance in our domestic affairs – say, for example, the car breaks down – we have to find out why. Unless we discover what has caused the problem, all our efforts will be useless. So if we want to free ourselves from the painful limitations of human existence, we must first ascertain their cause.

Analysis of the problem of suffering produces two widely divergent views. Most of us take the attitude, consciously or unconsciously, that 'I have a number of strong desires that I can't suppress – desires to possess this and to enjoy that. If my desires are fulfilled, I am happy; if not, I am miserable. Happiness must therefore consist in the full satisfaction of my desires, and suffering in the opposite. So I'm going to try as hard as I can to get hold of the things I want, and avoid the painful experiences I don't want. In this way I shall be able to escape pain and suffering.'

But the Buddha, considering the same problem, came to the opposite conclusion. He began by pointing out that all things are impermanent. This none of us can deny, since we experience it in one way or another every day. We may think that happiness and freedom from pain come from the satisfaction of our desires, but we cannot altogether ignore such unpalatable facts of life as sickness, old age, death, and separation – or at least not for long. Whatever we enjoy cannot last, and this is painful to us because we want it to last for ever. We want to be always in good health and spirits, but one day sickness is going to overtake us. We want to retain our youthful strength and vigour, but soon old age will steal imperceptibly upon us. We want to live for ever, but sooner or later we will have to die. Think how many painful separations we have to endure in the course of a single lifetime: from family, from dear friends, from possessions. All this causes us suffering. So our suffering cannot be avoided through the satisfaction of desire. Our solution of the problem is really no solution at all.

Many of us, sooner or later, do start to understand this. Of course, we do our best to ignore it. We try to convince ourselves that we are happy, that we *must* be happy, because we've got all the things that make people happy. But then a whisper comes from deep within our heart and says, and keeps on saying, 'But you're not really happy.' We don't like to listen to this little voice. We put our fingers in our ears and go off to pursue happiness in one way or another, smothering and stifling this nagging feeling. But it's there underneath, building up, painfully pressing, even festering like a secret wound. Stifling it only makes it worse. Rather, we should cherish our dissatisfaction, because it is this that makes us restless, and it is restlessness that makes us go in search of something higher, something more satisfying, some greater happiness.

Of course, we don't know at first what we are looking for. That's the absurdity of it, and the beauty of it too. But even though we don't know what we want, we start looking for it. There's just this vague restlessness, a groping around in all directions for we know not what. And eventually, if we go on looking long enough, we come into contact with something which, for want of a better term, could be called spiritual. (This is not an altogether satisfactory word, but it will have to do.) We come into contact with something higher, or at least a glimpse of something higher, something which is not of this world, even something which is 'out of this world'. It may be a symbol, an echo, a reflection: a book that speaks to you, a picture, a person. And when you come into contact with it, whatever the circumstances, at once you respond. In the depths of your heart you get a feeling, or at least an inkling, that this is what you have been searching for all the time, even though you didn't know it.

This response is what, in the context of Buddhist tradition, is called faith. And this is the next step of the spiral path: in dependence upon unsatisfactoriness arises faith. The Sanskrit word is *śraddhā*. We translate it as faith, but it isn't faith in the sense of believing to be true something which cannot be rationally demonstrated. *Śraddhā* can also be translated as confidence or devotion, and it refers to the whole emotional side of the spiritual life. The word comes from a verb which means 'to place the heart on'. So faith in the Buddhist sense means the placing of one's heart on the Unconditioned, on the Absolute, rather than on the conditioned. It is the reorientation of one's whole emotional life.

It is, in other words, the ethically wholesome counterpart of *tṛṣṇā*, craving or thirst. In dependence upon feeling – in this case feeling the unsatisfactoriness of the world – there arises not craving but faith – faith in something above and beyond the world, a sensitivity to a higher dimension of truth and reality. Perhaps the best definition of faith is that it is the response of what is ultimate in us to what is ultimate in the universe.

For Buddhists faith means specifically faith in the Three Jewels: the Buddha, the Enlightened teacher; the Dharma, the path leading to Enlightenment; and the Sangha, the spiritual community of those who have realized the higher stages of the transcendental path.[242] They are called the Three Jewels because just as jewels are the most precious things in the material world, the Buddha, the Dharma, and the Sangha are the three most precious things, the three highest values, in the spiritual world.

Faith – this intuitive, emotional, even mystical response to something higher, something supreme, something of ultimate value – is the first step on the spiral path, and the very beginning of the spiritual life. Then, in dependence upon faith, arises joy. This is the next step. You have found what you were looking for. You may not have been able to seize hold of it, but at least you've had a glimpse of it, like the sun through a cloud. So naturally, after perhaps a long period of searching, you are pleased and satisfied and contented.

More than that, this contact with higher values has begun to transform your life. It isn't just a theoretical thing. Your heart has actually been lifted up; this is what the word *śraddhā* literally means –

a lifting up of the heart. You have been lifted up to something higher, have touched something higher, have experienced, even if only for a moment, something higher. And on account of that contact, however brief, however electrical, as it were, a change begins to take place. You feel that you now have a definite aim in life. Before, you were just swept along aimlessly, driven in pursuit of this or that – education, promotion, marriage, a good pension, whatever it happened to be. But once faith has arisen, you have a definite aim in life: to develop your contact with the higher dimension to which you have become sensitive.

Of course, it isn't, usually, all plain sailing. Faith may arise but it may also subside. After an initial rush of enthusiasm for the spiritual life, and a phase of reading everything we can lay our hands on, and going to talks and meditation classes, we may suddenly lose interest. Perhaps our interest is caught by something else, or perhaps, frankly, we get fed up with trying to be 'spiritual' and just feel like living it up for a while. The pendulum may swing back and forth for quite some while, as our enthusiasm for spiritual life waxes and wanes, but as time goes by it swings less and less violently until it comes eventually to rest in the centre.

As one's faith strengthens, one gradually becomes a little less self-centred. One's egoity has been disturbed, shaken up, and as a result one begins to become just a little more generous, a little more outward-going. One tends not to hang on to things quite so tightly. What may be described as the lower part of one's nature, the part which is chiefly interested in things like food, sleep, and sex, starts coming under the conscious control of the higher part of one's nature. One begins to live more simply and harmlessly, and this makes one happier and more contented. More at ease within oneself, one doesn't rely so much upon external things. You just don't need them as much as you used to. You don't care if you haven't got a beautiful house in the suburbs, a flashy car and all the rest of it. Less concerned with all those things, much freer and more detached than you were before, you are at peace with yourself. You may not have explored fully what you have discovered, but you've made contact with it, you know it's there, and that contact has at least begun to transform your life.

You come naturally to start living a more ethical life, especially observing what in Buddhism are called the five precepts: not taking life, not taking what is not given, abstaining from sexual misconduct, speaking truthfully, and abstaining from intoxicating or stupefying drinks and drugs.[243] You have a more or less good conscience, and so you feel joyful. Joy, in other words, is the next stage of the spiral path.

JOY

The Buddhist attitude is that if you're leading a spiritual life, you should be happy, open, and carefree. Religious festivals and celebrations in particular are joyful occasions. When I came back to Britain after twenty years in the East I was surprised to find that the Buddhist movement was on the whole such a serious affair. People hardly dared even to smile when one made a joke in a lecture. But if you have found the precious thing that you were looking for, and if it has really begun to transform your life, why shouldn't you be happy? If you're not happier than other people who haven't found this source of inspiration, what's the use of being a Buddhist? What does being a Buddhist really mean? Joy, one could say, is the hallmark of the true Buddhist.

Buddhism attaches great importance to this stage of feeling happy and carefree and at peace with oneself, having a clear conscience, being able to go about with a song on one's lips. If for any reason one lapses from this state of joy – maybe through having done something one shouldn't have done – and one becomes all sad and serious, and starts beating one's breast and thinking one is a terrible sinner, the Buddhist view is that this is a very unhealthy state to be in, and the sooner one can get out of it the better.

It may possibly be that one actually has nothing to regret. In the West people only too often suffer from irrational feelings of guilt, especially perhaps with regard to matters of sex, about which certain beliefs may have been instilled by orthodox Christianity from an early age. Such feelings must be resolved, otherwise there is no real possibility of spiritual progress.

If you really have made a mistake, you need to admit it, try to make up for it, and resolve not to do it again. But having understood what you have done, and having tried to put it right, you can just put it out of your mind – just forget it and walk on, leave it behind; it won't do you any good to keep carrying it around.

Buddhist tradition prescribes various ways of bringing about this sort of psychological effect. If you feel weighed down by an unskilful thing you have done, large or small, you can just stand in front of the shrine and bow to the image of the Buddha, then think it all over and say to yourself, 'What a fool I've been. I shouldn't have done that, I really am sorry.' (This is especially important if what you have done has involved hurting someone else.) Then you say to yourself, 'All right, I won't do it again. I shall be very careful, I shall watch myself, I'll be aware, I'll be mindful.' And then you recite some texts, try to focus your mind on the Buddha's teaching, try to recollect the ideal, light some candles if you like, burn some incense, and in this way purge your mind of remorse and restore your clear conscience, your state of joy (the Sanskrit term is *prāmodya*) and happiness.[244]

RAPTURE

In fact, you can become even more joyful. In dependence upon joy arises rapture; this is the next stage of the path. Even joy isn't enough; one can become more positive still. 'Rapture' is the nearest we can get in English to translating *prīti*, which is a very powerful word in the original Sanskrit. *Prīti* is an intense, thrilling, ecstatic joy, which is so powerful that you feel it in your body as well as in your mind. When we listen to a beautiful symphony, or watch the setting sun, or have a heart-warming communication with a friend, we are sometimes so deeply moved that we experience not only an emotion, but also a physical response. One may be so greatly affected, for instance, that one's hair stands on end. Some people shed tears. You see people at symphony concerts wiping their eyes. This is *prīti*. In the full sense it is an overwhelming psychophysical experience of rapture and bliss and ecstasy which may even carry one right away; this is the sort of experience that will be generated as we follow the path.

This rapture is not unlike the surge of inspiration that artists feel welling up within them at the time of creation. What they are doing may be very difficult – it may be giving them all sorts of trouble, whether it's a painting or a poem or a piece of music they're creating – but at the same time there is a sort of rapture, a sort of ecstasy out of which they are creating, on account of which they are creating.

Prīti can be of five different kinds. First, there's the 'lesser thrill', as it's called. This is the sort of rapture that makes your hair stand on end, as can happen when you are very moved by something. Then there's the 'momentary rapture'; this is the rapture that comes just like a flash of lightning. It's so overwhelming that you can bear to experience it only for an instant. It touches you, reduces you to ashes, as it were, and then it's gone. You can't stand more of it than that – it just comes and goes. And then there's what's called the 'flooding rapture'. Just as the tide comes in to fill a cave on the seashore, so rapture floods in upon you, especially when you are meditating, and you feel almost carried away by it. Then there's what's called the 'all-pervading rapture', in which you feel just like a balloon, so light, so buoyant, almost as if you were lifted up. And lastly there's what's called the 'transporting rapture', which is said actually to cause levitation.[245]

People are often intrigued by the idea of levitation. It's a rather minor interest in Buddhism, but I have met various people who have experienced it. For example, many years ago I happened to be passing through a place called Kharagpur in India. Kharagpur is near a big railway junction, and I'd gone there from Calcutta to give a lecture. The lecture was scheduled for about eleven o'clock at night – they like to have their lectures late in those parts – so I was waiting for the one o'clock morning train to take me back to Calcutta. I was waiting on the station platform among a crowd of people, and we all got talking to pass the time until the train arrived. Of course, this being India, the train was late.

After a while someone brought forward a certain individual, an ordinary looking man in ordinary Indian dress, from the crowd, and they said, 'This man has a problem.' I thought perhaps his wife had run away, or his son hadn't passed an examination, or something of that sort. But they said, 'No. The trouble is that he levitates.' So I said, 'Do you mean that he literally levitates?' They said, 'Yes. He's a Kabirapanthi.' A Kabirapanthi is someone who follows the sect founded by Kabir, the great medieval Hindu-cum-Muslim yogi. And apparently every morning this man was practising certain breathing exercises, as a result of which he would just float up a few inches, or even a few feet, above the ground.

Naturally I said to these people, a little suspiciously, 'Has anyone seen this happening?' They said, 'Oh yes, we've all seen it every day. He just can't control it. He wants to meditate, but this levitation gets in the way. As soon as he does his breathing exercises he just starts going up into the air. So what should he do? How should he stop?' This, of course, is the sort of question one might be asked at any time in India.

I said, 'According to Buddhism levitation is brought about by excess of *prīti* – that is, rapture. So what one must do is cultivate the mental faculty of equanimity or tranquillity, *upekṣā*. If one does that, there will be a sort of counterbalancing force to the *prīti*, and levitation will not occur.' I never went to Kharagpur again, so I never heard whether the prescription was successful, but let us hope that it was.

I met another levitator when I was living in Kalimpong, up in the Himalayas. I was once entertaining to lunch an American couple and a Tibetan lama, rather a distinguished one. In the course of the lunch the American man said, with a rather knowing smile, 'I suppose you haven't heard of anyone who can levitate?' So the lama said modestly, 'Yes. In fact, I do a little myself.' At this the two Americans nearly fell off their chairs. They said, 'You can do it *yourself*?' He said, 'Yes. I don't think I could do it right now, but if I spend about six months meditating alone in the jungle, or in a secluded monastery, at the end of that time I can levitate.'

He was not really unusual – although my visitors certainly thought so. I have met a number of Tibetans who have either seen levitation done or who can do it themselves. It is all said to be due to an excess of *prīti*, or rapture, when one's experience, especially in meditation, becomes so intense that the body is quite literally lifted up. One finds records of this sort of thing not only in Buddhist life and literature, but also in the lives of some comparatively recent Christian mystics. But Buddhists would say it isn't a very important phenomenon or experience. This is still only the third stage of the path – it's essentially a mundane experience. If it happens one shouldn't take too much notice of it. It just means that one has accumulated rapture of sufficient intensity to produce this particular psychophysical effect.

To use modern terminology, one could say that rapture comes about as a result of the release of blocked energy – energy that is short-circuiting itself, as it were, or as if locked up. In the course of one's spiritual life, especially when one practises meditation, these blocks get dissolved. One digs down, one uncovers certain depths within oneself, and little complexes are resolved, so that the energy locked up in them is released and surges up. It's due to this upsurge of energy, felt throughout the nervous system as well as in the mind, that one experiences *prīti*.

CALM

Then, in dependence upon rapture there arises calm or peace. In Sanskrit this is called *praśrabdhi*. The word means 'calm, tranquillity, serenity', and it is the calming down of the physical side effects of rapture, so that you're left with a purely mental and emotional experience.

The physical experiences calm down not because the rapture is less but because it has become greater, beyond all possibility of physical expression. This is traditionally illustrated with the simile of an elephant stepping into a pond. In India, of course, there were and still are lots of elephants, and elephants are very fond of bathing. Almost every day, sometimes several times a day, they like to go down into a pool, pond, lake, or river and bathe, squirting water over themselves and one another. But suppose an elephant goes to bathe in a small pond, a pond which is perhaps not much bigger than the elephant himself. When this great beast gets into that little pond, because the elephant is so big, and the pond, in comparison, is so small, the water goes splashing out at the sides. This is like rapture. The experience is so great, and our capacity to receive it is so small, that some of it spills over, as it were, in the form of these physical side effects.

But then, suppose the elephant steps into a great pool of water, a huge lake, or even an enormous river. Then, even when he fully immerses himself in the water, there's hardly a ripple, because although the elephant is so big, the body of water is immeasurably bigger. In the same way, in this stage, even though the experience of rapture may be very great, you're more able to receive it, more able to bear it. The physical sensations therefore die down, leaving just the inner, purely mental experience of rapture.[246]

BLISS

In the fifth stage, in dependence upon calm – calm in the sense of this purely mental experience of rapture – there arises bliss, *sukha*. *Sukha* has various meanings in Buddhism. It can refer to pleasant bodily feeling, or to pleasurable emotion or happiness, whether hedonic or spiritual. Here it means the feeling of intense happiness that wells up within you when bodily awareness is transformed. The physical side of rapture has been refined away, and a purely mental or spiritual experience of bliss or happiness is left.

Given this progression of ever more positive mental states, from joy to rapture to calm or pacification, and now even to bliss, it seems extraordinary that some of the early books written in the West on

Buddhism described it as a gloomy, pessimistic, negative religion. Here we see the exact opposite. Bliss is described as a state of intense happiness that represents the complete unification of all our emotional energies. They are not divided, there's no split. They are all flowing together strongly and powerfully in a single direction, like a great river. There are no negative emotions. By the time you've risen to this stage there is no craving, no fear, no hatred, no anxiety, no guilt, no remorse, no negative emotion whatsoever. Whatever energy you had invested in those negative emotions now flows positively in the form of bliss, this intense happiness. In this way we rise higher and higher in the spiritual scale.

This points to an extremely important aspect of the spiritual life: the fact that we owe it to ourselves and to others to be emotionally positive whenever possible. In this way we shall contribute not only to the raising of our own level of consciousness and being but also to that of everybody with whom we come into contact. Unfortunately it is possible to be so bound up with negative emotions, so riddled with fear, anxiety, jealousy, possessiveness, hatred, and suspicion, that one's whole life is passed in a sort of dark cloud. To stop this from happening, one has to be very quick to prevent negative emotions from developing, and actively cultivate and encourage the positive emotions of love, joy, compassion, peace, and so on.

Only too often even religious life, organized religious life, is bound up with negative emotion. Without wishing to harp on this sort of theme – because preoccupation with negative emotion is itself negative – one has only to look back on the history of Europe, with its hundreds of years of religious persecution and witch-hunts, to see that this is so. The lesson to learn from all this is perhaps not to get caught up in group emotion, especially 'religious' group emotion.

It is no accident that what could be described as the motto of Buddhism is the phrase *sabbe sattā sukhī hontu*, which means 'May all beings be happy.' In a way, this is the sole wish of Buddhism – it's as simple as that. It's not just words, not just something to repeat and recite. The aspiration is that all beings should be emotionally positive, that everyone should be free from negativity, free to become happy, blissful, full of love, compassion, peace, joy, devotion, and faith.

Then sixthly, dependent upon this intense happiness arises *samādhi*. The word has several different meanings, but here it means concentration. This does not mean a forcible fixation of the mind on a single object, but a concentration which comes about quite naturally when, in that state of intense happiness, all one's emotional energies are flowing in the same direction. In other words, when we are completely happy, when all our emotional energies are unified, we are concentrated in the true sense. A concentrated person is a happy person, and a happy person is a concentrated person. The happier we are, the longer we shall be able to stay concentrated; and conversely, if we find it difficult to concentrate for very long, the reason will be that we are not happy with our present state. If we were truly happy we wouldn't need to do anything else – we could just stay still. But we are unhappy, dissatisfied, so we get restless and go searching for this or that, looking for some distraction, some diversion.

This connection between happiness and concentration is illustrated by another story from the scriptures. We are told that one day there was a discussion between a certain king and the Buddha. The king came to the Buddha to ask him about his teaching, and as they talked a question cropped up – the question of which of them was happier. Was the Buddha happier than the king, or was the king happier than the Buddha? Of course, the king was quite sure that he was the happier of the two by far. He said, 'Well, look, I've got all these palaces, I've got this army, I've got this wealth, I've got all these beautiful women. What have *you* got? Here you are sitting underneath a tree outside some wretched hut. You've got a yellow robe and a begging-bowl, that's all. Obviously I'm far happier than you.'

But then the Buddha said, 'Well, let me ask you a question. Could you sit here perfectly still for an hour, enjoying complete and perfect happiness?' The king said, 'Yes, I suppose I could.' Whereupon the Buddha said, 'All right. Could you sit here without moving, enjoying complete and perfect happiness, for six hours?' And the king said, 'That would be rather difficult.' Then the Buddha said, 'Could you sit for a whole day and a whole night, without moving, absolutely happy the whole time?' And the king had to admit, 'No, that would be beyond me.' Then the Buddha said, 'Well, I could sit here for seven days and seven nights without moving, without stirring, all the time experiencing complete and perfect happiness without any change, without any diminution whatsoever. So I think I must be happier than you.'[247]

The Buddha's happiness arose out of his concentration, and his concentration arose out of his happiness. Because he was happy he was able to concentrate; because he was able to concentrate he was happy. And the fact that the king could not concentrate showed that the king was not really as happy as he had thought, certainly not as happy as the Buddha.

This relates closely to the practice of meditation. We know that meditation begins with concentration, but many of us find this very difficult. It's no use thinking that concentration can be gained by force of will; although, of course, a lot of people do think this. It's quite usual to experience a train of thought along the lines of 'Here I am. This is my time for meditation. I've got a concentration technique I can use. My mind is buzzing, full of idle thoughts. There's traffic going up and down outside. I'm sure there's going to be a knock on the door at any minute. But I'm going to concentrate. I don't particularly want to, but I've made up my mind to do it, so I will.' Most people's approach to meditation is more or less like this. We try to fix the mind forcibly on a certain point, but then all sorts of disturbances arise – we get distracted – because there is a split within us, and our emotional energies are not integrated. But meditation is not just a question of the application of techniques, not even the right techniques. It's much more a matter of gradual growth.

It has to be said that the Buddhist scriptures don't always seem to bear this out. They recount many instances in which a monk goes along to see the Buddha, the Buddha says a few words, and the monk – or sometimes the lay person – becomes Enlightened.[248] Or they describe a monk living in the forest who sees a leaf fall from a tree, and from that gains an intense realization of impermanence which leads almost immediately to his becoming Enlightened.[249] So why doesn't this kind of thing happen to us? Why don't the Buddha's words, or the falling leaves, affect us in this way?

Partly, at least, it's because the ground has not been prepared. It's full of rocks and stones and weeds and garbage. Even if a few seeds are scattered haphazardly here and there, they don't stand a chance, even before considerations of rain and light come into play. So the ground must have been prepared. Faith, satisfaction, delight, rapture, and so on must be cultivated (both within and outside the meditation practice) before any concentration technique can be really fruitful. If concentration doesn't grow in this natural, spontaneous way, if we insist on making it a business of the forcible fixation of the mind on an object, the unregenerate or unsublimated portions of our psyche are liable to react against what we are doing.

We may manage through force of will deliberately, consciously, to hold the mind on a certain object – the breath, or an image of the Buddha, or a mantra. We may even succeed in keeping the mind on that object for a while. But we've done it with the energy of the conscious mind. The unconscious mind isn't cooperating, and sooner or later there's going to be a reaction, or even a sort of breakdown.

This doesn't mean that concentration exercises are not useful; they are. But they're much more effective when the ground has been cleared. If we haven't really stopped to think about the unsatisfactoriness of life, if no faith has arisen, if there isn't much joy, and certainly not much rapture or calm or bliss or anything like that, there's not much possibility of real concentration. It's significant that concentration in the sense of *samādhi* arises only at the sixth stage, halfway up the path. It's only then that we can really begin to concentrate, because our emotional energies have been unified, and we are now, perhaps for the first time in our lives, happy. So really one's whole life needs to be a preparation for meditation.

It is also important to prepare well for each individual meditation session – the same gradual approach applies here, although the timescale is different. You can't just sit down and switch your mind on to the object of concentration; you have to pave the way. First of all, you have to disengage your energies from other things, and direct them into one channel; then, when your preparations for meditation are complete, the concentration exercise – the mindfulness of breathing or whatever it is – will just put the finishing touch, and you're away.

But however elevated our meditation practice, however concentrated we are, at this point we are still on the level of the mundane. We're on the spiral but we're still subject to the gravitational pull of the round. However, with the arising of the next stage in the series we come to the second part of the spiral, which is purely transcendental and from which there is no possibility of regression.

Although this stage represents a radical change, it still arises in dependence on the previous stage of the path. There's a saying of the Buddha that comes into its own here: 'The concentrated mind sees things as they really are.'[250] When the mind is full of thoughts, when it isn't calm or harmonized or balanced, but pulled this way and that, it can't see things as they really are. But the concentrated mind – not the mind which is straining to stay on an object of concentration, but the mind which is naturally concentrated, with or without the help of a concentration exercise – is able to see the true nature of things.

KNOWLEDGE AND VISION OF THINGS AS THEY REALLY ARE

When the waters of a lake are still, they can reflect the face of the moon without distortion. But when the wind blows, making lots of tiny ripples, or even great waves, the reflection of the moon is broken up and distorted. The way we see things is like that – all in bits and pieces, broken up, twisted. It's only the concentrated mind that sees things as they are, that sees the full moon as it is, full and perfect and round. And this is the stage we come to next: in dependence upon *samādhi*, concentration, there arises *yathābhūta-jñānadarśana*: 'knowledge and vision of things as they really are'. This stage is of the utmost importance, because it marks the transition from meditation to wisdom, from the psychological to the spiritual. Once we've reached this stage, the stage of Stream Entry, there can be no falling back. According to the traditional teachings, the attainment of Enlightenment is now assured.

One way of putting it is to say that this 'knowledge and vision' is insight into the three characteristics of conditioned existence. First of all, one sees that all conditioned things are impermanent, that they're constantly changing, that they don't remain the same for two consecutive instants. Then, one sees that all conditioned things are ultimately unsatisfactory. They may give us some pleasure for a time, but they can't give permanent and absolute happiness, and to expect that from them is a delusion. And then, thirdly, one sees that all conditioned things are insubstantial, ultimately unreal. Not that we don't experience them, not that they're not there, empirically speaking, but we see them only superficially, we don't penetrate into what they really are.

Consequently this stage represents a direct perception: you actually *see through* the conditioned. Not only that; you see through the conditioned to the Unconditioned. Piercing through the impermanence of the conditioned, you see the permanence of the Unconditioned; piercing through the unsatisfactoriness of the conditioned, you see the perfectly satisfying nature of the Unconditioned; and piercing through the insubstantial, the unreal, you see that which is eternally and everlastingly real, that which Mahāyāna Buddhism calls the *dharmakāya*, the 'body of spiritual truth'.[251]

When you begin to see things in this way, your whole outlook changes radically. You are not the same as you were before. In Shakespeare's play, once Hamlet has seen the ghost stalking the battlements he's a changed man, because he's seen something from another world, another dimension. In the same way, but in a much more positive sense, once you've glimpsed something beyond, once you've seen through the passing show, once you've had a glimpse of that higher dimension, call it what you will, higher reality, the Absolute, even God if you must, once you've had a glimpse of that – not just an idea of it, not a concept, not a speculation, but a real glimpse, a real contact, a real communication – then you'll never be the same again. A permanent change takes place in your life. To use the Yogacārin expression, you've turned about, or begun to turn about, in the deepest seat of consciousness.[252]

WITHDRAWAL

Then, dependent upon knowledge and vision of things as they really are, there arises *nirveda*. This is sometimes translated as 'revulsion' or 'disgust', but that's too strong, too psychological a way of putting it; at this level you're far above and beyond any psychology in the ordinary sense, because you're above and beyond the psyche, the mind, in any ordinary sense. It's a purely spiritual withdrawal – calm, deliberate, and natural. This stage represents the clean, even serene, withdrawal from involvement in conditioned things. It's just like seeing a mirage in the desert. At first, seeing those palm trees and that oasis, you may hasten in their direction. But when you see that it's a mirage, you stop in your tracks. There is no point in going towards what isn't really there. Similarly, when you deeply see, when you really realize, on the basis of your experience of *samādhi*, that conditioned things, all the things with which you normally come into contact, are unsatisfactory, that they're going to pass away, and that there's no real truth or reality in them, you become less and less attached to them. You withdraw from them, you lose interest.

This stage of withdrawal is a sort of sitting loose to life. You still play the games that other people play – or at least some of them – but you know that they're games. A child takes his game very seriously because to him it is real, but the adult can join in the child's game while knowing that it's a game. If the child wins, the adult doesn't get upset, because it's only a game. In the same way, once you've seen through the games people play, you can go on playing the games, but you know that they're just games and you can withdraw from them, at least inwardly. You may be doing what is necessary objectively, but subjectively you're not caught up in it. This is what is meant by withdrawal. You're still part of the conditioned, but in your heart you've withdrawn from it.

In India fishermen sometimes catch fish in their hands. They poise themselves on the bank at the edge of a flooded rice-field and look down into the muddy water between the rice plants, watching for a sign of movement. Then suddenly they reach down and grasp something. But sometimes, when they bring what they have caught out of the water, they see that it isn't a fish at all, but a poisonous snake – and of course they drop it at once. The Buddhist texts say it's just like this with conditioned things. We grab hold of them, just as the fisherman grabs what he hopes is a fish. But then, just as the fisherman sees the marks that show that what he thought was a fish is a poisonous snake, so, when we see on all these mundane things that we've grasped the three marks of unsatisfactoriness, transitoriness, and insubstantiality, we just let go.[253]

DISPASSION

In dependence upon withdrawal arises *vairāgya*, which can be translated, approximately at least, as 'dispassion'. This stage differs from the previous one in that while withdrawal is the movement of detachment from conditioned existence, dispassion is the state of actually being detached. In this state you can't be moved or stirred or touched by any worldly happening. This isn't hardness or insensitivity, but a state of serene imperturbability, like that exemplified by the Buddha just before his Enlightenment.

According to legend, when the Buddha was sitting under the bodhi tree along came Māra, the embodiment of evil – or, it would be more accurate to say, the embodiment of *saṃsāra* – with his forces. In depictions of this episode in Buddhist art you see Māra leading his army, with elephants and horses and soldiers and all sorts of monstrous demon figures, and they're throwing great rocks and spitting fire and releasing arrows against the Buddha, hundreds and thousands of them swarming and swirling around. But the Buddha doesn't take any notice. He doesn't even see them, doesn't even look, doesn't even listen. He's in a state of complete imperturbability, complete dispassion.[254] And this is what this stage represents. You're so firmly fixed in the truth, your mind is so absorbed in the Unconditioned, that nothing can touch you.

There's a beautiful touch in these representations of the defeat of Māra in Buddhist art. As all the arrows, all the stones, all the flames that are hurled by these demon hosts close in on the Buddha, as they whizz through the air, when they touch the edge of his halo they turn into flowers and fall to the ground. So this is the state of dispassion. All the forces of Māra may rise up against you, all these weapons may come hurtling through the air, but as soon as they touch the edge of your halo, they just turn into flowers.

FREEDOM

In dependence upon dispassion there arises freedom – spiritual freedom, *vimukti*. Nowadays there's quite a lot of talk about freedom, and most people, it seems, think that it means the freedom simply to do as one likes. But the Buddhist conception of freedom is rather different. In the earliest Buddhist teaching it is twofold. Firstly there's *ceto-vimukti* – freedom of mind – which means complete freedom from all subjective emotional and psychological bias, from prejudice, from all psychological conditioning. And secondly there's *prajñā-vimukti* – the 'freedom of wisdom' – which means freedom from all wrong views, all ignorance, all false philosophy, all opinions.[255]

This complete freedom of heart and mind at the highest possible level is the aim and object of Buddhist life and practice. The Buddha once said, 'Just as the ocean has one taste, the taste of salt, so my teaching has one taste: the taste of freedom.'[256] This is the final objective, if you like, the end of Buddhism, this taste of complete spiritual freedom, freedom from everything conditioned, even from the very distinction between the conditioned and the Unconditioned, as the Mahāyāna goes on to say.

KNOWLEDGE OF THE DESTRUCTION OF THE *ĀSRAVAS*

But this freedom is not the culmination of the spiral path – not quite. Next, dependent upon freedom arises the stage called 'knowledge of the destruction of the *āsravas*'. It isn't even enough to be free. The next stage is to *know* that one is free. And one knows that one is free when one realizes that the *āsravas* have been destroyed. This is another of these untranslatable terms; it's a very expressive word which means a sort of mental poison that floods the mind. There are three *āsravas*: *kāmāsrava*, which means the poison of desire or craving for experience through the five senses; *bhavāsrava*, craving for any form of conditioned existence, even for existence as a god; and *avidyāsrava*, the poison of spiritual ignorance.²⁵⁷ When these poisons are extinct, and when one knows that they are extinct, then at last thirst or craving, *tṛṣṇā*, the emotional counterpart of spiritual ignorance, has been destroyed. You've broken the chain at its weakest and its strongest link. In dependence upon feeling there no longer arises any craving whatsoever. And at that stage you have reached the end of the spiral path, you have gained Buddhahood.

A NATURAL PROCESS OF GROWTH

The spiral path shows us that the spiritual life is a natural process of growth, each succeeding stage arising from the overflow, as it were, of the preceding stage. As soon as one stage reaches its fullness, it inevitably passes over into the next. One finds this in meditation. Sometimes people wonder how, when you've got to a certain stage in meditation, you go about progressing to the next stage. But there's really no need to ask. If you get to a certain stage and you go on cultivating that, so that it becomes more and more full, more and more complete, then out of its very fullness it will move forward, under its own momentum, to the next stage. Similarly, as each stage of the path reaches a point of fullness, it gives birth to the next stage. We don't really have to worry about the next step; we just need to cultivate the stage we're at. It's quite useful to have a theoretical idea of what lies ahead, but one doesn't need to bother about it too much. Once one stage is fully developed it will automatically pass over into the next.

The principle of conditionality isn't just an idea. Being aware that this is how life works can have a transforming effect on every aspect of the way we live. When any experience befalls us – when someone says something to us, or we read something, or we experience something through the senses – we can always ask ourselves whether our reaction is cyclical or progressive. If there's a cyclical reaction – say from pleasure to craving – then we go round and round on the wheel of life. But if there's a progressive response, however faint, however feeble – say from an experience of the unsatisfactoriness of life to a feeling for something higher – then at that very moment we place our foot, however hesitantly, upon the first step of the path to Enlightenment.

8

THE JOURNEY TO ENLIGHTENMENT

THE TRANSCENDENTAL EIGHTFOLD PATH

The fact that in terms of the spiral path permanent transformation begins with 'knowledge and vision of things as they really are' suggests that usually we do *not* see things as they really are. We see them only as they appear to be; we see them the wrong way round; we even see them upside-down. The Buddha identified four 'upside-down views' (*viparyāsas*) that represent the way we usually see things.²⁵⁸ One of these views is seeing the painful as pleasant; another is seeing the impermanent as permanent; the third is seeing real selfhood where there is no real selfhood; and the fourth is seeing the ugly as beautiful. And these four upside-down, topsy-turvy views stand between us and reality.

Let us, for instance, take a closer look at impermanence. In the case of something quite obvious, quite tangible, like a house or a car, we can become attached to it and start behaving as though that object is going to be there for ever. We start treating it as though it were permanent. This applies, of course, to our relations with people as well. Not that we actually *think* that our house or our car is permanent. If we were asked we would say, 'Well, of course it isn't permanent. I know that very well.' But our emotional attitude towards it is that it is permanent, and it's the emotional attitude, primarily, that constitutes the topsy-turvy view. When we are deprived of something to which we have become attached, towards which we are in the habit of behaving as though it will always be there, we experience suffering, to a greater or lesser degree, and this tells us that we have been seeing at least that particular thing, or indeed person, the wrong way up.

Similarly, we see what is really insubstantial, without selfhood or own-being – and this very much includes our view of ourselves – as having a self, something substantial and fixed amid, or somehow standing behind, the changing processes of life. And we imagine that what is in reality unsatisfactory is giving us satisfaction – or at any rate we imagine that it will give us satisfaction in the future. These three 'topsy-turvy views' are of course connected with the three *lakṣaṇas*, the three characteristics of conditioned existence.

The fourth *viparyāsa* – seeing what is in reality ugly as being beautiful – requires a little more explanation. The teaching isn't saying that we should regard a flower, say, as being essentially ugly. It is more that in comparison with the beauties of a higher plane of reality, the beauty experienced within conditioned existence pales into insignificance.

So we need to turn our view of things the right way up, or, as the Buddhist expression has it, to cultivate 'right view' or even 'Perfect Vision'. If you have Perfect Vision, you see the painful as painful, the impermanent as impermanent, and so on. You also see the truth of the four noble truths, and the truth of conditioned co-production. In other words, you see reality, at least to some extent.

Perfect Vision is the first step of the Buddha's Noble Eightfold Path, which, as it happens, was the Buddha's first ever description of the path to Enlightenment. We have seen how, having decided to teach the Dharma, he sought out his old companions with the intention of unfolding to them his great discovery. The way he put it to them, which resulted eventually in their realization of the truth, was in terms of the four noble truths: that life is unsatisfactory; that this is because of our craving; that it is possible to reach a state of complete peace and freedom from the painful tug of craving for things to be otherwise; and that one can reach that state by following a path. In this connection the Buddha outlined what has become known as his 'Noble Eightfold Path'.[259] Here I want briefly to introduce this formulation of the path – perhaps the best known throughout the Buddhist world – as well as two much less well-known descriptions: the seven factors of Enlightenment, and the seven *visuddhis* or purifications.

The first thing to say about 'the' Eightfold Path is that in fact there are two: the mundane Eightfold Path and the transcendental Eightfold Path.[260] You may perhaps have been thinking that Perfect Vision of reality is a strange place for a spiritual path to start; it's rather reminiscent of the Zen phrase, 'If you want to climb a mountain, start at the top.' But strictly speaking, it is the transcendental path to which one refers when one speaks of the Āryan Eightfold Path ('āryan' here means 'noble' or 'holy') and it is this path that starts with Perfect Vision. The mundane Eightfold Path is an Eightfold Path but it's not an Āryan Eightfold Path. Most accounts of Buddhism deal only with the mundane Eightfold Path, but they deal with it as though it was in fact the transcendental Eightfold Path, which can be rather confusing. Here I want to focus specifically on the transcendental Eightfold Path.

It is divided into two great sections. The first section consists of the first step only – that is to say, Perfect Vision – while the second section consists of all the other steps: Perfect Emotion, Perfect Speech, Perfect Action, Perfect Livelihood, Perfect Effort, Perfect Mindfulness, and Perfect *Samādhi*. These two sections are also known as the two paths: the Path of Vision or Path of Reality; and the Path of Transformation. The Path of Vision represents our initial vision of things as they really are – a glimpse that is sufficient to start in us the process of real, radical transformation – and the Path of Transformation represents the gradual transformation of every aspect of our being, every aspect of our life, in the light of that glimpse. At the same time, the more we are transformed – the more our life is transformed – the brighter that glimpse becomes.

Let us see, just briefly, how this works out in detail. Once one has taken the first step, Perfect Vision, then the Path of Transformation begins with – and I'm translating interpretively here – Perfect Emotion. This represents the transformation, in the light of Perfect Vision, of our entire emotional and volitional nature. Greed is transformed into generosity; we don't grasp or grab – we give. Aversion is transformed into loving-kindness, cruelty into compassion, and so on.

The third step of the path is Perfect Speech. Only too often speech is untruthful – not only that, it's often harsh, often frivolous, and often divisive. Perfect Speech is the exact opposite. It's truthful, of course, but it's also pleasant, affectionate, meaningful, and genuinely beneficial. In the *Dhammapada* the Buddha says, 'Better than a thousand meaningless words collected together is a single meaningful word on hearing which one becomes tranquil.'[261] Perfect Speech is also conducive to harmony, in the sense of bringing people together, creating friendship between them rather than dividing them.

The fourth stage of the transcendental Eightfold Path is Perfect Action. This consists in behaviour that is thoroughly ethical. It consists in abstention from violence, from misappropriation, and from unchastity; and in more positive terms it consists in actions expressive of love, generosity, and contentment. On the mundane Eightfold Path, this is a matter of conscious discipline. But Perfect Action as a factor of the transcendental Eightfold Path is natural and spontaneous; it is action as transformed in the light of Perfect Vision.

All these stages – Perfect Emotion, Perfect Speech, and Perfect Action – involve other people, at least to some extent. One can't be generous without someone to give to; one can't speak the truth without someone to speak it to. Thus Buddhist ethics is not just self-regarding, but also other-regarding. Indeed, we cannot really separate self from other in any case – and this is especially true of the next stage, Perfect Livelihood. Perfect Livelihood consists in earning one's living – in supporting oneself and one's family, if one has a family – in a way that does no harm to any living being. In contemporary terms we could say that Perfect Livelihood is livelihood that is ethically and ecologically sound. Buddhist tradition gives quite a number of examples of wrong livelihood: for instance, selling alcohol, manufacturing weapons, dealing in poisons, and so on.[262] Nowadays, of course, the list would be much longer, but the principle remains the same.

Modern economic life has become extraordinarily complex. Our livelihood, only too often, depends on the livelihoods of so many other people, and it's sometimes very difficult for *us* to be ethical if *they* are not ethical. So it's not enough for us to be *personally* ethical; we also have to try to transform the society in which we live into an ethical society. It's very difficult to be perfectly ethical in an unethical society. What this means in principle is that the Buddhist has not only to transform himself or herself. We have to try to transform the world in some degree, at least the society in which we happen to live, in collaboration with other like-minded people.

Then, sixthly, there's Perfect Effort. This is the effort, basically, to eliminate and prevent unskilful mental states as well as to develop and initiate skilful ones. This is an extremely important aspect of the spiritual life. Though it is spoken of as the sixth step of the Path, Perfect Effort really enters in at every stage. In fact, one could almost speak of the spiritual life itself as a life of Perfect Effort because there is never anything passive about it.

The seventh, penultimate step is Perfect Mindfulness or Recollection. This consists in knowing what we're doing, whether mentally, verbally, or physically, and also why we are doing it. In other words, this step consists in our being *aware* – aware of ourselves, aware of other people, aware of our environment, even aware of reality.[263]

And then eighthly and lastly is Perfect *Samādhi*. I'm using the Pāli/Sanskrit word here because in the context of the transcendental Eightfold Path there is really no equivalent English term. It usually means mental one-pointedness or concentration but here it represents the total absorption of one's subjective being in reality.

This, then, is the Path of Transformation. First we develop the Path of Vision – we obtain a glimpse of reality, the Dharma Eye opens at least a little,[264] we even enter the stream – and *then* we enter upon the Path of Transformation, transforming our own lives and the society in which we live. Of course, even if we have not developed the Path of Vision in the transcendental sense, we will have had at least a glimpse of a glimpse of reality, or we would not have set out on the Path at all. At the least, we can cultivate the intellectual counterpart of Perfect Vision, usually known as right view. And we can still work to transform ourselves in the light of what we have seen. We can still follow the mundane Eightfold Path. Our aim, however, should be to enter upon the transcendental Eightfold Path, to enter the stream that leads ultimately to the ocean of Nirvāṇa.

THE SEVEN FACTORS OF ENLIGHTENMENT

The seven factors of Enlightenment, or *bodhyaṅgas*, are: awareness; sorting out of mental states; energy; joy; calming down; *samādhi*; and equanimity.[265] After a brief glance at this list, one might be forgiven for concluding that we are now dealing with a very different path from the Eightfold Path we have just – at least in imagination – traversed. Gone are overt references to such matters as speech and livelihood; instead we are asked to consider 'sorting out mental states' and 'calming down'.

And indeed, this formulation of the path to Enlightenment is more akin to the spiral path, with which it shares several stages.

Bodhi means 'Enlightenment' (the word 'Buddha' comes from the same root) and *aṅga* means 'limb' or 'shoot'; so the seven *bodhyaṅgas* are the seven limbs or branches of the spiritual life, all of which are to be developed if *bodhi* is to be attained. Their name reminds us that we should not take the image of a path too literally as a description of the spiritual life. Sometimes it may help to see in one's mind's eye a path stretching ahead of one, or spiralling up the mountain and out of sight. But it is just as valid – and may be more useful sometimes – to see spiritual growth as being akin to the unfolding of the petals of a flower, or the growth of a sturdy tree. We are reminded of this by the fact that the 'factors' of Enlightenment are seven 'limbs' or 'shoots' – and in fact the eight aspects of the Eightfold Path are designated by this same word, *aṅga*.

The first of these 'limbs' is *smṛti*, which is usually translated 'recollection' or 'awareness'. The spiritual life, one could say, begins with awareness: simply knowing what is happening, knowing what is going on. Not that it is simple to do this. Four kinds of awareness are usually distinguished. In the first stage we are aware of what we are doing – that is, we are aware of bodily movement, and also of what we are saying. We are rarely fully aware of what we are doing, and very often we don't really know what we are saying either, because our minds are elsewhere, but this is a crucial aspect of awareness.

Then, we also need to know what we are feeling: whether we are happy or sad, greedy or contented, angry or loving. And we also need to become aware of what we are thinking. At first it may not be obvious that we need to make an effort to do this; surely we know what we're thinking, at least most of the time? But very often we don't. At this very moment, even, you may not really know what you are thinking. You may think you are fully absorbed in what you are reading – but are you? Or are you thinking about what you need to do next, or what you did yesterday, or what to have for supper? Unless we know what we are thinking from moment to moment, the mind will be scattered and confused. The fourth kind of awareness to be practised is awareness of the Dharma. Once we know – at least intellectually – the truth of how things really are, we must try never to forget it. Whatever we do, we must keep the Dharma in mind.

But we can start with the basics. We may find it impossible to keep the Dharma in mind much of the time. We may find it hard to stay aware of what we are thinking and feeling. But we can begin by at least trying to stay aware of what we are saying and doing. There's a story that illustrates the fundamental importance of this level of mindfulness. It's about a young Japanese Buddhist who wanted to learn meditation. Deciding he needed a meditation teacher, he searched for some months, and travelled many hundreds of miles, until he came to a temple where – so he had heard – a great meditation teacher lived. Having been granted an interview, the young man entered the teacher's room. First, though, he folded up the umbrella he was carrying, and put it to one side of the door.

The teacher asked him what he wanted, and he said, 'I want to learn to meditate. Please teach me.' The teacher said, 'All right. But first I want to ask you one or two questions.' The young man was quite pleased to hear this, thinking that he would be questioned about the theory of meditation. But the teacher asked, 'When you arrived just now, was it raining?' The young man replied, 'Yes, it was raining quite heavily.' Then the guru asked, 'Did you come carrying an umbrella?' The young man thought this rather an odd question. Why wasn't the teacher asking him anything about meditation? But anyway, he thought he'd better reply. 'Yes,' he said. 'I was carrying an umbrella.' Then the teacher asked, 'When you came into my room, on which side of the door did you leave it?' Try as he might the young man couldn't remember. There was nothing he could say. So the teacher said, 'You are not yet ready to practise meditation. First you need to learn mindfulness.' And away the young man had to go.[266]

Of course, we need not really put off learning to meditate until we have learned to be mindful. Indeed, meditation – especially the mindfulness of breathing – will help us to cultivate mindfulness. But our practice need not be – *should* not be – restricted to when we're sitting in meditation. We can practise mindfulness in all situations. Whatever we do, we should do it carefully, with proper thought. We may be studying, or cooking, or sweeping the floor, or mending the car, or driving, or talking with our friends – but whatever it is, we can try to do it with a clear mind, with *smṛti*, with recollection and awareness.

The second *bodhyaṅga* is *dharma-vicaya*. Usually the term Dharma or Dhamma means the Buddha's teaching, but, as we have seen, it can also mean 'mental state', and this is what it means here. Having become aware of your mental state, with *dharma-vicaya* you take the process a step further. *Vicaya* means 'distinguishing' or 'sorting out'; so this stage or limb of the path involves not just being aware of your mental states, but distinguishing them from one another, in particular distinguishing 'skilful' (*kuśala*) states from 'unskilful' (*akuśala*) ones.

The Buddhist meditators and scholars of certain traditions have made something of a speciality of the identification of different mental states; in its most systematized form, this is known as the Abhidharma.[267] But the crucial distinction is between skilful – that is, ethical – states, and unskilful states. It isn't enough just to let mental states happen. We have to keep watch over the mind; we have to sort out the skilful states we wish to develop from the unskilful ones we wish to get rid of.

We can think of it as a process of sifting or sorting out. In India one of the most time-consuming household tasks – and of course it is almost always done by the women of the house – is cooking. And more often than not, the meal involves cooking rice. So everywhere in India you will see cooks spreading rice out on a kind of wicker tray, and then going over it very carefully, putting the grains of rice on one side and the stones and bits of dirt on the other, until eventually there is a big heap of nice clean rice and a small pile of dirt and stones.

Of course, in the West our rice usually comes pre-packed and spotless, but the idea of this kind of sorting out persists in our language in phrases such as 'separating the wheat from the chaff'. And we can think of sorting out our mental states in a similar way. We can literally say to ourselves, 'This is skilful; that is unskilful. This I must cultivate and develop; that I must get rid of.' Just as rice is sorted from stones, one can purify one's mind by getting rid of unskilful mental states.

The third factor of Enlightenment is *vīrya*, which means 'energy'. Buddhists may sometimes be imagined to be rather passive and ineffectual, but in fact a Buddhist should be the embodiment of energy: physical energy, mental energy, emotional energy, and spiritual energy. Of course, this energy must be put to good use. The great Buddhist poet Śāntideva defines *vīrya* as 'energy in pursuit of the good'.[268] If you have a lot of energy but use it for a purpose that is not worthwhile, you are not practising *vīrya*.

Śāntideva likens a person with *vīrya* to an elephant – not a tame elephant but a wild elephant. The wild elephant is a playful beast, and one of the things he likes doing in hot weather is plunging into a pool, especially a lotus pool. After plunging into one pool and spending a few minutes there he comes out and plunges into another pool. Thus he goes on plunging into one pool after another, and in this way enjoys himself. Śāntideva says that the bodhisattva is like that. As soon as one task is finished he plunges joyfully into another.[269]

The fourth factor of Enlightenment is *prīti*, which, of course, we have already encountered as a stage of the spiral path. *Prīti* is joy or enthusiasm, and its development follows naturally from the development of energy. That energy radiates in all directions, so that you are full of life, bubbling over. You feel really wonderful. For an illustration of this we can look to Buddhaghosa, the great commentator on Pāli texts. *Prīti*, Buddhaghosa says, is like a great silken bag filled with air.[270] I suppose our modern equivalent is a balloon. When you are full of *prīti*, you feel very light, as though you were floating through the air, and very happy. And you get this sort of feeling especially when you meditate.

The fifth factor is *praśrabdhi*, 'calming down'; again, this is also a stage of the spiral path. The excitement, as it were, of *prīti* has died away, and you are left with a calm, steady feeling of pure happiness. To use a homely image, it is like what happens when a bee collects nectar from flowers. First it locates the flower, then it alights on it with a loud buzzing sound and crawls within the petals. So long as the bee has not found the nectar the buzzing sound continues, but as soon as it finds it, the sound stops. *Praśrabdhi* is like that.

Samādhi is the sixth factor. Of course, as we have seen, the word means much more than just 'one-pointedness of mind', but it does include this. We find an example of one-pointedness in the life of the Buddha himself. After his Enlightenment the Buddha was a wanderer all his life, and even when he was an old man he continued to walk from place to place, teaching the Dharma. And sometimes, of course, he felt quite tired and quite thirsty. On one such occasion he sat down at the side of the road and asked Ānanda to fetch some water from a nearby river. While Ānanda was away the Buddha passed the time in meditation. After a while Ānanda returned and told the Buddha that he was unable to get any water, because five hundred bullock carts had just crossed the river and made it very dirty. They had, in fact, passed along the road by the side of which the Buddha was sitting. But to Ānanda's surprise the Buddha said, 'I heard nothing at all.' Five hundred bullock carts had passed by right in front of him, but he had not heard a thing. This is what is meant by one-pointedness.[271]

As part of the process of developing *samādhi*, one makes a start by cultivating one-pointedness of mind. It's not necessary to adopt a wandering lifestyle or go and live in a cave in order to do this; it can be done in the affairs of everyday life, by trying to give one's whole mind to whatever one is doing, whether it is washing the dishes or contemplating the Dharma.

The seventh and final factor of Enlightenment is *upekṣā*, which is usually translated 'equanimity'. The word sometimes connotes no more than a psychological state of security, but here it is synonymous with Enlightenment itself. If you have *upekṣā* you are like a mountain, solid, massive, and unshakeable, even if the winds blow from all the corners of the earth. Whichever of the eight worldly winds – happiness or sorrow, praise or blame, loss or gain, fame or infamy – is buffeting us, we needn't let it affect us.[272] We can be just like the mountain. With the development of *upekṣā* in its fullest sense, the last of the seven factors of Enlightenment is present; and we become as unshakeable as the Buddha himself.

THE SEVEN *VISUDDHIS*

Towards the end of the fourth century CE a boy was born into a Brahmin family in the city of Magadha. Magadha was near the place which had become known as Bodh Gaya because, hundreds of years before, a man called Siddhārtha Gautama had sat to meditate beneath a tree by the river there, and had gained Enlightenment. But the Brahmin boy did not hear the Buddha's teachings until, as a young man well versed in the Hindu scriptures and keen on discussion and debate, he met a Buddhist elder called Revata. It was Revata who got him interested in Buddhist doctrine, especially the Abhidharma, which by that time had been in the process of development for more than five centuries. When the young man wanted to know more, Revata told him he could take things further only if he accepted ordination into the Buddhist tradition. This the young man did, eager as he was to learn, and he soon mastered the teachings of the three *piṭakas* of Buddhist doctrine.

The young man became known as 'Buddhaghosa' – 'he whose speech is like that of the Buddha' – and he went on to become the greatest of all commentators on Theravāda Buddhism. Of his many works, the most famous is the *Visuddhimagga*, or 'Path of Purity'.²⁷³ The work amounts to a complete exposition of Theravāda teaching, focusing particularly on meditation practice and technique. It is based, as its name suggests, on yet another formulation of the Buddhist path. The *Visuddhimagga*, the 'Path of Purity', is divided into seven stages which are outlined in the *Rathavinīta Sutta* of the *Majjhima Nikāya*, the collection of middle length sayings.²⁷⁴

So here is a way of thinking about the path to Enlightenment that emphasizes the point that spiritual practice is all about purifying the mind. In fact, we find that the path of the seven *visuddhis*, the seven purities, corresponds to the threefold path of ethics, meditation, and wisdom. The first *visuddhi* (they are listed in this chapter in their traditional Pāli form) is *sīla visuddhi*, purity of ethical conduct; the second is *citta visuddhi*, purity of mind, gained especially through meditation; and the remaining five *visuddhis* are a progressive approach to wisdom through five stages.

But before we investigate the seven *visuddhis*, it is worth having a look at a point that crops up in the *Rathavinīta Sutta* in which they are mentioned. The *sutta* recounts a dialogue between two of the Buddha's disciples, Śāriputra (whom we have already met) and Puṇya. It describes how Puṇya, having listened to the Buddha teaching, 'gladdened, roused, incited, and delighted', goes to meditate in a certain grove. Śāriputra follows Puṇya to the grove, hoping to converse with him, and when the two men have spent the day meditating beneath the trees of the grove, they start to talk. The subject Śāriputra chooses to raise is that of the seven *visuddhis*.

In particular, he is concerned with a kind of question that might well be asked about any formulation of the path to Enlightenment. He wants to know, 'Do we get to Nirvāṇa by means of *sīla visuddhi* (that is, the first of the seven stages of this particular path)?' And Puṇya answers no. Then Śāriputra asks, 'Do we get to Nirvāṇa without *sīla visuddhi*?' And again the answer is no. Then: 'Do we get to Nirvāṇa by means of *citta visuddhi*?' No. So he asks, 'Well, do we get to Nirvāṇa without *citta visuddhi*?' and again the answer is no. He asks the same question about all the other *visuddhis*, but each time the answer is no. You don't get to Nirvāṇa with them, and you don't get to Nirvāṇa without them. Puṇya – who at this stage doesn't know he's talking to the revered Śāriputra –

chooses to make the matter clear with the help of an illustration called the 'Relay of Chariots'. (This is how the *sutta* gets its name, incidentally; *Rathavinīta Sutta* means 'Discourse on the Relay of Chariots'.)

In ancient India, in the Buddha's day, most people had to walk everywhere, but if you were rich you might have a chariot, drawn by two or maybe four horses. The illustration given in the *sutta* is this. There is a king, and he wants to get to a certain city, but it is a long way away. So he gets into his chariot and drives his horses for many miles. When the horses are tired he jumps out of his chariot and gets into another which is waiting with some fresh horses, and drives on again. Some miles later, these horses too get tired, so he jumps out and gets into another chariot. In this way he changes chariot and horses seven times.

Hence the question arises, does the first chariot take the king to his destination? No, it does not. Does the second chariot take him to it, or the third? Again, the answer is no. But does the king get to his destination without the help of the first chariot, the second chariot, and so on? No, he does not. What happens is that the first chariot takes him to the second chariot, the second chariot to the third, and so on, until the seventh chariot carries him to his destination. In just the same way, *sīla visuddhi* takes you as far as *citta visuddhi*, *citta visuddhi* as far as *diṭṭhi visuddhi*, and so on. Then the seventh *visuddhi*, *ñāṇadassana visuddhi*, takes you as far as Nirvāṇa. Thus one doesn't gain Nirvāṇa by means of *sīla visuddhi* and so on, but one doesn't gain Nirvāṇa without it.

Śāriputra is well pleased with this answer – although Puṇya is rather embarrassed to discover that he has been holding forth to such a great Dharma teacher as Śāriputra. And the story is a useful illustration of the point that none of the stages of the path can be regarded as ends in themselves.

So let us return to consider the first of these seven 'chariots': *sīla visuddhi*. *Sīla* means 'ethical conduct', so at this stage of purification one pays attention to one's ethical life. Basically, there are five *sīlas*, five ethical precepts: not to harm living beings, not to take what is not given, not to commit sexual misconduct, not to speak falsehood, and not to take intoxicants.[275] If one can observe all these five precepts, one's ethical conduct is purified, giving one a strong basis for one's individual development, as well as the basis of a harmonious social life.

Once you are leading an ethical life, you find that it begins to have a purifying effect on your mind, so this first stage naturally flows into the second, *citta visuddhi*. *Citta* means 'mind', and this purification is somewhat similar to the stage of *dharma-vicaya* in the seven factors of Enlightenment. It means getting rid of *akuśala cittas*, unskilful states of mind – anger, jealousy, fear, ignorance – and replacing them gradually with positive, friendly, clear states. This is, of course, a central purpose of meditation.

If you purify your mind, it becomes very clear. No longer mentally confused, you can think clearly and straightforwardly. This leads to the third stage of purification, *diṭṭhi visuddhi*. This is the first of the five stages of purification which involve the progressive realization, in terms of actual experience, of the true nature of phenomenal, conditioned existence on the one hand, and Nirvāṇa on the other. *Diṭṭhi* (Sanskrit *dṛṣṭi*) simply means 'view'. Developing *diṭṭhi visuddhi* involves getting rid of wrong views and cultivating right views.

The Buddha had a lot to say about wrong views; he enumerated sixty-two different kinds.[276] Of these, three of the most fundamental are: 'everything is made by God'; 'everything is the result of fate or destiny'; and 'everything happens by chance'. Ultimately these wrong views can be traced back to our belief in a fixed, unchanging self or soul. Traditionally, therefore, the purification of views involves reflection – in the context of meditation – on the three characteristics of conditioned existence, the five *skandhas*, or another of the formulations of the Dharma that reflect the way things really are.

When you practise *diṭṭhi visuddhi* you purify your mind of these three wrong views. You see that when things happen, they happen because of certain definite causes and conditions – and that this holds good not only of the external world, but also of your own mind. The realization that we are not fixed beings, but can change if we make the effort, and that if we set up appropriate conditions, desirable consequences will follow, is the key to spiritual development. But if you don't realize this – if you think that your life is not in your own hands but controlled by God or fate or random circumstance – you can't take the spiritual initiative. We may think that 'abstract ideas' don't impinge much on 'real life', but in fact it is very important to establish right views.

The next stage of purification is closely related to the previous one. Having purified one's views, one may still be reluctant to act on the basis of right views. So the next step is 'crossing over by the overcoming of doubt' – *kankhāvitaraṇa visuddhi*. Here, doubt doesn't mean just enquiring into things. It is perfectly valid, indeed desirable, that one should doubt in this sense; one shouldn't take things on trust. But this is not what is meant here. This doubt is an unwillingness really to find out about things. You don't take the trouble to find out the truth because, to put it bluntly, you don't want to. If you find out the truth you may have to put it into practice, and that is going to mean change – by which it is natural to feel threatened. And one strategy one may use to defend oneself against change is to raise all sorts of unnecessary difficulties and objections. Underneath it all is the desire to keep things vague and unclear. If one allows to emerge a clear vision of how things are, one is going to have to act, one is going to have to change.

Highly educated people tend to suffer a lot from this sort of doubt because, with their active minds, they can raise all sorts of problems and difficulties. They enjoy the sort of talking that goes on all night and never comes to any conclusion – because if it doesn't come to any conclusion you don't have to take any action. It's very important to overcome this kind of doubt. It's not so difficult to see through wrong views (Pāli *micchā-diṭṭhis*), but if you're not careful, even after you have apparently got rid of the view, you bring it all back with your doubt. Unless one can overcome this sort of doubt, one's will is going to be completely paralysed.

The next *visuddhi* is 'knowledge and insight into what is the path and what is not the path'. (In Pāli this is *magga-amagga-ñāṇa-dassana*.) This, again, is a very important stage. It is one thing to be convinced, at least provisionally, that you can take responsibility for your own spiritual life, having cleared away doubt and confusion, at least for the moment. But if you are going to make spiritual progress, the next thing you need to do is commit yourself to a specific line of approach, and this is not easy in a world that offers so many spiritual and pseudo-spiritual options. Not only that. Once you have committed yourself, it isn't necessarily going to be obvious whether or not any particular action, practice, or initiative is actually conducive to spiritual growth.

Here one needs to bear in mind the Buddha's advice to his aunt Mahāprajāpatī Gautamī: that a reliable teaching will lead one towards dispassion, not passion; towards freedom, not bondage; towards simplicity of lifestyle, not covetousness; towards contentment, not discontent; towards energy, not laziness; towards solitude, not company; and towards delight in good, not delight in evil.[277] These are the criteria we need to apply and keep on applying, if we are to be able to distinguish the right path from the wrong path.

The next *visuddhi*, 'knowledge and vision of the path' (*paṭipadā-ñāṇa-dassana*), clearly follows from the previous one. Once you have established what is the right path and what is the wrong path, the next step is actually to tread the path for yourself. Then from your own experience you come to know that it is the path. It's no good distinguishing the right path from the wrong path if you don't then follow the right path. And, of course, this is easier said than done. Even when one can see clearly which is the right path to take, one is still held back by all the forces within one that resist change. This is what could be called the battleground of the spiritual life. As the *Dhammapada* says, 'Though one should conquer in battle thousands upon thousands of men, yet he who conquers himself is [truly] the greatest in battle.'[278]

The seventh and last of the *visuddhis* is called simply 'knowledge and insight' – *ñāṇa-dassana*. This is not ordinary knowledge, but an elevated, pure, supremely clear knowledge – the knowledge that sees things exactly as they are. It's a sort of wisdom (*prajñā*), and of course it is joined with *karuṇā*, with compassion. It is a knowledge that fills you with energy and enables you to work for the benefit of other people, even for the benefit of the whole world.

These seven stages of purification will carry us along the whole course of human development, to Enlightenment itself. Or rather, if we develop them, we will move under our own steam in the direction of Enlightenment. Above everything else, the Dharma is something to be practised. This is why it is spoken of as a path – a path which, as we have seen, is described in so many different ways. The idea is that we don't just gaze admiringly at the signpost that says 'Nirvāṇa this way'; we actually begin to follow the path to which the sign points. Whether we think in terms of the transcendental Eightfold Path, or the seven *bodhyaṅgas*, or the seven stages of purification, the idea is the same: that here is a path we must actually travel.

There are still more ways of thinking of the path. Sometimes, for example, it is called the *madhyama mārga*, or 'middle way' – that is, the middle way between extremes, especially the extremes of self-torture and self-indulgence;[279] of course, each of the formulations of the path we have considered is a middle way. Each of these formulations has its own use, its own emphasis. Perhaps the little-known path of the seven stages of purification in particular deserves to be more widely known, especially because it emphasizes that the Buddhist path is a path of beauty. As well as ethical purity, *visuddhi* means 'brightness, splendour, excellence'. It doesn't just mean purity in the ordinary sense; it means something much more than that. It means a beautiful path, a path that we should enjoy following. It's just like going along a track among beautiful hills. The higher you go, the more beautiful the view, the more open everything becomes, the more you enjoy it and the more free you feel.

9

THE PATTERN OF BUDDHIST
LIFE AND WORK

The subject of this chapter is the 'five spiritual faculties'. The chapter title
is intended to emphasize the overall purpose of these faculties, which is
the living of a Buddhist *life*. Buddhism is concerned with life. One might
even say that Buddhism is itself life – life in the sense of growth, in the
sense of realizing the potential of one's life. A Buddhist is someone who
is first and last alive – awake to life.

We often come across people who, while they may be present in
body, do not seem to be really mentally or emotionally present. They're
not fully alive to what is going on, not really alive to other people –
not alive even to themselves. But the most basic characteristic of a
Buddhist should be that they positively vibrate with presence, with
spiritual life, with a wakefulness to life. Everything else on the spiritual
path is secondary to this and follows from it.

I may say that this is one of the reasons why, when I was in India,
I was so much attracted to the movement of conversion to Buddhism
among the ex-Untouchables, and why I became so deeply involved in
it.[280] They were very poor and largely illiterate, and indeed many of them
still are, but one thing at least they had – and still have – and that is life.
They are completely alive. Their involvement with Buddhism means a
sort of enhancement, a refinement, of the vibrant life they already have.

Travelling to an Indian village usually involves a journey by train
followed by a ride on a bus or a bullock cart; then you finally approach
your destination on foot. It's a laborious business as a rule, but if you

have been invited to speak to the people of the village about the Dharma, they do everything they can to make the engagement a memorable and joyful one. You are often still a couple of miles out from the village when you are met by an enthusiastic party of twenty, thirty, perhaps forty men – young and old – who proceed to dance you into the village, such being their traditional mode of welcome for an honoured guest. A long brass trumpet is sounded, there is much banging of tambourines and rattling of castanets, and they dance and stamp energetically all the way to the village. There, some of the houses will be decorated in various ways – for example with chalk designs in front of the doors – and flags will be hung everywhere, especially the five-coloured Buddhist flag. And when they finally come together for the meeting, usually very late at night, everyone is agog to hear something about Buddhism. In short, everyone is alive to the occasion.

In the West we do things differently. We tend to lead rather separate, routine-filled lives. We are dominated by routines and responsibilities, and in such circumstances how is it possible to be spontaneous, to bubble with spiritual life? Routine – by which I don't mean a carefully thought-out, balanced programme of activities, but a dull, mechanical daily round – kills spontaneity, and without spontaneity there is no life in any meaningful sense. You might even go as far as to say that life *is* spontaneity, that spontaneity is life. This is why I am here characterizing the traditional Buddhist teaching of the 'five spiritual faculties' as the 'pattern of Buddhist life and work'. The five spiritual faculties should amount, in the end, to a spontaneous and enthusiastic engagement with life, and the work of life, in the fullest and deepest possible sense.

What, then, are these 'faculties'? In Sanskrit and Pāli they are called *indriyas*, and if we look at the etymology of this term we will find that it throws a great deal of light on the subject. *Indriya* denotes 'that which belongs to Indra' – Indra being, in Indian mythology, the ruler of the gods. So the *indriyas* are those things that pertain to Indra, the ruler, and thus the word translates as 'the governing – or controlling – principles'.

What is really interesting about this word, however, is its application to what we call 'the senses'. In the Indo-Aryan languages *indriyas* is the term given to the five senses (or six, if you include the mind). They are given this name, meaning 'governing, controlling, dominating principles', because the whole of human life as we normally live it is governed, controlled, dominated, by these senses.

Every living thing, whether vegetable or animal or human, belongs to a certain level of development. Every living thing, from the lowest to the highest, from the humblest to the most exalted, has its own place in the scale of evolution. And every sentient being is organized to function on its own particular level – which it does through the operation of its own particular range of senses: the *indriyas*.

This is quite a sobering thought. Most of the time we are controlled, dominated, governed completely by our senses – though these do include, according to the usual Buddhist way of reckoning them, the mind as a sense-faculty. We can see that this is the case most clearly, perhaps, first thing in the morning. During sleep the senses have been more or less in abeyance. But eventually we wake up, we open our eyes, sleepily turn over, and start becoming aware of the external world. As we do so the senses all begin to look for their respective objects and we start to act on the impulses to which they give rise: we make tea, we switch on the radio, we look for the newspaper, we decide to have another five minutes in the warmth of the bed. The senses of sight, hearing, smell, taste, touch, and mind are all moving out towards, and engaging with, various objects (including mind-objects), and this goes on all through the day. All the time we are being pulled by the senses, and therefore we identify ourselves with the senses and with the psychophysical organism to which they belong. And we function most of the time largely on that basic psychophysical plane of the *indriyas*.

However, this word *indriyas* denotes also the five *spiritual* faculties.[281] Edward Conze calls them the five 'cardinal virtues',[282] but this translation fails to register the fact that it is the same word as for the sense-faculties. The fact that the same word is used for both sets of faculties is significant because it indicates the overriding importance of the five spiritual faculties to the spiritual life. The suggestion is that the two sets of *indriyas* perform an analogous function. Just as the five sense-faculties govern and control and dominate mundane life, so, in the same way, the five spiritual senses govern and control and dominate spiritual life. Just as we find our way about the physical world with our sense-faculties, so, in the same way, we find our way about the spiritual world with the five spiritual faculties.

If our various senses are – to the extent that we have them at all – more or less fully functioning, our spiritual faculties are embryonic and in need of development. It is the development of these five spiritual senses or faculties that makes up the pattern of Buddhist life. They are: *śraddhā* or faith; *prajñā* or wisdom; *vīrya* or energy, vigour; *samādhi* or concentration; and *smṛti* or mindfulness. Let us take them one by one.

FAITH

I have known people who have been surprised to find that there is any such thing as faith in Buddhism. They have come into contact with Buddhism under the initial impression that it is essentially rational, that emotion is not really involved at all. This confusion arises out of two mistaken ideas: that emotion is essentially irrational, and that faith is the same thing as belief.

Belief – in the sense of accepting as true on authority something that one can never verify, or something that is even inherently absurd – is not faith, at least not in Buddhism. In Buddhism, as we have already seen in connection with the spiral path, *śraddhā* or faith covers the entire devotional or feeling aspect of spiritual life. Faith in Buddhism could never be said to be contrary to reason – or even beyond reason. Faith is the emotional counterpart of reason. What you understand with your intelligence you must feel also with your emotions. The two go together, and you can't really separate them.

Śraddhā in Buddhism is faith in the Three Jewels: the Buddha, the Dharma, and the Sangha. But it is especially faith directed towards the Buddha himself, because – at least from our point of view – the Buddha comes first. Even though the Dharma represents immemorial Truth, we would know nothing of it without the Buddha, and there would certainly be no Sangha without him. In Buddhism faith is essentially faith in the founder of Buddhism himself.

However, it's not just belief; it's not even just feeling. Faith in the Buddha is the sort of emotional response that you have when you are confronted by the embodiment of Enlightenment. This confrontation can take place in various ways. You can of course be confronted personally by some living human being who is the embodiment of Enlightenment. Alternatively, you can be confronted through literature, by reading about someone who was such an embodiment – if not the life of the Buddha himself, then perhaps the biography of the great Tibetan yogi, Milarepa, or that of Huineng, the sixth patriarch of Chan or Zen Buddhism. With any of the great masters or teachers, there is the possibility of an immediate emotional response to accounts of their lives – whether historical or legendary – a response that is not just sentimental, but engaged, challenging, personal, real.

Then again, you can be confronted by an image, an artistic representation – a painting or a statue – of someone who was Enlightened. Here I am reminded of a French Buddhist nun whom I knew in Kalimpong in the 1950s. She told me that in her student days in Paris she used to like visiting museums and art galleries, which is how she found herself eventually in the Guimet Museum of oriental art. She was a rather militant, aggressive woman; she told me that she used to go around with a pair of ice-skates with which to defend herself if she was attacked. 'Well, I thought if I carried these skates with me, if anyone tried to attack me I'd slash the blades across his face.'

But as she strode along the galleries of the Guimet – having left the skates in the cloakroom – looking to left and right rather fiercely as she usually did, suddenly she encountered an image of the Buddha. From her description I gather that it was an image from ancient Cambodia. She just turned a corner and there was the celebrated smile – faint and delicate and rather withdrawn – so characteristic of this Khmer style of sculpture. The whole expression of the face is intensely peaceful.

The face of this image just stopped her in her tracks. She told me that she stood looking at it without moving, almost without blinking, for forty-five minutes. She couldn't take her eyes off it. The impression of peace, tranquillity, and wisdom that emanated, that streamed as it were, from those features, was so strong that she couldn't pull herself away. She hadn't yet studied anything about Buddhism, but as soon as she saw this image, she felt compelled to ask herself, 'What is it that gives its expression to this image? What is it trying to tell me? What depths of experience does it come from? What could the sculptor have experienced, to be able to express something like this?'

Confronted by this embodiment of Enlightenment, she could not move away unchanged. In fact, it determined the whole subsequent course of her life. This is the kind of emotional response we can have to an embodiment of Enlightenment simply rendered in stone, let alone one in the form of a living person. And it is a response that amounts to faith.

What it is in fact is the response of our potential Enlightenment – our own deeply hidden capacity for Enlightenment – to the actual

Enlightenment with which we find ourselves confronted. There's something deep down within us that has a sort of affinity with what is fully realized, fully expressed, fully achieved, in that embodiment of Enlightenment. There's a sort of kinship. It's as though you have two stringed instruments side by side: if you sound the strings of one, the other starts softly vibrating too.

And what this response gives rise to is devotion. There are all sorts of different ways of expressing devotion, but traditionally it is done by means of prostration or worship, the offering of flowers, the lighting of candles and incense, and so on. Some people in the West are a little shy of Buddhist devotional practices. They would like to think that Buddhism had nothing to do with the kind of apparently superstitious activities that they were trying to get away from when they abandoned Christianity. They feel, perhaps, that these are practices for children, and that it is time to be grown-up and stop bowing and scraping and offering candles and the like.

However, if you leave out devotion you are closing the door on any emotional engagement with your spiritual ideal. A healthy spiritual life, just as much as a healthy psychological life, must include the expression of emotion.[283] Having said that, there is a balance to be maintained. Faith and devotion can go to extremes, and when they do so they become superstition, fanaticism, or intolerance. It is for this reason that, according to this teaching of the five spiritual faculties, faith – the whole emotional and devotional side of the spiritual life – should be balanced by wisdom.

WISDOM

Broadly speaking, in Buddhism *prajñā*, wisdom or knowledge, is coterminous with the Dharma understood as truth, principle, reality. More specifically, it consists in seeing things as they really are rather than as they appear to be. It consists in seeing all worldly existence as conditioned, and thus as unsatisfactory, impermanent, and without an ultimate and unchanging self. At the same time it involves seeing the Unconditioned, by contrast, as being blissful, permanent, and characterized by true individuality, unimpeded by the illusion of a separate and substantial self. Wisdom is further seen, in the Mahāyāna development of Buddhism, as consisting in the realization of the great *śūnyatā* or voidness – that is, the essential non-difference between the conditioned and the Unconditioned.

Technically speaking, wisdom is of three kinds. Firstly, there is *śruta-mayī-prajñā*: wisdom or knowledge or understanding that is derived from hearing (or reading). You are sufficiently interested to take the trouble to listen to someone speak about the Dharma or to pick up a book and read about it, and you are receptive enough to derive some understanding from what you hear or read. It makes sense to you and you take it in.

Secondly, there is *cintā-mayī-prajñā*: *prajñā* or wisdom 'based on thinking', i.e. your own individual thinking. You start reflecting on the Dharma, chewing it over rather than just swallowing it undigested. You start thinking on your own account, seeking to arrive at an understanding based on your own thinking, working out the implications of the Dharma yourself rather than having it interpreted for you by someone else.

The third level of wisdom is *bhāvanā-mayī-prajñā*. *Bhāvanā* means 'calling into being' or 'cultivating', and it is conventionally translated as 'meditation'; so this is wisdom based on one's reflections in the context of the experience of higher states of consciousness. It is not arrived at through intellectual thought. It is realized, intuited, seen, as a result of meditation, as a result of one's own spiritual – and especially transcendental – experience.[284]

Most of us have had some experience of all three kinds of wisdom. We have all come to some understanding as a result of hearing about the Dharma, or at least reading about it. We have all developed our understanding as a result of independent thought, however rudimentary. And many of us have had moments of direct vision, some glimpses of the truth as mediated by a higher state of consciousness, especially in meditation. But it is important to be clear about which category of wisdom our experience falls into, and especially about whether it is our own wisdom or someone else's. It's easy to imagine that we have reflected upon something ourselves when all we have done is juggle with someone else's thoughts and insights.

A useful and illuminating exercise is to survey one's ideas and views and perceptions and assess how many of them can be found to be the result of one's own individual reflections. Unless one is a very exceptional individual, it won't be many. Nearly everything we know comes by hearing, or reading, so ninety-nine per cent of our knowledge and understanding we get at second hand. Nearly all of us tend to consume large daily quantities of facts and opinions without giving much time to really thinking about them. Unless we earn a living by thinking, we probably feel we can't afford the time simply to sit and reflect upon things in such a way as to come up with a truly original thought.

Can you honestly say that you have ever had a truly independent thought? Have you ever really thought something out for yourself from beginning to end without any help at all? Have you ever thought something through and come up with an original idea? Have you ever had a significant thought – even a shade of a variation of one – that no one else has ever had? It happens of course, but *cintā-mayī-prajñā* is quite rare.

As for *bhāvanā-mayī-prajñā*, this is even more rare. We may imagine that we have had a direct, intuitive insight into something when all we have done is achieve a certain depth of reflection that has given us a clearer idea of it. The amount of wisdom we have developed while in higher meditative states is likely to be very small indeed.

All of this may sound unnecessarily discouraging, but it is in fact the reverse. If we never make these distinctions, we may flatter ourselves that the ideas and insights we embrace are our own thoughts, even our own experience. And if we do that, we will not be allowing ourselves the option of moving on to a deeper and more personal investigation of reality, and even perhaps eventually the possibility of an actual experience of the Truth, a truly transformative wisdom.

Prajñā represents the whole intellectual and doctrinal side of Buddhism. At least the first and second levels or kinds of wisdom do – the third, strictly speaking, is neither intellectual in a narrow sense, nor emotional, but represents a sort of fusion of the two. But the first two definitely represent an intellectual – as opposed to an emotional or devotional – approach to the goal of Buddhism. The development of *prajñā* can therefore, when taken to extremes, become a merely academic sort of knowledge. It can become, as a friend of mine once described the writings of a famous scholar of Buddhism, 'as dry as the last ounce of dust in desiccation'.

Unfortunately some people have a definite taste for this sort of thing. Another old friend, Lama Govinda, who originally came from

Germany, said of his own countrymen that their idea of a good lecture on Buddhism would be a discussion of all the different possible meanings of a certain term according to various dictionary definitions, followed by a close analysis of its meaning according to at least a dozen Buddhist scholars, before concluding judiciously that all these views were wrong. This, he said, was the way to fascinate a German audience. And he said that the English liked a different sort of lecture. What they wanted was the complete picture, a single perspective on the whole subject. Whether this would still be the case today is another matter, but it does illustrate the way that a strength – in this case the German tradition of intellectual rigour – can become a weakness when it is not balanced by anything else. For this reason, in the five spiritual faculties, faith and wisdom form a pair. The one must be balanced by the other. Neither must be allowed to outweigh the other; they must work together in harmony.

VIGOUR

As we saw when we considered *vīrya* as one of the seven factors of Enlightenment, it is defined by Śāntideva in the *Bodhicaryāvatāra*, the 'Guide to the Career of the Bodhisattva', as 'energy in pursuit of the good'.[285] Energy in the usual sense of the word – as applied to people who dance all night or pursue money and power vigorously – is not *vīrya* at all. *Vīrya* is energy applied to the goal of Nirvāṇa.

Vīrya can be of two kinds – objective and subjective. The objective aspect of *vīrya* consists in doing things to help others, things that may involve a certain amount of physical effort and trouble, even difficulty. In its subjective sense, that is, as applied to one's own mental content, it corresponds to *samyak vyāyāma*, right effort or Perfect Effort, the sixth step of the Noble Eightfold Path. Right effort consists of the 'four great efforts': firstly, the effort to eradicate unskilful states of mind; secondly, to prevent the arising of unskilful states that have not as yet arisen; thirdly, to maintain skilful states of mind that are already present; and fourthly, to bring forth skilful states that have yet to arise. This is the fourfold right effort.[286] It is the effort to eliminate all unskilful states of mind, all states that are rooted in greed and hatred and bewilderment or delusion, and to cultivate all skilful states, all states rooted in generosity, love, and wisdom.

Both these aspects of *vīrya*, objective and subjective, need to be cultivated, as the Buddha himself never tired of pointing out. His discourses are quite often about the importance of maintaining the momentum of one's practice. One presumes that he must have noticed his followers tending to let things slide from time to time, to stop putting in the effort, to stagnate.[287]

There is quite an arresting story from the *Jātaka* tales that would evidently have been recounted in order to awaken energy that was beginning to flag in this way. The *Jātaka* tales are a collection of stories about the activities of the Buddha-to-be in his previous lives, both human and animal. They're a kind of Buddhist folklore. This story concerns the god Indra, who happens to be on a journey when he comes to the banks of a great river, a river so broad that he can hardly see the further shore. Just down by the edge of the water he finds a squirrel that is behaving in a rather extraordinary manner. It is repeatedly dipping its big bushy tail into the water, and then lifting it up and sprinkling the water on the dry land.

Intrigued, the king of the gods asks the squirrel, 'What on earth are you doing?' The squirrel replies quite cheerfully, 'I'm emptying all the water of the river on to the dry land.' Indra of course is totally bemused at the scale of this ambition: 'You foolish creature! Do you really think you can fulfil such a task?' But the squirrel looks at him, unabashed: 'Certainly – it's only a question of going on long enough.' Indra is quite impressed by that, and the Buddha comments that although there may appear to be little progress taking place, and we may not seem to be getting very far, if we carry on long enough, anything may be achieved.[288]

If we keep putting one brick on top of another, a house may be built. If we keep reading one page after another, a particular subject will eventually be mastered. If we keep doing a regular meditation practice, day after day, our overall mental state will change. Indeed, it is the only way these things can be done, by steady persistence. From moment to moment, even from day to day, we may seem to be progressing by such tiny amounts that it can all seem to be a waste of time, but in the spiritual life, that is how we achieve anything: by regular, sustained, long-term effort.

However, there is no doubt that, like the other faculties, true vigour can turn into something much less helpful. It can become restlessness: energy in pursuit, not of the good, but of anything that will take us away from our experience of ourselves, anything that will distract us from our deeper task. If we can't settle down, if we're always wanting to be on the move, busy doing something, this is not vigour but a neurotic inability to sit still, a compulsion to avoid any kind of relaxed attentiveness to what is present before us. The result is activity that tends to be restless, agitated, and jerky, whereas real vigour is relaxed, easy, and smooth. Real vigour is achieved by not allowing one's energy to be one-sided – in short, by counterbalancing it with the spiritual faculty of *samādhi*.

ONE-POINTEDNESS OF MIND

As we have seen, *samādhi* covers the whole field of what we generally call concentration and meditation. *Samādhi* literally means the fixation of the mind on a single object – in other words, one-pointedness of mind. There is nothing forced about this concentration; it is more accurately described as a unification of the total energies of the psyche. Our energies are generally quite scattered – it is rarely that we are at once mentally, emotionally, and physically fully concentrated. *Samādhi* consists in drawing all of ourself together into a single focus of energy.

The Buddhist scriptures describe *samādhi* in terms of the four *dhyānas*. These are progressively purer and clearer states of superconsciousness which are attained as one's energies progressively become more and more unified. They are usually described, especially by scholars, in rather a dry, analytical manner – all one gets, very often, is a catalogue of different mental functions. This is unfortunate, because it does need to be emphasized that these are actual experiences attainable by living human beings like you and me. The spirit, the human experience, of these higher or more unified states of consciousness is brought out very well by the Buddha himself in four famous similes.

Of the first *dhyāna*, the Buddha begins, 'Suppose you take a plateful of soap powder. ...' By the way, this soap would have come – this may come as a surprise – from a soap tree: the tree has a large fruit that would have been dried and powdered, as it still is in parts of southern India, and used as soap. And the Buddha goes on, 'Suppose you then gradually mix your soap with water and knead it all together until you have a ball of soap absolutely saturated with water, so that there is not a single speck of soap powder that is still dry, and not a single drop of water trickling free of the ball. ...'

When you sustain this level of meditative concentration you are saturated with this higher consciousness: a blissful peace fills every part of your psychophysical organism. You are permeated by that super-subtle sense-experience, just as the powder is permeated by the water. There is no unintegrated energy draining away or drifting off.

'Well', the Buddha says, 'the first stage of *dhyāna* is like that.' It is a state of unified consciousness, the union of positive and negative forces – the yin and the yang principles, as the Chinese tradition would say – within one's conscious mind. It is a state of harmony, integration, and peace, in which the energies of the conscious and the energies of the unconscious mind are brought together, unified, and harmonized, just like the soap powder and the water in the Buddha's simile.

For the second *dhyāna*, the Buddha proposes the image of a pool of water – perfectly clear, pure water – being constantly refreshed and replenished by an underwater spring. The second *dhyāna* is a clear pure state of consciousness into which rapture and joy are bubbling up all the time from deep within you.

As for the third *dhyāna*, this is likened to lotus flowers immersed in a pond of fresh water. The whole plant – stalks, leaves, flowers, blossoms, seed pods – lives immersed in the water, permeated by the water, but still separate and distinct from it. Similarly we experience our consciousness as completely pervaded and fed by an all-encompassing bliss.

Finally, the Buddha describes the fourth level of higher consciousness through another typically Indian image. He invites you to imagine that in the heat of the day when you are very hot and dusty you go and bathe in a pool or a river, and then, on emerging from the clear fresh water, you wrap yourself in a clean, cool, white sheet, and you just sit there like that, enveloped from head to toe. In the same way, in the fourth *dhyāna* you wrap yourself in a purified consciousness that insulates you from all harm. The dust of the world cannot touch you.

Such are the Buddha's comparisons for the four successively purer and clearer states of *samādhi*.[289] However, although these are intensely positive and beneficial attainments, they too can be taken to extremes if they are practised on their own, without reference to anything or anyone else, without being balanced by energy and vigour. You can end up with inertness or passivity, even laziness or drowsiness. It is a particular danger for people who sit naturally and comfortably in meditation posture, and are happy to sit there, more or less undisturbed by gross mental activity, but not putting any effort into really deepening their awareness.

So *samādhi* must be balanced by *vīrya*, especially work that benefits other people, and especially physical labour. In the Zen monasteries of Japan, as in the pre-communist Chan monasteries of China, you get your full share of both meditation and work. However many hours of meditation you do, you will be expected to do almost an equal number of hours of hard physical work. It will involve being down on your knees scrubbing the floor or up to your elbows in water scouring pans, not just deliberating over the arrangement of a couple of flowers or taking a delicate paintbrush to a porcelain bowl.

A friend of mine, Peggy Kennett, who became a Zen teacher in Japan after many years of difficulties (being foreign and female), once wrote to me describing the daily programme in her small monastery, where she had three or four disciples. They began at four in the morning with hard physical work until nine, and then had a simple meal, after which they got down to four or five hours of meditation, and finally they had another light meal in the afternoon. That was their life, she said: physical labour and meditation.[290]

If they had been spending all their time in meditation you can be quite sure – in the case of the comparative novices, anyway – that they would have become just lazy. On the other hand, if they had been spending all their time in physical labour they would eventually have become – unless exceptionally gifted – more or less brutalized: just hewers of wood and drawers of water. So both must be there, at least to some extent: so much meditation, so much physical effort – a balance between the two.

Most people are naturally inclined either towards activity or towards meditation, depending on their psychology, on whether they are extrovert or introvert. Some people have suggested that Buddhism is particularly suitable for introverts because of its emphasis on meditation, but this is to fail to take account of the balance of qualities called for by this teaching of the five spiritual faculties.

Besides, once an individual has made some definite spiritual progress, they are beyond this sort of classification. You can say neither that they are introvert, nor that they are extrovert. It is important to balance a natural introversion, which may express itself in an affinity for meditation, with outward-looking activity and healthy work (or vice versa) – certainly in the earlier stages of one's spiritual career.

In the Buddhist tradition, as we have seen, mindfulness, or the development of awareness, is practised with regard to four areas of experience. Firstly, as regards the body and its movements and attitudes, one is mindful of whether one is walking, standing, sitting, or lying down. One brings full awareness to the whole body, whether moving or still, and one is mindful of what each hand and foot and every other part of the body is doing. Secondly, one practises mindfulness as regards feelings, whether pleasant, painful, or neutral – whether one is happy or sad, elated or depressed, pleased or displeased. Thirdly, one tries to sustain mindfulness of thoughts: whether one is thinking about dinner or friends or relations or the work to be done the day after tomorrow, one should know exactly where the mind is going, where it is straying, from minute to minute.

The fourth area of one's experience of oneself to which mindfulness is applied is one's higher spiritual ideals. Whatever one may be doing, wherever one may be going, even in sleep, one keeps up at least a sort of undercurrent of awareness or mindfulness of one's ultimate goal. This is one of the purposes of mantras.[291] Repeating a mantra to oneself throughout the day is a means of keeping in touch all the time with one's ideals. One may be out shopping or sitting down with a cup of tea, or talking to someone – but if the mantra is always there in the background, one never completely loses touch with one's ultimate objective. So this is what the practice of mindfulness entails – maintaining some level of awareness of all these different areas all the time.

There is no danger of getting caught up in an unbalanced over-enthusiasm for the practice of mindfulness. Unlike the other spiritual faculties, mindfulness or awareness does not need to be balanced by something else. If faith is not balanced by wisdom it becomes blind and fanatical. If wisdom is not balanced by faith it turns cold and dry as dust. If energy is not balanced by meditation it degrades into mere restlessness, and if meditation is not balanced by vigour it degenerates into sloth and apathy. But in the case of mindfulness and awareness there is no such danger. By its very nature it is incapable of degenerating when left to itself. It does not need to be balanced.

In fact, mindfulness is itself the balancing agent. It is only through mindfulness that you can balance faith and wisdom, energy and meditative concentration. Mindfulness is so pivotal to Buddhism because balance itself is so pivotal to Buddhism. The Buddhist spiritual life is the balanced life at the highest possible level, in the broadest possible sense. If we're not trying to be balanced then we're not really practising Buddhism. Being Buddhist really means always trying to avoid slipping into extremes, or rather rising above the tendency to slide to one extreme or the other. It means looking for a point of balance, the pivot or fulcrum, as it were, between, or rather above, the extremes. And we do this through the exercise of mindfulness.

All this is not to say that mindfulness can be said ever to stand alone in any literal sense. In practice you can't really have any one faculty without also having the others, even if in a lesser degree. They are all present. One of them may predominate, but the fact that it is there at all means that the others are there, at least embryonically. And the spiritual effectiveness with which any faculty operates will depend on the degree to which it is balanced by the others.

For instance, you may have a lot of devotional feelings – you may be fond of offering flowers, lighting candles, and waving sticks of incense – but this will not constitute faith in any real sense without some understanding of the significance of it all. There is no faith, properly speaking, without wisdom – and vice versa. There is no faith without spiritual energy, either, because when you participate in any devotional exercise a certain amount of effort is involved – at least you have to turn up. The same goes, too, for concentration: devotional practice and concentration go hand in hand. In the process of making offerings or chanting a mantra or reciting a puja or performing prostrations, you will, if you do these things with the appropriate faith and devotion, develop concentration – sometimes a deeper level of concentration than you might normally get even in meditation. And finally, of course, mindfulness must be there with faith, otherwise there can be no continuity to your faith, no possibility of sustaining it beyond a series of fitful impulses, unconnected to one another and therefore going nowhere.

So the pattern of the Buddhist life lies in the development of all the five spiritual faculties equally: faith and wisdom, energy and concentration, and above all mindfulness. In this respect it is interesting to compare these five spiritual faculties – or at least four of them – with the four principal yogas of Hinduism.

The word *yoga* in Hindu systems of thought means 'union' – that is, union with the higher self (according to the Vedanta), or union with God (according to the theistic forms of Hinduism). Thus each of the four yogas is a particular path to union with the higher self or with God. At the same time they correlate quite closely with four of the five spiritual faculties of Buddhism. *Bhakti* yoga, the yoga of devotion, corresponds to the spiritual faculty of faith. *Jñāna* yoga, the way to union through knowledge, is the Hindu equivalent of the spiritual faculty of wisdom. *Karma* yoga, the way of selfless work, matches up with the Buddhist faculty of spiritual vigour or energy. And *rāja* yoga, union through the royal science of concentration and meditation, is of course the Hindu version of the spiritual faculty of meditative concentration. The correlation is quite exact.

However, the significance of this comparison is to be found where the two systems part company, which is in the way they are applied. A Hindu teacher will tell a disciple who is very emotional to take up *bhakti* yoga – that is, to leave aside *jñāna, karma,* and *rāja* yoga, and seek liberation simply through being a devotee. Someone who is very intellectual, on the other hand, will be told to follow just the path of *jñāna*, the path of knowledge and study. Then again, a person who is very active will be advised to take up the spiritual path of unselfish work. In modern India politicians are often accorded the courtesy title of '*karma* yogins', because of course there is no one so unselfish, if we go by the tenor of their pronouncements, as a politician: they give up all their time, all their energy, for the public good. Someone, finally, who is introspective, and perhaps a bit uncommunicative – a loner – will be picked out as a natural *rāja* yogin, and will be set to meditate and not bother with knowledge, devotion, or outward activity.

Thus the Hindu approach is to follow the line of least resistance; they say that if your natural inclination is towards, say, devotion, then you should specialize in that. However, Buddhists take the opposite – and more demanding – approach. They say that one should pay attention to the faculty which is weak. If one's faith is strong, then one needs to cultivate wisdom – and vice versa, otherwise one's strength will become a weakness. If one is meditative, one needs to cultivate some outward-going energy – and vice versa. Developing one's strong point fully will actually depend upon developing one's weak point. Indeed, all four faculties – faith, wisdom, energy, and meditation – need to be developed; otherwise one's spiritual development will be lopsided.

The reason for this difference in approach may well lie in the one faculty that is missing from the Hindu system. It is quite astonishing to note that mindfulness is not stressed in Hinduism at all, but this is my own personal experience, having heard Hindu teachers and pandits speaking on hundreds of occasions. Amongst many addresses and discourses about devotion, spiritual knowledge, meditation, and so on, not once have I heard mindfulness or awareness mentioned. This may be one of the reasons why in Hinduism you have to choose between the four yogas. You can't unify them because they can be unified only through mindfulness or awareness. There was one great Hindu teacher, Sri Aurobindo, who did blend all the four classical yogas into what he called an 'integral yoga' – but even he says nothing about mindfulness or awareness.[292] Mindfulness does seem to be a distinctively Buddhist emphasis.

The environment for Buddhist life and work, for the growth and development of the five spiritual faculties, is provided by the spiritual community, the sangha in the broadest sense.[293] It provides spiritual friends to help us identify where we need to put our energy, whether into meditation, beneficial work, devotion, or study. (As for mindfulness, this is to be practised constantly as an aspect of everything we do.) The sangha also provides opportunities for us to help set up, support, and make use of facilities by which the spiritual faculties may each be developed. Traditionally, these facilities would have centred around viharas where the monks lived and practised and taught, but today in the West they often consist of public centres, retreat centres, right livelihood businesses, libraries, and so on.

NURTURING THE FIVE SPIRITUAL FACULTIES

The spiritual community is like a greenhouse. Seeds are sown in trays under glass during the cold weather, to be transplanted outside when they have germinated and the weather is a bit milder. Likewise, it is in the favourable environment of the spiritual community that our spiritual faculties will best develop. Of course, the plants are kept in the greenhouse only while they're comparatively vulnerable, and in a way it is the same with us: the point of the spiritual community is not to provide a closed shelter from the world. But our spiritual faculties are always liable to be crushed, or frozen, or dried and withered, or burnt up, if we do not have the spiritual community – a favourable context for intensifying spiritual practice – to support us.

This image of spiritual development as being like the growth of a plant is a very traditional one, going right back to the Buddha's vision of humanity as being like a bed of lotuses. It can be useful to think in terms of nurturing our spiritual faculties, helping them to grow and develop by making sure we have appropriate conditions. I would say that, just as there are five spiritual faculties, so there are also five conditions for spiritual growth – though this is a list of my own, not a traditional one.

For the growth of a plant, obviously, five things are needed. First of all there needs to be a seed; and then the seed needs soil, warmth, light, and water. Similarly if we are to grow, if we are to develop our spiritual faculties, five things are necessary.

First of all, the seed is the potentiality for Enlightenment – and according to traditional Buddhist teaching, all human beings, even all living beings, possess that. The seed is there. We can all become Enlightened if we make sufficient effort – of course, the effort involved is very great – and if conditions are propitious.

Then, just as the plant needs soil, we need circumstances that are favourable to spiritual growth and development. We can still develop to some extent if circumstances are unfavourable, but it's much more difficult. In particular we need leisure, health, and facilities of various kinds; and in the West we're very fortunate that usually these facilities do lie ready to hand.

Many Buddhists in India, for example, do not have access to the facilities that we enjoy. For them it's not easy to follow the spiritual life, for all sorts of reasons. I heard about a young woman who became a Buddhist and wanted to take up meditation, but she came from a family of eighteen people who all lived together in a hut that had only one room. But she was determined to meditate, so she got up very early and sat to meditate on a shelf to one side of the hut, and in that way she kept up her meditation practice. Not many of us in the West ever have to meditate sitting on a shelf in a small room occupied by seventeen other people, but this is what she did. I also heard of an old woman who wanted to go on a week's retreat. The cost of a retreat in India is very small, but this old woman – she was about seventy – didn't have even that small amount. So she worked for a month as a farm labourer, digging and carrying stones, to save up enough to go on a week's retreat.

We don't have such difficulties anywhere in the West. We have it very easy, and we don't always appreciate that. We have access to books.

We have free time. We have health. We have leisure. So we have to ask ourselves, do we really make the best use of all these facilities?

Then, corresponding to the warmth the seed needs, we need the warmth of spiritual friendship; this is very important in Buddhism. I usually distinguish between two kinds of spiritual friendship: what I call 'vertical' spiritual friendship, between the less and the more spiritually experienced, especially between pupil and teacher; and 'horizontal' spiritual friendship, the spiritual friendship that springs up within the sangha among those who are practically on the same level. We really need both. We can't always be in personal contact with our teacher, if we have one. Perhaps he or she has many disciples and doesn't have much time to spare for us. But in any case what we most need is just friendship, human friendship – and this we get from our peers. We all need this warmth in our spiritual lives.

And then, corresponding to the light that the seed needs if it is to grow, we need intellectual clarity, clear thinking. Not all Western Buddhist teachers, it has to be said, are celebrated for clarity of thought; only too often one comes across serious misunderstandings and mis-representations, even about quite basic Dharmic matters. Hence we need the light of intellectual clarity; we need clear thinking.

And then of course, more than anything we need the rain of the Dharma. And the rain of the Dharma must be pollution-free. It must not be an acid rain. In other words, the Dharma must not be mixed with non-Dharmic or even anti-Dharmic elements. Buddhist teachers in both East and West are becoming increasingly aware of this danger. We do need to engage in creative dialogue with the adherents of other religions and philosophies, but we need to be very clear about what the Buddha taught, what Buddhism teaches. We need the rain of the Dharma, desperately, more than ever before, but that rain needs to be pure, unmixed with Catholicism or Vedanta or secular ideologies. We need to saturate ourselves in the rain of the pure Dharma. In that way our spiritual faculties will grow and develop, and bear fruit: the precious fruit of Enlightenment.

10

THE THREEFOLD PATH: ETHICS

No one who has read in the Pāli scriptures the glowing descriptions of the life of the Buddha and his disciples can doubt that they were all supremely happy people. Their love, compassion, renunciation, happiness, and contentment profoundly impressed all who came within the orbit of their influence. Kings and courtiers, prostitutes and virtuous widows, soldiers and scholars, farmers and artisans, all sat at the feet of the Buddha in order to learn the secret of that radiant happiness. It is no wonder that among the many epithets by which he is known is the title *Sugata*, 'the happy one'.

But even during the lifetime of the Buddha there were many people who did not relish a reward as abstract as the peace and blessedness of Nirvāṇa, but craved a teaching that would show them how to satisfy their human desires and aspirations. The Buddha would encourage people who felt like this by pointing out that there were various heavens in which they could be reborn as a reward for virtuous deeds such as feeding the poor, providing for the sick, digging wells, and planting shady trees under which travellers could rest. But he did not omit to warn them that these celestial realms were temporary abodes. When their stock of merit is exhausted, the inhabitants of these heavens are caught again in the ceaselessly revolving wheel of change, to be born once more in the human realm, and live and suffer as before. Perhaps, the Buddha would point out, once one had experienced these vicissitudes a few times, one would become weary of transient happiness and resolve to win the lasting bliss of Nirvāṇa.[294]

The Buddhist ethical system also envisages a series of hells in which those who have behaved unskilfully are reborn as a result of their unskilful actions. But the hells are as transitory as the heavens. When their misdeeds have been expiated, the inhabitants of hell are born once more in the human realm, and have yet another opportunity to find the path that leads beyond the wheel of life.[295] In the Buddhist vision, all beings – even the bird and the flower, some would say – will ultimately become Enlightened.

THE LAW OF KARMA

All this, of course, follows from the law of karma. In its simplest and most widely accepted form, the doctrine of karma is merely an expression of the universal belief that as we sow, so do we reap: ultimately we ourselves will feel the effects of our actions. The doctrine of karma helps in some degree to explain the apparent discrepancies of fortune that exist in the world; but one has to be very careful here. Someone's suffering – or happiness – is not necessarily the result of their past actions. The law of karma is often much misunderstood in this respect. Here we come back again to the basic truth: conditionality. The Buddha identified five orders of conditionality, five *niyamas*, as Buddhaghosa subsequently called them: physical inorganic; physical organic (i.e. biological); psychological; karmic; and transcendental.[296] Unless one has the insight of a Buddha, one cannot be sure which *niyamas* have brought about what particular effect.

The example usually given is that of a fever. If one gets a fever, it may be a chill caused by a sudden change in temperature; or one may have caught a viral infection; or perhaps one has succumbed to illness as a result of some kind of mental strain; or it may have been caused by an unskilful action committed in the past; or it may even be the effect on one's system of transcendental insight. Thus the same end result may have been brought about by something physical, something biological, something psychological, something karmic, or something transcendental – or a combination of two or more of these.

Causality is a complex web; anything that happens or comes into being does so as a result not of one cause, but of many. Indeed –

and this is an aspect of the Buddha's insight into reality – if one reflects on the factors that have produced the coming together of any phenomenon, there is simply no end to them. Consider, for example, what has 'caused' the loaf of bread (or the bag of rice) in your kitchen. Think of the people involved – and what 'caused' them. Think of their ancestry, stretching back into beginningless time. Think of the sun and the rain and the earth; think of transportation and packaging materials. Really, there is nothing, and no one, who has not been involved in the coming into being – and into your kitchen – of that loaf of bread. This is, incidentally, another way of coming at the truth of *anātman*, 'no separate selfhood'. Reflection shows us that nothing has an 'own-being' separate from everything else; everything and everyone is interconnected. To illustrate this, Mahāyāna Buddhism gives us the image of Indra's net – an infinite net of jewels each of which reflects all the other jewels in the net.[297]

The many-stranded complexity of causality means that if someone is suffering in some way, it cannot be assumed that this is inevitably the result of unskilful behaviour on their part. It may be, but you just can't tell. Hinduism adopts a fatalistic view of the law of karma, and some Buddhists seem to say something similar, but the Buddhist doctrine of the five *niyamas* makes it clear that someone's present suffering cannot be assumed to imply past unskilfulness.

What we can be sure of is that present unskilfulness is almost certain to result in future suffering (although some minor unskilful actions are 'cancelled out' by skilful ones); and skilful action will bring us joy. Our *locus classicus* here is the very beginning of the *Dhammapada*:

> Experiences are preceded by mind, led by mind, and produced
> by mind. If one speaks or acts with an impure mind, suffering
> follows even as the cart-wheel follows the hoof of the ox (drawing
> the cart). Experiences are preceded by mind, led by mind, and
> produced by mind. If one speaks or acts with a pure mind,
> happiness follows like a shadow that never departs.[298]

This is the basis of Buddhist ethics, sometimes summarized as 'actions have consequences'. So here we have the law of conditionality as applied to the ethical sphere. The Buddhist tradition has many sets of precepts or training principles, the most universally practised of which is the list of five ethical precepts. They are not rules in any narrow, literalistic sense; it is more accurate to describe them as principles of ethical behaviour. They reflect the way an Enlightened person would naturally behave, so that in trying to behave in that way oneself, one moves gradually towards Enlightenment.

THE FIVE PRECEPTS

There are four basic precepts – together with a fifth which is equally basic but upon the practice of which not all Buddhists agree. This is the way they are expressed:

I undertake the training principle of abstaining from taking life.
I undertake the training principle of abstaining from taking the
   not-given.
I undertake the training principle of abstaining from sexual
   misconduct.
I undertake the training principle of abstaining from false speech.
I undertake the training principle of abstaining from taking drink
   and drugs that cloud the mind.[299]

These five precepts enshrine, broadly speaking, the principles of non-violence, non-appropriation, chastity, truthfulness, and mindfulness.

The principle of non-violence is that we should refrain from harming or hurting others and, in particular, from killing or injuring them. Fundamentally, violence is the assertion of one's own ego at the expense of another. In its most extreme form it means the physical elimination of another in one's own personal interest. Violence towards another human being thus represents a denial of fundamental human solidarity, a radical assertion of separative selfhood, and a failure to identify imaginatively with another person.

If you are capable of violence towards someone, it is because you are failing to put yourself in their position, to empathize with them, to feel their feeling as your own. To a violent person, another person is simply an object, a thing. Violence is thus the ultimate negation of ethical and spiritual life; and non-violence in some ways represents the fundamental principle of Buddhism. There is one text, in fact, the *Mahāvastu* of the Lokottaravādins, which says this – that non-violence is the supreme *dharma*.[300] The implication is that if you sincerely try to practise non-violence you will find, in the long run, that you are practising every other Buddhist virtue. In principle they are all contained in non-violence.

Non-violence means not just that we should abstain from acts of violence, but that we should work for the welfare and happiness of mankind by every means in our power. It is impossible to do this unless our hearts are full of love towards people. Non-violence – *ahiṃsā* – may be defined as 'love in action'. If we want our actions to be harmless and helpful we should at all times cultivate a loving state of mind. Without this it is impossible to do any real good. A hateful thought can work untold harm in the world; all deeds of violence were once hateful thoughts, just as all acts of charity were once thoughts of love. Love is the only force strong enough to overcome hatred, and for this reason it is the most powerful weapon in the world. Clearly the practice of *ahiṃsā* on an international scale would entirely preclude the possibility of war or any other form of bloodshed or butchery, including capital punishment and the slaughter of animals for food. The ideal of *ahiṃsā* is that it should be universal in practice and universal in application.

A clear statement of this is to be found in the *Mettā Sutta*, or 'Discourse on Divine Love', which is expressive of the very essence of *ahiṃsā*.

Now, may every living thing, or weak or strong,
Omitting none, tall, middlesized or short,
Subtle or gross of form, seen or unseen,
Those dwelling near or dwelling far away,
Born or unborn – may every living thing
Abound in bliss. Let none deceive or think
Scorn of another, in whatever way.
But as a mother watches o'er her child,
Her only child, so long as she doth breathe,
So let him practise unto all that live
An all-embracing mind. And let a man
Practise unbounded love for all the world,
Above, below, across, in every way,
Love unobstructed, void of enmity.

Standing or moving, sitting, lying down,
In whatsoever way that man may be,
Provided he be slothless, let him found
Firmly this mindfulness of boundless love.
For this is what men call 'the State Sublime'.
So shall a man, by leaving far behind
All wrongful views, by walking righteously,
Attain to gnostic vision and crush out
All lust for sensual pleasures. Such in truth
Shall come to birth no more in any womb.[301]

The second great principle of Buddhist ethics is the principle of non-appropriation. Violence is based on a strong sense of 'I' and appropriation is based on a strong sense of 'mine' – the two go together. So we must not take what belongs to others, either by force or by fraud – in other words, we must not steal. The traditional phrase is that we should not 'take the not-given'.

This is obviously going to mean not appropriating things that belong to other people, and this includes acquiring debts that one is unable to repay, and borrowing things without asking. But one can also take the not-given in the sense of taking people's time or energy without checking with them that they are willing to give it.

When it comes to the non-appropriation of material things, this includes the kind of thing that many people these days would hardly think of as theft at all. Living as we do in a world governed, even dominated, by institutions and multinational corporations, it is easy to feel that cheating them – perhaps fiddling our tax return or claim for social welfare, or taking home stationery from the office – is ethically insignificant, even justifiable in the face of what we may perceive as an unjust system.

This kind of attitude, though, fails to take into account the true nature of Buddhist ethics. Morality is not an end in itself. The altruistic aspect of ethical behaviour is obvious; what may not be so obvious is that our actions have their effect on us too. Each of the five precepts is expressed not just in 'negative' terms – 'I undertake the training principle of *abstaining* from taking the *not*-given,' for example – but also in positive terms:

With deeds of loving-kindness I purify my body.
With open-handed generosity I purify my body.
With stillness, simplicity, and contentment, I purify my body.
With truthful communication I purify my speech.
With mindfulness clear and radiant I purify my mind.

Here we are reminded that practising these precepts involves the cultivation and expression of positive qualities as well as abstention from doing harm. We are also reminded, through the emphasis on purification, that in behaving ethically we are refining and purifying our own mental states, and thus preparing the ground for the practice of meditation and the development of wisdom.

Whether we feel that our appropriation of what belongs to the government or our employer is going to make any difference to 'them' is, viewed from this perspective, not the point. If our aim is to see things as they really are, an aspect of this is going to be the attempt to break down the barrier between self and other. The practice of ethics gives us constant opportunities to do this, to go beyond the strong sense we have of the separation between 'me' and 'the world', or 'other people'. And, of course, we are reminded all the time these days that even actions that seem so small as to make no difference can in fact have a devastating cumulative effect: on wildlife, on weather systems, on the whole world.

The third precept relates to the principle of chastity. This is, obviously, about our sexual behaviour, and it means in the first place that we should not exploit others sexually, should not obtain sexual satisfaction by means of force, fraud, or misrepresentation. Sex, as everybody knows, is a very powerful urge indeed; the Buddha once said something to the effect that if there was another saṃsāric force that was as strong, we would have no hope of spiritual development.[302] If one takes one's practice of Buddhism seriously, therefore, one will naturally find oneself relegating sexual activity to the periphery of one's life rather than allowing it to occupy a central position, and one's aim will be eventually to achieve complete chastity of body, speech, and mind, even though – to be realistic – for many people this may be possible only towards the end of life.

But we can all aim to cultivate 'stillness, simplicity, and contentment' in this area of life, aiming to be contented with our situation, whether we are 'married' or single, homosexual or heterosexual, and whether we choose to be sexually active or not. The Buddha had no pronouncements to make about sexual orientation or behaviour; nothing is singled out either for special approval or for condemnation. What is important is that we should bring a spirit of non-harming to our sexual activities, and that we should steer clear of the modern Western tendency to glorify the sexual relationship – a tendency that has obviously caused a great deal of unhappiness.

The fourth principle is that of truthfulness. We should never in any way, either directly or indirectly, give our consent or approval to what we know is false. Truthfulness in its widest sense may be defined as unity of thought, word, and deed. In the Pāli scriptures the Buddha is often referred to not as 'the Buddha' but as 'the Tathāgatha'. There are various explanations of the meaning of this title, but one of them is that a Tathāgatha is one who acts as he speaks and speaks as he acts.[303] That this achievement constitutes almost a definition of Enlightenment itself shows how rare a quality complete truthfulness really is.

Without truthfulness there can be no such thing as commerce, no such thing as the administration of justice, and no such thing as politics in the true sense of the term. It is interesting that in the Pāli scriptures, when the Buddha refers to truthfulness, the illustration he chooses is from the judicial context.[304] If a witness commits perjury even after taking an oath, justice cannot be administered, and if justice cannot be administered the whole social fabric collapses. The speaking of truth in the courtroom is an example – almost a paradigmatic example – of truthfulness, because unless the truth is held to be sacred in such a context, there's really no social, human life. And, one might add, untruthfulness consists not merely in telling lies, but also in refraining from speaking the truth when this might remove ignorance and misunderstanding.

In Jonathan Swift's satire *Gulliver's Travels*, when Gulliver visits the country of the Houyhnhnms, he discovers that they are so virtuous that they don't have a word for 'lie'. Gulliver has to take great pains to explain what a lie is, and in response the Houyhnhnms coin a term in their own language: 'to speak the thing that is not'. So we 'speak the thing that is not' – we tell lies. But why? Untruthfulness is always based on negative mental states. We tell lies or suppress the truth, we exaggerate or minimize, either out of greed – to get something we couldn't otherwise get – or out of fear of punishment, or just out of vanity.

In some very rare circumstances, one may need to give up truthfulness for the sake of a still greater virtue. The classic illustration given by the Buddhist tradition is that of a monk who saw a man running to hide himself behind some bushes. Presently a band of ruffians with swords in their hands came dashing along the road in hot pursuit and asked the monk if he had seen the man they were looking for. And, of course, the monk said he had not. In such a case one can be excused from telling the truth since if one did so, one would incur responsibility for murder.

But most of us are unlikely ever to be caught on the horns of such a dilemma. The alternatives between which we are forced to choose are usually to tell the truth and so lose something, or to tell a lie and so be enriched. In modern life there are many occasions when one may be tempted to bend the truth, particularly when dealing with tax forms or other official business. This is another area of ethics in which it is easy to feel that the institutions of the state or the multinationals, impersonal as they are, will not feel the effect of our actions. This may or may not be true; but we ourselves will feel the effects of unskilful behaviour. We need to bear in mind the alienating effect of untruthfulness on our own mental states.

The fifth precept is broadly speaking the application of the principle of mindfulness. But – and this is why it is controversial in Buddhist circles – it is expressed in terms of abstention from 'drink and drugs that cloud the mind', and of course the most common of these is alcohol. There is some difference of opinion among Buddhists, even in the East, regarding this precept. Some believe that a Buddhist should abstain from alcohol totally. Others would say that one can take alcohol in moderation – that is to say, to the extent that it does not cloud one's awareness.

Personally I think that it is better if, as Buddhists, we can abstain totally. Even if the occasional drink doesn't do *us* any harm, what about the example we set? One has only to open the newspapers to see how much harm, how much damage, how much misery, how much loss of life, is caused by the abuse of alcohol. I think that Buddhists really need to set an example here. Some years ago one of my students, touring around some of the Buddhist centres in America, was shocked to find that some centres actually had their own bar, so that, whether before or after the meditation, you could go and have a drink, a cocktail or whatever. I think that, at the very least, alcohol should not be available at Buddhist centres or at Buddhist functions.

But there is more to this precept than the question of whether or not we drink alcohol, important though that question is. Mindfulness, one could say, is the characteristic virtue of the thinking or mental part of our make-up. It goes far beyond such practices as doing the washing-up mindfully, answering the telephone with awareness, and so on, although all such practices are valuable. Mindfulness means, above all, that every day of the week, every hour of the day, and every minute of the hour, we continually bear in mind the true nature of our situation. We need, in other words, to bear in mind the four noble truths: suffering, the cause of suffering, the cessation of suffering, and the way leading to the cessation of suffering.

We have seen – in the chapter on the gravitational pull – that virtuous behaviour alone cannot take us to Enlightenment. This is symbolized not just by the second circle of the wheel of life, with its light and dark halves, but also by the third circle, with its depiction of the six realms. Skilful action will result in pleasant consequences for us, symbolized by the realm of the gods, and unskilful action will have unpleasant consequences, symbolized by the hell realm. But in the Buddhist vision both heaven and hell are still within the round of mundane existence, within the conditioned; once we have experienced the karmic consequences of our actions, we will still be faced with the necessity of finding the way beyond the wheel of life. This is why ethics or morality is only the first stage of the threefold path.

At the same time, this idea that mindfulness can extend to mindfulness of our purpose in life – indeed, that this is a crucial aspect of the practice of mindfulness – suggests that practising ethics fully is going to take us on to the further stages of the path. In practice skilful behaviour as conceived by the Buddha only makes sense in the context of a commitment to the spiritual path. There is no God in Buddhism insisting on our following a list of commandments 'because he says so'. Ethics is conceived not as an end in itself but as a means to the attainment of Enlightenment.

THE THREE REFUGES

This connection between skilful behaviour and commitment to the path to Enlightenment is made explicit in a practice that is followed by Buddhists of all schools: the recitation of the Refuges and Precepts.

The Three Refuges are the Three Jewels of Buddhism: the Buddha, the Dharma, and the Sangha. The recitation of the Refuges is an expression of one's commitment to the Three Jewels, traditionally called 'Going for Refuge to the Three Jewels'. And then, straight after reciting these verses of commitment to the spiritual path, one chants or recites the five precepts. It is in the context of Going for Refuge, in other words, that ethical practice is most meaningful.

I want, therefore, to go into this question of Going for Refuge to the Three Jewels in a bit more detail. It presents us with another way of regarding the path to Enlightenment – indeed, I would say that it presents us with the most important, or at least the most fundamental, way of regarding that path. Going for Refuge to the Three Jewels, one could say, is the fundamental act of the Buddhist spiritual life.

Of course, to make sense of this one needs to understand what the Buddha, Dharma, and Sangha really are. For example, a Buddhist is one who goes for Refuge to the Buddha *as* the Buddha; he or she has faith in the Buddha as the Enlightened One, not something else. This may seem obvious, but it isn't to everyone. If, for example, one spends any time in India, one is sure to meet with pious, religious-minded Hindus. And if, in such company, one mentions the name of the Buddha, they say, 'Oh yes, we know all about him. He is the ninth incarnation of the Hindu god Vishnu.' As a Buddhist one has to disagree with this view of the Buddha. When I lived in India myself I frequently found myself having to say, 'No. The Buddha was not an incarnation of a god. He was a human being, a human being who gained Enlightenment by his own efforts.'

Similarly, we don't go for Refuge to the Buddha if we consider him to have been just a wise man like Socrates, or just an ethical teacher like Epictetus. If we have that sort of idea about the Buddha – if we have any idea about him other than that he is the Enlightened One – there's no Going for Refuge. Similarly, there's no Refuge if one simply admires the Buddha's personality from a safe distance, saying, 'Oh, how wonderful! The Buddha was so kind, so compassionate, so wise,' while not allowing oneself actually to be moved by his Enlightened qualities. No amount of simple admiration constitutes Going for Refuge.

In the same way, one has to understand what is really meant by 'Dharma' in order to go for Refuge to the Dharma. The Dharma is the transcendental path to Enlightenment. If one regards it just as a source of interesting and useful ideas, or of merely academic interest, then even if one knows quite a lot about it, especially in its historical manifestations, one is not Going for Refuge to the Dharma, one is not actually a Buddhist. Academic knowledge about Buddhism certainly has its own definite, though limited, value; but Going for Refuge to the Dharma is quite another matter.

Going for Refuge to the Sangha means Going for Refuge to the Āryasaṅgha, those men and women who have personally realized the higher stages of the transcendental path – Stream Entry and beyond. Sometimes it's said that one goes for Refuge to the *bhikkhu* sangha, to the order of monks, but this is not at all correct. The Sangha to which one goes for Refuge consists of both monks and lay-people; indeed, on this level the distinction between monastic and lay doesn't have much relevance.

By the way, I am quite deliberately using the expression *Going* for Refuge, not *taking* Refuge. Many Western Buddhists talk of taking refuge with Bhikkhu So-and-so or Lama So-and-so, but the original expression is definitely 'I *go*' – *gacchāmi*. This is quite an important difference, I think. The implication is that Going for Refuge is an action, something one does. It's a movement towards something infinitely greater than oneself. One can even speak of Going for Refuge as a surrender of oneself. But 'taking' Refuge has a rather different connotation. It suggests appropriation; it suggests trying to make the Three Jewels yours in an egoistic sense – even trying to grab them – rather than trying to make yourself theirs.

It may seem like quibbling to insist on saying 'Going for Refuge' rather than 'taking Refuge', but the use of the latter expression may be symptomatic of an unhealthy trend in contemporary Buddhism. Nowadays we are presented with marvellous opportunities for understanding and practising many different forms of Buddhism. Things were very different when I came in contact with Buddhism more than fifty years ago. At that time there was only one Buddhist group in London – and it was probably the only one in Britain – and it had perhaps a dozen active members. I can remember us meeting during the war, in a little room in central London not far from the British Museum. On one occasion we were sitting there, meditating – well, at least we were sitting there with our eyes closed, trying to experience some inner peace – and suddenly there was a terrific noise and the windows rattled. Of course, a bomb had fallen. But I am glad to say that nobody moved. Whether this was Buddhist equanimity or British phlegm I'm not sure – perhaps we were all waiting for somebody else to move first – but nobody moved. We just sat there and finished our meditation. That was Buddhism in Britain fifty years ago.[305]

Things are very different these days. There are at least a couple of dozen flourishing Buddhist groups just in London, and hundreds more throughout Britain, while in America there are probably several thousand groups representing nearly all the Eastern Buddhist traditions. These have all come to the West, at least as addressed to Westerners – I'm not referring here to the so-called ethnic Buddhist communities – within the last twenty or thirty years, in what amounts to a tremendous, radical cultural development. Before this happened, our knowledge of religion was pretty well limited to Christianity. Perhaps we'd just about heard of Islam, if we'd read about the Crusades. But now, well, not to speak just of Buddhism, we know, or at least we've heard of, so many different religions. There's been this vast expansion of our spiritual horizon.

But there's a danger – a danger of what could perhaps be called 'pseudo-spiritual consumerism'. Nowadays we're consumers almost by definition. 'I shop, therefore I am' just about sums up our philosophy. And there's a danger that we will bring this consumerist attitude with us when we approach Buddhism, especially when it is presented to us in so many tempting varieties, in so many mysterious, exotic, and fascinating forms. Only too often, I'm afraid, we just can't wait to get our sticky little paws on them. There's a sort of smorgasbord of spiritual goodies just waiting to be devoured, and the temptation is to pick and choose as the fancy takes us.

If we do this, we become not Buddhists, not people who go for Refuge, but consumers of Buddhism. And to be a consumer of Buddhism is the very antithesis of the transformation that Buddhism is all about. As 'consumers' we assimilate Buddhism to ourselves, at least in its externals, assimilate it to our own greed, hatred, and delusion. But if we are to transform ourselves, we need to assimilate ourselves to Buddhism.

This commitment to transformation is a progressive thing. In the process of a deepening commitment, a deepening Going for Refuge to the Three Jewels, it is possible to identify a number of levels, and I have come up with my own terms for these, to paraphrase the equivalents in Pāli and Sanskrit.

The first level is what I would call cultural Going for Refuge, or even ethnic Going for Refuge. In the Buddhist East there are tens, scores, perhaps even hundreds of millions of Buddhists, and in a sense they all go for Refuge. At least, they all repeat 'To the Buddha for Refuge I go; to the Dharma for Refuge I go; to the Sangha for Refuge I go,' either in Sanskrit or Pāli, or in their own language, so they all consider themselves to be Buddhists. But usually they repeat the Refuge-going formula without attaching any great significance to it; it's just a formality.

I have seen this myself many times. In the East, at the start of any Buddhist meeting, someone, usually a monk, recites or chants the Three Refuges and Five Precepts, and everybody repeats them after him. But rarely do people ask themselves, 'What are we doing? What does this mean?' It's just part of their culture, something they always do. It's the respectable thing to do, even; it's respectable to be a Buddhist and recite the Refuges and Precepts from time to time. But not much thought is given to it. It's something that you've inherited, something you do because your parents or grandparents do it or did it. This is cultural or ethnic Going for Refuge. Its significance is not really spiritual, but mainly cultural, or even sociological. This is the first, and lowest, level of Going for Refuge. And, of course, one need not depreciate that level. It's a starting point.

The next level is that of 'provisional' Going for Refuge. This is the level of someone who is genuinely interested in Buddhism – but only up to a point. They may try to observe the precepts – sometimes. They may meditate a little, or even quite a lot – sometimes. They may read books on Buddhism, even take a degree in Buddhist studies. Many Western people who would describe themselves as Buddhists go for Refuge on this sort of level. At this point they are not making a serious effort to develop insight into the truth, nor are they really orientating their lives towards the Three Jewels. In fact, on the contrary, they may well be trying to fit Buddhism into a quite ordinary, probably quite affluent, probably middle-class, lifestyle. This is provisional Going for Refuge – Going for Refuge up to a point.

Then comes 'effective' Going for Refuge. When your Going for Refuge is effective, you have given some thought to the matter. You know what is meant by the Buddha, Dharma, and Sangha, and you really and truly wish with your whole heart, your whole soul, to go for

Refuge. You wish to practise the Dharma, to follow in the Buddha's footsteps, to be an effective member of the sangha, to develop spiritually, even to gain Enlightenment. And you are determined, at least in your conscious mind, that you will do that. You commit yourself to the Three Jewels. You haven't as yet had any major spiritual experience, any transcendental breakthrough, but you're doing your best to be a real, authentic practising Buddhist of this tradition or that. This effective Going for Refuge is the level of Going for Refuge of the majority of sincere practising Buddhists.

Even in the Buddha's day there were many, many of his disciples who achieved only this level of Going for Refuge, and it is illustrated many times in the Pāli scriptures. Someone hears the Buddha teach, they are greatly impressed, and they accept the teaching sincerely – but they do not actually see reality. Nonetheless, they go for Refuge, saying 'To the Buddha for Refuge I go; to the Dharma for Refuge I go; to the Sangha for Refuge I go.'[306] And this is effective Going for Refuge. One has a theoretical understanding of the teaching; one tries to behave ethically; one practises meditation; and one does one's utmost to develop penetrative insight or clear vision. One does one's best to organize one's life in such a way as to make such things – especially meditation and the development of insight – possible. In short, one orients the whole of one's existence, as far as one possibly can, towards the Three Jewels. One gives Buddhism absolute priority in one's life. One is then effectively Going for Refuge.

And then there's what I've come to call real Going for Refuge, which is synonymous in traditional Buddhist terms with Stream Entry and also with what is called in the Buddhist texts the 'opening of the Dharma Eye'. Real Going for Refuge means that your faith in the Three Jewels has become unshakeable. The traditional phrase is that no śramaṇa, no brahmaṇa, not even Brahmā himself together with Māra the evil one, could shake your faith in the Buddha, the Dharma, and the Sangha.[307] It is absolutely unshakeable, like the Himalayas themselves. And your ethical practice is also firmly established. Moreover, in that real Going for Refuge, there is a distinct, unmistakable element of what is called vipaśyanā, or clear vision, which means a vision of the transcendental, not as something distant, but as something that is present, here and now, actually realized, at least to some extent. Vipaśyanā represents a sort of entry into, an approach to, the Unconditioned itself.

Again, there are a number of episodes in the Pāli Buddhist scriptures that illustrate this level of Going for Refuge. The Buddha wandered around India for many years, going on foot from village to village, town to town, city to city, sometimes travelling through vast tracts of jungle. And in his wanderings he came across all sorts of people. He might meet a wandering ascetic, or a learned Brahmin, or a poor outcast, or a prince. Whoever they were, more often than not he would get into conversation with them, and start telling them about the Dharma. Usually he took a gradual approach. He would start off by talking about the benefits of generosity, then about ethics, then about meditation. Only then, when the ground was thoroughly prepared, would he start speaking about his own specific teaching – conditionality – whether in the form of the four noble truths or in some other form. The person – whether ascetic or Brahmin or outcast or prince – listened, and sometimes it happened that he or she was absolutely overwhelmed. And this experience found expression in what became a sort of stock phrase, indeed, a phrase that has become common to the point of cliché in our own time. People said that they felt as though they had 'seen the light'. It was as though they had been living in darkness before, but now light had arisen, and was shining on them.[308] Another common way of putting it was that one felt as though one had been relieved of a great burden, a great weight – nowadays perhaps we'd describe this as the weight of anxiety, the anxiety that seems to pervade modern life.

This person's Dharma Eye would open. He or she would see reality, see the truth of conditionality, see that the whole of mundane existence is painful (at least potentially), transitory, and devoid of permanent unchanging selfhood. As a result of this insight the man or woman to whom the Buddha had spoken would be utterly transformed. And then, from the depth of their heart would come these words: *Buddham saranam gacchāmi; Dhammam saranam gacchāmi; Sangham saranam gacchāmi* – 'To the Buddha for Refuge I go; to the Dharma for Refuge I go; to the Sangha for Refuge I go.' This is the *real* Going for Refuge, the Going for Refuge that is consequent upon the opening of the Dharma Eye. It's sometimes called 'transcendental Going for Refuge', because it's the Going for Refuge of Stream Entrants and others on the higher, purely transcendental, part of the spiral path. But it is certainly a level to which all Buddhists may realistically aspire.

Going for Refuge is the central and definitive act of the Buddhist life. It is quite neglected in some Buddhist circles, but in more recent times there seems to have been a revival of interest in it, as serious practitioners have looked more deeply into the teachings of their traditions. Followers of the iconoclastic Zen tradition, for example, have discovered that the great Zen teacher Dōgen's faith revolved around Going for Refuge, pure and simple. As he was dying, apparently the last practice Dōgen did was to walk around a pillar upon which he had written 'Buddha, Dharma, Sangha'. And he said, 'In the beginning, in the middle, and in the end, in your life, as you approach death, always, through all births and deaths, always take refuge in Buddha, Dharma, Sangha.'[309]

THE REFUGES AND PRECEPTS

Wherever you hear the Three Refuges chanted, they will always be followed by a recitation of the (usually) five precepts. One can say that if Going for Refuge, or commitment to the Three Jewels, is one's lifeblood as a Buddhist, observance of the precepts represents the circulation of that blood through one's whole body. So the precepts are the expression of one's Going for Refuge. Not only that: they also support it, because one cannot truly go for Refuge while leading a thoroughly unethical life.

Of course, the precepts are a basic Buddhist practice. Once one has been a Buddhist for some time it is perhaps easy to find oneself thinking that there is no need to spend much time considering them; one may perhaps think that one knows them pretty well already. If one does think this then one has probably not given them any serious thought at all, and it may well be time to start making a practice of them.

It is easy to be distracted by the showier aspects of the Buddhist tradition, to be fascinated by Buddhist art and the mystery and glamour of the Tantra, or to be drawn into trying to disentangle beautiful knotty conundrums of Buddhist philosophy. It is also easy to forget basic things like the ethical precepts – which we do at our peril.

When I received Tantric initiations myself, I was told that initiation is a very secret, very sacred thing – it's not to be talked about. In fact, one of my Tibetan lama teachers told me that I was permitted to speak about a particular initiation I had received only with one other person whom he named. That was how secret it was in those days. But nowadays, in the West, Tantric initiation, even Anuttara Yoga Tantra, the 'Highest

Yoga Tantra', is being advertised. One enrols for a weekend course, one pays one's fee, and one gets initiated, perhaps along with several hundred other people. One doesn't have to prepare oneself, one doesn't even have to be a Buddhist.

This is certainly not in accordance with the Buddhist Vajrayāna tradition. I remember one of my teachers telling me that if one wanted to practise Anuttara Yoga Tantra one first of all had to practise the Hīnayāna (this was the term he used; nowadays we usually say 'Theravāda') – for twelve years; one then practised the Mahāyāna for six years; then one practised the Outer Tantra for six years; and only then would one be considered ready to receive Anuttara Yoga Tantra initiation. But nowadays it seems one can do it all in the course of a weekend. Of course, some teachers will justify this by saying that they are planting seeds that will mature in the future, but I must say that I personally reject this explanation as a shameful rationalization. If one really wants to plant seeds, one should teach Buddhist ethics.

I I

THE THREEFOLD PATH: MEDITATION

The Nuclear Age ... the Space Age ... the Age of Information ... the Post-Christian Era. ... Any attempt to characterize the presiding spirit of one's own times is bound to be a rash intellectual procedure. Particularly is this so today, when the sheer range and rapidity of cultural developments make it hard to foresee what will turn out to have been the most significant. But from the point of view of Buddhists in the West, the present age has perhaps most tellingly been described as the 'Age of Anxiety' or the 'Age of Psychology'. Whether it is called the Age of Psychology because it is called the Age of Anxiety or vice versa is hard to say, but the two terms reflect the fact that what we may call the mind, or consciousness, has been the subject of a great deal of investigation and reflection in the West during the twentieth century. In fact, simply from an empirical and mundane point of view, humanity at present probably knows more about the mind and its workings, its hidden recesses, than ever before in history.

Although poets and philosophers have long had some intimation of the existence of the subconscious mind, Freud succeeded in placing the whole concept on an irrefutably scientific basis, subsequently giving rise to a whole host of (often conflicting) psychological theories. As a result, a number of mental illnesses can be treated with some measure of success, and abnormal mental states generally are better understood. Furthermore, various hidden powers of the mind – clairvoyance, telepathy, and so on – have been given a scientific stamp of authenticity.

Research into drug-induced mental states has also changed the way in which we view the mind. Even mystical experience is no longer regarded as an unfortunate result of neurosis, brain seizures, or vitamin deficiency.

Thus ever more fascinating vistas are gradually being revealed to us. We used to have in the West a very limited and superficial view of the human mind. We thought of it as something relatively static, and we identified it with the conscious mind, with the individual consciousness, and with the physical body. But we are beginning to see that the range of the human mind, the possibilities open to the possessor of human consciousness, are far more extensive than we previously imagined.

We are often told, with the help of an image beloved of depth psychology, that the mind is like an iceberg, of which we see only a small part – the conscious tip, as it were – protruding above the waves. Underneath, like the vast submerged mass of the iceberg, there are layers and layers, levels and levels, of which normally we are simply not aware. This image presents us with an important half of the picture. For the other half we need to call upon a different image, that of a mountain, particularly a mountain of the Himalayas, towering up for thousands upon thousands of feet. The lower slopes, the foothills, are always visible, but most of the time you don't see the summit at all: it is hidden by an impenetrable blanket of mist and cloud. The mind is also like this: not only does it have depths of which we are unaware; it has heights of which we are unaware, too.

This growing psychological awareness in the West puts us in a better position to be able to meet Buddhism and understand what it is about. If we have come lately to an awareness of, and interest in, the nature and workings of the mind, Buddhism specifically addresses itself to these questions. In fact, we may go as far as to say that Buddhism is concerned with little else other than the mind. For instance, Zen is famously (though anonymously) defined as 'a direct pointing to the mind'. This is all that Zen does, in a sense: it just says 'Look at your own mind.' And almost every school of Buddhism is saying in one way or another, the same thing: 'Look at your mind. Look at yourself. Be aware of the heights and the depths of your own consciousness.'

Inasmuch as the emphasis of Buddhism is always on the practical more than the theoretical, Buddhists are more concerned with the heights than with the depths of the mind. Buddhism envisages heights of mind beyond mind with a view to climbing those heights – that is, with the expansion of awareness beyond its present upper limits to ever higher spheres of consciousness. And the way this is achieved – according to all schools of Buddhism – is through the practice of meditation. In fact, meditation may be defined, for general purposes, as the systematic expansion of awareness or consciousness.

The first and last thing to know about meditation is that it is something to be practised, to be experienced, rather than something to be talked about or read about. At the same time, we need to have a general idea of what we are supposed to be doing when we meditate. Without any clear sense of direction in our practice, we may get a definite benefit from it, but we may just as definitely feel that we are groping in the dark. The aim of the following introduction to meditation, to the systematic expansion of consciousness, is to offer some help to those who have begun actually to practise meditation, and to suggest how they may orient themselves more effectively in relation to their practice, as well as to give an idea of what meditation is to anyone new to the subject. We will approach meditation by way of a consideration of four principal themes: why we meditate; preparations for meditation; the five basic methods of meditation; and the three progressive stages of meditational experience.

WHY WE MEDITATE

A consideration of one's motivation for meditation is a good place to start, because motivation is an important and constant element in determining how effective one's meditation practice is, and even whether one continues to meditate at all. Having known a great many meditators, I would say that there are basically two types of motivation or approach. These may be provisionally designated as the 'psychological' approach and the 'spiritual' approach.

The basic psychological motivation for meditation is the search for peace of mind. People who are not particularly interested in Buddhism or philosophy or religion, or even in psychology, may still be looking for something that they call peace of mind. They find that the hurry and bustle of day-to-day living is a bit too much for them. The various strains and tensions to which they are subjected – financial pressures, personal difficulties, problems with relationships, even perhaps degrees of neurotic anxiety – all add up to a general feeling of unhappiness. They hear that meditation can give you peace of mind, and they have the impression that Buddhists are happy, tranquil people, so in this way they come to Buddhist meditation, looking for some inner tranquillity, for the peace which, it seems, the world cannot give.

As for the spiritual motivation for meditation, this is at root the desire or aspiration for Enlightenment. In wider terms, it encompasses the desire to understand the meaning of existence itself, the desire to come to some sort of intelligible terms with life, or even, more metaphysically, to know reality, to see the truth, to penetrate into the ultimate nature of things. In this way meditation may be approached as a stepping-stone to something higher – to an awareness, an understanding, an experience even, of ultimate reality itself.

These two approaches – the psychological and the spiritual – are not mutually exclusive. You can take up meditation with a psychological motivation, and then find that imperceptibly the sheer momentum of your practice carries you beyond the boundaries of the psychological into a world of spiritual experience. And on the other hand, even if your motivation is spiritual from the beginning, you will still need to establish a healthy psychological foundation for your practice, which may well involve a purely psychological approach in the early stages.

Indeed, it is not easy to draw a hard and fast line between the realm of the psychological and the realm of the spiritual. They shade into each other in such a way that you cannot always be sure which realm your experience and approach falls into. There is an overlap, a sort of common ground, between them. In terms of expanding consciousness, we could say that the psychological approach represents a partial and temporary expansion of consciousness, whereas the spiritual approach stands for a total and permanent expansion of consciousness. There is a difference of degree (in a certain sense), rather than a difference of kind, between the two.

However, they are, in the end, quite distinct realms, quite distinct approaches or motivations, and they should not be confused with each other more than we can help. If we identify the spiritual with the psychological, then we will be setting unnecessary limits on our practice and what we are capable of achieving with it.

These are essential. If we find ourselves dissatisfied with our progress in meditation – if the milestones are not exactly flashing by – it is probably because we have plunged straight in without doing the necessary preparation. If on the other hand we are really well prepared, we are virtually meditating already, whether we know it or not.

First – and most important – is ethics. Of course, all Buddhists try to observe five fundamental ethical precepts, i.e. to abstain from taking life, from taking what is not given, from sexual misconduct, from false speech, and from intoxication. But precisely how does ethics relate to one's practice of meditation?

Modern Indian meditation teachers usually speak of the ethical preparation for concentration and meditation in terms of bringing under control three things: food, sex, and sleep. As regards food, they say that you should never overload the stomach. At the same time you shouldn't ever leave it completely empty, unless you are deliberately undergoing a fast. The way they explain it, a quarter of your stomach should be for food, a quarter for water, and half of it should be empty. It is also said that you should avoid certain kinds of food – especially hot, spicy food, which is supposed to stimulate the passions (and of which Indian people are inordinately fond). However, one can probably take this idea of certain foods having particular psychological effects with a pinch of salt. Suffice it to say that heavy food, and food that is conducive to flatulence, should certainly be avoided. The atmosphere – and noise – created by a whole roomful of people who have dined 'not wisely but too well' on hot curry can seriously disrupt any attempt to meditate.

Moving on to the question of sex, it is said that celibacy is best, but this is simply not a realistic aim for everyone. So, instead, we can say that moderation at least – some degree of restraint – should be observed. Meditation calls for a great deal of nervous energy, particularly as you go into deep concentration, and this nervous energy is dissipated in sexual release. It is up to the individual to work out exactly where the most effective balance in this respect may be struck, according to their circumstances, and based on their own observation and reflection.

The third thing to be restrained is indulgence in sleep. This is not often mentioned in connection with meditation, but – again according to Indian meditation teachers – what we should find when we meditate is that we need to sleep a little less than before. If we sleep well as a general rule we probably tend to take it for granted, but of course sleep is a wonderful and mysterious thing indeed, as poets throughout the ages have testified. There is, for example, a beautiful and striking passage in Cervantes' *Don Quixote*, in which Sancho Panza sings the praises of sleep.[310] However, it is only recently that we have begun to understand the real purpose of sleep. It is not, as was formerly thought, just to rest the body. The generally accepted view nowadays is that you sleep in order also to be able to dream; and one purpose of dreaming is thought to be to sort out all the perceptions and impressions of the day and file them away for future reference.

When you meditate deeply, you aren't aware of the body, and therefore you are no longer taking in impressions, so you don't need to process so much data. There is much less sorting out and filing away to be done, and thus much less need to dream. In this way, deep meditation drastically reduces the number of hours you need for sleep.

This does not mean that one should necessarily sleep less in order to meditate more effectively. In fact, most people nowadays tend, if anything, to sleep rather less than they need to. It seems that since the widespread availability of electric light at the beginning of the twentieth century, people sleep, on average, an hour less than they did before then. There is no need to deprive oneself of sleep – this will lead to alienation. But wallowing in bed after one has had enough sleep will obviously promote lethargy and mental lassitude.

So ethical preparation is, in the first place, control of food, of sex, and of sleep. On top of these, however, and equally important, is the need to curb aggressiveness. Not just overt physical aggression, but any rude, harsh, domineering speech or posture (one sees this especially in the way many parents behave towards their children) will impede the development of positive mental states. And a vegetarian diet should be adhered to – conditions permitting – as an expression of one's dedication to a harmless way of life.

In summary, ethical preparation for meditation consists in leading, as far as possible, a quiet, harmless, and simple life. What is required is a peaceful life without loud noise, hectic social activity, or violent physical exertion. All these things can leave one's whole system too 'tingling', 'raw', and altogether too grossly stimulated to transmit the refined impulses that are generated by meditation.

I should add, though, that while strenuous exercise is not to be recommended as preparation for meditation, some kind of gentle exercise or relaxation technique – like hatha yoga or t'ai chi ch'uan – together with careful attention to finding a meditation posture that enables one to stay relaxed, comfortable, and alert, is very beneficial. One need not feel obliged, by the way, to adopt the classical cross-legged meditation posture. Sitting astride meditation cushions, or sitting on a chair, does just as well. The important thing is to experiment until one finds a comfortable way of sitting. One of the advantages of attending a meditation class is that one can get some help with establishing an appropriate and supportive meditation posture.

The issue of work, of livelihood, is also an aspect of preparation for meditation. Working at a certain job for six, eight, even ten hours a day, five or six days of the week, year after year, inevitably has an enormous cumulative effect upon the mind. You are being psychologically conditioned all the while by your occupation. Choosing a means of livelihood that is peaceful and beneficial in one way or another is crucial, not only as preparation for meditation, but as a basis for one's whole development as a healthy human being.

Checking through all these factors might seem like more than enough preparation to deal with. But there is more. A most important part of the ethical preparation for meditation is to be mindful and self-possessed. One needs to be aware of the body and its movements, aware of emotions and emotional reactions, aware of thoughts, aware of what one is doing and why one is doing it. One needs constantly to cultivate calmness, collectedness, mindfulness, in everything that one does, whether speaking or remaining silent, working or resting, cooking or gardening or doing the accounts, walking or driving or sitting still. One must always remain watchful and aware. This is the best preparation for meditation. Maintaining a constant level of awareness in this way means that as soon as you sit down to meditate, as soon as you summon up an object of concentration, you slip into a meditative state without any difficulty at all.

There are just two further points of importance. Learning meditation solely from books isn't enough, unless one is exceptionally gifted. By its nature, meditation is a personal, individual thing, for which no amount of general guidance and instruction can be enough. Moreover, a personal teacher will bring to bear upon our difficulties a degree of objectivity that we are unlikely to be able to achieve on our own. A teacher is needed at least until we have some advanced spiritual experience under our belt. Even then, there can arise all sorts of spiritual dangers that a teacher who knows us well can see us through.

Lastly, there is preparation by way of devotional exercises. These don't appeal to everybody, but for those who are devotionally – which can often mean emotionally – inclined, they may be very helpful indeed. They come in all sorts of different – and some very elaborate – forms, but at their simplest they involve making symbolic offerings to a *rūpa* or image of the Buddha before starting to meditate. Lighting a candle symbolizes the light of vision that we are about to try to light in our own hearts; flowers symbolize the impermanence of all worldly things; and finally incense, permeating the air all around us, represents the fragrance of the good, the beautifully-lived life, which influences the world around us wherever we go in subtle, imperceptible ways.

We have examined in some detail – even laboured over – the subject of preparation for meditation for a very good reason. If you are prepared to pay attention to all these details, then there will be very little more to do. One might almost say that you won't then need to meditate at all; you will have only to remain still and close your eyes and you'll be there – concentrated.

THE FIVE BASIC METHODS OF MEDITATION

Here I want to focus on five methods of meditation which correspond to the five 'mental poisons' that stand between us and our own innate Buddhahood.[311] Enlightenment is within us all, but it is shrouded in spiritual ignorance or *avidyā* – as the vast azure vault of the sky may be obscured from horizon to horizon by dark clouds. This obscuring factor of *avidyā*, when it is analysed, is found to consist of the aforesaid five mental poisons.

The first poison is distractedness, inability to control wandering thoughts, mental confusion; and the meditation practice that acts as its antidote is the mindfulness of breathing. Then the second poison is anger, aversion, or hatred; and its antidote is the meditation practice called in Pāli the *mettā bhāvanā*, the cultivation of loving-kindness. The third poison is craving or lust, and it is countered by the 'contemplation of decay'. Ignorance, in the sense of ignorance of our own conditionality, is the fourth poison; and it can be tackled by the contemplation of the twelve links of conditioned co-production. Finally, the fifth poison is conceit, pride, or ego-sense, whose antidote is the analysis of the six elements.

THE MINDFULNESS OF BREATHING

The mindfulness of breathing is the antidote to the mental poison of distractedness because it eliminates wandering thoughts. This is one of the reasons why it is generally the first practice to be learned; no other method can be practised until some degree of concentration has been mastered.

This practice is not about concentration in the sense of a narrow, willed application of the attention to an object. It involves gradually unifying the attention around one's natural breathing process, integrating all one's mental, emotional, and physical faculties by means of gently but persistently bringing the attention back to the experience of the breath, again and again. The point is not to *think* about the breath, or do anything about it at all, but simply to be aware of it. There are four stages to the practice. For beginners, five minutes to each stage is about right.

Sitting still and relaxed, with the eyes closed, we begin by bringing our attention to the breathing. Then we start mentally to count off each breath to ourselves, after the out-breath, one to ten, over and over again. There is no particular significance to the counting. It is just to keep the attention occupied with the breathing during the early stages of the practice while the mind is still fairly scattered. The object of our developing concentration is still the breath (rather than the numbers).

In the second stage we continue to mark the breaths by counting them, but instead of counting after the out-breath we now count before the in-breath. Ostensibly there may not seem to be any great difference between these first two stages, but the idea of the second is that we are attentive right from the start of each breath, so that there is a quiet sharpening of the concentration taking place. There is a sense of anticipation; we are being aware before anything has happened, rather than being aware only afterwards.

In the third stage we drop the support of the counting and move to a general and continuous (at least, as continuous as we can manage) awareness of the whole process of the breathing, and all the sensations associated with it. Again, we are not investigating or analysing or doing anything special with the breath, but just gently nudging the attention to a closer engagement with it. As our concentration deepens, it becomes easier to maintain that engagement, and the whole experience of the breath becomes more and more pleasurable.

In the fourth and final stage we bring the attention to a sharper focus by applying it to a single point in our experience of the breath. The point we focus on is the subtle play of sensation where we feel the breath entering and leaving the body, somewhere round about the nostrils. The attention here needs to be refined and quiet, very smoothly and intensely concentrated in order to keep continuous contact with the ever-changing sensation of the breath at this point. The practice is brought to an end by broadening our awareness again to include the experience of the whole of the breath, and then the whole of the body. Then, slowly, we bring the meditation to a close and open our eyes.[312]

THE *METTĀ BHĀVANĀ*

The cultivation of universal love, or *mettā bhāvanā*, is the antidote to anger or hatred. *Mettā, maitrī* in Sanskrit, is a response of care and warmth and kindness and love to all that lives, a totally undiscriminating well-wishing that arises whenever and wherever we come into contact with, or even think about, another living being. The practice is divided into five stages.

In the first stage we develop love towards ourselves, something that many people find very difficult indeed. But if one can't love oneself one will find it very difficult to love other people; one will only project on to them one's dissatisfaction with – or even hatred of – oneself. So we try to appreciate or enjoy what we can about ourselves. We think of a time when we were happy and content, or we imagine being in a situation where we would feel quite deeply happy being ourselves, and then we try to tune in to that feeling. We look for and bring awareness to elements in our experience of ourselves that are positive and enjoyable.

Then, in the second stage, we develop *mettā* or love towards a near and dear friend. This should be someone of the same sex, to reduce the possibility of emotional projections – and it should be someone towards whom we have no erotic feelings, because the point of the practice is gradually to develop a focus on a very specific positive emotion that is closer to friendship than to erotic love. For the same sorts of reasons, this person should be still living and approximately the same age as oneself. So we visualize, or at least we get a sense of, this person, and we tune into the feeling they evoke in us, looking for the same response of benevolence that we have been developing towards ourselves. Usually this second stage is the easiest, for obvious reasons.

In the third stage, whilst maintaining the sense of an inner warmth, a sort of glow that we have generated towards ourselves and our good friend, we bring to mind in their stead a 'neutral' person. This is someone whose face we know well, whom we see quite often, but whom we neither particularly like nor dislike. It may well be someone who plays a more or less functional role in our life, like a postman, a shopkeeper, or a bank-clerk, or it may be someone we see regularly on the bus. We apply to this neutral person the same benevolence and care that we naturally feel for our friend. It must be emphasized that what we are trying to develop in this type of practice is not a thought – not an *idea* – about developing a feeling, but the actual feeling itself. Some people may find this quite difficult to achieve – they feel dry and numb when they try to be aware of their emotions. It is as if their emotional life is so unconscious that it is simply unavailable to them to begin with. However, with time and practice it all starts to flow more easily.

In the fourth stage, we think of someone we dislike, even someone we hate – an enemy – someone who has perhaps done us harm or an injury – though to begin with it may be best to think of someone with whom we just don't get on. In the meditation we deliberately allow our heart to stay open to them. We resist the urge to indulge in feelings of hatred or animosity or resentment. It is not that we necessarily condone their behaviour; we may well need to criticize and even condemn it; but we stay in touch with a fundamental care for their welfare. In this way, by continuing to experience our friendly attitude even in relation to an enemy, our emotion starts to develop from simple friendliness into real *mettā*.

These first four stages are introductory. At the beginning of the fifth and last stage, we bring together in our mind all these four persons – self, friend, neutral person, enemy – and we cultivate the same love equally towards them all. Then we go a little further, we spread our vision a little wider, to direct this *mettā* towards all beings everywhere, starting with those close to us, either emotionally or geographically, and then expanding outwards to include more and more people, and excluding no one at all. We think of all men, all women, all ages, nationalities, races, religions; even animals, even beings, maybe, who are higher than human beings – angels and gods – and even beings higher than that: bodhisattvas and spiritual teachers, whether Buddhist or non-Buddhist; whoever is eminent in good qualities. We may also expand out beyond our own planet, sending *mettā* to whatever beings may live in other parts of the universe, or in other universes. We develop the same love towards all living beings.[313]

In this way we feel as though we are being carried out of ourselves in ever expanding circles; we forget ourselves, sometimes quite literally, becoming enfolded in an ever-expanding circle of love. This can be a very tangible experience for those who practise the *mettā bhāvanā*, even after a comparatively short time. Not for everyone, of course: it is very much a matter of temperament. Some people take to it like ducks to water and enjoy it immensely within a matter of minutes. For others it is a struggle to get a fitful spark of *mettā* going, and the idea of radiating it seems a joke – they don't see how they are ever going to do it. But they can, and they do. In the end, with a bit of practice, a bit of perseverance, it happens, it arises. If the potential for Buddhahood is within all of us, then the potential for *mettā* certainly is.

THE CONTEMPLATION OF DECAY

The contemplation of decay or impurity, which counteracts lust or craving or attachment, is not a practice that many people care to take up, though it is popular in some quarters in the East. There are three different forms of it. The first, and the most radical, is to go to a cremation ground and sit there among the corpses and charred remains. It may sound a drastic course of action, but it has to be so, in order to counteract the fierce power of craving. You look closely at what death does to the human body and you think, 'This is what will happen to me one day.'[314]

There is no special teaching here, nothing esoteric or difficult to understand. There is no big secret in this practice. You simply recognize that one day your own body will be swollen and stinking with putrefaction like this one, your own head will be hanging off, and your own arm lying there on its own, like that one, or that you too will be a heap of ashes in somebody's urn (cherished somewhere, we hope).

These are all clear models of our own end, so why not admit it? Why not face the fact? And why not change the direction of our life to take account of this fact? It is in order to bring out such a vein of self-questioning that monks in the East make their way – often quite light-heartedly – to the cremation ground and sit looking at one corpse after another: this one quite fresh, recently alive; that one a bit swollen; and that one over there – well, rather a mess. They go on until they get to a skeleton, and then a heap of bones, and finally a handful of dust. And all the time a single thought is being turned over in the mind: 'One day, I too shall be like this.' It is a very salutary practice which certainly succeeds in cutting down attachment to the body, to the objects of the senses, the pleasures of the flesh.

If this practice seems too drastic, or even just rather impractical, there is another way of doing it. Rather than literally going to the cremation ground, you can go there in your imagination and simply visualize the various stages of the decomposition of a corpse. Or even more simply, you can just reflect on the fact that one day you must die. One day your consciousness must be separated from this physical organism. One day you will no longer see, you will no longer hear, you will no longer taste, or feel. Your senses will not function because your body will not be there. You will be a consciousness on its own – you don't know where – spinning, perhaps bewildered, in a sort of void; you just don't know.

If even this sort of train of reflection seems a bit too harsh and raw, a bit too close to the bone, we can reflect on impermanence in general. Every season that passes carries its own intimations of impermanence. The sweetness of spring is all the more intense, all the more poignant, for its brevity, for no sooner are the blossoms on the trees in full bloom than they start to fade. And of course in autumn we can contemplate the decay and end of all things as we see the leaves turning yellow and falling, and our gardens dying back into the earth. This kind of gentle, melancholic contemplation, so often evoked in English poetry, particularly the odes of John Keats, and in the poetic tradition of Japan, can also have a positive effect in freeing us to some extent from our unrealistic perception of the solidity and permanence of things.

But there is no need to approach even the most drastic of these practices in a mournful or depressed spirit, because they are all about freeing ourselves from a delusion that just brings suffering in its wake. It should be exhilarating – if you take up this practice at the right time – to remind yourself that one day you will be free of the body.

I did the cremation ground practice myself once when I was a young monk in India. I went along to a cremation ground at night and sat there on the banks of the Ganges. There was a great stretch of silver sand, and at intervals funeral pyres had been lit and bodies had been burned, and there was a skull here and a bone there and a heap of ashes somewhere else. ... But it was very beautiful, all silvered over by a tropical moon, with the Ganges flowing gently by. The mood the whole scene evoked was not only one of serious contemplation, but also one of freedom and even exhilaration.

This sort of mood probably reflects the fact that the practice overcomes fear. It is said that the Buddha himself used it for this purpose. If you can stay alone in a graveyard full of corpses at night, you are unlikely ever to be afraid of anything again, because all fear, basically, is fear of losing the body, losing the self. If you can look death – your own death – in the eye, if you can absorb the full reality of it and go beyond it, then you'll never be afraid of anything again.

However, the more challenging forms of this practice are not for beginners. Even in the Buddha's day, we are told, some monks who practised it without proper preparation and supervision became so depressed through contemplating the impurity and decay of the human body that they committed suicide.[315] Normally one is advised to practise the mindfulness of breathing first, then the *metta bhavana*, and go on to contemplate corpses only on the basis of a strong experience of *metta*. But all of us can at least recall the impermanence of all things around us, and remember that one day we too will grow old and sicken, that we too must die, even as the flowers fade from the field and the birds of the air perish, to rot and return to the ground.

THE *NIDĀNA* CHAIN

The contemplation of the twelve links of conditioned co-production is the antidote to ignorance. We have already gone into the details of this chain of links – or *nidānas* – illustrating the principle of conditioned co-production in terms of human existence. In this meditation practice one consciously reflects on it, by means of the images that depict it in the outermost circle of the Tibetan wheel of life, as follows:

(1) Ignorance, *avidyā*: represented by a blind man with a stick; (2) volitions or karma formations, *saṃskāras*: a potter with a wheel and pots; (3) consciousness, *vijñāna*: a monkey climbing a flowering tree (we climb up into the branches of this world and reach out for its flowers and fruit); (4) mind and body, *nāma-rūpa* (i.e. name and form): a boat with four passengers, one of whom, representing consciousness, is steering; (5) the six sense-organs, *ṣaḍāyatana*: a house with five windows and a door; (6) sense-contact, *sparśa*: a man and woman embracing; (7) feeling, *vedāna*: a man with an arrow in his eye; (8) craving, *tṛṣṇā*: a woman offering a drink to a seated man; (9) grasping, *upādāna*: a man or woman gathering fruit from a tree; (10) becoming or coming-to-be, development, *bhava*: a man and a woman copulating; (11) birth, *jāti*: a woman giving birth; (12) old age and death, *jarā-maraṇa*: a corpse being carried to the cremation ground.

Here is the whole process of birth, life, death, and rebirth according to the principle of conditioned co-production. As a result of our ignorance, and of the volitions based upon our ignorance in previous lives, we are precipitated again into this world with a consciousness endowed with a psychophysical organism, and thus six senses, which come into contact with the external universe and give rise to feelings – pleasant, painful, and neutral. We develop craving for the pleasant feelings, and thus condition ourselves in such a way that inevitably we have to be born again and die again.

These twelve links are distributed over three lives, but at the same time they are also all contained in one life – even in one moment. They illustrate – whether spread over three lives or a day or an hour or a minute – the whole way in which we condition ourselves; how we make ourselves what we are by our own reactions to what we experience.

When we look at the wheel of life we are looking in a mirror. In all its circles and all its details, we find ourselves. When I contemplate anger, in the image of a snake at the centre of the wheel of life, it is not anger in general I am concerned with. When I contemplate greed, in the likeness of a cock, I am not considering the universal psychological phenomenon of greed. When I contemplate ignorance, in the form of a pig, I am not studying some category of Buddhist thought. It is me there, just me: the anger, the greed, and the ignorance – they're all mine.

Seeing, next, a circle of people either going from a lower to a higher state or slipping from a higher to a lower state, I recognize myself in them. I am never standing apart from that wheel: at any one time I am going either one way or the other, up or down.

Looking beyond these figures I may imagine that at last I am examining a representation of six different and separate realms of existence – which in a sense they are. The human realm is clearly my own, where people are communicating, learning, creating. But when I look at the realm of the gods I find there my own moments and dreams of bliss and joy, and in the realm of the titans, my own ambition and competitiveness. Grazing and snuffling with the animals is my own lack of vision, my own consumerism, my own dullness. In the realm of the hungry ghosts is my own desolate yearning for some solid satisfaction from the objects of my craving. And in hell are my own nightmares, my own moments of burning anger and cool malice, my own brief seasons of hatred and revenge.

Finally, in contemplating the twelve *nidānas* of the outermost circle we get a picture of how the whole process goes on, the mechanism of the whole thing. We see ourselves as a piece of clockwork, as indeed we are most of the time. Much of the time we are really no more free, no more spontaneous, no more alive, than a well-programmed computer. Because we are unaware, we are conditioned and therefore fettered. So in this practice we become aware of our conditionality, the mechanical, programmed nature of our lives, our tendency to react, our self-imprisonment, our lack of spontaneity or creativity – our own death, our spiritual death in a negative sense, our death-in-life. Almost everything we do is just tightening our bonds, chaining us more securely to the wheel of life. The contemplation of the twelve *nidānas* provides a traditional support for this kind of awareness.[316]

THE SIX ELEMENT PRACTICE

The analysis of the six elements is the antidote to conceit or pride or ego-sense: i.e. the antidote to the feeling that I am I, this is me, this is mine. In this practice we try to realize that nothing really belongs to us, that we are, in fact, spiritually (though not empirically) just nothing. We attempt to see for ourselves that what we think of as 'I' is ultimately (though not relatively) an illusion; it doesn't exist in absolute reality (even though clearly it does exist at its own level).

Before starting, we develop a degree of meditative concentration, and establish a healthy emotional basis for the practice to follow with perhaps a preliminary session of the *mettā bhāvanā*. Then we contemplate the six elements in an ascending order of subtlety: earth, water, fire, air, ether or space, and consciousness.

So first of all, earth – the earth upon which we're standing or sitting, and the earth in the form of trees and houses and flowers and people, and our own physical body. In the first stage of the practice we consider this element of earth: 'My own physical body is made up of certain solid elements – bone, flesh, and so on – but where did these elements come from? Yes, they came from food – but where did the food come from? Basically, the food from which my body is substantially made came in the first place from the earth. I have incorporated a portion of the earth into my physical body. It doesn't belong to me. I have just borrowed it – or rather, it is temporarily appearing in this form of myself. To claim that it is mine is, in a sense, theft, because it does not belong to me at all. One day I will have to give it back. This piece of earth that is my body is not me, not mine. All the time it is returning to the earth.' When we see this clearly enough we relinquish hold on the solid element in our physical body. In this way the sense of 'I' starts to lose its firm outlines.

Then we take the element of water, and we consider: 'So much of this world is water: great oceans and rivers, streams and lakes and rain. So much of my body, too, is water: blood, bile, spittle, and so on. This liquid element in me – where have I got it from? What I assume to be mine I have only taken on loan from the world's store of water. I will have to give it back one day. This too is not me, not mine.' In this way the 'I' dissolves further.

Now we come to a still subtler element: fire. In this stage we consider the one single source of light and heat for the whole solar system – the sun. We reflect that whatever warmth there is in our own physical body, whatever degree of temperature we can feel within us, all of it derives ultimately from the sun. When we die, when the body lies cold and still and rigid, all the warmth that we think of as our own will have gone from it. All the heat will have been given back, not to the sun of course, but to the universe. And as we do this the passion of being 'I' cools a little more.

Then, air: we reflect on the breath of life, on the fact that our life is dependent upon air. But when we breathe in, that breath in our lungs is not ours; it belongs to the atmosphere around us. It will sustain us for a while, but eventually the air we make use of so freely will no longer be available to us. When the last breath passes from the body we will give up our claim on the oxygen in the air, but in fact it was never ours to begin with. So we cease to identify ourselves with the air we are, even now, taking in; we cease to think, even tacitly: 'This is *my* breath.' And thus the 'I' gradually begins to evaporate.

The next element is called in Sanskrit *ākāśa*, a term translated either as 'space' or as 'ether'. It isn't space in the scientific sense, but rather the 'living space' within which everything lives and moves and has its being. We reflect that our physical body – made up of earth, water, fire, and air – occupies a certain space, and that when those constituent elements have gone their separate ways again, that space will be empty of the body that formerly occupied it. This empty space will merge back into universal space. In the end we see that there is literally no room for the sense of 'I'.

At this point we should, at least in principle, be dissociated altogether from the physical body. So sixthly and lastly we come to the element of consciousness. As we are at present, our consciousness is associated with the physical body through the five gross physical senses and through the mind. But when we die we are no longer conscious of the body; consciousness is no longer bound up with the material elements, or with physical existence at all. Then consciousness dissolves, or *resolves* itself, into a higher and a wider consciousness, a consciousness that is not identified with the physical body.

This higher and wider consciousness may be realized at many different levels. The individual consciousness, free from the body, may be expanded to a more universal, even collective, consciousness; from that to the *ālaya-vijñāna*, the repository or store-consciousness;[317] and from that we may even break through to the fringes of Absolute Mind. In this way our own petty individual mind is dissolved or resolved into the ocean of universal consciousness, so that we go completely beyond the sense of 'I', and become completely free from the sense of 'mine'.[318]

The five basic methods of meditation fall quite naturally into two important groupings (though there is some overlap between them). The mindfulness of breathing and the *mettā bhāvanā* are primarily concerned with developing *śamatha*, that is, tranquillity, calm, and expansion of mind or consciousness. Any technique of concentration on a simple object or developing a fundamental basis of positive emotion will fall into this category. And it should be said that some effective acquaintance with such techniques is essential before one attempts any more complex or advanced ones.

The other three basic practices are *vipaśyanā* practices – that is, they are concerned primarily with the development of insight, a deep, supra-rational understanding of reality. Any visualization or devotional practice or mantra recitation will also be concerned fundamentally with this goal.

The sheer wealth of different meditation techniques available may seem bewildering – or enticing. But in a way one needs to be wary of the very idea of a meditation 'technique'. All the five basic methods of meditation involve following certain tried and trusted procedures, and we need to be thoroughly familiar with these if we are to make progress in meditation. But the practice of meditation does not consist simply in the application of particular techniques. Meditation is not so much a science as an art, and in this art, as in all others, it is the inner experience rather than the technique that is all-important. It is even possible to become very proficient at the techniques of meditative concentration and yet realize nothing of the real spirit of meditation. Far better to master the spirit – as well as the technique – of just one practice, than manage the empty manipulation of a dozen of them.

THE THREE PROGRESSIVE STAGES OF MEDITATIONAL EXPERIENCE

These are, in Sanskrit, *śamatha, samāpatti,* and *samādhi. Śamatha* means literally 'tranquillity', so it stands for peace and calm and equanimity of mind. It is a state of perfect inward concentration, perfect equilibrium, in which mental activity of any kind, especially discursive mental activity, is minimal, or entirely absent. It corresponds to the four levels of superconsciousness known in the scriptures as *dhyānas* (or *jhānas* in Pāli).

However, *śamatha* may also be subdivided – according to a different principle from that which distinguishes the four *dhyānas* – into three levels or degrees. The first of these consists in concentration on a gross physical object, as when you have your eyes open and you are fully concentrated on some material object external to your own mind. The second is when you close your eyes and concentrate your mind on the subtle mental counterpart of that original gross material object. Here, the degree or level of concentration attained is much more refined, much more elevated. As for the third stage of *samatha* – the highest of all – with this you are totally absorbed in the object. There is no difference now between the concentrating mind and the object on which you are concentrating; you have become one with it. These are the three levels of *samatha*.

The second stage of meditational experience is *samāpatti*, which literally means 'attainment'. *Samāpatti* stands for those attainments we experience as a direct result of practising concentration. You may perhaps see an inner light or hear sounds – of mantras, divine voices, and so on – and you may even smell a sort of divine perfume pervading the room even though there is no physical cause for it. You may see beautiful landscapes or skyscapes unfolding themselves before your inner eye. This is *samāpatti*.

You may see figures of Buddhas, bodhisattvas, great teachers, mythological beings, and so on. You may experience changes in your bodily weight, or your temperature – and this last may be a change that is not just subjective; you may actually be particularly cool or warm to the touch. You may have an experience of telepathy (reading other people's thoughts) or of clairvoyance (seeing things at a distance) or of clairaudience (hearing things at a distance). All these things come under the heading of *samāpatti*. More significantly, you may experience intense rapture and joy, or a surpassing peace and bliss. And even more significantly, you may have flashes of insight, flashes of intuitive understanding of the nature of things, when at least momentarily you realize and become one with the truth.

All these experiences, from the highest to the lowest level, are *samāpatti*-type experiences. Inasmuch as people's temperaments and levels of development vary greatly, there is also a wide variety of experiences of this kind. This is an extraordinarily rich field. Nobody, however gifted, experiences all these different *samāpattis*, but everybody, in the course of their practice of meditation, will come across at least some of them.

The third and last stage of meditational experience is *samādhi*, which, as we know by now, is a more or less untranslatable term. In fact, it's difficult to say much about *samādhi* at all. The most you can say, really, is that it is a blissful state of transparent and luminous voidness, free from all thoughts, free from the dichotomy of subject and object. And the perfection of *samādhi*, *samādhi* in its fullness, *samādhi* at the highest possible level, is equivalent to Enlightenment, or, at least, one aspect of Enlightenment.

So when we develop *samādhi*, we have reached the fringes at least of Enlightenment; and there we come to the end of what we call meditation. Consciousness has been fully expanded. It has expanded from the individual to the universal, from the finite to the infinite, from the mundane to the transcendental, and from the consciousness of ordinary humanity to that even of supreme Buddhahood.

I2

THE THREEFOLD PATH: WISDOM

In the last few months of his life, there was one theme that the Buddha returned to again and again. The Pāli canon describes him wandering from place to place with Ānanda, his attendant, everywhere gathering his followers together and reminding them of the path to Enlightenment. And the theme he chose was the threefold path: ethics, meditation, wisdom. He would say, 'This is morality, this is concentration, this is wisdom. Concentration, when imbued with morality, brings great fruit and profit. Wisdom, when imbued with concentration, brings great fruit and profit. The mind imbued with wisdom becomes completely free from the corruptions, that is, from the corruption of sensuality, of becoming, of false views and of ignorance.'[319]

This way of putting it reminds us that the threefold path is progressive. There is no meditation, certainly not to any great extent, without ethics; and there is no true wisdom without meditation. This was very much emphasized by the great leader of India's new Buddhists, Dr B. R. Ambedkar. In his book *The Buddha and His Dhamma* he says, 'Prajñā (wisdom), without śīla (ethics), is dangerous.' Mere *prajñā*, Dr Ambedkar says – that is, *prajñā* in the sense of intellectual knowledge – is like a sword in the hand of an angry man.[320] Someone who is merely learned, who is just well-read, can do a lot of harm. *Śīla* and *samādhi* are also necessary.

Dr Ambedkar goes even further than this. He says that even *prajñā* in the full sense – wisdom based on a foundation of ethics and meditation

– is not enough. But what else, then, is necessary? What else *could* be necessary? What could one need beyond perfect wisdom? The answer is, of course, compassion. True wisdom, in fact, is always accompanied by compassion. The Mahāyāna says that, like a great bird, the Dharma needs both its wings – wisdom and compassion – if it is to fly.

THE DIFFERENCE BETWEEN *VIJÑĀNA* AND *JÑĀNA*

There are several Sanskrit words usually translated as 'wisdom' or 'knowledge', which can be rather confusing. To begin with, there are the words *vijñāna* and *jñāna*. Both these words come from the same verbal root: *jñā*, to know. But although they have a shared derivation, there is a clear distinction between them, a distinction that is of absolutely fundamental importance: for Buddhism, for spiritual life, even, ultimately, for civilization and culture itself.

The two words both have several meanings, but here I want to use them in the way they are used in the teaching of the four reliances, which occurs in a number of Mahāyāna texts.[321] The first of these reliances is that one should rely on the teaching, not on the person who teaches. Secondly, one should rely on the meaning, not on the expression. Don't be misled by the expression; try to find out what is really meant. And then, thirdly, one should rely on scriptures of definitive meaning, not on scriptures of interpretable meaning. Some passages in the Buddhist scriptures are obscure, even ambiguous, whereas others are clear and straightforward; so one interprets the obscure in the light of the clear and straightforward, the interpretable in terms of the definitive. And fourthly, one should rely on *jñāna*, not on *vijñāna*.

As this fourth reliance implies, although *jñāna* and *vijñāna* come from the same verbal root, there is a big difference between them; in fact, they are opposites. *Jñāna* sees things as they really are; *vijñāna* sees things only as they appear to be. *Jñāna* is free from greed, hatred, and delusion; *vijñāna* is completely ensnared in them. *Jñāna* is transcendental; *vijñāna* is mundane. *Jñāna* is of the nature of *nirvāṇa*; *vijñāna* is of the nature of *saṃsāra*.

The vast majority of people, of course, rely on *vijñāna*. To put it in the terms used in the Yogācāra tradition, their knowledge is determined by the physical senses, by the so-called rational mind, and by the ego mind or ego consciousness.[322] Very few people really rely on *jñāna*, on transcendental wisdom. Stream Entrants do, and so perhaps do the very greatest of the great poets and thinkers, but most people not only do not rely upon *jñāna*, they have no conception of *jñāna* as distinct from *vijñāna*. For them knowledge is essentially *vijñāna*, something empirical and rational, something of a sophisticated scientific type. People simply have no conception of the possibility of another kind of knowledge, no conception of the possibility of *jñāna*. One could therefore say that as a Buddhist one's greatest task in the West today is to explain, even insist upon, the difference between *vijñāna* and *jñāna*. Unless this difference is understood and acted upon, there can be no real spiritual life, no real Buddhism, no real – as distinct from effective – Going for Refuge.

So we must rely on *jñāna*, not *vijñāna*. But we cannot rely on *jñāna* unless we have at least some experience of it, and we cannot experience it unless we develop it. So how are we to develop it? Well, we develop it through the whole momentum of our whole spiritual life. We develop it as a result of meditation, ethics, spiritual friendship, Dharma study, Right Livelihood, and so on. In short, we develop *jñāna* and learn to rely upon it on the basis of effective Going for Refuge. One could say that our effective Going for Refuge is not really effective unless we're trying all the time to transform it into real Going for Refuge, unless we're trying to make the transition from *vijñāna* to *jñāna*, from the mundane to the transcendental.

PRAJÑĀ

But when one comes across 'wisdom' in Buddhist literature, the word being translated is usually neither *jñāna* nor *vijñāna*, but *prajñā*. *Prajñā* is also from the verbal root *jñā*, to know, and the prefix *pra* is simply an intensifier; so *prajñā* may be said to be 'knowledge proper', or even knowledge *par excellence*. Like *jñāna*, *prajñā* sees things as they really are, sees them according to reality. Like *jñāna*, *prajñā* is free from greed, hatred, and delusion; it's transcendental and of the nature of Nirvāṇa. Nonetheless there is a great difference between the two, *jñāna* representing a state that has been achieved, while *prajñā* represents a function or faculty. *Jñāna*, in a word, is static; *prajñā* is dynamic.

The nature of *prajñā* is illustrated by a passage in the *Platform Sūtra*, which is the foundation text of Zen Buddhism. Huineng, the sixth patriarch, says 'Samādhi is the quintessence of prajñā, while prajñā is the activity of samādhi.'[323] (In the context of the *Platform Sūtra*, *samādhi* does not mean concentration and meditation, but corresponds to *jñāna*.) At the same time we should not think that the two – that is to say, *jñāna* and *prajñā* – are really separate. As Huineng goes on to point out, they are like the lamp and its light. He says, 'With the lamp, there is light. Without it, it would be dark. The lamp is the quintessence of the light, and the light is the expression of the lamp. In name they are two things, but in substance they are one and the same. The same is the case with samādhi [i.e. *jñāna*] and prajñā.'

As we have already seen in considering wisdom as a spiritual faculty, according to Buddhism there are three progressive levels of *prajñā*: wisdom derived from hearing; wisdom based on thinking; and wisdom based on meditation. The attainment of this third level of wisdom – *bhāvanā-mayī-prajñā* – is the attainment of wisdom in the full sense.[324] In other words, it's *bhāvanā-mayī-prajñā* that makes a Buddha a Buddha.

WISDOM, COMPASSION, AND SKILFUL MEANS

As a Buddha, one's dearest wish is that others too should experience the freedom of heart and mind that comes with true wisdom. This does not mean that one goes around giving people little homilies on the true nature of existence – or not necessarily, anyway. A Buddha's wisdom is accompanied not only by compassion but also by what is known as 'skilful means' (the Sanskrit word is *upāya*). The historical Buddha, Śākyamuni, seems always to have been able to find the right way of putting things to people. There are many examples of this, but perhaps one of the most poignant is the story of his encounter with a young woman called Kisāgotamī.

Gotami was her clan name, and Kisā – which means 'thin' – was a sort of nickname. She had not been married long, and she was the mother of a small son. One day the boy was bitten by a snake and unfortunately he died. Kisāgotamī nearly went mad with grief. She refused to give up her son's body, but went from door to door asking people for medicine to bring him back to life. She wouldn't listen to reason, but eventually someone had the good sense to suggest to her that she should go to see the Buddha. He would surely be able to give her the medicine she wanted, they said. This was all Kisāgotamī needed to hear. She went straight to the Buddha, laid the body of her son at his feet, and said, 'Please give me the medicine. Please bring my son back to life.'

For a while the Buddha was silent, and then he said, 'All right, I'll give you the medicine. But first I want you to bring me something. I want you to go and get some mustard seeds.' Well, that sounded easy enough. Kisāgotamī leapt to her feet and was about to dash off, when the Buddha said – and we can imagine him saying this very kindly – 'There's just one more thing, just one condition. The seeds must come from a house where no one has ever died.'

We can imagine that Kisāgotamī scarcely heard this. As she hurried towards the village, one thought was uppermost in her mind: that if she could persuade someone to give her some mustard seeds, her son would live again. She stopped at the first house she came to, and explained what she wanted. Of course, when they heard her story, the people who lived there were ready to give her as many seeds as she wanted. But then she remembered the Buddha's one condition. 'Has anyone ever died in this house?' she asked. And the householders replied sadly, 'What is this that you are saying? The dead are many, the living are few.'

So she went to another house, and the same thing happened. Then to another; the same again. In the end, she understood. Death wasn't just something that had happened to her son. Death comes to all, to every man, to every woman. Everybody must die one day. She therefore left her son's body in the forest, came back to the Buddha, and knelt before him. Putting her hands together, she said, 'Lord, please give me a Refuge.' So the Buddha gave her a Refuge – in fact three Refuges: in the Buddha, the Dharma, and the Sangha. She left home, learned to meditate, and eventually that glimpse she had had of the true nature of existence flowered into Perfect Vision, wisdom in all its fullness.[325]

THE PERFECTION OF WISDOM

The importance that Buddhists have always attached to the attainment of wisdom is reflected in the fact that there is a whole school of Buddhist thought and practice devoted to the Prajñāpāramitā, the 'Perfection of Wisdom', which has been called a 'wisdom beyond words', or even a 'wisdom beyond wisdom'.

Of course, the Perfection of Wisdom tradition began with the Buddha; that's where the story starts. The Buddha attained Enlightenment under the bodhi tree at Bodh Gaya 2,500 years ago. He 'saw things as they really are'. And at first, as we have seen, he doubted if it would be possible for him to communicate his vision to other people. It was so – well, out of this world. So he was inclined to remain silent. But eventually, fortunately for us, he decided he would teach. Out of compassion he decided that he would teach the Dharma for the benefit of those whose eyes were covered with only a little dust.[326]

So the Buddha taught; and what he taught was an expression in concepts, images, and words of his Enlightenment experience. Not that he gave a definitive description of that experience. He didn't say much about it, in fact; he only hinted at it, he only pointed in its direction, saying, so to speak, 'If you go in that direction you will see what I saw.' As we have seen, he said that his teaching was like a raft. Just as one uses a raft to cross the river and get to the opposite shore, so one uses his teaching to cross the flood of *saṃsāra* and reach *nirvāṇa*. His teaching, he insisted, was only a means to an end, only a finger pointing to the moon.

But, as time passed, as the Buddha himself passed away, as one generation of disciples was succeeded by another, some of the Buddha's later followers didn't do what he had asked them to do. They didn't look from the finger to the moon; instead, they fastened their attention on the finger, so to speak. Or, reverting to the earlier metaphor, they made themselves at home on the raft, forgetting to use it to cross the flood.

This was particularly the case when it came to doctrine. The Buddha himself gave only hints, but in the course of centuries those hints hardened for some people into certainties, even into dogmas, elaborate doctrinal systems. The Abhidharma, which was the preoccupation of Indian Buddhist scholars for centuries, came to be regarded as literally embodying absolute truth, and is still so regarded in some Buddhist countries.[327]

But not all Buddhists agreed that the Abhidharma literally embodied absolute truth. Not all Buddhists agreed that *prajñā* and Abhidharma were identical. And some of these Buddhists produced a literature of their own, a literature that went beyond *prajñā* in the Abhidharma sense – or, one could say, a literature that went beyond literalism, that in fact fought literalism tooth and nail. This was the literature of the Prajñāpāramitā tradition.

This literature was produced over a period of several hundred years, until it eventually comprised about thirty-five independent texts, some of them very extensive indeed. But large or small, they are all known as *sūtras*; that is, they all purport to be discourses given by the Buddha himself, although one cannot take it that they were literally given by the historical Buddha and then written down exactly as he gave them. Their particular emphasis, however, especially their anti-literalism, goes back to the Buddha himself, and the Buddha's own teaching.

The main theme of all the Perfection of Wisdom *sūtras* is, as we have seen, emptiness, *śūnyatā*. Perhaps the best known is the *Vajracchedikā*, or 'Diamond-Cutter Sūtra', generally known simply as the *Diamond Sūtra*. Then there is the *Heart Sūtra*. There's a Prajñāpāramitā *sūtra* in 8,000 lines, one in 25,000 lines, and one in 100,000 lines – that's the longest of them all. And this vast literature, consisting of many volumes, was translated in its entirety into English by Dr Edward Conze – a feat for which all Buddhists can be profoundly grateful.

Gratitude is very much a Buddhist virtue. In fact – this may come as a surprise – even Buddhas feel gratitude. The *Prajñāpāramitā Sūtra in 8,000 Lines* says that the Tathāgatas or Buddhas

> treat the Dharma with respect, revere, worship and adore it,
> for they know that this essential nature of *dharmas* is just the
> Perfection of Wisdom. For the all-knowledge of the Tathāgatas
> has been brought about from this perfection of wisdom, and for
> that the Tathāgatas are grateful and thankful to her. With justice
> can the Tathāgata be called 'grateful and thankful'. In gratitude
> and thankfulness the Tathāgata favours and cherishes the vehicle
> on which he has come, and the path by which he has won full
> enlightenment. That one should know as the gratitude and
> thankfulness of the Tathāgata.[328]

If the Buddha is grateful to the Perfection of Wisdom, how much more grateful we should be, not just to the Perfection of Wisdom, but to the Buddha himself. We should in fact be grateful to all our spiritual friends, grateful to all those who have brought us into contact with the Dharma, or helped us to deepen our contact with it or understanding of it – and grateful to the translators of Buddhist texts, including Dr Conze, the translator of the Perfection of Wisdom *sūtras*. Gratitude, we may say, is one of the greatest of virtues.

Nowadays, sadly, it is a virtue that is rather neglected. Sometimes people are ashamed to feel or express gratitude. There's a sense perhaps that we've been given something we didn't deserve, or at least that we feel we didn't deserve. If we receive something from someone, this seems to put us in an inferior position, and we don't like to feel inferior. This would seem to be the sort of difficulty we have with the idea of gratitude.

When I first came into contact with Buddhism in 1942, Dr Conze had only just started translating the Perfection of Wisdom literature. There was, however, an English translation of a Chinese version of the *Diamond Sūtra*, and when I read this it made a tremendous impression on me, as did the *Platform Sūtra*, the *sūtra* of Huineng, which I read at about the same time. Reading these two works – I was sixteen at the time – I realized I was a Buddhist and in fact had always been one. I have therefore always felt intensely grateful to the translators of these two books – to William Gemmell, the translator of the *Diamond Sūtra*, and Wong Mow Lam, the translator of the *Platform Sūtra*. This is why when I published my book on Buddhist canonical literature, *The Eternal Legacy*, I dedicated it to their memory.

The Prajñāpāramitā texts have been described as 'dangerously disorienting to the unwary student'. They're disorienting because they completely upset our ideas about reality. In particular, they challenge our literalistic thinking. This is something that I've been given reason to think a lot about over the years. I would say that at least half the questions I get asked in seminars, and even in people's letters, are based on literalistic misunderstandings. If people could only realize that they were being literalistic, and quite how literalistic they were being, they wouldn't need to ask those particular questions. The Prajñāpāramitā texts perform the very useful function of challenging our literalistic thinking, especially our literalistic thinking about Buddhism itself. They compel us, oblige us even, to realize that a raft, even the raft of the Dharma, is just that: a raft. They insist on our looking not just at the finger but at the moon to which the finger is pointing.

As well as challenging our thinking, the Perfection of Wisdom texts encourage us to feel devotion, to take our understanding beyond the intellectual to something that is 'felt in the blood, and felt along the heart', to borrow Wordsworth's phrase.[329] In its opening lines, the *Ratnaguṇa-saṃcayagāthā* challenges us to 'call forth as much as you can of love, of respect, and of faith'.[330] The Mahāyāna tradition that produced the Prajñāpāramitā literature eventually came to venerate Perfect Wisdom in the form of a goddess, also called Prajñāpāramitā, a development that simply expanded on the sense of gratitude the Buddha felt for the wisdom through which he had gained Enlightenment. The goddess Prajñāpāramitā is visualized as gold in colour, and she holds a Perfection of Wisdom text to her heart; she is sometimes called 'the mother of all the Buddhas'. Perhaps – to end this brief series of reflections on wisdom – this hymn to the Perfection of Wisdom, from the *Prajñāpāramitā Sūtra in Eight Thousand Lines*, will give as good an idea of what is meant by 'wisdom' in Buddhism as we are going to find. In the text, Śāriputra addresses the Buddha, saying:

The perfection of wisdom gives light, O Lord. I pay homage to the perfection of wisdom! She is worthy of homage. She is unstained, the entire world cannot stain her. She is a source of light, and from everyone in the triple world she removes darkness, and she leads away from the blinding darkness caused by the defilements and by wrong views. In her we can find shelter. Most excellent are her works. She makes us seek the safety of the wings of enlightenment. She brings light to the blind, she brings light so that all fear and distress may be forsaken. She has gained the five eyes, and she shows the path to all beings. She herself is an organ of vision. She disperses the gloom and darkness of delusion. She does nothing about all dharmas. She guides to the path those who have strayed on to a bad road. She is identical with all-knowledge. She never produces any dharma, because she has forsaken the residues relating to both kinds of coverings, those produced by defilement and those produced by the cognizable. She does not stop any dharma. Herself unstopped and unproduced is the perfection of wisdom. She is the mother of the bodhisattvas, on account of the emptiness of own marks. As the donor of the jewel of all the Buddha-dharmas she brings about the ten powers (of a Buddha). She cannot be crushed. She protects the unprotected, with the help of the four grounds of self-confidence. She is the antidote to birth and death. She has a clear knowledge of the own-being of all dharmas, for she does not stray away from it. The perfection of wisdom of the Buddhas, the Lords, sets in motion the wheel of the Dharma.[331]

13

THE COSMIC SIGNIFICANCE OF
THE BODHISATTVA IDEAL

What is the Dharma? This is the question we have been pursuing, now from this angle, now from that, and the same question, of course, has exercised the Buddha's followers ever since the Buddha himself was alive. The Buddha, we know, lived and taught for some forty-five years before his final passing away, which is traditionally known as the *parinirvāṇa*, the attainment of supreme *nirvāṇa*, the ultimate peace, beyond conditioned things, eternal and complete and self-illuminating. And after the Buddha's *parinirvāṇa*, there arose among his disciples two groups, or two parties if you like.

One party was on the whole quite satisfied with the Buddha's verbal teaching. They were deeply interested in the different doctrinal formulations of the teaching: the four noble truths, the Eightfold Path, the seven stages of purification, the five *skandhas*, the twelve *nidānas*, and so on. In fact they concentrated on the verbal teaching so much that they came to regard it as being Buddhism, the whole of Buddhism. For them this *was* the Dharma.

But the other party was not quite satisfied with this. They accepted the Buddha's verbal teaching and all the doctrinal formulations, but they felt that this was not the whole story. Above and beyond – or if you like behind – the verbal teaching, the life and personality of the Buddha had also to be taken into consideration. What the Buddha himself was as a man, an Enlightened man, an Enlightened being, and what he did was at least as important as what he said. The verbal, doctrinal teaching gave expression to the Buddha's wisdom, but his life, his person, his activity, gave expression to his compassion.

In maintaining this, this group of Buddhists would have been able to cite many examples of the Buddha's generosity and kindness towards all those with whom he came into contact. The Buddha's lifetime was still within living memory, and the Buddhist community was taking great care to preserve all the many teachings, as well as all the anecdotes and stories about the Buddha, memorizing them and teaching them to others – for it would be several hundred years before any of it would be written down. But perhaps the most telling account of what the Buddha was really like is to be found in the records of his relationship with the man with whose name, as it happens, that oral tradition is most closely associated: Ānanda.

Ānanda was one of the Buddha's cousins, and his attendant for the last twenty years of his life. He is credited with having had perfect recall, so that when it came to memorizing the Buddha's many teachings for posterity, Ānanda was the main source of information. After all, he was with the Buddha all the time; he heard whatever he said and remembered it word for word. If he happened to miss a teaching, the Buddha would repeat it to him later. So Ānanda, perhaps more than anyone, is intimately associated with the Buddha's doctrinal teachings.

But as far as Ānanda himself was concerned, there was something else that was even more important to him. When the Buddha was close to death, Ānanda was found weeping, saying to himself again and again, 'The Master is about to pass away from me: he who is so kind.'[332] These words of Ānanda's, as he stood there by the door of the hut where the Buddha was lying ill, are of the very greatest significance. Ānanda had been with the Buddha for twenty years. He had heard the Buddha deliver hundreds of abstruse, philosophical, deeply mystical discourses. He had heard him answer thousands of questions. He must have admired his brilliance, his affability, the ease with which he handled difficult questions. And no doubt he had also witnessed all sorts of unusual things about the Buddha, all sorts of strange, supernormal happenings.

But what was the overall impression of the Buddha's character upon Ānanda after all those years, all those teachings? It is expressed in those few words that Ānanda uttered as he wept: 'he who is so kind'. This is very significant. Ānanda was not grieving for 'he who is so wise', or 'he who is so Enlightened', or ' he who has such a deep philosophical understanding', or ' he who is such a brilliant debater', or 'he who has worked so many miracles', or 'he who is so brave', or 'he who is so tireless'; but for 'he who is so kind'.

The Buddha's compassionate heart had to be taken into account as much as his wise mind – this is what the second party of his followers maintained. Buddhism comprises not just wisdom but also compassion, they said, and both of them together form the spiritual ideal. Yes, Buddhists should seek to gain Enlightenment – this gives expression to the wisdom aspect of the Dharma. But they should seek to gain Enlightenment for the sake of all sentient beings. It is this that gives expression to the Dharma's compassionate aspect.

From this instinct on the part of these early Buddhists eventually emerged what became known as the Mahāyāna school of Buddhism. It was the Mahāyānists who came up with the image we have already encountered: the bird of Enlightenment held aloft by the two wings of compassion and wisdom. And among the many teachings of the Mahāyāna, towering above them like a mountain peak above so many foothills, was its central conception: the bodhisattva ideal.[333] For in the bodhisattva wisdom and compassion are perfectly combined.

THE BODHISATTVA AND THE WILL TO ENLIGHTENMENT

But what is a bodhisattva? A bodhisattva is a being (*sattva*) who lives for the sake of Enlightenment (*bodhi*). Thus the bodhisattva ideal is nothing other than a statement of the Buddhist ideal itself, the ideal of the attainment of Enlightenment, the ideal of evolution from a state of unenlightened to a state of Enlightened humanity. But it is even more than that. The bodhisattva is further defined as one who seeks to gain Enlightenment not just for the sake of his or her own emancipation from suffering and ignorance, but in order that all sentient beings may also gain Enlightenment. This was the Mahāyāna's way of drawing in the compassionate aspect, the altruistic dimension, of the desire to gain Enlightenment.[334]

So the next question is: how does one become a bodhisattva? How does one embark on the realization of this ideal? The general Mahāyāna answer to this question is that one becomes a bodhisattva by the arising of what is called the *bodhicitta*. Some scholars translate *bodhicitta* as 'thought of Enlightenment', but this is exactly what it is not. It is not a thought about Enlightenment but an urge in the direction of Enlightenment, an urge of one's whole being. In fact, going even further than this, the great Mahāyāna teachers say that the *bodhicitta* is not a conditioned mental state or function at all. In traditional terms it is not included in the five aggregates (*skandhas*) that between them make up the whole of conditioned existence. The *bodhicitta* is something transcendental, something belonging to the Beyond, a reflection of the Unconditioned in the midst of the conditioned. It is perhaps best to translate it as the 'will to Enlightenment'.

We must not think that this will to Enlightenment is anybody's individual will. The *bodhicitta* is not individual. It arises in different bodhisattvas, but there are not as many *bodhicittas* as there are bodhisattvas. There is only one supreme, transcendental *bodhicitta*, in which individuals participate, or which individuals manifest, in varying degrees. It is a sort of cosmic will, a universal will to universal redemption. And those of whom it takes possession, in whom it arises or manifests, become – or are – bodhisattvas.

This is the metaphysical answer to the question of how one becomes a bodhisattva. But if one is going to take this ideal seriously, if one is going to regard following the path of the bodhisattva as a practical proposition, one is naturally going to need some idea of how to go about it. Strictly speaking, the bodhisattva's career begins with the taking of a vow. The *bodhicitta* is universal, but the bodhisattva is an individual, and the *bodhicitta* therefore expresses itself in his or her life and work in an individual manner. This individual expression, in and through the bodhisattva, of the cosmic, transcendental *bodhicitta* is known as the bodhisattva vow. This vow is not just a verbal expression, not just a statement of intent that you hope will galvanize you into action. By the time you take it, the whole momentum of your being will be behind your intention; it represents a reorientation of your entire being.

THE BODHISATTVA VOW

The bodhisattva vow is traditionally spoken of in the singular but it is really plural. There are quite a number of sets of vows, but the best known is that of the four great vows, which are still repeated, especially in Mahāyāna monasteries, all over the Buddhist world: 'May I deliver all beings from difficulties; may I eradicate all passions; may I master all *dharmas*; may I lead all beings to Buddhahood.'

But this is still not practical enough as far as we are concerned. Clearly to take these vows in full confidence that one could fulfil them, one would need already to have done a good deal of spiritual practice. The situation is analogous, in a way, to the relationship between the mundane Eightfold Path and the transcendental Eightfold Path. Once Perfect Vision in the full sense has arisen, one can perfect each of the remaining seven stages of the path. But one can work towards the arising of that Perfect Vision through following the path on a mundane level.

THE SIX PERFECTIONS

Similarly, once the *bodhicitta* has arisen in the bodhisattva, he or she can take the bodhisattva vow in full confidence that that vow will be fulfilled. Then, as the 'establishment aspect' – as it is called – of the arising of the *bodhicitta*, the bodhisattva practises six *pāramitās*, six perfections or transcendental virtues: giving, uprightness or ethics, patience, vigour, meditation, and wisdom.[335] But before the arising of the *bodhicitta*, when one is still aspiring to become a bodhisattva, one can undertake to develop these virtues as best one can, so that the practice of these six perfections may in fact be regarded as another formulation of the path to Enlightenment.

GIVING

The first of the perfections is *dāna*: giving or generosity – essentially a positive, outward-going attitude, an urge to give and to share. One can enumerate all the different kinds of things that can be given away – there are all sorts of lists and classifications in Buddhist literature – but potentially one can give away anything that can be possessed. One traditional list enumerates six kinds of giving that the would-be bodhisattva can practise.[336]

There is, to begin with, the obvious kind – obvious but very important: the giving of material things like food, clothing, and so on. Then there's a less obvious gift, the giving of fearlessness. Great importance is attached to this in Buddhist circles. The bodhisattva, by his very presence, creates in other people a positive attitude, an attitude of fearlessness, of freedom from fear. Anxiety, as we have already noted, is one of the great problems of today. You see it writ large on most people's faces, because most people's way of life conduces to anxiety and fear. This fear is often repressed; because it is repressed it becomes unconscious; and when one has unconscious fears one tends to project them so that they spread over the whole of one's life, and one feels threatened on all sides. But if you are a bodhisattva, by your presence, by your example, you counteract all this. Through your positivity you create confidence and freedom from anxiety wherever you go, and through your wisdom you help people to see that it isn't worth being attached to or bound down by conditioned things. You give them a new, larger perspective, indeed a cosmic perspective, and in this way you emancipate them from conditioned things and create in them an attitude of fearlessness.

Thirdly, the bodhisattva gives education and culture. These are considered to be very important in all Buddhist countries because it is understood that unless there is a certain level of education in the true sense, not just book learning, but culture in the sense of a refinement of spirit, no spiritual life is really possible. In practical terms this is expressed in a general encouragement of the arts and sciences.

Fourthly, the bodhisattva is ready to sacrifice, if necessary, life and limb. This is something that surpasses the scope of most of us today; few people are called upon actually to sacrifice their life or even their limbs for the sake of what they believe. But there have been times in the past when people have died for their beliefs, and there are areas of the world, even at present, where if you have spiritual principles and stand up for them in public, you may be risking your life. We shouldn't forget how fortunate we are in being able to profess publicly and follow those spiritual principles in which we believe. Under less favourable circumstances we might have to pay for our belief, or at least our profession of it, with our lives.

Then again, the bodhisattva is also prepared to give away his or her merits. In the Buddhist way of thinking, merits are something you acquire as the result of good deeds and generous actions; but we're told that the bodhisattva is quite ready to give away whatever merits he or she has acquired. If you're a bodhisattva you don't want to mark yourself off from other beings as being more meritorious or virtuous than they are. This is why, at the conclusion of a meditation or devotional ritual, Buddhists often recite verses 'transferring merit'.

The verses generally say something to the effect that you don't wish to keep the merits accruing from this spiritual practice to yourself; you wish to share them with all living beings whatsoever.

The sixth gift is the gift of the Dharma, the Truth, the Teaching. This is the greatest of all gifts. You can give people food and clothing but they may not lead a very noble life. You can give them fearlessness but even that may not carry them very far. Even if you give them education, culture, and so on, even if you share your merits with them, they still may not be leading a truly human life. But once you give the gift of the Dharma, once you open their spiritual eyes, once they can see things in a more universal perspective, once they can begin to see the pattern of it all and accord their lives with that pattern, once they are oriented in the direction of Enlightenment, then they truly begin to live, rather than merely existing. So the gift of the Dharma is the best gift of all.

At least, it is the best gift in a sense, according to the traditional sixfold classification. But there is another form of giving that is even higher or at least more comprehensive, a gift that includes all the others. This is the gift of oneself. In 'Song of Myself', the American poet Walt Whitman says, 'When I give, I give myself.'[337] It is easy to give material things but not give yourself with them. You can make other people fearless, you can free them from anxiety, and still not give yourself. It is even possible to give the gift of the Dharma but not give yourself. So to give oneself is the greatest of all gifts, the supreme gift that includes all others. And this gift too the bodhisattva gives. If you are a bodhisattva, you give yourself, you radiate yourself out towards all other living beings, not holding anything back. This is the ultimate form of giving – and certainly not one to be undertaken prematurely, before one has developed the inner resources to be able to give so unstintingly. But everyone can start to practise generosity in some way; it is the most basic of virtues. Indeed, it is often said in Buddhist countries that without a spirit of giving – which finds expression in practice – there is no spiritual life.

SKILFUL ACTION

The second perfection practised by the aspiring bodhisattva is the transcendental virtue of *śīla*. As we have already seen, *śīla* is sometimes translated as 'morality', but perhaps it is better to avoid this term with its unhelpful connotations. Morality in the Buddhist sense is 'skilful action' – action expressive of skilful mental states, states that are free from craving, aversion, and ignorance. There are various traditional patterns of skilful behaviour – for instance, the five precepts, the ten precepts, and the sixty-four precepts undertaken by bodhisattvas. As we have seen, these sets of precepts are not just lists of rules, but training principles to be applied with intelligence and awareness to all the different spheres of human life and activity. In this context – to add to the aspects of ethical behaviour that have already been discussed – I want to consider three very basic areas of life: food, work, and marriage.

First, a word about food. According to the Mahāyāna *sutras*, if you are a bodhisattva you should eat – since even a bodhisattva has to eat – just for the sake of health and vigour, not to satisfy neurotic cravings. You should also eat without causing harm to other living beings, which means in practice being vegetarian, as far as possible.[338]

The Buddhist tradition frequently oscillates between discussion of abstruse philosophy and consideration of much more homely matters such as diet. Some scholars of Buddhism tend to smile at such apparent lurches from the sublime to the ridiculous, and are surprised, for example, that in the *Lankāvatāra Sūtra*, in the midst of profound metaphysical and epistemological speculation, you suddenly find a chapter on the unskilfulness of eating meat.[339] And of course the scholars say, 'It must have been interpolated. The Buddha couldn't possibly have spoken on a subject like this. Someone must have added it later on.'

But not so. This sort of attitude simply betrays the lack of a sense of proportion. After all, we eat food every day, and it has a constant effect on our bodies and our minds, so it is much more important than we generally think. One might even go so far as to say that there is little point in calling oneself a Buddhist if one is going to continue having the same old meat and two veg for dinner. One of the things we have to appreciate, as we have seen again and again, is that taking up the Buddhist path isn't just about learning the philosophy. We have to start changing each and every aspect of our lives. And diet is one of those really basic things; you can hardly have anything more basic than food. So certainly when one starts following the spiritual path, an important and radical change may need to be made.

As far as work is concerned, whether one is simply working to earn money or whether one's work is vocational, the important thing is that the work should be in accordance with what is traditionally called Right Livelihood: that is, it shouldn't harm or exploit others, and it shouldn't degrade oneself, or narrow or mechanicalize the mind. I used to rather shock people when I was asked about work by saying, 'Do as little as possible.' And I would still say this if by work is meant work done simply for the sake of earning money. If one's work is also one's vocation, of course, there need be no limitation whatever – but to have a vocation is rare under modern conditions. Perhaps the best solution is to arrange to work part-time, if that is possible. Then one's free time can be used for creative activities, meditation, study, and the cultivation and development of friendship.

But these days I wouldn't necessarily say that one should work as little as possible, because a positive alternative has been opened up. In recent years a number of Western Buddhists have been experimenting successfully with the establishing of 'team-based right livelihood' businesses, creating a context in which Buddhists can work together, so that one's work is very much part of one's spiritual practice, and one's need to spend time meditating and studying the Dharma is recognized and taken into account as a matter of course. If one is able to find or create such a situation, one need place no limits on one's involvement in the work situation. Indeed, to be a little provocative, one might even say that in such circumstances one should work *as much* as possible.

The third area of ethical practice I want to mention here is marriage – although 'marriage' is another of those words I prefer to avoid, because it raises all sorts of misconceptions, and indeed it is somewhat outmoded these days. The Buddhist conception of marriage, so far as it has a conception at all, is entirely different from the Western Christian conception. To begin with, in Buddhism marriage is not regarded as a religious sacrament, or as legally binding and enforceable in a court of law; it is seen simply as a relationship between two people, a relationship that is known to and accepted by the family, friends, and social circle of the two people involved – and which can be ended, if appropriate, without any fuss and bother, as long as the welfare of all those concerned – especially children – is taken into account. In Buddhist countries there has never been any rigid or universal pattern of marriage relationship: monogamy, polygamy, and polyandry are all permitted. Homosexuality and heterosexuality are viewed in the same light; the only criterion is the quality of the human relationship involved.

PATIENCE

The third of the perfections the bodhisattva practises is *kṣānti*. *Kṣānti* is often translated as 'patience', but it covers a number of virtues – not just patience and forbearance, but also such things as gentleness, docility, even humility, as well as love, tolerance, and receptivity. Or, to put it another way, *kṣānti* consists in the absence of anger, and of all desire for retaliation and revenge. This is *kṣānti*, and it is one of the most beautiful of all the Buddhist virtues.

ENERGY IN PURSUIT OF THE GOOD

Fourthly, the aspiring bodhisattva practises *vīrya* or vigour, which is usually defined as 'energy in pursuit of the good' – 'the good' here meaning Enlightenment for the sake of all sentient beings. We have, of course, already come across *vīrya* as one of the five spiritual faculties and one of the seven factors of Enlightenment – and there is good reason for this, because without energy no spiritual life is possible. One might even say that the central problem of the spiritual life is finding enough energy – especially emotional energy – for it. It isn't something you can do without really trying, or if you're half-asleep.

But many people haven't got much energy. Exhausted or overwhelmed, dull or sluggish, they seem not to have any energy available to them. But why not? Where has the energy gone? What's happened to it? Well, the chances are – apart from the possibility that one is suffering from one of the debilitating illnesses that are becoming increasingly common – that one's energy isn't available either because it's blocked, or because it's wasted, or because it's too coarse. So, obviously, we have to learn to unblock our blocked energy, conserve our wasted energy, and refine our coarse energy. There are various ways of doing this: through awareness, through engaging in creative work, through communication, meditation, enjoyment of the fine arts, faith and devotion, and so on. In this way energy can be freed, released, made available for the spiritual life.

I need hardly say that according to the Mahāyāna tradition the bodhisattva himself or herself is the embodiment of energy. If you are a bodhisattva, your energy is wholly and totally available to you for the purposes of your spiritual career; there is a smooth, uninterrupted, harmonious flow of energy – indeed, you yourself are that flow of energy

– in the direction of Enlightenment. This free flow of energy means that the bodhisattva does many things and accomplishes a great deal, but there is no question of haste, strain, or tension.

MEDITATION

The fifth perfection of the bodhisattva is meditation. As we have already seen, there are three levels of meditation: the concentration and unification of one's energies; ascent into higher stages of consciousness – we could call this 'meditation proper'; and the turning of the mind to the contemplation of reality.

WISDOM

The sixth and last of the perfections of the bodhisattva is wisdom. In the Buddhist context wisdom means intuition, transcendental intuition if you like, of the Unconditioned. It means seeing reality face to face – not thinking about it or entertaining ideas about it, but seeing it directly and experiencing it for oneself. There are many ways of describing this wisdom, and a very popular way is in terms of what are called the five knowledges. These are the five principal aspects or modes of wisdom, just like five facets of a jewel. They are symbolized in Tibetan iconography by the mandala of the Five Buddhas, each Buddha of the mandala being associated with a particular facet of knowledge or wisdom.

First of all, there is what is known as the knowledge of the *dharmadhātu*. This is the basic knowledge, of which the other four are aspects. The *dharmadhātu* is the universe as the sphere of manifestation of reality, the gravitational field of reality – the whole universe being pervaded by reality just as space is pervaded by the sun's rays. So 'knowledge of the *dharmadhātu*' is knowledge of the whole cosmos as being pervaded by – indeed as being ultimately non-different from – Unconditioned reality itself. In the Mahāyāna, this knowledge is symbolized by the figure of Vairocana, the Illuminator, the white Buddha, the Buddha of the centre of the mandala.

Next there is the mirror-like knowledge, so called because the Enlightened mind sees everything. It pierces through all veils. It understands the true nature of everything, seeing it in its ultimate depth, its ultimate reality. And it sees with complete objectivity and impartiality.

Just as a mirror reflects without distortion whatever is placed in front of it and remains untouched, untainted, by the objects it reflects, so the mirror-like wisdom reflects all things, sees all things, knows all things, understands all things, pierces and penetrates all things, but it is not touched, not affected, by things – they don't stick to it. It's perfectly free, perfectly independent; there's no subjective reaction, but complete, pure, perfect objectivity. The mirror-like wisdom just reflects the whole of existence. It is symbolized by Akṣobhya, the imperturbable one, the one who cannot be moved, the dark-blue Buddha of the eastern quarter.

The third of these five knowledges is the knowledge of equality or sameness. Because the Enlightened mind sees everything with complete objectivity, without reacting, seeing the same reality in everything, it has the same attitude towards all, is even-minded towards all, has the same love and compassion towards all. Just like the sun's rays, it shines impartially without any differentiation or distinction. And this knowledge, the knowledge of equality, sameness, oneness, is symbolized by Ratnasambhava, the jewel-born Buddha, the yellow Buddha of the southern quarter.

After this comes the all-distinguishing knowledge. The mirror reflects everything equally, but it does not confuse or blur the distinctive features of things. It reflects a rose as a rose, a tree as a tree, a man as a man, a mountain as a mountain. It doesn't merge and blur them all together. This is very important. It means that the Enlightened mind sees things not only in their unity, but also in their diversity, and it sees them in both these ways together. It sees their unity, their common essence, but also sees them in all their unique, unrepeatable, ineffable individuality. For this reason, philosophically speaking, Buddhism is neither monistic nor pluralistic, but both and more than both. Unity does not obliterate difference, and difference does not obscure unity. Both are there together – unity in difference, difference in unity. This all-distinguishing knowledge is symbolized by Amitābha, the Buddha of infinite light, the red Buddha of the western quarter.

The fifth knowledge is the all-performing knowledge. The Enlightened mind devotes itself to the welfare of all living beings. It helps living beings in whatsoever way it can. It devises various 'skilful means' – ways of helping, methods of working – but it does all this naturally and spontaneously. It doesn't have to think things out. It just functions purely, simply, freely, spontaneously, and everything gets done. In a sense, it does nothing. In another sense, it does everything. This all-performing knowledge is symbolized by Amoghasiddhi, the infallible success, the green Buddha of the northern quarter.[340]

BALANCING THE PERFECTIONS

In this context wisdom can be seen as the sixth of the six perfections practised by the bodhisattva. Just as the five spiritual faculties can be considered to consist of two pairs, with a balancing fifth factor, the six perfections can be thought of in three pairs. Giving and uprightness represent between them the altruistic and the individualistic aspects of the spiritual life. Then the second pair, patience and vigour, represent – metaphorically speaking – the 'feminine' and the 'masculine' approaches to the spiritual life. And lastly, meditation and wisdom represent the internal and external dimensions, as it were, of the Enlightened mind. The bodhisattva synthesizes and balances all these pairs of opposites – individualistic and altruistic, 'feminine' and 'masculine', internal and external – in his or her own Enlightened or well-nigh Enlightened mind. In the bodhisattva's spiritual life there is no one-sidedness.

THE BODHISATTVA'S CAREER – TRANSCENDING TIME AND SPACE

In the course of his or her spiritual career, the bodhisattva passes through ten stages of spiritual progress. In the first stage the *bodhicitta*, the will to Enlightenment, arises, and manifests in or through you. In the eighth stage, you become 'irreversible': that is, you cannot fall back from the attainment of Supreme Enlightenment for all; there is no danger of your ever regressing to the comparatively lower ideal of Enlightenment for yourself alone. And in the tenth and last stage you attain Supreme Enlightenment itself, for the sake of all sentient beings.[341]

Now all this – the practice of the six perfections, the arising of the *bodhicitta*, the passage through all ten stages of spiritual progress – takes an immensely long period of time. Indeed, according to the tradition, the length of time it takes is absolutely unthinkable and awe-inspiring. We're told that it takes not less than three *kalpas*, or three aeons, and although there is no precise figure given, a *kalpa* is very lengthy indeed, a period of millions of years.[342] During this period the bodhisattva, passing through the stages of spiritual progress, also passes through many different lives in many different spheres, many different worlds, many different planes. But all the time he or she holds fast, as though to a golden thread, to the will to Enlightenment.

The bodhisattva ideal is of the very essence of the Mahāyāna form of Buddhism, and could well be called the finest flower of Buddhist spirituality. Its significance is not just individual or personal, but cosmic in the true sense of that much misused word. 'Cosmic' really means universal, pertaining to the cosmos or the universe as a whole, not limited to any one period of history, not even limited to this earth. And we find that the bodhisattva ideal, according to the Mahāyāna *sūtras*, is unlimited in time and unlimited in space.

Similarly, when the bodhisattva dedicates himself to the attainment of Enlightenment for the sake of all sentient beings, this expression is meant quite literally. By 'all sentient beings' – these words that reverberate through the entire Mahāyāna tradition, re-echoing like a great chorus throughout all the Mahāyāna *sūtras* – one means not just beings living on this earth, on this particular plane of conditioned existence, but the beings of all worlds, all planes, all spheres whatsoever.

We find a hint of this in the meditation practice called the development of universal loving-kindness, the *mettā bhāvanā* – which, incidentally, is often practised to help induce the arising of the will to Enlightenment. As we saw in the chapter on meditation, one starts this practice by developing love towards oneself, then towards a near and dear friend, then towards a neutral person, then an enemy. Then, in the final stage of the practice, one's *mettā* goes out in ever-widening circles. First of all you direct *mettā* to all the people in the room where you are meditating (if you are meditating with others), then to all the people in the locality, in the city, the country, all the continents one by one, then the beings of the whole earth, all human beings, animals, and so on, and then finally all living beings whatsoever in all the directions of space. Thus one develops *mettā* not just for the beings of this earth but for beings inhabiting other planets, other worlds, even other galactic systems. It goes as far, as wide, as universal, as this.

The expression 'all sentient beings', which occurs so often in the context not only of the bodhisattva ideal but of the Mahāyāna generally, as well as in the context of the loving-kindness practice, suggests three interrelated things. First of all, it makes it clear that according to Buddhism there is not just one world but a plurality, even an infinity, of worlds. Secondly, it leaves room for the possibility that some of these worlds, at least, are inhabited by other intelligent beings. And thirdly it suggests that these worlds and these other intelligent beings are not outside the scope of Buddhism, of the way to Enlightenment, either in theory or in practice.

Some years ago there arose a dispute among some German Catholic theologians. The question that arose was this. Suppose, as a result of the discoveries of modern science, we find that other worlds are inhabited. Suppose we find intelligent beings on Mars or Venus or even the Moon. Would the Christian scheme of redemption apply to those beings? Did Christ die for them? Or did he die only for the inhabitants of this Earth? This question was much discussed and, predictably, opinion was divided. Some held that Christ's salvation was for the benefit of the beings of this Earth only, while others believed that it was for the benefit of all sentient beings – to use the Buddhist expression – whatsoever.

But so far as Buddhism is concerned, the question of its scope was settled long ago, in fact from the very beginning. Buddhism can be described as a universal teaching in the fullest sense, a teaching applicable to all intelligent beings at any time, whether now, ten million years ago or ten million years hence, in any part of the universe, whether in this galactic system or any other. It is, as the *Tiratana Vandanā* says, *akāliko* – it is applicable at all times and in all places.

THE *LOTUS SŪTRA*

This is brought out strongly in some of the Mahāyāna *sūtras*, especially the *Saddharma Puṇḍarīka Sūtra*, the 'White Lotus of the True Teaching', often called simply the *Lotus Sūtra*. The *Lotus Sūtra* is the grandest of all the Mahāyāna *sūtras*. Others may be more profound in their teaching, or more subtle, but the *Lotus Sūtra* is the most awe-inspiring, the most colourful, the most impressive, the most dramatic. One might even go so far as to say that it is perhaps the grandest of all the spiritual documents of mankind. Of it, W. E. Soothill, who was a Christian missionary in China, and one of the first translators of the *sūtra* into English, says:

> From the first chapter we find the *Lotus Sūtra* to be unique in the world of religious literature. A magnificent apocalyptic, it presents a spiritual drama of the highest order, with the universe as its

stage, eternity as its period, and Buddhas, gods, men, devils, as the dramatis personae. From the most distant worlds and from past aeons, the eternal Buddhas throng the stage to hear the mighty Buddha proclaim his ancient and eternal Truth. Bodhisattvas flock to his feet, gods from the heavens, men from all quarters of the earth, the tortured from the deepest hells, the demons themselves crowd to hear the tones of the Glorious One.[343]

The scene of the *sutra* is the Vulture's Peak, that great rocky crag overlooking Rājagṛha in northern India. You can still go there today; I've stood there myself in the evening, looking out over the valley, and certainly a very peaceful and very solitary, very sublime spot it still is. It was the scene of many discourses given by the historical Buddha to his more intimate disciples. But in the *Lotus Sūtra* it isn't just an earthly mountain, it isn't just a rocky crag. It symbolizes the very summit of conditioned existence.

As the *sutra* opens, we see the Buddha surrounded by twelve thousand *arhants* – that is, twelve thousand 'saints' who, according to the traditional definition, have realized Nirvāṇa for their own sake alone, as well as by eighty thousand bodhisattvas, and tens of thousands of gods and other non-human beings with their followers. And on this occasion, seated on the Vulture's Peak, surrounded by this great congregation, the Buddha, Śākyamuni Buddha, delivers a discourse, at the conclusion of which, as so often happens in a Mahāyāna *sutra*, we're told that flowers rain down from the heavens and the whole universe shakes. Then the Buddha closes his eyes, the smile almost fades from his lips, and for a long, long time he remains immersed in meditation. And as he is in that state of profound meditation, a ray of white light issues from between his eyebrows and lights up the entire universe, revealing in the infinitude of space innumerable world systems in all directions. And in each of these world systems revealed by this white light is seen a Buddha teaching the Dharma to his disciples, and a bodhisattva sacrificing life and limbs for the sake of Supreme Enlightenment.

This great marvel, this apocalyptic vision, having taken place, the Buddha then reveals to the great assembly a higher, more esoteric, more profound teaching than has ever been given before. Some of the disciples are able to accept this teaching immediately, but others are not. Indeed, they react against it so strongly that they simply walk out – a very significant episode. But to the others, those who have been able to receive the teaching, the Buddha gives a prediction, a prediction of a particular kind typical of Mahāyāna *sūtras*.

This kind of prediction usually follows upon a bodhisattva's making his vow, whether in the form of the four great vows or any other form, in the presence of a living Buddha. The Buddha in whose presence the bodhisattva has made his vow then tells that particular bodhisattva what his name will be when he too becomes a Buddha, what the name of his Buddha-field will be, and what his aeon or *kalpa* will be called. On this particular occasion, Śāriputra, for example (who, of course, is in fact an *arhant* rather than a bodhisattva) is told that he will become a Buddha known as Lotus Radiance, that his Buddha-field will be called the Pure, and that his aeon will be called the Great Jewel-Adorned Aeon.

There are still greater revelations to come. A third of the way through the *sūtra* there occurs the most impressively dramatic scene of the whole pageant. Suddenly there appears a great stupa (a stupa being a sort of reliquary in which the relics of a Buddha are kept), springing up out of the earth and towering way up into the sky, like a huge mountain. It is made, we are told, of the seven precious things: gold, silver, lapis lazuli, crystal, and so on. Not only that; it is magnificently adorned, and from it come light, fragrance, and music, which fill the entire earth. While the disciples are still marvelling at this incredible sight, from the stupa there comes forth a mighty voice, praising Śākyamuni Buddha for preaching the *Lotus Sūtra*, and bearing witness to the truth of what he has said.

You can imagine the astonishment, even the consternation, of the disciples, advanced though they are, when all this happens. But after they've got over their surprise, one of them has the presence of mind to ask what it all means, and Śākyamuni Buddha explains that the stupa contains the intact body of an ancient Buddha called Abundant Treasures. Furthermore, he says that this Abundant Treasures lived millions of years ago, and made a great vow that after his *parinirvāṇa* he would appear whenever and wherever the *Lotus Sūtra* was taught and would bear witness to the truth of its teaching.

The disciples are very interested to hear this and they naturally wish to see the Buddha Abundant Treasures. But it seems that Abundant Treasures has made another vow, to the effect that if a Buddha in whose presence his stupa appears wishes to show Abundant Treasures to his disciples, a certain condition must first be fulfilled: the Buddha who wishes to open the stupa must cause all the Buddhas who have emanated from him and who are preaching the Dharma throughout the universe to return and assemble in one place.

This condition Śākyamuni Buddha, 'our' Buddha, fulfils. He emits another ray of light from his forehead that illuminates innumerable pure Buddha-fields in the ten directions of space, revealing all the Buddhas there. And all these Buddhas, in all the directions of space, realize the significance of the message. They all tell their own bodhisattvas that they must go now to the Sahā-world. (*Sahā* means 'endurance' or 'suffering', and our world is given this name because among all the worlds, according to the Mahāyāna *sūtras*, it is a particularly unpleasant one, and one is not at all fortunate to be born here.)

Our world is then purified, we are told, for the reception of those bodhisattvas. The earth is transformed into a pure blue radiance like that of lapis lazuli, marked off neatly in squares with beautiful golden cords, and it is adorned not just with ordinary trees but with trees made entirely of jewels, all bright and shining. Gods and men, we are told, other than those of the congregation, are transferred elsewhere, whatever that may mean. Villages, towns, mountains, rivers, and forests just disappear; and the earth smokes with incense, and is strewn with heavenly flowers.

When this process of purification has taken place, five hundred Buddhas arrive from these distant worlds or Buddha-fields, each attended by a great bodhisattva, and take their seats on magnificent lion thrones under jewel trees. But once these five hundred are seated the available space has been used up, and the Buddhas have hardly begun to arrive. What is Śākyamuni Buddha to do?

Well, we are told that he purifies and transforms untold millions of worlds in the ten directions of space to accommodate all the incoming Buddhas. And when this has been done, when they've all assembled, all the hundreds of thousands of them, Śākyamuni Buddha ascends into the sky as high as the door of the stupa, and draws the bolt of the door, with a sound like ten thousand thunders. The door opens, and inside is seen the intact body of the ancient Buddha Abundant Treasures. Śākyamuni takes his seat beside Abundant Treasures, and the whole congregation then scatters flowers on the two Buddhas.

So there's this great stupa, towering in the sky, with the Buddha Abundant Treasures seated in it and Śākyamuni Buddha seated beside him. But the congregation is still right down on the ground, and they all wish, we are told, to be raised to the level of those two Buddhas. Exerting his supra-normal power, Śākyamuni Buddha therefore raises the whole assembly into the sky, at the same time asking them, in a loud voice, a very important question.

I'm afraid we'll have to leave them there. I've already told more of the story than our present purpose really requires. But perhaps enough has been said to make it clear that in the Buddhist vision the activities of the bodhisattvas, like those of the Buddhas, are not confined to this world. Many people find episodes like these from the *Lotus Sūtra* rather surprising when they first come across them. Somehow they are not quite what one imagines that a Buddhist scripture will be like. Perhaps Buddhist literature is generally expected to be rather abstruse and philosophical and conceptual, not to say analytical and academic. But the *Lotus Sūtra* seems to read more like science fiction – transcendental science fiction of course.[344]

This reminds me of a time when I was staying in Bombay with a Polish friend of mine. One day he gave me a book called *Star Maker* by Olaf Stapledon – a comparatively early but good example of science fiction. And my friend said, 'You'll like this. It's just like a Mahāyāna *sūtra*.' And indeed when I read it I found that the comparison was a fair one. Of course, there is a great deal of difference between the Mahāyāna *sūtras* and even the best science fiction because the former have a definite spiritual, not to say transcendental, content. But there are a number of important resemblances too. Both the Mahāyāna *sūtras* and science fiction go beyond this particular planet; and both of them tend to show humanity as ranging backwards and forwards in time, and throughout space, from one side, as it were, to the other, which can be a very liberating experience even if only imaginatively realized.

Every so often these days there's a flurry of interest in unidentified flying objects. Some people believe that they originate from Venus or even more distant parts of the universe, and that they are sent or occupied by beings more highly evolved than ourselves. Many films and television programmes reflect the general interest in time and space travel. But one could say that all these modern myths have the same general significance: the extrapolation of consciousness beyond the usual frontiers into the universe at large.

The bodhisattva ranges not only from world to world, from one universe to another, but from one plane of existence to another. This is depicted in one particular version of the Tibetan wheel of life. Some paintings of the wheel show the bodhisattva Avalokiteśvara appearing in each of the realms: the realm of the gods, the titans, the animals, the hell-beings, the hungry ghosts, and the human realm. Avalokiteśvara's name means 'the lord who looks down in compassion', 'the hearer of the cries of the world'; he is the embodiment of compassion; and he appears among the beings of each plane, each realm, in a Buddha-form appropriate to their particular needs.

Among the gods he appears as a white Buddha playing a stringed instrument – a lute or a sort of guitar, to judge from the illustrations. And the music he plays is the melody of impermanence. The gods are very long-lived, and they have a happy life, so they tend to forget that one day it will come to an end and they will die. They have to be reminded of the impermanence of things, so that they will start thinking about and practising the Dharma. Hence among the gods Avalokiteśvara, the Bodhisattva of Compassion, appears as a white Buddha playing a sort of guitar – a rather unconventional image for a Buddha, it has to be said.

Then among the titans, those great war-like beings who are perpetually fighting with the gods for the possession of the wish-fulfilling tree, Avalokiteśvara appears as a green Buddha brandishing a flaming sword – the sword of knowledge. He is, as it were, saying to the *asuras*, the titans, 'All right, you are trying to defeat the gods, you are very warlike. Well, you don't have to give up fighting, but why don't you try to gain true victory – the true victory that is gained only through knowledge?' So he brandishes among them the flaming sword of spiritual knowledge that wins true spiritual victory, as it were saying to all these warring multitudes, these giants, even perhaps to the great nations of today, that one doesn't gain victory by conquering others. One gains victory by conquering oneself – that is the true spiritual victory.[345]

Then, among animals Avalokiteśvara appears as a blue Buddha, and he shows the animals a book. The book of course represents knowledge, understanding, culture, everything that distinguishes the human from the animal; and Avalokiteśvara shows it, as it were, not only to animals but to animal-like human beings, indicating the next stage, the next level of evolution, that will lead them on to the spiritual path.

Fourthly, Avalokiteśvara appears among the beings in states of suffering, states of torment, as a smoke-coloured Buddha, and he showers upon them ambrosia, which cools and alleviates their suffering. When people are suffering and tormented, there is no use in preaching to them. What you must do, the only thing you can do, is to try to alleviate their suffering.

Similarly, when Avalokiteśvara appears among the hungry ghosts as a red Buddha, he regales them with food and drink that they can actually consume. (Hungry ghosts are said to be in the very unpleasant predicament of being perpetually starving, but having mouths no bigger than pinheads. Any food or drink they manage to swallow turns to sharp daggers in their stomachs.) Swami Vivekananda once said, 'It's a sin to preach religion to a starving man.' Give him something to eat and drink first, and then give him the gift of the Dharma.

Lastly, Avalokiteśvara appears among human beings as a yellow Buddha, carrying the staff and begging-bowl of a religious mendicant. This symbolizes the spiritual life, the path to Enlightenment which only human beings are capable of following in its entirety. (To make spiritual progress, the beings of other realms or planes of existence must be reborn as human beings.)[346]

Avalokiteśvara is not the only archetypal bodhisattva who symbolizes compassion. There is also, for example, the bodhisattva Kṣitigarbha, who is one of the most popular bodhisattvas in the Far East. His name means 'earth-womb', and he is connected with the depths, in fact with hell. Kṣitigarbha's concern is to rescue those who appear to be irrecoverably lost. He descends into the depths of sentient existence, goes right down into the depths of insanity, despair, and torment, in order to remedy, even transform, conditions there. The figure of Kṣitigarbha, this great bodhisattva who descends into the depths of hell, represents the transforming power of the Buddha's influence, the bodhisattva's influence, even under the most difficult and unfavourable circumstances.[347]

Thus the bodhisattva ideal, as depicted in the Mahāyāna scriptures, is not limited by time or space. The bodhisattva traverses all time, all space, even all worlds, ascending into the highest heights and plumbing the lowest depths. The bodhisattva ideal exemplifies, more perhaps than any other spiritual ideal, the potential for Enlightenment of humanity, and it exemplifies it in the clearest, the most unmistakable, the most glorious manner possible. And even more than that. The bodhisattva ideal is not just an ideal for human life and conduct, though it includes that. The figure of the bodhisattva is a sort of force, the activity of which is not limited to this world or this plane, but which is at work throughout space, in all worlds. One can call it the *bodhicitta*, the will to Enlightenment; one can call it what one likes. One can, indeed, call it the Dharma, for that is what it is. But whatever one calls it, one may be sure that it works from eternity to eternity, leading not only this world, not only the human race, but the whole of existence, to higher and ever higher levels of being. It is the Unconditioned at work in the midst of the conditioned; it is light at work in the heart of darkness.

What is the Sangha?

PART I
THE GROUP AND THE
SPIRITUAL COMMUNITY

INTRODUCTION

I first came to know about Buddhism in the 1930s, when I was ten or eleven. What I learned – from a series of articles in an encyclopaedia – did not affect me very deeply at the time. However, when I was sixteen I read two Buddhist texts called the *Diamond Sūtra* and the *Sūtra of Huineng*, and these made a very deep impression on me indeed. In fact, I can go so far as to say that through them I had my first glimpse of what is known in the Buddhist tradition as Perfect Vision, my first direct insight into the true nature of reality. From that time onwards I considered myself a Buddhist, but it was fully two years before I came into direct contact with other Buddhists. For two years I was on my own – reading, learning, trying to understand, and even eventually writing about Buddhism. I read everything I could lay my hands on that might throw light on it, including material from many other spiritual traditions.[348]

Buddhism in the West has moved on a lot since then. For one thing, never before in the history of the world has it been possible to have translations of the great spiritual classics of East and West, all in cheap editions on one's own bookshelf, to read at one's leisure. All these spiritual traditions and teachings have suddenly found themselves in the melting pot together, all acting upon and influencing one another. And although there are many more Buddhist organizations these days, many people's first contact with the Buddha's teaching still comes about through reading; personal contact with Buddhists tends to come rather later. Those who live in big cities may be able to find Buddhist groups fairly easily, but beyond the main conurbations many people have to get on with their practice as best they can on their own, perhaps for many years. I have met individuals who have read about Buddhism, and even tried to practise meditation, for ten or fifteen years, without meeting a single Buddhist during that time.

We are conditioned by our experience, especially our early experience, and this is true even of our experience of Buddhism. If you have become accustomed to studying alone, meditating alone, thinking your own thoughts without testing them against the thoughts of others, or having any real communication with like-minded people, you may question the necessity of joining a group at all, even a Buddhist group. You may feel that you're not the kind of person who joins groups.

But, as I discovered myself when I did finally meet other practising Buddhists, contact with other people who are following the Buddhist path makes a world of difference to one's own ability to do so. Indeed, the sangha, the spiritual community, has from the very beginning of the Buddhist tradition been given an equal place with the two other great ideals of Buddhism: the Buddha, who represents the ideal of Enlightenment, and the Dharma, the way or teaching that leads to Enlightenment.

The term 'sangha' has come to mean a number of different things. In its most specific sense it refers to the men and women who, throughout Buddhist history, have gained Enlightenment through following the Buddha's teaching. It is also used in some Buddhist traditions to refer to the monastic community, as distinct from the laity; and it is perhaps most commonly used simply to signify the Buddhist community as a whole. But in considering the question 'What is the sangha?' we will be contemplating the essential nature of sangha – that is, the nature of the relationship between the individual Buddhist and the wider collectivity of Buddhist practitioners. As we will see, the sangha ideally consists of developing individuals, and its purpose is not to become a powerful organization, a group, but to further the development of the individual towards the ultimate goal of liberation for the sake of all beings.

To explore the nature of the sangha in these terms, we will need to examine some basic questions. For example, what is the difference between a group and a spiritual community? And what is it to be an individual? The first part of this book will be dedicated to drawing the distinction between the group and the spiritual community, and will include a brief history of spiritual communities, both Buddhist and non-Buddhist, as well as the beginnings of a definition of individuality. The second part will focus on the true individual – that is, what it is to be truly human – in the context of the evolution of consciousness, and will explore in various ways the qualities associated with individuality.

In its broadest sense, sangha can be said to be about communication, about relationships. The third and final part of this book will therefore consider some of the ethical implications of the individual Buddhist's relationship to others: friends, spouses, family, fellow workers, and spiritual teachers. And in our concluding chapters, we will consider briefly the relationship of the individual Buddhist and the spiritual community to the world as a whole, and at least open up the possibility that the Buddhist sangha may play a part in improving the situation in which, globally speaking, we find ourselves.

I

THE SANGHA JEWEL

THE THREE MOST PRECIOUS THINGS

Every religion or spiritual tradition has certain concepts, symbols, credal forms, and ideals that enshrine its highest values. The sangha is one of the three ideals that lie at the heart of Buddhism.

The first of these three is the ideal of Enlightenment, a state of wisdom that is one with compassion, and compassion that is one with wisdom: an intuitive understanding of ultimate reality in its absolute depth and in all its manifestations. This ideal is represented not by any kind of divinity – not by 'God' or a prophet or incarnation or son of God – nor simply by a wise and compassionate human being, but by a man who became what has come to be called a Buddha. The historical Buddha was an ordinary human being who, through his own efforts, transcended his human limitations, to become for Buddhists the symbol of reality itself. To accept the Buddha Jewel as an ideal is to acknowledge that it is relevant to us personally, and that we ourselves can aim to become Enlightened. The Buddha, in short, shows us what we can become.

The second great Buddhist ideal is that of the Dharma. The word has a bewildering number of meanings, including attribute, law, principle, custom, practice, tradition, duty, and ultimate element of existence.[349] But here it means the path to Enlightenment – the sum total of all those practices, procedures, methods, and exercises that help us towards the realization of Enlightenment.

This way of defining the Buddha's teaching is central to any clear understanding of Buddhism. It is very easy to fall into a doctrinaire attitude and start saying, 'Such and such a way of doing things *is* Buddhism', but someone from a different school of Buddhism might say just the opposite. Some Buddhists will tell you, 'It all depends on your own effort', while others will say, 'Any effort you make simply builds up the strength of your delusion – you just have to realize that there is no self to make an effort.' So how do we work our way through such conflicting messages? How do we get to what the Buddha truly meant to communicate? Fortunately for us, this question occurred to one of the Buddha's original disciples, his old foster-mother and aunt, Mahāprajāpatī – because differences of opinion as to what the Buddha actually taught existed even in his own day. She, of course, was able to go straight to the source of all these different ways of understanding the Dharma. She asked the Buddha himself, 'How do we judge what is the Dharma and what isn't?' And he said, 'It's very simple. Those teachings which when put into practice (not speculated about, but *put into practice*) lead to such things as detachment, decrease of worldly gains, frugality, content, patience, energy, and delight in good – these, you may be sure, are my Dharma. And the opposites of these things are not my Dharma.'[350]

The Buddha here sets out the goals of the spiritual life in precise terms, and the means to those ends have to be equally precise. They also have to be functional; by definition, Buddhist practice has to work. This is why the Buddha described the Dharma on another occasion as being like a raft;[351] without it there is no means of getting across the raging torrent of craving, hatred, and delusion, but still it is only the means – it is not an end in itself. Once it has carried you over to Enlightenment, so to speak, it can be discarded; it is no further use to you personally.

The Mahāyānists took the Buddha's advice to Mahāprajāpatī to a significant conclusion. Taking one of the rock edicts of the great Indian emperor Aśoka, which reads, 'Whatever the Buddha has said is well said,'[352] they reversed it, to say, 'Whatever is well said (*suvacana*) is the word of the Buddha (*buddhavacana*).'[353] This means, of course, that we have to be very careful about what we take to be 'well said'. The care with which the Dharma should be interpreted can be expressed by translating the term as 'the real truth'. An authentic expression of the Dharma will always express the real truth about human existence. This is the second great Buddhist ideal.

And the third great ideal of the Buddhist life is the sangha. The word sangha means 'association' or 'society'. It is not an exclusively Buddhist term, being common to many ancient and modern Indian languages. In the context of Buddhism, however, the sangha in its broadest sense is the ideal of spiritual community, the fellowship of those who follow basically the same path towards ultimately the same goal. It may come as a surprise that the spiritual community should be regarded as being so very important – as important, indeed, as the ideal of Buddhahood itself, and as the Buddha's teaching. But from the very beginning the Buddha clearly regarded the sangha as being of supreme importance. He set great store by his disciples, especially his Enlightened disciples, insisting that any honour he received should be shared with them. On one occasion, someone wanted to offer him some rather valuable robes, and he said, 'No, don't offer them to me; offer them to the sangha – the merit of such an offering will be the greater.'[354] The true significance of this is not that members of the sangha are to be treated as VIPs. Rather, it points to the great value the Buddha placed on spiritual community, and specifically on spiritual friendship. As we shall see – and, I hope, come to feel – spiritual friendship is, as the Buddha said, the whole of the spiritual life.

The ideals of the Buddha, Dharma, and Sangha are known in Sanskrit as the *triratna*, the Three Jewels or (as the Chinese translators put it) the three most precious things. They are called this because as far as the Buddhist tradition is concerned they embody the highest values of existence – or three aspects of the one ultimate value. Relating to them makes everything else worthwhile. Everything else exists for the sake of the essence, the reality, they represent. Every Buddhist subject or practice you could possibly think of is connected with one or more of these Three Jewels.

They come in a definite order. The Buddha Jewel came into existence first, when Siddhārtha Gautama gained Enlightenment under the bodhi tree. Then, two months later, when he delivered his first discourse to five old friends, the five ascetics, in the deer park at Sarnath, near Benares, the second Jewel, the Dharma, appeared.[355] And the Sangha Jewel arrived last of all, when those five ascetics, one by one, bowed to him and said, 'Accept me as your follower.'

This pattern tends to be repeated in the way Buddhism is introduced into a new part of the world. In Europe, for example, it was at the end of the eighteenth century that the Buddha became generally (though imperfectly) known. Gradually it was realized that the Buddha was an Indian teacher and that, for instance, the Buddha revered in Sri Lanka was the same as the figure known in China as Fo. But his teaching was not studied until the middle of the nineteenth century, and it still took quite some time for the people who had become interested in the Dharma to begin to form Buddhist societies, which constituted the rudimentary beginnings of a sangha. The Buddhist Society in Eccleston Square, London, founded in 1924, is probably the oldest of these. Even in the West today there is still some way to go in the formation of an effective Buddhist sangha. Indeed, not all Western Buddhists recognize the importance of sangha as providing the conditions necessary to support an effective Buddhist life.

WHAT IS THE BUDDHIST LIFE?

The question 'What is the Buddhist life?' can be answered in one word. It is a *committed* life. A Buddhist is not someone who has merely been born into a Buddhist family, or who has made an academic study of Buddhism and knows a great deal about its history and doctrines. Nor is a Buddhist someone who dabbles in Buddhism, who has a smattering of knowledge about it and airs their views on the subject, who mixes up Buddhism with Christianity, or Vedanta, or New Age ideas of one kind or another. A Buddhist is someone who is committed to the Three Jewels, who 'goes for Refuge' to them (in the traditional phrase) and who, as an expression of that going for Refuge, seeks to observe the ethical precepts of Buddhism. This is the heart of the matter.

Going for Refuge to the Buddha means accepting the Buddha and no other as one's ultimate spiritual guide and exemplar. Going for Refuge to the Dharma means doing one's utmost to understand, practise, and realize the fundamental import of the Buddha's teaching. And Going for Refuge to the Sangha means looking for inspiration and guidance to those followers of the Buddha, both past and present, who are spiritually more advanced than oneself.

Another term for the Three Jewels is the 'Three Refuges' (*triśaraṇa* in Sanskrit).[356] Referring to the Buddha, Dharma, and Sangha as jewels reflects how precious they are. But if you have really recognized their preciousness, that recognition will change you. If you truly regard something as valuable, you act as though it really is so. If you are convinced that the Three Jewels represent the three highest values of existence, you will act upon that conviction, and this act is what is known as Going for Refuge. It is equivalent to what in other religious systems is known as 'conversion'.[357]

In this context the word 'refuge', which is the literal translation of the original Sanskrit term śaraṇa, is not about running away, seeking escape from the harsh realities of life through losing oneself in pseudo-spiritual fantasies. Rather, it represents two great shifts in one's being. These are, firstly, the recognition that permanence, unchanging identity, unalloyed bliss, and pure beauty are to be found nowhere in mundane existence but only in the transcendental nirvāṇic realm; and secondly, the wholehearted resolve to make the great transition from the one to the other, from the mundane to the transcendental.

In many traditionally Buddhist countries this profound change of heart is institutionalized in the form of a ceremony called 'taking the Refuges'. In this form it tends to get trivialized. Any public meeting, even a political meeting, it is sad to say, will start with everyone 'taking' the Refuges and Precepts – that is, reciting them – just to show that they are all good Buddhists. Another way that Going for Refuge gets diminished is when it is taken as something you do once and for all, like baptism in Christianity, so that it is assumed that when you have 'taken the Refuges' from a monk, you are safely a Buddhist.

As a committed Buddhist one goes for Refuge – or tries to – all the time. As one's appreciation of the Three Jewels grows, one's Going for Refuge becomes correspondingly more profound, and this can sometimes have surprising results. It may mean that what brings you to Buddhism in the first place becomes not more but less important, as your deepening understanding comes to displace the comparatively superficial appreciation of Buddhism that was sufficient to get you going in the first place.

For instance, one may have heard it said that whereas Christianity is a religion of faith, Buddhism is a religion of reason, and one may be drawn to Buddhism on that basis. As one goes more deeply into it, one finds that while reason is given an honoured place in Buddhism, it is by no means enthroned as its governing principle, but one remains a

Buddhist because one has gone deep enough not only to be able to put reason in its proper place, but also to find other aspects of Buddhist practice profoundly meaningful.

Thus Going for Refuge is an experience that is deepening and growing more multidimensional all the time. One accepts the ideal of Enlightened humanity, exemplified by the historical Buddha, as being more and more relevant to oneself personally; one takes that ideal as one's personal goal in life more and more to heart; and one tries to practise the Dharma in such a way as to realize that ideal more and more effectively.

A famous south Indian teacher called Swami Ramdas, who died in the early sixties, was once asked, 'Why is it that so many people who take up the spiritual life don't make any real progress? Though they go on with it year after year, they just seem to be standing still. Why?' His answer was simple and uncompromising. 'There are two reasons,' he said. 'In the first place, they have no clearly defined ultimate objective towards which they want to work. Secondly, they have no clearly defined way of getting there.'

So far as Buddhism is concerned, that goal is Buddhahood, and the way of getting there is the Dharma. These are the two necessary ingredients of one's spiritual life as a Buddhist. They may even appear to be sufficient. Why, then, should one have to go for Refuge to the Sangha as well? How does Going for Refuge to a spiritual community help us?

WHY GO FOR REFUGE TO THE SANGHA?

It has been said that the history of Buddhist philosophy can be summed up as the struggle between Buddhism and the abstract noun. So, to guard against the ubiquitous enemy, abstraction, we should be clear that when we speak of the spiritual community, we are not referring to some ethereal entity apart from the people who comprise it. Membership of a community means relationship with people within that community. We can now put our question another way: how is it that entering into relationship with other people who hold a common ideal and follow a common path should help us in our spiritual life?

In a sense, it comes down to the simple saying: 'Birds of a feather flock together.' That is how they survive. There was an occasion when the Buddha addressed the Vajjians, a tribe from the Vaiśālī area who had come under some threat. Among other things, he told them that they would prosper as long as they continued to meet regularly, in full and frequent assemblies, conducting their business in harmony and dispersing in harmony. Afterwards he went on to apply the same criteria to the spiritual survival of the sangha.[358]

The heart of the sangha is *kalyāṇa mitratā*, a very beautiful phrase. It is less a philosophical term than a poetic one. *Kalyāṇa* means beautiful, charming, auspicious, helpful, morally good. Thus the connotations are aesthetic, moral, and religious. The term covers much the same ground as the Greek expression *kalos kai agathos*, which means 'good and beautiful'. *Mitratā* means simply friendship or companionship. *Kalyāṇa mitratā* therefore means something like 'beautiful friendship', or 'morally good companionship', or simply 'spiritual friendship'. There is an exchange between the Buddha and his disciple Ānanda which spells out its importance in the Buddha's eyes. Ānanda was the Buddha's cousin and became his attendant for the last twenty years of the Buddha's life. He accompanied the Buddha wherever he went, and they had an understanding that if by any chance Ānanda was not present when the Buddha delivered a discourse, or discussed the Dharma with anyone, when they were alone together the Buddha would repeat to Ānanda everything he had said. Ānanda had an astonishingly retentive memory. Indeed, it is said that we owe our knowledge of the Buddha's teachings to him. Because he made a point of listening to everything the Buddha said, storing it away in his memory so that he could repeat it later on for the benefit of others, his testimony was used to authenticate the teachings that were preserved after the Buddha's death.

On this particular occasion the Buddha and Ānanda were on their own when Ānanda suddenly came out with something to which he had obviously given a bit of thought. He said, 'Lord, I think that *kalyāṇa mitratā* is half the spiritual life.' And then one presumes that he sat back and waited for some kind of appreciative affirmation from the Buddha. It seemed to Ānanda that what he had said was incontrovertible: having like-minded people around you who are also trying to grow and develop must be half the battle won. But the Buddha said, 'Ānanda, you're wrong. *Kalyāṇa mitratā* is not half the spiritual life; it's the whole of it.'[359]

Why is this? Of course we learn from those we associate with, especially those who are more mature than we are, and learning will clearly be important if we are to make progress in the spiritual life. But in what does 'progress in the spiritual life' really consist? What are we *really* learning? The knowledge we need, in the end, is self-knowledge. And the real significance of the deep individual-to-individual contact that Going for Refuge to the Sangha involves lies in the simple fact that we get to know ourselves best in relation to other people. If you spent your whole life alone on a desert island, in a sense you would never really know yourself. As it is, though, we have all had the experience of clarifying our ideas through discussion – and even of discovering that we knew more than we thought we did – simply through trying to communicate with another person. It is as though trying to communicate activates an understanding that is already there but has never manifested until now, and even brings forth new aspects of oneself – aspects which one only ever discovers as a result of contact with another person. Through meeting the challenge of real communication, one comes to know oneself better.

It is not only a matter of activating one's understanding. Meeting certain people can disturb aspects of ourselves that had been rather deeply buried. We say that a particular kind of person 'brings out the worst in us'. Perhaps nothing is said, but they somehow touch a raw nerve. It can be a shock to realize what that individual has evoked in us, to find ourselves behaving in a way that we like to think is uncharacteristic of us, even expressing hatred or contempt towards the person who has triggered this behaviour. Of course, that unpleasant side of us was always there, but it needed that person to bring it to the surface. In this apparently negative but highly spiritually beneficial way too, other people can introduce us to ourselves. We cannot transform ourselves unless we have a full sense of what lies within us.

Conversely, certain people seem to 'bring out the best in us'. Again, nothing necessarily needs to be said, but just being with them makes us feel lighter, more cheerful, more energetic, more positive. Other people can also sometimes activate resources of kindness and decency that we didn't know we had in us. And in a specifically Buddhist context, there will be certain people who activate a quality of faith in us simply through contact with their own faith. Something that was not active before is stirred up.

The sangha is necessary, in short, because personal relationships are necessary for human development. This applies at all levels – cultural, psychological, and spiritual. The vast majority of people undoubtedly develop most rapidly, and even most easily, in the company of others – or at least in contact with others. Not that it is impossible to develop entirely on one's own; indeed, there is a Buddhist term for those who do so: *pratyekabuddhas*, private or solitary Buddhas.[360] However, although there are a number of canonical references to them, it is significant that all these solitary Buddhas are located in the remote and legendary past. There appear to be no historical examples.

We generally need the stimulation, reassurance, and enthusiasm of others who are going in the same direction as we are. We are naturally stimulated by someone who shares our special interest in something. Even though we still have to put in the effort ourselves, at least we see the point of it more clearly – we are less undermined by doubts. Membership of the sangha also gives us the opportunity to serve others, to express our generosity and helpfulness. Even in such a simple activity as providing tea and biscuits at a Buddhist festival, we can discover in ourselves the capacity for generosity, altruism, and general positivity.

Thus the sangha is there to help us know ourselves and express ourselves better. It is able to do this because everyone who participates in it is committed to the Buddha as the ideal of self-knowledge in the highest and deepest sense, and to the Dharma, the various principles and practices by which that self-knowledge may be achieved. A common allegiance to the first two Refuges constitutes the bond of unity between the members of the spiritual community. We are all following – albeit at different stages – the same path to the same ultimate goal.

By the same token, if one is not really aiming for Enlightenment, and not really trying to practise the Dharma, then one may say that one is committed to these ideals, but whatever one may say, one is no more a member of the sangha than a donkey following a herd of cows can be a member of that herd. This is the image used by the Buddha in the *Aṅguttara Nikāya*: as he puts it, 'The donkey may say, "I am a cow too, I am a cow too" … but neither in his horns nor in his hoofs is he anything like a cow, whatever he may say.' Likewise, simply reciting the Refuges does not make one a member of the sangha. The bond is inner and spiritual.[361]

At a certain point in our development, however much we may meditate and read books about spiritual practice, we have to recognize that these are not enough. There is no doubt that we can learn a lot on our own, but if we are to grow spiritually in a fully rounded way, we eventually have to experience the vital part that communication has to play in our spiritual life. The following verse comes from the *Dhammapada*, a very early collection of the Buddha's teachings, here quoted in the original Pāli:

Sukho buddhānamuppādo,
sukhā saddhammadesanā.
Sukhā saṅghassa sāmaggī,
samaggānaṃ tapo sukho.[362]

The first line means 'Happy – or blissful, or blessed (*sukho*) – is the arising of the Buddhas.' When someone becomes a Buddha, this is a happy thing for all humanity. The second line may be translated 'Happy is the preaching of the true doctrine.' The teaching of the Dharma is a blessing for the whole world. The third line is 'Happy is the spiritual community in following a common path.' In the fourth line *tapo* means 'heat' and refers to spiritual practices which are like a fire burning up all impurities. The line therefore runs, 'The blaze of spiritual practice of those on the same path is happy or blessed.'

It is not enough to have a distant idea of Enlightenment, the theory of the Buddha's teaching, or a Buddhist organization. There is no future for Buddhism without a truly united and committed spiritual community, dedicated to practising together. And when Buddhists do come together in the true spirit of the sangha, there is then the possibility of inhabiting, for a while at least, the *dharmadhātu*, the realm of the Dharma. In this realm, all we do is practise the Dharma, all we talk about is the Dharma, and when we are still and silent, we enjoy the Dharma in stillness and silence together. The clouds of stress and anxiety that so often hang over mundane life are dispersed, and the fountains of inspiration within our hearts are renewed.

2

THE TRADITIONAL SANGHA

CELEBRATING THE SANGHA REFUGE

It is easy enough to make a decision to commit oneself to the Three Jewels. However, it is by no means so easy to sustain that commitment. If we are not careful, the vision fades, we lose momentum, we become distracted and restless, or we get comfortable and settle down, and our commitment is lost. It is therefore absolutely essential that we should set up our lives to include regular reminders of our original commitment. There are many ways of doing this – in fact, one might argue that Buddhist practice in all its aspects is designed to do it – but one traditional reminder is the celebration of Buddhist festivals.

The Buddha's Enlightenment is commemorated on the full moon day of the Indian month Vaiśākha, which occurs in April or May. On this anniversary, otherwise known as Buddha Jayanti, we remind ourselves of what a human being is capable of attaining, and thus what we ourselves can aspire to. The Buddha's teaching, the Dharma, is celebrated on the full-moon day of the Indian month Āṣāḍha, in June or July, and this too is an anniversary, commemorating the Buddha's first discourse, his first teaching to humanity. As for the sangha, its festival, which reminds us of all those who have followed the path to Enlightenment before us, and celebrates the very existence of the spiritual community, comes on the full-moon day of Kārttika (October-November). Sangha Day is different from the other two major festivals in that it does not commemorate a specific event in the life of the Buddha. Instead, it recalls an annual event in the life of the early sangha.

If we go back in imagination to the first spiritual community that gathered around the Buddha, we find that it was composed of what I shall call part-timers and full-timers. In the Buddha's time there were many people who aspired to follow the Dharma but – by choice or through circumstance – remained at home. They married, brought up families, worked, and had civic and political responsibilities, and they meditated and practised the Dharma as best they could in those circumstances. They could therefore be described as part-timers. (They were later known as lay disciples.) Other factors being equal, they did not tend to develop spiritually as rapidly as the full-timers, but they did make some progress, and in some cases considerable progress – even more than many of the full-timers.

By contrast, full-timers, who became what we now know as monks and nuns, cut off all connection with home, left family and secular employment, renounced all civic and political duties, and signalled their lifestyle by staining their clothes saffron with an earth dye called *gerumati*, so that people could recognize them for what they were when they came round with their begging-bowls. These full-timers were entirely devoted to the practice of the Dharma. They studied together, they meditated, and they took upon themselves the task of preserving the teachings of the Buddha by memorizing them. Study did not of course involve reading, because there were no books to read. The only way to study the Dharma was to hear it from someone who could recite it to you, so that you could discuss it and eventually memorize it yourself. In the end you would become a sort of living, walking book.

At this time one of the most significant characteristics of these full-timers was that they were peripatetic, wandering from place to place rather than settling down where they found friendly and congenial lay supporters. This way of life was epitomized in an Indian saying:

The water is pure that flows;
The monk is pure who goes.[363]

However, there was a problem with always being on the move: the weather. Once the rainy season in India has arrived – usually sometime in July, but exactly when depends where in the country you are – it rains solidly, torrential rain drumming down for day after day, month after month, until October. It was not a time to be out of doors, unless you had rice to plant, and that would be the case only at the very beginning of the season. Obliged to take shelter like everyone else, the full-timers would stay in one spot during this period, usually in small groups. Thus an annual pattern developed of continuous wandering for eight or nine months, followed by three or four months in a cave, or some kind of shelter made of broad tropical leaves, or a bamboo and thatch cottage in someone's garden. In this way there arose the institution of the rainy-season retreat, the *varṣāvāsa*.

In the course of time quite a number of full-timers would gather together for this retreat – scores or even hundreds of them – all studying and meditating in one place. They would be joined from time to time by local part-timers, for whom the monsoon was also a period of enforced inactivity, and who therefore had more time on their hands than usual. Normally, part-timers were too busy to give very much attention to the Dharma; the instruction they received from wanderers passing through was brief and probably soon forgotten amidst the chores and pleasures of the daily round. The rainy season was therefore a golden opportunity for them to go more deeply into their practice under the spiritual direction of the full-timers.

At the end of the rainy season retreat there would be a great celebration, in two parts. First, the *pravāraṇā* was observed, a ceremony in which everyone begged everybody else's pardon. After three or four months cooped up together, there were inevitably some unresolved tensions and misunderstandings that needed to be cleared up. So the seniormost full-timer would begin the process, saying, 'Venerable sirs, if I have committed any mistake, or offended anybody, or said anything I should not have said in the course of the last three months, please accept my apologies.' Everyone else would then follow his example one by one down to the most junior person present.

The second ceremony of the day was the *kaṭhinacīvaradāna*. *Kaṭhina* means 'difficult', *cīvara* means 'dress' or 'robe', and *dāna* means 'giving' – hence this is the ceremony of 'the difficult giving of robes'. We say 'robes', but in fact everyone wore 'robes' at this time, so the full-timers did not wear some special ecclesiastical garment of the kind that the term 'robe' brings to mind nowadays. The part-timers would make themselves responsible for providing the full-timers with new clothes.

This was considered an especially meritorious offering at this particular time, after the rainy season, and it was called a 'difficult' offering because you had this one opportunity in the year to make it.

There is to this day a traditional procedure in Burma which makes the offering truly difficult. Every year the lay people – or rather the laywomen – set themselves the task of making the robes from scratch, all in the space of the day of the ceremony. They sit up all night spinning cotton into thread; then they weave the cloth from the thread, cut the cloth into strips and sew these together, and finally dye the finished robes ready for the ceremony – all within twenty-four hours. This feat is performed as a mark of their devotion to the sangha of full-timers.

Eventually, for one reason or another, the rainy season retreat began to extend beyond the rainy season itself. The full-timers would sometimes stay on for a while after the rain had stopped, perhaps to pursue some particularly challenging discussion of the Dharma to a conclusion. Then, perhaps, they would want to follow this up with a period of intensive meditation together. In the end they would linger on for so long that the next rainy season would be almost upon them, and they would decide there was little to be gained from going off just for a month or two of wandering. Gradually, their accommodation became less improvised, as temporary thatched huts or leaf shelters were replaced by more substantial dwellings. In this way monasteries came into being, and the full-timers became monks.

Although the full-timers began effectively to be on continuous retreat, or at least to be settled in one place all the time, the tradition of the rainy-season retreat continued to be observed, even – as the Buddhist world expanded – in the desert regions of Mongolia, Tibet, and northern China, where there was very little rain at all. But whether it was called a rainy season retreat or a summer retreat, it would be a time of intensified effort. It became the custom in some countries to give ordinations at the end of the retreat, and the conclusion would invariably consist in the celebration of the *kārttikapūrṇimā*, the full-moon day of Kārttika, or Sangha Day.

THE TRADITIONAL CATEGORIES OF THE SANGHA

The distinction between monks and lay people, full-timers and part-timers, shows that the sangha is not a single, homogeneous body. Indeed, this twofold model has been questioned by Reginald Ray, who in his book *Buddhist Saints in India* presents the sangha instead in terms of a threefold model: laymen, monastics and forest renunciants.[364] By its very nature the sangha comprises people at varying levels of commitment and spiritual attainment, whatever their lifestyle. In the most traditional terms, it is possible to distinguish, for example, what we could call a social level, an ecclesiastical level, and a spiritual level.

The *Mahāsaṅgha*

At the social level, there is the *mahāsaṅgha*, the great assembly, so called because it is great in size. It consists of all those who, with whatever degree of sincerity, go for Refuge to the Three Jewels, and who observe a greater or lesser number of ethical precepts. It is the collectivity of those accepting the spiritual principles or truths of Buddhism, regardless of lifestyle, whether they are monastic or lay, whether they have left the world or remain very much in the world, even, in many cases, very much *of* the world. Thus the *mahāsaṅgha* consists of both full-timers and part-timers, and even people who are no more than nominal Buddhists. This is the broadest level of sangha.

The *Bhikṣu-Bhikṣuṇī* Sangha

Then, at the ecclesiastical level, there is the *bhikṣu-bhikṣuṇī* sangha. The term 'sangha' is sometimes understood as referring specifically to the community of full-timers, usually thought of as the community of monks or the community of nuns. These terms monk and nun will certainly do for many full-timers throughout Buddhist history. The ancient Buddhist monasteries were vast, and until quite recently in Tibet a monastery of five hundred monks would have been considered small. But although a great many *bhikṣus* would have lived in monasteries, the *bhikṣu* sangha has never been a purely monastic order, which is why Reginald Ray includes in his account of the sangha settled monastics and forest renunciants. If we are going to use the term 'monk' in a Buddhist context we need to remember that it carries a broader meaning than it usually does in English.

Today there are two main branches of the monastic order: the Theravāda branch in Sri Lanka, Burma, Thailand, Cambodia, and Laos, and the Sarvāstivāda in Tibet, China, Vietnam, and Korea. There is little difference between the way of life and the rules observed by the monks of these two great traditions. However, Tibetan lamas are not to be confused with *bhikṣus*. 'Lama' simply means spiritual teacher; a lama may sometimes be a monk but not always, especially in the Nyingma and Kagyu Schools. Japan is rather a special case because although the *bhikṣu* ordination was introduced there, it died out and was replaced by the bodhisattva ordination.

There is also an order of nuns, *bhikṣunīs*. This died out in many parts of the Buddhist world even before it could be introduced into Tibet, so that neither Theravāda Buddhism nor Tibetan Buddhism currently has any *bhikṣunī* tradition. But the *bhikṣunī* ordination does survive in Vietnam, China, and Taiwan. (There is much discussion today about the desirability of reinstating the *bhikṣunī* ordination more widely, the controversy turning in part on the traditional subordination of nuns to monks.) Nuns observe roughly the same number of rules as monks, and are shown – at least they should be shown, according to Buddhist tradition – the same kind of respect as monks.

Whether one is living in a monastery, or as a wanderer or hermit, or as a kind of local priest, being a *bhikṣu* or *bhikṣunī* does not in itself signify a particular depth of Going for Refuge. What such members of the monastic sangha have in common is their particular set of ethical precepts. This is the sangha in an ecclesiastical sense: a group of people set apart, as it were, from the world and united as a religious order by a common way of life, especially by a common rule.

Novice monks observe just ten precepts, or thirty-two in some traditions, but when they receive *upasampadā*, full acceptance into the order, they have to follow 150 rules – and in some parts of the Buddhist world all 150 are indeed observed.[365] Many of these rules, however, are no longer relevant, having been devised in the specific conditions of life as a wanderer in northern India 2,500 years ago, and they are often tacitly dropped in modern times.

The four most important rules are the *pārājikas*.[366] *Pārājika* means 'defeat'. If one breaks one of these rules, one is permanently excluded from the order and will have to wait till another lifetime to rejoin it. The first *pārājika* is that one must not intentionally take the life of another human being. The second is that one must not take what is not given – that is, anything of such value that taking it could bring one before a court of law. The third is that one must abstain from any form of sexual intercourse.

These three *pārājikas* are straightforward enough, but the fourth requires a little more explanation. This is that one must not lay false claim to any spiritual attainments. Westerners seem to think nothing of asking people if they are Enlightened, or if they experience *samādhi*. But in the East it is considered spiritual bad manners to talk about one's personal attainments at all, except perhaps with one's closest friends and one's teachers.

The reason for this is illustrated by an episode from the Pāli canon, in which the Buddha's great disciple Sāriputta has apparently spent the whole afternoon in the forest meditating. When he emerges in the evening, he meets Ānanda, who remarks, 'Your face is wonderfully bright today; what have you been doing?' Sāriputta replies, 'I have been meditating in the forest; but while I was meditating, there did not come to me the thought, "I am meditating."'[367] The point he is making is that as long as this thought is there, you are not really meditating, because you haven't progressed beyond the level of the personal 'I', the subjective self. In a sense you are only meditating when there is no one doing it, when it just – as it were – happens.

Moggallāna comments on this by way of a little pun. 'This is how true people speak,' he says, 'They tell the essence – or gist – of the matter (*attha* in Pāli) but they don't bring in the self (*attā*).' With most of us, by contrast, whenever we meditate a bit, or muster a bit of generosity, the self always wriggles in somehow. A momentary inflation takes place as we think '*I* did that' or '*I* had that experience.'

The rest of the rules are secondary to these four basic ones, in the sense that if one breaks them one can make reparation by confessing one's breaches of them to one's fellow monks. Even if one is a hermit, therefore, one should not completely lose touch with the larger sangha.

Buddhist monks and nuns have various duties. Their first duty is to study the Dharma and practise it; they are especially enjoined to practise meditation. Secondly, they are meant to set a good example to the laity. Thirdly, they should preach and teach. Fourthly, they have the responsibility of protecting the local community from unwholesome psychic influences. In cultures where it is taken for granted that we are surrounded by occult forces, it is traditionally believed that while some of these forces are beneficial, others are malign, and that, by their austerities, meditations, and blessings, monks are able to ward off these malign forces and keep them from harming ordinary people. There isn't much call for this service in the West, but it is a very important monastic function in the East.

Finally, monks are supposed to give worldly advice. In the East, whenever things go wrong – your children get into trouble, or you have money problems, or drink problems, or neighbour problems, or relationship problems – it is customary to take your problem to the monks and ask their advice. By virtue of the fact that they don't have these problems themselves, being without wives or children or money, the monks can perhaps be expected to take a more objective view of the situation, just as a spectator has a better view of a football match than any of the players on the pitch.

The scholar Edward Conze once said that without a monastic order Buddhism has no backbone. What we can certainly say is that without full-timers, men and women who are fully committed to Buddhist practice, there will be nothing to build a sangha around. In Britain, the first monks appeared before Buddhist groups had been formed. The pioneer of the English monastic sangha was Allan Bennett, who was ordained as Ananda Maitreya in Burma in 1902 and returned to England in 1908.[368] But since then, in the West the categorization of monks as full-timers and laity as part-timers has largely broken down. And there is a further focus on the sangha that transcends any distinction of lifestyle whatsoever. This is the Āryasaṅgha.

The Āryasaṅgha

The term *ārya* was originally used to refer to a group of tribes who invaded India from the north-west. Owing to the high status of the conquering tribes, *ārya* came to mean 'noble' in a more general sense, and then gradually acquired a spiritual significance and thus came to mean 'holy' as well. The Āryasaṅgha is therefore the community of the noble or holy ones, those who are in contact with the transcendental, those who have a knowledge of the ultimate reality of things.

As it includes lay people as well as monks, the Āryasaṅgha may be said to constitute the spiritual as distinct from the merely ecclesiastical hierarchy of Buddhism. It cannot be categorized in terms of any formal scheme or organizational set-up, but represents an intermediate hierarchy between Buddhahood and unenlightened humanity. Its members may not be in physical contact – they may live not only in different places, but at different times – but the transcendental experiences or attainments they share unite them beyond space and time. The Āryasaṅgha is the sangha in the purely transcendental sense. That is, it is characterized essentially by the quality of wisdom or insight.

The Buddhist path is often divided into three basic elements: ethics, meditation, and wisdom.[369] All three are to be cultivated together, but they culminate in wisdom, as ethics and meditation may be cultivated without wisdom, whereas wisdom cannot be cultivated except on the basis of ethics and meditation. And in its turn, the cultivation of wisdom (*prajñā*) is also divided into three constituents.[370] The first level is that which comes by hearing: *śruta-mayī-prajñā*. The term originally referred to oral learning, characteristic of a preliterate society, but it can be taken to include knowledge picked up from books as well as from conversation and lectures. One learns about the nature of reality, and even about the nature of insight into the nature of reality. At this level, the aim is to get a clear conceptual idea of how things really are.

The second level of wisdom is wisdom that is acquired through one's own thought and reflection: *cintā-mayī-prajñā*. Having heard or read something about the true nature of things, you turn over in your mind what you have heard, and in doing so you start thinking seriously about it and – in time – develop your own insights. And thus you gain a deeper understanding.

The third level of wisdom is that which comes through meditation: *bhāvanā-mayī-prajñā*. This is wisdom above and beyond any purely intellectual insight. It is not thought out; it is not conceptual at all. In fact, it is only when the mind is completely still that true wisdom can begin to arise in the form of flashes of direct insight: intuitive, non-conceptual understanding. In the concentrated mental state which arises through meditation, truth or reality can flash upon the mind directly, unmediated by ideas, thoughts, or even feelings about that reality or truth.

The Āryasaṅgha consists only of those who have experienced this third level of insight. However, nothing in the spiritual life comes all at once. Any mastery, whether of ethics, meditation, or wisdom, comes by degrees. Whatever bumps and jolts we may experience in our spiritual life at times, real progress is steady and systematic. So it is with the experience of insight, and thus with one's progress as a member of the Āryasaṅgha – for there are levels of attainment even within this exalted company. You may experience no more than a feeble flash of insight if your meditation is too weak to sustain anything stronger. But if your concentration in meditation is more powerful, the flash of insight you experience when it comes may be brilliant enough to illumine the depths of reality. It is according to this varying degree of intensity of insight that the different kinds of *ārya pudgala* (noble or holy person) are distinguished.

But how can different degrees of insight be measured? Traditionally, there are two ways: a subjective way and an objective way. Subjectively, insight is measured according to the number of 'fetters' that it breaks. We will examine this approach at the beginning of the next chapter. Objectively, it is measured according to the number of rebirths remaining to be lived through once that level of insight has been attained. This is the measurement we find used to define the sangha in the *Tiratana Vandanā*, the salutation to the Three Jewels, chanted by Buddhists all over the world. In the third section of this the sangha is characterized as 'happily proceeding ... uprightly proceeding ... methodically proceeding ... correctly proceeding'.[371] And it is further declared that the sangha comprises persons at four distinct levels of spiritual development. Each of these levels has its own title:

1. A Stream Entrant or *śrotāpanna* is someone who no longer has to struggle against the current, so to speak. He or she cannot fall back from the course of spiritual progress, and it is said that he or she will gain full Enlightenment within, at the most, seven more rebirths.

2. A once-returner or *sakṛdāgāmin* is someone who will attain liberation in one more lifetime as a human being.

3. A non-returner or *anāgāmin* is someone who will not have to come back to the human plane at all, but will be reborn in the so-called 'pure abodes' (*śuddhāvāsa*) at the peak of the realm of pure form, the *rūpa-dhātu*. He or she attains Nirvāṇa from there.

4. An *arhant* (which means simply 'one worthy of worship') is one who has already reached the goal.

These purely spiritual categories comprise the Āryasaṅgha. But the Buddha also described the Āryasaṅgha in more colourful terms. Comparing the order of monks to a great ocean, he said that just as the great ocean was 'the abode of vast creatures', so the sangha likewise contained spiritual leviathans of its own.[372] These monsters of the deep, so to speak, make up the Āryasaṅgha.

Clearly it is good for the larger sangha to have regular contact with these leviathans, and this must have been one of the advantages envisaged by the Buddha when he directed the sangha to make a point of gathering together in large numbers and on regular occasions.[373] If you are used to living and working in the context of a small local Buddhist community, it is good from time to time to get a sense of the sangha as a whole, and see your own life and work within a much bigger context. It is salutary, if you are used to being a big fish in a small pond, to experience occasionally being a tiny fish in a great ocean. You may sometimes even get a glimpse of what seems to be a real monster – although, of course, who within the sangha is a shrimp and who is a whale is not always easy to tell.

THE BODHISATTVA HIERARCHY

The spiritual hierarchy of the Āryasaṅgha is outlined in the Pāli canon,[374] which is accepted by all schools, and in the Theravāda schools of Sri Lanka, Burma, and Thailand is understood as constituting the full extent of Buddhist canonical literature. All other Buddhist scriptures come under the broad heading of Mahāyāna Buddhism – sometimes called 'developed' Buddhism – as found in Tibet, China, Japan, Korea, Vietnam, and a number of other Eastern countries – and Western ones too, these days. The term Mahāyāna means 'great way', and those schools that did not accept the Mahāyāna scriptures were termed – though not by themselves, naturally – the Hīnayāna or 'little way'.

The concept of the Āryasaṅgha is common to all the different schools of Buddhism, but the Mahāyāna adds to this basic classification a further hierarchy. This is the hierarchy of bodhisattvas, those who are aiming for Enlightenment not just for their own sake, but for the sake of all living beings.[375] This is the bodhisattva ideal. As with the Āryasaṅgha, there are four grades of bodhisattva, according to the number of stages in their development (known as *bhūmis*) that they have traversed.

1. The novice bodhisattva, or *ādikarmika-bodhisattva*, has accepted the bodhisattva ideal in all sincerity, but has yet to achieve the first stage of the path, or any degree of transcendental insight.

2. Bodhisattvas 'of the Path' are those who are progressing between *bhūmis* one to six.

3. 'Irreversible' bodhisattvas are those who have attained the seventh *bhūmi* (out of ten). Just as the Stream Entrant cannot fall back into the lower realms of existence, the irreversible bodhisattva cannot fall back into seeking the goal of individual Enlightenment – a lesser achievement, from the Mahāyāna point of view – but is sure to sustain momentum towards Enlightenment for the sake of all beings.

4. Bodhisattvas 'of the *dharmakāya*'. This is a somewhat abstruse conception, referring to what may be described as personalized aspects of Buddhahood itself. Just as white light may be broken up into the seven colours of the spectrum as seen in a rainbow, the pure white light of Enlightenment may be broken up – as it were – into its own different colours, that is, into the different aspects of the Enlightened mind: love, wisdom, peace, freedom, knowledge, and so on. If the Buddha is a personification of Enlightenment itself, bodhisattvas of the *dharmakāya* represent personifications of individual aspects of that Enlightenment.

The two hierarchies – the Āryasaṅgha and the four levels of the bodhisattva path – clearly overlap to some extent, and some Mahāyāna texts refer to Stream Entrants as 'Hīnayāna bodhisattvas'.

Thus the sangha is a spiritual community existing at various levels, from the social and ecclesiastical level right up to the highest spiritual level, and you go for Refuge to the Sangha by joining it at whatever level you can. Firstly, you can join it at the level of the *mahāsaṅgha* just by being a member of the Buddhist community in a purely formal, external sense. Secondly, you can make a more definite commitment by receiving ordination. In the Theravādin tradition ordination means becoming a monk, but in the Mahāyāna, the bodhisattva ordination is in principle for monk and laity alike, although in practice one finds that the term 'sangha' is often used with reference to monks alone. And thirdly, you may be part of the sangha at the level of the Āryasaṅgha or bodhisattva sangha by virtue of your spiritual attainments.

This, at least, is the threefold sangha according to Buddhist tradition: the general Buddhist community, the monastic sangha, and the Āryasaṅgha of those who have attained Insight. But in practice today one might say that there is a fourth kind of sangha, or an alternative kind to the traditional monastic sangha. Remembering the difference that was evident even in the Buddha's day between full-timers and part-timers, one might call this fourth kind of sangha the full-time sangha or the effective sangha. In the order I founded, the Triratna Buddhist Order, for example, we have chosen to make a break with tradition in the sense that we have only one ordination, whatever one's lifestyle or gender. Finding the idea of a division between monastic and lay unhelpful, we instead lay the emphasis on being a full-time Buddhist, whatever one's way of life.[376] It is this full-time sangha, this effective spiritual community, which one could say consists of those who are effectively Going for Refuge, and provides the context for the individual man or woman's development towards what I would call true individuality.

3
INDIVIDUALITY: THE ESSENCE
OF SANGHA

So far, we have discussed the general principles of the sangha in traditional and historical terms, describing how its basic institutions and concepts have emerged. I now want to look behind those formal institutions and concepts and try to define the deeper principles of spiritual community, independent of any traditional Buddhist context.

The term Āryasaṅgha is usually translated as 'Sangha of noble – or superior – ones', but the translation of the Sanskrit term *ārya* I prefer is 'individual', or 'true individual'. The four kinds of individuals to which the *Tiratana Vandanā* refers are just that – individuals. The expression used is *purisapuggalā* – 'persons who are individuals'. A spiritual community consists, in essence, of individuals. And where non-individuals form an organization, it can never be a spiritual community, but only a group.

The idea that some people are radically more developed than others is not popular in our day, but it is absolutely fundamental to Buddhist thinking. It is vital that we appreciate how significant this distinction between the individual and the non-individual is. The development of true individuality is, comparatively, a very recent development in terms of world history, and we certainly cannot take it for granted.

But what is a true individual? Let's begin with the traditional Buddhist answer, which is usually put in terms of the ten fetters you need to break in order to gain ultimate freedom.[377] Of these, the most significant from our point of view are the first three. If you can break these, your continuous development towards Enlightenment is assured, and you become a Stream Entrant, a member (albeit at the humblest level) of the spiritual community in the highest sense. You become, in short, a true individual. It should be emphasized that this is a goal within the reach of any seriously practising Buddhist.

Notice, by the way, that I am making a distinction between an 'individual' and a 'true individual'. As I will explain in detail in Chapter 5, I usually use the word 'individual' in contrast to 'the group'. As a member of a group, one is an individual in a purely statistical sense. Through developing one's capacity to think and feel for oneself, one becomes more individual, and once one has strengthened one's individuality sufficiently, one is capable of making an individual commitment to the spiritual path. This is why, in the threefold puja I composed for use in the Triratna community, we say, 'As one by one we make our own commitment'. The decision to follow the spiritual path is one that can only be made by an individual. One could say that this level of individuality corresponds to what I have called effective Going for Refuge. True individuality, representing as it does a greater degree of individuality, corresponds to what I would call real Going for Refuge. This is what is called in the Theravāda Buddhist tradition Stream Entry, and it occurs, as I said, when one has broken the first three fetters.

The first of these fetters is *satkāya-dṛṣṭi*. *Sat* means real or true, *kāya*, body, and *dṛṣṭi* is view; the term as a whole is usually translated 'personality-belief'. This is the belief that one's present personality, one's self as it is here and now, is fixed, final, unchanging: an absolute fact. This belief is the first fetter that hampers one's growth as an individual.

Satkāya-dṛṣṭi is often explained, particularly in the West, in purely philosophical terms, as though it consisted in adherence to a particular school of thought with regard to the nature of the self, but it isn't really that at all. It is true that this fetter involves views. Indeed, it consists in holding one of two opposing extreme views. One of these is the belief that the self continues to exist after death as an essential entity, whether you believe that this entity goes to heaven or is reborn. The other is the belief that the self disappears altogether with the death of the physical body. The Buddhist view, in contrast to both of these, is that the various psychological and spiritual processes which constitute one's personality continue after death, but that there is no unchanging essence underlying this stream of psychical events.

However, this fetter is more like a deeply-rooted attitude than an intellectual viewpoint. It can be rationalized in philosophical terms, but it is essentially a largely unconscious attitude – one that says, in effect, 'I am what I am and there's nothing to be done about it.' If I have a bad temper, that's just the way it is. I was born that way and I must just live with it. And yes, I suppose others are going to have to live with it too.

Even if we admit the need for change in ourselves, we can probably conceive only of superficial changes. If we try to imagine ourselves radically changed and then look carefully at this imagined self, we will find that it bears a striking, fundamental, and detailed resemblance to the way we are now. Really to imagine the possibility of radically changing would involve letting go of whatever idea we have of ourselves as we are now. The true individual knows that progress of any kind involves change, and that change means that something must go, something must die – *you* must die. To produce a new self, there has to be a death of the old self. It is the only way. An individual happily accepts this death as a necessary condition of growth.

The second fetter is *vicikitsā*, usually translated 'doubt', 'perplexity', 'uncertainty', or 'scepticism'. Again, we are not concerned here with an intellectual position. *Vicikitsā* is less an intellectual uncertainty than an emotional inability to commit oneself, an unwillingness to make up one's mind, to think things through to a conclusion. It is a reluctance to put one's heart into what one does. It is not that honest doubt of which Tennyson speaks:

There lives more faith in honest doubt,
Believe me, than in half the creeds.[378]

Vicikitsā is lack of integration. One is literally not an individual but a loose congeries of selves. Out of this association of selves, one self will emerge to commit the whole 'person' to a decision; the next day another self, thinking better of it, will reverse that decision. One self gets enthusiastic about something, only to be replaced by another self that wonders what all the fuss was about. Thus one self follows another, like waves breaking on the shore of one's present state of mind. Everyone is familiar with this state of affairs, but it is particularly obvious to people who meditate. One self wants to meditate, another doesn't. One self gets going with its meditation dragging all the other selves protesting in its wake; but gradually it weakens and goes under, submerged in a welter of other selves (technically called 'distractions') which, if they can, will bring the meditation to an end altogether. In this way we drift through our meditation and through life, pulled now in one direction, now in another. As Shakespeare's Richard II comes to realize, wasting time is how we disintegrate:

I wasted time, and now doth time waste me.[379]

Only an individual, one who is integrated, a unified personality, can commit himself or herself in such a way as actually to make spiritual progress.

The third fetter is *śīlavrata-parāmarśa* – literally 'grasping (*parāmarśa*) moral rules (*śīla*) and religious vows (*vrata*)'. This does not exactly mean 'attachment to religious rites and ceremonies', which is how the expression was first translated into English towards the end of the nineteenth century. This was in the days of the great ritualist controversy: earlier in the century, adherents of the Oxford Movement had tried to bring the old Catholic rituals back into the Church of England, and they were vigorously opposed by the more Protestant wing of the church. It seems that the early translators of the Pāli canon could not help taking this fetter as some sort of anti-ritualist statement, and thinking of the Buddha as a proto-Protestant or even an early rationalist, opposed to the more colourful side of religion – a view of the Buddha that flies in the face of all the evidence. In fact, the fetter is dependence on ethical rules and religious observances *as ends in themselves*.

Even when we have translated the Pāli term correctly, it is still open to misinterpretation. Ethical and religious observances in no way constitute a fetter in themselves. What holds us back is our depending on them, treating them as ends in themselves rather than as means to Enlightenment. We are held back, in other words, by conventional morality and conventional religion. The idea that this should be a fetter is often thought of as a specifically Zen attitude, but it is basic Buddhism – and even basic Christianity: 'The Sabbath,' as Jesus says, 'was made for man, not man for the Sabbath.'[380] Likewise, ethics and practices are there to be useful, not to use us.

Why do we always miss this point (as to some extent we must if we are not Stream Entrants)? Yet again, we are concerned here not with a consciously maintained viewpoint but with an unconscious emotional attitude. It is to do with the fact that we tend to want to get something from our spiritual practice that has nothing to do with its true purpose. Often we derive from our practice some kind of status within the group, a measure of acceptance by other people, respectability, security, a sense of belonging. This is a well-known phenomenon of whatever spiritual tradition is dominant within a culture. In the West, it used to be virtually obligatory to go to church, and your church-going established your reputation in the community. Indeed, this was usually what people went to church for – not to worship God, but to create a good impression.

But even if you simply attend a small Buddhist group, which may do nothing at all for your conventional social standing, after a while you may find yourself going along mainly for the positive, friendly atmosphere. Despite your best intentions you will go through the motions of meditation, devotion, study, spiritual friendship, and so on, in order to get the kind of self-affirmation which, deep down, is what you really want from the group meeting. In order to break this fetter one needs to treat all these practices and activities – crucial as they all are – as means to a specific end, which is one's own development as an individual.

In this account of breaking the first three fetters,[381] I have spoken of one's *development* as an individual, and it is important to notice this. The metaphor of breaking the fetters may suggest a sudden breakthrough, but the first three fetters are, one might say, weakened by whatever one does to try to overcome the limitations of fixed self-view, lack of integration and going through the motions, and it is towards overcoming these that much of one's effort in following the spiritual path is directed. One is moving, one might say, from being a group member, to becoming an individual, to becoming a true individual, or Stream Entrant.

Beyond this point, according to tradition the once-returner has weakened the fourth and fifth fetters, while the non-returner is released from any further human rebirth by breaking them altogether. (An *arhant* breaks the last five as well, but we need not go into these, as they are of little immediate relevance to where most of us actually are.)

The fourth and fifth fetters are *kāma-rāga*, desire for sensuous experience, and *vyāpāda*, anger or animosity. These two are much stronger fetters than the first three. In fact, they bind us very tightly indeed, and it is sobering to reflect that even one so spiritually advanced as a Stream Entrant is still bound by them, at least in subtle forms. A little imagination shows us how it is that even a 'once-returner' has only weakened – not broken – these fetters. In the case of the fourth fetter, one has only to imagine what it would be like to go suddenly blind, say – not to see the light, and all the myriad details of the visual world around us that we take for granted – to realize with what inexpressible longing one would desire that visual world. Or suppose you suddenly went deaf, and were plunged into a totally silent world, with no voices, no music, none of the constant background of sound reminding you that you share the world with other living beings. You would probably long to have that sort of contact again, long for the beauty of the most simple music, more than anything else in the world. The same goes for the world of touch, and even taste.

The longing that would arise on being deprived of all our sense experience is almost literally unimaginable. But at the time of death this is what happens. The mind is torn from these things, suspended in a void that is truly dreadful for those who still desire contact with the external world through the five senses. *Kāma-rāga* is therefore what causes one's consciousness to seek expression in the form of another sense-based existence, and it follows that on the breaking of this fetter one becomes a non-returner.

As for the fetter of anger or animosity, it is more or less impossible to imagine being without some element of discontent, irritation, resentment, impatience, or ill-humour; these states almost constantly hover somewhere in the background of our experience. And this is not even to mention our more noticeable outbursts of anger, which draw on the apparently bottomless wellspring of animosity within us.

But even if we cannot as yet break these fetters, we can be aware of them, and of the need to weaken them through the practice of meditation, in which we attempt to withdraw from sense experience at least temporarily, and to let go of our animosity as well – this latter being the particular object of the *mettā bhāvanā* practice, the development of universal loving-kindness.[382]

We now have the traditional answer to the question of what makes one an *ārya* – that is, to use the translation I prefer, what makes one a true individual. If you are a true individual you are prepared to change, to let go of any fixed idea of yourself, even to die. You are integrated enough to be able to commit yourself wholly, and you do not confuse means with ends. These are the attitudes that we need to nurture if we are to break the first three fetters and achieve Stream Entry. Further to this, a true individual is aware of the influence that our sense experience has upon our minds, and of the need to reduce that influence through the practice of simplicity, contentment, and meditation. And a true individual tries to be aware of negative emotion, not expressing it in harmful ways, and trying hard to cultivate positive emotion.

This is one way of defining a true individual. We shall be exploring ways of becoming an individual and then developing true individuality in the second part of this book. For now, we will focus on the relationship between the individual and the spiritual community, a relationship that began with the emergence of the individual comparatively recently in our human history. Let us go on to look at the development of the individual – and the spiritual community – from a historical perspective.

4

THE HISTORY OF THE SPIRITUAL COMMUNITY

History is a perilous undertaking, an attempt to be objective about what happened in the past that has no real hope of success. Straightforward facts are hard to come by, and historians endlessly discuss their theories. Even when the facts are agreed upon, the study of history is these days more complex than it used to be. History is no longer simply 'the lengthened shadow of a man'.[383] There are all sorts of alternative perspectives to take. One may make broad sweeping generalizations, or undertake narrow, highly focused surveys of data. One may take a social view, a cultural view, an economic view, a feminist view ... and there are radically different and even contradictory angles that one may take within each of these and other areas of study. But having acknowledged that when it comes to history we have to be circumspect, I am now going to throw caution to the winds and consider a vision of history as a whole. I use the word vision deliberately because I want to convey in a few crude brush-strokes a vivid general impression.

Of course, such large-scale overviews of history tend to come and go just like anything else. Hegel saw history as the progressive manifestation of Spirit, and as a process, moreover, that moved from East to West, from ancient China to modern America.[384] Following on from Hegel, Karl Marx presented history in terms of economics and class conflict, and as passing through four great stages – a slave society, feudalism, capitalism, and communism – in accordance with who controls the means of production. Then came Toynbee's vision of the rise and fall of civilizations, which enumerated more than two dozen distinct civilizations, some of which survive only in the form of their monuments, as in Egypt, while others, like Hinduism, are still thriving, and some, as in Tibet before the Chinese invasion, exist only in what Toynbee calls a fossilized form (though most Buddhists would disagree with this particular assessment).[385] None of these visions of history has survived the twentieth century in very good condition, and Francis Fukuyama's recent attempt to predict the end of history already looks somewhat premature.[386]

However, the existentialist philosopher Karl Jaspers (1883–1969), in his conception of the Axial Age, affords us an insight into the historical emergence of widely scattered examples of a radically individualized consciousness that cannot be ignored in any discussion of the human ideal of individuality.[387] From this starting point we shall go on to a brief historical survey of spiritual communities – that is, individuals organizing themselves on a collective basis.

The history of mankind as a species covers hundreds of thousands, even millions of years. Much of this time is usually referred to simply as the prehistoric era. The emergence of specifically human consciousness produced for the first time a species that could not be defined in purely biological terms. Gathering roots, fruits, and seeds, and later hunting game, scattered family groups or tribes roamed through a world which was in a sense very much smaller than our own. Their views of the past and the future were narrow, and their view of the world around them was restricted to their immediate locality. What they were conscious of was immediate experience, here and now. What they knew, they knew directly and intimately. They were ignorant of more or less everything except how to survive, though this they knew very well indeed. At the same time, because their numbers were so few, the natural world through which they roamed must have seemed to them terrifying in its vastness.

We can imagine that they wandered through forest or savannah, lodging in caves, holes in the ground, or among the roots of trees. They had the use of nothing inherited from the past – no houses, villages, bridges, roads, or even huts or paths. There were no laws, nor was there any authority beyond that of the head of the family. There was no mechanical sense of the flow of time against which to measure your experience: you simply saw the sun rise and set, and watched the procession of the seasons. The bare trees budded and opened their fresh leaves to the light, and then you would see the same leaves turning yellow and fluttering to the ground. These changes went with changes of temperature, and changes in the way you went about getting food. But you knew nothing of the past, nothing of history. You knew your parents and grandparents, your children and grandchildren, but beyond that there was just a mist. You knew nothing about other human beings, living in other times or other places. There was no 'knowledge' in our sense of the term at all. Primitive man was ignorant and, as far as we know, happily ignorant. We can hardly imagine such a state of affairs; to us this age can only seem very remote.

However, in a sense it is not remote at all. The period of prehistory is virtually coterminous with the history of humankind itself. The ten to twenty thousand years of modern or historical humanity is no more than a full stop to the long, meandering palaeolithic and neolithic periods of our development. In fact, we are still living on the fringes of the Stone Age. Almost everything we value – higher culture, civilization, literature, science and technology, work, and leisure – has been completely unknown to our species for virtually its entire history. Our roots go very deep indeed. For almost our entire existence as a species we have been primitive and ignorant; and, under the surface, very largely we still are. Indeed, a great deal of our unconscious conditioning derives from the exigencies of primitive life.

These almost unimaginably vast and almost completely blank wastes of prehistory are sometimes termed, more poetically, the age of Prometheus, after the demigod who, according to Greek myth, stole fire from heaven for the use of humankind. As well as making use of fire, primitive human beings made stone tools and developed the beginnings of language and religion. The great cosmic or nature myths originated towards the end of this period, and along with religion came art, which until very recent times was not separate from religion.

Then suddenly – and it was, comparatively speaking, quite sudden – around 20,000 years ago this erstwhile hunter-gatherer species started to till the ground, to sow seeds and reap crops. With the development of agriculture, nomadic life gave way in some places to village settlements, and eventually towns and even cities, especially in the great river valleys of Asia and North Africa: the Nile, Tigris, and Euphrates, the Indus and

Ganges, the Huang He and Yangtze Kiang. Agriculture promoted the development of forethought; tilling the ground for the sake of a future harvest was a considered activity, not a spontaneous impulse, and it was thus the first step towards civilization.

The rate of development increased exponentially, and the Stone Age was followed in quick succession by the Bronze and Iron ages. Alphabets were invented; literature and history of a kind began to be written; basic geometry and astronomy were mastered; government, administration, and law took shape; and commerce, war, and conquest spread these developments further afield. Fertility myths replaced the old cosmic or nature myths. This whole period is known as the Age of Agriculture, the River Valley Age, or the Age of Divine Kingship.

Then, about 2,500 years ago, there was another major shift in consciousness, termed by Karl Jaspers the Axial Age, when the great religions came into being, together with a succession of great empires. We may identify a further revolution commencing around 500 years ago: the Age of Science and Technology, or the Age of Anxiety. But the crucial moment in the development of human beings, the moment at which the species fully realized its unique potential for the first time, was the Axial Age.

The term coined by Jaspers derives from Hegel, who speaks in his *Philosophy of History* of the axis of history, the point upon which the whole of human history turns.[388] For him, this point was the appearance of Christ, but, as Jaspers points out, such an interpretation can have meaning only for the believing Christian. If there is indeed an axis in history, it will be found to be a set of circumstances which has significance for everyone.

Jaspers finds this decisive turning point in a spiritual upheaval that he identifies as having taken place between 800 and 200 BCE. All over the world – or at least the more developed parts of the world – humanity seems suddenly to have awakened from the sleep of ages. At this time, individuals were born whose achievements and ways of looking at the world have profoundly influenced, directly or indirectly, almost the entire human race. Even after 2,500 years, many of these individuals are still revered household names, and their work is still appreciated, consulted, and discussed.

The *Analects* of Confucius (551–479 BCE) are probably still the greatest single influence on the Chinese character, while the *Daodejing*, composed by the altogether more mysterious figure of Laozi (?604–?531 BCE), is a perennial worldwide best-seller. These two are only the best known of a host of Chinese sages, including Mencius (372–289 BCE) and Zhuangzi (c.350–275 BCE). India can boast a galaxy of sages responsible for the wisdom teachings of the Upanishads, as well as the founder of Jainism, Mahāvīra, and of course Gautama the Buddha. More or less contemporaneously, Persia was graced by the figure of Zoroaster or Zarathustra (?628–?551 BCE), whom we know as the founder or refounder of Zoroastrianism, the faith of the Parsees. This was the religion of the Persian Empire, and it heavily influenced all the Semitic monotheistic religions: Judaism, Christianity, and Islam.

The tiny country of Palestine produced the great Jewish prophets: Amos and Isaiah, Jeremiah, the Second Isaiah, and a number of others, whose sublime moral insights were much later developed by Jesus of Nazareth, and indeed still resound throughout the Western world today.

Finally, in Greece there was an outburst of philosophical, spiritual, and artistic creativity unequalled anywhere else, before or since. A. N. Whitehead remarked famously, if a little boldly, that Western philosophy is little more than a series of footnotes to Plato.[389] Plato was the pupil of Socrates and the teacher of Aristotle, whose works dominated medieval Muslim and Christian thought. But these three represent only the highest point of a complex philosophical tradition.

The epic poetry of Homer, the lyric poetry of Pindar, the fables of Aesop, the poetic drama of Sophocles, Euripides, and Aeschylus, the comedies of Aristophanes, and the sculptures of Phidias and Praxiteles, represent the most sublime works of art still extant from within a culture of unimaginable richness, which also produced the first modern historians, Herodotus and Thucydides, and the physician Hippocrates, whose oath of medical ethics still has relevance for doctors of medicine in the West today. Finally, Thales, Anaximander, Pythagoras, Archimedes, and Euclid were just a few of the Greek thinkers who between them established the principles of mathematics and scientific method that two thousand years later would set off another intellectual explosion, giving us the modern world as we know it.

Simply reciting such a litany of names makes it clear that, as Jaspers observes, 'In this age were born the fundamental categories within which we still think today, and the beginnings of the world religions, by which human beings still live, were created.' Jaspers goes on: 'Myths were remoulded, were understood at a new depth during this transition, which was myth-creating after a new fashion, at the very moment when the myth as a whole was destroyed. ... Man is no longer enclosed within himself. He becomes uncertain of himself and thereby open to new and boundless possibilities. ... For the first time philosophers appeared. Human beings dared to rely on themselves as individuals.'[390]

When we ask what such a diverse array of individuals have in common, this is the obvious answer. It is not simply that they were seminal figures – founders of religions or of schools of thought or of forms of artistic expression. They certainly did not think of themselves in such terms, even though, when we look back on what happened as a result of their lives, we can see that many of them did become founders in one way or another. No – what they all have in common is that they are all true individuals. They stand out from the mass of humanity, not because of who they dominated, ruled over, or conquered, but because of who they were in themselves. Even across the gulf of millennia we recognize them as sharply defined individuals, and thus we can, in a way, enter into a personal relationship with them. They represent a new strain of human being that was simply not evident before this period. They thought independently. They were not psychologically dependent on the group. They were able to stand, if necessary, alone. Whether they were true individuals in the sense I used the term in the last chapter, as referring to Stream Entrants, as outlined in the last chapter, is not easy to assess, Stream Entry being defined in such clearly Buddhist terms, but that these extraordinary figures represented the emergence in history of a new kind of individuality is not in doubt.

THE HISTORICAL DEVELOPMENT OF SPIRITUAL COMMUNITIES

As a result of this new development we find, from a spiritual point of view, two forces henceforth working in opposition to each other throughout history: the group and the individual. To these, a third force should be added: spiritual communities. Because it is generally characteristic of the true individual to enter into relationship with other people who are committed to developing individuality, we usually find them working in the context of spiritual communities.

Thus in ancient Greece there appeared a number of schools of philosophy – the Milesian school, the Platonic school, the Neoplatonic, the Stoic, the Epicurean. These should not be thought of as academic schools of thought in the modern sense. They were founded as spiritual communities – at least in certain respects – of masters and disciples, searching for the truth together. Indeed, the school of one of the most influential of Greek thinkers, Pythagoras, was known explicitly as a mystical society. Such spiritual communities occurred throughout the Graeco-Roman world.

In Palestine at the same time communities such as the Essenes provided the soil in which Jesus of Nazareth planted the seed of his teachings, and subsequently, Christian communities spread rapidly all round the Mediterranean. Meanwhile, around the third century CE communities of Manicheans – followers of the prophet Mani – were to be found in what is now Iraq and Iran, and a little later, in the same area and beyond it, arose various Sufi communities. Throughout this period in India the Buddhist sangha was spreading, and to a lesser extent the Jain sangha as well. One might expect to find spiritual communities in China also, but until Buddhist sanghas were formed there in the second century CE one can point only to a literary élite as fulfilling such a role.

Three traditions of spiritual communities were, and still are, of particular importance on account of the number of individuals involved in them, the length of time they thrived, and their influence on the world. These are the Buddhist, Sufi, and Christian communities. Of these, the Buddhist sangha is the longest-lived. It is not often realized that the Buddhist sangha is, so to speak, the classic form of the spiritual community. Buddhists formed a spiritual community from the beginning, not as a sort of afterthought. Indeed, it could be said that Buddhism *is* essentially a spiritual community. The sangha is an integral part of the Three Jewels at every level. In the Theravāda the spiritual community tends to be identified with the monastic community, but in the Mahāyāna countries, where the great unifying factor, historically speaking, is not so much the Three Refuges as the bodhisattva ideal, it is identified with monastic and lay people alike.

The Sufi brotherhoods, while scattered all over the Muslim world, have at best an ambiguous relationship with orthodox Islam. Al-Ghazālī is probably the most distinguished and best known of all Sufi mystics. Sufi ideas derive from Neoplatonism, Manicheism, and even Hinduism and Buddhism, and therefore, from an orthodox Islamic viewpoint, Sufis are often heretical, and some have been executed for their heretical pronouncements. However, Sufi communities have continued to nourish the Islamic world to the present day.

The beginnings of the Christian church are shrouded in obscurity and controversy, and to begin with it clearly consisted of small communities of followers, but in the fourth century, Christianity became the official religion of the whole Roman Empire, and thus virtually ceased to be a spiritual community. It became an aspect of 'the group', the ecclesiastical wing of the state. Eventually it became a political power in its own right, claiming its own authority, with its own sphere of influence and control. Through the centuries it became, especially in the form of the Roman Catholic Church, increasingly authoritarian, intolerant, coercive, and persecuting.

It has to be said that the seeds of this degeneration were present in Christianity from the beginning – as they are, perhaps, in all forms of monotheism. However, within this official Christianity – and to some extent in protest against it – spiritual communities continued to arise in the form of monastic communities, where the real Christians, the real individuals, were to be found. The monasteries were islands of civilization and culture throughout the Dark Ages from the collapse of the Roman Empire in the fifth century until the reign of Charlemagne in the eighth, preserving much of the Latin and even some Greek literature.

In this connection the Benedictine order – founded by St Benedict in the sixth century in Italy – is of particular importance. In fact, it was less an order than a loose association of autonomous monasteries, each under its own abbot. In the course of time, some of these became economically and politically powerful and, as the original Christian church had succumbed in earlier times to the pressure this inevitably produced, by the eleventh century the monasteries had ceased to be spiritual communities and had become 'groups' – part of the church in the narrow, socio-political, ecclesiastical sense.

Once again, a need for reform arose, and this need was met initially by the Cistercian monastic movement and the Carmelites or White Friars in the twelfth century, followed in the thirteenth century by the Franciscans, the Dominicans, the Poor Clares, and the Austin Friars. These movements were the orthodox aspects of a spiritual ferment that gripped Europe during the Middle Ages, throwing up all kinds of more or less heretical movements – the Lollards, the Brethren of the

Free Spirit, the Taborites, and others – who were ruthlessly persecuted by the church and in many cases eventually stamped out.

But in the sixteenth century, Lutheranism arose. This was a heresy that could not be stamped out, but sparked off an explosion of heresies throughout central, western, and northern Europe which came to be called the Reformation. All kinds of spiritual movements emerged, large and small, all more or less Christian. Some of these lasted only a few months, some lasted for years, and a very few lasted for centuries. Of the movements that emerged out of the seventeenth-century Puritan revolution in England, for example, the Diggers lasted only for a few years in the late 1640s, while the Quakers have flourished to this day.

Thus it is clear that spiritual communities have played a significant part in European history. Indeed, one can say that for two thousand years in the West, a great battle has been fought between official religion, more or less tied in with the 'powers that be', and the spiritual community in a multiplicity of changing forms. It is a battle between power and love (or *mettā*, to use the Buddhist term), authority and spiritual freedom, stagnation and growth, reactivity and creativity. This battle is continuously being won and lost again, and there is no guarantee that any one spiritual community will survive for very long, nor any certainty that the spiritual family of which communities are a part will survive.

Manicheism is just one example of a spiritual tradition that lost the battle. Manicheism was a pacific, tolerant, almost eclectic teaching. Philosophically, it was a form of dualism – that is, it proposed the existence of two ultimate principles, light and darkness, neither of which could be said to originate from the other. The Manicheans believed that however far you went back, you would always find these two principles, independent of and sometimes in conflict with each other. The task of human beings, according to Mani, is to liberate the light within us from the darkness in or around us.

According to some scholars, Mani may have been influenced by Buddhism – he certainly refers to the Buddha's teachings in some places in his own writings – and Manichean spiritual communities appear to have been similar to Buddhist ones in many respects. There is even some evidence to suggest that central Asian Manicheism in turn influenced the later development of Mahāyāna and Vajrayāna Buddhism. For example, it is possible to detect touches of Manicheism in the life of

Padmasambhava, one of the founders of Tibetan Buddhism. One of the most striking features of Manicheism was its stress on the importance of beauty in the spiritual life. According to tradition, Mani was himself a painter – it seems that even now the word *mani* means painter in modern Arabic – and he encouraged the visual arts, including calligraphy.

Manicheism spread phenomenally quickly, from Iraq and Iran through the whole of the late Roman Empire, all over central Asia, to penetrate India, China, and even Japan. However, this popular, tolerant, and peaceful religion attracted a commensurate degree of vilification, intolerance, and persecution. In the West, it was mercilessly crushed throughout the Roman Empire by the orthodox Christian church. In the Middle East it was exterminated by fanatical renascent Zoroastrianism, and Mani himself was martyred by the Zoroastrians. Even in China Manicheans were persecuted, by Taoists and Confucians alike. The very literature of this worldwide spiritual community was destroyed so systematically that only fragments remain. Scholars have been able to reconstruct their history and teachings only from scraps and fragments, from scrolls discovered in the desert, and from the occasional dismissive or hostile reference in the literature of the Manicheans' enemies.

So here is an important lesson from history. A spiritual community can be as hugely successful as Manicheism was, and still disappear almost as if it had never existed. This is just one historical example of something that is an ever-present danger. Just as the world has seen the emergence of spiritual communities of various kinds, it has also seen the emergence of 'the group', by which I mean the various collectivities into which humanity has organized itself. If you are a member of a spiritual community it is important to remember that you are engaged in a constant battle with the group. So far as the spiritual community is concerned it is a non-violent battle; but the enemy will not be quite so particular, if the past is anything to go by. It is the distinction – and the relationship – between the spiritual community and the group that we must now go on to consider.

And that relationship, I should add, need not necessarily be such as to crush the possibility of the spiritual community out of existence. If it has been possible for the Axial Age to occur, then a still greater change may take place. If individuals and spiritual communities can emerge from time to time out of the group, then we must also believe in the possibility, however remote, that the spiritual community may one day outweigh the group, that light may overcome darkness. Also, there is such a thing as what I would call a 'positive group'. We need to define our terms. Let us go on to look in more detail at the group and the spiritual community.

5

THE GROUP AND THE SPIRITUAL COMMUNITY

As defined in terms such as those outlined in the last chapter, individuals are clearly in short supply. Spiritual communities are no less rare – because it is individuals who form them. Individuals sometimes exist in comparative isolation; more often, it seems, they are found together, though in very small numbers. When they come together, they make up between them a spiritual community. When non-individuals get together, though, what you have is a group. It is the distinction between the group and the spiritual community that we will be exploring here.

A group is basically a collection of people who are not individuals. There is no term in English for such people, interestingly enough, but the traditional Buddhist term is *pṛthagjanas* – 'ordinary folk' – and they are clearly distinguished from *āryas*, that is, from true individuals. But even when it comes to a less elevated degree of individuality than that of the *ārya*, this too is quite rare. According to Buddhist tradition, most of us are individuals only in a statistical sense. We are separate from one another, one could say, in every way except the one that really matters. We have separate bodies, and separate votes if we are lucky, but we can hardly say that we have separate minds. If we look carefully at where our opinions and decisions come from, we will see that only too often we don't have minds of our own at all. What we think and feel is determined by our conditioning, by the particular circumstances of our own particular existence. If we are self-conscious at all, it is in only the most vague and intermittent way; we tend to think and feel and act according to how others are thinking, feeling, and acting, and we will almost always accept, very often implicitly, the norms and values of the various groups to which we belong. At those times when we fail to act like individuals, our minds, such as they are, have been effectively submerged in a kind of collective, group mind.

THE CHARACTERISTICS OF THE GROUP

In axiomatic – if extreme – terms, we might say that, set against the individual, the group is always wrong. Why? In principle, a group comprises a number (and the nature of the group usually makes this a very large number) of 'statistical individuals' or 'social units'. That is, it consists of people who possess no true individuality, people with a comparatively low level of consciousness and self-awareness. Their emotions will tend to be crude and reactive, they will not like to be alone, they will need the support of others for their views and feelings, they will like to be part of a crowd or gang, and so on.

This is not to say that such people are of no account. Quite the opposite: they are of infinite – though as yet unrealized – account. It is precisely because all human beings are capable of becoming individuals that we need to be able to distinguish between those who are aiming to realize their potential and those who are not. (Not as yet, anyway.) We shall then have some idea of where we are going and where we are choosing not to go. The fact that the vast majority of people are not interested in developing as individuals, and in this life are unlikely ever to be so, does not mean that they do not have the capacity to become individuals.

The bonds that hold us as statistical individuals together in groups are usually more or less material (without necessarily attaching any deprecatory meaning to that word). People are united by ties of blood with their family or their tribe. They are united by ties of soil with those who live and work on the same land, through their common allegiance to the land that they and their ancestors have occupied for so long. They are united, especially in the case of larger groups, by ties of economic interest. And they are united by fear, by the need to defend themselves against larger, more powerful, more aggressive groups.

Since the Axial Age, individuals and spiritual communities have continued to emerge at irregular intervals and in different places. Much more marked, however, has been the development of the group. Starting with the family group, the tribe, the state, and the empire, we have inherited over the centuries a vast and complex web of groups to which we may be affiliated: schools, businesses and multi-national corporations, football clubs and Rotary clubs, councils, churches, committees and societies, pubs, interest groups, political parties, and so on. We also belong to a social group or class, an economic group, a religious group, a cultural group, a linguistic group, a racial group. We are born into some groups, but we have to join others by conscious choice, by paying a subscription, being initiated, joining the colours, or whatever it may be. These two categories overlap to some extent but, by and large, the groups into which one is born tend to be more group-like than those which one joins voluntarily.

Many of these groups are associated with their own distinctive symbols, so that to see the symbol is immediately to be reminded of the group it symbolizes. Totem poles, national flags, national anthems, and national dress all serve this function. There is also the old school tie, the fraternity pin, the union card, the party badge. With these symbols go slogans and sayings expressive of group loyalties: 'God's own country', 'Home sweet home', 'Land of hope and glory', 'Land of the free', 'Land of my fathers', 'The bulldog breed', 'Maybe it's because I'm a Londoner', 'The old firm', 'Don't let the side down', 'Workers of the world unite'. ...

Group feelings of loyalty go very deep indeed. That loyalty may not always be expressed, or even conscious, but it is there, deep down, and if someone's group loyalties are offended they can swiftly turn from a mild-mannered model citizen into a fanatical partisan, ready to tear limb from limb anyone who challenges their group, or questions their group loyalty.

At a football match or a rally, or when you are conscripted into the army, you find that the collective spirit of the group you have joined seems to take over and you become submerged in it. There's a sort of group mind or soul which you obey almost despite yourself – it seems to control you. This is not just occult mythology, but a widely-reported phenomenon.

So strong are the feelings involved, so ubiquitous, so invariable, so universally distributed amongst human beings, that some anthropologists and psychologists even go so far as to speak of a group instinct, no less compelling than the reproductive instinct. The group instinct quite simply impels us, they say, to get together with other people. Whether we can really speak of a group instinct is questionable – some psychologists say that the word 'instinct' is a red herring dragged across the path of psychological theory, and doesn't correspond to anything at all. However, what we can say is that the group consists of individuals in a statistical sense only – not true individuals, but people whose consciousness is an aspect of the group consciousness and whose thoughts, feelings, and behaviour conform to group patterns and norms.

Among animals, of course, groups fulfil a definite biological function. If it is bitterly cold, and you are in danger of being frozen to death, with no fire, artificial shelter, or clothes to supplement your fur, hair, or wool, you will huddle together with others to keep warm. As well as warmth, the group also provides safety; its fit and strong members will often protect those who are younger and weaker. Even a lion will only prey on the weaker animals if they are allowed to lag behind, and some herds of animals will surround the weaker members of the herd to make sure this does not happen. In this way the group on the animal level facilitates the survival of the species concerned.

Wanting to belong to a group is in our bones, in our blood. We have a long history of gathering together in groups. If we include our primate ancestors, we have about twenty million years of group conditioning, as ape-man, man-ape, and human. To begin with we used to live in something like an extended family group or small tribe of perhaps fifty individuals, with just occasional encounters with other small tribes. With the development of language we have been able to accommodate a somewhat larger tribal grouping than this. But almost all our relationships would have been within this home group, and in some ways this is the size of group that we would all naturally like to get back to.

It is only within the last few thousand years (which is really no time at all by comparison) that we have developed all sorts of much more complicated social groupings. Today we find ourselves struggling to get what we need from ever more distorted, even aberrant social institutions. It is more and more difficult to find groups of the right scale. On the one hand we have the isolated nuclear family, which can be so cramping as to be a breeding ground for neurosis; and on the other, we belong to a group – the nation state – which is so big as to be meaningless on a personal level. Between these two institutions we establish, in a partial and intermittent fashion, membership of or loyalty to all sorts of other groups, but none of these seem to satisfy our ancient need to belong to a small tribe of between thirty and sixty people, a group in which we can live and work, in genuine and continuous personal relationship with all its members.

We have all been born into groups, and we are all therefore subject to the conditioning arising from those affiliations. Our ideas, our views, our feelings, the way we react to people and situations, our convictions – all these will tend to be determined by group conditioning of one kind or another, except in so far as we become conscious of such conditioning and distance ourselves from its influence. The groups themselves often overlap or even cohere. And all these overlapping groups together make up 'the world'.

Groups fear individuality and all its manifestations, and always tend to discourage it. The group requires conformity. This is because it is based on power, which whether physical, intellectual, or economic is always the power of the strong over the weak, the power of those who have the resources, the cunning, or the knowledge to be able to impose their will on others, deploying brute force or subtle manipulation in order to exploit others for their own, usually selfish, purposes. The group consists of those who wield that power and those who give it to them. Such power is exercised within any group, whether political, cultural, tribal, familial, or even religious.

THE SPIRITUAL COMMUNITY

The purposes of a community of individuals, a spiritual community, are utterly different from those of the group. They are twofold: firstly, its members help one another to develop spiritually; secondly, in whatever way they can, they help others outside the community to develop their individuality. In essence, a spiritual community is a free association of individuals. To form one, therefore, the first requirement is a number of individuals. You can no more have a spiritual community without individuals than you can have an omelette without eggs. A spiritual community is not created by acquiring a building, an exotic form of dress, and a long list of rules. You don't need a building, you don't need an 'authentic tradition', you don't even need a religion. You need individuals: that is the basic ingredient. In other words, you need a number of people who are relatively emancipated from the group, relatively integrated and aware, and have an inner direction and positive purpose to their lives. Where there are no individuals, there will be no spiritual community, call it by whatever name you please.

Next, there should be regular personal contact between these individuals. This is not simply polite social interchange. Nor does it involve herding together in a group for psychological warmth and comfort and support. The spiritual community consists of individuals who are in deep personal contact with one another. It will challenge you to be yourself, and demand that you take further steps towards being a true individual. People within the spiritual community will do what they can to spark off real communication, genuine spiritual exchanges. Within the Buddhist tradition, such communication is called *kalyāṇa mitratā*, 'lovely friendship'. Yes, you are all trying to develop, but you are also trying to develop together. Not only that, you are also helping one another to develop.

Clearly such emergent individuals are not going to agree on everything. However, it is important that the members of a spiritual community share the same general approach to the spiritual life. There must be a common spiritual framework within which they are all trying to develop. This framework constitutes their medium of communication, without which they will find it difficult to help or even understand one another. It consists mainly of two things. Firstly, the spiritual community must have a common spiritual ideal, all of its members aiming ultimately for the same higher states of consciousness, the same realization. And secondly, they must have a common means of realizing that ideal, a common path or teaching, a common practice or method. They are walking the same way in the same way. As we have already seen, in Buddhism, these two things are known as the Buddha Jewel and the Dharma Jewel. The spiritual community itself of course is the Sangha, the third Jewel.

Members of a spiritual community may well choose to live under the same roof, to encourage closer personal contact, and thereby greater mutual helpfulness, between its members, and produce a more intensive situation than can otherwise be achieved. This is not to say that it is essential to be with one's spiritual friends all the time. Even after one has become a member of the spiritual community, it is good to be on one's own sometimes. Nevertheless, we definitely stand the best chance of developing spiritually if we have prolonged contact over a period of years with others who are progressing, and particularly with others who are more advanced than we are. The best kind of spiritual community will include at least one person who is more developed than the others, and who can provide some kind of direction for the rest of the community. Such a person is known traditionally as a *kalyāṇa mitra*, a spiritual friend, although on occasion all members of a spiritual community should be able to act as *kalyāṇa mitras* to one another.

Spiritual communities are by definition very small, and very few. It seems to be a law of human development that when a spiritual community reaches a certain size it starts to feel (so to speak) the gravitational pull of the group and tends to take on the characteristics of a group, and as it does so, it degenerates. Most traditional, orthodox religious bodies were once genuine spiritual communities that expanded and were then absorbed back into the group in a form that was more acceptable to the group. However, although true spiritual communities may be insignificant in size, they exert a powerful leavening influence on the 'doughy mass' of the general population.

HOW THE GROUP AND THE SPIRITUAL COMMUNITY AFFECT EACH OTHER

The group and the spiritual community are trying to do two quite different – even opposite – things. The group is trying to produce good group members: good family men, good wives and mothers, dependable employees, loyal citizens, obedient soldiers, party members who can be relied upon to toe the line. The spiritual community, by contrast, is trying to produce individuals. The group insists on conformity, while the spiritual community encourages freedom of thought. But this is not all. The defining principle of the spiritual community, as opposed to the group's insistence on conformity, is more than simply freedom of thought, important as that freedom may be. It is freedom to grow.

Limited though it is in so many ways, the power of the group cannot be overestimated. It governs the lives of the vast majority of people, and most people are happy for it to do so. We therefore need to ask ourselves what we are really looking for, and also to be clear about the nature of the alternatives before us. Are we really looking for a spiritual community, or do we simply want a group? The spiritual community is not a collectivity of any kind – it is a community of individuals. It is not even a substitute for a group, which in a time of transition like the present is what many of us are looking for. Many old established institutions, customs, and traditions are breaking up. The old groups are breaking up – starting with the family. Family ties are not nearly so significant as they used to be. Nowadays, who bothers to keep up connections with their second and third cousins? Well, you hardly know who they are sometimes. But formerly people kept track of every single person even remotely related to them.

In the East, the family still does rule people's lives. When I lived in India, someone would often be introduced with the words, 'This is my brother.' I soon learned that this did not mean quite what it appeared to mean. 'Oh,' I'd say, 'Same mother, same father?' 'Oh no, he is my great grandfather's sister's daughter's husband's brother's grandson.' People used to keep in touch with every single relation they had, sometimes even a couple of hundred of them. But in the West today the extended family has lost its importance for a lot of people.

The nation state is another group that is breaking up. To leave the country of your birth used to be a rare event; even to leave your village was a mark of some enterprise. In times past it was held up as an ideal to live out your days hearing the sounds of the next village, without ever wanting to go there. Today, however, people love to travel widely, and to go to live and work or study in another country is no longer regarded as a sad exile, unless you are a refugee driven from your home by force, and even then you may be more than happy to be given asylum in a prosperous foreign country.

Class loyalties too are breaking down. In the old days, if you were born a serf, you died a serf, and if you were born a nobleman, you died a nobleman, but nowadays, everything is much more fluid. People identify themselves less by their class than by what they do, and as they rise in their profession, many leave behind the social milieu into which they were born and lose touch with old friends.

The result of all these shifts is that many people, having moved away from family and friends and even their own country, find themselves with no social group. Naturally they feel lonely and isolated, and equally naturally, even unconsciously, they start looking round for a group to which they can belong. In this way they may come in contact with a spiritual community, formed by a number of individuals. Liking the positive atmosphere, the lonely person may want to join this community. But they are joining it not as a spiritual community, but as a group. They are not joining it in order to develop spiritually, but for the sake of warmth and companionship – perhaps because they just can't face the four walls of their cold apartment. In this way, the spiritual community becomes a substitute for the group. You haven't got a family? All right, join this spiritual community. You aren't a member of any club? Well, there's always that spiritual community down the road. You don't belong to a tribe, you haven't got a chief or a totem of your own? Don't worry, you'll find something that will do instead at your friendly neighbourhood spiritual community.

In this connection, certain developments in modern Japan are quite illuminating. Over the last hundred or more years, with the Meiji restoration, and the modernization and industrialization that followed, the feudal structures that used to be the focus of loyalty in Japan were swept away. As a result, the average Japanese person was left with nothing to belong to, nothing to be loyal to. The family was too small to satisfy the strongly felt need for a more clan-like structure, while the country as a whole – the Land of the Rising Sun – was too big.

Apparently, many modern Japanese have solved the problem by adopting the company they work for as their 'clan'. 'The lone peg gets hammered into the ground,' they say. In the West a young man or woman will often try all kinds of jobs, but that is not the way they do things in Japan. Quite simply, you never leave your job. You serve the firm unstintingly, and it takes care of every aspect of your life, from your mortgage to your marriage. You go on holidays organized by the firm, with fellow employees, and you look up to the chairman of the company with reverence, as a sort of clan chief, even to the extent of feeling you would give your life for him.

Religion has also been harnessed to the great Japanese need to belong. In the West you find well-meaning ecclesiastics calling for a renewal of faith to fill the spiritual void at the heart of our society – and few people listen. But in Japan, since the war, they have had a religious revival of epic proportions. New sects and even new religions have been mushrooming, many of them Buddhist in origin, drawing on Mahāyāna Buddhism in general, Nichiren Buddhism in particular, and most of all upon the *Lotus Sūtra*. But the teaching is apparently not really the point. What matters is the organization. Each of these sects has a founder, who takes the title of Patriarch or Archbishop – as they are styled by everyone, including the press – of whatever the sect is called. The founder usually has a wife, and together these two lead the sect. In other words, they are the archetypal father and mother, and are sometimes even called father and mother by their devoted followers, who not unusually number hundreds of thousands, even millions. Some of these devoted followers occupy important government positions. Naturally, there is a complex hierarchy, consisting of perhaps a dozen different grades of membership, all with their robes and uniforms, badges, sashes, and headgear. They erect huge temples, and mansions for their leaders. Some of them have their own department stores, and even their own railway stations.

Whether it's the company or the new religion, it comes to much the same thing: both fulfil the need to belong to a group. Clearly we should not use the spiritual community as a substitute for a group in this way. The only real danger facing the spiritual community is that it may be replaced by the group. The spiritual community as such cannot become a group; it can only wither away or disappear and be replaced by a group bearing the same name and having the same external appearance.

This happens on a grand scale when a universal religion degenerates into an ethnic religion, as occurs when a religion ceases to meet the spiritual needs of the individual, as all universal religions by their very nature profess to do, and starts providing for the collective needs of the group. Priests start guaranteeing fertility, blessing tanks, and so on. It is as if the group exerts a kind of gravitational pull on any spiritual community that is not vigilant.

The residential spiritual community is particularly vulnerable to this danger. When people are living together under one roof, the danger is that they will start to make themselves more and more comfortable, until the kitchen, rather than the shrine-room, becomes the focus of their life together. The fact is that prior to the attainment of Stream Entry, you can't stand still, you can't rest on your laurels. You can't ever feel, 'Well that's enough for this life, I'll put in some more work in my next life.' The minute you stop making an effort, you start slipping back.

All this may make it seem as if the group is the villain of the piece. It isn't really. We just need to be clear about what it is, and keep it in its rightful place. The desire to belong to a group is a basic human need which cannot simply be by-passed. Although the group and the spiritual community are trying to do two very different things, they are closely, even intimately, connected, and each exerts a strong influence on the other. The spiritual community has a refining and softening, even civilizing, influence on the group. By its very presence, it helps the group to be open to higher values, to be what we may call a positive group, a group within which individual development is possible, even if not actively encouraged.

If the spiritual community can exert a positive influence on the group, however, the influence of the group on the spiritual community always tends to be destructive. The group mentality invariably tries to turn the spiritual community into another group, and it always, eventually, succeeds. The spiritual community then has to be re-established by those individuals who realize what has happened. However, the spiritual community cannot cut itself off from the group entirely. Because its commitment to higher values includes compassion, it is committed to working with the group mentality and developing individuality from it. Another way of putting this is to say that you cannot be born into a spiritual community. A hereditary spiritual community is a contradiction in terms. The lower evolution may be determined by the replication of particular genes, but the higher evolution is not a biological process at all. (We will be examining in some detail what I mean by 'higher evolution' in Part Two.) The spiritual community has to be recruited afresh in every generation. This is its weakness but it is also its strength.

Hence it is not enough simply to create a spiritual community of developing individuals; it is also necessary to establish healthy groups within which it is possible for healthy group members – and thus potential individuals – to arise. Such groups will be based less on authority and power than on friendliness and love. In the next two chapters we will consider first the relation of authority to the spiritual community, and then, by contrast, the development of what I call the positive group.

6

AUTHORITY

The term 'authority' is very ambiguous. In ordinary parlance, it means the power that is exercised by a person by virtue of their office, their legal, social, or political position. Someone has authority in this sense not by virtue of their qualities as an individual, but merely by virtue of their position. Authority in this sense is very different from true individuality. The ambiguity comes in when we speak, for instance, of moral authority. Here the word carries a different shade of meaning, one closer to its original meaning (as derived from 'author'). But nowadays authority is generally understood to mean power exercised by virtue of one's office or one's position, and it is in this sense that I want to discuss it here.

The precise nature of authority in this sense is similar in principle to the idea of representing something apart from oneself – for example, an ambassador, a Member of Parliament or Senator, a trade union delegate, or even a salesman. In all these cases, someone is entrusted for certain purposes with the power of the group or organization to which he or she belongs. The group accepts or agrees to whatever he or she accepts or agrees to as that group's representative. The power that the representative exercises is not his or her own, however, but the power of the group that he or she represents.

It is much the same in the case of authority. Here also you exercise power not by virtue of what you are as an individual, but by virtue of the office or position you hold. Your qualities as an individual may fit you for that position, but the power you exercise in it derives from the position, not from your personal qualities. In other words, the power you exercise is not your own; it belongs to the group or organization that has created your office or position.

From all this there follows an important conclusion. When we deal with someone who is some kind of representative, or with someone occupying a position of authority, we are not dealing with them as an individual; nor are they functioning as an individual. And from this follows an even more important conclusion. As we have seen, we can deal with others within the spiritual community only as individuals; if we deal with them in any other way, the spiritual community ceases to exist. Within the context of the spiritual community, therefore, we cannot deal with others as representatives, or as occupying some kind of official position. Indeed, in the spiritual community there can be no representing, no official positions, and therefore no authority deriving therefrom.

If we deal with others as occupying positions of authority or as representatives, we are not dealing with them as individuals and therefore, *ipso facto*, we are functioning not within the spiritual community but within the group. Even within a Buddhist team-based right-livelihood situation there can be no authority. After all, who employs whom?

Sometimes people like to assume positions of authority; they like to speak for others. An individual will resist such roles as far as possible, although others may make this difficult. For example, I spent altogether nearly twenty years in India, and while there I had no other interest than to immerse myself in Buddhism. In pursuit of this sole interest I adopted the Indian way of life completely, to the extent of being sometimes mistaken for an Indian (sometimes, but not always, as we shall see). For years on end I never saw or spoke to any member of the European community. Nevertheless, some of the Indians with whom I came into contact persisted in regarding me as British – and, moreover, as in some way representing Britain. In 1956 I was asked more than once, 'Why have you invaded Suez?' People who asked that question did not see me, the individual, but only a representative of Britain, and they treated me as such.

The same sort of thing happened in reverse when I returned to England in 1964. Newspaper reporters used to come and see me, and they would ask me, in the nicest possible way, 'Why do you believe in self-mortification?' Once again, they didn't see me; there was no attempt to find out what I actually did believe. They saw me as a representative of what they understood Buddhism to be. There was no awareness of me as an individual at all.

What being a representative and holding authority have in common is power. You exercise power over others, or you have the power (sometimes thrust upon you) of speaking for others. This word, too, has an interesting ambiguity. Power can mean the ability – physical, mental, or moral – to act. It can also mean force or energy applied or applicable to work. But what we are concerned with here is power in the sense of the possession of a controlling influence over others, the capacity to coerce others, directly or indirectly, physically or psychologically.

Spiritual coercion is a contradiction in terms. Power in the sense of a capacity to coerce has no place in the spiritual community. Power has its place – it is in fact necessary – but it is necessary to the *group*. Indeed, the group is based on power, and cannot exist without it. Group issues are always political issues, and power is what politics is about; politics is essentially about who coerces whom. The spiritual community, on the other hand, cannot coexist with power. As soon as one exercises power, one ceases to treat others as true individuals, and when that happens the spiritual community ceases to exist.

The group consists of people who relate to one another in terms of power. The spiritual community, on the other hand, is the embodiment of a very different principle, and it consists of individuals who relate to one another in terms of that principle. The obvious place to look for this principle is in a universal religion, which is ideally a spiritual community (by contrast with an ethnic religion, which by very definition is a group religion). There should, again ideally, be no place in a universal religion for authority and power. Unfortunately, this is not always the case with religions as historical phenomena. Power tends to creep in, and to the extent that this happens, the religion ceases to be a spiritual community, and becomes a group. This seems to have happened more with some religions than with others. The theistic religions, those based on belief in God, tend to be corrupted by authority and power more markedly than are non-theistic religions, although the latter are not unmarked by such corruption.

The reason is quite simple. God does not appear or speak for himself to ordinary people, so he needs a representative to tell people what he wants them to do. A prophet or messenger of God is such a representative, and so is the incarnate Son of God, appearing in human form to tell people what to do, how to live and so on.

The representative not only tells us what God wants us to do; he has also been entrusted with God's power, so he has the right to coerce us into doing what God wants us to do, if we are unwilling to do it of our own free will. So the crucial question is, exactly what manner of being is the representative attempting to represent? In most theistic religions the concept of God is ambiguous, ambivalent, even self-contradictory, because they are attempting to combine two different Gods – the God of Power and the God of Love, or the God of Nature and the God of Morality – into one. The consequences of this can be distressing for the theist. If, for example, your nearest and dearest were to be struck dead by lightning, this would be an 'act of God' (and is still defined as such in English law) because lightning is a part of nature, and behind nature there is God. But this God of Nature is also the God of Love, so you have to interpret your dreadful loss as having been visited upon you and yours for your and their own good. The whole event has to be interpreted as an expression of God's love in some way. You experience the effects of power, but you have to convince yourself that they are the actions of a loving God.

So does God's representative represent both of these aspects of God? You can be entrusted with power and exercise it on behalf of a higher authority, but can you entrust your love to somebody? In popular parlance we say, 'Give so-and-so my love,' but can you really give love that is not your own? No, of course not. In other words, whereas power can be delegated, love is a quality of the individual.

A representative of God cannot, therefore, represent the God of Love, but only the God of Power. To reinforce his authority, he may claim to represent the God of Love, but that is not possible. The representatives of theistic religions always exercise power because that is all they can exercise. In consequence, the theistic religions always are – or tend to become – group religions, power structures.

This is strikingly evident in the case of Christianity, especially the Roman Catholic Church. Christians originally constituted, in the very early days, a kind of true spiritual community called the *ecclesia*, later known as the Church. It began as an underground movement – quite literally, because its members are said to have met in the catacombs beneath the city. Gradually this spiritual community of early Christians came out into the open and Christianity spread into most parts of the Roman Empire until in the fourth century it became the official religion of the entire Empire. Other religions were prohibited, and various heresies were proscribed, although it was never easy to determine what was and what was not heretical. To do all these things the Church had to assume and exercise temporal power.

According to three out of the four Gospels, Christ himself rejected temporal power. Power was one of the three things with which the Devil tempted him in the wilderness, and he rejected it. But the Church was unable to follow his example. This was not just out of human weakness, but due to the self-contradictory nature of Christianity itself. The Old Testament teaches a God of Power, a God of battles, a God who encourages his worshippers (in this case the children of Israel) to slaughter their enemies. But the New Testament teaches a God of Love; it teaches his worshippers to forgive their enemies. It is obviously impossible to follow both these directions at the same time. So which do you choose?

The Church was bound to follow the God of Power, to employ coercion in propagating its faith, and thus to turn from a spiritual community into a group, for two connected reasons. Firstly, as we have seen, a God needs a representative to interpret him, and you cannot represent love. Sometimes the Pope has been criticized for not representing the God of Love. For example, a play called *The Representative* written in 1963 by the German playwright Rolf Hochhuth attacked Pope Pius XII, who refused to condemn Hitler's massacre of the Jews, for just this reason. But such a criticism is beside the point, because a representative cannot represent the God of Love. He can only represent the God of Power.

Secondly, the Church started exercising temporal power, and it was only natural that it should come to represent a God in heaven that matched its own role in the world. This applies especially in the case of the Roman Catholic Church, which regarded itself as inheriting the political power of the Western Roman Empire. The head of the Roman Catholic Church, the Pope, was originally just Bishop of Rome, but after a few centuries he came to be known as the Vicar of Christ (vicar meaning 'representative'). Thus, from the Middle Ages right down to the nineteenth century, the popes have claimed to be vicegerents of God, with the literally God-given right to exercise complete control over kings and princes. At times they have actually raised armies, fought battles, and even led their troops into battle in person. They launched a number of crusades against the Muslims, and even against the unfortunate Albigenses of southern France. Worst of all, they founded the Inquisition, through which they tried to enforce uniformity of belief. In the course of centuries, many thousands of people were cruelly tortured and slaughtered by the Inquisition and other agencies of the Roman Catholic Church. During the Middle Ages and even afterwards the Church behaved in every way like a power structure of the worst type, and virtually the only trace of Christianity as a spiritual community was to be found in the monasteries. Thus the Roman Catholic Church provides us with the most prominent example of power creeping into and more or less taking over a spiritual community. But it has happened in the case of other religions too, including Buddhism, albeit in far subtler ways.

Within the spiritual community, by contrast, although some people may be more individual than others, they use their experience, and even their natural authority, not to dominate other people, nor even to impose their own vision on others, but to help them develop as individuals. But if the spiritual community is not a power structure, what is it built around? Clearly, if the principle that governs the group is power, the principle embodied by the spiritual community is love. However, the English word 'love' is a treacherously ambiguous word, because what is called love is all too often only a form of power. The appropriate word in Pāli is *mettā* (*maitrī* in Sanskrit). This is usually translated 'friendliness', but it is friendliness raised to the highest conceivable pitch of intensity, a sort of supercharged friendliness. When we feel *mettā* towards others we see them as individuals, and we treat them as individuals. The importance of *mettā* is reflected in the fact that many Buddhists regularly and systematically cultivate it in the form of a meditation practice, the *mettā bhāvanā*.

Mettā cannot be expressed with violence, through coercion, or by authority. The use of power may be necessary in all sorts of situations, but these situations by their very nature will not occur within the spiritual community. If *mettā* is present, force is unnecessary. Each individual sees for himself or herself what needs to be done – or they see it as soon as it is pointed out to them in a friendly manner – and seeing it, they are happy to do it.

One could go further and say simply that positive emotion in general is at the heart of the spiritual community: not only *mettā*, but also *karuṇā* (compassion), *muditā* (joy in the virtues and happiness of others), and *upekṣā* (peace or equanimity), as well as *śraddhā* (faith and devotion). The spiritual community embodies all these sublime, uplifting, animating emotions.

But even then there is something missing. There is a metaphysical or transcendental dimension that must also be present if the spiritual community is to be sustained. The ultimate principles governing the spiritual community are *mahāmaitrī*, the *great* friendliness, and *mahākaruṇā*, the *great* compassion: that is to say, friendliness or compassion conjoined with *prajñā*, transcendental wisdom. In other words, the principle governing the spiritual community is nothing less than what we call the *bodhicitta*, the cosmic will to Enlightenment,[391] as reflected in the hearts and minds of all the individuals who make up the spiritual community.

7

THE POSITIVE GROUP AND
THE NEW SOCIETY

It is difficult to imagine a community dominated by – or rather imbued with – wisdom and compassion. But as potential individuals we have experience of such a community from time to time, and to a limited extent; and there is no excuse for our not attempting to live by such light as we may have. Most of us, most of the time, are functioning as members of a group, and we are therefore accustomed to relating to one another in terms of power – not just direct, naked power, but also power in the form of fraud, exploitation, and manipulation. In our better moments we must want to change all that. We must want to learn to relate in terms of friendliness, compassion, and wisdom.

Another way of putting this is that we must want to relate on the basis of the *bodhicitta*. This term from Mahāyāna Buddhism refers to the will to Enlightenment that is immanent in each and every individual. When the *bodhicitta* (the word literally means 'Enlightenment-heart') has arisen in us, we are strongly motivated to gain Enlightenment, and that motivation has a definitely altruistic orientation; that is, we seek to gain Enlightenment not just for the sake of our own liberation and happiness, but for the benefit of others – indeed, as the traditional phrase has it, for the benefit of all sentient beings.

When we go for Refuge to the Buddha, Dharma, and Sangha, we go from the group to the spiritual community, from being governed by the power principle to being inspired by the principle of the *bodhicitta*, from the old society to a completely new, different kind of society. Buddhists speak in terms of moving from the world, *saṃsāra*, to Sukhāvatī, the Pure Land, a world in which conditions are entirely conducive to the practice of the Dharma. All of us surely, at least sometimes, feel dissatisfied with the world as it is, and would like to live in a better, more beautiful world than the one we at present experience, a world which supports and encourages what is best in us – our generosity, our kindness, and our awareness – instead of conspiring to undermine those qualities.

Many people throughout history have felt this same desire, of course, in the East as well as in the West. We can be sure that people felt it in the Buddha's own day, because we have, for instance, the story of Vaidehī, the wife of King Bimbisāra, who was the ruler of the north Indian kingdom of Magadha. Vaidehī's story is related in the *Amitāyur-Dhyāna Sūtra*, the *sūtra* on the meditation of the Buddha Amitāyus, the Buddha of Eternal Life.[392] (This is one of a group of three *sūtras* dealing with Sukhāvatī, the Happy Land, and its Buddha Amitābha or Amitāyus, the other two being the larger and the smaller *Sukhāvatī Vyūha Sūtras*.)

The story begins with Prince Ajātasatru seizing the throne of Magadha and imprisoning his own father, the righteous old King Bimbisāra, whom he intends to starve to death. But Vaidehī, the king's chief consort (and the mother, as it happens, of Ajātasatru) manages to smuggle food to her husband and thus keep him alive. When Ajātasatru finds out what she has been doing, he threatens to kill her, but in the end is satisfied with imprisoning her.

So there is Vaidehī, alone in prison, hated by her son and unable to supply food to her husband. Understandably, she is thoroughly miserable. But she does not just abandon herself to her misery. Completely disillusioned with being queen, and with worldly life in general, she gives up all thought of her fine palaces, considers her family as lost to her, and concentrates her mind on the Buddha, who is, as it happens, only a few miles away, on the Vulture's Peak. She even contrives to prostrate herself in his direction. And thereupon, the Buddha appears before her. Whether he appears quite literally in his physical form or in some sort of vision we are not told, but when the queen raises her head after paying homage to him, there he is. It is the world-honoured one Śākyamuni, his body glowing purple gold (according to the text), sitting on a lotus flower consisting of a hundred jewels, with Mahāmaudgalyāyana on his left and Ānanda on his right. Above him Vaidehī sees the gods who protect the world showering down heavenly flowers, making offerings to him.

At this sight Vaidehī again prostrates herself on the ground, sobbing, 'O World-Honoured One, what former sin of mine has produced such a wicked son?' But she is not just concerned with her own misfortune. She goes on, 'O Exalted One, what cause and circumstance has connected your life with that of Devadatta, your wicked cousin and once your disciple? My only prayer,' she says, 'is this. O World-Honoured One, please preach to me in detail of all the places where there is no sorrow or trouble, where I should go to be reborn. I am not satisfied with this world of depravities, with Jambudvīpa (that is, India) which is full of hells, of hungry ghosts and brutish life. In this world of depravities there assembles many a multitude of the wicked. May I not hear again the voice of the wicked. I pray that I may never again see a wicked person. Now I throw my entire body and limbs to the ground before you and seek mercy by confessing my sins. I pray for this only, that the sun-like Buddha may instruct me how to meditate on a world wherein all actions are pure.'

By his magical power, the Buddha shows Vaidehī a number of different Pure Lands where there is no suffering, where there is heard no voice of lamentation or even the echo of it. She sees them all in an extended vision, and she chooses to be reborn in Sukhāvatī, the Pure Land of Amitābha or Amitāyus, the land of bliss in the west. Then the Buddha proceeds to instruct her in what she must do to achieve this. She must go for Refuge, she must observe the ten precepts – in short, she must follow faithfully all the fundamental teachings of the Dharma. On top of this she should meditate on Amitāyus, the Buddha of Eternal Life, and his Pure Land, Sukhāvatī. She should visualize them, see them – at least in her meditation – in this very life, and the Buddha teaches her how to do this by way of a series of sixteen meditations.

The first meditation consists of concentrating on an image of the deep red disc of the setting sun. Then one visualizes a ground, foundation, or base of lapis lazuli, deep blue in colour, extending to infinity in all directions, criss-crossed with a network of golden cords. Next, from amidst the golden cords there spring up trees made of jewels, lakes made of jewels, lotuses made of jewels. And eventually, after a whole series of meditations, in the midst of all these brilliant forms of deep colour and dazzling light, one sees Amitābha himself, the Buddha of Infinite Light, attended by his two great bodhisattvas, Avalokiteśvara and Mañjuśrī, embodying his compassion and his wisdom.

The Buddha tells Vaidehī that having meditated in this way, when she comes to die she will be reborn in this higher realm upon which she has been so intensely focused. She will find herself sitting in the calyx of a beautiful lotus flower, the petals will open, and she will see Amitābha seated before her. She will hear his teaching from his own lips, face to face. And she will have nothing to do but practise it and meditate upon it.

Thus conditions in the Pure Land are archetypally ideal. Discourses on the Dharma are heard in the form of the music of the wind blowing through the jewelled trees, and the cries and calls of curlews and waterfowl and birds of paradise. Literally everything speaks to you of the Dharma, and all the conditions of life conduce to the attainment of Enlightenment. Even under these perfect circumstances it is not easy to attain Enlightenment, but at least nothing in your environment holds you back.

This picture, painted for the benefit of Vaidehī in her prison cell, is beautiful, but it may seem a little alien, so remote is it from the world we ordinarily inhabit. But Sukhāvatī is not just another world; our task is to create it, as best we can, on this earth. We have to improve things here, make the situation in which we live more and more conducive to the flowering of the spiritual life and the attainment of Enlightenment.

That is why, in 1967, I founded a new Buddhist movement, and why in the following year I ordained the first members of the Western Buddhist Order, as the spiritual community at the heart of the positive group. The idea was to create – and enable others to continue to create – our own Sukhāvatī, here in our own world, on howsoever small a scale. Over the years I have seen this movement grow slowly but steadily. Every year sees a new Buddhist centre, a new retreat community, or a new right-livelihood business being created somewhere around the world.

One of the most significant of these ceremonies was the opening of the London Buddhist Centre in Bethnal Green, East London, in 1978. On that occasion we conducted ten days of celebration and appreciation, culminating in the dedication of two shrine-rooms. In the larger of these, the focus of the ceremony was a more than life-size image of Amitābha, the Buddha of the West, the Buddha of Infinite Light, who – just as

Śākyamuni told Vaidehī – presides over the Pure Land called Sukhāvatī, 'the happy land' or 'the place of bliss' or simply 'abounding in bliss'. Sukhāvatī is the name given to the whole complex (community space and public centre) in Bethnal Green.

But what is Sukhāvatī, really? What were we really celebrating at the opening of the centre? Were we congratulating one another on having built a place where people can come along once a week to discuss Buddhism and listen to lectures given by someone who has read a great many more books on the subject than they have? Did we work so hard so that we could do a little therapeutic meditation and take a medicinal dose of Buddhism once in a while just so that we could keep going with our normal life in the same old way? ('Don't let them meditate for more than five minutes,' I was once told by a prominent English Buddhist. 'More than that is dangerous for Westerners.')

The name Sukhāvatī was chosen to signal an aspiration that this centre should serve a more noble, radical, even revolutionary function than simply giving people their spiritual vitamins to help them stagger along on the path of worldliness for another few days. Any centre associated with the movement I founded is intended to be nothing less than the nucleus of a new society.

'A new society'? The expression is not new – it was once even the name of a weekly magazine – but under the slogan is a simple but profound, sublime, and radical human aspiration. The new society is designed to allow people to develop as human beings. It will not try to do for people what they can only do for themselves; but it provides facilities, opportunities, and an environment of encouragement, as well as a social and spiritual context of human fellowship, which makes it easier for people to develop as human beings.

To speak of trying to create a new society within the old one is to acknowledge that the old society cannot function in this way, because most of its members are not interested in human development. Far from helping the spiritual aspirant, society at large makes it difficult for us to develop even if we want to, and much of the energy that should be going into the work of spiritual transformation gets frittered away in simply trying to resist society's counter-evolutionary forces, its oppressive, coercive, spirit-crushing influence. In an ideal society we would not have to be on the defensive all the time in order to preserve a little space within which we could grow. Our energies would be liberated for the purpose of our own spiritual development in free association with other like-minded people.

But how can a Buddhist movement function as a new society in miniature? What is its structure? How does it work? It is essentially a fellowship of people who are trying to develop as individuals. At least, a few of its members are doing so, keeping in more or less regular contact with one another and trying to develop together and help each other to develop. These individuals constitute the spiritual community within our movement; and they constitute also the heart of the movement. But we cannot expect that everybody connected with the movement will be making that kind of effort.

The movement therefore has two parts, two levels: a spiritual community proper, and what could be described as a healthy or positive group. First, there is the order, a spiritual community which is open to anyone who is sufficiently integrated as an individual as to be able to make a valid commitment to the path to Enlightenment, and who can thus seriously undertake the primary act of all Buddhists everywhere – Going for Refuge to the Three Jewels. The heart of the movement, therefore, consists of individuals. And the positive group is open to anybody who wishes to take part in its activities. These are the two distinct but overlapping – even interfusing – levels within the movement as a whole. Together they comprise what one could call a Buddhist group, although I prefer to use the expression 'movement' because this suggests that it is in its essence a dynamic process.

All the activities of this movement have one purpose, and one purpose only: to help people grow and develop as individuals. It has never been our aim to build up an organization in the ordinary sense, like that of some modern Japanese Buddhist sects. Our aim is not to march with banners through the streets of London and take over the Albert Hall, or to end up with just a self-serving institution. Indeed, the presence of the spiritual community in the midst of the positive group is intended to ensure that this does not happen.

When I say that members of the order are members of the spiritual community, I mean that they belong to the real, living, joyful spiritual fellowship of those practising the Teaching and following the Way. When I say that they are those who go for Refuge, I am not speaking simply of repeating the Refuge formula two or three times a year on the occasion of some Buddhist festival, as happens in so many parts of the Buddhist world, and even in some Buddhist groups in the West. By Going for Refuge I mean actually committing oneself full-time to the realization of the ideal of human Enlightenment in this very life, and being prepared to give up whatever stands in the way of that commitment.

This spiritual community is just a part of the wider positive group, and this in turn is a part of what is traditionally called the *mahāsaṅgha*, the spiritual community of the four directions – north, south, east, and west – and the three periods of time: past, present, and future.

Howsoever embryonic its development, we are forming the nucleus of a new society. We have initiated a society in which the idea that someone can represent the position or views of someone else, or claim special authority on account of their position, or seek to exert pressure upon or power over someone else, is absurd. In this society there can be room only for individuals living in free association with one another, inspired by the principles of great compassion and transcendental wisdom, and above all by the *bodhicitta*, the will to Enlightenment for the sake of all beings.

8

THE PATH OF DISSATISFACTION

So how do you join a spiritual community? Obviously, you can't do it just by paying a subscription. You can't even do it by kneeling in the snow outside closed monastery gates, Japanese Zen-style. Firstly, and essentially, it is a question of trying to become an individual, trying to develop spiritually. Then it consists in making contact with other individuals who are also trying to develop, and engaging in spiritual practice with them within a common spiritual framework. This is what joining the spiritual community really means.

To put it the other way round, one joins the spiritual community by leaving the group. One ceases to identify oneself with the group; one ceases to feel that one belongs to any kind of group. Nowadays, the pressure of our responsibilities may make it very difficult to do this literally; we cannot simply leave our responsibility for our dependants to be picked up by someone else. But this is no excuse for avoiding any kind of tangible renunciation of the group. There is always the possibility of self-deception. You may say, 'I can get on perfectly well without my home and family – I'm not emotionally dependent on them,' but there is no way of knowing this except by trying out how life feels without them. You may say, 'I'm not particularly attached to living in my native country – I'd be able to manage quite happily anywhere in the world,' but until you have tried coping with totally unfamiliar surroundings, weather, institutions, and customs, and speaking a foreign language for months at a time, you will never be sure. It is easy enough to feel that one is dissociating oneself from group attitudes, but as one's emotional dependence on the group tends to be somewhat unconscious, one will have difficulty proving this to oneself.

The Buddha himself effectively joined the spiritual community by leaving the group in the form of his family home. In the traditional accounts of the Buddha's life, this event is often related dramatically and beautifully. We are told how, one moonlit night, the Buddha, having made his fateful decision to leave everything in the world that he loved, set out alone for the first time in his life.[393] Before he left, he went into the inner apartment of the palace and saw his young wife asleep, with their child lying by her side. Tempted to wake them for a last farewell, he thought better of it – it would be so painful for his wife, and perhaps she would even try to prevent him from going. Standing in the doorway, he just looked at them for a few moments, then turned swiftly away. As well as his wife and child, he also left his father, who, as chief of the clan, was in a position to give him the best start in life, his foster-mother, who looked after him when he was a baby, and his friends. He became, for a number of years, a mendicant, known in those days as a *parivrājaka*, which means 'one who has gone forth' – gone forth, that is to say, from the household life into a life of homelessness, or even, one might say, grouplessness.

In the Buddha's day there were many men, and even a few women, wandering about as *parivrājakas* – rootless, homeless, groupless – all over northern India. They subsisted on alms, going early in the morning from door to door with an alms bowl, taking whatever food people cared to give them. These *parivrājakas* were the spiritual ancestors of the modern Indian sadhus, whom one can still see going from village to village on foot, sitting on the steps of temples and at the feet of great spreading banyan trees.

Going forth as the Buddha did, you cease to belong to the group and become a sort of lone wolf, an individual on your own. So far as the group is concerned, you no longer exist. In orthodox Hinduism this renunciation is marked in dramatic, even terrifying fashion by a special ritual in the course of which you officially become a wanderer. You kindle a sacred fire and pour libations into it while chanting mantras, and then you place on the fire certain personal possessions, finishing with two highly symbolic articles. The first of these is your *tiki*, a tuft of hair which every orthodox Hindu layman has growing on the crown of his head. You snip it off and place it in the fire. Then you take the sacred thread which, if you are a caste Hindu, you wear around your body, and put it on the fire as well. This is a tremendous thing to do because Hindu social life is pervaded by caste through and through – your caste is the most significant aspect of your identity. But you haven't come to the end of the ritual yet, by any means. You conclude by performing your own funeral ceremony. You act as the priest at your own cremation. Whoever you were before, that person is now dead. According to Hindu tradition (although not in modern India) you are officially dead. In terms of the group you don't exist; you have no legal or civil rights. This is the length to which Hindu renunciants traditionally used to go – and to some extent still do go – in order to sever at the root their connection with the group.

For the Buddha, complete dissociation from the world, and the renunciation of one's social identity, was an accepted practice in a way that it is not for us in the West. But we can try to emulate the Buddha's great renunciation as far as we can by going forth – to use the traditional Buddhist term – from as many groups as possible: from home and family, from social position, from national identity, and so on. Such a renunciation is all the greater in a society like ours which has no tradition of this kind. By doing so you have embarked on the transition from being a group member to being a true individual.

The Buddha only became Enlightened after six years of desperate struggle and unceasing search as a *parivrājaka*. When he began to make known what he had discovered, most of his disciples were recruited from the *parivrājaka* class (which was the classless class, you might say, as its members had all renounced their class along with all their other affiliations). In most cases they had been wanderers for many years before they came in contact with the Buddha, embraced his teaching, and were accepted by him – or by other disciples on his behalf – into the spiritual community.

Hence we can distinguish two separate phases of entry into the sangha. First, there is a phase of going forth from home, giving up the group, and wandering, without identifying oneself with any particular collection of people. The second phase consists in joining the spiritual community. These two, one might say, are the negative and positive aspects of one and the same process. Moreover, these two phases are reflected in the Buddhist ordination procedure even today. When you are ordained as what in the West we call a Buddhist monk (though 'monk' isn't an entirely appropriate term) there are two ordinations: the so-called lower ordination, the *pabbajjā* or going forth, and the higher ordination, the *upasampadā*. The going forth symbolizes breaking free of the group, cutting off biological ties, social ties, group loyalties, and political connections of every kind – being simply an individual, on one's own, even isolated; and the higher ordination represents the acceptance of that individual into the spiritual community. The individual is accepted on the basis of having been tried and tested, as it were, in the fires of solitude. He or she has not run back to the group, and can therefore be accepted not as someone taking refuge in a snug little religious coterie, but as an individual accepted by other individuals as a responsible member of the spiritual community.

But how, today, do we begin to make this transition from the old society to the new? One can of course approach any one of a number of traditional Buddhist organizations which more or less resolutely follow the mode of life of Eastern Buddhism in modern Western society. But assuming at least the nucleus of the new society to be already in existence, in the form in which I have described it, one can also make that all-important transition via a Buddhist centre. This is the bridge, the common ground, where these two worlds meet and overlap.

What one brings to the Buddhist centre, at least initially, is a sense of dissatisfaction. This might seem an unlikely attitude for Buddhists to encourage – we are all surely familiar enough with dissatisfaction. Anyone who has ever ordered some product by mail or online will know this feeling, despite the manufacturer's guarantee of full and complete satisfaction. When the thing finally arrives and you unwrap it, somehow it seems less glamorous, less luxurious, flimsier, smaller, than in the photograph. Sometimes it is even the wrong colour, or there's a part missing. Our disappointment may be such that we have no hesitation in sending the offending article, unsatisfactory as it is, back for a refund, perhaps accompanied by a strongly-worded note.

But we have all taken delivery of one article which, when we compare it with the design specifications, is clearly incomplete or botched, and yet we seem more than satisfied with it. That article is, of course, ourselves. We want everything else in our lives to be properly made, polished and shiny, but we cherish ourselves in our imperfect state. So how can we become dissatisfied? We need to compare ourselves as we are here and now with how we could be in the future. We become dissatisfied when we get a glimpse of a potential which is without any limit and see that by comparison we are at present distinctly unsatisfactory and limited. When we espouse that vision we are in a sense taking the first steps towards sending ourselves back in disgust and demanding a properly functioning human individuality.

Dissatisfaction – if it is not just disgruntlement but a genuine and creative mood of inner revolt – is a positive and powerful impulse. Indeed, such a mood is the starting point. You are dissatisfied, perhaps, with the quality of your relationships, with your work, with your leisure activities – and perhaps, more often than not, you are pretty fed up with yourself as well. You start looking around for a new direction, and you hear, perhaps, about Buddhism, and then about the Buddhist centre, about meditation classes, and you start going along to those classes, and to listen to talks. You may even go on a weekend retreat. And as a result of all this, you start to change.

Such change is quite noticeable. I have seen it taking place many times. One sees people visibly changing almost before one's eyes – and this, one might say, is a miracle: that people can change, not just piecemeal, but from top to bottom. Indeed, the Buddha himself referred to this as the greatest of all miracles. In general he condemned the display of so-called miracles or supernormal powers. The ancient Indians were very interested in these things, and even now people tend to perk up and take notice as soon as the subject comes up. The Buddha was often asked to demonstrate miraculous powers, and sometimes he did, if he saw good reason to do so. But for him they were entirely insignificant, and if he thought that they were being taken too seriously, he refused to have anything to do with them. He even went so far as to say, 'I condemn and abhor them, I look down upon them.' 'These,' he went on to say, 'are not real miracles. The real miracle is when someone who was following the dark path changes and starts following the bright path, the path of skilful activities, the path of the spiritual life.'[394]

It is a miracle that continues to occur – often, it seems, against all the odds. People come along quite literally off the street, looking hopeless and dejected, as if they carried all the cares of the world on their shoulders. They start meditating, they become more aware, and in the course of a few weeks, sometimes in the course of a weekend retreat away in the country, you see them beginning to look bright and cheerful. They begin to see something of the Buddha's vision of existence, and they change. One might think that when someone has travelled along the same old rut for decades, it is too late. But that is a great mistake. If you find the right sort of encouragement and the right sort of conditions, you can change at any time of your life.

After this initial positive change takes place, you will perhaps start to feel a deeper dissatisfaction. You may start feeling that you cannot go on living in the same old way. You begin to find your old relationships and old work very restricting. You experience, in short, something of what the Buddha himself experienced when he made the decision to go forth. At that point you might decide to take some action: to move into a residential community for a couple of weeks to see what it's like, for example, or to work in a Buddhist right-livelihood project for a trial period.

The whole process – from initial dissatisfaction to going forth – may only take two or three months, but it is more likely to take several years. It varies a great deal from one person to another. But when the transition from the old society to the new is finally made, you are henceforth part of the new society, and your strength as an individual strengthens that new society. From then on you live in a situation that is conducive to your development as a human being, one in which the possibility of growth is infinite. And that is a very rare opportunity indeed. As I know from my own experience, one seldom encounters such an opportunity in the Buddhist East, and one has had little hope at all of ever coming across it in the West until recent times, with the establishing of a number of effective spiritual communities. Having found such a context, one is well on the way to becoming a true individual. It is the nature of true individuality that we will now go on to consider.

PART II
THE TRUE INDIVIDUAL

INTRODUCTION

Am I an individual, or just a social unit? This is the central question of our personal lives, and it is one we need to keep asking ourselves, and keep trying to penetrate more deeply. It is also the key to the development of a sangha, a spiritual community. No individuals, no sangha. Any consideration of what the sangha is must therefore include as full an understanding as possible of the nature of individuality. So – what is an individual? There is no one answer to that question. We have seen already that the true individual can be defined in traditional Buddhist terms as someone who has broken through the first three fetters and has thus gained Stream Entry. We have also witnessed the emergence of the individual in the context of human history. In the following chapters we will be considering individuality from various other points of view.

First, we will take a brief look at the qualities typical of an individual. Then, in Chapter 9, we will broaden our scope to consider the development of individuality not just in terms of relatively recent history, but in the context of the evolution of consciousness as a whole. But then, having expanded our vision to take in such a broad and lofty perspective, we will narrow our focus to address a question that may already have occurred to you. Is it really legitimate, in terms of Buddhist doctrine, to speak of the 'individual'? Isn't Buddhism famous for its 'no-self' doctrine? It is worth taking some time to clarify the ways in which it is – and is not – appropriate to think of the spiritual life in terms of the development of individuality; this we will do in Chapter

10, 'The Integrated Individual'. And in Chapters 11 and 12 we will relate our developing conception of individuality to two other fields of thought and experience: Western philosophy, in the form of the thought of Friedrich Nietzsche, and the arts, in which context we will consider whether or not it is appropriate to think of the artist as a true individual.

But to begin with, what – in general – are the characteristics of the true individual? There are all sorts of qualities that the individual will tend to develop, and no account of them will ever encompass the full range of possibilities. Individuality cannot be measured or weighed or estimated in terms of any number of qualities or characteristics. It is unfathomable and inexhaustible, and the same can be said for its qualities and characteristics. There are, however, certain qualities of the individual that seem especially relevant to many people's experience and behaviour. To be an individual, before anything else perhaps, you need objectivity, clarity, and intelligence in the broad sense. You need to be aware that actions have consequences, that you are responsible for your actions and therefore responsible for their consequences too. This is a *sine qua non*, without which one cannot proceed further. You also need to be receptive – otherwise, again, you are stuck. But beyond these fundamentals, the following positive characteristics may be said to be typical of the individual.

Firstly, as an individual you are free – or at least comparatively free – from group conditioning, and you constantly try to see beyond your own conditioning. You are aware of how the world has come to be the way it is, aware of history. One way in which this kind of awareness can be developed is through travelling. As many people have discovered, the process of moving away from the familiar supports to one's views and experiencing the very different group conditioning of another country can make one realize that the way one is accustomed to look at the world is not the only way of seeing things.

Secondly, you have developed self-consciousness – not in the adolescent sense of feeling that everyone is looking at you, but in the sense of being aware of what you are doing and why. I use the word 'developed' here deliberately; it takes discipline and effort to develop self-consciousness, and indeed many of the traditional Buddhist practices are designed precisely to develop it. Primitive man was conscious but not self-conscious, not aware, and all too often the same goes for modern, 'civilized' man. But as an individual you are aware.

Broadly speaking, this awareness has four dimensions: awareness of self, of nature, of other people, and of reality. The first of these dimensions, awareness of self, includes many things. To begin with, you are aware of your physical body, and its position and movements. You are also aware of your emotions, whether positive or negative, and of your thoughts – of ideas, concepts, reflections, reasoning. You are aware of your conditioning too – your upbringing, your environment, your early experiences, your associations, your skills and tendencies, likes and dislikes. You are aware of your own basic motivations – you are able to be reasonably objective about yourself, to weigh yourself up fairly accurately.

Essentially, you are aware of your own uniqueness, aware that 'universal consciousness' has focused itself in you, and that as one of an infinite number of foci of that consciousness, you are irreplaceable. You are intensely, luminously aware. You feel the very vibration of your own individual existence. You are aware of yourself as sharply distinguished, differentiated, from the whole of the rest of nature. You are aware of your absolute unrepeatability – of how in the course of ages, through hundreds and millions of years, there will never be anybody else like you.

The second dimension of awareness is awareness of nature. You are aware of nature as something completely other, something which is not yourself, even though you have emerged from it, grown out of it. You are aware of your physical surroundings, the environment. With the third dimension of awareness you are aware of other people, particularly others who are also self-aware. You are aware of what is happening between you and others – that is, you are aware of the nature and quality of your relationships.

Finally, and above all, you cultivate the fourth dimension of awareness: awareness of reality. You are aware of the mysterious, elusive thread of unity that runs through the whole of the vast fabric of things. That is, you are aware – or seek to become aware – of absolute reality, of what is sometimes called the transcendental. You have a direct, personal relationship with the deeper reality of things. We can go so far as to say – somewhat poetically, perhaps – that the individual is one through whom the deeper reality of things, the truth behind appearances, functions or is present in the world. Through the individual is seen the universal: in fact, the individual and the universal coincide.[395]

If you are an individual, you know what you are doing. You are not reactive, or mechanical, or impelled; you are not driven, or dragged along by blind instinct. You are not the victim of your own unconscious urges. You are spontaneous and free.

Thirdly, and following on from this self-awareness, you are, if you are an individual, set apart from the mass of humanity. You are no longer submerged in the species, in the group. You are yourself. We may even say that each individual constitutes a distinct species. The Tibetan text called *The Precepts of the Gurus* lists 'ten signs of the superior man'; the ninth is as follows:

> To differ from the multitude in every thought and action is the sign of a superior man.[396]

This is not to say that you go out of your way to be different. An individual is not necessarily an eccentric. Nor is an individual to be confused with an individualist, or with someone with an inflated ego which they like to inflict on others. It is simply that you think for yourself and therefore, inevitably, that you think rather differently from others. You may respect the thoughts of others, and even make use of them, but at the same time you will give careful thought to the validity of other people's thinking.

It doesn't occur to you to desire to be different from others – it isn't that you want to 'stand out from the herd'. Nor do you set yourself 'above the herd'. An individual is certainly not someone who simply gets to the top of the social group, like kings, ministers, millionaires, film stars, and so on. An individual is different in kind, different in quality from others. You differ from others simply by being yourself.

Fourthly, you are not psychologically dependent on others. You do not require the approval of the group for your peace of mind. You don't mind differing from other people, you don't mind entertaining ideas that nobody else would dream of adopting. The disapproval of the group will not pressure you into conformity. If need be, you are prepared to go it alone. This doesn't mean going it alone as a matter of principle – on the contrary, the need to appear independent of others is just another form of dependency. Nor do you have to refuse help from others in order to be independent: elderly people who refuse to accept their objective limitations, saying, 'I've always been independent', do not thereby display real independence. Real independence is independence of mind: you are autonomous, you make your own choices.

With this freedom and self-determination goes creativity. One way to put this is to say that primitive humanity is reproductive, modern humanity is productive (i.e. producing material things – food, housing, clothing, artefacts), but the individual is creative. That is to say, what you create as an individual, even though it may be material in form, has a spiritual significance. Whether you are creating music, literature, philosophy, religion, or whatever, you are really creating yourself. The individual is his or her own greatest work of art. This is obvious in the case of men like the Buddha, Confucius, or Socrates. But in much later times we see it, perhaps on a diminished scale, in the case of, for example, Goethe. He is the greatest poet of the German language, but we may say, nevertheless, that his greatest poem was his life. This commitment to his own development as an individual comes out very well in his *Conversation with Eckermann*: he worked on his own character, his own personality, his own life, quite consciously, in the same spirit in which he created his literary works.

The French theatre director Antonin Artaud (1896–1948) expresses a similar commitment in very passionate terms in his 'Points':

> I hate and renounce as a coward every being who consents to having been created and does not wish to have recreated himself, i.e. who agrees with the idea of a God as the origin of his being, as of the origin of his thought.
>
> I hate and renounce as a coward every being who agrees not to have been self-created and who consents to and recognizes the idea of a matrix nature of the world as his already created body.
>
> I do not consent to having not created my body myself and I hate and renounce as a coward every being who consents to live without first having recreated himself.
>
> I hate and renounce as a coward every being who does not recognize that life is given to him only to recreate and reconstitute his entire body and organism.[397]

Fifthly, as an individual you may be, and you accept that you may be, unpopular. Unpopularity is not of course a characteristic as such of the true individual – it is just something that he or she often experiences.

The Buddha himself (before he became the Buddha) had to be prepared to lose the friendship and respect of his five followers on the path of asceticism, when he decided that self-torture was useless and started taking proper food again.[398] Even after his Enlightenment he was not at all popular in some quarters, because he challenged the vested interests of an entrenched hereditary priesthood. Fortunately, the Indians on the whole are a rather tolerant people. Other great individuals have not been so fortunate. Socrates was condemned to death, Confucius was driven from state to state, and almost died of starvation in a ditch. The prophets of Israel were liable to be stoned. As for the creative artist of modern times, he or she can still arouse fury in the mob.

Sixthly, the individual will develop emotions that are positive and refined. Everyone is capable of positive emotion – even Stalin was a kindly fellow from time to time, apparently – but it is clear from this example alone that you cannot rely on your natural human warmth to express itself as compassion, sensitivity, peace, and joy. Whether positive or negative, human emotion naturally tends to be crude, even violent. A positive, refined, focused emotional nature therefore needs to be consciously developed. You need to take full responsibility for your own mental states. You recognize that your emotional experience is self-created.

Seventhly, your energies flow freely and spontaneously, cleanly and harmoniously. There are no blockages, no inhibitions, no 'hang-ups'. All your energy is always available. You are therefore able to be creative in whatever you do.

Eighthly, you are alone. To be an individual in the midst of people who are not individuals is to be alone. To create in the midst of people who merely produce or reproduce is to be alone. As an individual you may feel this very intensely – and you may not know whether to be glad or sorry about it. You are glad because, having created yourself anew, you experience something you have not experienced before, but you are sorry because the greater your experience is, the harder it is for you to share it with others. The Buddha himself no doubt experienced aloneness, especially during the period between leaving home at the age of 29 and gaining Enlightenment six years later at the foot of the bodhi tree. Even after that, until he was able to share his experience of Enlightenment, he would have experienced his aloneness even more intensely. At one level or another, this is always the situation of the individual.

However, being alone is not your aim. The final characteristic of the individual I want to draw out here is that you encourage others to be individuals in their own way. You are willing to take responsibility in any situation in which you find yourself, to help make it a creative situation both for yourself and for others. This is, as we have seen, the basis upon which individuals create a spiritual community.

In all these ways you accept responsibility for yourself, for your own individual growth, for your own life, and for the effect that your life has on the life around you. And you act accordingly, because you see such growth as being the most important thing in life for each and every human being. You therefore commit yourself wholeheartedly to the process of individual development. In more traditional, more Buddhistic terms, as a true individual, you commit yourself to the Three Jewels.

9

THE EVOLUTION OF THE INDIVIDUAL

On the basis of the above description, who would not want to be a true individual? At the same time, we have already seen that individuals are extremely rare, which suggests that it is not easy to become one. So how do you become an individual? What is the process? We have seen how individuals first began to emerge during what Jaspers called the Axial Age. But how did that happen? We can explore this in terms of a concept that is in many ways the most significant idea in the whole range of modern thought: evolution.

The *locus classicus* of evolution as a concept is of course Darwin's great theory of natural selection and the origin of species. However, evolution need not be restricted to a specifically scientific application. In general terms, it refers to the way in which all processes, however much they appear on the surface to be fixed in their forms and functions, are conditioned and impermanent adaptations or sets of circumstances that have grown out of earlier sets of circumstances or less highly organized adaptations. This is perhaps the most significant use of the term evolution from a Buddhist point of view.

As a general principle, evolution can be applied to almost anything. It enables us to understand the whole of existence – from the formation of planets, to the central Darwinian concept of biological evolution, all the way through to human institutions, and even ideas themselves – as being in the process of some kind of unfolding, some kind of growth. The universe, we can say, is one gigantic process of becoming. And we are part of that process.

The model of evolution we know best is that of a blind, accidental, and ruthless groping towards ever more successful adaptations to ever-changing environmental circumstances. If one species develops a new genetic configuration which gives it an edge over its environment, then other species have to develop adaptations of their own to meet that challenge. Even what we know as the self can be explained as a more or less successful way in which a certain group of organisms have adapted themselves to their environment. It is, one might say, a development driven from underneath.

This model is an essentially mechanistic one, and it leaves all sorts of important questions unanswered. Some would even say that it is wisest to leave them unanswered, arguing that no such explanation can begin to dispel the essential mystery of things, particularly the mystery of consciousness and the self. It is to engage with this mystery that another, quite different model is sometimes invoked. According to this way of thinking, evolution is not so much driven from underneath as drawn up from above. Of course, generally speaking such ideas are the province of religion, which usually has a vitalist or teleological perspective on the whole principle of evolution. The very fact of evolution beginning to reflect upon its own workings is seen as indicating that the process is also a progress, and that it must be in some sense directed from above or beyond itself. That is, if progress is observed occurring within the process of evolution, it is assumed that this progress happens in relation to some identifiable goal, value, or principle above or beyond that whole process.

Neither of these models works altogether satisfactorily on its own, but they do not have to be set in opposition to each other. If one is not rigidly literalistic about either model, they may each be said to be relevant to particular aspects of our situation. Thus, in the faltering, unforeseeable steps of Darwinian evolution we could also read the progressive manifestation through time of an absolute, transcendent reality whose very presence makes possible the emergence of one new quality and characteristic after another in that evolutionary process. There is not, obviously – from a Buddhist perspective, anyway – some preordained grand plan behind the whole process of evolution, but we can say perhaps that this absolute reality is a kind of reservoir on which evolution, especially human evolution, continually draws.

The purpose of bringing evolution into a discussion of Buddhism is not so much to explain evolution in spiritual terms as to use the idea of evolution to throw light on the spiritual development of the individual. It is not meant to suggest anything merely scientific, historical, or even religious. It is a way of describing a process within ourselves as individuals. It concerns ourselves as continually growing – *evolving* – beings, as beings who are capable, indeed, of infinite development.

First, we can look back at how we have evolved. We are the product of billions of years of cosmic evolution, about half a million years of human evolution, and ten thousand years of cultural evolution. Biologically speaking, we have evolved from lower, simpler forms of life, and anthropologically we have evolved from savagery and barbarism to civilization and culture, while psychologically we have evolved from unconsciousness to simple consciousness, and from simple consciousness to the rudiments of self-consciousness. Secondly, we can look forward to what we are developing into – not as a group, not as a species, but as individuals. The dividing line between these two kinds of development is represented by self-consciousness, or awareness.

So we stand at this watershed. Human beings at their best – aware, responsible, intelligent, sensitive – stand at this turning point where a higher evolution emerges from the 'lower' evolution. Unfortunately, we are capable of sinking well below this point as well as of rising far above it. We like to think of ourselves as leading fully human lives, but it has to be said that most of the time our ingrained animality – our group-consciousness – is only fitfully illuminated by individual self-awareness. Real humanity, in other words, is an achievement rather than something with which we are born.

This is in no way to deny our common humanity. It is to remind us of what being human is about, of what distinguishes us from the lower evolution. The higher evolution is the evolution of our humanity, which must always be an ongoing process. The freedom we gain by virtue of our self-awareness necessarily allows us the freedom to surrender that freedom. But we are also capable as individuals of building upon that basic level of humanity. We have the capacity to evolve beyond the point of self-consciousness towards another crucial point. This is where transcendental awareness – direct awareness of reality – emerges; and this awareness propels us even further, towards what Buddhists call Enlightenment. It is in this way that we can see Buddhism not as a religion in the conventional and debased sense of the term, but as the path of the higher evolution, as the whole evolutionary process becomes self-conscious in human beings.

The Russian novelist Vladimir Nabokov, when asked what distinguishes us from the animals, answered as follows:

> Being aware of being aware of being. In other words, if I not only know that I am but also know that I know it, then I belong to the human species. All the rest follows: the glory of thought, poetry, a vision of the universe. In that respect, the gap between ape and man is immeasurably greater than the one between amoeba and ape. The difference between an ape's memory and human memory is the difference between an ampersand and the British Museum library.[399]

Though there is some continuity in the growth of the higher evolution from the lower evolution, there is one crucial discontinuity. The lower evolution is collective: a mutation must be shared amongst a whole group of organisms before it can be said that a new species has evolved. By contrast, the higher evolution is carried by the individual, because the growing point is the development of self-consciousness, awareness, mindfulness. To the extent that there is awareness, there is the higher evolution, and vice versa. Just as when you see a bud on the bare branch of a tree, you know that sooner or later there will be a leaf, and even a blossom, in the same way you know that if in anybody's life you see some glimmer of awareness, you may be certain that sooner or later they are going to develop beyond that level of awareness.

As a result of developing awareness, a single individual can ultimately develop qualities that are different from those found in the generality of people not just in degree, but in kind. He or she can become an entirely new kind of being – what the Buddhist tradition terms a Buddha, an Enlightened One. It is important to understand that the true purpose of any universal religion (as distinct from ethnic or tribal religions) is to produce such beings, and that they are not just the same old thing reissued in a new and improved edition, but an altogether new species of being, a fresh 'meta-biological' – so to speak – mutation.

The higher evolution being a matter for the individual, we have to think of it not in general, but in particular, even personal terms. Having looked at the vast processes of evolution as if through a telescope, we must take a microscope to the subject and examine how the individual evolves or develops. Under the microscope we shall be putting, in effect, ourselves.

Human beings consist, roughly speaking, of two broad divisions: the physical body and the mind or consciousness. The body belongs to the lower evolution. We have inherited this body, so wonderfully made, from a long series of animal ancestors, extending back into dim and distant ages. As for the mind – well, it would tie things up neatly if we could say that the human mind belongs essentially to the higher evolution. But we definitely cannot. Aristotle defines Man as a rational animal, but ordinary rational consciousness is not enough, in itself, to raise us above the lower evolution. Indeed, some of the higher mammals clearly possess rudimentary powers of reasoning of their own. All we can say is that the human mind has the *potential* to embark on the higher evolution. The development of both our powers, both the physical and the mental, is severely limited by our evolutionary genetic inheritance. But in the mind there lies the possibility of a continued development, of what I am calling a higher evolution. In a sense, we are mind rather than body, and if our future lies anywhere, it lies in the mind. In other words, the future evolution of humanity will be mainly, if not exclusively, psychological and spiritual.

Before we describe the stages of development through which consciousness passes, it would be appropriate to define what we mean by consciousness. Unfortunately, one has to confess at once that any definition would be tautological. Here is one dictionary's attempt at a definition of consciousness: 'A character belonging to certain processes or events in the living organism which must be regarded as unique and therefore as indefinable in terms of anything else, but which can perhaps be best described as a view of these processes or events as it were from the inside.'[400] The individual is, as it were, inside what is happening – that is as near as we can get to, if not a definition, at least a description, of consciousness. Consciousness, therefore, is synonymous with awareness, whatever that may be.

The difficulty we are faced with is that of differentiating successive stages in the development of something which is unique and indefinable. If consciousness at one stage is unique and indefinable, it will be equally so at every other stage. How can one unique and indefinable thing be distinguished from another?

The difficulty is more apparent than real. If consciousness is 'a view of certain processes or events in the living organism', where there is a view, there is obviously something viewed. The stages of development through which consciousness passes may therefore be distinguished on the basis of their respective objects. If we do this we can make out four degrees or levels of consciousness: simple consciousness, self-consciousness, transcendental consciousness, and absolute consciousness.[401] These terms are provisional – others might conceivably do just as well. Alternatively, for example, these levels could be called sense consciousness, subjective consciousness, objective consciousness, and universal consciousness.

The first level – simple consciousness – is synonymous with sense-based perception. It consists, that is to say, in awareness of sensations arising from contact between the sense organs and the external world. This is the level of consciousness we share with animals; it connects us with the vast process of biological evolution, a process of almost unimaginable extent, stretching from the simplest unicellular organism to the miraculous intricacies of our biological functions as primates.

The second level – self-consciousness – is not merely perceiving, or even conceiving (through the cognitive sense). You perceive that you perceive. You are aware that you are aware. Not only do you experience sensations, feelings, emotions, thoughts, and volitions, and so on; you experience yourself as experiencing them. Not only are you aware of what comes to you through your senses; you are able to stand aside, as it were, and be aware of yourself as being aware of the things you are sensing, rather than being immersed in them, identified with them.

It is in this reflexive form of consciousness – consciousness bending back on itself – that our humanity most characteristically resides. It connects us with the tens of thousands of years in which self-reflective consciousness has gradually allowed us to distinguish ourselves from the rest of the animal world. Here we find ourselves in the human realm proper, the realm explored in the cognitive and social sciences. This is the culmination of the lower evolution and the inauguration of the higher evolution. It stands as a watershed between the two, and is thus of crucial importance. However, this is not all we are capable of: we can go further still.

With the development of full self-consciousness we see ourselves as we truly are. With the development of the third level, transcendental consciousness, we see the world as it really is. This is where philosophy and religion come into their own. It is where we make some kind of connection with the nature of reality, culminating in an experience of transcendental awareness. This awareness is of the higher spiritual reality that embraces both oneself and all conditioned existence – the whole evolutionary process. It is described as transcendental because it transcends the distinction between subject and object.

At least, up to a point. At this stage an object is still perceived as an object, but it is as though the 'line' where subject and object meet and divide off from each other is replaced by a crack – which may widen into a clear gap – through which shines the light of absolute or universal consciousness. Starting off as a narrow flickering shaft of light, this is the flash of insight in the light of which we see the transcendental. And this light in which we see the transcendental is also the light in which the transcendental sees us. In other words, the awareness or consciousness by which we know the transcendental is identical with the awareness or consciousness by which the transcendental knows us.[402] Awareness is no longer wholly identified with the self and its subjective, psychological conditionings. It is for this reason that transcendental consciousness may also be spoken of as objective consciousness.

The fourth level, absolute or universal consciousness, is the gradual flowering of Buddhahood itself out of that experience of transcendental consciousness. It frees us from the whole cycle of human life and death, and may therefore be termed the supra-human level. The crack widens to become an aperture, and the aperture goes on opening out, expanding, as it were, to infinity. In this way consciousness becomes one with its object, which is infinite. Subject and object entirely disappear. Hence here there is nothing to be said.

The practical reality of how consciousness evolves – at least beyond the stages of the lower evolution – is obviously more various and uncertain than this account can suggest. There are all sorts of intermediate stages in the evolution of consciousness; I have delineated these four principal ones in order to give a clear, broad, and simple outline of the subject.

It has been suggested that the process of human gestation recapitulates in nine months the hundreds of millions of years of evolution that underlie the human species as a whole. The child also recapitulates in his or her early years the evolution of consciousness from simple consciousness to self-consciousness, from animal to primitive humanity. At the time of birth the child is an animal with merely animal needs;

but within about three years he or she develops reason, memory, and language, and the rudimentary self-consciousness that these accomplishments reflect and nurture.

However, progress slows down dramatically during those first three years. From traversing the equivalent of hundreds of millions of years in the womb we go on to cover just a few million years of evolution during our first three years outside it. And after that point there is practically no development at all, in comparison with the staggering development that takes place in those early years. In the remaining years allotted to us, we learn to read and write, we acquire knowledge – even a great deal of it; we perhaps learn to paint or play the piano, and we almost certainly learn to drive a car. In other words we recapitulate, more or less sketchily, the history of civilization. But in terms of consciousness we remain throughout life more or less where we were at the age of three.

Why is this? Why do we stop at this point of rudimentary self-consciousness? The reason is to be found in the distinction between the lower evolution, which is a collective process, and the higher evolution, which is an individual achievement. The higher evolution cannot be recapitulated in the way the lower evolution is recapitulated in the development of the foetus. You can inherit simple consciousness from your parents, but not self-consciousness – much less transcendental consciousness. Even if you were lucky enough to have parents endowed with transcendental consciousness, you yourself would still have to start again from the beginning. The good news is that the path of the higher evolution can be traversed within the limits of a single human life.

The lower evolution carries us up to the point of rudimentary self-consciousness, and then it leaves us there. From then on, our progress depends on our own conscious effort. Without that, no further progress is possible. This predicament is somewhat reminiscent of another crucial episode in evolution, when life was leaving the sea in which it began and beginning to invade the dry land. The tide washes on to the shore sea-creatures that are developing a capacity to make some very limited use of conditions on land – perhaps to lay their eggs. Then, when the tide retreats, it leaves these creatures stranded on the shore, to make their own way. The sea cannot do any more for their development. Our predicament, we may say, is a little like theirs. Life has swept us on to the shores of self-consciousness and left us there to fend for ourselves.

The general surge and flow of evolution can do no more for us. From here onwards it is all up to us individually.

We are therefore confronted with a choice – not a collective choice, not a choice facing us as a species, but an individual one. It confronts you and me. We – that is, you and I – can either stop where we now are, or continue the process of evolution. And if we do decide to continue, the evolution we embark on will mean one thing – the development of consciousness.

Moreover, if we continue the process of evolution, we can do so only by virtue of our individual determination and effort. Nature will not help us do it. A human existence is – and by definition must be – a struggle, even a fight. Life can seem just to drift along, and no doubt we can drift along with it. But if some aspects of life involve passively riding a prevailing current, the higher evolution is not one of them. Self-development – the development of consciousness to a higher level – is a struggle with some very recalcitrant material indeed.

This is because most of us, most of the time, think of self-development, if we think of it at all, in terms of physical or intellectual development. We may wake up in the morning and think, 'I'm going to get fitter today' or 'I'm going to read something about Buddhism today.' But how often do our aspirations include the objective of developing our consciousness – self-development in the fully and distinctively human sense of the expression? If the answer is 'Not very often, if at all,' we have to face the fact that we are failing to lead truly human lives.

There is no compulsion to follow the path of the higher evolution. In fact, most people are not even aware of the possibility of doing so, and most of those who are don't bother to take advantage of that awareness. Even being prepared to entertain such a question therefore puts one in a small minority. Any minority finds itself in a difficult position, and the minority who set out on the path of the higher evolution have the particular difficulty that it is a path from which it is very easy to be diverted.

The higher evolution is traditionally the concern of the universal religions – that is, the religions of the individual, the religions that speak not just to one particular ethnic group but, in principle, to all people. But today there is little to be gained from going to ministers, priests, and mullahs for guidance in how to develop one's level of consciousness. In most parts of the world – including Buddhist ones – the universal religions have become essentially ethnic in their concerns. They are part of the establishment, offering themselves as forms of community service and no more. There is probably more concern for the development of consciousness to be found within the sphere of the arts and some branches of psychology than in more conventional attempts to live a spiritual life.

There is a verse in the *Bhagavad Gītā*, the celebrated and popular Hindu text, in which Krishna (who, we may say, embodies absolute consciousness) is represented as saying that out of a thousand men, only one seeks him, and that out of a thousand who seek him, only one will find him.[403] So, according to Krishna, the goal will be attained by perhaps one person in a million – and this is probably rather a generous estimate.

The *Dhammapada* makes the same point from a less dramatic perspective. The Buddha says, 'It is difficult to attain the human state. It is difficult to hear the real truth. The arising of an Enlightened one is difficult.'[404] To paraphrase, we can say that it is difficult really to be a human being – it is easier to withdraw from that challenge into a more or less animalistic state. It is difficult to develop self-consciousness, and more difficult still to develop transcendental consciousness. It is difficult to be an individual, to go on making an effort to be aware.

The difficulty has to be emphasized, not to discourage us, but to give us some hope of success. So long as we realize that the process is difficult and take that difficulty seriously, we shall be able to overcome it. But if we don't allow ourselves to realize how difficult it is going to be, if we think it can't be as difficult as all that, then we won't be able to do so.

Although the odds are stacked against us, and the goal seems remote, our immediate task is clear. It is to develop our rudimentary self-consciousness into full self-consciousness, as well as to begin to develop the third level of consciousness, transcendental or objective consciousness. Though the third level cannot be perfected before the second is fully developed, the two are nonetheless developed together. The full development of self-consciousness perfects one's humanity; and with the full development of transcendental consciousness, this makes one a Stream Entrant, someone in whom the influence of the higher evolution outweighs that of the lower evolution.

The higher evolution is a formidable proposition and it will take all our energy. If we are going to concern ourselves with it, we will have to concern ourselves with it – with the development of consciousness – always and everywhere. We cannot dedicate half our time and energy to it. It is all or nothing. Whatever situation confronts us, whatever experience befalls us, whatever opportunity presents itself to us, we always have to ask ourselves: 'What bearing does this have – directly or indirectly – on the higher purpose I have set myself?' We have to raise this question in relation to our work, our personal relationships, our social, cultural, and sporting activities, our interests – the books we read, the music we listen to, the films we watch. The question is always the same: what effect is this going to have on my development as a human being?

Making the living of a religious or even spiritual life in a conventional sense our main consideration will not necessarily have any kind of positive impact on our development. But if we make the development of consciousness the primary motivation in everything we do, we will make sure progress. And if we don't – well, we won't.

10

THE INTEGRATED INDIVIDUAL

Innate within us is the desire to change, to grow, to evolve. That is what being human means. And yet, as we have seen, the evolution of consciousness is not an automatic process. As anyone who has ever aspired to change will know, it is hard to sustain the effort to do it. However inspired we sometimes are, we are only too likely to find it almost impossible to sustain that inspiration, or to translate it into consistent effort towards greater self-awareness.

Why is this? The reason is that we are not so much a self as a succession of selves, perhaps even a bundle of selves. We are not a unified, continually operative self, but a whole number of selves battling for supremacy, only one of which is in control at any one time. This explains why we so often fail to do what we have set out to do. For example, the assumption behind a decision to get up early in the morning is that the person who makes the decision and the person who will carry it out are one and the same. However, when we wake up we are apt to find that during the night another self has come on duty, a self who has no intention of getting up, but rather fancies a lie-in this morning. So we lie there, vaguely remembering the decision made the night before, and wondering what happened to our resolve.

Becoming an individual, therefore, is a process of integration. Somehow we have to find a way of unifying the different selves that are within us, integrating our total being, conscious and unconscious, intellectual and emotional. As well as this integration, which we could call 'horizontal', there is also 'vertical' integration to achieve: an integration with our own unrealized higher potential, which is achieved through allowing ourselves to experience our heights – and our depths. Thinking of the Buddhist life in these terms, we can see that committing ourselves to the observance of ethical precepts helps us to live in such a way that we mean what we say, and do what we mean to do; in other words, we develop integrity. The traditional Buddhist practice of mindfulness in all its forms also nurtures the integration of our many 'selves', as we make the effort to maintain continuous awareness throughout the activities of daily life. And meditation can be described as a direct method of integrating ourselves. Firstly, it brings about 'horizontal' integration, as our scattered selves are gradually drawn together through our focus on the object of concentration. Then, on the basis of that horizontal integration, we can engage in meditation practices in the course of which we reflect on and progressively experience higher truth, in a process of 'vertical' integration. Devotional practices and Dharma studies also help us to move towards this kind of vertical integration.

But even once we have understood the need to develop awareness in all senses, and have perhaps started trying to develop it through such methods, it is still not certain that we will develop it in the right way. There is a danger that we will develop instead what I think of as alienated awareness. In an age of transition, when there are no stable, universally accepted values upon which we can base our lives, many people lose any very solid sense of identity. Also, many people are conditioned to clamp down on their bodily sensations, especially those connected with sex, and to repress negative emotion, to feel what they are told they ought to feel rather than what they truly feel. So, for a variety of reasons, many of us find ourselves unable, or unwilling, to experience ourselves, especially our feelings and emotions. As a result, when we try to develop awareness, we may become aware of ourselves without actually experiencing ourselves. In a sense, we are aware of a non-experience of ourselves, of ourselves not being there.

This failure to experience ourselves is disastrous because it tends to create a split between the conscious and the unconscious, between that part of ourselves which we allow ourselves to experience continuously, and that part which we have made an unconscious decision not to experience and which we therefore experience only intermittently and partially, if at all.

But refusing to experience a certain part of oneself does not mean that the part in question has ceased to exist. Unacknowledged it may be, but it is still very much alive; and not only alive, but kicking. In one way or another, it will make its presence felt, typically in the guise of moods. Suddenly we feel depressed, or angry, or anxious; the mood seems to take possession of us, and we don't really know why. We sometimes even say, 'I didn't feel quite myself yesterday,' or, 'I don't know what's come over me today,' – almost as if we feel we are someone else for as long as that mood persists.

Unfortunately, the painful state of alienated awareness has in the past been aggravated by certain Eastern spiritual teachers who have made all sorts of statements that fail to take account of the differences between the modern Western mentality and the traditional Eastern way of seeing things. Buddhist teachers, for example, and many of their Western disciples, have been known to assert, on the authority of the Buddha's teaching of *anattā*, that we have no self, or that the self is an illusion. Hindu teachers, meanwhile, will tell you that you are not the body, you are not the mind, you are not your feelings or emotions or thoughts; you are, in fact, God.

True awareness, integrated awareness, is developed by learning to experience yourself more fully, to be more aware of what you experience in your physical body, and in your feelings and emotions, particularly those feelings that you like to think you don't experience. One of the basic but very important functions of the sangha is to provide a safe environment in which we may disclose ourselves to others and – in having our experience acknowledged by others – gradually learn to acknowledge more of it ourselves.

Another way the sangha plays a big part in all this is to help us to become aware of what is going on. It is obviously very difficult for us to tell whether there are aspects of our experience that we are not allowing ourselves to be aware of, as the problem is lack of awareness itself. But our spiritual friends may well be able to see what is going on better than we can ourselves, and will find ways – kind and sympathetic ways – to draw it to our attention. And, of course, we will be able to do the same for them.

In discussing all this, certain questions inevitably arise. If awareness is about experiencing oneself, what is to be understood by the term 'oneself'? Is the self identical with consciousness? What is the relation between the self and individuality? Are they two things or one and the same? Then again, what is personality – and where does the ego come in? A great deal has been said on all these subjects in the spiritual traditions of the world, and in the contexts of philosophy, both ancient and modern, and modern psychology. They are variants, in a sense, of that most basic question, 'Who am I?'

I do not propose to enter into a discussion in this context of the nature of the self, interesting and important though the subject certainly is. Here, I just want to make a simple point about terminology. All these terms – self, individual, personality, ego – tend to be used rather freely, but it matters a great deal what they mean. Questions such as 'What is the self?' are not just matters of semantics, not just quibbling over the meaning of words. Or rather, they are indeed semantic questions, but semantics happen to be of the greatest practical importance, even in the spiritual life.

No less a figure than Confucius attests to the value of semantics. In the China of his day (more or less the time of the Buddha) there were hundreds, even thousands, of small states, each administered by a prince or duke, and some of course were better run than others, giving rise to a certain amount of speculation and consulting of sages on the part of the more philosophical rulers as to how best to reform one's state. Confucius was once asked, 'If you want to create the ideal state, what is the first thing you need to attend to?' (Of course, Western sages like Plato and Thomas More have applied themselves to this same question.) One can easily imagine the kind of issues most people would start thinking about: defence, revenue, agriculture, education, law – even, at a stretch, religion or culture. But Confucius replied, 'The rectification of terms.'[405] This must come first. You have to start by being precise about what you are saying, by defining your terms; if you do this, orders will be unambiguous, and actions decisive.

This advice is relevant not only to the reformation of the state, but also if we want to reform ourselves, and it is particularly pertinent to us in the West today. We have so much advice to choose from. There are so many spiritual teachers, and they all use the same sort of language – but they use it to give quite contrary guidance. One of them may tell you just to ask yourself, 'Who am I?' Nothing more than that. When you are speaking, ask yourself, 'Who is speaking?' When you are listening, ask, 'Who is listening?' When you are thinking, ask, 'Who is thinking?'

When you are experiencing anything, don't bother about the object, concern yourself only with the subject; ask yourself 'Who is experiencing this?' The idea is that you just keep turning these questions over and over in your mind.

But another, equally authoritative teacher may say, 'No, give up all thought of the self. It's pure illusion. It's when we ask ourselves "Who am I?" that all the trouble starts.' Then again, another authority will say, 'Realize the great self, see that your true self is God, that you are this great self which is God.' And someone else will insist that you have to come down to earth and get on with your life, be yourself, cultivate your own personality, do your own thing, develop yourself from the roots up. But then someone else will say, 'No, you must tear up the ego by the roots, blow it up with dynamite if necessary.' One well-known British Buddhist once said in a lecture that you have to hack off great bleeding lumps of self to lighten your load for the spiritual ascent.

In this way we can become confused about what is a quite fundamental issue. We don't know who to believe, so we don't know what to do about the most central and at the same time most inchoate aspect of our experience. When we try to get to grips with it, we discover that we are just dimly aware that there is something around, and we call it 'I', we call it 'me'. We are pretty clear – at least most of the time – that there is something there, call it what you like; and it seems that this something we call 'I' or 'me' is the same something to which such terms as ego, self, and so on refer. But what is this something that all our experience dances around? And what should we do about it? We may find that there seems to be no clear consensus about this. But the experience of 'me', of 'I', is undoubtedly there, even if it ought not to be. Even if we tell ourselves that we only *think* it is there, that it doesn't really exist, still, the thought is there, deluded though it may be. If we want to get seriously confused we may even fall into thinking that we only think that we think it is there.

Still the practical question remains: what do we do about the something we call 'I' (or about the thought of 'I', for it comes to the same thing either way)? Should we cultivate it, refine it, idealize it, or reject it? And if we are going to reject it, should we eradicate it, or ignore it, or undermine it? Or should we just look at it gently and steadily until we see that it isn't really there at all? Unless we settle this issue, our spiritual life is more or less at a standstill.

I venture to propose that Confucius' political solution – the rectification of terms – can be applied to clear this spiritual impasse. Terms such as self, person, individual, and ego all have somewhat ambivalent meanings. Each of them is either to be cultivated or eradicated, depending on the sense in which the word is used. Indeed, we can draw out these ambivalent meanings into separate terms, so that we can identify more clearly what is to be cultivated and what eradicated. Thus, we get true individuality and false individuality; the higher self and the lower self; the person and the personality; being ego-directed and being ego-centred.

But what is the basis of the distinction between the positive and negative interpretations of these terms? If we go back to the question of alienated awareness, we shall see that it arises due to one's failure to experience oneself, especially one's feelings and emotions, and perhaps most especially one's negative feelings and negative emotions.

Pragmatically speaking, we don't have to concern ourselves with the reality or otherwise of the self or the individual in any metaphysical sense. We are self-aware and there is no doubt that this is our experience. The task ahead is to clarify and intensify that experience of self-awareness, to cultivate the higher self, true individuality, and ego-directedness, and become an integrated person.

This, then, is the basis for the distinction between the negative and the positive usages of the terms self, individuality, person, and ego. It is to do with the degree of integration or unification they refer to. True individuality is integrated; false individuality is not. One is to be developed, the other got rid of. The same applies to higher self and lower self, person and personality, and ego-directedness and ego-centredness. The first of each of these terms refers to the experience we try to cultivate through spiritual practice: an integrated experience of 'I' or 'me'. Jung gives a good sense of this in the following definition of the self (as summarized by one of his disciples, Violet de Laszlo): 'The self by definition comprises the full scope of a personality from its most individual traits to its most generic attitudes and experiences, actual as well as potential. Hence it transcends the existing personality. The archetype of wholeness or of the self can therefore be regarded as the dominant of psychic growth.'[406] We achieve this experience by recovering and acknowledging whatever aspects of ourselves we may have tried to disown, and allowing ourselves to experience them again.

This is what it takes to become a true individual. But, one might ask, is becoming an individual such a good thing? How does this idea of the development of individuality fit in with the Buddha's famous *anattā* ('no self')[407] or indeed with the general idea that a truly spiritual life entails becoming in some sense 'selfless'?

The Buddha's teaching of *anattā* is the apparently categorical denial that anything like a self exists. When I was studying Pāli, Abhidhamma, and Buddhist logic in Benares, my teacher used to be fond of pointing out that the word *anattā* (*anātman* in Sanskrit) is a compound expression, made up of the word *attā* (*ātman*) usually translated as 'self', prefixed by *an*, meaning 'no' or 'not'. He would go on to say that if one wanted to understand the meaning of the whole expression, one could do so only after having understood the meaning of *attā*. You can't realize the truth of non-self unless you first have some idea of what is being referred to by 'self'. This might seem obvious, but it apparently wasn't obvious to everybody. Some Theravādin monks were outraged at his point of view, which seemed to them utterly heretical.

But he was quite right. You cannot understand what is meant by non-self unless you know what particular conception of the self is being negated by that prefix. It is clear from the various contexts in which the word *anattā* occurs in the Buddhist scriptures that the Buddha was concerned to negate the brahmanical idea (which was current at the time) of a permanent unchanging self. He did not teach that our experience of ourselves is a complete and utter delusion and that we are not in reality here at all. He taught that the empirical self, the psyche, is not a fixed entity, that it is constantly changing, and that it is because it is changing that it can evolve. All that we know and experience and name as the self is in a state of constant flux – this is what is meant by *anattā*. Thus the purpose of the teaching of *anattā* is entirely practical. It should be taken not as a metaphysical statement, but as a means of keeping the path to Enlightenment clear. Only if we understand, not just intellectually but deep in our hearts, that there is nothing fixed at the heart of our experience, can we evolve.

11

OVERCOMING THE SELF

My principal aim in bringing forward my own favourite modern Western philosopher, Friedrich Nietzche, in this context is to introduce a concept from his thinking that elucidates the defining characteristic of the Buddhist path. It seems to me, speaking from a Buddhist perspective, that Nietzsche's work constitutes the most important of all the lines of thought that the modern West has produced. I therefore propose to give a brief outline of the life and work of Nietzsche and then compare his central concept of the superman or overman – and allied ideas, especially that of a continuing process of evolution within the individual – with Buddhism as the embodiment or exemplification of that continuing evolutionary process.

I became acquainted with Nietzsche's writings at the age of about eighteen, during my early army days, when I was still in England. One glorious summer's day, taking advantage of a day off, I went to Box Hill, a famous beauty spot in Surrey, and lay on the grass in the brilliant sunshine, reading *Thus Spoke Zarathustra*. The combination of profound thought and beautiful poetry in this, Nietzsche's most famous and popular work, made such a tremendous impression that as I looked up it seemed almost as though its words were written across the blue sky in scarlet letters. I have had something of a taste for Nietzsche ever since that day, and have continued to return to him every now and then.

Nietzsche was born in Germany in 1844, the son of a Lutheran pastor. (It was in fact Nietzsche who said that the Lutheran pastor was the father of German philosophy.) His father died in 1849, and Nietzsche spent the rest of his childhood surrounded by women – his mother, his sister, his grandmother, and two maiden aunts – until he was sent to boarding school. He went on to the universities of Bonn and Leipzig where he studied classical philology, and he was appointed to the Chair of Philology at Basle at the age of 24, before he had even graduated, on the recommendation of the eminent scholar and philologist Ritschl, who had been deeply impressed by Nietzsche's work as an undergraduate. At Basle Nietzsche took a particular interest in the philosophy of Schopenhauer and the music of Wagner, and in 1872 he published his first book, *The Birth of Tragedy*. Other works followed, but in 1879, when he was still only 35, he resigned his university post, terminating his academic career, and thereafter spent most of his active life in Switzerland and Italy.

It was a life of intense loneliness; indeed, no one who reads about the details of his isolated and pain-filled life can fail to be touched. He was almost completely on his own, understood by no one apart from one or two friends with whom he corresponded. He was also physically unwell, and sometimes in quite unbearable pain. He continued to write until 1888, and between 1883 and 1885 he produced *Thus Spoke Zarathustra*. But his work received hardly any recognition. When the fourth part of *Zarathustra* came out, only a few dozen copies were sold. Finally, in 1889, Nietzsche became insane and he died, still insane, in 1900, at the age of 55.

As far as Nietzsche's thinking is concerned, the term philosophy is a misnomer. Nietzsche fired off a number of illuminating ideas which certainly hang together – or at least the leading ideas among them do. However, he did not aim to come up with a logically consistent interpretation of all existence, or the whole of experience. His great predecessors – Kant, Hegel, Fichte, Schelling, Schopenhauer – had all attempted to build up a systematic philosophy, but Nietzsche was not a system builder. He did not aspire to erect a lone and gigantic edifice of thought within which everything could be accommodated. Indeed, he insisted on the iconoclastic paradox that 'the will to system is a will to lack of integrity'.[408]

Therefore, with the exception of *Thus Spoke Zarathustra*, all Nietzsche's later writings are simply strings of aphorisms. He is, one might say, the master of the aphorism. No one else seems to have been able to say so much in so few words. His only possible rival, as far as I can see, is William Blake, with 'The Proverbs of Hell' from *The Marriage of Heaven and Hell*, and here Blake is perhaps even more pithy than Nietzsche himself. But that was Blake's sole attempt at that particular form. He wrote 'The Proverbs of Hell' when he was quite young, and as he got older he became rather more prolix. Nietzsche, on the other hand, became increasingly aphoristic and brilliant, devastating and iconoclastic, as he got older, and his pronouncements became more and more like thunder-claps or hammer blows.

Nietzsche's aphoristic and unsystematic approach is not accidental. He is aphoristic because he chooses to be. Indeed, it is of the essence of his method. Some of his aphorisms have something of the spirit of the sayings of the Zen masters of China and Japan. Each of them penetrates deeply into the reality of existence from a particular point of view, and each stands on its own merits. The truth of one aphorism is not dependent on the truth of another; they are not logically connected in that way.

Coleridge once said of the great actor Charles Kean, 'To see him act is like reading Shakespeare by flashes of lightning.' Similarly, reading Nietzsche is like trying to make out the landscape of human existence by the fitful but brilliant illumination of flashes of lightning. For an instant, just in a few words, it is as though everything is flooded with light, and we see everything clearly from that particular angle. And then, absolute darkness. Then we read another aphorism, and another flash from another direction lights up another quarter of the sky, so that again everything is revealed, before the darkness descends once more.

Lightning-flashes seem to show us different landscapes. At some level we know that they are all the same landscape, but it is difficult to piece together the glimpses the lightning reveals into one coherent, all-embracing visual composition. The same goes for the writings of Nietzsche: they are inspiring reading, but very difficult indeed to expound systematically.

What this does mean, however, is that we can consider Nietzsche's aphorisms singly, without necessarily relating them to the rest of his work, and this is how I propose to proceed here. The aphorisms I shall be looking at in this chapter are those concerning his idea of the 'superman', 'self-overcoming', and the 'Will to Power'.

I have put the word 'superman' in quotation marks for two reasons; firstly, to indicate that it is not a literal translation of Nietzsche's original German term; and secondly, as a warning not to attach to Nietzsche's concept certain dubious connotations that have gathered around it ever since the Nazis made use of it for their own purposes (and of course to distinguish it from the comic-book hero of that name).

The term used by Nietzsche is *Übermensch*, which literally means not superman but overman; or even over-and-above-man. The Übermensch is the man who stands over and above – who transcends – human beings as they exist at present. One could even speak of the overman as 'transcendent man'. In other words, the Nietzschean superman is not just present-day humanity writ large, present-day humanity in a superlative degree, but a completely different type of humanity.

We will be stuck with the word superman as a popular rendition of Nietzsche's Übermensch for as long as George Bernard Shaw's play *Man and Superman* continues to be the English-speaking world's most prominent cultural expression of the Nietzschean concept. The chances of Shaw's work being supplanted in this respect were more or less nullified by the regrettable fact that after his death Nietzsche's whole way of thinking was hopelessly corrupted and debased in the popular understanding. It was debased, first of all, at the hands of his sister, and after that at the hands of those who tried to associate Nietzschean ideas with Nazi ideology. It is only in comparatively recent years that Nietzsche's thinking has been rescued from the most gross of these misinterpretations, and at last interpreted more accurately, notably by Walter Kaufmann.[409]

To begin to get a true flavour of Nietzsche we need to look at how he goes about presenting his material, which, as the title *Thus Spoke Zarathustra* intimates, is quite individual. Nietzsche's Zarathustra has very little to do with the Zarathustra – or as he is often known, Zoroaster – who is the historical founder of the ancient Zoroastrian faith. Nietzsche's Zarathustra is fictional; he is simply the mouthpiece for Nietzsche's own ideas. However, what the two Zarathustras do have in common is that they have a message for mankind.

The opening section of the work, entitled 'Zarathustra's Prologue', represents him as coming down from the mountain; this is of course symbolical and meant to be so. Zarathustra has been on the mountain for ten years, thinking and meditating, and now his wisdom has ripened and he wants to share it with mankind. On the way down he is recognized by a saintly hermit who has been living in the forest at the foot of the mountain for a long time, and who remembers seeing him years earlier on his way up. The hermit tries to persuade Zarathustra not to leave the mountain: 'People are so ungrateful, and distracted. Don't waste your time going down among them; better to be a hermit, to live in the forest with the birds and the beasts, to forget the world of men and simply worship God.' But Zarathustra leaves the hermit at his prayers in the forest, and as he goes on his way he says to himself, 'Could it be possible that this old saint in the forest has not yet heard anything of this, that God is dead?'[410]

The thunderous observation that God is dead constitutes one of Nietzsche's most important insights, and it echoed down the twentieth century, giving rise to a whole 'death of God' theological movement. Nietzsche was the first to see that God was no longer up there in the heavens. In fact he saw clearly something that many people have since come to see as well, although others would still declare that he was entirely wrong. He saw that orthodox Christian teaching, with its belief in a personal God, a Supreme Being, a Creator, and its doctrines of sin and faith, justification and atonement, and resurrection, was dead, finished, irrelevant. His declaration heralded the beginning of what some people would identify as a post-Christian age. And if God is dead, then the Christian conception of man is dead as well. The conception of man as a fallen being – a being who, having been disobedient and sinful, needs grace to redeem him, a being who will be judged and perhaps punished – is no longer relevant. All the old dogmas are exploded.

So we need a new conception of who and what we are as human beings. We find ourselves in a universe without God. We are on our own, and therefore have to try to understand ourselves afresh. We can't accept ready-made answers any more. We find ourselves here and now, in the midst of the starry universe, standing on the earth, surrounded by other living beings like ourselves, with a history behind us, and perhaps a future before us, and we each have to ask ourselves – not anybody else because there's nobody else to tell us – the crucial question, 'Who am I? What am I?'

Now that the old definitions are gone, we have to define ourselves anew, discover ourselves, know ourselves. This, anyway, is what

Zarathustra has done on the mountain. He has thought, meditated, and contemplated for ten long years, and now he knows what man is, and he is bringing the message of what he has learned to humanity. So Zarathustra comes to a town on the edge of the forest, he enters the town, and there in the market square he finds people gathered together. They haven't assembled to listen to him – they didn't even know he was coming. They have come to see a travelling tightrope-walker. But as this entertainer hasn't turned up yet, Zarathustra seizes the opportunity and speaks to them.

His initial statement, addressing the people in that market square, and through them all humanity, is this: 'I teach you the overman. Man is something that shall be overcome.' Then he asks, 'What have you done to overcome him?' – by which he means 'What have you done to overcome yourself?' Through the words of Zarathustra in this prologue, Nietzsche points out that evolution never stops. In the course of evolution every kind of being has created something beyond itself, given birth to something higher than itself in the evolutionary scale – and there is no reason to suppose that this process will stop with human beings. Nietzsche's view of evolution is rather primitive here, but it does not have to be taken literally for his conclusion to strike home.

As the ape in a sense created human beings, so we ourselves must now create a new kind of being. We do this by overcoming ourselves, and we begin to do that, Nietzsche goes on to say, by learning to despise ourselves, to be dissatisfied and discontented with ourselves. Only when we begin to look down on ourselves can we begin to rise above ourselves and be higher and greater and nobler than we were.

It should be emphasized again that Nietzsche's overman is not the product of evolution on anything resembling Darwinian lines. For Nietzsche the overman is not produced automatically, as a result of the general blind functioning of the evolutionary process. Nietzsche distinguishes sharply between what he calls the Last Man and the overman himself. The Last Man is simply the latest human product of the general, collective evolutionary process, not a higher type. The overman, by contrast, will be the product of the individual man or woman's effort to rise, even to soar, above himself or herself. It is on account of his distinction between the Last Man and the overman that Nietzsche is able to dissociate himself from superficial nineteenth-century ideas of human progress as an ongoing collective social development. As far as

Nietzsche is concerned, we have to do something about it ourselves, by our own individual choice.

Nietzsche is not always explicit on this point, but he seems to be saying that whereas Darwinian evolution is collective, this higher evolution, as I call it, is individual. He has a dramatic vision of humanity as a rope or bridge stretched over an abyss between the beast on the one hand and the overman on the other.[411] In other words, he is saying that there is an element of risk attached to being truly human. We represent something transitional, rather than a fixed end point. We must therefore live with insecurity, even live dangerously. We must not hanker after cosy comfort. We must live for something other than ourselves, if we are to be truly ourselves. This something other, for the sake of which each and every individual should and must live, is the overman.

For Nietzsche the turning point, the great watershed of the evolutionary process, comes not between animal and man, but between man who is still an animal and man who is truly human. The distinction is a sharp one; in fact, Nietzsche's views on what constitutes humanity are rather too radical and demanding for a Buddhist to be able to subscribe to them. He says, in fact, that the majority of human beings are not human at all, but animals.

From a Buddhist point of view, the human realm includes a wide range of development in terms of self-consciousness, or awareness. Most human beings regularly veer between their animal nature and states of mind characterized by human sympathies, and even occasionally the finer, more integrated states of mind that are traditionally associated with the realms of the gods. Nietzsche's definition of humanity is a lot narrower, and not very flattering to the average person, obviously. People don't like to hear that they fall short of true humanity.

It is therefore not surprising that when Zarathustra speaks to the people in the market place about the 'overman' they just laugh at him, and take more interest in the tightrope-walker. For Nietzsche the category of the truly human, the human realm proper, includes only philosophers, artists, and saints. And the overman, apparently, is superior even to them. Kaufmann, expounding Nietzsche, says of him, 'He maintains in effect that the gulf separating Plato from the average man is greater than the cleft between the average man and a chimpanzee.'[412]

In fact, Nietzsche distinguishes three categories. The first consists of the animal realm, including the majority of human beings – honorary human beings, we may say. The second consists of the human realm proper. And the third is the category of the overman. Nietzsche also speaks of what he calls 'prefatory men', who seem to be intermediate between the human realm and that of the overman; that is, they are those who are bent on seeking in all things for that aspect of themselves which must be overcome. However, he is not very clear about how they might differ from the already narrow category of the truly human. If the overman is Nietzsche's ideal, the truly human seem to be those who aspire to it, and are engaged in the process of self-overcoming – i.e. artists, philosophers, and saints.

One overcomes oneself by 'giving style to one's character'.[413] By this, Nietzsche means not accepting oneself ready-made. He complains that most people's characters have no particular style, almost as if they were somehow factory-made, or even no more than the raw materials out of which a real individual style might be formed. The attitude he is advocating is one of treating one's life and character as so much raw material, and making something of it.

Usually we think of our character, our temperament, our personal characteristics or qualities, as a set of givens. We imagine that we are stuck with who we are for the rest of our lives. If we have a tendency to get angry quickly, that is how we are, we're stuck with it. If we are sensitive or shy, again, that is how it is with us – it's no different in principle, we think, from being tall or short. But according to Nietzsche, we may have come off a long production line, consisting of our genetic inheritance and parental influence, our general social and educational conditioning, but we still have a long way to go. We are not the finished product. In fact, this is merely what we begin with.

Nietzsche says in effect that we should work upon ourselves, create ourselves out of whatever condition we find ourselves in, just as a potter makes something beautiful out of a lump of clay. Just as it is possible to take a heavy, sticky mass, get your fingers into it, and start shaping it into something, in the same way you can shape yourself. If you start by being honest with yourself and admitting that you are more or less unformed as a human being, you can start to form this untidy, shapeless, dough-like stuff into something better.

As an example of someone who gave style to their character, Nietzsche cites Goethe. Goethe, who lived from 1749 to 1832, was the greatest of German poets, a notable dramatist and novelist, as well as a thinker, scientist, and mystic, but Nietzsche admired him most of all because all the time he was trying to make something of himself. He was an individual. It is evident from biographies, and from the records of his conversations, that throughout his long life, he was always working upon himself, just as one might work upon a poem, a novel, or a scientific treatise. This was evident also to his contemporaries. When Napoleon saw Goethe for the first time, he exclaimed, quite spontaneously, 'Look, there is a man!' Considering that Napoleon had conquered Europe, while Goethe's political status was negligible (he was merely an ex-minister of a small German state), this suggests that Goethe succeeded in the central aim of his life. From the unpromising bundle of rakish passions and wild ideas that was his youthful self, Goethe created a man in the fullest and truest sense, as Napoleon observed him to be.

We have seen that Nietzsche arrived at the concept of the overman by a consideration of the general nature of the evolutionary process. According to the way he understood the nature of existence, life – not just human life, but all life – is that which must always overcome itself. It is never satisfied with itself. It must continually, at every stage, go beyond itself. Life, we may say, is a self-transcending process.

This innate urge is what Nietzsche calls the Will to Power.[414] This term, which Nietzsche introduced comparatively late in his writings, like 'superman' has been much misunderstood and lamentably misinterpreted as having dubious political or even military resonances. But by Power – with a capital P – Nietzsche does not mean anything material at all. Certainly he means nothing to do with politics. The Will to Power is the will to a more abundant, noble, and sublime mode of being, a qualitatively, dimensionally different life. Especially, it is the will to the realization of the overman.

Nietzsche emphasizes that this higher degree of being is attainable only to the extent that the lower degree of being is left behind, negated, even destroyed. This brings us to a vital aspect of the Will to Power, and Nietzsche's approach generally, which is that it involves an uncompromising iconoclasm. Nietzsche looked at commonly accepted values, generally held ideas of good and evil, and he called quite categorically and peremptorily for them to be thrown away as so much rubbish. Otherwise, he said, the overman cannot be brought into existence.

Nietzsche is therefore utterly ruthless and uncompromising in his condemnation of the average man and his subhuman requirements. We are accustomed to thinking of the Hebrew prophets – Amos, Jeremiah, and the Second Isaiah, for example – as terrible enough in their fulminations against the vanity of men, but they are mildness itself compared with Nietzsche. He is for shattering – as he puts it – all the old tablets of the law. He has no time whatever for the whole of modern civilization and culture. Nietzsche is almost certainly the most devastating – in the full, literal sense of that term – critic of itself that the human race has ever produced. He is wholesale and unmitigated in his denunciation of human beings as we know them, and all their works, and all their ways. He says simply that they must all go – not just out of personal negativity, but simply because they get in the way. They must be transcended; they must make way for the overman.

It is crucial to Nietzsche's iconoclasm that in negating existing values and modes of thought, there is no question of negating something external to oneself. It is a question of negating not other people's values but one's own. It is oneself that one must overcome. It is with oneself that one must ruthlessly engage in battle. Nietzsche's fondness for the terminology of warfare is another source of misunderstanding, but the enemy is always oneself.

From the *Dhammapada* we have the Buddha's own exhortation to join this uncompromising struggle: 'Though one should conquer a thousand men in battle a thousand times, yet he who conquers himself has the more glorious victory.'[415] But how much further can we press a resemblance or even a comparison between the teaching of Nietzsche and that of the Buddha? Nietzsche did know something of Buddhism, but in his day very few Buddhist texts had been translated, and he did not know enough to be in a position to arrive at a balanced judgement about it. He had little conception, for example, of the positive content of the ideal of Buddhahood, and there is little such positive content in his conception of the overman. This is hardly surprising, in view of the fact that Nietzsche's overman is the product of thought. It is the product of a brilliant intellect, penetrating to the point of intuitive genius, but it is still an intellectual intuition, not the product of transcendental realization. Hence the conception of the overman by no means equals that of the Buddha – of Enlightened humanity.

However, the conception of the overman certainly points in the same general direction, and Nietzsche's rope stretched over the abyss between the beast and the overman therefore corresponds in a general way to the Buddhist path, because this path is ourselves. We are not static entities, but evolving, developing beings. According to Buddhism as well as Nietzsche, we follow this path by continually overcoming ourselves and rising to successively higher levels.

If we want to be bold, we can even say that the Will to Power corresponds in a general way to the Will to Enlightenment. Both are active. Both are powerful volitions. Both are concerned not just with thinking about the highest realizable ideal, but with actually attaining it. One is the ideal of the overman, while the other of course is the ideal of Buddhahood, Supreme Enlightenment for the sake of all living beings. And the achievement of both ideals requires the overcoming of our lesser identities, our lower selves, our smaller values, baser ideas of every kind.

With this clear similarity established, we can make out two equally clear differences. The Will to Enlightenment, the *bodhicitta*, is more altruistic, more other-regarding, more cosmic.[416] It is the manifestation in the individual of a universal, cosmic principle. Of course, the figure of Zarathustra, who is meant to exemplify the overman, does want – presumably as an essential aspect of his attainment – to share his wisdom with mankind. But the Will to Power is essentially more individualistic than the Will to Enlightenment.

The second difference between the Buddha's teaching and Nietzsche's thinking is to do with method. Nietzsche brings out the necessity for discontent with ourselves, and for overcoming ourselves so that the overman may be created, with blinding clarity, more so than any other Western philosopher or thinker. But he fails miserably – though nobly – to show us how to do it. He says, 'Overcome yourself,' but he doesn't say anything about how to go about it. There are no practical instructions – we are left with the empty exhortation. Buddhism, on the other hand, as an ancient spiritual tradition, has many methods, exercises, and practices for self-overcoming.

This makes a big difference. It is not so difficult to see that someone is ill, but only a skilled physician can prescribe the method of treatment they need to get well. Nietzsche certainly paints a grim and vivid picture of the disease of modern humanity, the disease which, in a sense, *is* humanity, and he also gives us an acute diagnosis. He then goes on to paint a glowing and inspiring picture of the patient restored to perfect health. But nothing is offered to link these two compelling pictures together. Nietzsche is not alone in this; almost the whole of modern Western philosophy suffers from the same missing link. It is rich in abstract thought, and some of this thinking, like Nietzsche's, pulses with intellectual energy, but it generally lacks any practical content.

Fortunately, in Buddhism we find not only the abstract ideal but also practical means for its realization; a way of life is prescribed. Nonetheless, Buddhists can learn a great deal from Nietzsche's uncompromising vision of human potential, rightly understood. Nietzsche's powerful vision allied with Buddhism's clear path of practice and supportive conditions (the sangha) together give us the possibility of the complete transformation of humanity that Nietzsche so desired. This is just one of the ways in which cooperation between Western philosophy and Eastern spiritual traditions can bear precious fruit.

12

THE ARTIST AS THE TRUE INDIVIDUAL

In the last few chapters we have begun to build up a picture of the true individual. We have seen the emergence of the individual in the context of evolutionary growth and change. We have also noted two contrasting, even apparently contradictory, stages in the growth of the individual: first, the necessity to acknowledge and integrate all aspects of oneself, including those one would rather *not* acknowledge; and then, on the basis of that integration, the need to set about going beyond oneself – 'self-overcoming', as Nietzsche put it. Moreover, we have seen that Buddhism can be considered as the path of the higher evolution, and as offering specific methods and practices whereby the individual can form himself or herself.

It may seem strange to be placing so much emphasis on the qualities of the individual in a book about spiritual community, but, as we have seen, in its essence the sangha is not about organizations or ecclesiastical status, but purely and simply about communication between individuals. It is thus of the greatest importance that we understand the nature of individuality.

In the final part of the book, we will broaden our field of inquiry to explore the kinds of relationships that are central to the life of any individual Buddhist – a consideration of sangha in the broadest sense. But before we do so, I want to introduce one last aspect of individuality. We have seen that the true individual is characterized by self-consciousness or awareness, positive and refined emotions, independence of mind and freedom from group conditioning, creativity and free-flowing energy, aloneness and frequent unpopularity. It strikes me that these characteristics can be said to be shared by a kind of person who is perhaps not generally associated with spiritual matters: the artist.

As we have seen, it was the artist (together with the philosopher and the saint) whom Nietzsche identified as being capable of self-overcoming. But why? What is the connection between art and spiritual growth? (The term 'art' should be taken in this context to cover all the fine arts – painting, sculpture, poetry, music, architecture, and so on.) I want to suggest that, as well as being related to the spiritual life through the production of works of art with sacred significance, the artist represents a particular aspect or manifestation of the higher evolution itself. This is not of course to say that one cannot participate in the higher evolution of humanity without being an artist. But one cannot be an authentic artist of any kind without at the same time participating in the higher evolution, in the spiritual life.

To some people this may seem like an unacceptable glorification of the artist. Many people don't see that art and artists are of much value in comparison with what they recognize as important or serious activities. The arts are sometimes seen as glamorous but trivial activities, or as the arcane luxury of a privileged élite, and of little relevance to the rest of us. It has to be said that a consideration of the lives of some artistic coteries, past and present, does seem to bear this view out. For example, the multi-talented Sitwell family, who seem to have formed a literary set all by themselves, are captured in the many-volumed autobiography for which Osbert Sitwell is chiefly known. His upbringing among a brilliant and eccentric family in a vast and rambling old mansion provided him with some good stories to tell, and he tells them very well. But one of his little stories illustrates just how alienated the work of the artist had become from the values of most ordinary people.

It seems that Osbert lived in one wing of this mansion, while his sister Edith lived in another, with long, long corridors in between, regularly traversed by a small regiment of servants. One morning he rang the bell to call a maidservant and passed her a note to give to his sister 'if she isn't busy'. 'But,' he warned the maid, 'if she is doing something, don't disturb her; just bring the note back to me.' About fifteen minutes later, the maidservant returned without the note, and Osbert asked her, 'Was my sister unoccupied, then?' To which the maid replied, 'Yes indeed, sir, she wasn't doing anything at all; she was just writing.'

Despite the respect accorded to certain great works of art of the past, for most people creative work is still 'doing nothing at all', and the activity of the artist is therefore misunderstood. Certainly it is seldom understood that – as I believe – art is part of the spiritual life, and that the artist is, or at least can be, the true individual. But a little thought reveals that the great artist does indeed share the characteristics we have identified as being aspects of individuality.

First of all, the artist is more alive than other people. The evidence for this is in the artist's sensitivity in the best sense of the term. The painter, for example, is much more keenly aware of differences of shape, contour, and colour, than are other people. If you go for a country walk in the company of an artist, you will notice that they tend to see more than you do. They will call your attention to the outline of a tree against the sky, or the precise colours of a fallen leaf, or a withered flower, or the blue shadows cast by trees on the grass. The painter awakens the rest of us to our surroundings with a sharper awareness of what is going on in the outside world of shapes and forms and colours.

The musician has a correspondingly keen ear. He or she can detect distinctions of musical pitch and rhythm that hardly exist for the rest of us. For example, the subtleties of the tabla-playing in Indian music can be astonishingly difficult to follow, even for a trained ear. The drum can be played with such unbelievable delicacy and refinement that it sounds like whispering voices, moving occasionally into a sort of grumbling, interspersed with other, sharper voices. If one has the training and the sensitivity to hear it, one can get the definite impression that the drum is speaking, communicating, while someone without that degree of aural development will be unable to hear its language.

The poet, of course, is equally sensitive to the different tones and rhythms of words. We all use words all the time, but we tend to use them in a careless, coarse way, without being fully aware of their meanings and sensuous qualities, their textures. Edith Sitwell, for example, described the different values of words in a way that revealed her exceptional sensitivity to them. Some words, she said, were 'rough' or 'hairy' or 'heavy', while others were 'smooth' or 'light'; such awareness of the distinctive qualities of words goes well beyond the range of most of us.[417]

Not only are artists acutely aware of the external world of sensuous impressions; they are particularly aware of their own responses to all these things, their own mental and emotional states. It isn't just that they reflect upon these states more than other people do – they actually experience them much more intensely. Furthermore, the artist is usually more aware of other people. This is graphically displayed in the work of the great portrait painters, dramatists and novelists, in which people are truly alive. There is a kind of spiritual biography in a great portrait. For example, the famous portrait of Pope Innocent x by Velázquez is a detailed reading of a very wicked man. You feel you can see in that face – in his cold eyes, the texture of the skin, the shape of the mouth, and his grim, fixed expression – everything he had ever done. Such a face can belong only to someone who has got where he is by corruption; and yet you can see, too, that his path of advancement is built out of a wealth of other human qualities and frailties. The painter has seen it all and put it down on the canvas.

In the plays of Shakespeare and the novels of George Eliot is to be found the same ability to see with such intensity as to be able to realize with absolute conviction the life of another human being. Turning briefly to an artist who comes somewhere in between being a painter and a novelist, I must confess that when I was much younger, I used to imagine that Hogarth's serial depictions of the London life of his time, like *A Rake's Progress* and *Marriage à-la-mode*, were caricatures, that in his satires he was exaggerating for effect. But after I had seen a bit more of life and observed people a little more closely, I came to the conclusion that Hogarth was being deadly accurate, and that people really were like that. He saw people as they were, and as they were he depicted them in his paintings and engravings, with terrifying candour.[418]

The artist, therefore, is aware of the external world, of himself or herself, and of other people. And the artist is also aware of something beyond all these things. He or she is aware in some incomprehensible way of reality itself – not in the sense of considering the concept of Reality with a capital R, but in the sense of being deeply and resonantly sensitive to the meaning and mystery of existence. The artist feels the presence of this mystery, whether cosmic or human.

As a result of this heightened and cultivated sensitivity and awareness, the artist is often distinguished by positive and refined emotions, particularly an ability to empathize with others, and to capture his or her own most fleeting and subtle mental impressions.

The true artist is also independent in spirit, and to a large extent free from group conditioning. Artists don't hesitate to go their own way, to be themselves. In fact, they have long been notorious for flouting convention, refusing to conform, refusing to do what is expected, or what will cause least fuss. In taking this kind of attitude, they are not just being eccentric or perverse or difficult. They are simply trying to lead their own life and to be themselves.

Then, of course, the artist is creative. Most importantly, the artist is creative of new values, such as did not exist or which were not experienced or perceived before. However, as well as this, artists are quite simply productive, and in the case of the very greatest artists, immensely productive. Their energies flow with extraordinary vitality. Shakespeare, Goethe, and Lope de Vega were all prolific writers, and the ancient Greek dramatists produced very many more plays than have survived intact. Bach, Handel, Haydn, Mozart, and Schubert all turned out a more or less unstoppable avalanche of music, while Titian, Rubens, and Rembrandt each left behind them a huge number of canvases.

Reading the life of any great artist, one is struck, sometimes with wonder, by the spectacle of this uninterrupted flow of creativity. You wonder how on earth they managed to fit all that work into what is in so many cases, like that of Mozart, a very short lifetime; or in other cases, like that of Bach, who fathered twenty children, a very busy lifetime; or in the case of a great many artists, altogether rather unfavourable domestic circumstances. Whatever way you look at it, such creativity implies a great deal of hard work. These artists did not twiddle their thumbs waiting for inspiration to strike. They just got on with it, morning, noon, and night. They were at their desks or easels at first light, and they would work all the hours they could, every day, in some cases without a break for years on end, right into old age.

Finally, artists are essentially alone, isolated from the masses on account of their greater awareness, their greater individuality and even their greater creativity. Only too often the ordinary person cannot understand why the artist should take such pains with words, with sounds, with line and colour and form. Surely one word or shade of colour will do as well as another very similar word or shade – why take so much trouble over it? Does the precise detail of that musical progression really matter, in the larger scheme of things? If you put that comma in or take that full stop out, what difference does it really make? Isn't it all a bit petty and precious? But to the artist, these things are all of the first importance.

As a result of the almost total lack of sympathy and understanding ordinary people have for what he or she is doing, the artist is usually unpopular, and sometimes not recognized at all. In one way or another, the greatest artists are ahead of their time, even ahead of other comparatively ordinary artists. Sometimes it takes the rest of humanity centuries to catch up. Only too often we find that the artist is condemned in his or her own generation only to be praised in generations to come. It is as though the voice of the ordinary people will honour an artist only after he or she is dead, as though the only good artist is a dead artist. This is all so well known that it is not necessary to insist upon it. The artist will often feel even more alone than does the religious genius or mystic.

If we look at what makes a true individual we find that the true artist tends to have essentially the same characteristics. But what defines someone as an artist? The definition will of course depend on the nature of what he or she creates. So – to plunge straight into one of the most vexed and debated questions in the history of Western thought – what is art?

This question has also been discussed in the East, especially in India, but the debate there has followed such different lines that one cannot even begin to compare it with Western arguments on the subject. It is a question that used to occupy a good deal of my own time and energy in the days before I took on responsibilities that put a limit on the amount of reflection I could devote to such an issue. I found that there are numberless definitions of art, some of them quite extraordinary. The eminent art critic Herbert Read came up with 'Art is an attempt to create pleasing forms.' Even more succinct is Clive Bell's definition, very famous indeed in its day, and the subject of his best-known work: 'Art is significant form.' As for the great Italian critic and statesman, Benedetto Croce, his offering seems a little vague: 'Art is intuition.'[419] Indeed, all the definitions I found seemed rather unsatisfactory – too broad, too narrow, or just incomplete. So eventually I decided to formulate my own.

I wrote my own short work on the subject, *The Religion of Art*, in the early 1950s, when I lived in Kalimpong, and in it I defined art as follows: 'Art is the organization of sensuous impressions that express the artist's sensibility and communicate to his audience a sense of values that can transform their lives.'⁴²⁰ The reason I find this definition particularly satisfying is that it takes a definitely spiritual perspective on art. It is from this angle specifically that I want to examine it here in a little more detail.

The primary assertion – 'Art is the organization of sensuous impressions' – should be obvious enough, but it is still worth making. One book on poetry that I consulted began by saying that we must never forget that poetry consists of words (and if there are people who do forget this, no doubt this author is right to remind them). But let us go even further: if poetry consists of words, of what do words consist? What is the raw material of poetry? Words consist of sounds, vibrations in the air, sounds associated in varying degrees – and sometimes only marginally – with conceptual meaning. The raw material of painting is simply visual impressions: shape and colour, light and shade. Likewise, music is made of auditory impressions: sounds and rhythms, whether loud or soft, harmonious or discordant. Indeed, all the arts have sensuous impressions as their raw material, their basic stuff. This is where art begins, with the impressions pouring in upon us all the time through our five physical senses (to which the Buddhist tradition adds mental activity as a sixth).⁴²¹

The artist organizes this chaos of impressions into a pattern, a shape, something whole, and in so doing creates a world, which is the work of art. There are various ways of organizing sensuous impressions, some very simple, others highly sophisticated. The key point is that the resulting work of art does not exist apart from the artist. The artist's shaping of sensuous impressions expresses his or her sensibility. That is to say, works of art express or embody the awareness of artists, their experience of life as a whole, their experience of themselves, of other people, and even of reality.

The sensibility expressed in the work of art reflects the level of consciousness of the individual artist. Not all artists have access to particularly high levels of consciousness, but even simple folk art – making and building things oneself, broadly following traditional patterns – expresses the rudiments of an artistic sensibility in a way that mass-produced goods do not. And just a few artists may be said even to penetrate, at least occasionally, beyond the furthest reaches of ordinary human consciousness, into the experience of transcendental consciousness.

The true artist has access to higher levels of consciousness, awareness, and even understanding, than the ordinary person. He or she is further advanced in the evolutionary development of humanity, and this is one of the reasons why he or she is an artist. At this point, I expect some readers will be shaking their heads with bemusement at the bold claim that the true artist represents a higher type of humanity than the ordinary, decent citizen. They will say that my rosy-tinted idea of the artist is fiction, and that only too often the artist is wicked, depraved, and selfish. Perhaps we should look into this question a little.

Admittedly, painters, poets, and musicians can be rather difficult to live with. This, I think, is often due to the fact that artists are rightly concerned to safeguard their privacy and working conditions from intrusion. There will always be well-meaning people who will try to make artists conform, make them behave, dress, look, talk, and even write or paint like other people. It is only natural that in such circumstances artists will rebel – sometimes even violently – against the efforts of kindly folk who only want them to be happy and successful. Rather ungratefully, the artist will insist upon being himself.

Besides this, the artist is, more often than not, in revolt against conventional morality. This is especially conspicuous in the case of a poet like Shelley, who flouted the moral canons of his day, and was ostracized for so doing. The real question is not whether the artist is immoral, but whether flouting conventional morality is wrong. Only too often it is clear that conventional morality itself is at fault, and that the artist's rejection of it is simply an expression of his or her own healthier and more balanced mental attitude.

Not, of course, that the artist is always 'balanced'; far from it. We have seen that we all tend to be – at least until we have embarked on the process of integration – not a unified self, but a bundle of selves. This is all too true of the artist. Indeed, the artist is only too often a deeply divided person, and sometimes it seems that the greater the artist is, the more deeply divided he is within himself. This deep cleft in the depths of his own being can make him tense and unbalanced, bordering even on madness. The artist can be said to have access to deeper states of consciousness than almost anyone else, but this does not mean that he has access to them all the time. As Shelley says in his 'Song', 'Rarely, rarely, comest thou, Spirit of Delight.'

This spirit of delight – the experience of a higher mode of being and consciousness – does indeed visit the creative artist all too rarely. The artist does not enjoy such states continuously, and in this he differs from the true mystic, who tends to dwell in them much of the time. Slipping and veering between these higher states and more ordinary states of mind, it can seem as though the artist were two people. It is a sad but unfortunately common experience to read a wonderful book and then find that the author is nothing like as wonderful in person as his book led you to believe he would be. You finally get to meet him, and you approach him full of gratitude and admiration, with the sense that certain books give you that the author is practically a friend already, that they have already revealed their soul to you, but then you are confronted with some dry, withered, mean little man, and you are sorry that you ever set eyes upon him, you are so disappointed.

It is as though the artist has two separate identities – an artistic self and an ordinary self. Hence the idea of the artist's inspiration coming down to him from on high, that it is not his own work. The eighteenth-century composer Haydn apparently had precisely this experience. Listening to a performance of his oratorio *The Creation*, written in his old age, he cried out, 'Not I, but a Power from above created that!' Now that he was back in his ordinary state of consciousness, Haydn the ordinary person had to disclaim the achievement of Haydn the artist.

This is also one of the reasons why we traditionally refer to the artist – and anyone who depends on some kind of higher power – as a genius. The word genius originally meant one's guardian deity, which translated into Christian terms as one's guardian angel. A genius represented the higher powers overshadowing you and guiding you, directing your steps; to put it another way, it represented your own higher self, conceived of as an independent or quasi-independent personality that was your ordinary self's source of guidance and inspiration. The same idea lies behind the classical concept of the Muses. At the beginning of the *Iliad*, for example, Homer invokes the goddess to 'sing of the baneful wrath of Achilles'. The *Odyssey*, likewise, begins: 'Tell me, Muse, of the man of many wiles. ...' For any classical poet this was the conventional opening. Following in their footsteps, Milton does likewise at the beginning of *Paradise Lost*, except that he invokes what he calls the heavenly muse, which he distinguishes from the profane muse. But the idea is the same. You are invoking some higher power which seems to be outside you but which in truth is your own highest self, whence any true artistic creation proceeds.

Nowadays the word genius tends to be used very freely, with no awareness of its original significance, and is applied to any moderately gifted person. Asked whether he saw himself as a genius, the novelist Vladimir Nabokov replied:

> The word 'genius' is passed around rather generously, isn't it? At least in English, because its Russian counterpart, *geniy*, is a term brimming with a sort of throaty awe and is used only in the case of a very small number of writers – Shakespeare, Milton, Pushkin, Tolstoy. To such deeply beloved authors as Turgenev and Chekhov, Russians assign the thinner term, *talant* – talent, not genius. It is a bizarre example of semantic discrepancy – the same word being more substantial in one language than in another. Although my Russian and my English are practically coeval, I still feel appalled and puzzled at seeing 'genius' applied to any important story-teller, such as Maupassant or Maugham. Genius still means to me, in my Russian fastidiousness and pride of phrase, a unique, dazzling gift – the genius of James Joyce, not the talent of Henry James.[422]

Whether or not one agrees with his estimation of Henry James, the force of the distinction he is making between talent and genius is very much in line with the kind of revaluation of what art means and what it means to be an artist that I am attempting here, in my own definition of art.

We have seen that art is the organization of sensuous impressions that express the artist's sensibility (at whatever level of refinement that may be). The definition goes on: 'and communicate to his audience a sense of values that can transform their lives'. How does this happen? And what is meant by 'a sense of values that can transform our lives'?

If we agree that the artist experiences a more comprehensive, more powerful degree of awareness than ordinary people, then the work of art not only expresses that degree of awareness but communicates it, in the sense that when the communication succeeds, we experience for the time being, to a lesser degree, the state of consciousness in which the artist produced it. This is the communication of the artist. Temporarily at least, we are raised to his or her level; we become a true individual. Temporarily, we share his or her sense of values and insight, and this can transform our lives.

This is ultimately what the evolution of our humanity is about. Transformation *is* evolution. It is not an outward change but a change of level. Artists, therefore, are not only more highly evolved themselves but, through the art by which they communicate their experience of themselves, they contribute to the higher evolution of other people.

Enjoyment of great works of art broadens and deepens our own consciousness. When we listen to a great piece of music, see a great painting, read a great poem – when we really experience it, allow it to soak into us – we go beyond our ordinary consciousness. We become more generous in our sympathies; our whole life is subtly but deeply modified. If we persist in pursuing an interest in the arts, our whole mode of being may be affected, and our lives may even be transformed.

Today, traditional religion – in the form of Christianity, at least – has lost its unquestioned hold on the minds of many people in the West. The astonishing architectural monuments to Christianity are still around us, but however glorious some of them may be, for most people they are empty shells. For the vast majority of people, orthodox religion is no longer a means of grace. It no longer uplifts us, or moves us, or transforms us, much less still transfigures us. People aren't even against it any more.

As the title of my own book on art is meant to suggest, for many people the place and function of religion has been taken over by art. This is one of the reasons, I think, for the immense popularity today of all the fine arts – for despite all the grumbling one hears about the decay of culture, the fine arts are hugely popular as they have never been before. Formerly the enjoyment of works of art was the privilege of a few. Five hundred years ago in England, most of us would have been living in miserable hovels. We would never have seen any paintings except perhaps one or two in the local church, and we would have heard little music of any quality. As for reading, hardly anyone read for pleasure, or even at all. Enjoyment of high culture was the privilege of no more than a few wealthy ecclesiastics and noblemen. Even as late as the eighteenth century, how many people heard the works of Bach, Haydn, or Mozart performed? A few tens of thousands at the very most – and sometimes only a few hundred bored aristocrats.

But nowadays the artistic heritage of the ages is within the reach of practically everyone. The music of the great composers may be heard and enjoyed over and over again, by millions of people throughout the world. High culture is being disseminated on an unprecedented scale.

What results this is likely to have we can only guess, but there must be some possibility that the sudden mass availability of high culture will start to exert a slow and steady refining influence on a considerable and influential section of the population.

If it is true that the arts have taken the place of religion, this is because they form an integral part, not of religion in the narrow sense, but of the spiritual life. And if I am right in this analysis, we should encourage all the fine arts, as an integral part of the spiritual life and the evolution of our humanity.

One final question remains to be addressed, and it concerns the psychology of artistic creation. How and why is it that, for the artist, the production of works of art should be a means – even *the* means – of higher evolution? What happens when the artist creates?

In brief, when artists create, they objectify. And when you objectify, you can assimilate. This is not unlike what happens in the process of traditional Buddhist visualization exercises. When, for instance, in meditation, we visualize the Buddha, we close our eyes and we see – we try actually to see rather than just think about – first, an expanse of green, with an expanse of blue sky above it, and in between, a bodhi tree. Then at the foot of the bodhi tree, we see the figure of the Buddha in orange robes. We see the supremely peaceful features, the golden complexion, the gentle smile, the curly black hair, the colours of his aura. We see all this as vividly as if the Buddha himself was sitting before us. And in what we visualize we recognize the spiritual qualities of the Buddha; in his face we see wisdom, compassion, tranquillity, fearlessness, and so on. Drawing gradually nearer to the visualized image, and thus to those qualities, we feel as if the visualized image was drawing nearer to us. We feel that we are absorbing within ourselves the Buddha's own qualities.[423]

If we persevere in this exercise, if we keep it up not just for a few days, but for months, even years, eventually a time will come when we fully assimilate all these qualities of the Buddha, and become one with him in that meditation experience. When that happens, the unenlightened being is transformed into the Enlightened being, and we realize our own Buddha nature. But in the course of this practice, in the process of this exercise, what has really happened?

What has happened is that our own potential – that is to say Buddha-hood – which was there all the time, unknown and unrecognized, in the heart of our own being, the depths of our own nature, has become actual; it has been realized. But it has been realized by being objectified, by being seen 'out there' (even though it is 'in here'). Having been objectified in this way, it has been gradually assimilated, more and more, until we become one with it.

The same sort of thing happens in the case of artistic creation. When we say that the artist creates out of his or her experience of some higher level of being, it is not quite as simple and straightforward as that makes it sound. It is not that the artist has the experience itself fully and perfectly and completely before creating anything. Someone who did that would not be an artist at all, but a mystic, which is something else and, at least potentially, something higher. The artist's starting point is a vague sense of something that he or she clarifies and intensifies in the process of creating the work of art. The original creative experience of the artist is like a seed which is bursting with life but whose nature is fully revealed only when the flower blooms, when the work of art itself stands complete and perfect. But however fine the objects one creates, whatever their transforming power, the highest aim of any artist must be the same as that of any human being. Each of us must aim to be ourselves our own finest work of art, to 'give style to our character' in Nietzsche's phrase – to become, that is, a true individual.

PART III
THE NETWORK OF PERSONAL
RELATIONSHIPS

INTRODUCTION

Some verses I once composed for the dedication of a Buddhist shrine-room include the aspiration: 'May our communication with one another be sangha.'[424] This reflects the very great importance that has always been given in Buddhism to the quality of communication both between members of the sangha and in the context of all the relationships an individual Buddhist has with other people. The Buddha had a great deal to say about communication – about the importance of truthful, kindly, meaningful, and harmonious speech, and about the necessity to pay attention to one's relationships in general, making sure that one is relating in ways that accord with one's Buddhist principles.

The reasons for this are quite obvious. To be human is to be related to other human beings. We cannot live our lives in isolation; whatever efforts we make to develop as individuals are continually tested in the fires of our relationships with other people. However calm, kind, and wise we may feel in the privacy of our own hearts or shrine-rooms, the true test of how fully we have developed these qualities comes when we are faced with the realities of life as represented by the challenges 'other people' represent.

The first human being to whom we are related is of course our mother. That relationship is very intimate, and it affects us for the whole of our lives. After that, our father comes into view, and perhaps brothers and sisters as well, together with grandparents, if we are fortunate. A little later we may also become aware of aunts, uncles, and cousins. This is usually the extent of our family circle. But then there are neighbours, and from the age of four or five there are teachers, schoolfellows, and friends. Later, there may be a husband or wife, and perhaps children. On top of these relationships we will probably have connections with employers and workmates, perhaps even employees. And we will also, sooner or later, have to have relationships of a kind with government officials, bureaucrats, even rulers, whether in our own country or abroad. By the time we reach maturity, we will find ourselves in the midst of a whole network of relationships with scores, perhaps hundreds, of people, and connected indirectly or distantly to very many more.

This network of relationships is the subject-matter of a Buddhist text known as the *Sigālaka Sutta*, which is to be found in the *Dīgha Nikāya*, the 'Collection of Long Discourses', in the Pāli canon.[425] It is a comparatively early text, the substance of which, we can be reasonably certain, goes back to the Buddha himself. It is called the *Sigālaka Sutta* because it is a discourse given by the Buddha to a young man called Sigālaka. One translator describes the *sutta* as 'Advice to Lay People'. In it the Buddha lays down a pattern for different kinds of relationships, explaining how each should be conducted. All this is set forth with such clarity and succinctness that it remains of considerable interest today – and we will be using it as the framework for the final section of this book.

Sigālaka is a young Brahmin, which means that he belongs to the priestly caste, the highest and most influential caste of Indian society. The introduction to the *sutta* reports that the Buddha happens to meet Sigālaka early one morning. Sigālaka's clothes and hair are still dripping wet from his purificatory ritual bath. (This is something you can still see today – Brahmins standing in the holy Ganges at Varanasi, dipping into the water and reciting mantras.) Having taken his bath, Sigālaka is engaged in worshipping the six directions: north, south, east, west, the zenith, and the nadir.

He is doing this, so he informs the Buddha, in obedience to his father's dying injunction, in order to protect himself from any harm that might come from any of the six directions. The Buddha thereupon tells Sigālaka that although worshipping the six directions is right and proper he is not going about it in the right way, if he wants such worship to protect him effectively. He then proceeds to explain what the six directions really represent.

The east, he says, means mother and father (in Indian languages mother comes before father) because one originates from them just as the sun – or at least the day – originates in the east. So the first relationship the Buddha refers to is that between parent and child. As for the other directions, they refer to the other key relationships in life: the south to the relationship between pupil and teacher; the west to that between husband and wife; the north to friends and companions; the nadir to the relationship between 'master and servant' (employer and employee, in modern terms); and the zenith to the relationship between lay people and 'ascetics and Brahmins'.

True worship of the six directions, the Buddha explains, consists in carrying out one's duties with regard to these six kinds of relationship. Such ethical activity is naturally productive of happiness, and it is in this sense that one protects oneself through this kind of 'worship'. Here the Buddha envisages the individual as being at the centre of a network of relationships, out of which he enumerates just six. The Buddha seems to give equal emphasis to these six primary relationships, which represent a fairly wide spread of human interaction, and in this respect he is characteristic of his culture, that of north-east India in the sixth century BCE.

But most other cultures emphasize one kind of human relationship rather more than the others. For example, a similar list to the one the Buddha gave Sigālaka can be found in Confucianism, according to which there are five standard relationships: between ruler and subject (sometimes described as prince and minister), between parent and child, between husband and wife, between brother and brother, and between friend and friend. But in ancient China particular emphasis was always placed on the relationship between parents and children, and especially on the duties of children towards parents. According to some Confucian writers, filial piety is the greatest of all virtues, and in classical times sons and daughters who were conspicuous examples of it were officially honoured by the government with a title, or a grant of a large piece of land, or a monument erected in their honour. The whole idea can only seem rather strange to us now, living as we do in very different times, when independence from one's parents is the goal as far as most people are concerned.

Turning to the ancient Greeks, we find no particular list of significant relationships. However, if we take Plato's account of the teachings of

Socrates as representative of the highest Greek ideals, it is clear that for them the relationship between friend and friend was the most significant. The moving description of Socrates' death puts this emphasis into stark perspective. Some time before his death we find him bidding a rather formal farewell to his wife and children, who are nevertheless described as sobbing bitterly. He then dismisses them, and devotes his last hours to philosophical discussion with his friends.[426]

In medieval Europe, on the other hand, the emphasis was placed on the relationship between master and servant, particularly that between the feudal lord and the vassal. Such was the centrality of this relationship that a whole social system was built around it. In the feudal system the great virtue was loyalty, especially to the person directly above you in the social pecking order. If you were a great lord it would be the king; if you were a small landowner it would be the local lord; if you were an ordinary servant or serf it would be your knight. And you would be prepared and willing to die for your feudal superior.

In the modern West, of course, we find the main emphasis placed upon the sexual or romantic relationship. One may move from one such relationship to another, but through all these ups and downs, their current sexual relationship nevertheless remains the central relationship for most people, giving meaning and colour to their lives. The romantic relationship is the principal subject-matter of films, novels, plays, and poems, and as an ideal it is all-consuming – lovers commonly declare that they cannot live without each other, even that they are prepared to die for each other. Thus for most people in our culture, the sexual/romantic relationship is the central and most important one – an idea which people of the ancient civilizations would probably have found ridiculous. This is not to say that they would necessarily have been right, but we can at least remind ourselves that people have not always felt as we feel today.

In the modern West other relationships often tend to be superficial because they are simply not given the same weight. We tend to neglect our relationships with our parents and with our friends, rarely taking these relationships as seriously as we do our romantic liaisons. That, we think, is the way things are meant to be. We tend to think that the tremendous value we give to this particular relationship compared with the lesser value we accord to others is perfectly normal; indeed, we are apt to assume that it has always been like that everywhere in the world.

But that, as we have seen, is not really the case. On the contrary, our position is a distinctly abnormal one. I am not aware of another society that has raised the sexual relationship so high above all others.

Quite apart from the neglect of other relationships, our attitude has the unfortunate result of overloading the romantic relationship. We come to expect from our sexual partner far more than he or she is able to give. If we are not careful we expect him or her to be everything for us: sexual partner, friend, companion, mother, father, adviser, counsellor, source of security – everything. We expect this relationship to give us love, security, happiness, fulfilment, and the rest. We expect it to give meaning to our lives, and in this way it becomes like an electrical cable carrying a current that is too much for it. The result is that the poor, unfortunate sexual relationship very often blows a fuse – it breaks down under the strain. The obvious solution is to work at the development of a greater spread of relationships, all of which are important to us, and to all of which we give great care and attention.

But one can see it the other way round too. As well as contributing to the decline of other relationships, the present-day centrality of the sexual or marital relationship also reflects the fact that other relationships have become more difficult or have tended to fall into abeyance. Teacher–pupil, employer–employee, and ruler–subject relationships have all been seriously depersonalized – indeed, often they are not seen as relations that should involve a personal element at all. But this was not the case in older societies. Centuries ago – as little as 150 years ago, in some areas of Europe – if you were a servant or an apprentice, you would probably have lived with your master under the same roof. You would have shared in his day-to-day existence, eating the same food at the same table, just as though you were a member of the family, albeit one who knew his or her place. Under the traditional apprenticeship system, a very close personal relationship could grow up between master and apprentice or servant, or in modern terms, between employer and employee.

The novels of Dickens, which date from the 1840s, by which time the industrial age was well under way, could still portray the relation between master and servant in distinctly feudal terms, because those terms were still a reality for many people. When in *The Pickwick Papers* Sam Weller, Mr Pickwick's faithful servant, wants to get married, Mr Pickwick naturally offers to release Sam from his service. Sam declares his intention to stay with Mr Pickwick, who says, 'My good fellow, you are bound to consider the young woman also.' But Sam says that she will be happy to wait for him. 'If she don't, she's not the young woman I take her for, and I give her up with readiness.' His duty, he says, is to serve Mr Pickwick.[427]

In this way he was harking back to the situation where you served a feudal chief who led you in battle, who was more powerful than you, who protected you, and to whom you were unconditionally loyal. This commitment made it a truly personal relationship, and very often the most important relationship in a man's life, even emotionally, and one for which other relationships would be sacrificed if necessary.

This attitude was still around to some extent in the East when I was there in the 1950s. In Kalimpong I sometimes had to engage Tibetan or Nepalese cooks, handymen, or gardeners, and it was noticeable that they quickly became very loyal. They weren't interested in just getting the money at the end of the month. Some of them didn't even want to work for money at all. They were much more concerned to have a decent relationship with a good master.

Nowadays, for better or worse, all this is on the way out, with the steady incursion of Western values. The very word 'master' makes people today feel slightly uneasy. The result is that you cannot generally have any truly personal relationship with your employer. You work not for a master but for a department in a company, and your work is overseen by people who have more power than you have, but no loyalty or commitment to you. Only in truly archaic situations, like an army regiment, in which loyalty and devotion to duty is the key to success, do you still find anything like this sort of relationship. Likewise, we have a very remote, impersonal relationship with those who are meant to protect our interests, and we certainly don't think in terms of serving them. You may get round to shaking hands with your local Member of Parliament or Congressman, but usually that's about as close to them as you are likely to get.

One might think that the relation between teacher and pupil would be a naturally personal one; it certainly can be so in the tutorial system of some universities. However, in general, teaching these days is a businesslike process of passing pupils from one teacher to another in the hope that a balanced ingestion of facts will result. Under the usual classroom system, one teacher sometimes has to address as many as forty pupils, and then moves on to teach another large group of pupils. A relationship is necessarily an individual thing, and it is virtually impossible to develop such relationships with every pupil in your care in such circumstances. Nor can you have favourites, as this will lead to resentment.

Anyway, most of us come in contact with teachers only when we are comparatively young, so that any relationship we might have with a teacher never gets a chance to mature. We don't generally think in terms of learning anything beyond the point at which we stop accumulating qualifications; that is the end of the teacher–pupil relationship for us, although certain relationships later on may involve an unofficial mentoring element which can have a profound effect on our development.

In modern life, relationships between friends are not, in the case of men anyway, meant to go deep enough to produce problems. We tend to keep such relationships at an easygoing, undemanding level, probably because in many people's minds there is a fear of homosexuality. Any strong emotional relationship between two people of the same sex, especially between two men, tends in our times to be rather suspect.

We can also say that relationships among brothers and sisters are much less important than formerly. One obvious reason for this is that some of us don't have brothers and sisters. It is all too common to find oneself an only child – very different from the large families of earlier times, when (especially before the advent of the Welfare State) members of the family would be expected to care for one another.

The fact that these various kinds of relationship have become more superficial means that we are left with only two effective personal relationships in our lives nowadays. The ancient Indians had six, the ancient Chinese had five, but we, for all practical purposes, have two: the parent–child relationship, and the husband–wife or boyfriend–girlfriend relationship. And of these two, it is the second that is for many people by far the more important.

Of course, there are various complicating factors in sexual relationships, the most obvious one being sex itself. Under the conditions of modern life, sexual needs are not only biological but also psychological. For example, a man will tend nowadays to associate the expression of his manhood less with his activity in the world than with his sexual activity, particularly if his work is fairly meaningless and undemanding.

Another complicating factor is that, as in most civilizations, the man–woman relationship is institutionalized – whether as marriage or as cohabitation. Apart from the parent–child relationship (which is on a rather different basis), marriage is the only one of our relationships that we legalize and institutionalize in this way. It is not just a personal understanding between two people; it involves a legal obligation, which under certain circumstances is even enforceable in a court of law. It is not always easy to make changes in such a relationship, and this can lead to difficulties.

When a conflict arises between our need to develop as an individual on the one hand and our sexual relationship on the other, the psychological pressure can build up to create intense distress. Indeed, any personal relationship has the potential to get in the way of our attempts to grow spiritually. There is something of a paradox here. On the one hand, personal relationships are absolutely necessary for human development. On the other hand, if we are committed to spiritual development, it is much easier to sustain a personal relationship with another person who is also trying to lead a spiritual life. Problems are likely to arise – especially in the context of a sexual relationship – when one of the two people wishes to engage in spiritual practice and the other does not, and such problems are difficult to resolve because we are unlikely to be completely wholehearted in our commitment to the spiritual life anyway. Part of us, so to speak, is likely to side with the other person against our spiritual aspiration, so that we may find ourselves agreeing that setting aside time to meditate, for example, is simply selfish.

Some people find that as they get involved with spiritual practice, the importance to them of their old personal relationships diminishes, at least for a time. This can be very difficult to accept. It sounds unbearably harsh to say that as you grow, you just have to leave family and friends behind in some sense. But in a way this is only to be expected. Spiritual life does involve an element of going forth, as we have already seen. And if you are interested in things that your friends and family have little or no knowledge of or interest in, you can't help losing contact with them to some extent.

However, many people find that as they mature in their spiritual practice, their increased positivity, sensitivity, and sense of gratitude brings them into much deeper and closer relationship, especially with their families, and this is very much to be welcomed, and indeed consciously worked on. After all, as the Buddha reminded Sigālaka, our parents gave us this life, which we increasingly feel to be very meaningful and precious; great love and respect is due to them for that, whatever has happened since. At the same time, as we move more deeply into spiritual practice, we will be forming new personal relationships with other people who are trying to live a spiritual life – in other words, we are likely to join or help form a spiritual community.

In the following chapters, we shall take a look at each of the six relationships that the Buddha encouraged Sigālaka to associate with the six directions. Each chapter looks at the relationship in question from a particular angle, so this is not intended to be a comprehensive account (which would hardly be possible in any case), but simply to give an opportunity to reflect on the nature of each relationship in turn. Having considered all six relationships, we will consider something that pertains to all of them, and is also a quality of the true individual: gratitude. We will conclude with two chapters that offer some thoughts on the individual Buddhist's relationship with the wider world. After all, far from being a rationalization for selfishness, as some people assume it to be, the Buddhist life can only be fully lived in the light of the realization of our interconnectedness with all life, and the commitment to act with compassion and vigour on that basis.

13

BEING A BUDDHIST PARENT

According to the Buddha's advice to Sigālaka, one of the six relationships to be honoured and respected is that between parents and children. We get a sense that this was something Sigālaka already knew something about, in that he was worshipping the six directions in the first place in deference to his father's wishes, but there is a great deal to be said about the duties of children to their parents. Here, however, I will be focusing on the duties of parents to their children.

I am not a parent myself, but I have certainly had occasion to observe the nature of parenthood, through my communication with friends and disciples who are parents, through my observations of what goes on around me, and through my reading and contact with the media generally. On the basis of such experience – albeit vicarious – as I have had, I will venture to offer a list of points that any Buddhist parent would do well to consider. I will not be going into the question of whether one should or should not have children. It is simply an established fact that many people, including many Buddhists, have them, and that there is a need, therefore, to consider how best to handle this important relationship.

The observations I want to make – many of which are simple common sense – are expressed in the form of fifteen points, the first of which is this:

1. REMEMBER THAT YOU ARE A BUDDHIST FIRST AND A PARENT SECOND

If one is both a Buddhist and a parent, it is important to think of oneself as a Buddhist who is a parent, rather than as a parent who happens to be a Buddhist. There is a great deal of difference between these two positions. In saying this, I am certainly not encouraging Buddhists to put their children second. If you want to go on retreat and your son or daughter happens to be ill, I am not suggesting you should leave him or her to someone else's tender mercies and go off on retreat. Not at all. Buddhism comes first in the sense that it is from Buddhism that you derive the very principles in the light of which you are trying to be a *Buddhist* parent, not just a parent.

Human beings share parenthood with practically the entire animal species; just becoming a parent is no great achievement, and almost all human beings do it. But although it is easy to become a parent, to be a good parent is very difficult indeed, and to be a Buddhist parent is still more difficult, because it involves applying, or trying to apply, Buddhist principles to your relations with your children. This point underlies all the others I want to make.

2. DON'T BE AFRAID TO TEACH YOUR CHILDREN BUDDHISM

These days there is a great deal of confused thinking about what children should be taught. People often say that we mustn't interfere with anybody's thinking; we should encourage people to think for themselves. Children should not be indoctrinated, but should be allowed to grow up with open, free, almost blank minds. Then, when they are old enough, they will decide for themselves whether they want to be Christian or Buddhist or agnostic or Muslim or Hare Krishna, or whatever appeals to them.

This way of thinking is totally unrealistic. While you are carefully refraining from teaching your children about Buddhism, refraining from indoctrinating them, as you may see it, all sorts of other agencies are going to be hard at work indoctrinating your children with quite different values from your own, whether you like it or not. Children are indoctrinated all the time: in school or playgroup, by television, by films, by the general atmosphere of our society. Don't think that if you refrain from 'indoctrinating' your children, they will be completely free to make up their own minds about things when they grow up.

Don't be afraid, therefore, to teach your children Buddhism – or rather, to communicate to them something of the spirit of the Dharma. Society in the broadest sense is going to be communicating all sorts of other messages, some of which may have a definitely negative effect on them, so don't hold back from giving them the positive influence of the Dharma. You don't have to try to teach them abstruse Buddhist doctrines. You can start very early by showing them picture books about the life of the Buddha, or the traditional stories of the Buddha's previous lives. Every child loves stories, and it is to be hoped that television is not excluding storytelling in the home altogether. In this way you can introduce them to the world of Buddhist culture, and give them something of the feel of Buddhism.

Something else you can do is set an example. When, as your children get older, you begin to communicate your values to them – your commitment to ethical speech, for example – it is important that you should be demonstrating that commitment in the way you live. As any parent will know, children are very quick to pick up on discrepancies. It's no use telling your son or daughter that it's wrong to tell lies and then saying, when someone comes to the door, 'Just say I'm not in.'

You also communicate to your children something of the spirit of the Dharma through the atmosphere that prevails in your home. It is important that when children come home from school or some other activity, they should feel that home is a good place to be: perhaps peaceful or perhaps quite lively, but happy and positive, with an atmosphere of affection and security. Perhaps they will eventually realize that this atmosphere has something to do with the fact that you are a Buddhist and that you meditate; but whether or not they make this connection, they will feel the benefit of living in a positive environment.

3. REALIZE THAT YOU ARE UP AGAINST IT

No parent will need reminding that as a parent one is up against it in the sense that bringing up children is expensive, or that children can be difficult, or that one has sleepless nights. But one is up against it in other senses too – up against the world in the broadest sense. As a Buddhist parent, you are trying to bring up your children in accordance with Buddhist principles, but those principles are far from being acknowledged in the outside world. You are saying one thing, as it were, to your child, but the world is usually saying something quite different, even quite opposite.

Any Buddhist has to fight to sustain their principles, but as a parent you have to fight the battle on your children's behalf as well as your own. The extent to which children should be shielded from outside influences, especially when they are very young, is a big question; and in any case it is only possible to shield them to a certain degree. But it is important and helpful to acknowledge that to try to bring children up in accordance with Buddhist principles is a tremendous challenge, because the outside world – consciously or unconsciously, intentionally or unintentionally – is all the time having a quite different influence on them, and on you as well.

4. JOIN A PARENT–TEACHER ORGANIZATION

Here we come to something much more specific. Sooner or later, your child will start going to school. My fourth point is therefore: join a parent–teacher organization. Don't just leave the education of your children during school hours to their teachers. It could almost be said that education is too important to be left to teachers, just as it is sometimes said that politics is too important to be left to politicians. The teachers may well be doing an excellent job, but they are up against it too – being a teacher is in some ways just as difficult as being a parent.

If you have school-going children, it is a good idea, therefore, to make contact with their teachers. Talk to them about your children, and children in general at the school, and also discuss with them the problems they themselves face as teachers. These days teachers have a very difficult time. There are more and more cases of teachers being physically attacked by students, and this sort of thing makes life very difficult for them indeed. If you join a parent–teacher organization or association, you can contribute some ideas and suggestions, so that the school may become a better place for all the children who are attending it. You may even get the opportunity to become a school governor, and thereby an even greater opportunity to influence the school in a positive and creative way.

5. COMMUNICATE WITH YOUR CHILDREN

Some people would say that this point should be addressed more to fathers than to mothers, but I am not going to make any such distinction. It is very important, if you are a parent, to communicate with your children. Talk to them seriously – don't talk down to them. If they ask a question, take it seriously. If you do so, you may be surprised to find how difficult it is to answer. Even quite small children are intelligent and perceptive, and can come up with quite extraordinary questions sometimes.

One of my happiest memories of my own childhood, back in the late 1920s and early 1930s, is of my father spending time talking to me. He would get home from work – when he was in work, because those were days of unemployment – at about six or seven o'clock, and come to my room – I'd be in bed already – and sit on my bed and talk to me for half an hour or an hour. Sometimes my mother would get impatient because she had his dinner ready and it was getting cold, but he was more interested in talking to me. He used to talk about all sorts of things, especially his wartime experiences – he had been seriously injured in the First World War, which had ended only a few years before. Not only did my father talk to me; as I grew older, I always found it very easy to talk to him.

So, talk to your children. Share your serious thoughts with them, to the extent that they are able to understand them. That means finding time to spend with them. Don't be too busy to talk to your own children. Even set aside a time, if you're very busy, just as you would set aside time to see a friend. Not, of course, that you should sit the children in front of you and say, 'Come on, we're going to have a little talk.' You must catch them on the wing. They may not always feel like talking when you've got time.

6. RESTRICT TELEVISION

It is difficult, if not impossible, to sustain a clear and positive mental state – to remain mindful, as Buddhists would say – unless you do something to limit the extent to which you absorb all the stimulating input of modern life. And, of course, nowadays a lot of input comes from television. There is a big debate going on as to whether or not there is a causal connection between violence as seen on television and violence in the home and in the street. Some experts say there is no real connection, others say there is, and it is very difficult for the layman to know the truth of the matter.

But from a Buddhist point of view we can be sure of one thing. Whether or not seeing violence on television results in actual violence, it certainly does not improve the mental state of the viewer. To spend several hours every week, or even every day, watching programmes that contain a large component of violence can only be to the detriment of one's mental state, whether one is an adult or a receptive and susceptible child.

Some people will say that children have rights, including the right to watch television whenever they like. But, as I have mentioned elsewhere,[428] I think it is better not to use the language of rights, but instead to think in terms of duties. And parents – Buddhist parents especially – have a duty to restrict the television viewing of their children.

The restriction should apply not just to what they watch, but also to how much time they spend sitting in front of the television. Surveys have found that many children in the West are overweight. This is partly because of an unhealthy diet – that is the subject of my next point – but also because they don't take enough exercise. And they don't take enough exercise because – apparently – it is much more interesting to be parked in front of the television set. Tests have shown that watching television also impairs the imagination – essentially because while one is passively taking in whatever the television producers choose to present, one is simply not having to use one's imagination.

Of course, restricting the watching of television is going to be difficult. One Buddhist mother I know said her children felt deprived because they didn't have a television in the house, and therefore felt different from all the other children at school because they couldn't join in discussions about what they had been watching the previous night. In the end their mother reluctantly had to give in to their persistent pressure, although she did manage to restrict their viewing to some extent. Obviously strong forces are at work. Nonetheless, one should take a firm line on this matter.

7. GIVE YOUR CHILDREN A HEALTHY DIET

This point may seem obvious, but again, contemporary conditions are against it. Living in the city and keeping my eyes open, one of the things

I notice is children eating in the street. And, of course, they are usually eating junk food: chocolate, ice creams, burgers, and chips. Parents need to do what they can to counter this widespread habit. There is no need to be faddish or fanatical in the way we were in the sixties, when we were all into macrobiotics. But whoever does the cooking for the family should try to give the family a balanced diet, and discourage snacking between meals.

And, of course, children should be discouraged from smoking. Another thing I notice as I walk around is how many schoolchildren smoke. I see them coming straight out of school – they can't be more than twelve or thirteen – and they pull out a packet of cigarettes and light up straightaway. So again, Buddhist parents need to take a firm line with their children when they come to that particular age.

It was very different when I was a child. I hadn't even thought of smoking when I was young, but when I reached the age of sixteen, my father said to me, 'Son, you're sixteen now. You can smoke if you want to.' I didn't, though – not until I joined the army. Even then I only smoked for a short while, because I didn't enjoy it, and I haven't smoked since. It's really very discouraging to see such small children, both boys and girls, already having acquired the smoking habit. So please discourage your child from smoking – well, don't discourage them, just stop it. Exert your parental authority. I know that parental authority has been reduced to shreds and tatters these days, but whatever pitiful remnants of it are left, exert it in this respect.

8. SOCIALIZE YOUR CHILD

This is a point I particularly want to emphasize. Your children don't belong just to you. They aren't just members of the family. They are, or will be, members of society, part of the wider community, and they need to be brought up, even trained, in such a way that they can function in a positive manner as members of that society. Again, this obviously involves the exercise of a certain amount of discipline. Children have to be brought up, for example, to respect other people's property, and to consider other people's feelings. Otherwise, they are going to have a very tough time in the world later on. You may put up with tantrums and bad behaviour and inconsiderate conduct, but the world will not.

So socialize your children. And don't inflict them on other people. One does see parents doing this. Little Jimmy or Mary is misbehaving, and being very inconsiderate where other people are concerned, but the parents just smile indulgently and other people are supposed to put up with it, or even think it's sweet. In fact, of course, other people are much more likely to be thinking, 'What a dreadful little brat!'

Good manners are rather unpopular nowadays, associated as they are with bourgeois values, middle-class upbringing, and all that sort of thing; the tendency is to throw the baby of good manners out with the bathwater of sociological fashion. But we have to do what we can to retrieve the baby. Recent research has even identified a definite connection between bad manners and juvenile crime, and this suggests that the aspect of socialization which consists in teaching children good manners is not to be underestimated.

9. DON'T BE POSSESSIVE

Of course, your child is your child, with all that that means, and you are legally responsible for him or her up to a point. But try to avoid thinking, 'This is *my* child.' Don't develop the attitude that no one else is allowed to speak to your children, or tell them off if they are misbehaving. In a healthy, positive community, it should be possible for any adult to tell off any child who is misbehaving anywhere. Unfortunately, in Western society at present, this is not possible. One sees it happening in India, but in the West people seem to resent anybody interfering, as they would call it, with their children.

Buddhist parents obviously shouldn't have this sort of attitude, partly because as Buddhists we try not to be attached, or at least to reduce our attachments, and partly because Buddhist parents are part of the Buddhist sangha. You shouldn't mind if a fellow Buddhist thinks it appropriate to remonstrate with your child for some misdemeanour. If your child is visiting the Buddhist centre with you, and while you are doing something, the child is racketing around the centre, any fellow Buddhist should be able to say, 'Come on Tommy, don't make such a noise,' without your resenting it or feeling offended.

A very important aspect of non-possessiveness is letting your children go when the time comes for them to leave the parental nest and go forth into the wider world. You should have brought them up in such a way that they can go forth freely, easily, without feelings of guilt, and with self-confidence, while you feel – yes, a little sad, that's inevitable – but on the whole quite pleased and happy, even, perhaps, if you'll admit it, a little relieved to see them go, and willing and ready to put the old relationship on a new basis.

There is a very interesting verse on this subject in the Hindu *Manusmṛti*. The verse refers to fathers and sons, but it applies to all parent–child relationships. It says, 'When your son is sixteen, cease to regard him as a son, and treat him as a friend.' And that, of course, becomes all the more possible when the child leaves home. When your son or daughter comes to visit you, try to see him or her not as your child returning to the nest for a bit of comfort, but as a good friend coming to see you for a good talk.

10. TEACH YOUR CHILDREN TO SPEAK PROPERLY

Sometimes when I'm out and about and I overhear people talking – not only children but adults as well – I am astonished at the sheer poverty of their vocabulary. Standards do seem to be dropping as regards language and verbal communication in general. It is therefore very important that children should be encouraged to extend their vocabulary and speak grammatically. Speech is our principal medium of communication with one another; unless we master it, we will simply be unable to communicate beyond a certain level.

Make sure, therefore, that your children grow up not just talking, but really *speaking* their language, speaking correctly and elegantly, with some attention to grammar and the correct use of words. Don't be afraid of correcting them. Some teachers maintain that children should never be corrected, because that would undermine their self-confidence, but it's a rather puny self-confidence that can be undermined in that way. If one is not corrected, one will go on making mistakes, and those mistakes will become habits. So correct your children when they pick up incorrect expressions from school friends – and, of course, when they show any tendency to use bad language.

Speech is such a wonderful thing, one of the greatest creations of the human race. We should use it, and teach our children to use it, as fully and effectively and beautifully as we can. Teaching our children to speak properly gives them access to something that is very precious indeed.

11. TAKE YOUR CHILDREN TO SUITABLE BUDDHIST FESTIVALS

It is best to steer a middle course here. Rather than invariably leaving your children at home when there is a Buddhist festival on, or invariably taking them with you, try to find out which festivals or celebrations might be suitable. Not all of them will be. A programme involving a lot of meditation, for instance, will not suit small children; it is unfair to expect them to sit still for such long periods of time, or even more than a few minutes.

But children do like to join in, and they like to do things, so if the celebration is going to include a festive puja, by all means take them along – in consultation, obviously, with whoever is organizing the festival. I have noticed that children like to make offerings to the shrine: that's something they can do, it's simple and poetic, and they enjoy it. They could even prepare the offerings themselves beforehand and bring them along and offer them in their own way.

Don't insist that the children should take part in everything – there are certain occasions when it may not be appropriate – but whenever possible, include them. Perhaps there could even be a special children's festival occasionally.

12. INTRODUCE CHILDREN TO YOUR BUDDHIST FRIENDS

This may seem obvious, but it doesn't always happen. With reference specifically to English people, there is a saying that an Englishman's home is his castle, and we tend not to let down the drawbridge. It's part of our English character that we tend to keep a bit separate from other people, and to keep our domestic life separate from our social life. But if you have children, it's a good idea to make sure they spend time with your Buddhist friends, or at least have some contact with them. Very often this happens naturally and spontaneously, but one may need to make some effort to make sure it does.

It is important partly because it helps compensate for the nuclearness of the nuclear family. In some parts of the world – India, for example – most parents still live as part of an extended or joint family of ten or fifteen or more members. But, in England, our castles have become very small indeed. The nuclear family is getting more nuclear every day, it seems, and that isn't healthy, either for the parents or parent, or for the children or child. Some families these days consist of just two people: one parent and one child – a rather constricting, even claustrophobic, situation. Introducing your children to your Buddhist friends helps to modify the potentially claustrophobic nature of the nuclear family.

Being accustomed from an early age to meeting adults from outside the immediate family circle definitely helps children develop self-confidence, and that is obviously a tremendous asset. One of the things I noticed when I came back to the West after many years in Asia was that people generally seemed to lack self-confidence. Parents have to do whatever they can to make sure that their children grow up with plenty of self-confidence – not the sort of confidence that finds expression in antisocial activity, but self-confidence of a positive and even creative kind. And it does help in the development of a child's self-confidence if he or she is accustomed to interacting with adults from beyond the family circle.

13. TEACH CHILDREN TO CARE FOR THE ENVIRONMENT

Children are quite often to be seen blithely discarding sweet wrappers and so on in the street, apparently unaware of what they are doing, or perhaps accustomed to thinking that someone else is going to tidy up after them, that it isn't their responsibility to keep the streets litter-free. And this, of course, is symptomatic of an attitude that potentially has far-reaching consequences for the environment.

Even in the planet's younger days, at the time of the Buddha, the environment was very much a concern for the practising Buddhist, and the Buddha himself had quite a lot to say about it. As a Buddhist parent, one will want to bring up one's children to care for and respect the environment, which is after all *their* environment. As they get older, you can discuss environmental issues with them – as well as issues of other kinds, of course, but environmental issues do have a very immediate practical application.

14. TEACH CHILDREN TO EMPATHIZE

This is very important indeed. In recent years in England there has been much discussion of the distressing case of James Bulger, a toddler who was murdered by two very small boys. In a radio discussion after the trial, someone said that the reason the two boys had committed that terrible crime was that they had not been brought up to know the difference between right and wrong. But there was a woman psychologist taking part in this discussion, and she disagreed. She pointed out that the two boys had been found guilty of murder – in other words, it had been ascertained that they knew the difference between right and wrong. And she went on to make the very important point that it isn't enough to know the difference between right and wrong; one has to be able to empathize with other living beings. Without empathy, one's recognition of the difference between right and wrong will be purely abstract and conceptual, and will not necessarily influence one's behaviour.

Of course, you can't give lessons in empathy; it can't be made part of the school curriculum. Here again the example of parents comes in. Children can be taught to empathize with people, and with animals too, taught to realize that animals feel pain just as they do themselves. There is an incident in the Pāli canon where the Buddha finds some boys tormenting a crow, and says to them, 'If you were tormented in that way, how would you feel?' Of course, they say they wouldn't like it. And the Buddha said, 'Well, if you would feel pain if you were treated in that way, don't you think the crow feels pain too?' And they have to admit that yes, it does. In other words, they start empathizing with the crow.[429]

In the well-known series of engravings by William Hogarth called 'The Four Stages of Cruelty', the first engraving depicts some boys tormenting a dog and a cat. In the next stage, one of the boys commits a murder. In the third stage, the boy who committed the murder is being hung. And in the last stage, his body is being dissected by some surgeons. Hogarth seems to be saying that this life of violence, which ends in the hanged man experiencing violence himself, begins with tormenting animals, having a lack of empathy with other living things.

Some people are so sensitive that they feel empathy even with plants, not liking to pick flowers because they feel that the plant is being injured in some way. Not everybody can empathize to that extent, but we should at least empathize with animals and with other human beings. This is one of the most important things we can teach our children.

It isn't easy being a parent. Even though I'm not a parent, I know that very well, because sometimes parents confide in me, and I keep my ears and eyes open. It's very difficult being a parent, whether a mother or a father – more difficult now than ever before, in some ways at least. There are so many variables, so many decisions you have to take without being able to know all the relevant facts. And things may go wrong, despite your good intentions.

Even apart from that, children are individuals. They bring their own karma with them. You may bring your child up beautifully, and he or she may turn out to be a monster; you may bring them up very badly, and they may turn out very well. I have lived long enough now to be able to see karma descending from one generation to another. For example, I have known children who were brought up very badly but who were themselves very good parents.

So there is karma to take into account. Quite apart from chromosomes, you don't know what karma your child brings with them. Things may turn out very differently from the way you expected them to turn out. Even apart from that, you yourself are a fallible human being. You're not omniscient. Maybe you mustn't tell your children that too early, but even parents don't know everything, and they can make mistakes.

Provided that you have really done your best for your children, and at every stage have made what you felt at the time was the best decision, if things do seem to have gone wrong, try to learn from that, but don't blame yourself too much. Don't feel guilty. If later on in life your child does something dreadful, don't agonize about it. Don't think that if only you hadn't done this or hadn't done that, it might have turned out different. You don't know. You can't work it out. You just have to do the best you can in the present, here and now. The rest is karma, chance, circumstances, society. So don't feel guilty if it does turn out that you've made mistakes, and don't even be too ready to think that what happens is due to your mistakes. Maybe it isn't. You don't know. But either way, don't blame yourself. You did your best at the time. That should be sufficient for you and for others.

Some parents feel they have to apologise to their children for the way they have brought them up. If you've done something definitely, unmistakably wrong, which has clearly caused the child suffering, say you're sorry when the child is old enough to understand. But apart from that, bear in mind that once your children reach adulthood, they are responsible for their own lives. If anything goes wrong, or if your son or daughter does something wrong, he or she can't blame you for that. Your children are responsible for themselves, just as you are responsible for yourself. You are responsible for them only to a limited extent, and for a limited period of time.

These are just a few of the things to be considered about the relationship, from a Buddhist point of view, between parents and children. It goes without saying, I hope, that all these considerations are to be understood within the overall understanding that as a Buddhist parent you relate to your child with love and care, and that everything you try to do – including the times you need to bring in some discipline – is done in that loving spirit.

14
IS A GURU NECESSARY?

The second of the relationships that 'protect the six directions', as the Buddha tells Sigālaka, is the relationship between pupil and teacher. Here we will be considering in particular the relationship between the disciple and the spiritual teacher, often thought of as a 'guru'. But is a guru necessary? This question connects with some of our earlier considerations about whether it is necessary to live one's spiritual life in the context of a spiritual community. The question is not likely to have occurred to Sigālaka or any of his contemporaries; at that time, the first question anyone would ask you would have been 'Who is your teacher?' not 'Do you think a teacher is necessary?'

But this question will inevitably arise sooner or later for any modern Westerner who genuinely tries to develop as an individual, to be authentically himself or herself. In particular, it is likely to arise if one attempts quite specifically and consciously to follow what we usually refer to as the spiritual path, and it will demand an answer all the more imperatively when one tries to follow that spiritual path in one or another of its oriental forms.

However, before we address the question itself, we must banish the haze of imaginative associations that gather around the magic word 'guru'. We must, unfortunately, dispel the vision of brilliant blue skies, beautiful white snow peaks, and, just above the snow line, the snug little caves which are in the popular imagination the natural habitat of that rare creature, the guru. We must come down to earth from those

inaccessible valleys of Shangri-la in which benign and wise old men with
long white beards and starry eyes pass on the secret of the very highest
teaching to a very few devoted disciples. We must ruthlessly dismiss
any notion of those lucky disciples effortlessly floating up to Nirvāṇa
on the strength of having secured the most advanced techniques from
the most esoteric lineage holder.

We need to consider the whole question of the guru in as sober and
matter-of-fact a fashion as possible, and try to understand what a guru
is, and what a guru is not. On that basis, it should become clear to what
extent and in what way a guru is necessary, if at all. We can also consider
the attitudes it may be appropriate to adopt in relation to the guru.

Let us begin by seeing what a guru is not. First of all, a guru is not
the head of a religious group. By a religious group I do not, of course,
mean a spiritual community, but rather a number of non-individuals
organized into a power structure around the forms or conventions of
some kind of religious practice. Religious groups are of many kinds –
sects, churches, monasteries, and so on – and they each have someone
at their head. Such heads are regarded with great veneration by other
members of the group, but there is likely to be something unfocused or
off-key about this devotion. They are venerated not for what they are
in themselves, as individuals, but for what they represent, what they
stand for, even what they symbolize.

It might seem obvious that they should stand for or symbolize
something spiritual; and in a superficial sense they do. But in fact they
represent the group itself. That they are the head of a group is their
principal significance. It is easy to see when this is the case; you just
have to wait for the head of a group to be criticized or even vilified, as
in course of time will inevitably happen. Members of groups usually
feel that an attack on the head of their group is an attack on them. Any
disrespect shown to the head of the group by those outside the group
is interpreted by group members as lack of respect for the group itself.

The Buddha refused to countenance any such attitude among his
followers. The *Brahmajāla Sutta* of the *Dīgha Nikāya* tells the story of
how the Buddha and a great crowd of his followers were once travelling
on foot between Rājagṛha and Nālandā, and found themselves in
company with a wanderer called Suppiya and a follower of his, a young
man called Brahmadatta. These two, in the hearing of the Buddha and
his followers, began to argue, and kept arguing as they walked. And

the subject of their argument, one can imagine, must have upset some of the Buddha's disciples considerably. For Suppiya, the text tells us, was finding fault in all sorts of ways with the Buddha, the Dharma, and the Sangha – though Brahmadatta was praising them just as strongly. All the travellers found themselves staying in the same place overnight, and still Suppiya and Brahmadatta kept on arguing.

Not surprisingly, when dawn came, the Buddha's followers gathered together and started talking among themselves about this disconcerting behaviour on the part of their fellow travellers. Coming to join them, the Buddha asked them what they had just been talking about, and they told him. Reading between the lines, we can gather that they were somewhat upset, even angry, at what had happened. But the Buddha said:

'Monks, if anyone should speak in disparagement of me, of the Dharma or of the Sangha, you should not be angry or displeased at such disparagement; that would only be a hindrance to you.'

Nor did the Buddha let the matter rest there. He said, 'If others disparage me, the Dharma or the Sangha, and you are angry or displeased, can you recognize whether what they say is right or not?' And the monks had to admit that, in those circumstances, they would be in no state to think about things objectively.

So the Buddha said, 'If others disparage me, the Dharma or the Sangha, then you must explain what is incorrect as being incorrect, saying, 'That is incorrect, that is false, that is not our way, that is not found among us.'[430]

If one reflects on this episode, one realizes that the Buddha is pointing out to his disciples a tendency that is all too human. If they had become angry, they might have thought their anger had arisen because the Buddha was being criticized, but in fact it was much more likely that anger had arisen because the group to which they belonged was being criticized, and so, in effect, *they* were being criticized. A disciple in that position might well feel that his wisdom in being a member of that group, and a follower of the person being criticized, was being called into question.

Examples of such sensitivity are not confined to the Pāli canon. I have come across Buddhists who would hunt through books on comparative religion, dictionaries of religion and philosophy, and the like, to see if they could find unfavourable references to Buddhism. When they found them, they would write off to the publishers, call public meetings, and organize protests and demonstrations. The most interesting aspect of the whole business was that the Buddhists who thus spluttered and seethed with rage were invariably convinced that they were thereby demonstrating their devotion to the Dharma. What they were exhibiting, however, was their group spirit – a thing that has nothing to do with the spiritual life or the Buddha's teaching.

Hence a guru is not the head of a religious group. Nor is he an ecclesiastical superior, someone higher up in the power structure of a religious group. When prominent religious personalities come from the East, they are sometimes heralded by advance publicity in which one is told that this particular personality is in charge of an important group of monasteries, or that he is second-in-command of an ancient and historic temple. Sometimes in India one is told simply that he is very wealthy. I was once in Calcutta at a time when preparations were being made for the arrival of a monk from a famous temple in Sri Lanka, and I was told by the head monk of the temple where I was staying that I ought to go and see him, as he was very important and influential. Naturally I asked, 'In what way is he important?' The head monk replied, 'He's the richest monk in Sri Lanka.' It was on that basis that I was expected to go and pay my respects to him.

This is an extreme example, but it is representative of a general expectation that one should be impressed by people who are higher up in the ecclesiastical structure, and regard them as gurus. But a guru is not this sort of figure at all. Someone who is organizationally important or influential is not thereby a guru.

A guru is not a teacher either – a statement that may come as something of a surprise. It is comparatively easy to understand that a guru is not the head of a religious group, but it is quite usual to think that a spiritual teacher is just what a guru is supposed to be. But what is meant by a teacher? A teacher is one who communicates information. A geography teacher teaches facts and figures about the Earth; a psychology teacher teaches facts and figures about the human mind. In the same way, a teacher of religion may teach the general history of all the different religions of the world, or the theology or doctrinal system of a particular tradition. But a guru, as such, doesn't teach religion. In fact, he or she doesn't necessarily teach anything at all.

People may ask questions, and he may answer those questions – whether or not he does so is up to him. But he has no vested interest in teaching. If nobody asked him any questions, he probably wouldn't bother to say anything. The Buddha himself made this perfectly clear. In several places in the Pāli scriptures he is reported as saying that he has no *diṭṭhi* – no view, no philosophy, no system of thought. 'There are lots of other teachers,' he says, 'who have this system of thought to expound, or that philosophy to teach; but I have none. I have no "view" to communicate. The Tathāgata (Buddha) is free from views, liberated from doctrines, emancipated from philosophy.'[431]

Outside the Pāli canon the Buddha is further reported as saying that he has no Dharma to impart. The great *Diamond Sūtra* describes innumerable bodhisattvas and disciples sitting and waiting for the Buddha to teach them the Dharma. But the Buddha tells them, 'I have nothing to teach.'[432] In another celebrated Mahāyāna text, the *Laṅkāvatāra Sūtra*, the Buddha goes so far as to say that he has never taught anything. 'Whether you have heard me speaking or not, the truth is that from the night of my Enlightenment, all through the forty-five years until the night of my *parinirvāṇa*, the night of my passing from the world, I have not uttered a single word.'[433] So the Buddha, the ultimate Buddhist guru, has no view, no teaching to impart. He is not a teacher.

Something else that the guru is not relates to one of the most striking facts about the human race as a whole, which is that the majority of its members do not grow up. People develop physically, of course, and they also develop intellectually in the sense that they learn how to organize their knowledge more and more coherently. But they don't grow up spiritually, or even emotionally. Many people remain emotionally immature, even infantile. They want to depend on someone stronger than themselves, someone who is prepared to love and protect them absolutely and unconditionally. They don't really want to be responsible for themselves. They want some authority or system to make their decisions for them.

When one is young, one depends on one's parents, but as one grows older, one is usually obliged to find substitutes for them. Many people find such a substitute in a romantic relationship, which is one of the reasons marriage is so popular, and also, often, so difficult. Others find their parent-surrogate in a concept of a personal God. One might even follow Freud in saying that God is a father-substitute on a cosmic scale. The believer expects from God the kind of love and protection that a child expects from his or her parents. It is highly significant that in Christianity, God is addressed as 'our Father'.

The role of father-substitute is often played by a guru – or rather a pseudo-guru. Mahatma Gandhi, for instance, was a great Indian politician, thinker, activist, even revolutionary, but it is rather significant that as a religious figure for much of his life he was addressed by his disciples as Bapu, 'Father'. Nor was this sort of title at all unusual in India. When I lived there I was in contact with quite a number of religious groups and their gurus, many of whom liked to be addressed as Dadaji, or 'Grandfather'. Their disciples, it seemed, were only too happy to fall in with their wishes in this respect.

This rather amused me, and when I was in Kalimpong and had some pupils of my own – most of them Nepalese rather than Indian – I asked them out of curiosity how they regarded me. At that time I was about thirty, and they were in their late teens and early twenties, so when they clasped their hands together and said with great fervour, 'Oh sir, you are just like our grandfather,' I was taken rather by surprise.

In India I also met a number of female gurus, and they were invariably addressed as Mataji, 'Mother', or even Ma, which means 'Mummy'. One of these gurus, who was well into middle-age when I first got to know her, was surrounded by young male followers, most of whom, as I discovered later, had lost their mothers. In the evenings they would gather in the meeting-hall to sit gazing up at 'Mummy' and singing in chorus the word Ma – nothing else, just that word, 'Mummy' – to the accompaniment of drums and cymbals. They would keep it up for two or three hours at a time: 'Ma, Ma, Ma, Ma, Ma'.[434] They believed that what they called 'Ma-ism' was a radical new development in religious history, and that the worship of Mother – this particular mother, anyway – would be the future religion of humanity. I was not at all surprised to find that there was intense competitiveness and jealousy among her disciples, as if they were all vying with one another to be the favourite, if not the only, son. It was also noticeable that they tended to disparage other groups. In the same way that children will say, 'My daddy is much stronger/richer than your daddy,' or 'Our house is bigger than your house,' they would maintain that in comparison with their own guru, other gurus were insignificant.

Fortunately, I have known gurus who knew how to manage their followers in a much more healthy manner – particularly certain Tibetan gurus. A story about three great lamas I knew personally in Kalimpong will illustrate this. All three were eminent lamas of deep and genuine spiritual experience, and they all had many disciples. Though they all belonged to the predominantly 'Red Hat' tradition, their characters were very different. One wore a sheepskin robe, dyed red, and was always on the move, so that it was difficult to catch him. Another lived with his wife and son, and gave initiation to thousands of people – initiations that were said to be particularly powerful. The third was the scholarly head of an important monastery.

The story I was told by one of their disciples – and they had a number of disciples in common – was that a discussion had once arisen among the disciples as to which of the three gurus was the greatest. In the end, one of the bolder spirits plucked up courage and approached one of the gurus. He said, 'Look, there's been a lot of discussion as to how the three of you would place yourselves with respect to each other. We all have immense veneration for all three of you, but we would appreciate it if you could clear up this point: Which of you is the greatest? Who has gone furthest? Who is nearest to Nirvāṇa?' So the guru smiled and said, 'All right, I'll tell you. It is true that among us three there is one who is much more highly developed than the other two. But none of you will ever know which one that is.'[435]

A real guru does not fall into the role of a father figure. This is not to say that people do not need father-substitutes, at least for a while. Such a projection may be necessary for their psychological development. One must also allow that the function of the guru is analogous to that of the true father: the guru fulfils the same function on a spiritual level that the true father fulfils on the ordinary human level. But the guru is not a substitute for a father where the father has been lacking, or where he is still required.

Neither should a guru be taken for a problem-solver. This brings us to a distinction that I find it helpful to draw between a problem and a difficulty. The difference is that a difficulty can be overcome or resolved with effort, whereas a problem cannot. If you put a lot of effort into what I call a problem, you only make it more problematic. It's like finding a knot in a piece of string and pulling on the two ends in order to untie it. You can pull as hard as you like, but you'll only succeed in tightening the knot. The genuine guru may help people overcome their difficulties, but he will not attempt to grapple with their problems.

There are fundamentally two kinds of problem: doctrinal problems and personal, usually psychological, problems. The problems of Westerners tend to be of the second type, whereas in the East people's problems are often doctrinal – they want to resolve technical questions to do with Nirvāṇa, the *skandhas*, the *saṃskāras*, and so on. However, even such doctrinal problems are very often psychologically motivated, or at least psychologically oriented. One asks even the most abstract theoretical question ultimately for personal psychological reasons, though usually one is not conscious of this.

If you have a problem, it embodies a self-contradictory situation; it cannot be solved on its own terms. But if you bring it to your guru, you are in effect asking him or her to solve the problem on its own terms. For instance, a woman comes along in great distress, so upset that she can hardly speak. Eventually she tells her guru that she just can't live with her husband any longer. She's had enough. If she has to put up with any more, she'll go stark staring mad. She's just got to leave him. But her problem is that if she leaves her husband, she will have to leave her children too – because the children cannot be taken away from their father – and leaving her children is no less impossible than continuing to live with her husband. She will go mad if she has to stay with her husband, but she will also go mad if she has to leave her children. 'What am I to do?' she asks her guru expectantly.

Then somebody else comes along and complains of lack of energy: 'I'm always tired,' he says. 'I feel exhausted all the time. I can't do a thing. I don't seem able to work up any interest in anything; I just lie around all day like a limp, wet rag. I can watch a bit of television or listen to the radio, but that's it. I feel utterly drained all the time. There's just one thing that I know will help: meditation. I can get energy through meditation – I'm convinced of that.' So the guru says, 'Well, why don't you meditate?' And the unfortunate disciple replies wearily, 'I just don't have the energy.'

But if the guru has to send this person away with his problem still unresolved, there are still more problems waiting in the wings. To take yet another example, someone comes along and says that he just wants to be happy. That's all he asks from life. And he feels that he could be perfectly happy if only someone would give him a satisfactory reason for being happy. He has examined all the reasons offered by religions, philosophies, and friends, but none of them has proved truly convincing.

Can the guru do better? If anyone has the answer, surely the guru will. Surely a guru is there to provide the answers to the big problems. Of course, the guru knows quite well that every reason he can produce will be rejected as unsatisfactory. But still the man demands an answer.

If you asked any of these people what they are really looking for, all of them would say that they want to find a solution to their problem. That is why they have come to the guru. They firmly believe he can solve their problems if he chooses to do so. But, in fact, this is not the situation at all. What these people really want to do is defeat the guru. They present their problem in such a way that the guru cannot solve it without their consent or cooperation – which they have no intention of giving.

Such people are sometimes very cunning. Especially in the East they will very often approach the guru with a great show of devotion and humility, bearing presents, making offerings, bowing, and declaring their unshakeable faith in the guru. They say, 'I've taken this problem of mine to lots of other gurus, to all the most famous teachers and masters, and not one of them could solve it. But I've heard so much about you, and I'm sure that you are the one person who can.'

Only a guru who lacks experience, or isn't a true guru, will be taken in by all this. The true guru will see what is going on at once, and will refuse to play the role of problem-solver, even if, as is very likely, the person with the problem goes away disgruntled, and starts saying that the guru cannot be a true guru because he hasn't got the down-to-earth compassion to deal with his disciples' problems. Some gurus are rewarded with quite damaged reputations for refusing to play this sort of game.

So a guru is not the head of a religious group, or a teacher, or a father-substitute, or a problem-solver. This does not mean that he or she may not, from time to time, function in these ways, and in many others. A guru can function, for instance, as a physician, a psychotherapist, an artist, a poet, a musician, or even just a friend. But he or she will not identify with any of these roles.

The guru may be the head of a religious group, although this rarely happens, because the qualities that make a guru are not those that assist promotion within an ecclesiastical system. Much more often, particularly within the Buddhist sangha, the guru may be a teacher – that is, he or she may function outwardly as a teacher. But it remains important to distinguish the teacher from the guru as such. Some gurus may be teachers, but by no means all teachers are gurus. A guru may even function as a provisional father-substitute or problem-solver, but the emphasis is on 'provisional'. As soon as possible, he or she will discard this role and function as a guru.

But if the guru is none of these things, what is a guru? Aristotle said that there are many different ways of being wicked, but only one way of being good[436] (which in the eyes of some people makes goodness seem rather dull). One could also say that there are many misconceptions about the guru, but only one true conception. There is therefore much that can be said about what a guru is not, but comparatively little to be said about what he or she positively is. Of course, this doesn't mean that it is any less important. Indeed, from a spiritual point of view, the more important a thing is, the less there is to be said about it.

Perhaps, above all, the guru is one who stands on a higher level of being and consciousness than ourselves, who is more evolved, more developed, more – in a word – aware. Also, a guru is someone with whom we are in regular contact. This contact may take place at different levels. It may take place on a higher spiritual plane – that is, telepathically – as the direct contact of mind with mind. There may be contact between the guru and the disciple in dreams or during meditation. But for the ordinary disciple, it generally takes place on the physical plane – that is, on the ordinary social plane, in the ordinary way. The relatively undeveloped disciple will need regular and frequent physical contact with the guru. According to Eastern tradition, ideally he or she would be in day-to-day contact with the guru, even living under the same roof.

Contact between the guru and the disciple should be 'existential' – that is, there should be real communication between them – not just the sharing of thoughts or ideas or feelings or experiences, even spiritual experiences, but communication of being, or, if you like, action and interaction of being. The guru and the disciple need to be themselves as fully as possible in relation to each other. The guru's business is not to teach the disciple anything, but simply to be himself in relation to the disciple. Nor, as the disciple, is it your business to learn. You simply have to expose yourself to the being – and to the effect of the being – of the guru, and at the same time, be yourself in relation to him.

Spiritual communication, like integration, can be thought of as being of two kinds: 'horizontal' and 'vertical'. Horizontal communication takes place between two people who are on more or less the same level of being and consciousness. Because their states of mind fluctuate from day to day, sometimes one of them will be in a better state of mind than the other, but the next day it may be the other way round. Vertical communication, on the other hand, takes place between people one of whom is on a consistently higher level than the other, quite apart from any ups and downs. It is such vertical communication that takes place between guru and disciple.

In all communication, whether horizontal or vertical, there is mutual modification of being. In the case of horizontal communication, in the course of communication anything one-sided or unbalanced in one's nature is corrected. People who really communicate gradually develop a similarity of outlook, responding to things in the same spirit; they have progressively more in common. At the same time, paradoxical as it may seem, they become more truly themselves.

Suppose, for example, a very rational person were to engage in true communication with a very emotional person. If they sustained this communication long enough, the emotional person would become more rational, and the rational person more emotional – each rubbing off on the other. At the same time, if you are the rational person (to take that example) you do not just have emotionality added to you from without. Through communicating with the emotional person, you are enabled to develop your own undeveloped emotionality which has been there all the time (as it were) beneath the surface. A quality emerges that was there, but not active. The communication has simply enabled you to become more yourself, more whole, more complete. And it's the same, obviously, if you are, at least to begin with, the emotional one of the two.

Vertical communication is different. The disciple grows in the direction of the guru's higher level of being and consciousness, but the guru does not become correspondingly more like the disciple. The principle of mutual modification of being does not mean that the guru slips back in his development as a result of his communication with someone less developed. He does not meet the disciple halfway, as it were. In the intensity of his or her communication with the guru, the disciple is in a sense compelled to evolve. He or she has no choice, unless they break off the relationship altogether, and a real disciple cannot even do that. It is said that the true disciple is like a bulldog puppy. When offered a towel, the puppy will snap at it and not let go, even if the towel was lifted off the ground with his jaws still attached to it. The true disciple has that sort of tenacity.

As a result of his vertical communication with the disciple, the guru also grows spiritually. The only guru who doesn't do this is a Buddha, a fully and perfectly enlightened one, and even among gurus a Buddha is extremely rare. It is sometimes said in Tantric circles that disciples are necessary to a guru's further development, that nothing helps a guru so much as having a really good disciple – not an obedient, docile disciple, but one who really engages in communication, one who is really trying to grow. A good disciple may give the guru quite a lot of trouble, sometimes more trouble than all the other disciples put together. It also occasionally happens that the disciple overtakes the guru, and a reversal of roles takes place. This situation is less problematic than it might seem from the outside, because the relationship is not one of authority or power, but of love and friendship.

So is a guru necessary? Well, to grow spiritually without any contact with a guru is extremely difficult. Generalizing, one might say that for most people spiritual growth does not take place without at least two factors being present: the experience of suffering, and contact with a more highly developed person or persons. Why? Because personal relationships and real communication are necessary to human development. Not only that – we need real communication that includes a vertical element. Through communication with our friends, we develop horizontally – we become more whole, more ourselves. But most people seem to need communication with a guru to enable them to rise to a higher level of being and consciousness. Just as a child develops into an adult mainly through contact with his or her parents, regular contact with at least one person who is more highly developed than we are is necessary for our spiritual development. Not that it is absolutely impossible to make progress without being in contact with such a person, but that kind of contact certainly speeds up and intensifies the whole process.

But if a guru is necessary, how do you go about choosing one? How do you know whether someone is more highly evolved than you are? Obviously, it is important not to make any mistake in this matter. The problem is that it is very difficult indeed to know if someone is really more advanced – perhaps impossible, without prolonged contact. Some gurus in the East say not only that it is impossible for the disciple to choose the guru, but that it is quite presumptuous for the disciple to think that he can do so, or that he can know whether someone is more developed than himself. What actually happens, they say, is that the guru chooses the disciple. You may think that you are choosing a guru, but in fact the only choice you are capable of making is of a religious group (with the guru as its head), or a religious teacher, or a father-substitute or problem-solver. You are not choosing a guru as such, because you are not equipped to see who is of greater spiritual attainment.

As a would-be disciple, what are you to do? All you can do is make as much progress as possible by yourself so that you can recognize and make contact with a spiritual community (as distinct from a religious group). Then you must hope that some member of that community will take you on as a friend, or refer you to somebody else who can. In any case, you should always be ready and receptive for the advent of the guru.

Sometimes the guru just grabs you by the scruff of the neck, as it were. You may not even have thought about the spiritual life; you may not have any interest at all in religion; you may not have any problems; you may be quite happy as you are; but the guru sees your potential, and takes you on anyway – he makes you a disciple regardless of your protests.

There is a well-known story of the Buddha himself adopting a disciple in such a peremptory manner. The disciple in question was his own cousin, a young man called Nanda – nicknamed Sundarananda, or 'Handsome Nanda'. The occasion was Nanda's marriage to a very beautiful girl, and it seems that the Buddha had been invited to the marriage feast. The Buddha had produced his begging-bowl and been served along with everyone else; then after the feast, he prepared to go back into the depths of the forest. Calling for Nanda, he said, 'Nanda, would you mind carrying my bowl just a little way for me?' And, rather pleased to get this special attention from his illustrious relation, Nanda followed him, carrying his bowl.

As the Buddha paced sedately on, Nanda came after him rather less sedately because he kept looking back at his new wife, entranced by the long shimmering tresses of her hair as she waved to him. After a few hundred yards, he found himself going deeper and deeper into the forest. He started to become a little uneasy, having heard all sorts of strange stories about his cousin. A mile or so into the forest he became really worried, but he was too much in awe of the Buddha to say anything, so he just stumbled on after him, still clutching his bowl. Mile after mile they went on in this way until eventually they emerged into a clearing where they found a circle of huts occupied by a group of the Buddha's disciples.

Wasting no time on introductions, the Buddha took the bowl from his cousin – who was by that time trembling with fear and confusion – and directed the other monks to ordain him. So they seized hold of Nanda, forced him down on to his knees, shaved his head, and stripped off his white robes, giving him yellow ones to wear instead. Finally he was instructed in the rules of the order of monks and taught how to meditate, and then left to sit under a tree and get on with it.

The story does, however, have a good outcome for Nanda, in that after undergoing further trials he eventually becomes an *arhant*, an Enlightened One.[437] Thus it is possible for a guru, if they know what they are doing, to go so far as virtually to hijack someone – an extreme example of the basic principle that it is the guru who chooses the disciple, not the other way round.

In a way, the guru cannot be overvalued. Nothing can be more valuable than the person who helps you to develop spiritually. All the same, it is true to say that in the East the guru often tends in a sense to be overvalued, while in the West he is usually undervalued. What can happen in the East is that a false and inflated value is attached to the guru. People in India sometimes say that the guru is God. This is asserted not just as a figure of speech, but quite literally. If you are sitting in front of the guru, you are not just looking at a human being, seated on a cushion on the floor. You're sitting in front of God – in fact, all the gods rolled into one, the all-powerful, the all-knowing himself. He may look just like an ordinary human being, but he knows everything that is going on in the whole universe, including everything going on in your mind. He can read your thoughts like an open book. If you've got a problem, you don't have to tell him – he knows already. He can do anything he likes. He can bless you, give you riches, promotion, fame, children, all with just a word of blessing. He can give you Enlightenment if he wants to. It is all in his hands – it's all the 'grace of the guru', as they say.

All the disciple has to offer is faith in the guru, faith that the guru is God. If the disciple only has enough of this kind of faith, the guru can work miracles on his behalf. Such faith is therefore regarded as of the very greatest importance. There are, of course, little difficulties. It sometimes happens that the guru appears not to know something, or to forget something you have told him, and you may get a bit upset by this. But the true disciple isn't bothered at all because he knows that these apparently human limitations and failings are tests of faith. The guru is only pretending to have slips of the mind to see if your faith is still firm and sound, just as a potter taps a pot after it's been baked, to see whether or not there's a crack in it.

It is no wonder that over the years the disciple comes to inhabit a fantasy world in which whatever happens is seen to do so on account of the guru's 'grace' and the guru's will. If the guru isn't careful, he may come to inhabit this fantasy world too, especially if he isn't a real guru. After all, it isn't easy to escape such a fantasy world if you yourself are at the centre of it. If someone comes and tells you that their child was sick and has now recovered due to your blessing, you may not be inclined to dispute that interpretation, even if you hadn't given the child a moment's thought.

The problem from the guru's point of view is that sooner or later it will dawn on certain of his more perceptive disciples that he isn't really God. While he may have a deep level of insight and spiritual experience, he also has some quite human limitations. Perceiving this, they are likely to conclude that he isn't a true guru, and go off to look for someone who is a true guru, someone who *is* God. If they do that, the same thing will inevitably happen all over again. They will start noticing little discrepancies, get disillusioned, and see that this guru too is 'only' a human being after all. And so the merry-go-round continues.

This happens among Buddhists as well to some extent. A Tibetan friend of mine, a lama and guru living in Kalimpong, recalled that when he first arrived there, the local Nepalese Buddhists used to flock to see him, bringing him wonderful offerings and eager to take initiations from him. But after a few years they got a bit tired of him. They continued to come to pay their respects, but he was amused to observe that they didn't bring quite such big offerings as before. Then a new lama arrived on the scene (he was a friend of the first one) and everybody abandoned my friend to get their new initiations from the new lama – to the amusement of both lamas. Eventually, as the Chinese communists seized power in Tibet, more and more gurus started to arrive in town, which was very bewildering for the local community. No sooner had they identified a supremely powerful guru and rushed to make him offerings, than another one arrived, who – according to some people – was even more eminent and accomplished. In the end they must have run through perhaps twenty gurus, looking for the 'real' one.

Clearly, the guru is overvalued in this manner in the East because he is regarded as an idealized parent figure: all-knowing, all-powerful, infinitely loving and tolerant. The disciple in such cases wants to adopt an attitude of infantile dependence. Gurus are usually very popular in India, but there is one thing demanded of them, regardless of almost anything else: they must always be kind and affectionate, soft-spoken and gentle. What they teach and how they live are side-issues by comparison.

In the West we have traditionally gone to the opposite extreme. Here, far from overvaluing the guru, we have hardly any concept of the guru at all. This is no doubt largely due to the influence of Christianity. On the one hand you have belief in God with all his various attributes, and on the other you have submission to the head of the particular religious group to which you belong, your ecclesiastical superior, but there seems to be no room for the guru in the true sense.

The gurus who do appear – who may eventually be identified as saints – are usually subject to the rule of the ecclesiastical authorities. In medieval times, even a great saint sometimes had to submit to a bad pope. Perhaps that didn't do the saint much harm, but it was bad for the pope, and for the Church as a whole. However, we must not imagine that the Christian tradition is the only spiritual tradition the West has ever known. Nor should we accept the assumption that the concept of the guru in the Eastern sense is alien to the Western mentality. There were certainly gurus in ancient Greece and Rome – for example Plato, who maintained a sort of school or academy, Pythagoras, who founded spiritual communities, Apollonius of Tyana, and above all perhaps, Plotinus. From Porphyry's life of Plotinus, especially the description of his later life in Rome, one gets the definite impression of a sort of spiritual community, set up more along the lines of an Indian ashram than in a manner typical of the kind of institution one might think of as characteristic of the later Roman Empire.[438]

Such great figures of classical times were gurus in the true sense of the term. And in modern post-Christian times there are signs that the importance of the guru is again beginning to be appreciated in the

West, despite our democratic and egalitarian prejudices, our modern belief that no one should be seen as better than anybody else. Even in modern cultures so apparently hostile to the possibility of spiritual development, there are signs that people are beginning to appreciate the significance of those who are more highly developed than the average person.

Such people may not be appreciated in spiritual terms; more often they are lauded as geniuses or heroes. A noticeable phenomenon in the United States is the academic guru figure, who travels from one university campus to another and attracts crowds of students to his lectures. Young people who may have no interest in gurus from the East are beginning to feel or even think quite consciously that there is not much to be gained from books, and that the conventional voices of religion, politics, and even the arts, don't say very much to them. They are therefore looking for some kind of guru figure. They want to be taught by someone wiser than themselves, someone they can look up to, someone who will shed a clear light to guide them on their path. There were some obvious examples of this phenomenon in the sixties – Buckminster Fuller, Allen Ginsberg, Timothy Leary, and Richard Alpert, who went on to become a guru in an overtly Eastern sense as Baba Ram Dass. Today, the 'guru' is a widespread feature of Western intellectual life.

As Buddhists, we have to follow a middle way. We have to recognize above all that we are capable of evolving from our present state of being and consciousness to a more fully developed degree of self-consciousness and even to a realization of transcendental consciousness, leading to what, without really being able to understand it, we can only call absolute consciousness. In order to do this, we have also to recognize that different human beings are at different stages of this great process of spiritual development. Some are lower down than we are, while others are higher up, even a great deal higher up. We have to recognize that those who are higher up in the scale of the evolution of humanity are in a position to help us, and that we will develop through communication with them. It is gurus in this sense whom we need to recognize as being superior. The kind of guru we don't need is one to whom we give an unrealistically inflated value, and onto whom we project our desire for an idealized father-figure. It is a great mistake to expect from a guru what we can only get, ultimately, from ourselves.

The Buddha did not ask anybody to regard him as a god or as God. He never asked anybody to have faith – much less to have absolute faith – in him. In fact, this is a very important aspect of Buddhism. The Buddha never said, 'You must believe in me, and believe what I say, if you want to be saved, or if you want to realize your own true nature.' Again and again in the Buddhist scriptures he is presented as saying, 'Let any reasonable man come to me, one who is willing to learn; I will teach him the Dharma.'[439] All he asks is that we should be rational and open-minded. All he requires is reasonable and receptive human contact. He seems to have been quite convinced that he could introduce anyone to the spiritual life without making any appeal for absolute faith and devotion, but purely by rational and empirical means. On this basis alone he could awaken anyone to the truth that the path to Enlightenment is the most worthwhile thing to which as human beings we can possibly devote ourselves.

15

FIDELITY

One of the five ways in which, according to the *Sigālaka Sutta*, husband and wife should 'minister' to each other is by not being unfaithful;[440] and fidelity is our theme here. I do not propose to treat the subject exhaustively, or even systematically; I just want to put together a few observations. As well as commenting on the nature of the relationship between husband and wife (or the modern equivalent), I want to explore the theme of fidelity because I have come to the conclusion, the more I have thought about it, that fidelity should be one of the qualities of what I call the true individual – that is, of one who is trying to become a truly human being.

So far as I can see, all the different kinds of fidelity can be included under three main headings: fidelity to oneself, fidelity to ideals, and fidelity to other people. Arguably, one could make fidelity to one's given word into a fourth heading, but this is perhaps best considered as an aspect of fidelity to oneself, although it obviously involves fidelity to others as well. Fidelity to oneself could also be described as being true to oneself, as in the famous advice of Polonius to his son Laertes, in Shakespeare's *Hamlet*:

> This above all: to thine own self be true,
> And it must follow, as the night the day,
> Thou canst not then be false to any man.[441]

Being true to oneself means consistently acting, speaking, and thinking in accordance with what is best in oneself. It involves seeing oneself objectively – not in a cold-blooded fashion, but in the sense of seeing clearly one's own real interests, in the highest and fullest sense, and being consistently faithful to them.

Fidelity to ideals is not so easy to explain. It does not necessarily mean fidelity to ideas. In fact, to understand what it does mean we have to be clear about the difference between an ideal and an idea. An ideal may be defined as a regulative model for human existence. But – and this is the important point – this model is not imposed upon human existence from outside. It is derived from human existence itself. An ideal brings the basic trend, the true nature, of that existence more clearly into consciousness, and thus intensifies, or even elevates, that basic trend. Ideals, therefore, are instruments of human development.

Someone holding an ideal can of course lose touch with the concrete situation, become detached from human experience, and when that happens the ideal ceases to function as an ideal. It becomes a dead ideal, and thus not really an ideal at all. Dead ideals are simply ideas, and as such they should indeed be rebelled against and rejected.

So fidelity to ideals means consistently acting, speaking, and thinking in accordance with the regulative models of human existence, being true to the basic trend or true nature of that existence, especially as that trend is reflected, intensified, and amplified in consciousness or awareness. Fidelity to ideals eventually becomes virtually indistinguishable from fidelity to oneself. It is, one might say, the objective counterpart of fidelity to oneself.

Fidelity to other people is perhaps easier to understand, at least superficially. In feudal society, there is the fidelity of the retainer to his overlord. In domestic life there is the fidelity of wife and husband to each other, and of servant to master. And in the broader sphere of social life there is fidelity between friends. Fidelity to other people means consistently behaving, speaking, and thinking in accordance with the way in which one has defined oneself in relation to those other people. It means behaving as one has undertaken to behave towards them.

Fidelity is thus the consequence of a voluntary act. One can speak of a good mother or a good slave, but one cannot speak of a faithful mother or a faithful slave, because the relation of mother to child or of slave to master is not one that is entered upon voluntarily. It is imposed – by nature in the one case, by society in the other.

But what makes fidelity a quality of the individual, or, indeed, part of the very way in which we should define the true individual? We have seen that the first and most fundamental quality, the essence, of the individual is self-awareness or reflexive consciousness, the ability to see oneself objectively. Being self-aware is seeing ourselves as others see us – not quite in Robert Burns's sense, perhaps,[442] but in the sense of seeing ourselves in the same sort of way that others see us, as an object of awareness. We can become the object of our own thought.

Thought is not limited, in the way that our body is limited, by time and space. Through thought we can abstract ourselves from the conditions under which we at present exist. In particular, we can form an idea of ourselves as having existed in the past and as having an existence to come in the future. Self-consciousness therefore involves a degree of separation from the present, a sort of standing back from it. It is because we have self-consciousness that we can project our idea of ourselves into the future; and it is because we can do this that we can say in the present that we will do something in the future. In other words, it is because we have self-consciousness that it is possible for us to make a promise.

When we say that fidelity involves consistency – consistently behaving in a certain way – this implies continuity in time. Consistency means behaving in the same way over a period of time. Indeed, it means more than this. It means consciously and deliberately behaving in the same way over a period of time. And to be able to do this, we must have self-awareness, we must be individuals.

If our self-awareness is weak, we will not be able to keep a promise. We may say the appropriate words because they are expected of us, but they will not have the significance of a promise if we are not able to keep that promise. If we don't keep a promise it is because in truth we never made it in the first place.

It is lack of self-awareness, lack of individuality, that gets in the way of our being faithful. This applies to our capacity to be faithful to ourselves and our ideals, but here I will discuss it in terms of fidelity to other people – in fact, in terms of fidelity to one other person. And, of course, the form of fidelity to another person with which we are most familiar, and about which we are usually most exercised, is sexual fidelity.

We all know what sexual fidelity means, at least in a superficial sense. It means confining one's sexual activity to one person. Most of us would also agree that the antithesis of fidelity is promiscuity. There are, of course, degrees of promiscuity, and most people understand the precise degree to be determined by the number of sexual partners one has (at different times in one's life, usually). But properly defined, promiscuity consists not in the multiplicity of one's sexual relations, but in non-continuity. The essence of promiscuity is that one does not have sexual relations with the same person twice consecutively. The most completely promiscuous person would therefore be the one who, over however long a period, never had sexual relations with any partner more than once.

With respect to sexuality, there are three possible lifestyles: the monogamous (or polygamous where that is an option), the promiscuous, and the celibate. The degree of approval accorded by 'the group' towards the way people express their sexuality is based, by and large, on these choices of lifestyle. (The group may also reserve degrees of disapproval for what it considers to be perverse expressions of sexuality.) But so far as the development of the individual is concerned, there are just two forms of sexual lifestyle: a neurotic form and a non-neurotic or psychologically healthy form. Someone who is trying to be an individual may follow any one of these lifestyles, provided he or she follows it in its non-neurotic form.

But how does this square with the idea that fidelity is a quality of the true individual? It would seem that there is a certain contradiction here. Are we, or are we not, saying that it may be ethical for the individual to follow a sexually promiscuous lifestyle? The difficulty is more apparent than real. The essence of the matter is that it is quite impossible for all the relationships of one's life to be continuous. However, some of them must be, otherwise one can hardly be self-aware at all. To the extent that one limits the continuity of one's relationships, to that extent one will not continue to grow as an individual. Having sexual relationships which are non-continuous need not be a problem if we have non-sexual relationships that are central to our life and which are continuous – i.e. in relation to which we practise fidelity. At the same time, if our non-continuous sexual relationships are more important to us than our continuous non-sexual relationships, we are obviously in serious difficulties.

But – to return to our main theme – how does one sustain fidelity to one person? There are two enemies of such fidelity: a 'near enemy', attachment, and a 'far enemy', distraction.[443] Distraction could be described as something that forces itself on our attention when we do not really want to pay attention to it. Of course, we experience distraction almost every time we try to meditate. We may be trying to concentrate on the process of our breathing, but the noise of the traffic outside intrudes and it seems that we just can't help listening to it. Sometimes the thing that forces itself on our attention is something to which at another time we would be very glad to pay attention. It may be something of which we are very fond or even something by which we are fascinated, something that appeals to our most basic interests and desires. I hardly need spell out the kinds of thing this might be. The distraction then becomes very difficult to resist.

In meditation, the distractions that present themselves to us come in the form of memories and fantasies, but in daily life we are confronted by distracting objects that are all too obviously and literally present. This is what makes it difficult for us to practise fidelity. The distracting object – or, generally, person – is present, whereas the person to whom we intend to be faithful may not be. Of course, the impression produced by something present is very vivid, by comparison with the impression produced by something that is not present (other factors being equal). Thus, a person who is present may cause us to forget – at least for the time being – a person who is absent, or even to act as if the absent person did not exist at all. There occurs a breach of continuity in our relationship with that other person, and this is the essence of infidelity. Present impressions have triumphed over our sense of continuity, in respect of our relation with that other person through past, present, and future.

We usually say that someone who yields too easily to the impressions of the moment has a weak character. They have very little continuity of purpose and, being so easily distracted, they don't have much individuality either. Such a person cannot practise fidelity. Of course, the reality of the situation is not so neat and abstract, although it can be described so succinctly. We are talking about some of the messier aspects of human life, and the human messiness involved should not be forgotten.

The near enemy of fidelity is attachment. It is called the near enemy because fidelity and attachment look very much alike, at least to the superficial observer. But where there is a neurotic degree of attachment to another person, there can be no fidelity, because there is no real self-awareness in that attachment, and therefore no real individuality. One's attachment to someone in the present excludes consciousness of past or future, and is simply prolonged indefinitely. One does not experience such a relationship as persisting through time. One is therefore incapable of fidelity.

But how does one know if one is capable of being faithful? How is fidelity tested? A test is a situation or experience that exposes the true nature of a thing, which reveals whether it is the genuine article or only a poor imitation. Thus, for example, fire reveals whether a certain yellow metal is gold or just something that looks like it.

Our fidelity to another person is, of course, tested by physical separation. When we are separated from someone, the relationship is transferred, at least for the time being, from the physical to the mental plane. Its continuity becomes exclusively mental (the term 'mental' being understood as including the emotional aspect of the psyche). It is much more difficult to live on the mental plane than on the physical plane, because sense consciousness is much stronger than self-awareness. Consequently, when as a result of separation our relationship has to exist on the mental plane, it is only too easy for that relationship to be interrupted by a relationship with someone else on the physical plane. In other words, it is only too easy for us to be unfaithful. Fidelity is possible only to the extent that we can envisage our relationship with the person from whom we are separated continuing into the future. This ability to project ourselves into the future is in turn possible only to the extent that we are self-aware.

Thus separation is also the test of self-awareness. Indeed, it is because it is the test of self-awareness that it is the test of fidelity. Separation reveals the level at which our relationship with another person really exists – whether it is predominantly physical or both physical and mental; and fidelity is possible only to the extent that a relationship is mental (and emotional). Physical separation can therefore be taken as an opportunity for developing and intensifying the non-physical side of a relationship along with one's self-awareness. This in turn will enhance one's individuality in the true sense of the term.

The most extreme form of separation, obviously, is death, and death is therefore the ultimate test of fidelity. One might even say that fidelity includes awareness of death, as indeed does self-awareness. If you can imagine yourself existing in the future, you can also imagine yourself not existing in the future. To be self-aware, to be human, to be an individual, is therefore to be aware of death.

Fidelity is also tested by isolation, in the sense of being in a minority, even in a minority of one. This kind of test applies particularly to fidelity to ideals, although it can also apply to fidelity to another person. It is very difficult really to stand alone. It is very difficult to hold on to your ideals – whatever those ideals may be – when everyone around you is trying to persuade you to abandon them, because they think those ideals are wrong, or inopportune, or out of date, or no fun. You are in a very difficult position when your most precious values cut you off from everyone else, whether from your family, your neighbourhood, your country, your culture – even, it may sometimes seem, from everyone in the whole world. If you happened to believe in God and your ideals also seemed to cut you off from him, so much the worse. Human beings will do almost anything to avoid the terrible isolation of being derided by others on account of their ideals, and most people will be tempted to give up those ideals under that sort of pressure.

A good example of isolation as the ultimate test of fidelity to ideals is to be found in Milton's *Paradise Lost*. In one passage, the angel Abdiel finds himself by a mischance among the rebel angels, and thus in the uncomfortable position of disagreeing with their rebellion against God. He is in fact the only one in the whole vast assembly of millions of rebel angels who so disagrees. After Abdiel, all alone, denounces Lucifer and the rebel angels, Milton comments on his noble fidelity, thus:

> So spake the seraph Abdiel, faithful found.
> Among the faithless, faithful only he;
> Among innumerable false, unmoved,
> Unshaken, unseduced, unterrified,
> His loyalty he kept, his love, his zeal;
> Nor number, nor example, with him wrought
> To swerve from truth, or change his constant mind,
> Though single, from amidst them forth he passed,
> Long way through hostile scorn, which he sustained
> Superior, nor of violence feared aught;
> And, with retorted scorn, his back he turned
> On those proud towers to swift destruction doomed.[444]

I will end this chapter with two stories, both concerned with both fidelity and death. The first comes from Beethoven's opera *Fidelio*, which was composed at the beginning of the nineteenth century. Fidelio means 'faithful one', and it is the name assumed by Leonora, the wife of a Spanish nobleman called Floristan. Floristan has aroused the enmity of Pizzaro, the governor of a gloomy medieval fortress which functions as a prison for political offenders, and Pizzaro seizes him and casts him in the deepest and darkest dungeon of the fortress, meanwhile spreading abroad a report of Floristan's death. Everybody believes this report – everybody, that is, except Leonora. Refusing to accept that her husband is dead, she plans a ruse to gain entry to the fortress and save him. Disguising herself as a young man, taking the name of Fidelio, she gets work in the fortress as assistant to the chief jailer, called Rocco. Of course, Rocco has a daughter who falls in love with the supposed young man, giving rise to the mandatory operatic complications.

Condensing the story to its essentials, it runs as follows: Pizzaro learns that Fernando, the minister of state, is coming to inspect the fortress, and decides to murder Floristan before Fernando arrives. He posts a trumpeter on the battlements to give warning of Fernando's approach, and orders Rocco, the chief jailer, to kill Floristan. Rocco refuses. Pizzaro then orders him to go and dig Floristan's grave and says that he will kill Floristan himself, with his own hands. So Rocco digs the grave ready for Floristan, and Fidelio (Leonora) as his assistant has to help him dig it, although she is digging the grave of her own husband. The scene then changes to Floristan's cell, where Pizzaro is on the point of stabbing Floristan. At this moment Leonora throws herself in front of him and says he must kill her first. As she does so, the famous trumpet call is heard. The minister of state arrives, Pizzaro is arrested, and Floristan and Leonora are reunited.

It has been said that 'as a drama and as an opera *Fidelio* stands almost alone in its perfect purity, in the moral grandeur of its subject and in the resplendent ideality of its music'.[445] As for the moral grandeur of its subject, this obviously refers to the opera's exploration of the theme of fidelity. When Floristan disappears and is rumoured to be dead, Leonora doesn't start looking for another husband, but goes in search of Floristan and risks her own life to save him. Her fidelity is tested by death in more ways than one, and she passes the test. The opera is not staged very often, although the various 'Leonora' overtures are familiar orchestral fare.

Whether this is because the 'moral grandeur of its subject' is a bit much for modern audiences, and fidelity is out of fashion, it is impossible to say. But if so, perhaps the fact is of significance. If we want to cultivate the qualities of the true individual, we may not get very much help from our society as far as fidelity is concerned.

Passing from a Western story to an Eastern one, and from an opera to a *sūtra*, we come again to the *Amitāyur-Dhyāna Sūtra*, the *sūtra* of the meditation on Amitāyus, the Buddha of Infinite Life.[446] Here we find another fortress, another dungeon, another prisoner, and another faithful wife – added to which we get some extra ingredients: the Buddha, the Dharma, and the Sangha. We have encountered this story before, in our consideration of the spiritual community and the Pure Land. As we have already seen, when this *sūtra* opens – in Rājagṛha, the capital of Magadha – King Bimbisāra has just been deposed by his wicked son Ajātasatru, who has shut him up in prison, hoping that there he will starve to death. In fact, he isn't just hoping – he conveniently forgets to give orders that his father should be supplied with food. But Vaidehī secretly takes food to her husband and keeps him alive day after day, week after week, month after month. In other words, she remains faithful.

Eventually, Ajātasatru becomes suspicious about the fact that his father is not dying as expected. Setting watch on the comings and goings at the prison, he eventually discovers that he has his mother to blame for his father's irritating survival. Ajātasatru is clearly not a dutiful son at the best of times, and in his fury he draws his sword on his mother, and is only restrained from matricidal violence by his ministers. They say, 'In our royal traditions there are many records of kings who have killed their fathers, but none yet of a king who has killed his mother. Desist from this unspeakably bad action.' Ashamed, the king sheathes his sword and contents himself with ordering that his mother should be imprisoned too. In prison she prays to the Buddha – for she is not only a faithful wife, but also a faithful disciple of the Buddha – and begs him to send his disciples, Ānanda and Mahāmaudgalyāyana, to visit her.

Hearing her plea with his divine ear, the Buddha does more than she asks. Together with Ānanda and Mahāmaudgalyāyana, he appears before her, resplendent with rainbow light, filling the darkness of the prison cell. Vaidehī tells him that she is dissatisfied with this world (as well she might be) and asks the Buddha to teach her how to meditate on a better world. The Buddha does as she asks, and the description of these meditations makes up the greater part of the *sūtra*.

In this story too we see how fidelity is tested by separation, even by death. Vaidehī remained faithful to Bimbisāra even at the risk of her own life. Possessing the quality of fidelity, she was an individual; and because she was an individual, she could go for Refuge to the Buddha, the Dharma, and the Sangha. She could see the Buddha and his disciples before her, and she could hear the Dharma. Ultimately, in fact, fidelity means fidelity to these three ideals. Fidelity to oneself is ultimately fidelity to the Buddha. Fidelity to ideals is ultimately fidelity to the Dharma. And fidelity to other people is ultimately fidelity to the Sangha.

Fidelity of this supreme kind is embodied in the figure of the female bodhisattva Tāra, sometimes called Samayatāra (which, according to Lama Govinda, translates as 'the faithful Tāra'). All bodhisattvas, however, are embodiments of perfect fidelity. They are faithful to all beings, and their fidelity is without limit in space and time. They are, we may say, individuals in the fullest and highest sense.

Hence if we want to be bodhisattvas, if we want to be individuals, we should practise fidelity. We should be faithful to ourselves, to our word, to our promise. We should be faithful to our ideals, to our experience, to our work, to the path of human development. We should be faithful to other people: not just to our lovers, but to our friends, fellow workers, and teachers. And ultimately we should be faithful to the Three Jewels. Without fidelity there is no continuity, without continuity there is no development, and without development there is no spiritual life. Fidelity is a human need because development is a human need. And fidelity is part of human nature because development is part of human nature.

16

THE MEANING OF FRIENDSHIP

In the modern world, friendship is arguably the most neglected of all the primary human relationships. But as we have seen, according to the Buddha himself, friendship has a direct connection with the spiritual life. Speaking to Sigālaka on the subject, he says that friends and companions are to be served and looked after in five ways.[447] In other words, we have five duties towards our friends, and if we perform these, our friendships will flourish.

First of all, it is our duty to be generous. We should share with our friends whatever we have. This should ideally be taken quite literally. Some Buddhist residential communities live on the basis of a common purse, pooling all their resources. This isn't easy to do, of course – some people find it difficult even to share a book – but it reflects the ideal relationship between friends. Ideally, your friend should not even have to *ask* you for money. If you take the principle of sharing seriously, you share everything: time, money, resources, interest, energy – everything. You keep nothing back for yourself.

The second duty is never to speak harshly or bitterly or sarcastically to our friends, but always kindly and compassionately. Speech is taken very seriously in Buddhism. The five basic Buddhist precepts include just one speech precept – to refrain from false speech – but it is not enough just to speak truthfully, and this is reflected in the ten precepts taken by some Buddhists. These include no less than four speech precepts, because it is so easy to fall into harmful, destructive speech, to speak in an indifferent, careless, or even callous way.[448]

Our third duty to our friends is to look after their welfare, especially their spiritual welfare. As well as seeing that they are all right in terms of their health and economic well-being, and helping them with any difficulties they have, we should help them in whatever way we can to grow and develop as human beings.

Fourthly, we should treat our friends in the same way we treat our own self. This is a very big thing indeed, because it means breaking down the barrier between oneself and others. One of the most important Mahāyāna texts, the *Bodhicaryāvatāra* of Śāntideva, deals with this topic in great depth and considerable detail.449

And fifthly, we should keep the promises we make to our friends. We should keep our word. If we say we will do something for a friend, we just do it, come what may. If we are careless about fulfilling our promises, it is usually because we make them carelessly. We therefore have a duty to make our promises so mindfully that we treat them as serious obligations. Once we have given our word, that should be that.

Just as we have these five duties towards our friends, they have the same duties towards us; it's a two-way thing. Our friends and companions minister to us, serve us, reciprocate our friendship. Having listed our duties towards our friends, the *Sigālaka Sutta* therefore gives a list of five ways in which our good friends look after us. Firstly, according to the *sutta*, they take care of us when we are sick. Secondly, they watch over our property when we are neglectful; in other words they take more care of our possessions than we do ourselves – that is a sure sign of friendship. Thirdly, they are our refuge in time of fear: they can allay our anxiety, and if we have genuine cause for fear they help us deal with the situation. Fourthly, they do not forsake us when we are in trouble; as the proverb says, 'A friend in need is a friend indeed.' And lastly, they show concern for our dependants. If we have children, our friends are just as concerned for their welfare as we are ourselves, and the same goes for the welfare of our disciples, if we happen to have disciples.450

These, in brief, are the duties of a friend. Clearly they represent a very high ideal of friendship, and they repay careful reflection. Here I will just point out one or two salient features. It is interesting, for example, that the first four duties are identical with another well-known list that occupies an important place in Mahāyāna Buddhism: the four *samgrahavastus*, usually translated as the four elements of conversion.[451] These form part of the seventh *pāramitā*, the seventh of the ten perfections to be practised by the bodhisattva: *upāyapāramitā*, the perfection of *upāya* or skilful means. The four *saṃgrahavastus* are thus an aspect of the bodhisattva's skilful means.

The fact that these elements of conversion are the same as the first four duties of a friend says something deeply significant about how the sangha operates at its best. It suggests that the best way of converting people is simply by being friends with them. Some people try to convert others to their point of view or their religion almost forcibly, but this is not the Buddhist way. Buddhists should convert people – if that is really the right word – simply by being friendly. We make friends and that's an end of it. There is no need to preach to people, to knock on their doors and say, 'Have you heard the word of the Buddha?'

As a Buddhist one should not be thinking about 'converting' someone, or in any way manoeuvring them on to the path that one follows oneself. One's business is just to be a friend, to be generous, to share whatever one has, to speak kindly and affectionately, to show concern for one's friend's welfare, especially their spiritual welfare, to treat them in the same way that one treats oneself, and to keep one's word to them.

However, the fact that these four things are elements of conversion means that in themselves they constitute a communication of the Dharma. You communicate the Dharma itself by practising friendship in this way. One could even go so far as to say that friendship *is* the Dharma. William Blake, the great English poet, artist, and mystic, said, 'Religion is politics,' but he went on to say, 'Politics is brotherhood.'[452] Religion, therefore, is brotherhood. We can say, following him, that the Dharma is friendship. If you are practising friendliness you are not only practising the Dharma, but communicating it.

One further issue raised by the duties of friendship has particularly important implications. It concerns the fourth duty: treating our friends and companions like our own self. The Sanskrit term here is *samānārthatā – samān* meaning equal. A friend is one whom you treat equally. But what does this mean? A clue is to be found in the etymology of the word friend, which is apparently cognate with the word free. Friendship is a relationship that can exist only between two or more free people – that is to say, people who are equals. Understanding this, the Ancient Greeks maintained that there could be no friendship between a free man and a slave.

We can take this metaphorically as well as literally. Friendship, we can conclude, can never involve any kind of power relationship. The relation between master and slave is based upon power, and where one person has any kind of power over another, there can be no friendship, because friendship is based upon love – to use the word love in the sense of the Pāli term *mettā* rather than in the sharply differentiated sense of the term *pema*, which is love as sticky attachment or possessiveness. *Pema* is fundamentally selfish, and it can easily turn into hatred; sexual love, of course, is often of this kind. But *mettā* is unselfish or non-attached, concerned only with the happiness and well-being of others.

The Pāli word for friend, *mitta* (Sanskrit *mitra*), is closely related to the term *mettā* (Sanskrit *maitrī*). And *mettā* is of course the quality developed in one of the most important Buddhist meditation practices, the *mettā bhāvanā*, the development of friendliness towards all living beings. This practice begins with the development of *mettā* towards yourself. In the next stage you develop *mettā* towards a near and dear friend (not a sexual partner or someone to whom you are sexually attracted). In the third stage you direct that same feeling of *mettā*, which by this time should be quite well-established, towards a neutral person – someone you know fairly well but whom you neither particularly like nor dislike. Next, in the fourth stage, you develop that same *mettā* towards an 'enemy' – someone whom you regard as an enemy or perhaps who regards you as an enemy, or both. It might sound incredible that you could develop deep friendliness towards an enemy, but anyone who has done the *mettā bhāvanā* practice with any regularity will know from their own experience that it is possible.

Finally, in the fifth stage, you develop *mettā* towards all these four people – to yourself, your friend, the neutral person, and the enemy – and then you start expanding the range of your *mettā*, cultivating it towards anyone upon whom your attention falls. You start with people who are close by – those meditating with you, or those in the same house or street – and then allow your *mettā* to radiate further and further, to include everyone in the neighbourhood, the city, the whole world. You can include within the scope of your *mettā* all kinds of people as well as other living beings, even gods and animals.

With the help of this meditation practice we can develop a friendly attitude. In other words, we shift from operating in the power mode to operating in the love mode. There are many ways of operating in the power mode – that is, focusing on getting what we want in a situation that involves other people. Usually, if we are clever enough, we don't have to use force. Subtly and indirectly we manipulate other people into doing what we want them to do, not for their good but for our own purposes. Some people are very good at this. They are so subtle, they seem so unselfish and so frank, that you hardly know that you are being manipulated, and it's so indirect that they may not even realize they're doing it. But in one way or another we deceive people, and ourselves, as to our real motives. We cheat, we lie, we commit emotional blackmail. But in *mettā*, in friendship, there is none of this, but only mutual concern for each other's happiness and well-being.[453]

Thus, friendship has a definitely spiritual dimension, and the Buddha has other things to say on the subject in other places. In chapter four of the *Udāna*, which may be an even earlier text than the *Sigālaka Sutta*, we find the Buddha staying at a place called Cālikā, accompanied by his attendant, who is at this time a monk called Meghiya. The two of them are alone together one day when Meghiya, who seems to be quite a young monk, happens to see a lovely grove of mango trees. In India you often get these on the outskirts of a village; the trees are very beautiful, with an abundance of dark green leaves, and they grow close together, so that as well as producing mangoes, they provide cool shade in the hot Indian summer.

Meghiya thinks to himself, 'What a beautiful grove of mango trees! And what a very fine place in which to sit and meditate – so cool and refreshing!' He therefore asks the Buddha if he may go and spend some time there. The Buddha, however, asks him to wait a while until some other monk arrives, because, for one reason or another, the Buddha needs someone to be with him. But Meghiya is not concerned with what the Buddha needs. Instead, he comes up with a clever and apparently unanswerable argument. He says, 'It's all very well for you – you've reached the goal of Enlightenment – but I have a long way to go in my practice. It's such a beautiful mango grove, I really want to go there and meditate.' In the end the Buddha has to agree, and off Meghiya goes, leaving the Buddha on his own. However, although Meghiya has got what he wanted, and the mango grove turns out to be just the peaceful place he thought it was going to be, he finds that he can't settle into his meditation at all. Despite his enthusiasm and energy, as soon as he sits down his mind is overwhelmed with greed, jealousy, anger, lust, false views – the lot. He just doesn't know what to do.

In the end he trudges back to the Buddha and reports on his abject failure. The Buddha doesn't scold him, but he gives him a teaching. He says, 'Meghiya, when you are spiritually immature there are five things that conduce to spiritual maturity. And the first of these is spiritual friendship. The second thing is the practice of ethics; and the third is serious discussion of the Dharma. Fourthly, you need to direct energy towards eliminating negative mental states and developing positive ones. And fifthly, you must cultivate insight in the sense of a deep understanding of universal impermanence.'454

The Buddha marked out these five things as necessary for the spiritually undeveloped, and of course he was implying that Meghiya should put spiritual friendship first. If you have a spiritual friend, whether the Buddha or someone much less eminent, they cannot be disregarded in the careless way that Meghiya has brushed off the Buddha. But like Meghiya, we are often unaware of the extent to which we are dependent spiritually on having personal contact with our spiritual friends, particularly those who are more developed than we are. It is very difficult to make any spiritual progress without them. The Buddha himself is no longer around, but most of us, like Meghiya, would not be ready for such a friend anyway. We would probably act rather as Meghiya did.

We may not have the Buddha, but we do have one another. We can help one another, encourage one another in our practice of the Dharma. We can confess our faults and weaknesses to one another. We can share our understanding with one another. We can rejoice in one another's merits. In these ways we can make a practice of spiritual friendship.

No one else can practise the Dharma for us; we have to practise it ourselves. But we do not have to practise it *by* ourselves. We can practise it in the company of other like-minded people who are trying to do the same, and this is the best way – in fact, the only effective way – to practise.

As the Buddha was to say to his disciple and cousin Ānanda, some years later at a place called Sakka, 'Spiritual friendship is the whole of the spiritual life.'455 But how are we to take this? We can understand that friendship is important, but the idea that friendship, even spiritual friendship, should be the whole of the spiritual life, does seem hard to swallow. But let us look a little more closely at what is being said here.

The Pāli word I have translated as 'spiritual life' is *brahmacariya*, which sometimes means celibacy or chastity – that is to say abstention from sexual activity – but in this context it has a much wider meaning. It consists of two parts. *Brahma* means high, noble, best, sublime, and real; it also means divine, not in the theistic sense but in the sense of the embodiment of the best and noblest qualities and virtues. And *cariya* means walking, faring, practising, experiencing, even living. Hence *brahmacariya* means something like 'practising the best' or 'experiencing the ideal'; we could even render it 'the divine life', or just 'spiritual life', as I have done.[456]

There is a further aspect to the term *brahmacariya* that brings us to a deeper understanding of what it means in this context. In early Buddhism there is a whole series of terms beginning with *brahma*, and one of these is *brahmaloka*, which means the sublime realm, the divine world, or simply the spiritual world in the highest sense. So the *brahmacariya* or spiritual life is that way of life that leads to the *brahmaloka* or spiritual world. But how is it able to do this? For the answer, we must turn to yet another early Buddhist text: the *Mahāgovinda Sutta*. Without going into the background to this *sutta* – it's a long story – we find in it this very question being asked: 'How does a mortal reach the immortal *brahma* world?' In other words, how can one pass from the transient to the eternal? And the answer given is short and simple. 'One reaches the *brahma* world by giving up all possessive thoughts, all thoughts of me and mine.' In other words, one reaches the *brahmaloka* by giving up egoism and selfishness, by giving up all sense of 'I'.[457]

Thus the intimate connection between spiritual friendship and spiritual life starts to come into focus. Spiritual friendship is a training in unselfishness, in egolessness. You share everything with your friend or friends. You speak to them kindly and affectionately, and show concern for their welfare, especially their spiritual welfare. You treat them in the same way you treat yourself – that is, you treat them as being equal with yourself. You relate to them with an attitude of *mettā*, not according to where the power between you lies. Of course this is very difficult; it goes against the grain, because we are naturally selfish. The development of spiritual friendship is very difficult. Leading the spiritual life is very difficult. Being a Buddhist – a real Buddhist – is very difficult. We need help.

And we get that help not only from our teachers but also from one another. We can't be with our spiritual teacher all the time, but we can be with our spiritual friends all the time, or at least much of the time. We can see them regularly, perhaps live with them, perhaps even work with them. If we spend time with spiritual friends in this way, we will get to know them better, and they will get to know us better. We will learn to be more open and honest, we will be brought up against our weaknesses, and in particular we will be brought up against our natural tendency to operate in accordance with the power mode. If we have spiritual friends, they will try not to relate to us in this way and they will expect us to operate in the love mode as well, to relate to them with *mettā*. Learning to relate to our friends in this way, we will gradually learn to respond to the whole world with *mettā*, with unselfishness. It is in this way that spiritual friendship is indeed the whole of the spiritual life.

17

BUDDHISM AND BUSINESS
RELATIONSHIPS

The principle of non-exploitation should ideally hold good in all the relationships of life. It should be possible for us to take what we need, whether food, clothing, education, or anything else, and give whatever we can. There is no need for there to be any connection between what we give and what we receive. Unfortunately, however, the way things usually work is that each person involved in any transaction, whether as the giver or as the receiver, thinks only of himself or herself, giving as little as possible in exchange for as much as possible. This is how ordinary life generally works: we negotiate transactions in which what we give is determined by what we can get for it, not by any regard for the consequences of the transaction for other people.

Beyond a certain point, any commercial profit made is necessarily at the expense of someone else; but the plight of the losers in the game does not generally bother the winners. A particularly brazen form of this universal phenomenon is to be found in poor places like India, where hugely wealthy dealers in grain, especially rice, hoard their stocks, refusing to admit that they have anything to sell, so as to force prices up. This may go on for weeks at a time, especially in remote parts of the country, to the point where people are actually starving, yet the merchants will hold on to those stocks as long as they possibly can, before slowly releasing them at extortionate prices on the black market. The poor have then to scrape together every penny in order to buy enough food to live on. Such exploitation happens –

albeit usually in more subtle ways – in all walks of life, in all parts of the world.

The idea of non-exploitation is clearly related to the second of the five precepts (the precepts which form the basis for the ethical life of all Buddhists). In trying to live in accordance with the second precept, one undertakes not to take what is not given. This is more than simply a roundabout way of saying 'not to steal'. Not stealing isn't enough. It leaves too many loopholes. Someone may be a perfectly honest person according to the letter of the law, but they may still build up their business in all sorts of irregular, dubious, or downright shady ways. Thus a great deal of wealth is amassed through highly unethical means without the breaking of any conventional ethical codes.

But the Buddhist precept is an undertaking not to take something unless those who are its present owners, whether individuals or the community as a whole, are willing and ready to give it to you. If it has not been given to you, you do not take it. I mentioned that there should be no connection between what we give and what we take. However, what we take must at the same time be given – in this respect giving and taking are two aspects of the same action. In some Buddhist countries monks are supposed to be so strict in the observance of this precept that when food is given to them on formal occasions, they are not allowed to eat it unless the plate containing the food is lifted up and actually placed in their hands.

The same principle finds application in the fifth stage of the Buddha's Noble Eightfold Path: right or perfect livelihood.[458] The very fact that right livelihood is included in the list suggests the importance given within Buddhism to the way one earns one's living. People may talk of getting the perfect job, but we can guess that this is not what is meant by 'perfect livelihood'. But how does something so apparently mundane as employment find a place in this august collection of ideals?

We all have to earn a living – those who are not monks, anyway – but however we do it, no harm should come either to others or to ourselves through the work we do. The early scriptures even offer a rough and ready guide to right livelihood in the form of a list of occupations that are prohibited for those following the spiritual path.[459] The first of these concerns any commercial activity that involves trading in living beings, whether humans or animals. Slavery is and always has been condemned and prohibited in Buddhist countries – Buddhists did not have to wait until the eighteenth or nineteenth century for a clear line on this issue. Of course, trading in human beings still goes on in the world today, but even more widespread is trading in animals for slaughter, also prohibited in Buddhist societies: you will never find a Buddhist butcher or slaughterman. This form of livelihood is harmful not only to the animals being slaughtered, but also to those doing the slaughtering. To spend eight hours a day killing pigs, cows, sheep, or chickens will necessarily bring about some degree of mental or emotional damage to the slaughterman, as a result of stifling his natural feelings of compassion for other living beings.

Another early Buddhist prohibition was placed upon trade in poisons – not of course medicinal poisons, but poisons used to take life. Before the days of autopsies, this was an almost foolproof way to dispose of someone; a dealer in poisons would give you a phial of the requisite potion – whether fast or slow working, painful or painless – and you would then dose that inconvenient person's curry with it. Like slavers, dealers in poisons are, in a sense, found less frequently today than they used to be. But, of course, the modern equivalent – the widespread dealing in what are called class A drugs (like heroin and cocaine) – is just as harmful. Also, many people are involved in the manufacture and sale of cigarettes and other indisputably harmful drugs, including advertising them and dealing in shares in them.

The third prohibition was against making or trading in weapons. For the early Buddhists this meant bows and arrows, spears and swords. From these primitive beginnings of the arms trade, however, our more advanced cultures have made considerable progress – so they would say – in the development of wonderfully safe and refined methods of ensuring victory over the enemies of civilized values. But any involvement in making these means of destruction, however 'intelligent' they may be, is to be condemned as wrong livelihood. There is no question of justifying any war, any idea that weapons are a deterrent, any bombs, however 'smart'.

These prohibitions are of course directed at the laity, but there are also certain ways of earning a living which are forbidden specifically to monks. For example, various forms of fortune-telling, of which there were very many in the Buddha's day, are enumerated and roundly condemned in the scriptures.[460] However, all over the Buddhist world monks to this day are relied on by the laity to foretell the future, and unfortunately many monks take advantage of this trust in their powers of prognostication.

Monks are also prohibited from earning a living through the display of psychic powers, or by promising psychic powers to others. The reason for this is obvious, really. People are naturally very interested in psychic phenomena, supernormal powers, and so on. Such things are generally taken more seriously on an everyday level in the East, but in certain circles in the West there is also an intense and unhealthy fascination with the idea of acquiring mysterious and occult powers that other people don't possess. If you dangle psychic powers in front of someone's nose, you can, if they are easily led, lead them almost anywhere.

I was once presented with the opportunity of doing this myself. When I lived in Kalimpong in the 1950s, an Englishman arrived on my doorstep one evening in the midst of the rainy season. I was quite accustomed to unexpected visitors, so I invited him in and he introduced himself. He was a medical man who had trained in Dublin. Quite soon I got round to asking him what had brought him to Kalimpong. He said straight out, 'I want to develop psychic powers.' This was not the first time someone had expressed to me this kind of interest, so I just said, 'What sort of psychic powers do you want to develop?' He said, 'I want to be able to read other people's thoughts, and to see the future.' He was not at all coy about it; he was quite open about what he wanted. I then asked him, 'Why do you want to develop these powers?' He simply said, 'It will help me in my work.' What that work turned out to be is not germane to this specific issue; I will mention only that he had been a disciple of Lobsang Rampa, who wrote a lot of books about the more fabulous and fanciful aspects of Tibetan Buddhism. Inspired by one of the most successful of these books, *The Third Eye*, my visitor was searching for a Tibetan lama who could perform an operation to open his third eye. It involved, he believed, drilling a little hole in the middle of his forehead and thereby endowing him with the clairvoyant vision he wanted.

One can see the temptation that this kind of person puts in the way of monks and lamas. He could have been milked by any unscrupulous teacher who was ready to pander to his desire for developing psychic powers. What he said to me made this very clear: 'If anyone can teach me these things I'm quite prepared to place at their disposal a very large sum of money.' He came to an untimely end, unfortunately, but before he did so, several people got quite a lot of money out of him in one way or another.

So much for general prohibitions as regards earning a living. However, the Buddha did not leave it at that, for, as we know, the economic relationship is one of the commonest fields of exploitation in the whole range of human life. Employers exploit employees if they can, and employees exploit their employers whenever they get the chance. We tend to think that problems of suspicion and exploitation between management and workforce, capital and labour, boardroom and factory floor, are peculiarly modern, but the Buddha gave considerable attention to this issue in his advice to Sigālaka as recorded in the *Sigālaka Sutta*. In the section of the discourse devoted to the employer–employee relationship the Buddha enumerates five duties of the employer towards the employee, and five duties of the employee towards the employer.[461] Together, these amount to a general guide to capital and labour relationships, and a business code of economic ethics for Buddhists.

Taking the duties of the employer first, the Buddha says that the employer must give the employee work according to his bodily and mental strength – that is, work he or she can do without injury. Unfortunately, 2,500 years later, this principle is still not being observed – certainly not in India. In India today, thousands of men and women earn their living as coolies, that is, as unskilled labourers. They are treated as beasts of burden, carrying heavy loads on their backs, or more usually on their heads. Coolies are at the very bottom of the economic ladder, and they have virtually no hope of rising above that level, even though they may have to support a growing family as well as themselves.

The problem from the point of view of the merchant hiring a number of coolies to carry, say, sacks of rice is that some coolies cannot carry as much as others, and they do not move as fast, particularly if they are old or unwell. It is shocking to say that the solution for a great many well-to-do merchants is to make sure they get their money's-worth out of all their coolies equally. This is a pitiable sight indeed – some old man, old before his time, staggering along, his veins standing out, muscles stretched like whipcord, and the perspiration streaming down, under loads which he has no business to be carrying at all. It's the same with the rickshaw pullers that you used to find all over Asia (though not any more, I am glad to say). Their life-expectancy was no more than a few years. They used to start pulling rickshaws when they were fifteen or sixteen; by the time they were twenty-five they usually had tuberculosis, and that would be the end of them within a few months. Their inadequate diet and the huge physical stress of their work quite literally killed them.

But for a very long time it was not an issue that bothered anyone. I remember vividly the first time I was in Sri Lanka, taking a ride in a rickshaw – rather against my will. As we moved smartly through the streets I kept telling the coolie to go slower, but he didn't understand me – he thought I was telling him, as most of his fares must have done, to go faster. The more I expostulated with him, the faster he went, until I had to tell him to stop altogether. Thereafter I used a rickshaw only in an emergency; and even then I would pick someone who was fairly strong and sturdy, and insist that he went at a reasonably leisurely pace. In retrospect, I should not, probably, have used them at all, but at the time it seemed there was no other work for them to do. However, the Buddha was quite clear that no human being should be hired to work beyond his natural capacity.

Secondly, the Buddha said that the employer should give the employee sufficient food and pay. This is still the custom in certain parts of India. If you employ someone you give them food and clothes, plus some cash, rather than a salary. But the operative principle is to give enough food and wages to enable the employee to live a full and decent human existence, not simply sufficient in relation to the work done. There shouldn't be any correlation between the amount of work done and the amount of pay received. Even if the employee is strong and healthy, and his output is prodigious, he should not get paid more than his weaker or even lazier fellows; he should just get what he needs by way of remuneration. We have become accustomed to thinking in terms of rewarding hard work and penalizing those who underperform: so much work done, so much pay received. But while this is an effective incentive to invention and enterprise, a Buddhist should ideally find that incentive somewhere else. If the incentive is greed, you are feeding that mental poison.

The employee is enjoined by the Buddha to work as faithfully as he can, and the employer is enjoined to provide for the employee's needs. These needs constitute not just a bare subsistence, but the means to live a richly human existence. We no longer have a society that divides quite so rigidly into employer and employee as the society of the Buddha's day, but the Buddha was not of course recommending the particular social structure of his day, he was simply pointing out the essential principle by which the people in his society could make an economic relationship an essentially human one.

We have to try to do the same within our own society. One radical plan that used to get an airing from time to time, and did seem to express the principle of non-exploitation very effectively, is the idea that on the attainment of their majority everyone should be given by the government a basic stipend to cover the cost of food, clothing, and shelter, regardless of whether they work or not. If they want more than this – if they want to travel, buy expensive electronic equipment, go out to cinemas and restaurants, have the luxury lifestyle that most people see as a virtual necessity – they will have to work. But in a luxury culture people should work because they want to – because they want to make a creative contribution to their society, or because they want a few extras, or both – not simply in order to live. In this way the state would support the spiritual community, enabling individuals who wanted to devote themselves to creative but financially unremunerative activity – to meditation, study, even the arts – to do so, if they were prepared to live a very simple, even monastic life.

Thirdly, the Buddha says that the employer should provide the employee with medical treatment and support after retirement. This we do have nowadays, with pensions, insurance, and so on, but it has taken two millennia for us to get round to this scheme of the Buddha's. Fourthly, the Buddha says that the employer should share with the employee any extra profit he makes. That is, you don't take the profits for your own purposes while telling your employees that they must make do with a basic level of support. Once again, we have caught up with this idea rather late in the day, in the form of bonus schemes. Fifthly and lastly, it is the duty of the employer, according to the Buddha, to grant the employee holidays and special allowances – and this, too, has something of a modern ring to it. However, we should not lose sight of the essential principle expressed in the Buddha's advice – that of establishing the human dimension of the economic relationship – which is not always what bonus schemes, holiday allowances, and pension schemes are about.

So much for the five points made by the Buddha for the guidance of the employer in relationship to the employee. The employee also has certain duties. The first of these is that he or she should be punctual. The Buddha's principle here is not just about clocking in on time, but of not needing to clock in at all. Indeed, the Buddha suggests that you try to be already working before your employer arrives: you are not coming to work simply to be seen to be working.

Secondly, the employee should finish work after the employer. You should try to become free of the whole clock-watching mentality. You don't fling down your tools as soon as the clock strikes. Thirdly, the employee should be sincere and trustworthy. This is quite obvious, as is the fourth point, which is that the employee should perform his or her duties to the satisfaction of the employer. Fifthly, the employee should speak in praise of his employer. The Buddha must have been aware of how readily workers abuse the boss behind his or her back, and it's the same now. Employees may be dutiful and respectful during working hours, but what you hear outside the company gates can tell a different story.

The Buddha is reminding us that, as with any relationship, the economic relationship should not be one of antagonism, in which all you feel you can express is impotent frustration. Ideally, it is a happy, harmonious relationship, in which there is no exploitation on either side. Each takes from the other what he or she needs, without causing harm, and gives what he or she can. If you are an employer, you make use of the labour and skills of your workers, and also take responsibility for seeing that their needs are met. And if you are an employee, you work to the best of your ability and take what you need from that work situation. There is then no need for a grim, protracted bargaining between employers and unions, as though they were in opposite camps, arranging a truce between opposing armies. As the Buddha says to Sigālaka, 'In this way the nadir is covered,' (the nadir being the direction that denotes the relationship between 'master and servant') 'making it at peace and free from fear.'

18

NON-EXPLOITATION

Let the silent sage move about in the village as the bee goes taking
honey from the flower without harming colour or fragrance.[462]

This verse comes from the *Dhammapada*, an ancient and deeply loved
anthology of verses which was the first Buddhist text to be translated
from the original Pāli into a European language (in this case Latin).[463]
It is characteristic of Buddhist scriptures to draw all sorts of beautiful
illustrations, metaphors, similes, and parables from day-to-day life in
India, and so it is with this verse from the *Dhammapada*, which is taken
from the chapter called 'Flowers', so-called because each verse mentions
a flower of some kind, or flowers in general, by way of illustration.

Anyone who has lived in India or in any of the Buddhist countries of
South-east Asia will be familiar with the timeless scene evoked in these
lines – the monk going for alms in the village. It was a scene I participated
in myself in my own wandering days as a monk, when I went around on
foot from place to place. But I have seen it as an observer often enough,
and will describe it here from that viewpoint. Usually the monks go out
for alms very early in the morning, because in India there is no such thing
traditionally as a midday meal. People eat what we would call lunch at
about nine o'clock in the morning; it is a huge meal, consisting mainly
of rice. After that – in the villages at least – people go off to work in
the fields and don't come back home again to eat until five or six in the
evening. So if the monk wants to fill his bowl, he has to be off at the crack

of dawn, leaving the monastery and moving silently along the deserted streets, stopping briefly at each house.

The Buddhist custom is that throughout his alms collection tour, as it is called, the monk should stand silently at each door with his begging-bowl, not asking for anything. But people are usually on the lookout for monks at this time, so it may be that a child runs inside and says, 'Mummy, the monk is here,' and the mother says, 'All right, ask him to wait.' Then she quickly ladles out some rice and curry, and takes it outside to put in the monk's bowl. The monk then recites a verse of blessing in Pāli, and moves on to stand at the door of the next hut.

The idea is not to get the whole meal from any one house, but to take a little here and a little there. In India even today Hindu sadhus follow this custom. It is called *madhukari bhikṣā*, which means collecting alms just like the bee collects honey. Just as the bee collects a little pollen from each flower it visits, in the same way the monk accepts a little food from one house, a little food from another, until he has enough to sustain him for the day.

Food is just one of four things that the monk is traditionally entitled to expect from lay supporters. The other three are clothing, especially in the form of the saffron robe; shelter, whether a temporary hut, a monastery, or some arrangement in between; and medicine. When the monk is ordained he is told that this is all he should expect from the lay people, and all he can accept from them.

The idea is that the monk or nun – that is, the person devoted to the religious life – should accept from lay supporters only what is necessary to keep him or her going, so that he or she can practise meditation, study, and teach the Dharma, and make progress towards Enlightenment. Inevitably, after 2,500 years of Buddhist history, a few things have been added to the list of requisites. The most significant addition is perhaps books; in modern times a collection of a few books tends to count as a fundamental requisite.

Buddhist monks still ideally lead an exceedingly simple life, making do with one or at most two meals a day, quite basic accommodation in cottages or huts, the minimum of clothing (easy enough in a tropical country), and very simple medicines. Incidentally, this medicine is supposed to be made of gallnuts and cow's urine. This is less bizarre than it sounds; you can make a sort of ammonia out of cow's urine which is efficacious in a number of ways.

But people in the West often say, 'Well, that's all very well. It's a great arrangement from the monk's point of view: he gets his food and clothing, he gets housed, perhaps in a beautiful monastery, he gets medicine when he is sick. Everything is provided for him, so that he can quietly get on with his studies, his meditation, his literary work, or his preaching, as he thinks fit. But what does he give in return?'

The traditional answer to this question is: nothing. He gets all he needs and he does absolutely nothing in return. Nobody even expects anything in return, and it does not occur to the monk that he should give anything in return. Anything you give to monks or nuns is given for the support of the sangha, not as payment for teaching. Correspondingly, teaching is not given in return for that support. The monk accepts what he needs, and he gives what he can, but there is no relationship between the two, no equivalence between what you give and what you get. When you can give, you give. When you need, you accept. There is no question of a bargain being struck. Just as the bee takes the nectar it needs from the flower to make its honey, without injuring the flower in any way, in the same way, the monk quietly and gently accepts what he needs without doing any harm to the village. In both cases, there is no exploitation.

This, then, is ideally the nature of the relationship between the layperson and 'ascetics and Brahmins' which the Buddha lists as the last of the six relationships to which Sigālaka (and all of us) should pay attention. Perhaps this relationship is more obscure to us than the others; many Western Buddhists do not think along the traditional lines of monastic and lay, although we may find it easier to relate to the full-timer/part-timer distinction we considered in an earlier chapter.[464] But this verse of the *Dhammapada* is not really just about monks, although some translations fail to make this clear.

The first problem with using the word 'monk' is that in Buddhism there is nothing resembling the Western conception of a monk. This problem is further compounded by the fact that 'monk' is the standard translation of the term *bhikṣu*, whereas the word in this verse of the *Dhammapada* is not *bhikṣu* but *muni*. In some contexts *muni* means monk in the sense of *bhikṣu*, but not always. A *muni*, essentially, is a wise man, or holy man, or sage. One of the Buddha's many titles was Śākyamuni, 'sage of the Śākya tribe'. *Muni* is also related to the term *mauna*, which in Sanskrit, as well as in the modern languages of northern

India, means 'silence'. So a *muni* is one who is silent, or even one who observes a vow of silence. In order to bring out this double meaning, some translators render *muni* as 'the silent sage'.

This combination of meanings suggests that silence and wisdom go together. Whether the *muni* is wise because he is silent or silent because he is wise, or both, it may be difficult to say. In any case, it is clear that we are talking about more than just monks here. This verse is very ancient, one of the earliest of all Buddhist scriptures (along with some passages of the *Sutta Nipāta*), and certainly predates the monastic sangha. Some scholars believe that *muni* was the original term used by Buddhists for the disciple of the Buddha who is himself Enlightened. According to this theory, the word *arhant* – the term for this ideal which has become so familiar – came later.

We can therefore get a much broader, more universal meaning from this verse by replacing the line 'so let the monk move about the village' with 'so let the wise person live in the world'. In this way, what appears to be an injunction restricted to those who are at least technically monks becomes applicable to everybody who lives in the world. It establishes a fundamental principle of the ethical and spiritual life, which is that the wise person does not exploit anyone or anything. This may seem very simple to understand, but if it were to be thoroughly and systematically put into practice, the effects would be far-reaching indeed.

If we are wise, we take from society, from others, and from our environment, what we objectively need in order to sustain life, to work, and to progress spiritually, while doing no harm to individuals, to society at large, or to the environment. And we give what we can. However unrealistic this ideal may seem, one does occasionally come across reflections of it in real working relationships, and there is no reason why it cannot be held up as an aspiration in the context of any working environment. Moreover, the principle of non-exploitation extends far beyond the field of economics. It has psychological and even spiritual implications which can be extended to cover the whole field of personal relationships, especially our more intimate relationships.

We don't just decide to like someone on a whim. We like them because they fulfil a certain need we have – a need of which we are not usually conscious, although we can become conscious of it if we try. If we don't try to become conscious of what our needs are, we tend to rationalize our liking for someone: we say we like them because they are considerate and kind, or because they love animals as we do, or because they are interested in Buddhism as we are. But behind these rational appraisals there is often something quite different at work. Perhaps that person satisfies our need for attention, our psychological need to be at the very centre of things. As long as that need continues, we shall continue to want it to be satisfied. And if we get from someone the attention we need, then obviously we will want that relationship to continue.

But how are we going to ensure that it does continue? Most of us, whether we realize it or not, find that the best way of doing this is to find out what the other person needs, and make sure that we are the person who satisfies that need. They may have, say, a deep lack of self-worth that manifests as a craving to be appreciated. Latching on to this, we start saying, 'What a wonderful writer you are – I wish I had such a way with words!' or 'Did you really paint this yourself? How do you manage to achieve such magical effects?' We give them what we sense they need, so that they become dependent on us for the satisfaction we give them, just as we have become dependent on them for the satisfaction of our own needs. In short, together we create a relationship of mutual dependence and exploitation. An unconscious bargain is struck; this is the basis of most human relationships. Because the whole process is more or less unconscious, neither party to the bargain questions whether the need is valid, or whether it is an artificial and unhealthy need which it would be better not to encourage. In this situation, the relationship is likely either to terminate catastrophically or to settle down into an increasingly boring routine.

Does this mean that we should never look to another person to fulfil our needs? Do we not have some valid psychological needs? The answer to this question lies in this same verse from the *Dhammapada*. Yes, we do have valid needs – material needs, psychological needs, and spiritual needs – but we should fulfil them as the bee takes pollen from the flower, without exploiting the person who fulfils those needs.

There are two kinds of need. Under the influence of one kind, we unconsciously negotiate a situation of mutual exploitation. The other kind of need is one of which we are more conscious, more aware. It is not bargain-hunting, but an ever-deepening spirit of mutual giving, without any thought of return. It happens between parents and children at their best. The parents give freely to the children without thinking that the children are going to reward them later for their efforts. The children, likewise, give what they can to their parents, not thinking about everything their parents have done for them, but simply giving to them because they love them.

This principle of non-exploitation and mutual generosity is the key to the Buddha's philosophy of personal relations, whether in political, religious, economic, or more intimate personal relationships. It is a principle the Buddha himself exemplified. He spent forty-five years going around north-eastern India on foot, teaching. All that he took from people was one meal a day, a few yards of yellow cloth, a little hut somewhere – perhaps in somebody's garden – which he borrowed from time to time, and occasional supplies of medicine.

What he took was infinitesimal. But what he gave was – is – incalculable: indeed its nature is that it cannot be measured out and bartered. The gifts he gave – compassion, understanding, sympathy, wisdom, guidance, love – by their very nature can only be given with no thought of return. His was the perfect example of his philosophy of personal relationships. He took only what he needed; he gave everything he had to give. Ranged against this philosophy is a sort of shopkeeper's mentality, which is the bane of the human race. And in all our relationships we can choose between these two attitudes.

19
GRATITUDE

Usually, influenced by books or even Buddhist scriptures, we think of the Buddha's Enlightenment as having taken place at a particular time, roughly 2,500 years ago – which, of course, in a sense, it did. We also tend to think of it as having taken place on a particular day, at a particular hour, even at a particular minute, at the instant when the Buddha broke through from the conditioned to the Unconditioned.

But a little reflection, and a little further study of the scriptures, will show us that it didn't happen quite like that. Here we can consider the distinction between the Path of Vision and the Path of Transformation – a distinction usually made in connection with the Noble Eightfold Path. On the Path of Vision one has an experience of the transcendental, a profound insight into the true nature of reality that goes far beyond any merely intellectual understanding. This insight comes gradually to pervade and transform every aspect of one's being – one's body, speech, and mind, to use the traditional Buddhist classification. It transforms all our activities. It transforms one, in fact, into a very different kind of person – a wiser and more compassionate person. This process is known as the Path of Transformation.[465]

Something like this takes place in the spiritual life of each and every one of us. And we see the same sort of thing happening, on a much more exalted plane, in the case of the Buddha. The Buddha's vision is unlimited, absolute, and all-embracing, and his transformation of body, speech, and mind can therefore be described as total, even infinite. But all the same, it did take a little time for this final transformation to take place. Buddhist tradition speaks of the Buddha as spending seven – or nine – weeks (accounts vary) in the vicinity of the bodhi tree, the tree beneath which he attained Enlightenment. In the course of each of those weeks something of importance happened. We could say that the Buddha's experience of Enlightenment started percolating through his being, until by the end of the last week (whether the seventh or the ninth) the process of transformation was at last complete.

One week a great storm arose, and the Buddha was sheltered from the rain, so the story goes, by the serpent king Mucalinda, who spread his sevenfold hood over the Buddha's head as he meditated.[466] Another week, Brahmā Sahāmpati, the ruler of a thousand worlds, requested the Buddha to teach the Dharma, saying that at least some of the beings in the world would be capable of understanding it, their eyes being covered with only a little dust.[467] And the Buddha, out of compassion, agreed to teach.

But here I want to focus on another episode, one that occurred quite early in the period after the Buddha's attainment of Enlightenment – during the second week, according to one source. According to this tradition, the Buddha stood at a distance to the north-east of the bodhi tree and remained for one week gazing at the tree with unblinking eyes.[468]

Centuries later, a stupa was erected on that very spot, to mark the place where the Buddha had gazed at the bodhi tree. It was known as 'the stupa of unblinking eyes', and Xuanzang, the great Chinese pilgrim, saw it when he visited India in the seventh century CE. In the memoirs he dictated to his disciples in his old age back in China, he described it thus: 'On the left side of the road, to the north of the place where the Buddha walked, is a large stone on the top of which, as it stands in a great vihara, is a figure of the Buddha with his eyes raised and looking up. Here in former times the Buddha sat [he says 'sat' but the source text says 'stood'] for seven days contemplating the bodhi tree.'[469]

Perhaps the Buddha didn't literally stand or sit there for a whole week, but we may take it that he gazed at the bodhi tree for a very long time. And the source text makes it clear why. He did it because he was grateful to the tree for having sheltered him at the time of his attainment of Enlightenment. According to the scriptures, the Buddha demonstrated gratitude in other ways too. After Brahmā Sahāmpati had made his request that the Buddha should teach the Dharma, and the Buddha had decided to do so, he then wondered to whom he should teach it. He thought first of his two old teachers, from whom he had learned to meditate not long after he left home. Finding their teaching insufficient, he had left them, but they had been helpful to him at a particular stage of his career, and after his Enlightenment he remembered that. It's as though he had a spiritual debt to them that he wanted to repay. But he quickly realized that his old teachers were dead.

He then thought of his five former companions. They too were people he knew from an earlier period of his spiritual quest, from the time of his experiments in asceticism. After leaving his first two teachers, he started practising extreme self-mortification, in the company of five friends who became disciples of his and admired him greatly because he had gone further in his self-mortification than anybody else at that time. But eventually the Buddha-to-be saw the futility of asceticism, realized that this was not the way to Enlightenment, and gave it up. When he started taking solid food again, just a few handfuls of rice to sustain himself, the five ascetics left him in disgust, saying, 'The śramaṇa Gautama has returned to luxurious living.' But this parting was not what remained in the Buddha's mind. Having realized that his two old teachers were dead, he reflected, 'The five ascetics were of great help to me when I was practising the penances. I would like to preach the Dharma to them.'[470] So this is what he did. He went to them, he taught them, and eventually they too realized the Truth that he had realized. And he did this out of gratitude.

So the newly Enlightened Buddha was a *grateful* Buddha, an idea which is perhaps unfamiliar to us. We think of the all-wise Buddha, the compassionate Buddha, the resourceful Buddha, but we don't usually think of the grateful Buddha. But one of the very first things the Buddha did after his attainment of Enlightenment was show his gratitude to those who had helped him. He was even grateful to a tree.

This incident gives us food for thought. The Buddhist scriptures contain a number of references that show that the Buddha and his disciples regarded trees and stones not as inanimate dead matter, but as living things. They would even have a relationship with them; they would talk to a tree or a flower, or rather to the spirit – the *devatā*, as they called it – inhabiting it. It is surely much better to have this attitude, to be an animist, than to think that trees and flowers and rocks and stones are just dead matter. The Buddha certainly didn't think in that way, and it was therefore possible for him to be grateful even to a tree.

It is not surprising, given that this was the Buddha's attitude, that gratitude finds a place in his ethical and spiritual teaching. It is found, for example, in the *Maṅgala Sutta*, the 'Sutta of Blessings or Auspicious Signs'. This short *sutta*, found in the Pāli canon, is often regarded as summarizing the whole duty, as we may call it, of the serious-minded Buddhist, and it enumerates gratitude as one of the auspicious signs. According to the *Maṅgala Sutta*, it is a sign that you are making spiritual progress.[471]

But what is gratitude? To find this out, we can turn to the dictionaries – and, of course, we should be very grateful to the makers of dictionaries. I am personally very grateful to Samuel Johnson. His historic dictionary is always at my elbow in my study, and when I am writing I sometimes consult it several times a day. Johnson defines gratitude as 'duty to benefactors' and as 'desire to return benefits'. Coming to more modern dictionaries, the *Concise Oxford* says, 'being thankful; readiness to show appreciation for and to return kindness', and *Collins* has 'a feeling of thankfulness or appreciation, as for gifts or favours'.

These definitions of the English word give us some understanding of what gratitude is, but from a Buddhist point of view we need to go further, and look at the Pāli word being translated as gratitude: *kataññutā*. *Kata* means that which has been done, especially that which has been done to oneself; and *aññutā* means knowing or recognizing; so *kataññutā* means knowing and recognizing what has been done to one for one's benefit. These definitions indicate that the connotation of the Pāli word is rather different from that of its English translation. The connotation of the English word gratitude is emotional – we speak of *feeling* grateful. But the connotation of *kataññutā* is rather more intellectual. It makes it clear that what we call gratitude involves an element of *knowledge*: knowledge of what has been done to us or for us for our benefit. If we do not know that something has benefited us, we will not feel grateful.

The Buddha knew that the bodhi tree had sheltered him, and he knew that his five former companions had been helpful to him, so he felt gratitude towards them. Not only that: he gave expression to that feeling. He acted upon it by spending a whole week simply gazing at the bodhi tree, and then by going in search of his five former companions so that he could communicate to them the truth that he had discovered. The important implication is that it is a perfectly natural thing to feel grateful for benefits we have received.

But the benefit has to be recognized as a benefit. If we don't feel that someone or something actually has benefited us, we won't feel grateful to them or to it. This suggests that we have to understand what is truly beneficial, what has really helped us to grow and develop as human beings. We also have to know who or what has benefited us, and remember that they have done so – otherwise no feeling of gratitude is possible.

In Buddhism there are traditionally three principal objects of gratitude: our parents, our teachers, and our spiritual friends. We have already considered some aspects of each of these relationships. Here I want to reflect a little on gratitude in relation to each of them.

I came back to England after spending twenty years uninterruptedly in the East studying, practising, and teaching the Dharma. When I came back, I found that much had changed. Quite a few things struck me as unusual – I hadn't encountered them in India, or at least not to the same extent – and one thing that definitely surprised me was finding out how many people, at least among those I knew, were on bad terms with their parents. Perhaps I noticed this especially because I was in contact with people who were concerned about their spiritual development, and wanted to straighten themselves out psychologically and emotionally.

If one is on bad terms with one's parents, something is quite seriously wrong. Perhaps it wouldn't even be an exaggeration to say that one's whole emotional life is likely to be affected, indirectly at least, by this state of affairs. I therefore used to encourage people to get back into positive contact with their parents, if it happened that they were estranged from them for any reason. I encouraged people to be more open with their parents and to develop positive feelings towards them. This was especially necessary in connection with the practice of the *mettā bhāvanā*, the development of loving-kindness. People had to learn to develop *mettā* even towards their parents, and for those who had had difficult childhoods, or had even suffered at the hands of their parents in some way, this was not easy. But even so, it was necessary in the interests of their own emotional, psychological, and spiritual development to get over whatever feelings of bitterness or resentment they were harbouring.

Some people, I discovered, blamed their parents in all sorts of ways for all sorts of things – an attitude that is reflected in a well-known little poem by Philip Larkin called 'This Be The Verse'. In this poem, Larkin gives expression in rather crude language to what he thinks your mum and dad have done to you, and he draws a rather depressing conclusion from that. The last verse of the poem reads:

Man hands on misery to man,
It deepens like a coastal shelf;
Get out as early as you can,
And don't have any kids yourself.

What a grim, nasty little poem! In 1995, however, it was voted one of Britain's favourite poems, coming in between Thomas Hood's 'I remember, I remember' and D. H. Lawrence's 'The Snake'. The fact that Larkin's poem should be so popular among intelligent poetry readers gives food for thought, suggesting as it does that negative attitudes towards parents are fairly widespread in our society.

The Buddha himself had quite a lot to say about our relation to our parents. In the *Sigālaka Sutta* he is represented as saying that there are five ways in which a son should minister to his mother and father as the eastern direction. He should think, 'Having been supported by them, I will support them, I will perform their duties for them. I will keep up the family tradition. I will be worthy of my heritage. After my parents' deaths I will distribute gifts on their behalf.'[472] The same applies, of course, to a daughter. She too should minister to her mother and father as the eastern direction, she too should think in this manner.

There is a lot that could be said about the five ways in which one should minister to one's parents. Here, though, I want to touch on something even more fundamental – so fundamental that in this *sutta* the Buddha seems to take it for granted. It is hinted at, however, in the imagery of the *sutta*. The Buddha explains to Sigāla that one pays homage to the east by ministering to one's parents in five ways. But why the east?

The reason is perhaps obvious. The sun rises in the east, it has its origin in the east, so to speak, and similarly we owe our origin to our parents – leaving aside questions of karma, of which perhaps parents are only instruments. If it were not for our parents, we would not be here now. They have given us life, they have given us a human body, and in Buddhism the human body is regarded as a very precious thing. It is precious because it is only in a human body (whether male or female) that one is able to attain Enlightenment. In giving us a human body, our parents are therefore giving us the possibility of attaining Enlightenment and we should be intensely grateful to them for that, especially if we are actually practising the Dharma.

Not only do our parents give us a human body; despite Larkin, they bring us up as best they can. They enable us to survive, they educate us. They may not always be able to send us to university and all that, but they teach us to speak, and this is the basis of most of the things we subsequently learn. Usually it's our mother who teaches us our first words, and this gives us the expression 'mother tongue'. It is through our mother tongue that we have access to all the literature that has been written in the language we learn in our earliest days, and we can enjoy that literature fully because it is in our mother tongue, rather than in a language we learn in later life.

Not everybody cares to acknowledge their debt to their parents. The classic example in English literature is the character Mr Bounderby in Charles Dickens' *Hard Times*, which happens to be one of my favourite Dickens novels. Mr Bounderby is a successful industrialist, and he is very fond of telling everybody that he is a self-made man. He tells them this on every possible occasion and at great length. He describes in vivid detail how he was abandoned by his mother, how he was beaten by a drunken grandmother, how he lived in the gutter as a child and had to fend for himself, how nobody had ever helped him and how he had made his own way in the world and become a rich man entirely by his own efforts. In the course of the novel, however, it transpires that all this is completely false. In truth he had a loving mother who brought him up carefully and educated him and helped him as much as she possibly could. In fact, his mother is still alive, but he keeps her at a distance in the country somewhere and won't allow her to visit him. In other words, Mr Bounderby is a monster of ingratitude.

We will consider the question of why people are so ungrateful later on. First, though, let us turn to the second of the principal objects of gratitude in Buddhism: our teachers. By teachers here I mean not Dharma teachers, but all those from whom we derive our secular education and culture. Here our school teachers obviously have an important place.

From them we derive the rudiments of such learning as we have, and we therefore have to be grateful to them. The fact is that we have found out very little of what we know, or what we think we know, as a result of our own efforts. Practically everything we know has been taught to us in one way or another. If we think of our knowledge of science or history, for example, few of us have even performed a single scientific experiment – or discovered a single historical fact – that no one else had performed, or discovered, before. All our work in this field has been done for us by others. We have benefited from their efforts, and our knowledge is little more than the echo of theirs.

As well as learning from living teachers, we also learn from people who have been dead for hundreds of years, from the writings they have left and the records of the words they spoke. It is not just a question of learning from them in a purely intellectual sense, acquiring information. Among those books are great works of the imagination – poems, novels, dramas – and these works are a source of infinite enrichment, without which we would be immeasurably poorer. They help us deepen and enlarge our vision. We should therefore be grateful to the great men and women who have produced them. We should be grateful to Homer and Virgil, Dante and Milton, Aeschylus and Kālidāsa, Shakespeare and Goethe. We should be grateful to Murasaki Shikibu, Cervantes, Jane Austen, Dickens, Dostoyevsky, and hundreds of others, who have influenced us more than we can possibly realize. The American critic Harold Bloom has gone so far as to claim that Shakespeare is the creator of human nature as we know it,[473] which is a very big claim indeed (though he gives his reasons for it).

Of course, our experience is also deepened, and our vision enlarged, by the visual arts and by music. The great painters, sculptors, and composers are also among our teachers. They too have enriched our lives, and to them too we should be grateful. I won't mention any names in this connection because there are simply too many to choose from – both ancient and modern, Eastern and Western – certainly not because I think that the great artists and composers are any less important than the great poets, novelists, and dramatists.

Thus by 'teachers' I mean all those who between them have created our collective cultural heritage, without which we would not be fully human. Remembering what we owe them, and feeling grateful to the great artists, poets, and composers, we should not only enjoy their work but also celebrate their memory and share our enthusiasm for them with our friends.

Before we go on to consider the third principal object of gratitude, our spiritual friends, I want to make the general point that we need not think of these three objects of gratitude as being completely separate and distinct from one another. There's a certain amount of overlap between the first and second, and between the second and third. Our parents are also our teachers to an extent. In Buddhist tradition parents are called *porāṇacariyas*, which means 'former (or ancient) teachers'. They are called this because they are the first teachers we ever had, even if they only taught us to speak a few words. We can be grateful to our parents not only for giving us life but also for giving us at least the rudiments of knowledge, and initiating us into the beginnings of our cultural heritage.

Similarly there is some overlap between teachers and spiritual friends. The very greatest poets, artists, and composers can inspire us with spiritual values, help us rise to spiritual heights. In the course of the last few hundred years, great changes have taken place, at least in the West. Previously, Christianity as represented by the Church was the great, even the sole, bearer of spiritual values. But now, having lost faith in Christianity, many people look elsewhere to find meaning and values, and they find them in great works of art: in the plays of Shakespeare, the poetry of Wordsworth, Baudelaire, and Rilke, the music of Bach, Beethoven, and Mozart, the great painters and sculptors of the Italian Renaissance. These great masters become, as it were, our spiritual friends, especially if we remain in contact with them and with their work over many years. Learning to admire and love them, we feel intensely grateful to them for what they have given us. They are among our spiritual friends in the broadest sense.

But now let us come to our spiritual friends 'proper'. Here, as with the word gratitude, we have to go back to the Sanskrit words behind the English equivalent. As we have already seen, the Sanskrit phrase translated as 'spiritual friend' is *kalyāṇa mitra*. *Mitra* comes from the word *maitri* (Pāli, *mettā*), and *maitrī* is strong, unselfish, active love, sharply distinguished in Buddhist tradition from *prema* (Pāli, *pema*), in the sense of sexual love or attachment. A *mitra* or friend is therefore one who feels a strong unselfish active love towards one. And *kalyāṇa* means firstly 'beautiful, charming,' and secondly 'auspicious, helpful, morally good'. Thus *kalyāṇa mitra* has a much richer connotation than the English phrase 'spiritual friend'.

Our spiritual friends are all those who are spiritually more experienced than we are. The Buddhas are our spiritual friends. The *arhants* and the bodhisattvas are our spiritual friends. The great Buddhist teachers of India and China, Tibet and Japan, are our spiritual friends. Those who teach us meditation are our spiritual friends. Those with whom we study the scriptures are our spiritual friends. Those who ordain us are our spiritual friends. And all these spiritual friends should be the objects of our intense, heartfelt gratitude. We should be even more grateful to them than we are to our teachers.

Why? Because from our spiritual friends we receive the Dharma. We have not discovered or invented the Dharma. We have received it as a free gift from our spiritual friends, from the Buddha downwards. In the *Dhammapada* the Buddha says, 'The gift of the Dhamma surpasses all gifts.'[474] The greater the gift, the greater the gratitude we should feel. We should not only feel that gratitude in our hearts; we should give expression to it in words and deeds. We can do this in three ways: by singing the praises of our spiritual friends, by practising the Dharma they have given us, and by passing on that Dharma to others to the best of our ability.

The greatest of our spiritual friends is the Buddha Śākyamuni, who discovered – or *re*discovered – the path that we as Buddhists follow today. It is to him that we go for Refuge, it is the Dharma he taught that we try to practise, and it is with the support of the sangha he founded that we are able to practise the Dharma. We therefore have reason to be intensely grateful to him – more grateful, in principle, than we are to anyone else. Our parents have indeed given us life, but what is life without the gift of the Dharma? Our teachers have given us knowledge, education, and culture, but what value do even these things have without the Dharma? It is because they are so intensely grateful to the Buddha that Buddhists perform pujas in devotion to him, and celebrate his life in the context of the various Buddhist festivals.

But people don't always find it easy to be grateful to their parents, or their teachers, or even their spiritual friends. Why is this? It is important to understand the nature of the difficulty. After all, gratitude is an important spiritual quality, a virtue exemplified and taught by the Buddha and many others. Cicero, the great Roman orator and philosopher, said that gratitude is not just the greatest virtue, but the mother of all the rest.[475] Ingratitude therefore represents a very serious defect. On one occasion the Buddha said that ingratitude was one of the four great offences that bring about *niraya* in the sense of rebirth in a state of suffering – a very serious and weighty statement.[476]

But why are we ungrateful to our parents, our teachers, our spiritual friends? One would have thought that as Buddhists we would be simply bubbling over with gratitude to all these people. A clue is to be found in the Pāli word that we translate as gratitude, *kataññutā*. As we have seen, it means knowing or recognizing what has been done for one's benefit. Similarly, *akataññutā* (*a* being the negative prefix), ingratitude, means not knowing or recognizing what has been done for one's benefit.

There are a number of reasons for ingratitude. Firstly, one may fail to recognize a benefit as a benefit. There are some people who do not regard life itself as a benefit, and hence do not feel grateful to their parents for giving them life. Sometimes people say things like, 'Well I didn't ask to be brought into this world.' If you believe in karma and rebirth, of course, this isn't quite true – but anyway, it is what people say. In a few cases, they may not regard life as a benefit because they experience it as painful, even predominantly painful, and therefore don't appreciate its value, don't realize the immense potential of human life. In Buddhist terms, they don't realize that it is possible for a human being, and only for a human being, to attain Enlightenment, or at least to make some progress in that direction.

Similarly, there are people who don't regard knowledge or education or culture as benefits. They feel no gratitude towards their teachers, or towards those who at least try to teach them something. They may even feel resentment. They may feel that education or culture is being imposed upon them. Such people are unlikely to come into contact with spiritual values, with the Dharma, or with spiritual friends, and even if they do, such contact will be external and superficial. They will not be able to recognize it for what it is. They may even see those who try to be their spiritual friends as enemies, and therefore the question of gratitude will not arise.

This was true of some people's responses to the Buddha himself. Not all those who heard him speak or teach felt grateful to him, by any means. There were many people in his day who saw him as a rather eccentric, unorthodox teacher. They certainly didn't feel any gratitude towards him for the gift of the Dharma. Sometimes people slandered him, and some people even tried to kill him.[477]

On the other hand, we may recognize benefits as benefits, and even recognize that they have been given to us by other people, but we may take those benefits for granted. Not realizing that they are a free gift, we may think that they are owed to us, that we have a right to them, and that therefore in a sense they belong to us already, so that we have no need to be grateful for them.

This attitude is widespread in society today. People tend to think that everything is due to them, that they have a right to everything. Parents, teachers, or the state have a duty to provide them with whatever they want. Even spiritual friends, they may think, have a duty to provide them with what they want. If they don't get what they want from one spiritual friend, or teacher, or guru, and get it quickly, in the way they want it, off they will go, to try to get it from someone else. Once again, the question of gratitude doesn't arise. Of course, parents, teachers, and friends have a duty to bestow benefits to the best of their ability. But it should be recognized that those benefits have been *given*, and that the response to them should therefore be one of gratitude.

Another reason for ingratitude is egoism. Egoism takes many forms, and has many aspects. Here I mean by it an attitude of chronic individualism: the belief that one is separate from others, not dependent on others in any way, and that one therefore does not owe anything to others. One feels that one is not obliged to them, because one can do everything oneself. Dickens's Mr Bounderby is a good example of this sort of attitude, but there are other examples in literature, like Satan in Milton's *Paradise Lost*, and 'Black Salvation' in *The Life and Liberation of Padmasambhava*. The person who is egoistical in this sense is incapable of feeling gratitude, and cannot admit that they have been benefited by others. They may not actually say so in the way Mr Bounderby does, but this is their underlying attitude.

This attitude sometimes finds expression in the sphere of the arts. Some writers and artists don't like to think that they owe anything to their predecessors. Wanting to be original, to strike out on a completely new path, they don't like to think that there is such a thing as cultural heritage, or a literary canon. In some circles this attitude has taken an extreme, even a virulent form, and has resulted in an attempt to repudiate the greater part of our literary and artistic heritage on ideological grounds. This is an extremely unfortunate, even potentially disastrous development, and it is to be resisted wherever possible. Egoism in the sense in which I am using the word also finds expression in the sphere of religion. It happens when we don't acknowledge the sources of our inspiration, or when we try to pass off as our own a teaching or practice that we have in fact learned from our spiritual friends.

The fourth and last reason for ingratitude that I want to mention here is forgetfulness. There are two main reasons for forgetfulness of benefits received. First, there is simply the passage of time. Perhaps the benefits were given to us a long time ago – so long ago that we have no distinct recollection of them, and no longer feel grateful to whoever bestowed them upon us, even if we did originally feel grateful. This is perhaps the principal reason for our not feeling actively grateful towards our parents. Over the years so much has happened in our life: early memories have been overlaid by later ones, other relationships have assumed importance, and perhaps we have moved away from our parents, geographically, socially, or culturally. And the result is that – practically speaking – we forget them. We forget the numerous ways in which they benefited us when we were young, and we cease therefore to feel grateful. The other possible reason for our 'forgetting' to be grateful is that we did not feel the positive effects of the benefits very strongly in the first place, and therefore did not feel much gratitude. In such circumstances, it is easy for the gratitude to fade away and be forgotten altogether.

These, then, are the four most important general reasons for ingratitude: failure to recognize a benefit as a benefit, taking benefits for granted, egoism, and forgetfulness. Ingratitude is, unfortunately, liable to crop up in various ways in the context of the life of a practising Buddhist. Beyond a certain point of spiritual progress, it is simply impossible to feel ungrateful. A Stream Entrant is incapable of it, and in fact will be overflowing with gratitude to parents, teachers, and spiritual friends. But until we have reached that point, we are in danger of forgetting to be grateful.

Over the years – more than thirty, at the time of writing – since I myself founded a Buddhist movement, I have received many, many letters, perhaps thousands, from people who have recently discovered the Dharma through one of the centres of the movement I founded, or through contact with individual members of the order. Every year I receive more and more of these letters. They come from young people and old people, from people in many different walks of life, from many different cultural backgrounds and nationalities. And all these letters say, among other things, one and the same thing. They say how glad the writers are to have discovered the Dharma. Not only that, the writers of the letters want to express their gratitude to the Three Jewels and to the Buddhist movement, and to me personally for having founded it. Some people express their feeling of gratitude very strongly indeed. They say that the Dharma has changed their lives, given their lives meaning, saved them from despair, even saved them from suicide.

Such letters of gratitude reach me nearly every week, and they make me think that I have not altogether wasted my time all these years. But over the years I've also noticed that while some people, perhaps the majority, stay grateful, and even become more and more grateful, in the cases of a few people, unfortunately, the feeling of gratitude weakens. They start forgetting the benefits they have received, and even start questioning whether they really were benefits at all. No longer knowing or recognizing what has been done for them, they become ungrateful. Feeling ungrateful to their spiritual friends, they may even start finding fault with them. This is a very sad state of affairs indeed, and in recent years I have given some thought to it and have come to certain conclusions about how it happens.

It seems to me that people forget the benefits they have received because they no longer actually feel them. And they no longer feel them because for one reason or another they have put themselves in a position where they cannot receive them. Let me give a concrete example. Suppose you have started attending a meditation class. You learn to meditate, and you achieve some success. You start practising at home. But one day, for one reason or another, you stop attending the class and then you gradually stop practising at home. You cease to meditate. Eventually you forget what meditative experience was like. You forget the peace and the joy you felt. You forget the benefits of meditation. So you cease to feel grateful to those who introduced you to the practice. The same thing can happen with regard to retreats, Dharma study, spending time with spiritual friends, taking part in pujas, and attending Buddhist celebrations. People can get out of touch. They can forget how much they did, once upon a time, benefit from those activities, and therefore they can cease to feel grateful to those who made the activities possible.

Sometimes people reconnect after a while; they start attending the meditation class again, or go on retreat again, perhaps after many years. I have known people who have re-established contact after anything up to twenty-two years – rather a long time in anybody's life. When this happens, they nearly always say the same thing: 'I had forgotten how good it was.' And therefore they feel renewed gratitude.

This is entirely appropriate. It is appropriate that we should be grateful, that we should recognize the benefits we have received. It is appropriate that we should be grateful to our parents, with all their admitted imperfections – parents are not perfect any more than children are. It is appropriate that we should be grateful to our teachers, to our spiritual friends, and to the Buddhist tradition. Above all, it is appropriate that we should be grateful to the Buddha, who, as we have seen, was himself utterly and instinctively full of gratitude.

CONCLUSIONS:
CAN THE SPIRITUAL COMMUNITY
SAVE THE WORLD?

20

A BUDDHIST VIEW OF CURRENT
WORLD PROBLEMS

In 1943 I was posted to India as a signals operator, and after the war I stayed on to spend the next twenty years in the East, seventeen of them as a Buddhist monk. During this time I attended a large number of public meetings of the kind that are very popular in India – open air meetings held late at night under the glare of arc-lights, which tend to go on and on. In fact, the bigger they are, and the longer they go on, the better. I thus used to hear a lot of speeches, and some of the topics – and even their treatment – became very familiar to me indeed. A favourite topic was Buddhism and world peace, and whoever was giving the talk, it was practically always the same.

First of all you would be treated to a graphic description of the terrible plight of mankind in the modern world. You would be reminded of the prevalence of flood, fire, pestilence, and war; then you would be led through the various incontrovertible signs of a universal and unprecedented breakdown of moral and spiritual values, focusing in particular on the behaviour and attitudes of young people today. Then, when you were judged to be fully reconciled to an altogether bleak prospect culminating in nuclear holocaust and no solution in sight, Buddhism would be brought in to save the day. Buddhism, you would be told, teaches non-violence; it teaches peace, love, and compassion. If everybody in the world followed the teachings of the Buddha we would have world peace, and all our problems would be solved. And that would be it – end of talk. Spontaneous applause would break out, the speaker would sit down, beaming with satisfaction, and the audience would clap away, happy in the knowledge that there was hope for the world after all. And, of course, the world would go on just as before.

The problem with this sort of analysis of our situation is not that it isn't true. If everybody in the world meditated every day and tried to develop kindness and love and compassion and joy, and worked at the precepts and followed the Noble Eightfold Path, then – well, we wouldn't just have peace, we'd have heaven on earth. No, the problem with this line of argument is that it's an over-simplification of both problem and solution. In the abstract, it's beautiful, but that is where it remains: in the abstract.

Another difficulty with talking about Buddhism and world peace is that Buddhists are not the only people with values that support world peace. If everyone in the world followed the teachings of Jainism, or Taoism, or certain forms of Hinduism, you would still get world peace, without any need to mention Buddhism. There's no need, in fact, to bring in any religion at all – religions don't have a monopoly on peaceful values. If everybody followed the teachings of Plato, or even Bertrand Russell, you would have world peace on the spot.

So if one is not simply going to offer Buddhism as a universal panacea for the world's ills, what *does* it offer? One cannot talk about *the* Buddhist view of world problems because there isn't an official Buddhist party line on these or any other issues. All one is left with is *a* Buddhist view of world problems. One can talk about world problems only from one's individual standpoint. And as a Buddhist standpoint, its validity can only be measured by how deeply one has been influenced by Buddhist teachings.

There is still, however, the question of what an individual Buddhist can have to say that is truly relevant to world problems. All I can say for myself is that the work I have engaged in as a Buddhist has arisen, to some considerable extent, out of the view I take of current world problems. This topic is not of academic or peripheral interest to me. In approaching it I am in some sense trying to make clear the *raison d'être* of my own existence as a practical working Buddhist; that is, as a Buddhist not just inwardly, in faith and conviction, but also as far as outward activities are concerned. My view of current world problems constitutes a sort of philosophical autobiography, even a confession of faith. It will, I hope, show where I stand and perhaps, to some extent, why I stand there.

We can probably all make our own list of world problems, and we hardly need reminding of them: most of them have been with us since the dawn of history, and the news industry keeps us abreast of those that are of more recent provenance. What is new about the problems of today is the very fact that we hear about them. They are global in character, world-scale problems. It really is as though we live in a global village, and although this is a matter of common knowledge, even a truism, it perhaps does not sink as decisively and deeply into our awareness as it should.

The result of globalization is that all world problems affect all of us in some way, either directly or indirectly, either potentially or in actuality. Not very long ago, the vast majority of people knew absolutely nothing about the problems of people who lived just a few valleys away, let alone people on the other side of the world. Catastrophic events hardly impinged at all on the lives of those who were not directly and immediately involved. Even in a country ravaged by years of terrible warfare there would be peasants within its borders going about their everyday lives knowing nothing whatsoever about it.

But not any more. We have the world's problems at our fingertips. The real problem for us is how to respond to them personally. How do we ensure that every individual citizen in the world grows up healthy and sound in body and mind? What can be done about the apparently increasing incidence of mental illness in the West? What is the role of women – and what is the role of men – in modern society? How do people with jobs avoid making themselves ill through overwork? How do people without work make the best use of their enforced leisure? How do we ensure that people are not discriminated against or abused on account of their racial origin? How do we reconcile the claims of law and order with those of individual freedom? How do we reconcile the conflicting interests of sovereign nation states? How can we all get along with one another?

Fresh outbreaks of hostilities between rival factions in some former European colony, food shortages and unrest in some ex-communist state, inner-city deprivation and crime, drug dependency and alcoholism, child labour, racial violence, industrial pollution, nuclear accidents, disease, drought, famine, starvation, 'ethnic cleansing' – these are just a few of the problems and crises that confront us, or at least pluck at our sleeves every now and then, and are recorded for us on the television and analysed for us in the newspapers. No doubt there are many others, equally pressing, that I have failed to mention. We all have our own pet world problems that seem more crucial than others. But the central problem for all of us is: how do we ourselves, individually, react to whatever we perceive to be the world's problems?

Sometimes our initial reaction will be very strong. For a while we may get quite carried away by our indignation: we are outraged; this should never be allowed to happen; something must be done; those responsible – if particular perpetrators can be identified – should be brought to justice; and so on. And we may be anxious on our own account, if the problem seems likely to affect us directly at some point. In the end, however, when that initial reaction has exhausted itself, we are overtaken – overpowered – by a different kind of reaction: helplessness. The problem is too big, too involved, for us to do anything about it. So we try to forget about it and get on with our own lives, and deal with our own personal problems. We are very sorry that others suffer, but at least we can try to enjoy our own lives.

This is, I suspect, how many people react to world problems. However, my own view is that such a withdrawal from public concerns into purely personal ones is not worthy of a human being – not worthy, at least, of someone who is trying to be a human being in the full sense of the term. It represents an abdication of responsibility. So, given that one is helpless to effect any kind of solution to these large issues, and given too that one can't turn aside and ignore them either, what is one to do?

World problems, by their very nature, are essentially group problems, as they always have been. What is new today is the size of the groups involved and the destructive power available to them. But whatever their size, the problems arising from these groups cannot be solved on the group level. All that can be achieved on the level of the group is a precarious balance of power between conflicting interests. And that balance, as we know only too well, can be disturbed at any moment.

The only hope for humanity is therefore necessarily a long-term solution, involving more people becoming clearer about how they need to develop as individuals and cooperating in the context of spiritual communities in order to make, in their various ways, a significant impact on the world, or on 'the group'. The alternatives before us are, in my opinion, evolution – that is, the higher evolution of the individual – or extinction. That would be my overall diagnosis of the situation facing us. As for practical ways to effect a remedy, I would prescribe four courses of action for the individual to undertake.

1. SELF-DEVELOPMENT

By this I mean the development of the mind, the raising of consciousness to ever higher levels of awareness. Human development essentially consists in this, and for most people the route to achieving it is through meditation. The practice of meditation essentially involves three things. Firstly, it involves concentration, the integration of all our energies, conscious and unconscious. Secondly, it involves the raising of consciousness to supra-personal states, leaving the ego-realm for higher, wider, even cosmic dimensions. And thirdly, it involves contemplation: the direct insight of the uncluttered mind – the mind in a state of higher consciousness – into the ultimate depths of existence, the seeing of reality face to face. Meditation is concerned with achieving all this. There are many different methods; you just need to find a teacher who will introduce you to one or two of them. After that, you stick with the methods and practise them regularly. That's all there is to it, really.

The more demanding aspect of self-development consists in what one does with the rest of one's life in order to support one's meditation practice. One will look after one's health. One will simplify one's life as far as possible, dropping all those activities, interests, and social contacts which one knows to be a waste of time. One will try to base one's life, and in particular one's livelihood, on ethical principles. One will make time – perhaps by working part-time – for study; for study of the Dharma, of course, but also for study of other subjects of general human interest: philosophy, history, science, comparative religion. Finally, one will find opportunities to refine and develop one's emotions, especially through the fine arts.

Self-development always comes first. However active you might be in all sorts of external areas – political, social, educational, or whatever – if you are not trying to develop yourself, you are not going to be able to make any truly positive contribution to anything or anyone.

2. JOIN A SPIRITUAL COMMUNITY

This does not necessarily mean joining some kind of organized body or living under the same roof as other aspiring individuals. It simply means being in personal, regular, and substantial contact with others who are trying to develop as individuals. It means being able to enjoy, and seeking out, not just the psychological warmth of the herd, but the challenge of real communication, genuine spiritual exchange.

3. WITHDRAW SUPPORT FROM ALL GROUPS OR AGENCIES THAT DISCOURAGE, DIRECTLY OR INDIRECTLY, THE DEVELOPMENT OF THE INDIVIDUAL

Groups derive their strength from their members, so it is a basic first step to weaken the power of the group by removing yourself from among its contributing members. Otherwise you are pulling in two directions at once: on the one hand trying to be an individual, and on the other lending your support to the very forces that hinder this process. If you wanted to take this principle to its ultimate conclusion you would withdraw support from the state, as the ultimate group of groups, though this would clearly be extremely difficult, however desirable from one point of view; and in practice we need also to bear in mind our responsibilities as citizens.

4. ENCOURAGE THE DEVELOPMENT OF INDIVIDUALITY WITHIN ALL THE GROUPS TO WHICH ONE UNAVOIDABLY BELONGS

It may be that one cannot help having a circle of friends or acquaintances, whether at home or at work, who are not interested in any kind of self-development. One may have to remain very nominally a member of a group. Still, one can stand up for what one believes in, and speak up whenever it is appropriate to do so. It is always possible to act in accordance with one's ideals even when others cannot – or do not appear to – understand what one is doing. The way to disrupt a group is simply to encourage people within it to think for themselves, develop minds of their own. So in the context of the group one can still work to undermine it. Even in the enemy camp, so to speak, one need not surrender one's individuality.

These, then, are the four strategies to get under way in order to begin to make a meaningful impact on world problems. A network of spiritual communities of all kinds, many of whose members would be in contact with one another, could exert a significant degree of influence, such as might – just possibly – shift the centre of gravity in world affairs. Spiritual communities have had a crucial impact in the past, and they may, with sufficient vitality, do so again.

It doesn't matter how humble a level we are operating at, or how undramatic our work may be. The true individual is not so much the king of the jungle as the indefatigable earthworm. If enough earthworms burrow away under the foundations of even the most substantial building, the soil begins to loosen, it starts to crumble away, the foundations subside, and the whole building is liable to crack and collapse. Likewise, however powerful the existing order may seem, it is not invulnerable to the undermining influence of enough individuals working – whether directly or indirectly – in cooperation.

A spiritual community is necessarily small, so the best we can hope for is a multiplicity of spiritual communities, forming a sort of network through personal contact between their members. A silent, unseen influence is exerted in this way, which we must hope will be able, at some point, to shift the centre of gravity in world affairs from the conflict of groups to the cooperation of communities. If this were achieved, if the influence of the spiritual community were to outweigh that of the group, then humanity as a whole would have passed into a new, higher stage of development, a kind of higher evolution as I like to call it – into what we might even describe as a fifth period of human history.

Such a shift in the governing values of the world is probably all that can save us from extinction as a species in the not very distant future. There are certainly signs of hope, but there is also perhaps little time left. In this situation it becomes the duty of every thinking human being to take stock of his or her position, and the responsibilities that it throws up. We have to appreciate that it is, without exception, the most important issue we shall ever face, either individually or collectively. It is certainly more important than any merely religious question, anything that concerns Buddhism in the sense of a formal or established religion. It concerns both the purpose and the very survival of human life.

21

BUDDHISM AND WESTERN SOCIETY

This is a bold title for such a short chapter, and I don't intend to deal with the subject systematically. Instead I shall take an altogether subjective approach, basing myself on my own experience of attempting to introduce Buddhism into Western culture.

During my time in India I became used to leading a simple life within the context of a traditional culture. Returning in 1964 to an England of postwar prosperity I found a culture that was quite different not only from the one I had become used to, but also from the one I had left twenty years previously. People spoke differently, they dressed differently, they behaved differently. Manners and morals had changed – to be frank, not always for the better.

There was already a Buddhist presence in that society. Indeed, I first returned to England in order to take up the position of resident monk in the Hampstead Buddhist Vihara. However, when in 1967 I founded a new Buddhist movement, I did so with few preconceived ideas of how Buddhism might be introduced most effectively into this – as it seemed to me then – quite strange society.

My initial point of interaction was meditation. I started conducting weekly meditation classes in a tiny basement room in central London. This setting was, I feel now, quite appropriate for my earliest forays into alien territory, into a culture devoted to values that are largely inimical to my own. In some sense one had to work below the surface, as an underground movement, rather like the early Christians in Rome who are supposed to have met in the Catacombs to take refuge from persecution. We are very fortunate in the West that we are not subject to overt persecution; but modern values which are antipathetic to religious faith of any kind – like materialism, consumerism, and relativism – are enforced in subtle but pervasive ways that make them all the more difficult to resist.

In these 'underground' meditation classes, I taught two methods of meditation: the mindfulness of breathing, known in Pāli as *ānāpanasati*,[478] and the cultivation of universal loving-kindness, the *mettā bhāvanā*. Quite soon, people attending these classes regularly were becoming noticeably calmer, clearer, and happier – as was only to be expected. There are many ways of defining meditation, but in very simple terms we can say that it enables the mind to work directly on itself in order to refine the quality of one's conscious experience, and in this way to raise one's whole level of consciousness. This process may be augmented by various indirect methods of raising consciousness, such as hatha yoga, t'ai chi ch'uan, and similar physical disciplines, together with the practice and appreciation of the arts. Thus the integration of Buddhism into Western society begins with at least some members of that society raising their levels of consciousness both directly through meditation, and indirectly through various other disciplines.

After a few months, we held our first retreat in the countryside, for just one week. It was attended by fifteen or twenty people who had been coming along regularly to these weekly meditation classes. On this retreat we meditated together, engaged in various devotional practices together, and discussed the Dharma together. Some of the retreatants were there to deepen their experience of meditation, and this they were able to do. But all of them discovered that simply being away from the city, away from the daily grind of work and home life, and being in the company of other Buddhists, with nothing to think about except the Dharma, was sufficient to raise their level of consciousness. So here was another point of interaction: changing the environment, changing the conditions in which people lived. That is, consciousness can be raised, at least to some extent, by changing society.

The integration of Buddhism into Western society therefore involves changing Western society. Inasmuch as our level of consciousness is affected by external conditions, it is not enough for us to work directly on the mind itself through meditation. We cannot isolate ourselves from society or ignore the conditions in which we and others live. We must make it easier for anyone within that society who wants to live a life dedicated to the Dharma to do so. To the extent that Western society has not been changed by Buddhism, to that extent Buddhism has not been integrated into Western society. In order to change Western society it is necessary to create Western Buddhist institutions and Western Buddhist lifestyles.

Thus, after a few retreats had been held, some of the people who had taken part in them decided to do what they could to prolong that experience. They set up residential spiritual communities so that they could live with other Buddhists, and have more time and space for their practice of the Dharma, and for support and encouragement. Some of our communities today comprise just two or three people living together; others consist of anything up to thirty people. Some members of communities have ordinary jobs like anyone else; others work full-time within Buddhist institutions and businesses. The most successful and typical kind of community is the single-sex community. Communities of men and women living together, sometimes with children, have been tried out, but rarely with great success. Clearly, such an arrangement is always going to involve additional complications.

Perhaps the most characteristic Western Buddhist institution is what we call the team-based right livelihood business or project. However, the way one earns one's living is a matter to which all Buddhists attach a great deal of importance. 'Right means of livelihood' is, as we have seen, the fifth step of the Buddha's Noble Eightfold Path. So here the interaction with Western society is economic.

The way it happened in our case was that some of the people living in communities felt they would be happier if they could work with other Buddhists as well as living with them. This team-based aspect of work became an important principle of our businesses. But the fundamental principle of Buddhist work is that it should be ethical, and when a number of people found their ordinary jobs not ethical enough, they resolved to create enterprises that were, and which could therefore be called 'right livelihood projects'. The third factor that went into establishing the founding principles of businesses came out during the creation of the complex of Buddhist centre and community in Bethnal Green in East London. The large sums of money required to complete the work were raised not simply by appealing for funds to generous patrons, welcome as such donations always are, but also by setting up cooperative right livelihood businesses – as they were then called – which donated their profits towards the creation of the Buddhist centre.

As they became established, right livelihood businesses came to do four things. They provided those working in them with material support, they enabled Buddhists to work with one another, they conducted themselves in accordance with Buddhist ethical principles, and they gave financial support to Buddhist and humanitarian activities.

In general, this Buddhist movement tries to create conditions that are conducive to human development. It does this in three main ways corresponding to three central aspects of ordinary human life which on balance are not conducive to spiritual development – the conventional nuclear family, work, and leisure activities. The idea is to open up and revolutionize these keystones of modern life, and where appropriate offer a more positive alternative to them.

Firstly, residential communities are meant to offer an alternative to stagnant relationships, particularly those of the tightly-knit family unit – or rather, the claustrophobic and neurotic closed system of a couple who no longer communicate with each other, orbited by one or two children, two cars, three television sets, a dog, a cat, and a budgerigar. Secondly, team-based right-livelihood projects are meant to offer an alternative to earning money in ways which are harmful to one's own development and which exploit others. And thirdly, the various activities provided and promoted by the spiritual community, both those that are directly Dharmic and those that are more indirectly helpful to spiritual growth, give us something positive to do with our free time. They give us an alternative to activities which merely enable us to pass the time, to forget about the stresses of work or family life, and all too often to forget about our own selves. These three things between them constitute the nucleus of the new society; they represent the transformation of conditions that tend to be unconducive to spiritual development into conditions that are conducive.

How each project goes about this work is up to the individuals concerned. Every one of these institutions is meant to function auto-nomously. Those who run it have to make their own decisions and take responsibility for them. At the same time, as an aspect of the development of this sangha, people with similar responsibilities for similar institutions make sure that they meet regularly to swap notes, and support and advise each other.

During the first few years of this movement's existence I was also delivering public lectures in which I sought to communicate the fundamental concepts of Buddhism in a way that was both intelligible to a Western audience and faithful to the Buddhist tradition. This was yet another point of interaction with Western society: the introduction of Buddhist ideas into Western intellectual discourse. By Buddhist ideas I do not mean doctrinal refinements or philosophical subtleties. I mean ideas so fundamental that Buddhists themselves often take them for granted, and fail to realize their full significance. Such, for example, is the idea that religion does not necessarily involve belief in the existence of God, of a creator and ruler of the universe. Another, related, idea is that it is possible for us to lead an ethical life, to raise the level of our consciousness, and to realize a transcendent reality, without invoking the aid of any outside supernatural power. If Buddhism is to be integrated into Western society, ideas of this fundamental kind will have to become familiar to all educated Westerners.

However, the most important kind of integration – without which the other kinds cannot exist – is the integration of the individual Buddhist into Western society. It is, after all, the individual Buddhist who meditates – meditation does not exist in the abstract. Likewise, it is the individual Buddhist who goes on retreat, who works in a right livelihood business, who communicates the fundamental ideas of Buddhism. Without the individual Buddhist there can be no integration of Buddhism into Western society.

The individual Buddhist is, as we have seen, someone who goes for Refuge to the Three Jewels. He or she does so not in isolation but in the company of other individuals who are also Going for Refuge. That is, he or she belongs to the sangha or spiritual community in the widest sense. It is this sangha rather than the individual Buddhist which will raise the level of consciousness of people living in Western society, which will change that society by creating Buddhist social and economic institutions, and which will introduce fundamental Buddhist ideas into Western intellectual discourse. It is this wider spiritual community that will effect the psychological, social, economic, and intellectual integration of Buddhism into Western society. This is what the sangha is really for; this is what the sangha really is.

NOTES

WHO IS THE BUDDHA?

CHAPTER I

1 In the first verse of Rudyard
Kipling's poem 'The English
Flag'.

2 The issue of the 'two cultures',
first debated by T. H. Huxley
and Matthew Arnold in
1881–2, came to a head in a
crusty confrontation between
C. P. Snow and F. R. Leavis in
1959.

3 The story of this lady (her
name was Mrs Crisp) is told
in Sangharakshita's memoir
Facing Mount Kanchenjunga,
Windhorse Publications,
Glasgow 1992, pp. 241–3
(*Complete Works*, vol. 21).
and in that context he reflects
further on the incident in
which Mrs Crisp hid the
teapot.

4 Pierre Teilhard de Chardin
(1881–1955) was a

Jesuit priest and also a
palaeontologist and geologist
who developed a theology
of evolution of the form
known as teleological
orthogenesis, that is, the
idea that evolution is
directed by an inner force
towards a particular end.
He called this culmination
the Omega Point, a kind of
supreme consciousness. He
outlined this in, for example,
The Phenomenon of Man,
published in 1955.

5 The theory of the descent
of species is fully developed
in Immanuel Kant, *Critique
of Judgement,* part 2, trans.
J. C. Meredith, Oxford 1952.
Nineteenth-century theories
of evolution, especially
Darwin's, added factual details
to Kant's theory without

changing anything in its basic framework.

To paraphrase Stephen Houlgate in *An Introduction to Hegel: Freedom, Truth and History* (Blackwell 2005, pp. 173–4), Hegel rejects outright the doctrine of the evolution of species. He would have known nothing of Darwin's *Origin of Species*, but would have been familiar with Lamarck, who asserted that lower organisms were generated spontaneously and higher organisms then gradually developed from them. Hegel wrote (in the introduction to *Philosophy of Nature*): 'It is completely empty thought to represent species developing successively, one after the other, in time...' Hegel was interested in the logical rather than temporal relations between phenomena in nature. He does note that 'the species of animals are exposed to contingency', hence the myriad of transitional forms found in the animal world. Hegel was interested in rational distinctions between animal species and in comparative anatomy, an interest quite compatible with the idea that species evolved from one another. See Hegel, *The Philosophy of Nature, Preliminary Concepts*, p. 194: 'Nature is to be viewed as a system of stages, in which one

stage necessarily arises from another.'
Aristotle classified all living organisms hierarchically in his Great Chain of Being, from plants through lesser animals to human beings at the pinnacle of creation. But natural selection holds the idea of change by common descent from a shared ancestor, while Aristotle sees each species as formed individually with its own purpose and place in nature. No species evolves into a new species. Aristotle, *The Works*, vol. iv: *History of Animals*, ed. David Ross, 1910, 588b.

6   The G. K. Chesterton epigram is given in various forms, one (said to derive from a combination of remarks in Chesterton's Father Brown stories) being 'The first effect of not believing in God is to believe in anything.' Although variants of this epigram are widely attributed to Chesterton, the specific origin of the phrase is evidently a mystery.

7   See p. 92.

8   *Aggañña Sutta*: 'On the Knowledge of Beginnings', *Dīgha Nikāya* 27; M. Walshe (trans.), *The Long Discourses of the Buddha*, Wisdom Publications, Boston 1995, pp. 407–15; or T. W. Rhys Davids (trans.), *Dialogues of the Buddha*, part 3, Pali Text Society, Oxford 1991, pp. 77–94. See also a dramatically

told account of the 'Genesis of the World' in J. J. Jones (trans.), *Mahāvastu*, vol. i, Pali Text Society, London 1987, pp. 285–301.

9 'Ode on Melancholy', third stanza.

10 For more on the spiral mode of conditionality, see pp. 258ff.

11 The four noble truths feature in some of the accounts of the Buddha's first discourse but not others. For one example, see section 28 of the *Ariyapariyesanā Sutta*, *Majjhima Nikāya* 26 (i.163); see Bhikkhu Ñāṇamoli and Bhikkhu Bodhi (trans.), *The Middle Length Discourses of the Buddha*, Wisdom Publications, Boston 1995, p. 265; or I. B. Horner (trans.), *Middle Length Sayings*, vol. i, Pali Text Society, Oxford 1957, pp. 216–7.

12 *Dhammapada* 276 (trans. Sangharakshita): 'By you must the zealous effort be made. The Tathāgatas (i.e., the Buddhas or Enlightened Ones) are only proclaimers (of the Way).' *Dhammapada* verse 165 (trans. Sangharakshita): 'Purity and impurity are matters of personal experience: one man cannot purify another.'

13 *Ehipassiko* is one of the attributes of the Dharma listed in the text chanted as the *Tiratana Vandanā* in many parts of the Buddhist world. The text is found in several places in the Pāli canon, for example in the

Mahāparinibbāna Sutta section 2.9, *Dīgha Nikāya* 16 (ii.93–4), where it is called the Mirror of the Dharma. See M. Walshe (trans.), *The Long Discourses of the Buddha*, Wisdom Publications, Boston 1995, p. 241; or T. W. Rhys Davids (trans.), *Dialogues of the Buddha*, part 2, Pali Text Society, Oxford 1977, pp. 99–100. For the list of attributes see also section 25 of the *Mahātaṇhasaṅkhaya Sutta*, *Majjhima Nikāya* 38 (i.265), Bhikkhu Ñāṇamoli and Bhikkhu Bodhi (trans.), *The Middle Length Discourses of the Buddha*, Wisdom Publications, Boston 1995, p. 358; or I. B. Horner (trans.), *Middle Length Sayings*, vol. i, Pali Text Society, Oxford 1957, p. 321.

14 'O Bhikṣus, my words should be accepted by the wise, not out of regard for me, but after due investigation – just as gold is accepted as true only after heating, cutting and rubbing.' *The Tattvasaṅgraha of Shāntarakṣita*, trans. Ganganatha Jha, Motilal Banarsidass, Delhi 1986, vol. ii, p. 1558, text 3588.

15 Vinaya Piṭaka ii.258–9 (*Cullavagga* 10.5). See I. B. Horner (trans.), *The Book of the Discipline*, part 5, p. 359. See also *Aṅguttara Nikāya* iv.280, in Bhikkhu Bodhi (trans.), *The Numerical Discourses of the Buddha*, Wisdom Publications, Boston

2012, p. 1193; or E. M. Hare
(trans.), *Gradual Sayings*,
vol. iv, Pali Text Society,
Oxford 1995, pp. 186–7.

16 The Buddha is recorded as
describing the four *brahma
vihāras* in the *Tevijja Sutta*
sections 76–9, *Dīgha Nikāya*
13 (i.251). See M. Walshe
(trans.), *The Long Discourses
of the Buddha*, Wisdom
Publications, Boston 1995,
p. 194; or T. W. Rhys Davids
(trans.), *Dialogues of the
Buddha*, part 1, Pali Text
Society, Oxford 1977, pp. 317–
8. Acharya Buddhaghosa
described in detail how to
practise the *brahma vihāras* in
the *Visuddhimagga* (317–25);
see Pe Maung Tin (trans.),
The Path of Purity, Pali Text
Society, London 1975, ch. 9,
pp. 365–75.

17 Thus the human life of a
Buddha must be seen in an
entirely different perspective:
it becomes a mere fraction
of a far bigger and more
important development, in
which the human element
is essentially the vehicle
for the rediscovery of the
universal (and in this sense
"transcendental") character
of mind or consciousness,
which according to the
Prajñāpāramitā Sūtra is
"inconceivable in its true
nature".

Lama Anagarika Govinda,
'The Buddha on the Ideal
of the Perfect Man and the

Embodiment of the Dharma',
Maha Bodhi Journal,
Vaishakha number, April 1954.

CHAPTER 2

18 *Nidānasaṃyutta*, *Saṃyutta
Nikāya* ii.105–6; see Bhikkhu
Bodhi (trans.), *Connected
Discourses of the Buddha*,
Wisdom Publications, Boston
2000, p. 603; or C. A. F. Rhys
Davids (trans.), *The Book
of the Kindred Sayings*, part
2, Pali Text Society, Oxford
1997, p. 74. This translation is
from Bhikkhu Ñāṇamoli, *The
Life of the Buddha*, Buddhist
Publication Society, Kandy
1972, p. 27.

19 It isn't certain which carving
this refers to, but a scene very
like the one described here is
depicted on the Great Stupa
at Sanchi, India, which was
originally commissioned by
the emperor Aśoka in the
third century BCE. In that
carving, the Buddha is indeed
in symbolic form, being
represented by a bodhi tree. At
that early date the Buddha was
never represented in human
form, but always symbolized
by an image such as a pair of
footprints, an umbrella, or, as
here, a bodhi tree.

20 The story of Queen Māyā is
told in many of the legendary
accounts of the Buddha's life.
See, for example, the *Nidāna-
kathā*, published as T. W. Rhys
Davids (trans.), *Buddhist
Birth-stories (Jātaka Tales): The
Commentarial Introduction*

entitled *Nidāna-kathā, the Story of the Lineage*, Routledge, London n.d., pp. 152–5. See also J. J. Jones (trans.), *Mahāvastu*, vol. i, Pali Text Society, London 1987, pp. 115–9; and the *Acchariya-abbhūta Sutta, Majjhima Nikāya* 123; see Bhikkhu Ñāṇamoli and Bhikkhu Bodhi (trans.), *The Middle Length Discourses of the Buddha*, Wisdom Publications, Boston 1995, pp. 979–84; or I. B. Horner (trans.), *Middle Length Sayings*, vol. iii, Pali Text Society, Oxford 1957, pp. 163–9. Also Aśvaghoṣa, *Buddhacarita*, book 1, verses 15–26.

21 The Buddha is represented as telling a simple account of his realization under the rose-apple tree in section 31 of the *Mahāsaccaka Sutta, Majjhima Nikāya* 36 (i.246); see Bhikkhu Ñāṇamoli and Bhikkhu Bodhi (trans.), *The Middle Length Discourses of the Buddha*, Wisdom Publications, Boston 1995, p. 340; or I. B. Horner (trans.), *Middle Length Sayings*, vol. i, Pali Text Society, Oxford 1957, p. 301. An embellished version of the story is found in later texts like the *Mahāvastu* and the *Nidāna-kathā*, and it is these that add the detail of how the shadow of the rose-apple tree did not move. See, for example, the *Nidāna-kathā*, published as T. W. Rhys Davids (trans.), *Buddhist Birth-stories (Jātaka Tales)*, Routledge, London n.d., pp. 164–5.

22 Discrimination against lower castes is illegal in India under article 15 of its constitution. However, societal stratification, and the inequality that comes with it, still exists. Government policies aim at reducing this inequality by a reservation quota, but paradoxically also have thus created an incentive to keep this stratification alive. It was this caste discrimination that motivated Dr Ambedkar and his followers to become Buddhist and leave the Hindu caste system entirely; see *Complete Works*, vol. 9.

23 The story of Asita's encounter with the infant Buddha is told in many places in the traditional literature, for example in the *Nālaka Sutta* of the *Sutta-Nipāta* (3.11); but it is the more legendary accounts that include the two possibilities: that Siddhārtha may become either a great ruler or a great sage. See *Lalitavistara Sūtra* in Gwendolyn Bays (trans.), *The Voice of the Buddha*, vol. i, Dharma Publishing, Berkeley 1983, pp. 150–63; or Aśvaghoṣa, *Buddhacarita*, trans. E. H. Johnston, Motilal Banarsidass, Delhi 1984, book 1, verses 54–85, pp. 12–18.

24 See *Sukhamāla Sutta, Aṅguttara Nikāya* i.144, in Bhikkhu Bodhi (trans.), *The Numerical Discourses of the Buddha*, Wisdom Publications, Boston 2012, pp. 239–40; or F. L. Woodward (trans.), *The*

Book of the Gradual Sayings,
vol. i, Pali Text Society,
Oxford 1995, p. 128; see also
Aśvaghoṣa, Buddhacarita,
E. H. Johnston (trans.),
Motilal Banarsidass, Delhi
1984, book 2, verses 29–32,
pp. 25–6.

25 The story of the birth of the
Buddha's son and his being
named Rāhula is told in
T. W. Rhys Davids (trans.),
Buddhist Birth-stories (Jātaka
Tales), Routledge, London n.d.,
p. 169.

26 It is Aśvaghoṣa's Buddhacarita
that describes the effect of the
sights on Siddhārtha as being
'like a bull on hearing the
crash of a thunderbolt nearby';
see E. H. Johnston (trans.),
Buddhacarita (iii.34), Motilal
Banarsidass, Delhi 1984,
part 2, p. 38.

27 The four sights are not
mentioned in the Pāli canon
as concrete encounters
of the historical Buddha.
They are presented as 'the
thought occurred to me
…': see Sukhamāla Sutta,
Aṅguttara Nikāya i.144, in
Bhikkhu Bodhi (trans.), The
Numerical Discourses of the
Buddha, Wisdom Publications,
Boston 2012, pp. 239–42; or
F. L. Woodward (trans.), The
Book of the Gradual Sayings,
vol. i, Pali Text Society, Oxford
1995, p. 128; also section 13
of the Ariya-pariyesanā Sutta,
Majjhima Nikāya 26 (i.163);
Bhikkhu Ñāṇamoli and Bhikkhu
Bodhi (trans.), The Middle

Length Discourses of the
Buddha, Wisdom Publications,
Boston 1995, p. 256; or
I. B. Horner (trans.), Middle
Length Sayings, vol. i, Pali Text
Society, Oxford 1957, p. 207. In
early Pāli sources the legendary
account of the four sights is only
described in connection with
the Buddha Vipassi; see sections
2.1 to 2.14 of the Mahāpādana
Sutta, Dīgha Nikāya 14
(ii.22–8); M. Walshe (trans.),
The Long Discourses of the
Buddha, Wisdom Publications,
Boston 1995, pp. 207–210;
or T. W. Rhys Davids (trans.),
Dialogues of the Buddha, part
2, Pali Text Society, Oxford
1991, pp. 18–22. In later
texts, for example the Nidāna-
kathā, Buddhavamsa, and
Lalitavistara, the story is applied
to the Buddha. The Mahāvastu
gives a particularly graphic
account of the four sights; see
J. J. Jones (trans.), Mahāvastu,
vol. ii, Pali Text Society, London
1987, pp. 145–53. See also
Aśvaghoṣa, Buddhacarita, book
3, verses 26–62.

28 See, for example, T. W. Rhys
Davids (trans.), Buddhist
Birth-stories (Jātaka Tales),
Routledge, London n.d.,
p. 173.

29 A stirring account of
Siddhārtha's leaving the palace
is given in the Mahāvastu; see
J. J. Jones (trans.), Mahāvastu,
vol. ii, Pali Text Society,
London 1987, pp. 155–6. See
also Aśvaghoṣa, Buddhacarita,
book 5. But the detail of

how the charioteer held on to the horse's tail is given in T. W. Rhys Davids (trans.), *Buddhist Birth-stories (Jātaka Tales)*, Routledge, London n.d., p. 174: 'The Future Buddha rode on the mighty back of the mighty steed, made Channa hold on by the tail, and so arrived at midnight at the great gate of the city.'

30 In most legendary accounts Siddhārtha gives his clothes to his charioteer, Channa, though in Aśvaghoṣa's version, the clothes are swapped with those of a hunter who serendipitously appears. See E. H. Johnston (trans.), *Buddhacarita* (iii.34), Motilal Banarsidass, Delhi 1984, pp. 89–90.

31 This description comes from L. Adams Beck, *The Life of the Buddha*, Collins, London n.d., p. 146. The Buddha described the great lengths he went to in practising austerities in the *Mahāsaccaka Sutta, Majjhima Nikāya* 36 (i.242–6): see Bhikkhu Ñāṇamoli and Bhikkhu Bodhi (trans.), *The Middle Length Discourses of the Buddha*, Wisdom Publications, Boston 1995, pp. 337–40, or I. B. Horner (trans.), *Middle Length Sayings*, vol. i, Pali Text Society, London 1967, pp. 297–301. An account of the austerities is also given in the *Mahāvastu*; see J. J. Jones (trans.), *Mahāvastu*, vol. ii, Pali Text Society, London 1987, pp. 120–6.

32 One version of the story of how Siddhārtha fell into a river is told in the *Fo-Sho-Hing-Tsan-King (A Life of Buddha)*, by Aśvaghoṣa, published as vol. 19 of the *Sacred Books of the East* series, trans. Samuel Beal, Motilal Banarsidass, Delhi 1998. p. 144.

33 The story of how the Buddha-to-be settled down to meditate by the river comes from a number of sources. See, for example, J. J. Jones (trans.), *Mahāvastu*, vol. ii, Pali Text Society, London 1987, pp. 126–7. See also the *Lalitavistara Sūtra*, in Gwendolyn Bays (trans.), *The Voice of the Buddha*, vol. ii, Dharma Publishing, Berkeley 1983, pp. 433–7.

34 For example, in the *Ariyapariyesanā Sutta* the Buddha describes the experience of Enlightenment in terms of the realization of freedom and that 'this is the last birth for me'; see *Majjhima Nikāya* 26; Bhikkhu Ñāṇamoli and Bhikkhu Bodhi (trans.), *The Middle Length Discourses of the Buddha*, Wisdom Publications, Boston 1995, p. 260; or I. B. Horner (trans.), *Middle Length Sayings*, vol. i, Pali Text Society, Oxford 1957, p. 211. In the *Mahāsaccaka Sutta*, Enlightenment is described in terms of the 'three true knowledges'; see *Majjhima Nikāya* 36 (i.249); Bhikkhu Ñāṇamoli and Bhikkhu Bodhi (trans.), *The Middle*

Length Discourses of the Buddha, Wisdom Publications, Boston 1995, pp. 341–2; or I. B. Horner (trans.), *Middle Length Sayings*, vol. i, Pali Text Society, Oxford 1957, pp. 303–4.

35 *Bhayabherava Sutta, Majjhima Nikāya* 4 (i.22); see Bhikkhu Ñāṇamoli and Bhikkhu Bodhi (trans.), *The Middle Length Discourses of the Buddha*, Wisdom Publications, Boston 1995, p. 105; or I. B. Horner (trans.), *Middle Length Sayings*, vol. i, Pali Text Society, Oxford 1957, pp. 21–30.

36 Shakespeare, *The Tempest*, act i, scene ii.

37 *Mahāsaccaka Sutta, Majjhima Nikāya* 36 (i.248); see Bhikkhu Ñāṇamoli and Bhikkhu Bodhi (trans.), *The Middle Length Discourses of the Buddha*, Wisdom Publications, Boston 1995, p. 341; or I. B. Horner (trans.), *Middle Length Sayings*, vol. i, Pali Text Society, Oxford 1957, p. 303.

38 The 'knowledge of the destruction of the *āsravas*' is described at the end of ch. 7, 'The Spiral Path', in *What is the Dharma?*, p. 278.

CHAPTER 3

39 The parable is addressed to Śāriputra. See Bunnō Katō et al. (trans.), *The Threefold Lotus Sūtra*, Kosei Publishing, Tokyo 1975, ch. 3, pp. 85–7; also Sangharakshita, *The Drama of Cosmic*

Enlightenment, ch. 3 (*Complete Works*, vol. 16).

40 *Ariyapariyesanā Sutta, Majjhima Nikāya* 26 (i.161); see Bhikkhu Ñāṇamoli and Bhikkhu Bodhi (trans.), *The Middle Length Discourses of the Buddha*, Wisdom Publications, Boston 1995, pp. 254; or I. B. Horner (trans.), *Middle Length Sayings*, vol. i, Pali Text Society, London 1967, p. 204.

CHAPTER 4

41 See ch. 1, section 10, 'The Positive Aspect of Nirvāṇa', in Sangharakshita, *A Survey of Buddhism* (*Complete Works*, vol. 1), which explains that 'it would be wrong to assume that in the Pāli texts no positive symbolical indications of the goal of the Āryan Eightfold Path are given' and proceeds to give examples. The Pāli canon also outlines positive approaches to the practice of the precepts. See, for example, the Buddha's teaching to Cunda the silversmith of the ten precepts in the *Aṅguttara Nikāya* v.264–8; Bhikkhu Bodhi (trans.), *The Numerical Discourses of the Buddha*, Wisdom Publications, Boston 2012, pp. 1518–23; or F. L. Woodward (trans.), *The Book of the Gradual Sayings*, vol. v, Pali Text Society, London 1972, pp. 178–80. See also Sangharakshita, *The Ten Pillars of Buddhism*, section 2 (*Complete Works*, vol. 2).

The positive mental states resulting from the practice of meditation are also described in colourful detail. See, for example, the descriptions of the *dhyānas* found in the Pāli canon in sections 76–82 of the *Sāmaññaphala Sutta*, *Dīgha Nikāya* 2 (i.73–5); M. Walshe (trans.), *The Long Discourses of the Buddha*, Wisdom Publications, Boston 1995, pp. 102–3; or T. W. Rhys Davids (trans.), *Dialogues of the Buddha*, part 1, Pali Text Society, Oxford 1977, pp. 84–6.

42 This saying is variously ascribed. Montaigne (1533–1592) said: '*Peu d'hommes ont esté admirés par leurs domestiques.*' Madame Cornuel (who died in 1694) wrote to the same effect: '*Il n'y a pas de grand homme pour son valet de chambre.*'

43 *Dhammapada* 103, trans. Sangharakshita.

44 In Vajrayāna Buddhism Trailokya Vijaya became a wrathful deity, sometimes a Buddha (a form of Vairocana), sometimes a *deva*. Some Vajrayāna archetypal figures were also depicted making a *trailokya vijaya mudra* or gesture. In Japan, Vajrasattva is known as 'the Subduer of the Three Worlds'.

45 Lama Anagarika Govinda, *Psycho-cosmic Symbolism of the Buddhist Stūpa*, Dharma Publishing, Berkeley 1976, p. 79.

46 For example, in the *Sela Sutta*, *Majjhima Nikāya* 92 (Sn 101–12), the Brahmin Sela asks the Buddha, 'supreme king of the Dhamma', who is his general, the disciple who helps him turn the wheel of Dhamma, and the Buddha tells him that his general is Sāriputta. See Bhikkhu Ñāṇamoli and Bhikkhu Bodhi (trans.), *The Middle Length Discourses of the Buddha*, Wisdom Publications, Boston 1995, p. 759; or I. B. Horner (trans.), *Middle Length Sayings*, vol. ii, Pali Text Society, London 1967, pp. 332–9.

47 This story is told in ch. 12 of the *Lalitavistara Sūtra*; see Gwendolyn Bays (trans.), *The Voice of the Buddha*, vol. i, Dharma Publishing, Berkeley 1983, pp. 211–38.

48 T. W. Rhys Davids (trans.), *Buddhist Birth-stories (Jātaka Tales)*, Routledge, London n.d., p. 180:

The great man collected mixed food. And when he perceived there was enough to support him, he left the city by the gate at which he had entered. And seating himself, facing toward the East, under the shadow of the Paṇḍava rock, he began to eat his meal. His stomach, however, turned, and made as if it would come out of his mouth. Then, though distressed by that revolting food, for in that birth he had never even beheld such food with his eyes, he himself admonished himself, saying: 'Siddhattha, it is true thou wast born in a family where food and drink were easily obtainable, into a state of life where thy food was perfumed third-season's rice, with various curries of the finest kinds. But ever since thou didst see one clad in a mendicant's garb, thou hast been thinking: "When shall I become like him, and live by begging my food? Would that that time were come!" And now that thou hast left all for that very purpose, what is this that thou art doing?' And overcoming his feelings, he ate the food.

49   See *Ariyapariyesanā Sutta*, *Majjhima Nikāya* 26 (i.167–70); Bhikkhu Ñāṇamoli and Bhikkhu Bodhi (trans.), *The Middle Length Discourses of the Buddha*, Wisdom Publications, Boston 1995, pp. 256–9; or I. B. Horner (trans.), *Middle Length Sayings*, vol. i, Pali Text Society, London 1967, pp. 207–10.

50   The Buddha describes his fear in the forest in the *Bhayabherava Sutta*, *Majjhima Nikāya* 4 (i.20–1). See Bhikkhu Ñāṇamoli and Bhikkhu Bodhi (trans.), *The Middle Length Discourses of the Buddha*, Wisdom Publications, Boston 1995,

p. 104; or I. B. Horner (trans.), *Middle Length Sayings*, vol. i, Pali Text Society, London 1967, pp. 26–7.

51   The Buddha's description of his austerities is recorded in, for example, sections 20–9 of the *Mahāsaccaka Sutta*, *Dīgha Nikāya* 36 (i.242–6); see Bhikkhu Ñāṇamoli and Bhikkhu Bodhi (trans.), *The Middle Length Discourses of the Buddha*, Wisdom Publications, Boston 1995, pp. 337–40, or I. B. Horner (trans.), *Middle Length Sayings*, vol. i, Pali Text Society, London 1967, pp. 297–301. A famous Gāndhāran stone carving of the emaciated Siddhārtha is to be seen in the museum at Lahore, Pakistan.

52   See section 33 of the *Mahāsaccaka Sutta*, *Majjhima Nikāya* 36 (i.247); Bhikkhu Ñāṇamoli and Bhikkhu Bodhi (trans.), *The Middle Length Discourses of the Buddha*, Wisdom Publications, Boston 1995, p. 340, or I. B. Horner (trans.), *Middle Length Sayings*, vol. i, Pali Text Society, London 1967, pp. 301–2.

53   These dramatic words are from the *Lalitavistara Sūtra*; see Gwendolyn Bays (trans.), *The Voice of the Buddha*, vol. ii, Dharma Publishing, Berkeley 1983, p. 439. See also Aśvaghoṣa, *Buddhacarita*, E. H. Johnston (trans.), Motilal Banarsidass, Delhi 1984, p. 186; and the *Appaṭivāna*

Sutta, Aṅguttara Nikāya i.50; see Bhikkhu Bodhi (trans.), *Numerical Discourses of the Buddha*, Wisdom Publications, Boston 2012, p. 142; or F. L. Woodward (trans.), *The Book of the Gradual Sayings*, vol. i, Pali Text Society, Oxford 2000, p. 45.

54 See, for example, section 27 of the *Dvedhāvitakka Sutta, Majjhima Nikāya* 19 (i.118); Bhikkhu Ñāṇamoli and Bhikkhu Bodhi (trans.), *The Middle Length Discourses of the Buddha*, Wisdom Publications, Boston 1995, p. 210, or I. B. Horner (trans.), *Middle Length Sayings*, vol. i, Pali Text Society, London 1967, p. 152. See also *Saṃyutta Nikāya* iv.133 & v.157; Bhikkhu Bodhi (trans.), *Connected Discourses of the Buddha*, Wisdom Publications, Boston 2000, p. 1212 & pp. 1639–40; or F. L. Woodward (trans.), *The Book of the Kindred Sayings*, Pali Text Society, Oxford, part 4, p. 85 and part 5, pp. 136–7.

55 A typical exhortation is to be found in the *Bhikkhunīpassaya Sutta* of the *Saṃyutta Nikāya* (v.154); see Bhikkhu Bodhi (trans.), *Connected Discourses of the Buddha*, Wisdom Publications, Boston 2000, p. 1638; or F. L. Woodward (trans.), *Kindred Sayings*, part 5, Pali Text Society, London 1979, pp. 136–7: 'Whatever is to be done by a teacher with compassion for

the welfare of students, that has been done by me out of compassion for you. Here are the roots of trees. Here are empty places. Sit down and meditate. Don't be lazy. Don't become one who is later remorseful.' One of the most famous passages in which the Buddha asks his disciples about their spiritual progress is the story of his visit to Anuruddha, Nandiya, and Kimbila, who say they are getting along 'as milk and water blend'; see *Cūḷagosinga Sutta, Majjhima Nikāya* 31 (i.207); Bhikkhu Ñāṇamoli and Bhikkhu Bodhi (trans.), *The Middle Length Discourses of the Buddha*, Wisdom Publications, Boston 1995, pp. 301–6; or I. B. Horner (trans.), *Middle Length Sayings*, vol. i, Pali Text Society, London 1967, pp. 257–62.

56 Dr Ambedkar quotes this saying of the Buddha in *The Buddha and his Dhamma* (Siddharth Publications, Bombay 1991, p. 327) and Christmas Humphreys also quotes it in *Zen Buddhism* (Unwin Paperbacks, London 1984, p. 27), but in neither case is a source given, and so far it has not been traced, although Christmas Humphreys avers that it is of the canon of the 'Southern School' of Buddhism.

57 *Aṅguttara Nikāya* v.33: 'The Lion: This, monks, is a name for the Tathāgata, the Arahant, the Fully Enlightened One.

When, monks, the Tathāgata expounds the Dhamma in an assembly, that is his lion's roar.' See Bhikkhu Bodhi (trans.), *The Numerical Discourses of the Buddha*, Wisdom Publications, Boston 2012, p. 1362; or F. L. Woodward (trans.), *The Book of the Gradual Sayings*, vol. v, Pali Text Society, Oxford 1972, pp. 23–4. But would the Buddha ever literally have heard a lion roar? Quite possibly. The Asiatic lion formerly occurred in south-eastern Europe, Black Sea basin, Caucasus, Mesopotamia and wide parts of India. Lions are depicted on top of some Aśoka pillars, for example the one at Sarnath.

58 There is a Mathuran standing Buddha in the Metropolitan Museum, New York, and another in the Government Archaeological Museum at Mathura, Uttar Pradesh.

59 There are several similar references in the *Dhammapada*; for example, verse 40 (trans. Sangharakshita): 'Perceiving the body to be (fragile) like a clay pot, (and) fortifying the mind as though it were a city, with the sword of wisdom make war on Mara.'

60 For example, in Edward Conze (trans.), *The Large Sūtra on Perfect Wisdom*, University of California Press, Berkeley 1975, ch. 2, p. 46, the bodhisattva is described as 'associated with resolute intention, and like the new moon'.

61 The bodhisattva ideal and the six perfections are described on p. 367ff., and also in Sangharakshita, *The Bodhisattva Ideal (Complete Works*, vol. 4).

62 A sense of the potential scope of the practice of the *pāramitās* from a Mahāyāna perspective is given by the section on the six perfections in Sangharakshita's *A Survey of Buddhism*, Windhorse Publications, Birmingham 2001, pp. 466–90 (*Complete Works*, vol. 1).

63 Edward Conze (trans.), *The Perfection of Wisdom in Eight Thousand Lines*, Four Seasons, Bolinas 1973, pp. 223–4.

CHAPTER 5

64 In his 1810 introduction to *Theory of Colours*, Goethe wrote:

> If the eye were not sensitive
> to the sun
> It could not perceive the
> sun.
> If God's own power did not
> lie within us,
> How could the divine
> enchant us?

This echoes the earlier Plotinus:

> Never did the eye see the
> sun unless it had at first
> become sun-like, and never
> can the soul have vision of
> the First Beauty unless itself
> be beautiful.

(*Enneads* i.6.9.)

65 Vinaya Piṭaka iii.3–4 (*Pārājika* 1.1) in I. B. Horner (trans.), *The Book of the Discipline*, part 1, Pali Text Society, Oxford 1996, pp. 6–7. Also Edward Conze et al. (eds.), *Buddhist Texts through the Ages*, Oneworld Publications, Oxford 1995, p. 60.

66 *Khandasaṃyutta, Saṃyutta Nikāya* iii.66; see Bhikkhu Bodhi (trans.), *Connected Discourses of the Buddha*, Wisdom Publications, Boston 2000, p. 901; or F. L. Woodward (trans.), *Kindred Sayings*, part 3, Pali Text Society, London 1975, p. 58.

67 *Lakkhaṇa Sutta, Dīgha Nikāya* 30 (iii.142–79); see M. Walshe (trans.), *The Long Discourses of the Buddha*, Wisdom Publications, Boston 1995, pp. 441–60; or T. W. Rhys Davids (trans.), *Dialogues of the Buddha*, part 3, Pali Text Society, Oxford 1991, pp. 137–53.

68 The Hindu *Law of Manu* states, 'Even an infant king must not be despised, from an idea he is a mere mortal; for he is a great deity in human form.' Trevor Ling, *The Buddha*, Temple Smith, London 1973, p. 54.

69 Vinaya Piṭaka ii.188 (*Cullavagga* 7.3) in I. B. Horner (trans.), *The Book of the Discipline*, part 5, Pali Text Society, Oxford 1992, p. 264.

70 Causing a schism in the sangha (Pāli *saṅghabheda*) was named in the early Buddhist tradition as one of the five 'heinous crimes', the other four being to murder one's father intentionally, to murder one's mother intentionally, to kill an *arhant*, and to wound a Buddha. These actions are said to bring immediate and disastrous karmic consequences (Sanskrit *ānantarya-karma*, Pāli *ānantarika-kamma*), with no possibility of any other mitigating karmic factors. In section 13 of the *Bahudhātuka Sutta, Majjhima Nikāya* 115 (iii.64–5), the Buddha is recorded as saying that it would be impossible for someone possessing right view to commit any of these five acts. See Bhikkhu Ñāṇamoli and Bhikkhu Bodhi (trans.), *The Middle Length Discourses of the Buddha*, Wisdom Publications, Boston 1995, pp. 928–9; or I. B. Horner (trans.), *Middle Length Sayings* vol. iii, Pali Text Society, London 1967, p. 108. It was a schism in the sangha of this disastrous sort that Devadatta attempted to cause, and which is described in the *Itivuttaka*:

There is one thing, bhikkhus, which, when it appears in the world, appears to the detriment of many persons, to the misery of many persons, to the loss, detriment and suffering of devas and humans. What is that one thing? It is disunity in the Sangha. When the Sangha is divided there are mutual quarrels, mutual recriminations, mutual denigrations and mutual expulsions. In this situation those who are unsympathetic are not converted and some who are sympathetic change their minds.

One who divides the Sangha Abides in a state of misery, in hell,
For the aeon's full duration.
Delighting in dissent, unrighteous,
He is deprived of security from bondage;
By dividing a unified Sangha He suffers in hell for an aeon.'

Itivuttaka 18 – this translation is from John D. Ireland (trans.), *The Udāna and the Itivuttaka*, Buddhist Publication Society, Kandy 1997, pp. 162–3.

However, in a seminar on Gampopa's *Precepts of the Gurus*, Sangharakshita, following the writings of Nalinaksha Dutt (see, for example, Dutt, *Buddhist Sects in India*, Motilal Banarsidass, Delhi 1998, pp. 37–8), draws a distinction between *saṅghabheda* of this sort and a skilful division in the sangha, the kind of natural split that began to occur even in the early days of Buddhism. 'If there's a sort of natural division in the sense that certain people are inclined to do things in this way, and certain people are inclined to do things in that way, let them separate positively and harmoniously.' He points out, though, that 'in more recent times *saṅghabheda* has been an absolute bugbear and the positive aspect of it has been quite forgotten in most Buddhist countries'. (This seminar, *Precepts of the Gurus* 1, held in September 1978, is available at www.freebuddhistaudio.com.)

71 These two incidents are described in the Vinaya Piṭaka ii.193–5 (*Cullavagga* 7.3); see I. B. Horner (trans.), *The Book of the Discipline*, part 5, Pali Text Society, Oxford 1992, pp. 271–4. The boulder did not harm the Buddha except that a splinter injured his foot, and the mad elephant let loose by Devadatta (the elephant's name was Nālāgiri) was pacified by the Buddha. The story of Devadatta's downfall is also told at Vinaya Piṭaka ii.202–3 (*Cullavagga* 7.3); ibid., pp. 283–5. See also the *Devadatta Sutta, Aṅguttara Nikāya* iv.160; E. M. Hare (trans.), *The Book of the Gradual Sayings*, vol. iv, Pali Text Society, Oxford 1996, pp. 109–10, and also Eugene Watson Burlingame (trans.), *Buddhist Legends*

(Dhammapada Commentary),
part 1, Pali Text Society, Luzac,
London 1969, p. 240.

72 In ch. 12 of the *White Lotus
Sūtra*, 'Devadatta', the Buddha
says that in a former life,
'through the good friendship
of Devadatta I was enabled
to become perfect in the Six
Pāramitās' and foretells that
Devadatta will become a
Buddha called Devarāja, 'King
of the Gods'. See Bunnō Katō
et al. (trans.), *The Threefold
Lotus Sūtra*, Weatherhill,
New York & Tokyo 1978,
p. 209; Leon Hurvitz (trans.),
*Scripture of the Lotus Blossom
of the Fine Dharma*, Columbia
University Press, New York
1976, p. 196.

73 The two merchants were called
Tapussa and Bhallika, and this
incident is described at Vinaya
Piṭaka i.4 (*Mahāvagga* 1.4);
see I. B. Horner (trans.), *The
Book of the Discipline*, part 4,
Pali Text Society, Oxford 1992,
pp. 5–6. However, it is Bhikkhu
Ñāṇamoli (*The Life of the
Buddha*, Buddhist Publications
Society, Kandy 1978, p. 34)
who has the merchants offer
the Buddha 'honey and rice
cakes'; I. B. Horner gives
the rather less appealing
translation 'barley-gruel and
honey balls'.

74 *Garava Sutta*: 'Reverence',
Saṃyutta Nikāya i.139. This
translation is from C. A. F.
Rhys Davids (trans.), *The Book
of the Kindred Sayings*, part 1,
Pali Text Society, Oxford 1989,

pp. 175–6. For an alternative
translation, see Bhikkhu
Bodhi (trans.), *The Connected
Discourses of the Buddha*,
Wisdom Publications, Boston
2000, pp. 234–5.

75 The twelve positive *nidānas*
are listed in the *Nidānavagga*,
Saṃyutta Nikāya ii.29; see
Bhikkhu Bodhi (trans.), *The
Connected Discourses of the
Buddha*, Wisdom Publications,
Boston 2000, pp. 553–6.

76 Section 29 of the *Cūḷavedalla
Sutta*, *Majjhima Nikāya* 44
(i.304); see Bhikkhu Ñāṇamoli
and Bhikkhu Bodhi (trans.),
*The Middle Length Discourses
of the Buddha*, Wisdom
Publications, Boston 1995,
p. 402; or I. B. Horner (trans.),
Middle Length Sayings, vol. i,
Pali Text Society, London 1967,
p. 367.

77 The six *gāravas* are listed in
the *Paṭhamāparihāna Sutta*,
Aṅguttara Nikāya iii.331; see
Bhikkhu Bodhi (trans.), *The
Numerical Discourses of the
Buddha*, Wisdom Publications,
Boston 2012, pp. 895–6; or E.
M. Hare (trans.), *The Book of
the Gradual Sayings*, vol. iii,
Pali Text Society, Oxford 1995,
pp. 232–3.

78 Alexander Pope, *Satires,
Epistles, and Odes of Horace*,
satire i, book 2, 1740.

CHAPTER 6

79 The story of Brahmā
Sahāmpati's request is told
in various places in the
scriptures, for example

in the *Ariyapariyesanā Sutta, Majjhima Nikāya* 26 (i.167–70); see Bhikkhu Ñāṇamoli and Bhikkhu Bodhi (trans.), *The Middle Length Discourses of the Buddha*, Wisdom Publications, Boston 1995, pp. 260–2; or I. B. Horner (trans.), *Middle Length Sayings*, vol. i, Pali Text Society, London 1967, pp. 211–3. Another version is to be found at *Saṃyutta Nikāya* i.137; see Bhikkhu Bodhi (trans.), *The Connected Discourses of the Buddha*, Wisdom Publications, Boston 2000, pp. 232–3; or C. A. F. Rhys Davids (trans.), *The Book of the Kindred Sayings*, part 1, Pali Text Society, Oxford 1997, p. 173. The exact translation 'but little dust in their eyes', used to describe those whose vision might readily be cleared by the Buddha's teaching, is also used in the translation of another well-known incident in the Buddha's life, the time when he sent his followers out to teach the Dharma: 'For, monks, there are beings who are pure, undefiled, with but little dust in their eyes, but who, because they have not heard the Dharma, are losing ground.' See J. J. Jones (trans.), *Mahāvastu*, vol. iii, Luzac, London 1956, p. 416.

80   The commentators on this verse interpret 'release their faith' in two different ways. It could mean 'let them let go of their wrong faith,' i.e. let them give up their faith in teachings that do not lead to Enlightenment. But it could also mean 'let them release their right faith,' i.e. let them free up their faith in teachings that do lead to Enlightenment. For example, translating *Saṃyutta Nikāya* i.137, C. A. F. Rhys Davids (*The Book of the Kindred Sayings*, part 1, Pali Text Society, Oxford 1989, p. 174) has 'Let those that hear renounce their faith', while Bhikkhu Bodhi (*Connected Discourses*, p. 233) has 'Let those who have ears release faith.' The story also appears at Vinaya Piṭaka i.7 (*Mahāvagga* 1.5), in which I. B. Horner gives the translation 'Let them renounce their faith' (*The Book of the Discipline*, part 4, Pali Text Society, Oxford 1996, p. 9). See also K. R. Norman, *The Group of Discourses* vol. ii, Pali Text Society, Oxford 1992, p. 390, in which he comments on a similar phrase in the *Sutta-Nipāta*. In the Brahmā Sahāmpati episode, he says, the phrase *pamuñcantu saddhaṃ* might mean 'proclaim their faith' or 'give up their (old) faith', i.e. wrong beliefs, or 'give up their desire' – the ambiguity is possibly intentional.

81   See, for example, the *Lalitavistara Sūtra* in Gwendolyn Bays (trans.), *The Voice of the Buddha*, Dharma Publishing, Berkeley 1983, vol. ii, p. 570; or the

Abhiniṣkramaṇa Sūtra in Samuel Beal (trans.), *The Romantic Legend of Śākya Buddha*, Motilal Banarsidass, Delhi 1985 (first published 1875), p. 237. This tradition is also preserved in the *Sinhala Thūpavaṃsa*.

82 See Vinaya Piṭaka i.9–14 (*Mahāvagga* 1.6), in I. B. Horner (trans.), *The Book of the Discipline*, part 4, Pali Text Society, Oxford 1996, pp. 13–21.

83 For example, in the *Ariyapariyesanā Sutta*, *Majjhima Nikāya* 26 (i.172), the Buddha describes his meeting with his first five disciples and how knowledge and vision arose in them as a result of his teaching, but says nothing of the content of his teaching; see Bhikkhu Ñāṇamoli and Bhikkhu Bodhi (trans.), *The Middle Length Discourses of the Buddha*, Wisdom Publications, Boston 1995, pp. 264–6; or I. B. Horner (trans.), *Middle Length Sayings*, vol. i, Pali Text Society, London 1967, p. 216.

84 *Kūtadanta Sutta*, *Dīgha Nikāya* 5; see M. Walshe (trans.), *The Long Discourses of the Buddha*, Wisdom Publications, Boston 1995, pp. 133–141; or T. W. Rhys Davids (trans.,) *Dialogues of the Buddha*, part 1, Pali Text Society, Oxford 1977, pp. 173–185.

85 This is the story of the farmer Kasi-Bhāradvāja, told in *Sutta-Nipāta* 1.4.

86 The name of the Buddha's critic on this occasion was Suppiya. See sections 1.1 to 1.6 of the *Brahmajāla Sutta*, *Dīgha Nikāya* 1 (i.1–3); M. Walshe (trans.), *The Long Discourses of the Buddha*, Wisdom Publications, Boston 1995, pp. 67–8; or T. W. Rhys Davids (trans.,) *Dialogues of the Buddha*, part 1, Pali Text Society, Oxford 1977, pp. 1–3.

87 The lay follower's name was Kevaddha. See sections 1 to 8 of the *Kevaddha Sutta*, *Dīgha Nikāya* 11 (i.211–4); M. Walshe (trans.), *The Long Discourses of the Buddha*, Wisdom Publications, Boston 1995, pp. 175–6; or T. W. Rhys Davids (trans.), *Dialogues of the Buddha*, part 1, Pali Text Society, Oxford 1977, pp. 276–9.

88 The novice monks were called Vāseṭṭha and Bhāradvaja. See sections 1 to 9 of the *Aggañña Sutta*, *Dīgha Nikāya* 27 (iii.80–4); M. Walshe (trans.), *The Long Discourses of the Buddha*, Wisdom Publications, Boston 1995, pp. 407–9; or T. W. Rhys Davids (trans.), *Dialogues of the Buddha*, part 3, Pali Text Society, Oxford 1977, pp. 77–81.

89 This was King Ajātasattu. See sections 1 to 12 of the *Sāmaññaphala Sutta*, *Dīgha Nikāya* 2 (i.47–50); M. Walshe (trans.), *The Long Discourses of the Buddha*, Wisdom Publications, Boston 1995, pp. 91–3; or T. W. Rhys

Davids (trans.), *Dialogues of the Buddha*, part 1, Pali Text Society, Oxford 1977, pp. 65–8.

90 *Kosambiya Sutta, Majjhima Nikāya* 48 (i.320–5); see Bhikkhu Ñāṇamoli and Bhikkhu Bodhi (trans.), *The Middle Length Discourses of the Buddha*, Wisdom Publications, Boston 1995, pp. 419–23; or I. B. Horner (trans.), *Middle Length Sayings*, vol. i, Pali Text Society, Oxford 1957, pp. 383–8.

91 This is the story of Suppabuddha, told in *Udāna* 5.3; see John D. Ireland (trans.), *The Udāna and the Itivuttaka*, Buddhist Publication Society, Kandy 1997, pp. 66–9.

92 This is the story of Visākhā, told in *Udāna* 8.8; see John D. Ireland (trans.), *The Udāna and the Itivuttaka*, Buddhist Publication Society, Kandy 1997, pp. 114–5.

93 Sections 5.23 to 5.30 of the *Mahāparinibbāna Sutta, Dīgha Nikāya* 16 (ii.148–52); see M. Walshe (trans.), *The Long Discourses of the Buddha*, Wisdom Publications, Boston 1995, pp. 267–9; or T. W. Rhys Davids (trans.), *Dialogues of the Buddha*, part 2, Pali Text Society, Oxford 1977, pp. 164–9.

94 The story of the golden flower is told in *The Gateless Gate*, case no. 6; see Mumonkan, *The Gateless Gate*, in K. Sekida (trans.), *Two Zen Classics*,

Weatherhill, New York 1996, p. 129; or Paul Reps, *Zen Flesh, Zen Bones*, Penguin 1972, p. 100.

95 The Vinaya Piṭaka is published by the Pali Text Society as *The Book of the Discipline*, parts 1–6, Sacred Books of the Buddhists vols. x–xv.

96 Translations of both the *Long Discourses (Dīgha Nikāya)* and the *Middle Length Discourses (Majjhima Nikāya)* are available from the Pali Text Society (as *Dialogues of the Buddha* and *Middle Length Sayings*) and Wisdom Publications (as *The Long Discourses of the Buddha* and *The Middle Length Discourses of the Buddha*) and also online.

97 The *Saṃyutta Nikāya* is published as Bhikkhu Bodhi (trans.), *The Connected Discourses of the Buddha*, Wisdom Publications, Boston 2000; and also *The Book of the Kindred Sayings*, parts 1–5, by the Pali Text Society, Oxford.

98 The *Aṅguttara Nikāya* is published by the Pali Text Society in five volumes as *The Book of the Gradual Sayings*, and by Wisdom Publications as *The Numerical Discourses of the Buddha*.

99 The story in which the Buddha-to-be was a robber is told in *Jātaka* no. 318, in H. T. Francis and R. A. Neil (trans.), *The Jātaka*, vol. iii, Pali Text Society, London 1973, pp. 39ff.

100 T. W. Rhys Davids, *Buddhism: Its History and Literature*, G. P. Putnam, London 1896, p. 78.

101 The Theravāda school of early Buddhism has preserved a collection of Pāli Abhidhamma teachings, and the Sarvastivāda and Yogācāra schools also have their Abhidharma collections. For an introduction to the literature of the Abhidharma, see ch. 7, 'The Fundamental Abhidharma', in Sangharakshita, *The Eternal Legacy* (*Complete Works*, vol. 14).

102 Edward Conze (trans.), *The Perfection of Wisdom in Eight Thousand Lines and its Verse Summary*, Four Seasons Foundation, San Francisco 1995.

103 Translations of the *White Lotus Sūtra* include W. E. Soothill (trans.), *The Lotus of the Wonderful Law*, Curzon Press, London 1987 and Bunnō Katō et al. (trans.), in *The Threefold Lotus Sūtra*, Kosei, Tokyo 1995. For Sangharakshita's commentary on the *sūtra*, see *Complete Works*, vol. 16.

104 For more about the 'turning about', the *parāvṛtti*, see Sangharakshita, *The Meaning of Conversion in Buddhism*, ch. 4 (*Complete Works*, vol. 2).

105 The *Gaṇḍavyūha* is the final section, 'Entry into the Realm of Reality', of the *Avataṃsaka Sūtra*, published as Thomas Cleary (trans.), *The Flower Ornament Scripture*, Shambhala Publications, Boston and London, 1993.

106 The *Lalitavistara Sūtra* is published as Gwendolyn Bays (trans.), *The Voice of the Buddha*, Dharma Publishing, Berkeley 1983.

107 *Maggasaṃyutta*, *Saṃyutta Nikāya* v.2; see Bhikkhu Bodhi (trans.), *The Connected Discourses of the Buddha*, Wisdom Publications, Boston 2000, pp. 1524–5; also F. L. Woodward (trans.), *The Book of the Kindred Sayings*, part 5, Pali Text Society, London 1979, p. 2.

CHAPTER 7

108 The Buddha is widely referred to by this title, which literally means 'Thus-come' or 'Thus-gone', so it means one who has 'gone beyond' conditioned existence – who leaves no trace.

109 A *śramaṇa* is someone who has taken up a homeless religious life. *Śramaṇa* literally means 'one who is washed, purified,' and it shares this literal meaning with the words 'Sufi' and 'Cathar'.

110 This story is told at Vinaya Piṭaka i.39 (*Mahāvagga* 1.23); see I. B. Horner (trans.), *The Book of the Discipline*, part 4, Pali Text Society, Oxford 1996, pp. 52–4.

111 Thomas Gray, 'Elegy in a Country Churchyard', 1750.

112 *Mahāsaccaka Sutta*, *Majjhima Nikāya* 36 (i.248); see Bhikkhu Ñāṇamoli and Bhikkhu Bodhi

(trans.), *The Middle Length Discourses of the Buddha*, Wisdom Publications, Boston 1995, p. 341; or I. B. Horner (trans.), *Middle Length Sayings*, vol. i, Pali Text Society, Oxford 1957, p. 303.

113 The five *niyamas* are listed in the Abhidharma in, for example, the *Aṭṭhasālinī*, Buddhaghosa's commentary on the *Dhammasaṅgani*, published as Pe Maung Tin (trans.), *The Expositor*, Pali Text Society, London 1921, p. 360.

114 *Aṅguttara Nikāya* iii.415; see Bhikkhu Bodhi (trans.), *The Numerical Discourses of the Buddha*, Wisdom Publications 2012, p. 963; or E. M. Hare (trans.), *The Book of the Gradual Sayings*, vol. iii, Pali Text Society, Oxford 1995, p. 294.

115 For more about the sevenfold classification of karma, see Sangharakshita, *The Three Jewels*, Windhorse Publications, Birmingham 1998, pp. 63–6 (*Complete Works*, vol. 2).

116 This distinction is found in the Theravādin commentarial tradition; for more about it, see Sangharakshita, *A Survey of Buddhism*, Windhorse Publications, Birmingham 2001, p. 170.

117 This story (of the abbot reborn as a donkey) is told by Alexandra David-Neel in ch. 1 of *Magic and Mystery in Tibet*, Corgi Books, London 1971,

pp. 45–6. The name of the hermit in the story was Dugpa Kunlegs, and Alexandra David-Neel says that 'his eccentricities – sometimes coarse ... have given birth to a number of stories in the style of Rabelais, much appreciated in Tibet'.

118 The *arhant* who was born a dwarf was Lakuṇṭaka Bhaddiya Thera. There are many stories about him in the commentarial tradition. According to one of them, found in the *Theragāthā* commentary (i.469ff.) and in the *Apadāna* (ii.489f.), in Kassapa Buddha's day he was the chief architect entrusted with the building of the stupa over the Buddha's relics, and when a dispute arose as to how big the stupa should be, he decided in favour of a small one; hence his small stature in his last life.

119 For weighty karma, see the *Abhidhammattha Saṅgaha*, published as Narada Maha Thera (trans.), *A Manual of Abhidhamma*, Buddhist Missionary Society, Kuala Lumpur 1987, pp. 294–5.

120 See Sangharakshita, *The Three Jewels*, Windhorse Publications, Birmingham 1998, pp. 65–6 (*Complete Works*, vol. 2).

121 'Burnt Norton', *Four Quartets*, 1944.

122 There is a chapter on this theme, 'The Evidence for Rebirth', in Nagapriya, *Exploring Karma and Rebirth*,

Windhorse Publications,
Birmingham 2004, pp. 111–7.

123 Nagapriya has made a start on
this work in *Exploring Karma
and Rebirth*, Windhorse
Publications, Birmingham
2004.

124 See, for example, section 29
of the *Bhayabherava Sutta,
Majjhima Nikāya* 4 (i.22);
Bhikkhu Ñāṇamoli and
Bhikkhu Bodhi (trans.), *The
Middle Length Discourses of
the Buddha*, pp. 105–6; or
I. B. Horner (trans.), *Middle
Length Sayings*, vol. i, Pali Text
Society, Oxford 1957, pp. 28–
9. See also section 40 of the
*Mahāsaccaka Sutta, Majjhima
Nikāya* 36 (i.248); Bhikkhu
Ñāṇamoli and Bhikkhu Bodhi
(trans.), *The Middle Length
Discourses of the Buddha*,
Wisdom Publications, Boston
1995, p. 341; or I. B. Horner
(trans.), *Middle Length
Sayings*, vol. i, Pali Text
Society, Oxford 1957, p. 303.

125 The six *abhijñās* (Pāli
abhiññās) consist of five
mundane (*lokiya*) powers
which are attainable through
concentration (*samādhi*):
the ability (1) to travel any
distance or take on any form at
will, (2) to see everything, (3)
to hear everything, (4) to know
another's thoughts, and (5) to
recollect former existences;
and a sixth which is attainable
through insight (*vipassanā*),
the extinction of the *āsavas*.
The *abhiññās* are enumerated
in many places in the Pāli

canon; for example, in the
*Ākankheyya Sutta, Majjhima
Nikāya* 6 (i.34–5); see Bhikkhu
Ñāṇamoli and Bhikkhu
Bodhi (trans.), *The Middle
Length Discourses of the
Buddha*, Wisdom Publications,
Boston 1995, pp. 116–7; or
I. B. Horner (trans.), *Middle
Length Sayings*, vol. i, Pali
Text Society, Oxford 1957,
pp. 43–4.

CHAPTER 8

126 *Anuradha Sutta, Saṃyutta
Nikāya* iii.257; see Bhikkhu
Bodhi (trans.), *The Connected
Discourses of the Buddha*,
Wisdom Publications,
Boston 2000, p. 1033; or
F. L. Woodward (trans.), *The
Book of the Kindred Sayings*,
part 3, Pali Text Society,
London 1975, p. 204.

127 The account of the Buddha's
last days is given in the
*Mahāparinibbāna Sutta, Dīgha
Nikāya* 16; see M. Walshe
(trans.), *The Long Discourses
of the Buddha*, Wisdom
Publications, Boston 1995,
pp. 231–77; or T. W. Rhys
Davids (trans.), *Dialogues
of the Buddha*, part 2, Pali
Text Society, Oxford 1977,
pp. 78–191.

128 Section 2.25 of the
*Mahāparinibbāna Sutta, Dīgha
Nikāya* 16 (ii.100); see M.
Walshe (trans.), *The Long
Discourses of the Buddha*,
Wisdom Publications, Boston
1995, p. 245; or T. W. Rhys
Davids (trans.), *Dialogues*

of the Buddha, part 2, Pali Text Society, Oxford 1977, pp. 107–8.

129   Sections 4.13 to 4.20 and section 4.42 of the *Mahāparinibbāna Sutta, Dīgha Nikāya* 16 (ii.126–8); see M. Walshe (trans.), *The Long Discourses of the Buddha*, Wisdom Publications, Boston 1995, pp. 256–7 and p. 261; or T. W. Rhys Davids (trans.), *Dialogues of the Buddha*, part 2, Pali Text Society, Oxford 1977, pp. 137–9 and p. 148.

130   Section 5.17 of the *Mahāparinibbāna Sutta, Dīgha Nikāya* 16 (ii.146); see M. Walshe (trans.), *The Long Discourses of the Buddha*, Wisdom Publications, Boston 1995, p. 266; or T. W. Rhys Davids (trans.), *Dialogues of the Buddha*, part 2, Pali Text Society, Oxford 1977, p. 161.

131   Sections 5.13 and 5.14 of the *Mahāparinibbāna Sutta, Dīgha Nikāya* 16 (ii.143–4); see M. Walshe (trans.), *The Long Discourses of the Buddha*, Wisdom Publications, Boston 1995, p. 265; or T. W. Rhys Davids (trans.), *Dialogues of the Buddha*, part 2, Pali Text Society, Oxford 1977, pp. 158–9.

132   Section 6.7 of the *Mahāparinibbāna Sutta, Dīgha Nikāya* 16 (ii.156); see M. Walshe (trans.), *The Long Discourses of the Buddha*, Wisdom Publications, Boston 1995, p. 270; or T. W. Rhys

Davids (trans.), *Dialogues of the Buddha*, part 2, Pali Text Society, Oxford 1977, p. 173.

133   These descriptions of the *dhyānas* are found in the Pāli canon in, for example, sections 75 to 82 of the *Sāmaññaphala Sutta, Dīgha Nikāya* 2 (i.73–6); see M. Walshe (trans.), *The Long Discourses of the Buddha*, Wisdom Publications, Boston 1995, pp. 102–4; or T. W. Rhys Davids (trans.), *Dialogues of the Buddha*, part 1, Pali Text Society, Oxford 1977, pp. 84–6.

134   The idea of five methods of meditation as antidotes to the five poisons or *kleśas* identified in the Mahāyāna tradition was first suggested to Sangharakshita by his teacher C. M. Chen, whom he knew in Kalimpong. For Mr Chen's own account, see C. M. Chen, *Buddhist Meditation, Systematic and Practical*, published by Dr Yutang Lin, El Cerrito 1989, chapter 8, 'The Five Fundamental Meditations to Cure the Five Poisons', pp. 326–30). See also Sangharakshita, *The Purpose and Practice of Buddhist Meditation*, Ibis Publications, Ledbury 2012, pp. 29–35; or volume 5 of the *Complete Works*.

135   The Buddha describes these twelve links in sections 1 to 9 of the *Mahānidāna Sutta, Dīgha Nikāya* 15 (ii.55–8); see M. Walshe (trans.), *The Long Discourses of the*

Buddha, Wisdom Publications,
Boston 1995, pp. 223–4; or
T. W. Rhys Davids (trans.),
Dialogues of the Buddha, part
2, Pali Text Society, Oxford
1977, pp. 50–5.

136 The last line of *The Light of
Asia*, by Sir Edwin Arnold.

137 'The Tibetan Tradition: Its
Presiding Idea' is ch. 9 of
Marco Pallis, *The Way and
the Mountain*, Peter Owen
Limited, London 1961.

138 The six element practice
is found in, for example,
the *Mahāhatthipadopama
Sutta, Majjhima Nikāya*
28 (i.184–91); Bhikkhu
Ñāṇamoli and Bhikkhu
Bodhi (trans.), *The Middle
Length Discourses of the
Buddha*, Wisdom Publications,
Boston 1995, pp. 278–85; or
I. B. Horner (trans.), *Middle
Length Sayings*, vol. i, Pali
Text Society, Oxford 1957,
pp. 230–8.

CHAPTER 9

139 This story is found in the
Doṇa Sutta, Aṅguttara Nikāya
iii.223: see Bhikkhu Bodhi
(trans.), *The Numerical
Discourses of the Buddha*,
Wisdom Publications 2012,
pp. 425–6; or F. L. Woodward
(trans.), *The Book of the
Gradual Sayings*, vol. ii, Pali
Text Society, Oxford 1995,
pp. 43–4. It resembles a story
told in the *Ariyapariyesanā
Sutta, Majjhima Nikāya* 26
(i.170–1) about a meeting
between the Buddha and the

first person who met him
after his Enlightenment, a
man by the name of Upaka,
but the details of the story
make it clear that in this
case the meeting with
Doṇa is meant; Bhikkhu
Ñāṇamoli and Bhikkhu
Bodhi (trans.), *The Middle
Length Discourses of the
Buddha*, Wisdom Publications,
Boston 1995, pp. 263–4; or
I. B. Horner (trans.), *Middle
Length Sayings*, vol. i, Pali
Text Society, Oxford 1957,
pp. 214–5.

140 In the *Aggivacchagotta Sutta,
Majjhima Nikāya* 72 (i.484–5),
the Buddha is asked a whole
range of speculative questions
of this kind by the wanderer
Vacchagotta; see Bhikkhu
Ñāṇamoli and Bhikkhu
Bodhi (trans.), *The Middle
Length Discourses of the
Buddha*, Wisdom Publications,
Boston 1995, pp. 590–1; or
I. B. Horner (trans.), *Middle
Length Sayings*, vol. ii, Pali
Text Society, Oxford 1957,
pp. 162–5.

141 *Dhammapada* 179, trans.
Sangharakshita.

142 This is E. M. Hare's translation
of verse 1076 of the *Sutta-
Nipāta*, in *Woven Cadences*,
Oxford University Press 1945,
p. 155.

143 Ibid., verse 1070, p. 154.

144 This story is told briefly
in section 1.16 of the
*Mahāparinibbāna Sutta,
Dīgha Nikāya* 16 (ii.82); see
M. Walshe (trans.), *The Long*

Discourses of the Buddha,
Wisdom Publications,
Boston 1995, pp. 234–5; or
T. W. Rhys Davids (trans.),
Dialogues of the Buddha, part
2, Pali Text Society, Oxford
1977, pp. 87–9. For another
perspective on the story, see
the *Sampasādanīya Sutta,
Dīgha Nikāya* 28 (Walshe,
pp. 417–25), in which,
following this exchange with
the Buddha, Sāriputta embarks
on a fervent and extended
rejoicing in the way the
Buddha teaches the Dharma.

145 The Buddha's ten powers
are described in the
*Mahāsīhanāda Sutta,
Majjhima Nikāya* 12 (i.69–
71); see Bhikkhu Ñāṇamoli
and Bhikkhu Bodhi (trans.),
*The Middle Length Discourses
of the Buddha,* pp. 166–7; or
I. B. Horner (trans.), *Middle
Length Sayings,* vol. i, Pali
Text Society, Oxford 1957,
pp.93–5. The ten powers and
eighteen special attributes are
listed in J. J. Jones (trans.),
Mahāvastu, vol. i, Pali Text
Society, London 1987,
pp. 125–6.

146 Here, the intersection of
the timeless moment
Is England and nowhere.
Never and always.

'Little Gidding', *Four
Quartets,* 1944.

147 Wong Mou-Lam's translation,
in Dwight Goddard (ed.), *A*

Buddhist Bible, Beacon Press,
Boston 1970, pp. 517–8:

While there is only one
system of Dharma, some
disciples realise it quicker
than others but the reason
why the names, 'Sudden'
and 'Gradual', are given is
because some disciples are
superior to others in their
mental dispositions. So far
as the Dharma is concerned,
the distinction of Sudden
and Gradual does not exist.

148 The story of Aṅgulimāla's
encounter with the Buddha
is told in the *Aṅgulimāla
Sutta, Majjhima Nikāya* 86;
see Bhikkhu Ñāṇamoli and
Bhikkhu Bodhi (trans.), *The
Middle Length Discourses of
the Buddha,* pp. 710–7; or
I. B. Horner (trans.), *Middle
Length Sayings,* vol. ii, Pali
Text Society, Oxford 1957,
pp. 284–92.

149 For more about the *trikāya*
doctrine, see ch. 2, section 6,
of Sangharakshita, *A Survey
of Buddhism,* Windhorse
Publications, Birmingham
2001, pp. 282–97 (*Complete
Works,* vol. 1).

150 *Diamond Sūtra* 7.i; see
Edward Conze (trans.),
Buddhist Wisdom Books,
Unwin Hyman, London
1988, pp. 62–3. For further
comment on these verses,
see Sangharakshita, *Wisdom
Beyond Words,* Windhorse
Publications, Birmingham

2000, p. 170 (*Complete Works*, vol. 14).

151 The story of Vakkali is told in different ways in the Pāli literature. The central message of each of the stories is the same – that he who sees the Dhamma sees the Buddha – but the context is different. It is the *Dhammapada* commentary that describes Vakkali's fascination with the Buddha's form; see Eugene Watson Burlingame (trans.), *Buddhist Legends, Translated from the Original Pali Text of the Dhammapada Commentary*, Harvard University Press 1921, part 3, xxv.11, pp. 262–3. In this version, the Buddha's advice is not enough to satisfy Vakkali; when forbidden to keep following the Buddha around, he threatens suicide and is only pacified when the Buddha creates an image of himself specially for Vakkali. After the Buddha says a few more words, Vakkali attains arhantship. In the *Saṃyutta Nikāya* (iii.120) the story is rather different. Vakkali is ill, and the Buddha visits him. It is when Vakkali says how he has wanted for a long time to set eyes on the Buddha that the Buddha tells him that 'he who sees the Dhamma sees me'. The Buddha reassures Vakkali that he will have a good death. The text says that after the Buddha's departure, Vakkali 'used the knife' (Bhikkhu Bodhi's translation). The Buddha, seeing a swirl of black smoke in the distance, says that it is Māra looking for Vakkali's consciousness, but he won't find it, because Vakkali has attained Nibbāna. See Bhikkhu Bodhi (trans.), *The Connected Discourses of the Buddha*, Wisdom Publications, Boston 2000, pp. 938–41; or F. L. Woodward (trans.), *The Book of the Kindred Sayings*, part 3, Pali Text Society, London 1975, p. 101–6.

WHAT IS THE DHARMA?

INTRODUCTION

152 D. T. Suzuki, *The Essence of Buddhism*, Buddhist Society, London 1947, p. 40.

153 *Dhammapada* 5, trans. Sangharakshita.

154 *Dhammapada* 279, trans. Sangharakshita.

155 The *Mahāmaṅgala Sutta* (the fourth *sutta* of the Minor Chapter in the *Sutta-Nipāta*) doesn't mention the eight worldly *dhammas* specifically. The eleventh verse of the *sutta* refers to 'worldly vicissitudes' in H. Saddhatissa's translation, (*Sutta-Nipāta*, Curzon Press, London 1985, p. 30) and 'all terrestrial happenings' in another; this is understood to refer in particular to the eight worldly *dhammas* enumerated

here. The scriptural *locus classicus* is the *Lokavipatti Sutta, Aṅguttara Nikāya* iv.157–9: see Bhikkhu Bodhi (trans.), *The Numerical Discourses of the Buddha*, Wisdom Publications 2012, pp. 1116–9; or E.M. Hare (trans.), *The Book of the Gradual Sayings*, vol. iv, Pali Text Society, Oxford 1995, pp. 107–9. They are also enumerated by Buddhaghosa at *Visuddhimagga* 683; see Buddhaghosa, *The Path of Purity*, trans. Pe Maung Tin, Pali Text Society, London 1975, p. 838.

156   The text of the *Tiratana Vandanā* is found in several places in the Pāli canon, notably in the *Mahāparinibbāna Sutta, Dīgha Nikāya* 16 (ii.93), in the section called the Mirror of the Dharma. See M. Walshe (trans.), *The Long Discourses of the Buddha*, Wisdom Publications, Boston 1995, p. 241; or T. W. Rhys Davids (trans.), *Dialogues of the Buddha*, part 2, Pali Text Society, Oxford 1977, pp. 99–100. Buddhaghosa discusses the elements of the text in great detail in the *Visuddhimagga* (198–221): see *The Path of Purification*, trans. Bhikkhu Ñāṇamoli, Buddhist Publication Society, Kandy 1991, pp. 192–218; or or Pe Maung Tin (trans.), *The Path of Purity*, Pali

Text Society, London 1975, pp. 227–56.

157   The full canon has been translated into English and published by the pioneering Pali Text Society (founded in 1881); other translations have become available in recent years, notably those published by Wisdom Publications, and by the website accesstoinsight. org.

158   Two monks [it is related] of fine cultivated language and fine eloquent speech, came to the Buddha and said: 'Lord, here monks of various names, clan-names, races [or castes] and families are corrupting the Buddha's words by repeating them in their own dialects. Let us put them into Vedic (*chandaso aropema*).' The Lord rebuked them: 'Deluded men! How can you say this? This will not lead to the conversion of the unconverted.'… And he delivered a sermon and commanded all the monks: 'You are not to put the Buddha's words into Vedic. Whosoever does so shall be guilty of an offence. I authorise you, monks, to learn the Buddha's words each in his own dialect (*sakkaya niruttiyā*).'

Vinaya Piṭaka ii.139 (*Cullavaga* 5.33). This translation is given by

Franklin Edgerton in *Buddhist Hybrid Sanskrit Language and Literature*, Benares 1965, p. 5. See also I. B. Horner (trans.), *The Book of the Discipline*, part 5, Pali Text Society, Oxford 1992, pp. 193–4.

159 O Bhikṣus, my words should be accepted by the wise, not out of regard for me, but after due investigation – just as gold is accepted as true only after heating, cutting and rubbing.

The *Tattvasaṅgraha of Shāntarakṣita*, translated by Ganganatha Jha, Motilal Banarsidass, Delhi 1986, vol. ii, p. 1558. text 3588.

160 See, for example, section 15 of the *Aggivacchagotta Sutta, Majjhima Nikāya* 72 (i.486); Bhikkhu Ñāṇamoli and Bhikkhu Bodhi (trans.), *The Middle Length Discourses of the Buddha*, p. 592; or I. B. Horner (trans.), *Middle Length Sayings*, vol. ii, Pali Text Society, Oxford 1957, pp. 164–5.

161 See D. T. Suzuki, *The Laṅkāvatāra Sūtra*, 3.61, George Routledge, London 1932, pp. 124–5.

162 Plato, *Phaedrus and the Seventh and Eighth Letters*, translated with an introduction by Walter Hamilton, Harmondsworth 1975, p. 136.

163 See sections 13 and 14 of the *Alagaddūpama Sutta, Majjhima Nikāya* 22 (i.134–5); Bhikkhu Ñāṇamoli and Bhikkhu

Bodhi (trans.), *The Middle Length Discourses of the Buddha*, Wisdom Publications, Boston 1995, pp. 228–9; or I. B. Horner (trans.), *Middle Length Sayings*, vol. i, Pali Text Society, Oxford 1957, pp. 173–4.

164 This story of Mahāprajāpatī Gautami is to be found at Vinaya Piṭaka ii.258–9 (*Cullavagga* 10.5); see I. B. Horner (trans.), *The Book of the Discipline*, part 5, Pali Text Society, Oxford 1992, p. 359; and *Aṅguttara Nikāya* iv.280–1, in E. M. Hare (trans.), *Gradual Sayings*, vol. iv, Pali Text Society, Oxford 1995, pp. 186–7; and Bhikkhu Bodhi (trans.), *The Numerical Discourses of the Buddha*, Wisdom Publications, Boston 2012, p. 1193.

165 The Jōdō Shinshū school of Buddhism, founded by the Japanese monk Shinran in the thirteenth century CE makes a distinction between the path of dependence on 'self-power' (*jiriki*) and the path of dependence on 'other-power' (*tariki*), which it itself follows. See the essay 'Religion as Revelation and as Discovery' in Sangharakshita, *Crossing the Stream*, Windhorse Publications, Glasgow 1987 (*Complete Works*, vol. 7).

166 The Bhabra Rock Edict in N. A. Nikam and R. McKeon (trans.), *The Edicts of Ashoka*, Asia Publishing House, Bombay 1959, p. 61.

167   *Adhyāśayasasaṃcodana Sūtra.*
     Quoted by Śāntideva. See
     Compendium of Teachings
     (*Śikṣā-samuccaya*), Cecil
     Bendall and W. H. D. Rouse
     (trans.), Motilal Banarsidass,
     Delhi 1971, p. 17.

     CHAPTER I
168   See Vināya Piṭaka i.21
     (*Mahāvagga* 1.11), in
     I. B. Horner (trans.), *The Book
     of the Discipline*, part 4, Pali
     Text Society, Oxford 1996,
     p. 28.
169   See Vināya Piṭaka i.39–41
     (*Mahāvagga* 1.23), in
     I. B. Horner (trans.), *The Book
     of the Discipline*, part 4, Pali
     Text Society, Oxford 1996,
     pp. 52–4.
170   A *sūtra* (Sanskrit) or *sutta*
     (Pāli) is a 'discourse', and is
     the most characteristic of the
     literary forms found in the
     Buddhist scriptural canons.
     They vary in length from a few
     lines to several volumes. Most
     sūtras purport to be records
     of the Buddha's own teaching,
     but some are teachings given
     by his leading disciples and
     later affirmed by the Buddha.
171   *Saṃyutta Nikāya* i.138; see
     Bhikkhu Bodhi (trans.), *The
     Connected Discourses of the
     Buddha*, Wisdom Publications,
     Boston 2000, p. 233; or C. A.
     F. Rhys Davids (trans.), *The
     Book of the Kindred Sayings*,
     part 1, Pali Text Society,
     Oxford 1989, p. 174.
172   See, for example, Bunnō
     Katō et al. (trans.), *The

Threefold Lotus Sūtra,
Kosei Publishing Co., Tokyo
1995, pp. 129–134; and
see also Sangharakshita's
commentary in *Complete
Works*, vol. 16.
173   *Aṅguttara Nikāya* iv.274–6;
     see Bhikkhu Bodhi (trans.),
     *The Numerical Discourses
     of the Buddha*, Wisdom
     Publications, Boston 2012,
     pp. 1189–90; or E. M. Hare
     (trans.), *Gradual Sayings*,
     vol. iv, Pali Text Society,
     Oxford 1995, pp. 181–5.
174   *Aṅguttara Nikāya* i.23–6; see
     Bhikkhu Bodhi (trans.), *The
     Numerical Discourses of the
     Buddha*, Wisdom Publications,
     Boston 2012, pp. 109–111;
     or F. L. Woodward (trans.),
     Gradual Sayings, vol. i, Pali
     Text Society, Oxford 2000,
     pp. 16–21.
175   The story of Aṅgulimāla –
     his name means 'necklace
     of fingers' – is told in the
     *Aṅgulimāla Sutta, Majjhima
     Nikāya* 86; see Bhikkhu
     Ñāṇamoli and Bhikkhu
     Bodhi (trans.), *The Middle
     Length Discourses of the
     Buddha*, Wisdom Publications,
     Boston 1995, pp. 710–7; or
     I. B. Horner (trans.), *Middle
     Length Sayings*, vol. ii, Pali
     Text Society, Oxford 1957,
     pp. 284–92.
176   Milarepa's extraordinary life
     story is told in L. Lhalungpa's
     The Life of Milarepa, London
     1987. See also Sangharakshita,
     Complete Works, vols. 18
     and 19.

177 For the story of King Aśoka, see John S. Strong, *The Legend of King Aśoka: A Study and Translation of the Aśokavādana*, Princeton University Press, Princeton 1983.

178 *Nidānasaṃyutta, Saṃyutta Nikāya* ii.92; see Bhikkhu Bodhi (trans.), *The Connected Discourses of the Buddha*, Wisdom Publications, Boston 2000, p. 594; or C. A. F. Rhys Davids (trans.), *The Book of the Kindred Sayings*, part 2, Pali Text Society, London 1979, p. 64.

179 For more about these myths, see, for example, Vessantara, *Meeting the Buddhas*, Windhorse Publications, Birmingham 1994, pp. 198–210 and p. 146.

180 For example, section 22 of the *Mahātaṇhāsaṅkhaya Sutta, Majjhima Nikāya* 38 (i.264); see Bhikkhu Ñāṇamoli and Bhikkhu Bodhi (trans.), *The Middle Length Discourses of the Buddha*, Wisdom Publications, Boston 1995, p. 357; or I. B. Horner (trans.), *Middle Length Sayings*, vol. i, Pali Text Society, Oxford 1967, p. 320.

181 See Vinaya Piṭaka i.10 (*Mahāvagga* 1.6) in I. B. Horner, *The Book of the Discipline*, part 4, Pali Text Society, Oxford 1996, p. 15. The *Maggasaṃyutta, Saṃyutta Nikāya* v.1–62, contains many teachings connected with the Noble Eightfold Path; see Bhikkhu Bodhi (trans.), *The Connected Discourses of the Buddha*, Wisdom Publications, Boston 2000, pp. 1523–66; or F. L. Woodward (trans.), *The Book of the Kindred Sayings*, part 5, Pali Text Society, London 1979, pp. 1–50. See also Sangharakshita, *The Buddha's Noble Eightfold Path (Complete Works*, vol. 1).

182 *Saṅgīti Sutta, Dīgha Nikāya* 33 (iii.209); see M. Walshe (trans.), *The Long Discourses of the Buddha*, Wisdom Publications, Boston 1995, p. 480; or T. W. Rhys Davids (trans.), *Dialogues of the Buddha*, part 3, Pali Text Society, Oxford 1991, p. 202.

183 The originators of what has become known as the Tibetan wheel of life were followers of the Sarvastivāda school of Indian Buddhism, which formed around the third century BCE; its adherents used to paint images of the wheel of life inside the gateways to their monasteries. For a fuller description of the *bhavacakra*, the 'wheel of becoming', see pp. 192ff.

184 There are many references to the twelve cyclical *nidānas* in the Pāli canon. For example, sections 17–21 of the *Mahātaṇhāsaṅkhaya Sutta, Majjhima Nikāya* 38 (i.261–4); see Bhikkhu Ñāṇamoli and Bhikkhu Bodhi (trans.), *The Middle Length Discourses of the Buddha*, Wisdom Publications, Boston 1995,

pp. 353–7; or I. B. Horner (trans.), *Middle Length Sayings*, vol. i, Pali Text Society, Oxford 1967, pp. 318–9. Alternatively see sections 1 to 9 of the *Mahānidāna Sutta*, *Dīgha Nikāya* 15 (ii.55–9): M. Walshe (trans.), *The Long Discourses of the Buddha*, Wisdom Publications, Boston 1995, pp. 223–4; or T. W. Rhys Davids (trans.), *Dialogues of the Buddha*, part 2, Pali Text Society, Oxford 1977, pp. 50–5. The positive *nidānas* are less frequently enumerated, but are to be found at *Saṃyutta Nikāya* ii.29–32; see Bhikkhu Bodhi (trans.), *The Connected Discourses of the Buddha*, Wisdom Publications, Boston 2000, pp. 553–6; or C. A. F. Rhys Davids, *Book of the Kindred Sayings*, part 2, Pali Text Society, Oxford 1997, p. 27.

CHAPTER 2

185 The pioneer of translations of Buddhist works into Western languages was Eugene Burnouf, the French philologist whose work suddenly drew Buddhism to the attention of the Western world. (His French translation of the *Lotus Sūtra* was published in 1852.) In 1879 Sir Edwin Arnold published his epic poem *The Light of Asia*; it was this work that formed the popular view of the Buddha's life and personality. See Stephen Batchelor, *The Awakening of the West*, Parallax, Berkeley 1994, ch. 14.

186 An example of someone who had this attitude was Vakkali, whose story is told in chapter 9 of *Who is the Buddha?*; see p. 150.

187 Several different sets of *nidānas* are enumerated in the *Nidānasaṃyutta*, *Saṃyutta Nikāya* ii.1–132; see Bhikkhu Bodhi (trans.), *The Connected Discourses of the Buddha*, Wisdom Publications, Boston 2000, pp. 533–620; or C. A. F. Rhys Davids, *Book of the Kindred Sayings*, part 2, Pali Text Society, Oxford 1997, pp. 1–93. The five *nidānas* are craving, grasping, existence, birth, ageing/death; the ten are the twelve minus ignorance and formations, and there are many other chains of *nidānas*, longer and shorter. For more on why there are these different sets of *nidānas*, see Sangharakshita, *A Survey of Buddhism*, Windhorse Publications, Birmingham 2001, pp. 128ff. (*Complete Works*, vol. 1).

188 The water of the Ganges may wash away past sins, but there is a saying that sins perch on the top of trees. When a man comes out of the Ganges and stands under a tree, the sins drop over his shoulders and seize upon him; these old sins ride him, as it were.

Original Gospel of Ramakrishna, abridged Alexander Lipski, World Wisdom Inc. 2011, p. 5.

189 *Skandha* literally means 'heap' or 'aggregate'. The Buddha taught that what we think of as the self or personality is made up of five 'heaps': *rūpa* (form); *vedanā* (feeling); *samjñā* (perception); *saṃskāras* (volitions); and *vijñāna*. There is no aspect of 'self' that does not fall into one of these categories, and they are all characterized by the three *lakṣaṇas*: impermanence, unsatisfactoriness, and insubstantiality. It is our clinging to the notion of a self which is somehow exempt from these characteristics that is the cause of our suffering. In the *Dhammacakkappavattana Sutta*, *Samyutta Nikāya* v.421, the Buddha is recorded as saying, after a description of the ways in which suffering occurs, 'in brief, the five aggregates subject to clinging are suffering'; see Bhikkhu Bodhi (trans.), *The Connected Discourses of the Buddha*, Wisdom Publications, Boston 2000, p. 1844; or F. L. Woodward (trans.), *Book of the Kindred Sayings*, part 5, Pali Text Society, Oxford 1979, p. 357). This is what is being referred to at the beginning of the *Heart Sūtra*: 'The Bodhisattva of Compassion, when he meditated deeply, saw the emptiness of all five *skandhas*, and sundered the bonds that caused him suffering.' The *Samyutta Nikāya* (iii.1–188) has a whole section on the *skandhas* (Pāli *khandas*), the *Khandasamyutta*; see Bhikkhu Bodhi, ibid., pp.853–983; or *Book of the Kindred Sayings*, part 3, Pali Text Society, London 1975, pp. 1–154.

190 The Tibetan name for the work usually known as the *Tibetan Book of the Dead* is *Bardo Thödol*, which literally means 'the liberation through hearing in the in-between state'. The text, said to have been composed by the eighth-century guru of Tibet Padmasambhava, is traditionally spoken to a corpse, guiding the consciousness of the deceased through the experience of the *bardo*. See *The Tibetan Book of the Dead*, Francesca Fremantle and Chogyam Trungpa (trans.), Shambhala Publications, Boston and London 1987.

191 *Bhagavad Gītā*, 2.20.

192 The *satkāryavāda* line of reasoning was 'held at the time of Nāgārjuna by the [Hindu] Sāṃkhya School ... it may be regarded as the representative Brahminical view of causation'; the *asatkāryavāda* 'was upheld by the Sarvāstivādins and Sautrāntikas, and is the representative Hīnayāna view.' Sangharakshita, *A Survey*

of Buddhism, Windhorse
Publications, Birmingham
2001, p. 352 (*Complete
Works*, vol. 1).

193 This is implied by
Buddhaghosa at
Visuddhimagga 602: 'There
is no doer of a deed/ Or one
who reaps the deed's result;
/ Phenomena alone roll
on – / No other view than
this is right.' See Bhikkhu
Ñāṇamoli (trans.), *The Path
of Purification*, Buddhist
Publication Society, Kandy
1991, p. 622; or Pe Maung Tin
(trans.), *The Path of Purity*,
Pali Text Society, London
1975, p. 726.

194 Reference to these four kinds
of attachment is made in
*Nidānasaṃyutta, Saṃyutta
Nikāya* ii.3; see Bhikkhu
Bodhi (trans.), *The Connected
Discourses of the Buddha*,
Wisdom Publications, Boston
2000, p. 535; or C. A. F. Rhys
Davids, *Book of the Kindred
Sayings*, part 2, Pali Text
Society, Oxford 1989, p. 4.

195 *Saṃyutta Nikāya* ii.29–32; see
Bhikkhu Bodhi (trans.), *The
Connected Discourses of the
Buddha*, Wisdom Publications,
Boston 2000, p. 553–6; or
C. A. F. Rhys Davids (trans.),
Book of the Kindred Sayings,
part 2, Pali Text Society,
Oxford 1989, p. 27.

CHAPTER 3

196 Sections 13 and 14 of the
*Ariyapariyesanā Sutta,
Majjhima Nikāya* 26 (i.163);

see Bhikkhu Ñāṇamoli and
Bhikkhu Bodhi (trans.), *The
Middle Length Discourses
of the Buddha*, Wisdom
Publications, Boston 1995,
p. 256; or I. B. Horner (trans.),
Middle Length Sayings, vol. i,
Pali Text Society, Oxford 1957,
p. 207.

197 The legendary account of
Siddhārtha's going forth
describes how the hooves of his
horse Kanthaka were held by
the non-human beings so that
he could leave without waking
anyone. For example, the
Mahāvastu says: 'But the four
guardians of the world, in their
brilliant diadems and flowing
garlands, put their hands that
were as the red lotus under
the hoofs of Kanthaka.' See
J. J. Jones (trans.), *Mahāvastu*,
vol. i, Pali Text Society, London
1987, p. 124.

198 See, for example, *Aśvaghoṣa,
Fo-Sho-Hing-Tsan-King (A
Life of Buddha)*, Samuel Beal
(trans.), Motilal Banarsidass,
Delhi 1998, pp. 38–46, the
section called 'Putting away
desire'.

199 Section 45 of the *Mahāgovinda
Sutta, Dīgha Nikāya* 19
(ii.241); see M. Walshe (trans.),
*The Long Discourses of the
Buddha*, Wisdom Publications,
Boston 1995, p. 308; or
T. W. Rhys Davids (trans.),
Dialogues of the Buddha, part
2, Pali Text Society, Oxford
1991, pp. 273–4.

200 The three *lakṣaṇas* (Pāli
lakkhaṇas) are enumerated

and discussed in many places in the Pāli canon. For example, *Samyutta Nikāya* iii.20–4; see Bhikkhu Bodhi (trans.), *The Connected Discourses of the Buddha*, Wisdom Publications, Boston 2000, pp. 867–71; or F. L. Woodward (trans.), *Book of the Kindred Sayings*, part 3, Pali Text Society, Oxford 1989, pp. 19–23. See also *Udāna* iii.10 in John Ireland (trans.), *The Udāna and the Itivuttaka*, Buddhist Publication Society, Kandy 1997, p. 49. The *locus classicus* is *Dhammapada* 277–9.

201   Of the many canonical references, see especially section 18 of the *Mahāsatipaṭṭhāna Sutta*, *Dīgha Nikāya* 22 (ii.305–7)): M. Walshe (trans.), *The Long Discourses of the Buddha*, Wisdom Publications, Boston 1995, pp. 344–6; or T. W. Rhys Davids (trans.), *Dialogues of the Buddha*, part 2, Pali Text Society, Oxford 1991, pp. 337–45.

202   From *De Profundis*; see, for example, Oscar Wilde, *The Soul of Man and Prison Writings*, Oxford World's Classics, Oxford 1999, p. 106.

203   Shakespeare, *Measure for Measure*, act 3, scene 1.

204   For example, section 38 of the *Alagaddūpama Sutta*, *Majjhima Nikāya* 22 (i.140); see Bhikkhu Ñāṇamoli and Bhikkhu Bodhi (trans.), *The Middle Length Discourses of the Buddha*, Wisdom

Publications, Boston 1995, p. 234; or I. B. Horner (trans.), *Middle Length Sayings*, vol. i, Pali Text Society, Oxford 1957, p. 180.

205   See, for example, *Itivuttaka*, section 100: 'Bhikkhus, I am ... an unsurpassed physician and surgeon.' John Ireland (trans.), *The Udāna and the Itivuttaka*, Buddhist Publication Society, Kandy 1997, p. 226.

206   For example, *Dhammacakkappavattana Sutta*, *Samyutta Nikāya* v.421; see Bhikkhu Bodhi (trans.), *The Connected Discourses of the Buddha*, Wisdom Publications, Boston 2000, p. 1844; or F. L. Woodward (trans.), *Book of the Kindred Sayings*, part 5, Pali Text Society, Oxford 1989, p. 357.

207   See Edward Conze, *Buddhism*, Cassirer, Oxford 1957, pp. 46–8.

208   For the story of the hawk with the piece of meat, see H. T. Francis and R. A. Neil (trans.), *The Jātaka: or Stories of the Buddha's Former Births*, vol. iii, book 4: *Catukanipāta* no. 330, *Sīlavīmamsa-Jātaka*, Pali Text Society, London 1973, pp. 66–8.

209   For more on this theme, see Sangharakshita's essay 'Desire for the Eternal' in *Crossing the Stream*, Windhorse Publications, Glasgow 1987 (*Complete Works*, vol. 7).

210   *Samyutta Nikāya* ii.94; see Bhikkhu Bodhi (trans.), *The Connected Discourses of the*

Buddha, Wisdom Publications, Boston 2000, p. 595; or C. A. F. Rhys Davids, *Book of the Kindred Sayings*, part 2, Pali Text Society, Oxford 1989, pp. 65–6.

211 Of the many texts that bear the name Upanishad, there are thirteen principal ones. They originate from the eighth to fourth centuries BCE, and form the basis of the school of Hindu philosophy known as the Vedanta. The *ātman* is one of their main themes.

212 The Tantra in particular sees things in this way, with its teaching of the *sahaja* or innate nature of reality; see p. 206.

213 For example, Buddhaghosa goes into them in some detail in the *Visuddhimagga* (656–9); see Bhikkhu Ñāṇamoli (trans.), *The Path of Purification*, Buddhist Publication Society, Kandy 1991, pp. 678–82; or Pe Maung Tin (trans.), *The Path of Purity*, Pali Text Society, London 1975, pp. 802–5.

CHAPTER 4

214 For example, *Jambukhādakasamyutta, Samyutta Nikāya* iv.251; see Bhikkhu Bodhi (trans.), *The Connected Discourses of the Buddha*, Wisdom Publications, Boston 2000, p. 1294; or F. L. Woodward (trans.), *Book of the Kindred Sayings*, part 4, Pali Text Society, Oxford 1989, p. 170.

215 *Dhammapada* 204: *nibbānam paramam sukham*, 'Nirvana is the highest bliss.'

216 *Kleśa nirvāṇa* is synonymous with the attainment of arhantship; *skandha nirvāṇa* is synonymous with *parinirvāṇa* ('full' *nirvāṇa*), a term which is usually used to refer to the death of the Buddha but in fact is applicable to the death of any *arhant*.

217 This is from Blake's poem 'London', in *Songs of Innocence and Experience*.

CHAPTER 5

218 In Zen Buddhism the 'Great Death' is synonymous with absolute *samādhi*. See, for example, Mumonkan, *The Gateless Gate*, in *Two Zen Classics*, trans. K. Sekida, Weatherhill, New York 1996, p. 129.

219 Har Dayal quotes the *Avadāna-śataka*, which says of the Bodhisattva, 'He had torn the eggshell (of ignorance) by his knowledge'; *The Bodhisattva Doctrine in Buddhist Sanskrit Literature*, Motilal Banarsidass, Delhi 1975, p. 15.

220 Herbert V. Guenther and Leslie S. Kawamura (trans.), *Mind in Buddhist Psychology*, Dharma Publishing, California 1975, p. xviii.

221 The Perfection of Wisdom *sūtras* are all available in English translation. For an introduction, see Sangharakshita, *Wisdom*

Beyond Words, Windhorse Publications, Glasgow 1993 (*Complete Works*, vol. 15).

222 See Edward Conze (trans.), *The Large Sūtra on Perfect Wisdom with the Divisions of the Abhisamayālaṅkāra*, part 1, Oriental Studies Foundation Inc, London 1961, pp. 129–30.

223 The followers of the Tathāgatagarbha doctrine, whose ideas are outlined in a Mahāyāna text called the *Mahāparinirvāṇa Sūtra*, especially adhered to the idea of the true, real, or great self. See Paul Williams, *Mahāyāna Buddhism*, Routledge, London and New York 1989, pp. 98–100.

224 *Dhammapada* 204.

225 Kosho Yamamoto (trans.), *Mahāyana Mahāparinirvāṇa Sūtra*, Karinbunko, Japan 1974, vol ii, p. 565.

226 In *The Book of the Gradual Sayings*, vol. ii (Pali Text Society, Oxford 1995, pp. 21–2), F. L. Woodward mistakenly translates *Aṅguttara Nikāya* ii.21:

> So he to whom the self is dear,
> Who longeth for the Great Self – he
> Should homage unto Dhamma pay
> Remembering the Buddha-word.

Woodward explains in a note that 'Great Self' is a translation of *mahatta*. However, he notes

also that his translation goes against the commentary, which says *mahantabhāvaṃ*, 'being great'. Woodward appears to be mistaken here, since *mahatta* just means 'greatness' (*mahā* + abstract suffix *-tta*), as the commentary says. Hence in Bhikkhu Bodhi's 2012 translation (*Numerical Discourses of the Buddha*, Wisdom Publications, Boston 2012, p. 408):

> Therefore one desiring the good,
> aspiring for greatness,
> should revere the good Dhamma,
> recollecting the Buddhas' teaching.

To complete the picture, Woodward's 'he to whom the self is dear' translates *attakāma*, but as Woodward himself notes, this should be read *atthakāma*, 'desiring the good', which is what Bhikkhu Bodhi also reads. Why Woodward translates in terms of self is unclear, as it is not congruent with anything else.

227 Ch. 13, verse 8 of Nāgārjuna's *Mūlamadhyamakakārikā*, trans. Kenneth K. Inada, Hokuseido Press, Tokyo 1970, p.93:

> The wise men (i.e. enlightened ones) have said that sunyata or the nature of thusness is the relinquishing of all false views. Yet it is said that those who adhere

to the idea or concept of
sunyata are incorrigible.

In Candrakīrti's
commentary on the
Mūlamadhyamakakārikā, the
Prasannapadā, published in
Mervyn Sprung (trans.), *Lucid
Exposition of the Middle
Way*, Routledge & Kegan
Paul, London 1979, pp.151–2,
Candrakīrti says:

> As the illustrious one said
> in the *Ratnakūṭa Sūtra*,
> 'those, Kāśyapa, who seize
> on the absence of being as
> an object they assail the
> absence of being and such,
> I say, are hopelessly lost.
> Indeed, Kāśyapa, it were
> better if one resorted to a
> belief in the reality of the
> individual as unshakable
> as Mount Sumeru, than
> to hold to a theory of the
> absence of being through
> the stubborn belief in the
> unreality of things. Why
> is that, Because Kāśyapa,
> the absence of being is the
> exhaustion of all theories
> and view.
>
>   One for whom, in
> turn, the absence of being
> itself becomes a dogmatic
> view I call incurable. It is,
> Kāśyapa, as if a sick man
> were given a medicine by a
> doctor, but that medicine,
> having removed his ills,
> was not itself expelled but
> remained in the stomach.
> What do you think,
> Kāśyapa, will this man

> be freed of his sickness?
> No indeed, illustrious one,
> the sickness of this man
> in whose stomach the
> medicine, having removed
> all his ills remains and is not
> expelled, would be more
> violent. The illustrious one
> said: 'In this sense, Kāśyapa,
> the absence of being is the
> exhaustion of all dogmatic
> views. But the one for whom
> the absence of being itself
> becomes a fixed belief, I call
> incurable.

See also Sangharakshita,
Wisdom Beyond Words,
Windhorse Publications,
Birmingham 2000, p. 128
(*Complete Works*, vol. 14).

CHAPTER 6

228 The verse is *Dhammapada*
183. This story of the
encounter between the sage
and the man of worldly power
has been variously attributed.
According to Dōgen, this
exchange took place between
Haku Kyo-i, the governor of
Hangzhou, and Zen master
Choka Dorin. See Master
Dōgen, *Shobogenzo*, book 1,
Gudo Nishijima and Chodo
Cross (trans.), Windbell,
Woking 1994, pp. 106–8.
Also quoted in Thomas
Cleary (trans.), *Rational Zen:
The Mind of Dōgen Zenji*,
Shambhala Publications,
Boston 1995, pp. 91–4.

229 See the beginning of ch. 2
in Sangharakshita, *The*

Buddha's Noble Eightfold Path (*Complete Works*, vol. 1).

230   For a brief introduction to the Five Buddhas of the mandala, see pp. 373ff.

231   The threefold way – ethics, meditation, and wisdom – is the threefold division of the Noble Eightfold Path, sometimes called the threefold training. The Buddha is said to have expounded the threefold way many times during his last teaching tour; see, for example, section 1.12 of the *Mahāparinibbāna Sutta, Dīgha Nikāya* 16 (ii.81): M. Walshe (trans.), *The Long Discourses of the Buddha*, Wisdom Publications, Boston 1995, p. 234; or T. W. Rhys Davids (trans.), *Dialogues of the Buddha*, part 2, Pali Text Society, Oxford 1977, pp. 85–6.

232   This distinction is found in the Theravādin commentarial tradition; for more about it, see Sangharakshita, *A Survey of Buddhism*, Windhorse Publications, Birmingham 2001, p. 170 (*Complete Works* vol. 1).

233   See verse 9 of the *Ratana Sutta* (*Sutta-Nipāta* 230), H. Saddhatissa (trans.), Curzon Press, London 1985, p. 25 for an encouraging example:

'Those who comprehend clearly the noble truths well taught by him who is endowed with

profound wisdom, however exceedingly heedless they may be, they do not take birth for the eighth time.'

See also *Aṅguttara Nikāya* iv.381; Bhikkhu Bodhi (trans.), *Numerical Discourses of the Buddha*, Wisdom Publications, Boston 2012, p. 1266; or E. M. Hare, *The Book of the Gradual Sayings*, vol. iv, Pali Text Society, Oxford 1995, p. 381.

234   Section 6.7 of the *Mahāparinibbāna Sutta, Dīgha Nikāya* 16 (ii.156); see M. Walshe (trans.), *The Long Discourses of the Buddha*, Wisdom Publications, Boston 1995, p. 270; or T. W. Rhys Davids (trans.), *Dialogues of the Buddha*, part 2, Pali Text Society, Oxford 1977, p. 173.

235   Among the many references to Stream Entry in the Pāli canon, the *Saṃyutta Nikāya* (v.342–413) has a whole section devoted to the subject. See Bhikkhu Bodhi (trans.), *The Connected Discourses of the Buddha*, Wisdom Publications, Boston 2000, pp. 1788–1837; or F. L. Woodward (trans.), *Kindred Sayings*, part 5, Pali Text Society, Oxford 1979, pp. 296–351.

236   'The breeze of His Grace is blowing night and day over thy head; unfurl the sails of thy boat (mind), if thou wantest to make rapid progress through the ocean of life.'

Swami Abhedananda, *The Sayings of Sri Ramakrishna*, no. 454, Cosimo Inc., 2010, p. 159.

237 Matthew 5:48.

238 The ten fetters are enumerated in, for example, sections 2.1 (7–8) of the *Saṅgīti Sutta, Dīgha Nikāya* 33 (iii.234); see M. Walshe (trans.), *The Long Discourses of the Buddha*, Wisdom Publications, Boston 1995, p. 495; or T. W. Rhys Davids (trans.), *Dialogues of the Buddha*, part 3, Pali Text Society, Oxford 1991, p. 225. See also *Saṃyutta Nikāya* v.61; Bhikkhu Bodhi (trans.), *The Connected Discourses of the Buddha*, Wisdom Publications, Boston 2000, p. 1565; or F. L. Woodward (trans.), *Kindred Sayings*, part 5, Pali Text Society, Oxford 1979, p. 49.

CHAPTER 7

239 The story of Śāriputra and Aśvajit is told at Vinaya Piṭaka i.39 (*Mahāvagga* 1.23); see I. B. Horner (trans.), *The Book of the Discipline*, part 4, Pali Text Society, Oxford 1996, pp. 52–4. See also p. 93 above.

240 Hebrews 13:14.

241 See pp. 36ff.

242 For example, the *Ratana Sutta, Sutta-Nipāta* 224–35, refers to the Buddha, the Dhamma, and the Sangha as precious jewels. See H. Saddhatissa (trans.), *Sutta-Nipāta*, Curzon Press, London 1985, pp. 24–5.

243 The five precepts are enumerated many times in the Pāli canon, for example, *Aṅguttara Nikāya* iii.212: see Bhikkhu Bodhi (trans.), *Numerical Discourses of the Buddha*, Wisdom Publications, Boston 2012, p. 792; or E. M. Hare, *The Book of the Gradual Sayings*, vol. iii, Pali Text Society, Oxford 1995, ch. 18, 'The Lay Disciple', p. 155.

244 For more about confession in the Buddhist tradition (which is very different in conception from the Christian practice of confession), see Sangharakshita, *Transforming Self and World*, ch. 2 (*Complete Works*, vol. 16).

245 Buddhaghosa lists these five kinds of *prīti* (Pāli *pīti*) in the *Visuddhimagga* 143–4; see Bhikkhu Ñāṇamoli (trans.), *The Path of Purification*, Buddhist Publication Society, Kandy 1991, pp. 140–2; or Pe Maung Tin (trans.), *The Path of Purity*, Pali Text Society, London 1975, pp. 166–7.

246 One use of this image is to be found in a story told about the Vedanta master of the early twentieth century, Swami Vivekananda. His biographer reports:

Witnessing the religious ecstasy of several devotees, Narendra one day said to the Master that he too wanted to experience it. 'My child,' he was told, 'when a huge elephant enters a small pond, a great commotion is set up, but when it plunges into the Ganga, the river shows very little agitation. These devotees are like small ponds; a little experience makes their feelings flow over the brim. But you are a huge river.'

Another version of this simile is found in the *Himavant Sutta, Samyutta Nikāya* v.63:

Monks, the nāgas depend on the king of snowy mountains to increase their substance, and account for their power. Increased and empowered they descend into small pools, then into large pools; then they descend into small rivers, and then into large rivers; and finally they descend into the great gathered waters of the ocean. Thus their body becomes great and full. Just like that, monks, the monk depending on virtue, supported by virtue, seriously takes up the practice of, and produces, the seven factors of awakening and attains the greatness and fullness of them.

Here, the mythic *nāgas* are the ones making the progress. In Pāli, *nāga* frequently means elephant, but it can also mean any large or particularly impressive animal.

The image of overflowing water to describe the transition from one positive mental state to another is given in the *Upanisa Sutta, Samyutta Nikāya* ii.32; see Bhikkhu Bodhi (trans.), *Connected Discourses of the Buddha*, Wisdom Publications, Boston 2000, p. 556; or C. A. F. Rhys Davids (trans.), *The Book of the Kindred Sayings*, part 2, Pali Text Society, Oxford 1997, p. 27.

247 Sections 20–2 of the *Cūladukkhakkhandha Sutta, Majjhima Nikāya* 14 (i.94); see Bhikkhu Ñāṇamoli and Bhikkhu Bodhi (trans.), *The Middle Length Discourses of the Buddha*, Wisdom Publications, Boston 1995, pp. 188–9; or I. B. Horner (trans.), *Middle Length Sayings*, vol. i, Pali Text Society, Oxford 1957, pp. 123–4.

248 An example of someone who responded so readily to the Buddha's words is Bahiya of the Bark-cloth. Urgently requesting the Buddha for a teaching, he was told, 'In the seen, only the seen. In the heard, only the heard', and, according to the text, 'the mind of Bahiya of the Bark-cloth was immediately freed from the taints without grasping'. In other words, Insight immediately arose. See *Bahiya Sutta, Udāna* 1.10 (i.6–9) in John D. Ireland (trans.), *The Udāna and the Itivuttaka*, Buddhist Publication Society, Kandy 1997, pp. 19–22. Likewise,

the wealthy layman Anāthapiṇḍika gained Insight immediately upon first meeting the Buddha: Vinaya Piṭaka ii.154–7 (*Cullavagga* 6.4); see I. B. Horner (trans.), *The Book of the Discipline*, part 5, Pali Text Society, Oxford 1992, pp. 216–20. It is noteworthy that according to the Pāli canon accounts, both of these men were very keen to meet the Buddha urgently – as though they were ripe to hear and understand the truth.

249   Darīmukha seeing the garden now empty came and sat on the royal seat in the garden. A withered leaf fell before him. In it he came to see the principles of decay and death, grasped the three marks of things, and making the earth re-echo with joy he entered on *paccekabodhi*. At that instant the characters of a householder vanished from him, a miraculous bowl and frock fell from the sky and clave to his body, at once he had the eight requisites and the perfect deportment of a centenarian monk, and by miracle he flew into the air and went to the cave Nandamūla in the Himālaya.

H. T. Francis and R. A. Neil (trans.), *The Jātaka,* vol. iii, Allen & Unwin, London 1897, no. 378, *Darīmukha-Jātaka*, p. 157.

250   For example, section 2.2 of the *Dasuttara Sutta, Dīgha Nikāya* 34 (iii.288; see M. Walshe (trans.), *The Long Discourses of the Buddha*, Wisdom Publications, Boston 1995, p. 519; or T. W. Rhys Davids, *Dialogues of the Buddha*, part 3, Pali Text Society, Oxford 1991, p. 262.

251   This is a reference to the Mahāyāna *trikāya* (literally 'three bodies') doctrine, according to which a Buddha appears on the material plane as the *nirmāṇakāya*, the 'body of form', on the archetypal plane as the *sambhogakāya*, the 'glorious body', and as an unconditioned consciousness beyond space and time, the *dharmakāya*, or 'body of truth'. For more about the *trikāya* doctrine, see ch. 2, section 6, of Sangharakshita, *A Survey of Buddhism*, Windhorse Publications, Birmingham 2001, pp. 282–97 (*Complete Works*, vol. 1).

252   For more about the 'turning about', the *parāvṛtti*, see Sangharakshita, *The Meaning of Conversion in Buddhism*, ch. 4 (*Complete Works*, vol. 2).

253   Buddhaghosa uses the simile of the poisonous snake in this way at *Visuddhimagga 652;* see Bhikkhu Ñāṇamoli (trans.), *The Path of Purification*, Buddhist Publication Society, Kandy 1991, p. 675; or, Pe Maung Tin (trans.), *The Path of Purity* Pali Text Society, London 1975, p. 797.

254   It is the Mahāyāna accounts of the Buddha's life that recount the mythical attack of 'Māra's hordes' on the Buddha-to-be as he was nearing Enlightenment. See, for example, Aśvaghoṣa, *Buddhacarita*, ch. 13, and the *Lalitavistara Sūtra*, published as Gwendolyn Bays (trans.), *The Voice of the Buddha*, Dharma Publishing, Berkeley 1983, volume ii, p. 480. See also Sangharakshita's talk, 'The Buddha's Victory', published in the collection of talks of that name, in *Complete Works*, vol. 11.

255   In his *Buddhist Dictionary* (Buddhist Publication Society, Kandy 1980), Nyanatiloka translates *ceto-vimutti* (Pāli) as deliverance of mind, and *paññā-vimutti* as deliverance through wisdom, saying that deliverance of mind, in the highest sense, is that kind of concentration (*samādhi*) which is bound up with the path of arahantship; and deliverance through wisdom is the knowledge (*ñāṇa*) bound up with the fruition of arahantship. These two deliverances are often paired – as in, for example, section 19 of the *Mahāsīhanāda Sutta*, *Majjhima Nikāya* 12 (i.71), in which they are jointly described as the tenth of the ten powers of a Tathāgata:

    'Realizing for himself with direct knowledge the Tathāgata here and now enters upon and abides in the deliverance of mind and deliverance by wisdom that are taintless with the destruction of the taints';

    see Bhikkhu Ñāṇamoli and Bhikkhu Bodhi (trans.), *The Middle Length Discourses of the Buddha*, Wisdom Publications, Boston 1995, p. 166; or I. B. Horner (trans.), *Middle Length Sayings*, vol. i, Pali Text Society London 1976, p. 95.

256   This is the sixth of the eight qualities of the great ocean described by the Buddha in the *Uposatha Sutta*, Udāna 5.5. See John D. Ireland (trans.), *The Udāna and the Itivuttaka*, Buddhist Publication Society, Kandy 2007, p. 68. See also Sangharakshita's talk 'The Taste of Freedom' (*Complete Works*, vol. 11).

257   The three *āsavas* (Sanskrit *āsravas*) are listed in many places in the Pāli canon. For example, section 43 of the *Mahāsaccaka Sutta*, *Majjhima Nikāya* 36 (i.249); see Bhikkhu Ñāṇamoli and Bhikkhu Bodhi (trans.), *The Middle Length Discourses of the Buddha*, Wisdom Publications, Boston 1995, p. 342; or *Middle Length Sayings* vol. 1, Pali Text Society, London 1976, p. 303. A few sources list a fourth *āsava*, *diṭṭhāsava*, the mental poison of wrong views; for example, section 1.12 of the *Mahāparinibbāna Sutta*,

Dīgha Nikāya 16 (ii.81); see
M. Walshe (trans.), *The Long
Discourses of the Buddha*,
Wisdom Publications, Boston
1995, p. 234; or T. W. Rhys
Davids (trans.), *Dialogues
of the Buddha*, part 2, Pali
Text Society, Oxford 1977,
pp. 327–37.

CHAPTER 8

258   The four *viparyāsas* (Pāli
vipallāsas) are listed in the
*Vipallāsa Sutta, Aṅguttara
Nikāya* ii.52; see Bhikkhu
Bodhi (trans.), *The Numerical
Discourses of the Buddha*,
Wisdom Publications,
Boston 2012, pp. 437–8; or
F. L. Woodward (trans.), *The
Book of the Gradual Sayings*,
vol. ii, Pali Text Society,
Oxford 1995, pp. 60–1. See
also ch. 11 of Sangharakshita,
The Three Jewels, Windhorse
Publications, Birmingham
1998, p. 72ff. (*Complete
Works*, vol. 2)

259   See the
*Dhammacakkappavattana
Sutta, Saṃyutta Nikāya* v.421;
Bhikkhu Bodhi (trans.), *The
Connected Discourses of the
Buddha*, Wisdom Publications,
Boston 2000, p. 1844; or C. A.
F. Rhys Davids (trans.), *Book
of the Kindred Sayings*, part 5,
Pali Text Society, Oxford 1979,
p. 357.

260   'When practised by the holy
ones, technically known as
Āryans, of whom there are
four kinds, it is known as the
transmundane (*lokottara*)
or transcendental Eightfold
Way; when practised by
non-Āryans, that is to
say by *pṛthaflanas* (Pāli
puthujjanas) or worldlings,
it is known as the mundane
(*laukika*) eightfold way.
The point of this distinction
is the difference between
a virtue consciously and
deliberately practised, with
more or less success, as a
discipline, and a virtue that
is the natural expression, the
spontaneous overflow, of an
inner realization.'

Sangharakshita, *A Survey
of Buddhism*, Windhorse
Publications, Birmingham
2001, p. 161 (*Complete
Works*, vol. 1).

261   *Dhammapada* 100, trans.
Sangharakshita.

262   For this list of kinds of wrong
livelihood, see, for example,
Aṅguttara Nikāya iii.208; see
Bhikkhu Bodhi (trans.), *The
Numerical Discourses of the
Buddha*, Wisdom Publications,
Boston 2012, p. 790; or E. M.
Hare (trans.), *The Book of the
Gradual Sayings*, vol. iii, Pali
Text Society, Oxford 1995,
p. 153.

263   For more on the four levels of
awareness, see Sangharakshita,
*The Buddha's Noble Eightfold
Path* ch. 7 (*Complete Works*,
vol. 1). These four levels
of awareness are not to
be confused with the 'four
foundations of mindfulness':

awareness of the body, feelings, consciousness, and mental objects – outlined in, for example, the *Mahāsatipaṭṭhāna Sutta*, *Dīgha Nikāya* 22; see M. Walshe (trans.), *The Long Discourses of the Buddha*, Wisdom Publications, Boston 1995, pp. 335–50; or T. W. Rhys Davids (trans.), *Dialogues of the Buddha*, part 2, Pali Text Society, Oxford 1977, pp. 327–37.

264 The Dharma Eye is one of the 'five eyes' of the Buddhist tradition; for a description of them see Sangharakshita, *Complete Works*, vol. 9, pp. 251–2.

265 The seven *bodhyaṅgas* are enumerated in, for example, the *Mahāsatipaṭṭhāna Sutta*, *Dīgha Nikāya* 22 (ii.303–4); see M. Walshe (trans.), *The Long Discourses of the Buddha*, Wisdom Publications, Boston 1995, p. 343. See also the *Ānāpānasati Sutta*, *Majjhima Nikāya* (iii.85–7); Bhikkhu Ñāṇamoli and Bhikkhu Bodhi (trans.), *The Middle Length Discourses of the Buddha*, Wisdom Publications, Boston 1995, pp. 946–8; or I. B. Horner (trans.), *Middle Length Sayings III*, Pali Text Society, London 1967, pp. 128–9.

266 This story is about Tenno, a disciple of Nanin. He had become a teacher when Nanin asked him this question, after which he went back to being a pupil. The story is told in *Zen Flesh, Zen Bones*, compiled by Paul Reps, Penguin Books, Middlesex 1971, p. 43.

267 The Abhidharma (the word simply means 'about Dharma', though its adherents came to think of it as 'the higher Dharma') began as an attempt to systematize the Buddha's teachings, and became a scholastic enterprise which lasted several hundred years and involved an exhaustive analysis of mind and mental events. See Sangharakshita, *The Eternal Legacy*, ch. 7, 'The Fundamental Abhidharma' (*Complete Works*, vol. 14).

268 'What is vigour? The endeavour to do what is skilful.' Śāntideva, *Bodhicāryāvatāra*, ch. 7, 'The Perfection of Vigour', verse 2.

269 Śāntideva, *Bodhicāryāvatāra*, ch. 7, 'The Perfection of Vigour', verse 65.

270 Buddhaghosa lists five kinds of *prīti* (Pāli *pīti*) in the *Visuddhimagga* 143–4; see Bhikkhu Ñāṇamoli (trans.), *The Path of Purification*, Buddhist Publication Society, Kandy 1991, pp. 140–2; or Pe Maung Tin (trans.), *The Path of Purity*, Pali Text Society, London 1975, pp. 166–7. The fourth kind is the 'silken bag' (sometimes translated 'bladder').

271 *Dīgha Nikāya* (ii.130); see M. Walshe (trans.), *The Long Discourses of the Buddha*, Wisdom Publications, Boston 1995, p. 258, or T. W. Rhys

Davids (trans.), *Dialogues of the Buddha*, part 2, Pali Text Society, London 1971, pp. 141–2. This is in fact a story told to the Buddha by Pukkusa the Malla about his teacher Āḷāra Kālāma.

272 The scriptural *locus classicus* for the eight worldly winds is the *Lokavipatti Sutta, Aṅguttara Nikāya* iv.157–9: see Bhikkhu Bodhi (trans.), *The Numerical Discourses of the Buddha*, Wisdom Publications 2012, pp. 1116–9; or E.M. Hare (trans.), *The Book of the Gradual Sayings*, vol. iv, Pali Text Society, Oxford 1995, pp. 107–9. They are also enumerated by Buddhaghosa at *Visuddhimagga* 683; see Bhikkhu Ñāṇamoli (trans.), *The Path of Purification*, Buddhist Publication Society, Kandy 1991, pp. 708–9; or Pe Maung Tin (trans.), *The Path of Purity*, Pali Text Society, London 1975, pp. 838.

273 Buddhaghosa's *Visuddhimagga* is available in translation as Ñāṇamoli (trans.), *The Path of Purification*, Buddhist Publication Society, Kandy 1991; or Pe Maung Tin (trans.), *The Path of Purity*, Pali Text Society, London 1975.

274 *Rathavinīta Sutta, Majjhima Nikāya* 24; see Bhikkhu Ñāṇamoli and Bhikkhu Bodhi (trans.), *The Middle Length Discourses of the Buddha,* Wisdom Publications,

Boston 1995, pp. 240–5; or I. B. Horner (trans.), *Middle Length Sayings*, vol. i, Pali Text Society, Oxford 1957, pp. 187–94.

275 The five precepts are enumerated many times in the Pāli canon, for example, at *Aṅguttara Nikāya* iii.212; see Bhikkhu Bodhi (trans.), *Numerical Discourses of the Buddha*, Wisdom Publications, Boston 2012, p. 792; or E. M. Hare (trans.), *The Book of the Gradual Sayings*, vol. iii, ch. 18, 'The Lay Disciple', Pali Text Society, Oxford 1995, p. 155.

276 For a list of the sixty-two wrong views, see sections 1.29–3.24 of the *Brahmajāla Sutta, Dīgha Nikāya* 1 (i.12–38); M. Walshe (trans.), *The Long Discourses of the Buddha*, Wisdom Publications, Boston 1995, pp. 73–86; or T. W. Rhys Davids (trans.), *Dialogues of the Buddha*, part 1, Pali Text Society, Oxford 1977, pp. 30–52.

277 This story of Mahāprajāpatī Gautami is to be found at Vinaya Piṭaka ii.258–9 (*Cullavagga* 10.5); see I. B. Horner (trans.), *The Book of the Discipline*, part 5, Pali Text Society, Oxford 1992, p. 359; also *Aṅguttara Nikāya* iv.280, in E. M. Hare (trans.), *Gradual Sayings*, vol. iv, Pali Text Society, Oxford 1995, pp. 186–7; or Bhikkhu Bodhi (trans.), *The Numerical Discourses of the Buddha*,

Wisdom Publications, Boston
2012, p. 1193.

278 *Dhammapada* 103, trans.
Sangharakshita.

279 For one of the first accounts
of the Buddha's teaching
of the middle way, see
*Dhammacakkappavattana
Sutta, Saṃyutta Nikāya* v.421;
Bhikkhu Bodhi (trans.), *The
Connected Discourses of the
Buddha*, Wisdom Publications,
Boston 2000, p. 1844; or
F. L. Woodward (trans.), *Book
of the Kindred Sayings*, part
5, Pali Text Society, Oxford
1989, p. 357; also I. B. Horner
(trans.), *The Book of the
Discipline*, part 4, Pali Text
Society, Oxford 1996, p. 15.

CHAPTER 9

280 For thousands of years the
people at the bottom of
the Hindu caste system,
who in the past were called
Untouchables, suffered terrible
prejudice on the part of those
of higher castes. Since 1956
many of them have converted
to Buddhism, inspired
not only by the Buddha's
rejection of caste, but also
by the example of Dr B. R.
Ambedkar. Dr Ambedkar
was an Untouchable who,
through talent, luck, and
force of character, became
independent India's first
Law Minister, and drew up
the Indian Constitution, in
which Untouchability was
declared illegal. Despite
this, ex-Untouchables are

sometimes still subject to
crippling social restrictions.
When, in 1956, Dr Ambedkar
converted to Buddhism, so
did 380,000 of his followers.
Ambedkar's death just weeks
after his conversion left the
new Buddhists without a
leader. Sangharakshita rallied
Ambedkar's followers, forging
a link that eventually led
to the establishment of the
TBMSG (Trailokya Bauddha
Mahasangha Sahayak Gana),
in relationship to the Friends
of the Western Buddhist
Order, which was developing
at around the same time.
In 2010 all the elements of
this international Buddhist
movement were given the same
name: the Triratna Buddhist
Community.

281 Among many canonical
references to the five
indriyas, the *Saṃyutta
Nikāya* (v.193 ff.) describes
them in various ways in a
section on the faculties; see
Bhikkhu Bodhi (trans.), *The
Connected Discourses of the
Buddha*, Wisdom Publications,
Somerville 2000, pp. 1668ff.,
also F. L. Woodward (trans.),
*The Book of the Kindred
Sayings*, part 5, Pali Text
Society, London 1979,
pp. 169ff. See also 'The Five
Spiritual Faculties', section 2
of chapter 3 in Sangharakshita,
A Survey of Buddhism,
Windhorse Publications,
Birmingham 2001, pp. 315–30
(*Complete Works*, vol. 1).

282 Edward Conze, *The Way of Wisdom: the Five Spiritual Faculties* (*The Wheel*, no. 65/66), Buddhist Publication Society, Kandy, first published in 1964 (available at accesstoinsight.org).

283 For a detailed look at the place of devotion in Buddhism, see Sangharakshita, *Ritual and Devotion in Buddhism* (*Complete Works*, vol. 11).

284 The three levels of wisdom are enumerated in, for example, section 1.10 (43) of the *Sangiti Sutta*, *Dīgha Nikāya* 33 (iii.219); see *The Long Discourses of the Buddha*, Wisdom Publications, Boston 1995, p. 486; *Dialogues of the Buddha*, part 3, p. 212.

285 'What is vigour? The endeavour to do what is skilful.' Śāntideva, *Bodhicāryāvatāra*, ch. 7, 'The Perfection of Vigour', verse 2.

286 For a canonical reference to the four right efforts, see section 21 of the *Mahāsatipaṭṭhāna Sutta*, *Dīgha Nikāya* 22 (ii.311); M. Walshe (trans.), *The Long Discourses of the Buddha*, Wisdom Publications, Boston 1995, p. 348; or T. W. Rhys Davids, *Dialogues of the Buddha*, part 2, Pali Text Society, Oxford 1977, p. 344. For more on the four right efforts, see Sangharakshita, *The Buddha's Noble Eightfold Path*, ch. 6 (*Complete Works*, vol. 1).

287 A typical exhortation is to be found in the *Bhikkhunīpassaya Sutta*, *Saṃyutta Nikāya* v.154; Bhikkhu Bodhi (trans.), *Connected Discourses of the Buddha*, Wisdom Publications, Boston 2000, p. 1640; or F. L. Woodward (trans.), *Kindred Sayings*, part 5, Pali Text Society, London 1979, pp. 136–7: 'Whatever is to be done by a teacher with compassion for the welfare of students, that has been done by me out of compassion for you. Here are the roots of trees. Here are empty places. Sit down and meditate. Don't be lazy. Don't become one who is later remorseful.' One of the most famous passages in which the Buddha asks his disciples about their spiritual progress is the story of his visit to Anuruddha, Nandiya, and Kimbila, who say they are getting along 'as milk and water blend'; see the *Cūḷagosinga Sutta*, *Majjhima Nikāya* 31 (i.207); see Bhikkhu Ñāṇamoli and Bhikkhu Bodhi (trans.), *The Middle Length Discourses of the Buddha*, Wisdom Publications, Boston 1995, pp. 301–6; or I. B. Horner (trans.), *Middle Length Sayings*, vol. i, Pali Text Society, London 1967, pp. 257–62.

288 This could be the *Kalandaka Jātaka* which is preserved in Sri Lanka; Indra is probably given the name Sakka. There is a similar story in the Hindu *Rāmāyaṇa*, in which Rāma

encounters a squirrel carrying pebbles in its mouth in an effort to build a bridge across the sea.

289 These images for the *dhyānas* are given in sections 15–18 of the *Mahā-Assapura Sutta, Majjhima Nikāya* 39 (i.276–9); see Bhikkhu Ñāṇamoli and Bhikkhu Bodhi (trans.), *The Middle Length Discourses of the Buddha*, Wisdom Publications, Boston 1995, pp. 367–9; or I. B. Horner (trans.), *Middle Length Sayings*, vol. i, Pali Text Society, Oxford 1957, pp. 330–2. See also sections 25–8 of the *Mahāsakuludāyi Sutta, Majjhima Nikāya* 77 (ii.15–17), Bhikkhu Ñāṇamoli and Bhikkhu Bodhi (trans.), *The Middle Length Discourses of the Buddha*, Wisdom Publications, Boston 1995, pp. 641–2; or I. B. Horner (trans.), *Middle Length Sayings*, vol. ii, Pali Text Society, Oxford 1957, pp. 216–7.

290 Peggy Kennett (1924–1996), later known as Jiyu Kennett Roshi, after training in Japan, became a teacher of Zen in the UK and North America, and founded the movement now known as the Order of Buddhist Contemplatives.

291 The word 'mantra' means, according to one etymology at least, 'that which protects the mind'. A mantra is said to be the sound symbol that expresses the Enlightened qualities of a Buddha or Bodhisattva in sonic form. Reciting a mantra, therefore, as well as being a means of concentration, helps one to sustain a connection with the transcendental. For more on mantras, see ch. 7 of Sangharakshita, *Creative Symbols of Tantric Buddhism* (*Complete Works*, vol. 13).

292 Sri Aurobindo (1872–1950), having been educated in England, was for a while politically active in the protest against British rule in India, but after having mystical experiences in prison he began his spiritual work, especially developing the method of practice he called integral yoga.

293 The word sangha, strictly speaking, refers to the Āryasaṅgha – the community of those men and women – past, present, and future – who have gained insight into the transcendental, but the term is also used much more broadly, as here, to refer to the greater (*mahā*) sangha, which can be said to consist of all those who follow the path taught by the Buddha.

CHAPTER 10

294 For example, *Saṃyutta Nikāya* i.33; see Bhikkhu Bodhi (trans.), *The Connected Discourses of the Buddha*, Wisdom Publications, Somerville 2000, pp. 122–3, also C. A. F. Rhys Davids (trans.), *The Book of the*

Kindred Sayings, part 1, Pali Text Society, London 1989, pp. 45–6.

295 Some Buddhists are happy to take it that the heavens and hells of Buddhist tradition exist literally, while others prefer to take the teaching more symbolically, seeing that even within the sphere of human life it is possible to lead a heavenly, hellish, or animal-like existence, and so on.

296 The five orders of conditionality, or *niyamas*, are enumerated by Buddhaghosa in his commentary on the 'Dhammasangani', the first book of the Abhidhamma Piṭaka, vol. ii. See Pe Maung Tin (trans.), *The Expositor*, ch. 10, ed. C. A. F. Rhys Davids, Pali Text Society, London 1921, p. 360; and also in his commentary on the *Dīgha Nikāya*, ed. W. Stede, Pali Text Society 1920, p. 360 (not available in English translation). Sangharakshita's source is C. A. F. Rhys Davids, *Buddhism: a study of the Buddhist norm*, Williams and Norgate, London 1912, pp. 118–9.

297 This image is associated especially with the *Avataṃsaka Sūtra* or *Flower Ornament Scripture*, available in translation by Thomas Cleary (Shambhala Publications, Boston & London 1993). Although Indra's Net is not specifically described in the *sūtra*, the feeling of it is strongly present in, for example, the verses in ch. 30 (Cleary pp. 891–904), and was elaborated in the Hua-yen school of Buddhism. For example, Francis H. Cook, *Hua-yen Buddhism: The Jewel Net of Indra*, Pennsylvania State University Press, 1977, p. 2:

Far away in the heavenly abode of the great god Indra, there is a wonderful net which has been hung by some cunning artificer in such a manner that it stretches out infinitely in all directions. In accordance with the extravagant tastes of deities, the artificer has hung a single glittering jewel in each 'eye' of the net, and since the net itself is infinite in dimension, the jewels are infinite in number. There hang the jewels, glittering 'like' stars in the first magnitude, a wonderful sight to behold. If we now arbitrarily select one of these jewels for inspection and look closely at it, we will discover that in its polished surface there are reflected all the other jewels in the net, infinite in number. Not only that, but each of the jewels reflected in this one jewel is also reflecting all the other jewels, so that there is an infinite reflecting process occurring.

298 *Dhammapada* 1–2, trans. Sangharakshita.

299 The five precepts are enumerated many times in the Pāli canon. For example, *Aṅguttara Nikāya*: iii.212; see Bhikkhu Bodhi (trans.), *Numerical Discourses of the Buddha*, Wisdom Publications, Boston 2012, p. 792; or E. M. Hare (trans.), *The Book of the Gradual Sayings*, vol. iii, ch. 18, 'The Lay Disciple', Pali Text Society, Oxford 1995, p. 155.

300 See J. J. Jones (trans.), *The Mahāvastu*, vol. ii, Luzac, London 1952, p. 96.

301 This is Sangharakshita's translation of the *Karaniya Mettā Sutta*, which is *Sutta-Nipāta* 1.8.

302 This is in the text from the Chinese Buddhist tradition called *The Sūtra of Forty-Two Sections*, which according to tradition was the first Buddhist text to be translated into Chinese. In section 23, the Buddha is represented as saying,

> 'Of all the lusts and desires, there is none so powerful as sexual inclination. This is so strong that there is no other worth speaking of beyond it. Suppose there were two of the same character, then under the whole heaven no flesh could be saved (or, be in possession of reason).'

This translation is by Samuel Beal in *A Catena of Buddhist Scriptures*, Trubner & Co., London 1871, p. 198.

Sangharakshita commented on this verse in two seminars on this *sūtra* given in the early 1980s, one in New Zealand and one at Padmaloka in the UK. At the latter, given in 1982, he described this verse as giving 'a paradigm of the dualistic situation'. Both seminars are based on the translation of the *sūtra* by John Blofeld, published by the Buddhist Society, London, in 1977. Blofeld (p. 18) translates this verse as: 'Of all longings and desires, there is none stronger than sex. Sex as a desire has no equal.' Sangharakshita's seminars are available at freebuddhistaudio.com.

303 *Aṅguttara Nikāya* ii.23; see Bhikkhu Bodhi (trans.), *Numerical Discourses of the Buddha*, Wisdom Publications, Boston 2012, p. 410; or F. L. Woodward (trans.), *The Book of the Gradual Sayings*, vol. ii, Pali Text Society, Oxford 1995, p. 25.

304 Someone, abandoning false speech, abstains from false speech; when summoned to a court, or to a meeting, or to his relatives' presence, or to his guild, or to the royal family's presence, and questioned as a witness thus: 'So, good man, tell us what you know,' not knowing, he says, 'I do not know,' or knowing, he says, 'I know'; not seeing, he says, 'I do not see,' or seeing, he says, 'I see'.

Section 13 of the *Sāleyakka Sutta, Majjhima Nikāya* 41 (i.288); see Bhikkhu Ñāṇamoli and Bhikkhu Bodhi (trans.), *The Middle Length Discourses of the Buddha*, Wisdom Publications, Boston 1995, p. 382; or I. B. Horner (trans.), *Middle Length Sayings*, vol. i, Pali Text Society, Oxford 1957, p. 347.

305 For more about the context of this incident, see Sangharakshita, *The Rainbow Road*, ch. 9 (*Complete Works*, vol. 20).

306 The Kālāmas are an example of a group of people who accept the Dharma but do not immediately see reality; see the *Kālāma* or *Kesaputtiya Sutta, Aṅguttara Nikāya* i.188–93; see F. L. Woodward (trans.), *Gradual Sayings*, vol. i, Pali Text Society, Oxford 1995, pp. 170–5; or Bhikkhu Bodhi (trans.), *The Numerical Discourses of the Buddha*, Wisdom Publications, Boston 2012, pp. 279–83. And an example of an individual who becomes a very sincere follower of the Buddha but does not gain Insight is King Pasenadi; his discussions with the Buddha are recorded in the *Kosalasaṃyutta, Saṃyutta Nikāya* i.68–102; see C. A. F. Rhys Davids (trans.), *The Book of the Kindred Sayings*, part 1, Pali Text Society, Oxford 1997, pp. 93–127; or

Bhikkhu Bodhi (trans.), *The Connected Discourses of the Buddha*, Wisdom Publications, Somerville 2000, pp. 164–94.

307 For example, section 9 of the *Aggañña Sutta, Dīgha Nikāya* 27 (iii.84); see M. Walshe (trans.), *The Long Discourses of the Buddha*, Wisdom, Boston 1995, p. 409; or T. W. Rhys Davids (trans.), *Dialogues of the Buddha*, part 3, Pali Text Society, Oxford 1991, p. 79.

308 The Pāli canon uses stock phrases to express people's response to the Buddha's teaching. The response (here as translated by Maurice Walshe at the end of the *Tevijja Sutta, Dīgha Nikāya* 13 in *The Long Discourses of the Buddha*, Wisdom, Boston 1995, p. 195) is:

'Excellent, Reverend Gotama, excellent! It is as if someone were to set up what had been knocked down, or to point out the way to one who had got lost, or to bring an oil-lamp into a dark place, so that those with eyes could see what was there. Just so the Reverend Gotama has expounded the Dhamma in various ways.'

309 This story of Dōgen was told by Abbot Tenshin Anderson in 'Speaking the Unspoken', Talk One, *Shambhala Sun*, June 1993, p. 31.

CHAPTER 11

310 'All I know is that so long
as I am asleep I have neither
fear nor hope, trouble nor
glory; and good luck betide
him that invented sleep, the
cloak that covers over all
a man's thoughts, the food
that removes hunger, the
drink that drives away thirst,
the fire that warms the cold,
the cold that tempers the
heat, and, to wind up with,
the universal coin wherewith
everything is bought, the
weight and balance that
makes the shepherd equal
with the king and the fool
with the wise man. Sleep, I
have heard say, has only one
fault, that it is like death;
for between a sleeping man
and a dead man there is very
little difference.'

Cervantes, *Don Quixote*,
ch. 68.

311 The idea of five methods of
meditation as antidotes to
the five poisons or *kleśas*
identified in the Mahāyāna
tradition was suggested to
Sangharakshita by his teacher
C. M. Chen, whom he knew
in Kalimpong. For Mr Chen's
own account, see C. M.
Chen, *Buddhist Meditation,
Systematic and Practical*,
published by Dr Yutang Lin,
El Cerrito 1989, chapter
8, 'The Five Fundamental
Meditations to Cure the Five
Poisons', pp. 326–30. See also
Sangharakshita, *The Purpose*

*and Practice of Buddhist
Meditation*, Ibis Publications,
Ledbury 2012, pp. 29–35
(*Complete Works*, vol. 5).

312 The mindfulness of breathing
is described in many places
in the Pāli canon. See, for
example, the *Ānāpānasati
Sutta, Majjhima Nikāya*
118 (iii.82–5); Bhikkhu
Ñāṇamoli and Bhikkhu
Bodhi (trans.), *The Middle
Length Discourses of the
Buddha*, Wisdom Publications,
Boston 1995, pp. 943–6;
or I. B. Horner (trans.),
Middle Length Sayings, vol.
iii, Pali Text Society, London
1967, pp. 124–6. Also the
*Satipaṭṭhāna Sutta, Majjhima
Nikāya* 10 (i.55–6); Bhikkhu
Ñāṇamoli and Bhikkhu
Bodhi (trans.), *The Middle
Length Discourses of the
Buddha*, Wisdom Publications,
Boston 1995, pp. 145–6; or
I. B. Horner (trans.), *Middle
Length Sayings*, vol.i, Pali Text
Society, London 1967, pp. 71–
2. Also the *Mahāsatipaṭṭhāna
Sutta, Dīgha Nikāya* 22
(ii.291), see M. Walshe
(trans.), *The Long Discourses
of the Buddha*, Wisdom
Publications, Boston 1995,
pp. 335–6, or T. W. Rhys
Davids (trans.), *Dialogues of
the Buddha*, part 2, Pali Text
Society, London 1971, p. 328.
Also the *Ānāpānasaṃyutta,
Saṃyutta Nikāya* v.311, in
Bhikkhu Bodhi (trans.), *The
Connected Discourses of the
Buddha*, Wisdom Publications,

Somerville 2000, pp. 1765–6, also F. L. Woodward (trans.), *Kindred Sayings*, part 5, Pali Text Society, London 1979, pp. 275–80.

Counting the breaths is first mentioned by Buddhaghosa in the *Visuddhimagga* (278–80); see Pe Maung Tin (trans.), *The Path of Purity*, Pali Text Society, London 1975, ch. 8, pp. 319–21. This is a commentary by Buddhaghosa on the Buddha's words in the *Satipaṭṭhāna Sutta*. See also Sangharakshita *Living with Awareness*, Windhorse Publications, Birmingham 2003 (*Complete Works*, vol. 15).

313 This meditation is described by Buddhaghosa in the *Visuddhimagga* (295–7); see Pe Maung Tin (trans.), *The Path of Purity*, Pali Text Society, London 1975. pp. 342–3. See also Sangharakshita, *Living with Kindness* (*Complete Works*, vol. 15).

314 This practice is described in, for example, sections 7–10 of the *Mahāsatipaṭṭhāna Sutta, Dīgha Nikāya* 22 (ii.295–7); see M. Walshe (trans.), *The Long Discourses of the Buddha*, Wisdom Publications, Boston 1995, p. 338–9; or T. W. Rhys Davids (trans.), *Dialogues of the Buddha*, part 2, p. 332.

315 This is related at Vinaya Piṭaka iii.68 (*Pārājika* 3.1); see I. B. Horner (trans.), *The Book of the Discipline*, part 1, Pali Text Society, Oxford 1996, p. 117.

316 This meditation practice is a recapitulation of the process the Buddha describes himself as having experienced just before his Enlightenment:

'I thought: What is there when ageing and death come to be? What is their necessary condition? Then with ordered attention I came to understand: Birth is there when ageing and death come to be; birth is a necessary condition for them.'

In this way he traced back each of the links of conditioned co-production. The translation quoted here is part of a passage in Bhikkhu Ñāṇamoli, *The Life of the Buddha*, Buddhist Publication Society, Kandy 1972, pp. 25–7. See also the *Nidānasaṃyutta, Saṃyutta Nikāya* ii.10; Bhikkhu Bodhi (trans.), *The Connected Discourses of the Buddha*, Wisdom Publications, Somerville 2000, pp. 537–40, also C. A. F. Rhys Davids (trans.), *The Book of the Kindred Sayings*, part 2, Pali Text Society, London 1997, pp. 6–7.

317 For an explanation of the *ālaya-vijñāna*, see Sangharakshita, *The Meaning of Conversion in Buddhism*, ch. 4 (*Complete Works*, vol. 2).

318 A canonical reference to the 'six element practice' is to be found in sections 8–17 of the *Mahārāhulovāda Sutta, Majjhima Nikāya*

62 (i.421–4); see Bhikkhu Ñāṇamoli and Bhikkhu Bodhi (trans.), *The Middle Length Discourses of the Buddha*, Wisdom Publications, Boston 1995, pp. 528–30; or I. B. Horner (trans.), *Middle Length Sayings*, vol. ii, Pali Text Society, Oxford 1957, pp. 92–5.

CHAPTER 12

319 Section 1.12 of the *Mahāparinibbāna Sutta*, *Dīgha Nikāya* 16 (ii.81); see M. Walshe (trans.), *The Long Discourses of the Buddha*, Wisdom, Boston 1995, p. 234; or T. W. Rhys Davids (trans.), *Dialogues of the Buddha*, part 2, Pali Text Society, Oxford 1977, p. 86.

320 'Prajna is like a sword in the hand of a man. In the hand of a man with sila it may be used for saving a man in danger. But in the hand of a man without sila it may be used for murder.'

B. R. Ambedkar, *The Buddha and his Dhamma*, Siddharth Publications, Bombay 1991, p. 210.

321 See, for example, the *Vimalakīrti-nirdeśa* in Robert A. F. Thurman (trans.), *The Holy Teaching of Vimalakīrti*, Pennsylvania State University, 1983, p. 99. And see also 'The Four Great Reliances: Criteria for the Spiritual Life', chapter 8 of Sangharakshita, *The*

Inconceivable Emancipation (*Complete Works*, vol. 16).

322 For more on *vijñāna* see Sangharakshita, *The Meaning of Conversion in Buddhism*, ch. 4 (*Complete Works*, vol. 2).

323 See A. F. Price and Wong Moulam (trans.), *The Diamond Sūtra and the Sūtra of Hui-neng*, Shambhala Publications, Boston 1990, p. 94.

324 The three levels of wisdom are enumerated in, for example, section 1.10 (43) of the *Sangiti Sutta*, *Dīgha Nikāya* 33 (iii.219); see Maurice Walsh (trans.), *The Long Discourses of the Buddha*, Wisdom Publications, Boston 1995, p. 486; T. W. Rhys Davids (trans.), *Dialogues of the Buddha*, part 3, p. 212.

325 See *Poems of Early Buddhist Nuns* (*Therīgāthā*), trans. C. A. F. Rhys Davids and K. R. Norman (trans.), Pali Text Society, Oxford 1997, pp. 88–9.

326 The story of Brahmā Sahāmpati's request is told in various places in the scriptures, for example in the *Ariyapariyesanā Sutta*, *Majjhima Nikāya* 26 (i.167–70); see Bhikkhu Ñāṇamoli and Bhikkhu Bodhi (trans.), *The Middle Length Discourses of the Buddha*, Wisdom Publications, Boston 1995, pp. 260–2; or I. B. Horner (trans.), *Middle Length Sayings*, vol. i, Pali Text Society, London 1967, pp. 211–3. Another version is to be found at *Saṃyutta*

Nikāya i.137; see Bhikkhu
Bodhi (trans.), *The
Connected Discourses
of the Buddha*, Wisdom
Publications, Boston 2000,
pp. 232–3; or C. A. F. Rhys
Davids (trans.), *The Book
of the Kindred Sayings*, part
1, Pali Text Society, Oxford
1997, p. 173.

327   The Abhidharma (the word
simply means 'about Dharma',
though its adherents came
to think of it as 'the higher
Dharma') began as an attempt
to systematize the Buddha's
teachings, and became a
scholastic enterprise that
lasted several hundred years
and involved an exhaustive
analysis of mind and mental
events. See Sangharakshita,
The Eternal Legacy,
ch. 7, 'The Fundamental
Abhidharma' (*Complete
Works*, vol. 15).

328   Edward Conze (trans.), *The
Perfection of Wisdom in
Eight Thousand Lines and its
Verse Summary*, Four Seasons
Foundation, San Francisco
1995, p. 178.

329   Line 29 of 'Lines Written
a Few Miles above Tintern
Abbey' (1798).

330   Preliminary admonition to
'The Perfection of Wisdom
in Eight Thousand Lines';
see Edward Conze (trans.),
*The Perfection of Wisdom in
Eight Thousand Lines and its
Verse Summary*, Four Seasons
Foundation, San Francisco
1995. Sangharakshita's

commentary is in *Wisdom
Beyond Words* (*Complete
Works*, vol. 15).

331   Edward Conze (trans.), *The
Perfection of Wisdom in
Eight Thousand Lines and its
Verse Summary*, Four Seasons
Foundation, San Francisco
1995, p. 135.

CHAPTER 13

332   Section 5.13 of the
Mahāparinibbāna Sutta, *Dīgha
Nikāya* 16 (ii.143); see M.
Walshe (trans.), *The Long
Discourses of the Buddha*,
Wisdom Publications, Boston
1995, p. 265; or T. W. Rhys
Davids (trans.), *Dialogues of
the Buddha*, part 2, Pali Text
Society, Oxford 1977, p. 158.

333   The bodhisattva ideal, the
bodhicitta, the six perfections
and the bodhisattva vow
are discussed in detail
in Sangharakshita, *The
Bodhisattva Ideal* (*Complete
Works*, vol. 4).

334   A distinction is made between
'historical' bodhisattvas,
men and women who have
undertaken the commitment
to gain Enlightenment,
and 'archetypal' bodhisattvas,
archetypal figures who
embody Enlightened
qualities.

335   The perfections are
enumerated many times in
the traditional literature.
See, for example, the
Pañcaviṃśatisāhasrikā 194–5,
quoted in Edward Conze,
Buddhist Texts Through the

336 One famous list of the gifts a Bodhisattva aspires to give is to be found in Śāntideva's *Bodhicaryāvatāra*, ch. 3, verses 6–21 (e.g. Kate Crosby and Andrew Skilton (trans.), Windhorse Publications, Birmingham 2002, pp. 27–9), but the tradition includes many and various discussions not only of what to give but the way in which gifts should be given and the consequences of giving. One passage even includes what one translation calls 'fried vegetable stalks' among the gifts listed; see *Aṅguttara Nikāya* iii.50, in E. M. Hare (trans.), *Gradual Sayings*, vol. iii, Pali Text Society, Oxford 1995, p. 41; or Bhikkhu Bodhi (trans.), *The Numerical Discourses of the Buddha*, Wisdom Publications, Boston 2012, p. 669.

337 *Leaves of Grass*, 'Song of Myself', part 40, line 9.

338 For example, in the *Vimalakīrti-nirdeśa*, Vimalakīrti challenges Subhūti: 'Take this food if, without abandoning desire, hatred, and folly, you can avoid association with them.' See Robert A. Thurman (trans.), *The Holy Teaching of Vimalakīrti*, Pennsylvania State University Press 1976, p. 27.

339 D. T. Suzuki (trans.), *Laṅkāvatāra Sūtra*, Motilal Banarsidass, Delhi 1999, ch. 8 'On Meat Eating', pp. 368–71.

340 For more about the five Buddhas of the mandala, see Sangharakshita, *Creative Symbols of Tantric Buddhism*, ch. 8 (*Complete Works*, vol. 14).

341 The ten *bhūmis* are enumerated in many Mahāyāna texts; for a particularly elaborte and beautiful description, see book 26 of the *Avataṃsaka Sūtra*; Thomas Cleary (trans.), *The Flower Ornament Scripture*, Shambhala Publications, Boston and London 1993, pp. 695–811.

342 Traditionally, the length of a *kalpa* is illustrated by the following simile: suppose that every hundred years a piece of silk is rubbed once on a solid rock one cubic mile in size; when the rock is worn away by this, one *kalpa* will still not have passed.

343 See W. E. Soothill (trans.), *The Lotus of the Wonderful Law*, Curzon Press, London 1987, p. 13.

344 For more about the *Lotus Sūtra*, see Sangharakshita, *The Drama of Cosmic Enlightenment* (*Complete Works*, vol. 16).

345 See *Dhammapada* 103: 'Though one should conquer in battle thousands upon thousands of men, yet he who conquers himself is (truly) the greatest in battle.' (trans. Sangharakshita)

346 For more about the Tibetan wheel of life, see Sangharakshita, *Creative Symbols of Tantric Buddhism* ch. 1, 'The Tibetan Wheel of Life' (*Complete Works*, vol. 13).

347 For more about Kṣitigarbha, see Vessantara, *Meeting the Buddhas*, Windhorse Publications, Birmingham 1994, pp. 199–201.

WHAT IS THE SANGHA?

PART 1: INTRODUCTION

348 For more about these experiences, see the first few chapters of Sangharakshita, *The Rainbow Road* (*Complete Works*, vol. 20).

CHAPTER 1

349 For more on these definitions, see pp. 158ff.

350 This story of Mahāprajāpatī Gautami is to be found at Vinaya Piṭaka ii.258–9 (*Cullavagga* 10.5); see I. B. Horner (trans.), *The Book of the Discipline*, part 5, Pali Text Society, Oxford 1992, p. 359. See also *Aṅguttara Nikāya* iv.280, in E. M. Hare (trans.), *Gradual Sayings*, vol. iv, Pali Text Society, Oxford 1995, pp. 186–7; or Bhikkhu Bodhi (trans.), *The Numerical Discourses of the Buddha*, Wisdom Publications, Boston 2012, p. 1193.

351 See sections 13–4 of the *Alagaddūpama Sutta, Majjhima Nikāya* 22 (i.134–5); Bhikkhu Ñāṇamoli and Bhikkhu Bodhi (trans.), *The Middle Length Discourses of the Buddha*, Wisdom Publications, Boston 1995, pp. 228–9; or I. B. Horner (trans.), *Middle Length Sayings*, vol. i, Pali Text Society, London 1967, pp. 173–4.

352 Bhabra Rock Edict, N. A. Nikam and R. McKeon (trans.), *The Edicts of Ashoka*, Asia Publishing House, Bombay 1959, p. 61.

353 *Adhyāśayasaṃcodana Sūtra.* Quoted by Śāntideva. See *Śikṣā-samuccaya*, Cecil Bendall and W. H. D. Rouse (trans.), Motilal Banarsidass, Delhi 1971, p. 17.

354 Sections 1–2 of the *Dakkhiṇāvibhaṅga Sutta, Majjhima Nikāya* 142 (iii.253); see Bhikkhu Ñāṇamoli and Bhikkhu Bodhi (trans.), *The Middle Length Discourses of the Buddha*, Wisdom Publications, Boston 1995, p. 1102; or I. B. Horner (trans.), *Middle Length Sayings*, vol. iii, Pali Text Society, Oxford 1993, p. 300.

355 The story of the Buddha's first discourse is told at Vinaya Piṭaka i.6–14 (*Mahāvagga* 1.5–6); see I. B. Horner (trans.), *The Book of the Discipline*, part 4, Pali Text Society, Oxford 1996, pp. 8–21. Also the *Dhammacakkappavattana*

Sutta, Saṃyutta Nikāya
v.420–4; see Bhikkhu Bodhi
(trans.), *The Connected
Discourses of the Buddha*,
Wisdom Publications, Boston
2000, pp. 1843ff; or C. A. F.
L. Woodward, *Book of the
Kindred Sayings*, part 5, Pali
Text Society, Oxford 1979,
pp. 356ff.

356 The language of refuge has
been used in Buddhism
since the earliest times.
According to the Vinaya
Piṭaka, the first two people to
encounter the Buddha after
his Enlightenment (they were
two merchants called Tapussa
and Bhallika) declared: 'We go
for refuge to the Blessed One,
and to the Dhamma.' Vinaya
Piṭaka i.4 (*Mahavagga* 1.4);
see I. B. Horner (trans.), *The
Book of the Discipline*, part 4,
Pali Text Society, Oxford 1996,
pp.5–6. See also *Dhammapada*
188–92.

357 For more on this way of
seeing Going for Refuge, see
Sangharakshita, *The Meaning
of Conversion in Buddhism*,
ch. 1 (*Complete Works*, vol. 2).

358 Section 1.4 of the
Mahāparinibbāna Sutta,
Dīgha Nikāya 16 (ii.73);
see Maurice Walshe (trans.),
*The Long Discourses of the
Buddha*, Wisdom Publications,
Boston 1995, p. 231; or
T. W. Rhys Davids (trans.),
Dialogues of the Buddha, part
2, Pali Text Society, Oxford
1977, p. 79.

359 *Upaddha Sutta, Saṃyutta
Nikāya* v.2; see Bhikkhu
Bodhi (trans.), *The Connected
Discourses of the Buddha*,
Wisdom Publications,
Boston 2000, pp. 1524–5;
or F. L. Woodward (trans.),
Kindred Sayings, part 5, Pali
Text Society, Oxford 1979, p. 2.

360 For an account of the
pratyekabuddhas, see Reginald
Ray, *Buddhist Saints in India*,
Oxford University Press,
Oxford and New York 1994,
ch. 7.

361 Suppose, monks, an ass
follows close behind a herd
of kine, thinking: I'm a cow
too! I'm a cow too! But he
is not like cows in colour,
voice or hoof. He just follows
close behind a herd of kine
thinking: I'm a cow too! I'm
a cow too! Just in the same
way, monks, we have some
monk who follows close
behind the Order of Monks
thinking: I'm a monk too! I'm
a monk too! But he has not
the desire to undertake the
training in the higher morality
which the other monks
possess, nor that in the higher
thought, nor that in the higher
insight which other monks
possess. He just follows close
behind thinking: I'm a monk
too! I'm a monk too!

*Gadrabha Sutta, Aṅguttara
Nikāya* i.229; see Bhikkhu
Bodhi (trans.), *The Numerical
Discourses of the Buddha*,
Wisdom Publications,

Boston 2012, p. 315; or
F. L. Woodward (trans.),
Gradual Sayings, vol. i, Pali
Text Society, Oxford 1995,
p. 209.

362   *Dhammapada* 194.

CHAPTER 2

363   This seems not necessarily to
be a reference to a specifically
Buddhist saying. In his
Complete Works the Vedanta
scholar Swami Vivekananda
quotes it just as 'a well-known
saying'.

364   See Preface to Reginald Ray,
Buddhist Saints in India,
Oxford University Press,
Oxford and New York 1994.

365   These rules comprise the
prātimokṣa, the set of training
rules recorded in the Vinaya
Piṭaka of the Pāli canon. (The
rules are to be found in the
Suttavibhaṅga; see I. B. Horner
(trans.), *The Book of the
Discipline*, part 1, Pali Text
Society, Oxford 1996.) The
versions of the *prātimokṣa*
followed by different Buddhist
traditions vary slightly.
See ch. 17, 'The Monastic
Order', in Sangharakshita,
The Three Jewels, Windhorse
Publications, Birmingham
1998, pp. 185ff (*Complete
Works*, vol. 2).

366   The *pārājikas* are listed in the
Vinaya Piṭaka; see the first
four sections of I. B. Horner
(trans.), *The Book of the
Discipline*, part 1, Pali
Text Society, Oxford 1996,
pp. 1–191 and part 3, Pali

Text Society, London 1983,
pp.156–76.

367   *Sāriputtasaṃyutta*, *Saṃyutta
Nikāya* iii.235; See Bhikkhu
Bodhi (trans.), *The Connected
Discourses of the Buddha*,
Wisdom Publications,
Boston 2000, p. 1015; or
F. L. Woodward and C. A. F.
Rhys Davids (trans.), *The
Book of the Kindred Sayings*,
part 3, Pali Text Society,
Oxford, 1975, p. 186.

368   Allan Bennett was a mentor
of Aleister Crowley and
taught him white magic. They
met when they were both
members of the Hermetic
Order of the Golden Dawn.
Having travelled to the East
for the sake of his health,
he studied Buddhism in Sri
Lanka and Burma before
returning to England. It is said
that he intended to travel on
to America, but if that was
his plan, it was thwarted by
the First World War, and he
lived out his life in his native
England until his death in
1923 at the age of 51. His
approach to the Dharma is
expressed in Allan Bennett,
The Wisdom of the Aryas,
Kegan Paul, London 1923.

369   The Buddha often described
the path to Enlightenment
in these terms and according
to the Pāli canon he did so
many times in the last days of
his life. For example, section
1.12 of the *Mahāparinibbāna
Sutta*, *Dīgha Nikāya* 16 (ii.81);
see Maurice Walshe (trans.),

The Long Discourses of the Buddha, Wisdom Publications, Boston 1995, p. 234; or T. W. Rhys Davids (trans.), *Dialogues of the Buddha*, part 2, Pali Text Society, Oxford 1977, p. 86. For an exposition of the threefold path, see *What is the Dharma?*, chapters 10–12, pp. 315ff. above.

370 The three levels of wisdom are enumerated in, for example, section 1.10 (43) of the *Saṅgīti Sutta*, *Dīgha Nikāya* 33 (iii.219); see *The Long Discourses of the Buddha*, Wisdom Publications, Boston 1995, p. 486; T. W. Rhys Davids (trans.), *Dialogues of the Buddha*, part 3, Pali Text Society, London 1991, p. 212. See also pp. 301ff. above.

371 The Buddha is recorded as making this fourfold classification on many occasions, for example, in the 'Mirror of Dhamma' he gave to Ānanda in the last days of his life; see section 2.9 of the *Mahāparinibbāna Sutta*, *Dīgha Nikāya* 16 (ii.93): Maurice Walshe (trans.), *The Long Discourses of the Buddha*, Wisdom Publications, Boston 1995, p. 241; or T. W. Rhys Davids (trans.), *Dialogues of the Buddha*, part 2, Pali Text Society, Oxford 1977, pp. 99–100. See also section 1.11 (14c) of the *Saṅgīti Sutta*, *Dīgha Nikāya* 33 (iii.227); Walshe, p. 491. The list of the eight

individuals, the four pairs of persons, is

'the stream-enterer and the one who is on the way to realizing the fruit of stream-entry, the once-returner and the one who is on the way to realizing the fruit of once-returning, the non-returner and the one who is on the way to realizing the fruit of non-returning, the arahant and the one who is on the way to arahantship',

as given in *Udāna* 5.5 (*Uposatha Sutta*); see John D. Ireland (trans.), *The Udāna and the Itivuttaka*, Buddhist Publication Society 2007, pp. 69–74.

372 The last of the eight qualities of the great ocean described by the Buddha in *Udāna* 5.5 (*Uposatha Sutta*) is that it is 'the abode of vast creatures' in F. L. Woodward (trans.), *The Minor Anthologies of the Pali Canon*, part 2, Pali Text Society, London 1985, p.65; and similarly the Dharma is the abode of mighty beings like the Stream Entrant, the once-returner, and so on (see previous note). See John D. Ireland (trans.), *The Udāna and the Itivuttaka*, Buddhist Publication Society 2007, p. 65.

373 Section 1.6 of the *Mahāparinibbāna Sutta*, *Dīgha Nikāya* 16 (ii.76–7); see Maurice Walshe (trans.), *The Long Discourses of the Buddha* Wisdom Publications,

Boston 1995, p. 233; or
T. W. Rhys Davids (trans.),
Dialogues of the Buddha, part
2, Pali Text Society, Oxford
1977, p. 82.

374   This hierarchy is found in
numerous places throughout
the Pāli canon: to take one
of very many examples,
see sections 42 to 45 of
the *Alagaddūpama Sutta*,
Majjhima Nikāya 22 (i.141);
Bhikkhu Ñāṇamoli and
Bhikkhu Bodhi (trans.), *The
Middle Length Discourses
of the Buddha*, Wisdom
Publications, Boston 1995,
pp. 235–6; or I. B. Horner
(trans.), *Middle Length
Sayings*, vol. i, Pali Text
Society, Oxford 1954,
pp. 181–2.

375   See Sangharakshita, *The
Bodhisattva Ideal*, ch. 7,
'The Bodhisattva Hierarchy'
(*Complete Works*, vol. 4).

376   For some of Sangharakshita's
writings on this theme see
Sangharakshita, *Forty-Three
Years Ago*, Windhorse
Publications, Glasgow
1993, especially p. 43, and
*The History of My Going
for Refuge*, Windhorse
Publications, Glasgow 1998,
especially pp. 110–5 (*Complete
Works*, vol. 2).

CHAPTER 3

377   The ten fetters are enumerated
in, for example, sections 2.1
(6–7) of the *Saṅgīti Sutta*,
Dīgha Nikāya 33 (ii.234):
M. Walshe (trans.), *The Long*

Discourses of the Buddha,
Wisdom Publications, Boston
1995, p. 495; or T. W. Rhys
Davids (trans.), *Dialogues of
the Buddha*, part 3, Pali Text
Society, Oxford 1991, p. 225.
Also *Saṃyutta Nikāya* v.61;
see Bhikkhu Bodhi (trans.),
*The Connected Discourses
of the Buddha*, Wisdom
Publications, Boston 2000,
p. 1565; or F. L. Woodward
(trans.), *Kindred Sayings*, part
5, Pali Text Society, Oxford
1979, p. 49.

378   Alfred Lord Tennyson, 'In
Memoriam A. H. H.' canto 96.

379   *Richard II*, act 5, scene 5.

380   Mark 2:27.

381   For more on the first three
fetters, see Sangharakshita,
The Taste of Freedom, ch. 1
(*Complete Works*, vol. 11) in
which these three fetters are
described as habit, vagueness,
and superficiality.

382   The Buddha speaks of
extending *mettā* in all
directions in verse 150 of the
Karaniya Mettā Sutta, *Sutta-
Nipāta* 1.8; see K. R. Norman
(trans.), *The Rhinoceros Horn
and Other Early Buddhist
Poems*, Pali Text Society,
London 1985, p. 24, and in
verse 76 of the *Tevijja Sutta*,
Dīgha Nikāya 13 (i.250–1);
see M. Walshe (trans.), *The
Long Discourses of the
Buddha*, Wisdom Publications,
Boston 1995, p. 194; or
T. W. Rhys Davids (trans.),
Dialogues of the Buddha, part
1, Pali Text Society, London

1973, pp. 317–8. Buddhaghosa, who lived almost a thousand years after the Buddha, wrote extensively on the practice of the *mettā bhavanā*; see *Visuddhimagga* 295–307 in Bhadantacariya Buddhaghosa, *The Path of Purification*, Bhikkhu Ñāṇamoli (trans.), Buddhist Publication Society, Kandy 1991, pp. 288–99, and especially sections 11–12 on p. 290. For a brief account of the practice, see also pp. 342ff. above.

CHAPTER 4

383   This phrase comes from T. S. Eliot's poem 'Sweeney Erect', which has the lines:

The lengthened shadow of a man
Is history, said Emerson.

In fact, Emerson wrote, in his essay 'Self-Reliance': 'An institution is the lengthened shadow of one man'.

384   See Georg Wilhelm Friedrich Hegel, *The Philosophy of History*, Dover Publications, New York 1956.

385   See Arnold J. Toynbee, *A Study of History: The Geneses of Civilizations*, Oxford University Press, New York 1962.

386   See Francis Fukuyama, *The End of History and the Last Man*, Avon Books, 1997.

387   See Karl Jaspers, *The Origin and Goal of History*, Routledge and Kegan Paul, London 1953.

388   Georg Wilhelm Friedrich Hegel, *The Philosophy of History*, Dover Publications, New York 1956, p. 319.

389   'The safest characterization of the European philosophical tradition is that it consists of a series of footnotes to Plato.' A. N. Whitehead, *Process and Reality*, 1929, part 2, ch. 1.

390   Georg Wilhelm Friedrich Hegel, *The Philosophy of History*, Dover Publications, New York 1956, pp. 2–3.

CHAPTER 6

391   See Sangharakshita, *The Bodhisattva Ideal*, ch. 2: 'The Awakening of the Bodhi Heart' (*Complete Works*, vol. 4).

CHAPTER 7

392   See *Amitāyur-Dhyāna-Sūtra* in *Buddhist Mahāyāna Texts*, ed. E. B. Cowell et al., Motilal Banarsidass, Delhi 1997, pp. 161–201. See also Ratnaguna and Śraddhāpa, *Great Faith, Great Wisdom*, Windhorse Publications, Cambridge 2016.

CHAPTER 8

393   Traditional accounts vary. In the *Majjhima Nikāya* (see section 14 of the *Ariyapariyesanā Sutta*, *Majjhima Nikāya* 26 (i.163); Bhikkhu Ñāṇamoli and Bhikkhu Bodhi (trans.), *The Middle Length Discourses of the Buddha*, p. 256; or I. B. Horner (trans.), *Middle Length Sayings*, vol. i, Pali

Text Society, Oxford 1957, p. 207) the Buddha simply says that

'though my mother and father wished otherwise and wept with tearful faces, I shaved off my hair and beard, put on the yellow robe, and went forth from the home life into homelessness'.

But other biographies, notably those of the Mahāyāna, describe in great detail, as suggested here, the Buddha's sorrowful leave-taking. It is this latter version of the story that Sir Edwin Arnold used in his epic poem about the Buddha's life, *The Light of Asia*.

394   This is what the Buddha calls 'the miracle of instruction'. See section 8 of the *Kevaddha Sutta, Dīgha Nikāya* 11 (i.214); M. Walshe (trans.), *The Long Discourses of the Buddha*, Wisdom Publications, Boston 1995, pp. 176; or T. W. Rhys Davids (trans.), *Dialogues of the Buddha*, part 1, Pali Text Society, London 1977, p. 279.

PART 11: INTRODUCTION

395   For more on this way of describing awareness, see Sangharakshita, *The Buddha's Noble Eightfold Path*, ch. 7, 'Levels of Awareness' (*Complete Works*, vol. 1).

396   See Dwight Goddard, *A Buddhist Bible*, Beacon Press, Boston 1970, p. 612.

397   Jack Hirschman (ed.), *Antonin Artaud Anthology*, City Light Books, San Francisco 1965, p. 222.

398   Section 33 of the *Mahāsaccaka Sutta, Majjhima Nikāya* 36 (i.247); see Bhikkhu Ñāṇamoli and Bhikkhu Bodhi (trans.), *The Middle Length Discourses of the Buddha*, p. 340; or I. B. Horner (trans.), *Middle Length Sayings*, vol. i, Pali Text Society, Oxford 1957, pp. 301–2.

CHAPTER 9

399   Vladimir Nabokov in conversation with James Mossman, *The Listener*, 23 October 1969.

400   James Drever, *A Dictionary of Psychology*, Penguin, Harmondsworth 1966, p. 49.

401   For more on these levels of consciousness see Robin Cooper, *The Evolving Mind*, Windhorse Publications, Birmingham 1996, ch. 6.

402   There is clearly scope for wondering whether this conception of a 'transcendental awareness' is not more or less the same thing as a conception of an absolute being. For more reflection on this theme, see ch. 2, 'The Awakening of the Bodhi Heart', in Sangharakshita, *The Bodhisattva Ideal* (*Complete Works*, vol. 4).

403   *Bhagavad Gītā*, ch. 7, verse 3.

404   *Dhammapada* 182.

CHAPTER 10

405 *Analects* 13.3.
406 Violet de Laszlo, *The Basic Writings of C. G. Jung*, Modern Library, 1959, pp. xxii–xxiii.
407 See Vinaya Piṭaka i.13–4 (*Mahāvagga* 1.6), in I. B. Horner (trans.), *The Book of the Discipline*, part 4, Pali Text Society, Oxford 1996, pp. 20–1.

CHAPTER 11

408 'The will to a *system*: in a philosopher, morally speaking, a subtle corruption, a disease of the character; amorally speaking, his will to appear more stupid than he is.'

Walter Kaufmann, *Nietzsche: Philosopher, Psychologist, Antichrist*, Princeton University Press, 1975, p. 80.
409 Ibid.
410 Friedrich Nietzsche, *Thus Spoke Zarathustra*, Penguin, London 1961, p. 41.
411 Ibid., p. 43.
412 Walter Kaufmann, *Nietzsche: Philosopher, Psychologist, Antichrist*, Princeton University Press, 1975, p. 151.

413 'Giving style' to one's character – a great and rare art! It is exercised by those who see all the strengths and weaknesses of their own nature and then comprehend them in an artistic plan until

everything appears as art and reason.

Quoted ibid., p. 251.
414 Ibid., ch. 6.
415 *Dhammapada* 103.
416 For more on the *bodhicitta*, see Sangharakshita, *The Bodhisattva Ideal*, ch. 2: 'The Awakening of the Bodhi Heart' (*Complete Works*, vol. 4) and above, pp. 365–6.

CHAPTER 12

417 See 'Some Notes on my own Poetry' in Edith Sitwell, *Collected Poems*, Macmillan, London 1957, pp. xv–xlvi.
418 These engravings by William Hogarth are to be seen in the National Gallery, London.
419 'Art is an attempt to create pleasing forms.' Herbert Read, *The Meaning of Art*, Faber and Faber, London 1943. 'Art is significant form.' Clive Bell, 'Art', 1914. 'Art is intuition.' Benedetto Croce, *The Essence of Aesthetic*, Heinemann 1921.
420 Sangharakshita, *The Religion of Art* (*Complete Works*, vol. 26).
421 There are examples of the mind being classified as a sense organ throughout the Pāli canon. See, for example, the Buddha's famous 'Fire Sermon': *Ādittapariyāya Sutta*, *Saṃyutta Nikāya* iv.19–20, in which, having declared that the eye, the ear, the nose, the tongue, and the body are 'burning', he says,

'The mind is burning, ideas are burning, mind-

consciousness is burning,
mind-contact is burning,
also whatever is felt as
pleasant or painful or
neither-painful-nor-pleasant
that arises with mind-
contact for its indispensable
condition, that too is
burning. Burning with
what? Burning with the fire
of lust, with the fire of hate,
with the fire of delusion. I
say it is burning with birth,
aging, and death, with
sorrows, with lamentations,
with pains, with griefs, with
despairs.'

Bhikkhu Bodhi (trans.), *The
Connected Discourses of the
Buddha*, Wisdom Publications,
Boston 2000, p. 1143; see also
F. L. Woodward (trans.), *The
Book of the Kindred Sayings*,
part 4, Pali Text Society,
London 1980, p. 10.

422 Vladimir Nabokov in
conversation with James
Mossman, *The Listener*, 23
October 1969.

423 For a further description of
how visualization practices
work, see Vessantara, *Meeting
the Buddhas*, Windhorse
Publications, Birmingham
1993, ch. 2: 'The Development
of Buddhist Visualization'.

PART III: INTRODUCTION

424 See *Puja*, Windhorse
Publications, Birmingham
1999, p. 37.

425 *Sigālaka Sutta, Dīgha Nikāya*
31; see M. Walshe (trans.),

*The Long Discourses of the
Buddha*, Wisdom Publications,
Boston 1995, pp. 461–9; or
T. W. Rhys Davids (trans.),
Dialogues of the Buddha, part
3, Pali Text Society, Oxford
1991, pp. 173–84.

426 See Plato, *The Last Days
of Socrates*, Christopher
Rowe (trans.), Penguin,
Harmondsworth 2010.

427 Charles Dickens, *The
Pickwick Papers*, ch. 61.

CHAPTER 13

428 See 'Rights and Duties' in
Sangharakshita, *Crossing
the Stream*, Windhorse
Publications, Glasgow 1987
(*Complete Works*, vol. 7).

429 In *Udāna* 5.4, the Buddha
tells this story and draws
from it exactly this moral,
though in that story the
boys are tormenting some
fish, not a crow. See John D.
Ireland (trans.), *The Udāna
and the Itivuttaka*, Buddhist
Publication Society 2007,
p. 66.

CHAPTER 14

430 Section 1.5 of the *Brahmajāla
Sutta, Dīgha Nikāya* 1 (i.3);
see Maurice Walshe (trans.),
*The Long Discourses of the
Buddha*, Wisdom Publications,
Boston 1995, p. 68; or
T. W. Rhys Davids (trans.),
Dialogues of the Buddha, part
1, Pali Text Society, Oxford
1977, p. 3.

431   See, for example, section
15 of the *Aggivacchagotta
Sutta, Majjhima Nikāya* 72
(i.486); Bhikkhu Ñāṇamoli
and Bhikkhu Bodhi (trans.),
*The Middle Length Discourses
of the Buddha*, Wisdom
Publications, Boston 1995,
pp. 592; or I. B. Horner
(trans.), *Middle Length
Sayings*, vol. ii, Pali Text
Society, Oxford 1957, p. 165.

432   Subhūti, what do you
think? Has the Tathāgata
attained the consummation
of incomparable
enlightenment? Has the
Tathāgata a teaching to
enunciate?
    Subhūti answered: As
I understand Buddha's
meaning there is no
formulation of truth
called consummation of
incomparable enlightenment.
Moreover, the Tathāgata
has no formulated
teaching to enunciate.
Wherefore? Because the
Tathāgata has said that
truth is uncontainable and
inexpressible. It neither is
nor is not.

A.F. Price (trans.), *The
Diamond Sūtra*, Shambhala
Publications, Boston 1990,
p. 24.

433   See D. T. Suzuki (trans.), *The
Laṅkāvatāra Sūtra*, George
Routledge, London 1932.

434   An account of Sangharakshita's
meeting with Anandamayi, 'the
blissful mother', is to be found
in *The Rainbow Road*, ch. 20
(*Complete Works*, vol. 20).

435   Sangharakshita also tells this
story in the preface to *Precious
Teachers* (*Complete Works*,
vol. 22). The three lamas were
Chattrul Rinpoche, Jamyang
Khyentse Rinpoche, and
Dudjom Rinpoche, and they all
feature in *Precious Teachers*.

436   Aristotle, *Nicomachean Ethics*,
book 2, 1105.b9.

437   The story of Nanda's
ordination on what would
have been his wedding day
is told in the *Dhammapada
Commentary*; see Eugene
Watson Burlingame
(trans.), *Buddhist Legends
(Dhammapada Commentary)*,
part 1, Pali Text Society, Luzac,
London 1969, pp. 218–9.
The better known sequel, in
which Nanda, now ordained,
is pining for his wife and
wants to leave the order of
monks, is told in the same
volume, pp. 220–3, and also
in *Udāna* 3.2; see John D.
Ireland (trans.), *The Udāna
and the Itivuttaka*, Buddhist
Publication Society 2007,
pp. 35–9.

438   Porphyry, *Plotinus*,
A. H. Armstrong (trans.),
Heinemann, London 1966.
vol. i, pp. 3ff.

439   Section 22 of the *Udumbarika-
Sīhanāda Sutta, Dīgha Nikāya*
25 (iii.55); see Maurice
Walshe (trans.), *The Long
Discourses of the Buddha*,
Wisdom Publications, Boston
1995, p. 393; or T. W. Rhys

Davids (trans.), *Dialogues of the Buddha*, part 3, Pali Text Society, Oxford 1991, p. 50.

CHAPTER 15

440   Section 30 of the *Sigālaka Sutta, Dīgha Nikāya* 31 (iii.190); see M. Walshe (trans.), *The Long Discourses of the Buddha*, Wisdom Publications, Boston 1995, p. 467; or T. W. Rhys Davids (trans.), *Dialogues of the Buddha*, part 3, Pali Text Society, Oxford 1991, pp. 181–2.

441   *Hamlet*, act 1, scene 4.

442   From 'To a Louse: on seeing one on a lady's bonnet, at church 1780': 'O wad some Power the giftie gie us/ To see oursels as ithers see us!'

443   The language of near and far enemies is derived from *Visuddhimagga* 319–20, in which Buddhaghosa identifies the near and far enemies of emotions such as loving-kindness and compassion. A far enemy is clearly opposite and inimical to the positive quality one wishes to cultivate: thus, ill will is the far enemy of loving-kindness. A near enemy, by contrast, is sufficiently like the desired quality to be mistaken for it: thus, sticky or needy affection (*pema*) is said to be the near enemy of loving-kindness. See Bhikkhu Ñāṇamoli (trans.), *The Path of Purification*, Buddhist Publication Society, Kandy 1991, p. 311–2.

444   *Paradise Lost*, book 5, lines 896–907.

445   George P. Upton, *The Standard Operas: their plots, their music, and their composers*, A. C. McClurg and Company, Chicago 1897, p. 41.

446   See *Amitāyur-Dhyāna-Sūtra* in E. B. Cowell et al. (eds.), *Buddhist Mahāyāna Texts*, Motilal Banarsidass, Delhi 1997, pp. 161–201.

CHAPTER 16

447   Section 31 of the *Sigālaka Sutta, Dīgha Nikāya* 31 (iii.190); see M. Walshe (trans.), *The Long Discourses of the Buddha*, Wisdom Publications, Boston 1995, pp. 467–8; or T. W. Rhys Davids (trans.), *Dialogues of the Buddha*, part 3, Pali Text Society, Oxford 1991, p. 182.

448   The four speech precepts are among the list of ten precepts first referred to in section 16 of the *Kūṭadanta Sutta, Dīgha Nikāya* 5 (i.138–9); M. Walshe (trans.), *The Long Discourses of the Buddha*, Wisdom Publications, Boston 1995, p. 137; or T. W. Rhys Davids (trans.), *Dialogues of the Buddha*, part 1, Pali Text Society, Oxford 1991, p. 179. They enjoin abstention from false, harsh, frivolous, and slanderous speech and encourage truthful, kindly, meaningful, and harmonious speech. Sangharakshita's comments on the four speech precepts are to be found in

The Ten Pillars of Buddhism (*Complete Works*, vol. 2).

449 Śāntideva, *Bodhicaryāvatāra*, ch. 8, verses 112 ff.

450 Section 31 of the *Sigālaka Sutta*, *Dīgha Nikāya* 31 (iii.190); see M. Walshe (trans.), *The Long Discourses of the Buddha*, Wisdom Publications, Boston 1995, pp. 467–8; or T. W. Rhys Davids (trans.), *Dialogues of the Buddha*, part 3, Pali Text Society, Oxford 1991, p. 182.

451 See Sangharakshita, *The Inconceivable Emancipation*, ch. 3 (*Complete Works*, vol. 16).

452 Are not religion and politics
    the same thing? Brotherhood
    is religion,
    O demonstrations of reason,
    dividing families in cruelty
    and pride!'

    William Blake, *Jerusalem*, plate 57, lines 10–11.

453 For more on the love mode and the power mode, see Sangharakshita, *The Ten Pillars of Buddhism*, part 2, section 1, on the first precept (*Complete Works*, vol. 2).

454 *Meghiya Sutta*, *Udāna* 4.1 in John D. Ireland (trans.), *The Udāna and the Itivuttaka*, Buddhist Publication Society, Kandy 1997, pp. 50–4.

455 *Maggasaṃyutta*, *Saṃyutta Nikāya* v.2: see Bhikkhu Bodhi (trans.), *The Connected Discourses of the Buddha*, Wisdom Publications, Boston 2000, pp. 1524–5; also F. L. Woodward (trans.), *The*

Book of the Kindred Sayings, part 5, Pali Text Society, London 1979, p. 2.

456 See Sangharakshita, *The Ten Pillars of Buddhism*, part 2, section 3, on the third precept (*Complete Works*, vol. 2).

457 Section 45 of the *Mahāgovinda Sutta*, *Dīgha Nikāya* 19 (ii.241); see M. Walshe (trans.), *The Long Discourses of the Buddha*, Wisdom Publications, Boston 1995, p. 308; or T. W. Rhys Davids (trans.), *Dialogues of the Buddha*, part 2, Pali Text Society, Oxford 1991, p. 273.

CHAPTER 17

458 For more on right livelihood as a limb of the Noble Eightfold Path, see Sangharakshita, *The Buddha's Noble Eightfold Path*, ch. 5: 'The ideal society' (*Complete Works*, vol. 1).

459 This list of prohibited occupations is to be found at *Aṅguttara Nikāya* iii.208; see Bhikkhu Bodhi (trans.), *The Numerical Discourses of the Buddha*, Wisdom Publications, Boston 2012, p. 790.

460 For example, *Brahmajāla Sutta*, *Dīgha Nikāya* 1; see M. Walshe (trans.), *The Long Discourses of the Buddha*, Wisdom Publications, Boston 1995, pp. 71–2; or T. W. Rhys Davids (trans.), *Dialogues of the Buddha*, part 1, Pali Text Society, Oxford 1977, pp. 16–9.

461 Section 32 of the *Sigālaka Sutta*, *Dīgha Nikāya* 31 (iii.191); see M. Walshe (trans.), *The Long Discourses*

of the Buddha, Wisdom
Publications, Boston 1995,
pp. 468; or T. W. Rhys Davids
(trans.), *Dialogues of the
Buddha*, part 3, Pali Text
Society, Oxford 1991, p. 182.

CHAPTER 18

462 *Dhammapada* 49, trans.
Sangharakshita.

463 This Latin translation was
published by Michael Viggo
Fausböll, a Danish pioneer of
Pāli scholarship, in 1855.

464 See p. 404.

CHAPTER 19

465 For more on the Path
of Vision and the Path
of Transformation, see
Sangharakshita, *The Buddha's
Noble Eightfold Path*, ch. 1
(*Complete Works*, vol. 1).

466 See *Mucalinda Sutta, Udāna*
2.1, in John D. Ireland (trans.),
The Udāna and the Itivuttaka,
Buddhist Publication Society,
Kandy 1997, p. 23. The story
of Mucalinda's protection
of the Buddha is also told in
Vinaya Piṭaka i.3 (*Mahāvagga*
1.3), in I. B. Horner (trans.),
The Book of the Discipline,
part 4, Pali Text Society,
Oxford 1996, p. 4.

467 The story of Brahmā
Sahāmpati's request is told
in various places in the
scriptures, for example
in the *Ariyapariyesanā
Sutta, Majjhima Nikāya*
26 (i.167–70); see Bhikkhu
Ñāṇamoli and Bhikkhu
Bodhi (trans.), *The Middle*

*Length Discourses of the
Buddha*, Wisdom Publications,
Boston 1995, pp. 260–2; or
I. B. Horner (trans.), *Middle
Length Sayings*, vol. i, Pali
Text Society, London 1967,
pp. 211–3. Another version
is to be found at *Saṃyutta
Nikāya* i.137; see Bhikkhu
Bodhi (trans.), *The Connected
Discourses of the Buddha*,
Wisdom Publications, Boston
2000, pp. 232–3; or C. A.
F. Rhys Davids (trans.), *The
Book of the Kindred Sayings*,
part 1, Pali Text Society,
Oxford 1997, p. 173.

468 See, for example, the
Lalitavistara Sūtra in
Gwendolyn Bays (trans.),
The Voice of the Buddha,
Dharma Publishing, Berkeley
1983, vol. ii, p. 570; or the
Abhiniṣkramaṇa Sūtra in
Samuel Beal (trans.), *The
Romantic Legend of Śākya
Buddha*, Motilal Banarsidass,
Delhi 1985 (first published
1875), p. 237.

469 Xuanzang, *Buddhist Records
of the Western World*,
Samuel Beal (trans.), Motilal
Banarsidass, Delhi 1981
(first published 1884), part 2,
p. 123.

470 See Vinaya Piṭaka i.7
(*Mahāvagga* 1.6), in
I. B. Horner (trans.), *The Book
of the Discipline*, part 4, Pali
Text Society, Oxford 1996,
p. 11.

471 'Reverence, humility,
contentment, gratitude and
timely hearing of the Dhamma;

this is the most auspicious performance.' *Mahāmaṅgala Sutta* in *Sutta-Nipāta* verse 265. This translation by H. Saddhatissa, Curzon Press, London 1985, p. 29.

472 From the *Sigālaka Sutta* (also known as the *Sigālovāda Sutta*), *Dīgha Nikāya* 31 (iii.188). This translation is from M. Walshe (trans.), *The Long Discourses of the Buddha*, Wisdom Publications, Boston 1995, p. 467. For an alternative translation, see T. W. Rhys Davids (trans.), *Dialogues of the Buddha*, part 3, Pali Text Society, Oxford 1991, p. 180.

473 Harold Bloom, *Shakespeare: The Invention of the Human*, Fourth Estate, London 1998.

474 *Dhammapada* 354, trans. Sangharakshita.

475 '[Of] all the virtues, there is no quality I would sooner have, and be thought to have, than gratitude. For gratitude not merely stands alone at the head of all the virtues, but is even mother of all the rest.'

'Pro Cnaeo Plancio', in N. H. Watts (trans.), *Cicero: The Speeches, with an English Translation*, Loeb Classical Library, Heinemann, London 1923, p. 513.

476 Ingratitude is listed as one of the four great offences at *Aṅguttara Nikāya* ii.226; see Bhikkhu Bodhi (trans.), *The Numerical Discourses of the Buddha*, Wisdom Publications, Boston 2012, p. 597; or F. L. Woodward (trans.), *The Book of the Gradual Sayings*, vol. ii, Pali Text Society, Oxford 1995, p. 234.

477 For example, according to tradition, the first person whom the Buddha met on the road after his Enlightenment – his name was Upaka – despite being impressed by the Buddha's appearance, having questioned him and been told that he was indeed Enlightened, simply said, 'May it be so, friend,' and walked away. See *Ariyapariyesanā Sutta, Majjhima Nikāya* 26 (i.172); also Bhikkhu Ñāṇamoli and Bhikkhu Bodhi (trans.), *The Middle Length Discourses of the Buddha*, Wisdom Publications, Boston 1995, pp. 263–4; or I. B. Horner (trans.), *Middle Length Sayings*, vol. i, Pali Text Society, London 1967, pp. 214–5. The Buddha often gave his followers advice on how to handle abuse, and on one occasion demonstrated this himself when a Brahmin called Akkosaka Bhāradvāja 'insulted and cursed him with rude, harsh words'. The Buddha points out that, just as if the Brahmin offered him food and he declined to accept it, the food would remain the Brahmin's property, on this occasion he declines to accept the Brahmin's abuse. See *Akkosa Sutta, Saṃyutta*

Nikāya i.161–3; Bhikkhu
Bodhi (trans.), *The Connected
Discourses of the Buddha*,
Wisdom Publications, Boston
2000, pp. 255–7; or C. A.
F. Rhys Davids (trans.), *The
Book of the Kindred Sayings*,
part 1, Pali Text Society,
Oxford 1997, pp. 200–3. And
the person who famously tried
to kill the Buddha was his
cousin Devadatta; see p. 63
above.

CHAPTER 21

478 For example, the *Ānāpānasati
Sutta*, *Majjhima Nikāya*
118 (iii.82–5); see Bhikkhu
Ñāṇamoli and Bhikkhu
Bodhi (trans.), *The Middle
Length Discourses of the
Buddha*, Wisdom Publications,
Boston 1995, pp. 943–6; or
I. B. Horner (trans.), *Middle
Length Sayings*, vol.iii, Pali
Text Society, London 1967,
pp. 124–6. See also the
Satipaṭṭhāna Sutta, *Majjhima
Nikāya* 10 (i.55–6); Bhikkhu
Ñāṇamoli and Bhikkhu
Bodhi (trans.), *The Middle*

*Length Discourses of the
Buddha*, Wisdom Publications,
Boston 1995, pp. 145–6;
or I. B. Horner (trans.),
Middle Length Sayings, vol.
i, Pali Text Society, London
1967, pp. 71–2. See also the
Mahāsatipaṭṭhāna Sutta, *Dīgha
Nikāya* 22 (ii.291); M. Walshe
(trans.), *The Long Discourses
of the Buddha*, Wisdom
Publications, Boston 1995,
pp. 335–6; or T. W. Rhys
Davids (trans.), *Dialogues of
the Buddha*, part 2, Pali Text
Society, London 1971, p. 328.
See also *Ānāpānasaṃyutta*,
Saṃyutta Nikāya v.311, in
Bhikkhu Bodhi (trans.), *The
Connected Discourses of the
Buddha*, Wisdom Publications,
Somerville 2000, pp. 1765–6;
or F. L. Woodward (trans.),
Kindred Sayings, part 5,
Pali Text Society, London
1979, pp. 275–80. See also
Sangharakshita, *Living
with Awareness*, Windhorse
Publications, Birmingham
2003 (*Complete Works*,
vol. 15).

SOURCES

The chapters in each of the three books in this volume were woven together from talks given by Sangharakshita between 1966 and 1994.

WHO IS THE BUDDHA?

First published in 1994 by Windhorse Publications

First published in 1998 by Windhorse Publications

First published in 2001 by Windhorse Publications

Part 1

Introduction
The Individual and the Spiritual Community (1970)
Buddhism, Nietzsche and 'The Superman' (1969)

1   The Integration of Buddism into Western Society (1992)
    The Individual, the Group, and the Community (1971)
2   The Individual, the Group, and the Community (1971)
3   The Individual, the Group, and the Community (1971)
4   A Vision of History (1978)
5   The Individual and the Spiritual Community (1970)
6   Authority and the Individual in the New Society (1979)
7   Authority and the Individual in the New Society (1979)
8   The Individual, the Group, and the Community (1971)
    Authority and the Individual in the New Society (1979)
    Buddhism, Nietzsche and 'The Superman' (1969)

Part 11

Introduction
The Axial Age and the Emergence of the New Man (1969)

9   Individuality, True and False (1970)
     How Consciousness Evolves (1970)
     Art and the Spiritual Life (1970)
10   Individuality, True and False (1970)
11   Buddhism, Nietzsche and 'The Superman' (1969)
12   Art and the Spiritual Life (1969)

Part III

Introduction
The Meaning of Friendship in Buddhism (1992)
The Problem of Personal Relationships (1970)

INDEX

rose-apple tree experience 22–3
going forth 29
gratitude 360, 596–8
old age 288–9
symbols of 137–8
Buddha Day, *see* Wesak
Buddha Jewel 393, 395, 439
Buddha-fields 243, 379–80
Buddhaghosa 288, 289, 316
Buddhahood 9, 12, 46, 54, 62–3, 395, 398, 502–3
buddha-kṣetra, *see* Buddha-fields
Buddha-mind 78–81, 91
Buddha-to-be, *see* Siddhārtha Gautama
Buddhavacana 78, 80–3, 89–90, 394
Buddhist art 45, 48–9, 53–4, 152, 179, 277, 331
Buddhist countries 15, 19, 50, 359, 368–9, 371, 582, 589
Buddhist life 71, 182, 268, 277, 296–314, 331, 395–6, 487
Buddhist parents 531–44
Buddhist path 15, 34, 45, 60, 290, 295, 493, 503
Buddhist philosophy 81, 101, 163, 183, 220, 231, 241–2, 331
Buddhist practice xi, xv, 14, 70–1, 394, 398, 403, 410
Buddhist world 19, 93, 115, 174–5, 281, 366, 406, 408
Burma 8, 19, 45, 89, 406–7, 410, 413
burning house, parable of 35
business relationships 581–8

Calcutta 50, 267, 548
castes 23, 49, 53, 77, 142, 158, 461, 522
causality 316–17
causation 99, 197–8
celibacy 337, 579
ceremonies 22–3, 194, 255, 397, 405–6, 419, 455
cetanā 99
change 12–13, 119, 148–9, 180–1, 254–6, 292–3, 418, 463–4
Channa 29, 118
charioteer 25–9, 207
chastity 318, 321, 579
childhood, growing up from 36
children, duties of 523, 531
China 241, 308, 377, 396, 406, 408, 413, 429, 432, 489, 495, 596
Christ 45–6, 49, 151, 189–90, 230, 426–7, 429, 449

Christianity 44–5, 189–91, 396–7, 427, 430, 448–50, 515, 603
crucifixion 230
death of 497
resurrection 230–1
view of Buddhism 151
Christianity-substitute 190–1
Cicero 604
cinta-mayī-prajñā 302–3
citta visuddhi 290–2
citta-niyama 98–9
clinging 41, 129, 193, 199, 201, 203, 255–6
commitment 324–5, 327, 331, 403, 471, 526, 528–9, 533
communication 90, 140, 164, 181–2, 514, 521, 554–6
enlightened 78–81
horizontal 554–5
real 140, 275, 390, 400, 439, 554, 556, 618
vertical 555–6
community, spiritual, *see* sangha
compassion 73, 132, 177–8, 355, 357, 364–5, 382, 451–2
composers 515, 602–3
concentration 123–4, 271–4, 306, 310–11, 337, 341, 351–2, 354
exercises/techniques 165, 272–4
meditative 54, 109, 307, 309, 311, 349, 351
conditionality 13, 94, 97–8, 100–101, 111, 182–6, 197–8, 330
implications 183–4
law/principle of 94, 98–101, 175, 181, 204, 279, 317
spiral mode of 13–14, 97, 101, 185, 203, 258
universal 92, 176, 183, 192, 194
conditioned co-production 12–14, 67, 69, 81, 92, 94, 175–6, 187, 192–3, 281
chain of, *see nidana* chain
links of 185, 243, 341, 346
conditioned existence 32, 48, 85, 213, 215–16, 220–1, 243–4, 292
conditioning
group 437–8, 468, 506, 509
psychological 52, 73, 129, 131, 142, 149, 277, 481
confession 265–6
conformity 438, 440, 470
Confucius 426, 471–2, 489, 491
confusion (*moha*) 7, 73, 83, 195, 259, 293, 340

consciousness 113–14, 129–31, 136–7,
   195–6, 333–6, 349–51, 479–83,
   554–6
  absolute 480, 484, 561
  acts of 216–17
  and being 101–2, 247, 512
  development of 16, 483–5
  evolution of 391, 467, 481, 486
  higher 53, 85, 136, 307, 617
  higher states of 70, 80, 107–9, 114,
   123, 126, 302, 439
  individual 112, 334, 350
  level of 114, 246, 270, 480, 483–4,
   511, 621, 624
  objective 480–1, 484
  states of 101–2, 104, 114, 123, 307,
   512, 514
  transcendental 480–2, 484, 561
  universal 136, 350, 469, 480–1
consumerism 348, 621
  pseudo-spiritual 327
contact, personal 63, 144, 314, 389,
   439, 578, 619
contemplation 123, 129, 134, 136,
   246–7, 341, 346, 348
contentment 15, 102, 104, 167, 283,
   293, 315, 321
continuity 148, 310, 478, 565–8, 572
control
  by the group 436
  by the senses 298
  of food, sex, and sleep 337–8
  of mind 124, 218, 264, 340
conventional morality 102, 245
conversion 208, 296, 397, 575
Conze, Edward 213–15, 298, 360–1
coolies 585–6
cooperation 41, 504, 553, 619
corpse, contemplation of 125–7,
   344–6
corruptions 354; see also āsravas
cosmos 35, 88, 164, 373, 376
counteractive karma 109
covetousness 15, 293
craving 14, 128–9, 184, 199, 201–3,
   259, 278–9, 347–8
creativity 38, 348, 431, 471, 506, 509
cremation grounds 125–6, 344–7
crime 99, 105, 615
cultural groups 39, 224, 436
culture 39, 162, 368–9, 427, 430,
   523–4, 604–5, 620
cyclical mode 97, 185, 258

dāna 367, 405
darkness 431, 433
  spiritual 61, 130, 193, 362
Darwin, Charles 10, 12, 189, 475–6, 499
death 27–8, 92, 94–8, 107–10, 199–201,
   346–8, 417–18, 568–72
  awareness of 127, 568
  and birth 92, 97–8, 117, 232, 258,
   362
  of Buddha 116–38
  and decay 130, 200–201
  fear of 211, 346
  mystery of 94, 96, 113
  recollection of 120, 124, 126–9
  spiritual 123, 230, 348
death-proximate karma 107–9
Deathless
  door to 74, 75, 98, 176–7
  quest for 208
decay, contemplation of 125–6, 345–6
  and death 130, 200–201, 207–8
deer park 75, 395
defilements 85, 118, 123, 128, 143,
   223, 362
delight 13, 15, 29, 167, 176, 238, 293,
   512
delusion 31, 244, 274, 304, 346, 355–6,
   362, 394
dependence 13–14, 67, 129–30, 185,
   196–200, 255, 263, 276–8
dependent origination, see conditioned
  co-production
depression 126–7, 258
Devadatta 63, 85, 454
devas 141–3, 152
development
  of consciousness 16, 483–5
  human 20, 59, 70, 556, 564, 572,
   617, 623
  spiritual 11, 59, 62, 311, 313, 561,
   599, 623
devotion 62, 66, 103, 144, 189, 191,
   301, 310–12, 372, 451, 546, 548
devotional practices 63, 310, 351, 487,
   621
dhamma, see Dharma
Dhammadinnā 68
Dhammapada xi, 48, 54, 84, 159, 589,
   591, 593
Dharma 66–70, 72–8, 157–65, 175–80,
   358–63, 393–6, 401–6, 604–8
  Eye 284, 329–30
  meaning 157–60, 167–9
  nature 160–3
  rain of the 178–81, 314

Enlightenment (*cont.*)
    Buddha's 19, 21, 32, 52, 92–3, 137,
        145, 148
    embodiment of 299–301
    experience 64, 66–7, 73, 97, 133,
        157–8, 178, 182
    journey to 252, 280–95
    way to 18–33
    will to, *see bodhicitta*
enthusiasm 264, 288, 401, 577, 603
equanimity 16, 85, 126, 184, 192, 199,
    284, 289
eternal life 223, 244, 249
eternity 145–6, 148–50, 164, 238, 378,
    384
ethics 53, 100–102, 104–5, 190–2,
    200, 264, 291, 315–32, 337,
    354, 370, 411, 582, 624
everyday life 186, 202, 260, 289
evil 13, 15, 52, 84, 137, 242, 277, 293
evolution 9–10, 13, 16–17, 20, 475–9,
    481–3, 498, 515–16
    biological 10–11, 59, 475, 480
    of a Buddha 3–17
    of consciousness 391, 467, 481,
        486
    higher 12–16, 18, 59–62, 444,
        477–80, 482–4, 505–6, 515–16
    of individual 475–85
    lower 12–16, 59, 61, 444, 477–82,
        484
evolutionary process 12, 16, 476, 478,
    481, 493, 498–9, 501
existence, human 8, 213, 261, 347,
    395, 483, 564, 586
experience
    human 4, 13, 306, 564
    meditation 31, 109, 120, 122, 335,
        351–2, 516, 608, 621
    sensuous 32, 199, 202, 420
    spiritual 166, 169, 175, 258, 329,
        336, 551, 559
exploitation 452, 581, 585, 588, 591, 593
external world 129, 134–5, 198, 246,
    292, 298, 421, 507–8
extinction 223, 617, 619
extremes 52, 75, 202, 294, 301, 303,
    307, 310

factors of Enlightenment, seven 186,
    242, 281, 284–9, 292, 304, 372
faculties 55, 57, 115, 296–9, 305,
    310–11, 356
    spiritual 233, 298, 306, 309, 311–14,
        357

faith 203, 263–4, 273, 299–301,
    309–11, 329, 400
    ethical counterpart of craving 263
false speech 318, 337, 573
family 24–5, 37–8, 55–6, 211–12,
    261–2, 441–2, 527–8, 537
fathers 600
father-substitute 549–51, 553, 557
fearlessness 53–4, 367–9, 516
feelings 199, 347
    consideration of others' 537
    devotional 310
    erotic 342–3
    group 436–7
    inability to experience 487, 491
    irrational 265
    learning to experience 488
    mindfulness of 203, 309, 480
    pleasant 129, 202–3, 347
    positive 104, 599; *see also mettā*
    reactions to 203, 260
    unpleasant 202–3
festivals, Buddhist 18, 19, 119, 401,
    403, 457, 540, 604
fetters 24–5, 199, 253–6, 412, 416–22,
    467
    breaking 253–7
Fidelio 570–1
fidelity 563–72
    to ideals 563–4, 569, 572
    to oneself 563–4, 572
    to other people 563–5, 572
five ascetics, *see* ascetics, five
five *niyamas* xiv, 98–101, 111, 316–17
five precepts 255, 264, 291, 318–25,
    328, 331, 370, 582
five *skandhas* 195, 198, 200, 292, 363
five spiritual faculties 186, 296–8, 301,
    304, 306, 308–14, 372, 375
fly-whisk 48–9
food
    borrowed from the earth 349
    the Buddha's reaction to alms food
        50–1
    for children 536–7
    effect on meditation 337–8
    employer's duty to provide 586–7
    gift of 369–70
    monastic 590–1
four noble truths, *see* noble truths
four sights 25–9, 34–6, 42, 207
freedom 15, 67, 277–8, 281, 368, 440,
    471, 477
friendliness 56, 90, 125, 179, 343, 444,
    450–2, 576

friendship 70–1, 314, 343, 371, 399, 472, 556, 573–80
  spiritual 90, 312, 314, 356, 360, 395, 399, 420, 439–40, 578–80, 599, 603–9; see also kalyāṇa mitratā
  the whole of the spiritual life 90, 395, 578–80

games 95, 276, 553, 581
Gaṇḍavyūha Sutra 88
gandharva 141–3
Ganges 162, 194, 346, 426
gāravas, six 69–71
Gautama, Siddhārtha 18, 21–30, 33–6, 38–43, 51–2, 149, 151, 207–8
generosity 15, 54, 55, 105, 245, 264, 282–3, 367, 367–9, 401, 409, 515, 573, 575
genius 57–60, 513–14
gifts xiii, 13, 367, 369, 594, 598, 604, 606
giving, see generosity
goals 73, 75, 193, 195, 224–8, 250, 394–5, 484
God
  death of 497
  of Love 448–9
  of Nature 448
  personal 152, 193, 497, 549
  of Power 448–9
Goethe, J.W. von 58, 471, 500–501, 509, 602
Going for Refuge 69, 153, 325–31, 356, 396–8, 400, 417, 457–8; see also Three Refuges
going forth 36–9, 42, 460–1, 528
gold, tested in the fire 15, 163
Govinda, Lama 17, 48, 303–4, 572
grasping 129, 199, 201, 225, 347, 419
gratitude 43, 64, 74, 360–2, 513, 528–9, 595–609
  objects of 599, 601, 603
gravitational field 244–5, 254, 373
gravitational pull 186, 241–57, 273, 324, 440, 443
gravity 100, 244, 619
great self 234–5
greatness 62, 235
group conditioning 437–8, 468, 506, 509
group loyalties 436, 462
group-consciousness 437, 477
groups
  cultural 39, 224, 436
  economic 38–9, 436
  positive 433, 444, 452, 455, 457–8

religious 6, 224, 546, 548, 550, 553, 557, 560
  social 5, 38, 436, 441, 470
  and spiritual community 434–44
growth, spiritual 258–9, 285, 293, 313, 506, 556, 623
guidance 41, 132, 134, 150, 483, 489, 587, 594
guilt 214, 227, 265, 270, 538, 543
gurus xiv, 70, 89, 162–3, 286, 470, 545–62, 606

habitual karma 108–9
happiness 97, 102, 225, 227, 258–9, 261–2, 269, 271–2
harmony 58, 90–1, 121, 283, 304, 307, 399
Haydn, J. 509, 513, 515
health 27, 97, 173, 313–14, 370, 574, 617
Heart Sūtra 233, 360
heavens 162, 167, 169, 230, 315–16, 378, 495, 497
Hegel, G.W. 9, 44, 423, 426, 494
hell 63, 182, 243, 316, 324, 348, 383, 495
hermits 88, 103, 125, 408–9, 497
heroes 46–7, 49, 55–7, 59–60, 177
heroic ideal 44–56
hero-worship 46, 57–71
hierarchy 10–11, 49, 413–14
higher consciousness 53, 85, 136, 307, 617
higher evolution 12–16, 18, 59–62, 444, 477–80, 482–4, 505–6, 515–16
higher self 310–11, 491, 513
higher states of consciousness 70, 80, 107–9, 114, 123, 126, 302, 439
hindrances 123, 256–7, 547
Hindu teachers 311–12, 488
Hinduism 310–12, 317, 424, 429, 614
Hindus xii, 97, 151, 162, 206, 217, 311, 325
history 389, 391, 396, 398, 423–6, 428, 432, 467–8
homeless life 34, 36, 42, 208, 460
Homer 96, 427, 513, 602
honour 19, 55, 65–6, 69–71, 105, 395, 510, 523
Huineng 146, 299, 356–7, 361, 389
human beings 62–3, 177–8, 180–1, 383, 425–8, 477–9, 496–500, 561–3
human body 190, 215, 344, 346, 601

labels 46, 143, 151, 232
laity 390, 409–10, 414, 583
lakes 18, 121, 269, 274, 349, 454
Lalitavistara 88
lakṣaṇas 209, 216–17, 220, 281; *see
    also* characteristics
lamas 134, 233, 268, 408, 551, 559,
    584
language 145, 151, 161, 164–5, 206,
    536, 539, 601
Laṅkāvatāra Sūtra 87–8, 370
levitation 267–8
liberations 85, 118, 133, 175, 223,
    311, 390, 412
    three 218–21
life
    Buddhist 71, 268, 277, 296–7, 299,
        310, 312, 395–6
    eternal 223, 244, 249
    ethical 53, 264, 291, 582, 624
    everyday 186, 202, 260, 289
    religious 256, 270, 590
    spiritual 263–5, 284–5, 296–9, 372,
        375, 398–9, 528–9, 578–80
    wheel of, *see* wheel of life
lifestyle 293, 328, 404, 407, 410, 415,
    566
Light of Asia, The 88
lightning 266, 448, 495
links, *see* nidānas
Lion's Roar 53
livelihood 283–4, 339, 583, 617
    perfect 282–3, 582
    right 222, 356, 370–1, 582
    and suffering 211–2
    wrong 283, 583
loka dharmas 159–60
Lokajyeṣṭha 61
Lotus Sūtra 35, 87, 91, 178, 377–84,
    443
lotuses 74, 177–8, 180, 313, 454
love 159, 319, 342–4, 448–50, 549,
    569–70, 576, 594
loving-kindness, see *mettā*
lower evolution 12–16, 59, 61, 444,
    477–82, 484
loyalty 436, 438, 442, 524, 526,
    569
Luther, Martin 194

Magadha 151, 289, 453, 571
Mahāgovinda Sutta 209, 57
Mahāprajāpatī Gautami 15, 22, 167,
    293
Mahāsaṅgha 407, 458

Mahāvastu 318
Mahāyāna 87–8, 235–6, 275, 278, 365,
    373, 376, 413–14
    scriptures 63, 182, 203, 231, 383,
        413
    sūtras 86–7, 89, 168, 178, 182, 235,
        370, 376–81
    tradition 86, 243, 361, 372, 376
Majjhima Nikāya 68, 84, 175, 207,
    209, 290
mandala of the Five Buddhas 243,
    373–5,
Mani 431–2
Manicheism 429, 431–2
Mañjughoṣa/Mañjuśri 54, 90–1, 455
mantras 127, 204, 249, 273, 309–10,
    352
Māra 52, 54, 84, 137,329
    attack on the Buddha 277
marriage 24, 264, 370–1, 442, 528, 549
Maudgalyāyana 84, 93, 173, 180
meat-eating 213–4, 215
medicine 83, 210, 237, 357–8, 427,
    590–1, 594
meditation 107–9, 119–24, 126–30,
    246–8, 286, 308–13, 333–54,
    409–12, 621
    aims of 123, 335–6, 617
    classes 264, 339, 463, 608–9, 620–1
    definition 120–1, 335
    experience 351–2, 516, 621
    levels 120–5, 351–3
    methods of 120, 123–5, 134, 621
        five basic 124, 335, 340–8, 350–1
    mettā bhāvanā 125, 340, 342, 344,
        346, 349, 351, 376
    mindfulness of breathing 124–6, 273,
        286, 340–2, 346, 351, 621
    motivations 335–6
    nidāna chain 130–1, 346–7
        preparations for 273, 335, 337–40
    recollection of death 120, 124,
        126–9, 346
    recollection of impermanence 128–9,
        345
    recollection of impurity/decay 125–6,
        344–5, 346
    samāpatti 122, 351–2
    śamatha 351–2
    side effects 122, 351–2
    six element practice 134–6, 348–51
    stupa visualization 176–7
    as weighty karma 109
meditative concentration 54, 109, 307,
    309, 311, 349, 351

Meghiya 577–8
memoirs 47, 596
mental activity 99, 111, 121, 195, 250, 351, 511
mental poisons, *see* poisons
mental states 104, 107, 216, 287, 317, 321, 323, 536
  positive 13, 67, 104, 269, 338, 535
  skilful 102, 104, 195, 244–5, 370
  unskilful 101, 195, 247, 283, 287, 292, 304
merchants 119, 178, 581
mettā 118, 125, 209, 282, 321, 342–4, 346, 376, 421, 450–1, 576–7, 579–80, 599, 621
mettā bhāvanā 125, 340, 342, 344, 346, 349, 351, 376
Mettā Sutta 319
Milarepa 103, 180, 299
Milton, John 513–14, 569, 602
mindfulness 70, 120, 286, 309–10, 312, 318, 320–1, 323–4
  of breathing 124–6, 273, 286, 340–2, 346, 351, 621
miracles 23, 76, 365, 463
misconceptions 31, 44–5, 151, 371, 554
misery 100, 102, 225, 227–8, 323, 453, 600
mistakes 90, 228, 233, 238, 539, 543, 556, 561
misunderstandings, safeguards against 83
moderation 323, 337
monasteries 50, 86, 406–8, 430, 546, 548, 551, 590
monks 19–20, 83–4, 323, 406–8, 410, 414, 582–4, 589–92
  order of 90, 326, 412, 558
moon 54, 161, 274
  finger pointing to the 166–7, 169, 238, 359, 361
morality 99, 102, 244–5, 248, 252, 354, 369–71, 512
  conventional 102, 245
  natural 102, 245
motivation 229, 335–6, 452
mountains 114, 282, 285, 289, 334, 374, 379–80, 496–8
movement 68, 185, 203, 244, 276, religious 296, 430–1, 455–7
Mozart, W.A. 58, 509, 515, 603
Mucalinda 596
murder 94, 107, 147, 323, 542
music 36, 39, 57–8, 421, 509, 511, 515, 602–3

mystery
  of death 94, 96, 113
  of life 6, 96, 113
  of the void 229–38
myths 5, 34, 41, 87, 178, 182, 230–1, 427–8

Nabokov, Vladimir 478, 514
Nāgārjuna 237
Nanda 557–8
natural morality 102, 245
natural world 424–5, 597–8
negative emotions 52, 270, 422, 487, 491
neutral persons 343, 376, 576
new society 456–8, 462, 464, 623
nidāna chain 68, 129–31, 134, 193, 200, 259, 346–7
nidānas 67–9, 129, 192–3, 195, 199, 201, 346, 348
  positive xiv, 67–8, 258–79
Nietzsche, F. xii, 61, 493–506
Nirvāṇa 116–17, 131–3, 184–5, 222–9, 234–6, 249–50, 290–2, 355–6
niyamas, five xiv, 98–101, 111, 316–17
Noble Eightfold Path 9, 14, 76, 184, 186, 242, 259, 281, 282, 284–5, 363
noble quest 208, 236
noble truths, four 8, 14, 76, 183, 199, 281, 324, 330
noise 212, 326, 337–8, 538, 567
non-exploitation 581–2, 587, 589–94
non-returners 254, 412, 420–1
non-self/no-self 60, 235, 492; *see also* anātman
non-violence 318–19, 613
novels 46, 508, 524–5, 602
nuclear family 540–1, 623
nuns 20, 83, 85, 88, 404, 407–9, 591

offerings 20, 64, 222, 310, 454, 540, 553, 559–60
old age 26, 92, 94, 97, 207, 210, 213, 262
om 80
once-returners 253, 412, 420–1
one-pointedness of mind 288–9, 306–12; *see also* mindfulness
opanayiko 163
opposites 97–8, 101, 184–5, 237, 355, 375, 394
ordinations xvi, 83, 289, 406, 414–15, 462
oscillation 68, 97, 184–5

overman 493, 496, 498–503
own-being 219, 281, 317, 362

pain
  mental, *see* suffering
  physical 117, 184, 210–1
painters 107, 432, 507–8, 512, 602–3
Pāli 15, 18, 98–9, 217–18, 293, 327–8, 589–90, 603
  canon/scriptures 117, 119, 179, 182, 184, 235, 322, 549
paṇṇatti-sīla 102
parables 87
  burning house 35–6
  raft 165–7, 252
  raincloud 178–81
pārājikas 408–9
pāramitās, see perfections
parāvṛtti 88, 275
parents 37, 70, 523–4, 527–9, 593–4, 603–7, 609
  gratitude to 599–601
parinirvāṇa 19, 76, 116–19, 137, 363, 379, 549
  difference from Nirvāṇa 117
Parinirvāṇa Day 119–20
parivrājakas 460–1
part-timers 404–7, 410
Path of Reality 282
Path of Transformation 282, 284, 595
Path of Vision 282, 284, 595
patience 54, 367, 372, 375, 394
paṭisanthāra 69–71
peace 72–3, 77, 79, 264–5, 270, 335–6, 351–2, 613–14
  world 613–14
perceptions 38, 41, 96, 115, 129, 149, 213, 216–17
Perfect Action 282–3
Perfect Effort 282–4, 304
Perfect Emotion 282–3
perfect livelihood 282–3, 582
Perfect Mindfulness 282, 284
Perfect *Samādhi* 282, 284
Perfect Speech 282–3
Perfect Vision 281–2, 284, 358, 367, 389
Perfect Wisdom 87, 355
perfection, human 62
perfection of wisdom 55, 87, 220, 233, 358, 360, 362
perfections 54, 353, 361–2, 367, 369, 372–3, 375, 575
  balancing 375
  six 54, 242, 259, 367–75

personal contact 63, 144, 314, 389, 439, 578, 619
personal God 152, 193, 497, 549
personal relationships 400, 428, 469, 519, 526, 528, 592, 594
personality 150, 188, 363, 417, 471, 489–91, 548
philosophers 58, 164, 333, 499–500, 506, 605
  Buddha not a philosopher 163–5
philosophy 5, 7, 58, 113, 182–3, 231–2, 549, 594
  Buddhist 81, 101, 163, 183, 220, 231, 241–2, 331
  Western 164, 427, 468, 504
physical body 117, 119, 136, 143, 145, 150, 216–17, 349–50
physical pain 117, 184, 210
'Pickwick, Mr' 525–6
plants 70, 109, 178, 180–1, 258, 307, 312–13, 542
Platform Sūtra 356–7, 361
Plato 44, 59, 164, 427, 489, 499, 523, 560
Plotinus 560
poems xvi, 58, 88, 266, 515, 524, 600, 602
poetry 36, 58, 86, 478, 506, 511, 603
poets xvi, 57–8, 84, 333, 338, 507, 512, 602
point of no return 68, 241, 250–3
poison 118, 237, 283, 583
poisons, mental
  āsravas 32–3, 67–8, 278, 354
  five 123–36, 340–1
    antidotes to 123–37, 340–2, 346, 348, 362
  three root 131, 134, 202–3, 243
political power 214, 261, 430, 449
politics 10, 47, 161, 322, 447, 501, 534, 561
positive emotions 15, 125, 270, 343, 351, 422, 451, 472
positive group 433, 444, 455, 457–8
  and new society 452–8
positive mental states 13, 67, 104, 269, 338, 535
positive *nidānas* xiv, 67–8, 258–79
power 215, 438, 444–50, 452, 501, 503, 576, 584
  God of Power 448–9
  mode 576–7, 580
  political 214, 261, 430, 449
  structure 448, 450, 546, 548
  supernormal 73, 463, 584

praise 19, 76, 151, 159–60, 179, 222, 289, 588
prajñā 53, 233, 294, 299, 302–3, 354, 356–7, 359; *see also* wisdom
Prajñāpāramitā (female Buddha) 362
Prajñāpāramitā Sūtra 55, 360, 362
prāmodya 266
praśrabdhi 268–9, 288
prātimokṣa 83
pratītya-samutpāda, see conditioned co-production
preaching 379–80, 383, 402, 591
precepts
   ethical 109, 255, 331, 396, 407–8, 487
   five 255, 264, 291, 318–25, 328, 331, 370, 582
pride 57, 134, 136, 341, 348, 514
princes 29, 119, 178, 330, 450, 489, 523
prison 453, 570–1
prīti 266–8, 288
problems 551, 553–4, 557
progress, spiritual 248, 250, 375, 383, 398, 412, 419, 598, 607
promiscuity 566
psyche 41–2, 196–7, 273, 275, 306, 492, 568
psychic powers 63, 84, 584
psychological conditionings 52, 73, 129, 131, 142, 149, 277, 481
psychology 99, 105, 224, 275, 308, 333, 335, 484
psychophysical organism 129–30, 198, 200, 230, 298, 307, 347
punishment 99–100, 114, 322
Puṇya 290–1
pupils 77, 314, 427, 523, 525–7, 545, 550
Pure Land 8, 244, 249, 453–6, 571
purification 186, 242, 259, 281, 291–2, 294–5, 321, 363
purity 33, 85, 167, 290, 295

raft, parable of the 165–7, 232, 252, 359, 361, 394
Rāhula 24
rain of the Dharma 314
raincloud, parable of 178–81
rainy season retreats 83, 209, 405–6
rapture 67, 97, 185, 259, 266–9, 273, 307
Rathavinīta Sutta 290–1
Ratnasambhava 374

Ray, Reginald 407
reality
   absolute 16, 237, 349, 469, 476
   conditioned 206, 234–5
   texture of 205–21
   transcendental 10, 151, 236, 476, 624
   two realities 206–9
   unconditioned 206, 234, 373
rebirth 129–32, 134, 187–8, 190, 192, 195–201, 249, 412
   good 195
   and karma xii, 92–115, 165, 187–8, 192, 605
   in Western Buddhism 188–92
recollection of death 120, 124, 126, 128
refined emotions 505, 508
refuge 153, 324–31, 356, 358, 396–8, 400–401, 414–15, 457–8
Refuges, Three 324–31, 358, 396–7, 429
relationships 371, 390–1, 521–9, 531, 544–5, 566–8, 587–8, 591–4
   business 581–8
   parents and children 338, 523, 531–44
   personal 400, 428, 469, 519, 526, 528, 592, 594
   romantic relationships 524–5, 549
   same-sex 321–2, 371, 527
   sexual 39, 321–2, 524–5, 527–8, 566
   sibling 527
reliances, four 355–6
religions
   theistic 11, 447–8
   universal 443, 447, 478, 483
religious groups 6, 224, 546, 548, 550, 553, 557, 560
religious life 256, 270, 590
religious observances 200, 253, 255, 419
remorse 180, 211, 266, 270
renunciation 55, 133, 315, 459–61
requisites, monastic 590–1
residential communities 83, 464, 573, 623
resources 56, 400, 438, 573
responsibilities 23, 25, 293, 459, 472–3, 616, 618–19, 623
restlessness 253, 262, 305, 309
retreats xi, xiii, xvi, 313, 405–6, 532, 608–9, 621–2
   rainy season 83, 209, 405–6
Revata 289
reverence 62–3, 69–71, 105, 137, 442

A GUIDE TO THE COMPLETE
WORKS OF SANGHARAKSHITA

Gathered together in these twenty-seven volumes are talks and stories, commentaries on the Buddhist scriptures, poems, memoirs, reviews, and other writings. The genres are many, and the subject matter covered is wide, but it all has – its whole purpose is to convey – that taste of freedom which the Buddha declared to be the hallmark of his Dharma. Another traditional description of the Buddha's Dharma is that it is *ehipassiko*, 'come and see'. Sangharakshita calls to us, his readers, to come and see how the Dharma can fundamentally change the way we see things, change the way we live for the better, and change the society we belong to, wherever in the world we live.

Sangharakshita's very first published piece, *The Unity of Buddhism* (found in volume 7 of this collection), appeared in 1944 when he was eighteen years old, and it introduced themes that continued to resound throughout his work: the basis of Buddhist ethics, the compassion of the bodhisattva, and the transcendental unity of Buddhism. Over the course of the following seven decades not only did numerous other works flow from his pen; he gave hundreds of talks (some now lost). In gathering all we could find of this vast output, we have sought to arrange it in a way that brings a sense of coherence, communicating something essential about Sangharakshita, his life and teaching. Recalling the three 'baskets' among which an early tradition divided the Buddha's teachings, we have divided Sangharakshita's creative output into six 'baskets' or groups: foundation texts; works originating in India; teachings originally given in the West; commentaries on the Buddhist scriptures; personal writings; and poetry, aphorisms, and works on the arts. The 27th volume, a concordance, brings together all the terms and themes of the whole collection. If you want to find a particular story or teaching, look at a traditional term from different points of view or in different contexts, or track down one of the thousands of canonical references to be found in these volumes, the concordance will be your guide.

1. FOUNDATION

What is the foundation of a Buddhist life? How do we understand and then follow the Buddha's path of Ethics, Meditation, and Wisdom? What is really meant by 'Going for Refuge to the Three Jewels', described by Sangharakshita as the essential act of a Buddhist life? And what is the Bodhisattva ideal, which he has called 'one of the sublimest ideals mankind has ever seen'? In the 'Foundation' group you will find teachings on all these themes. It includes the author's *magnum opus, A Survey of Buddhism*, a collection of teachings on *The Purpose and Practice of Buddhist Meditation*, and the anthology, *The Essential Sangharakshita*, an eminently helpful distillation of the entire corpus.

2. INDIA

From 1950 to 1964 Sangharakshita, based in Kalimpong in the eastern Himalayas, poured his energy into trying to revive Buddhism in the land of its birth and to revitalize and bring reform to the existing Asian Buddhist world. The articles and book reviews from this period are gathered in volumes 7 and 8, as well as his biographical sketch of the great Sinhalese Dharmaduta, Anagarika Dharmapala. In 1954 Sangharakshita took on the editing of the *Maha Bodhi*, a journal for which he wrote a monthly editorial, and which, under his editorship, published the work of many of the leading Buddhist writers of the time. It was also during these years in India that a vital connection was forged with Dr B. R. Ambedkar, renowned Indian statesman and leader of the Buddhist mass conversion of 1956. Sangharakshita became closely involved with the new Buddhists and, after Dr Ambedkar's untimely death, visited them regularly on extensive teaching tours.

From 1979, when an Indian wing of the Triratna Buddhist Community was founded (then known as TBMSG), Sangharakshita returned several times to undertake further teaching tours. The talks from these tours are collected in volumes 9 and 10 along with a unique work on Ambedkar and his life which draws out the significance of his conversion to Buddhism.

3. THE WEST

Sangharakshita founded the Triratna Buddhist Community (then called the Friends of the Western Buddhist Order) on 6 April 1967. On 7 April the following year he performed the first ordinations of men and women within the Triratna Buddhist Order (then the Western Buddhist Order). At that time Buddhism was not widely known in the West and for the following two decades or so he taught intensively, finding new ways to communicate the ancient truths of Buddhism, drawing on the whole Buddhist tradition to do so, as well as making connections with what was best in existing Western culture. Sometimes his sword flashed as he critiqued ideas and views inimical to the Dharma. It is these teachings and writings that are gathered together in this third group.

4. COMMENTARY

Throughout Sangharakshita's works are threaded references to the Buddhist canon of literature – Pāli, Mahāyāna, and Vajrayāna – from which he drew his inspiration. In the early days of the new movement he often taught by means of seminars in which, prompted by the questions of his students, he sought to pass on the inspiration and wisdom of the Buddhist tradition. Each seminar was based around a different text, the seminars were recorded and transcribed, and in due course many of the transcriptions were edited and turned into books, all carefully checked by Sangharakshita. The commentaries compiled in this way constitute the fourth group. In some ways this is the heart of the collection. Sangharakshita often told the story of how it was that, reading two *sūtras* at the age of sixteen, he realized that he was a Buddhist, and he has never tired of showing others how they too could see and realize the value of the '*sūtra*-treasure'.

5. MEMOIRS

Who is Sangharakshita? What sort of life did he live? Whom did he meet? What did he feel? Why did he found a new Buddhist movement? In these volumes of memoirs and letters Sangharakshita shares with his readers much about himself and his life as he himself has experienced it, giving us a sense of its breadth and depth, humour and pathos.

6. POETRY, APHORISMS, AND THE ARTS

Sangharakshita describes reading *Paradise Lost* at the age of twelve as one of the greatest poetic experiences of his life. His realization of the value of the higher arts to spiritual development is one of his distinctive contributions to our understanding of what Buddhist life is, and he has expressed it in a number of essays and articles. Throughout his life he has written poetry which he says can be regarded as a kind of spiritual autobiography. It is here, perhaps, that we come closest to the heart of Sangharakshita. He has also written a few short stories and composed some startling aphorisms. Through book reviews he has engaged with the experiences, ideas, and opinions of modern writers. All these are collected in this sixth group.

In the preface to *A Survey of Buddhism* (volume 1 in this collection), Sangharakshita wrote of his approach to the Buddha's teachings:

> Why did the Buddha (or Nāgārjuna, or Buddhaghosa) teach this particular doctrine? What bearing does it have on the spiritual life? How does it help the individual Buddhist actually to follow the spiritual path?... I found myself asking such questions again and again, for only in this way, I found, could I make sense – spiritual sense – of Buddhism.

Although this collection contains so many words, they are all intent, directly or indirectly, on these same questions. And all these words are not in the end about their writer, but about his great subject, the Buddha and his teaching, and about you, the reader, for whose benefit they are solely intended. These pages are full of the reverence that Sangharakshita has always felt, which is expressed in an early poem, 'Taking Refuge in the Buddha', whose refrain is 'My place is at thy feet'. He has devoted his life to communicating the Buddha's Dharma in its depth and in its breadth, to men and women from all backgrounds and walks of life, from all countries, of all races, of all ages. These collected works are the fruit of that devotion.

We are very pleased to be able to include some previously unpublished work in this collection, but most of what appears in these volumes has been published before. We have made very few changes, though we have added extra notes where we thought they would be useful. We have had the pleasure of researching the notes in the Sangharakshita Library at 'Adhisthana', Triratna's centre in Herefordshire, UK, which houses his own collection of books. It has been of great value to be able to search among the very copies of the *suttas*, *sūtras* and commentaries that have provided the basis of his teachings over the last seventy years.

The publication of these volumes owes much to the work of transcribers, editors, indexers, designers, and publishers over many years – those who brought out the original editions of many of the works included here, and those who have contributed in all sorts of ways to this *Complete Works* project, including all those who contributed to funds given in celebration of Sangharakshita's ninetieth birthday in August 2015. Many thanks to everyone who has helped; may the merit gained in our acting thus go to the alleviation of the suffering of all beings.

Vidyadevi and Kalyanaprabha
Editors

THE COMPLETE WORKS OF SANGHARAKSHITA

WINDHORSE PUBLICATIONS

Windhorse Publications is a Buddhist charitable company based in the UK. We produce books of high quality that are accessible and relevant to all those interested in Buddhism, at whatever level of interest and commitment. We are the main publisher of Sangharakshita, the founder of the Triratna Buddhist Order and Community. Our books draw on the whole range of the Buddhist tradition, including translations of traditional texts, commentaries, books that make links with contemporary culture and ways of life, biographies of Buddhists, and works on meditation.

To subscribe to the *Complete Works of Sangharakshita*, please go to: windhorsepublications.com/sangharakshita-complete-works/

THE TRIRATNA BUDDHIST COMMUNITY

Windhorse Publications is a part of the Triratna Buddhist Community, an international movement with centres in Europe, India, North America and Australasia. At these centres, members of the Triratna Buddhist Order offer classes in meditation and Buddhism. Activities of the Triratna Community also include retreat centres, residential spiritual communities, ethical Right Livelihood businesses, and the Karuna Trust, a UK fundraising charity that supports social welfare projects in the slums and villages of India.

Through these and other activities, Triratna is developing a unique approach to Buddhism, not simply as a philosophy and a set of techniques, but as a creatively directed way of life for all people living in the conditions of the modern world.

For more information please visit thebuddhistcentre.com